Advance Praise for The VaR Implementation Handbook

A valuable survey of the latest developments in VaR methodology. This book will be of interest to both academics and practitioners working in the arcane field of financial market risk management.

—**Professor Moorad Choudhry**, Department of Economics, London Metropolitan University

The current VAR book edited by Professor Gregoriou is a serious and well-thought contribution to the finance academic literature. Today Value-at-Risk is considered by many academics as an immense area of research with continued explosive growth. The content of the book is designed to advance the knowledge of scholars worldwide, while guiding practitioners through the modern techniques of risk measurement.

—**Dr. Sotiris K. Staikouras**, Associate Professor of Banking & Finance and Director Undergraduate Programmes, Cass Business School, London

This timely book contains in-depth analyses of VaR measurement and modeling, as well as useful discussions of various managerial applications. I highly recommend this book for anyone wanting to deepen their understanding of VaR theory and practice.

—**Paul Brockman**, Matteson Professor of Financial Services, University of Missouri, College of Business

To successfully manage even the strongest market turbulences like the subprime credit crises market participants need efficient instruments to continuously measure their risk. This book perfectly helps practitioners to qualify and to quantify the specific types of risk exposure by providing the tools for modelling the uncertainties inherent in their portfolios. However, Value at Risk is a value adding compendium not only in difficult times."

—**Christian Hoppe**, Senior Specialist Securitization and Credit Derivatives, Commerzbank AG

This book provides a broad overview of different Value-at-Risk applications for the banking and insurance sector as well as for the portfolio management especially for alternative investments.
Professor Gregoriou has collected an excellent composition of articles which feature advanced Value-at-Risk applications and their usage in different fields of the financial industry.
—**Oliver Schwindler**, Investment Analyst Hedge Funds at Feri Institutional Advisors GmbH

THE VaR IMPLEMENTATION HANDBOOK

THE VaR IMPLEMENTATION HANDBOOK

GREG N. GREGORIOU

EDITOR

New York   Chicago   San Francisco
Lisbon   London   Madrid   Mexico City
Milan   New Delhi   San Juan   Seoul
Singapore   Sydney   Toronto

This publication is designed to provide accurate and authoritative information in regard to the subject
matter covered. It is sold with the understanding that neither the author nor the publisher is engaged in
rendering legal, accounting, futures/securities trading, or other professional service. If legal advice or
other expert assistance is required, the services of a competent professional person should be sought.

—*From a Declaration of Principles jointly adopted by a Committee
of the American Bar Association and a Committee of Publishers*

Neither the editors nor the publisher can guarantee the accuracy of individual chapters. All authors are
responsible for their own written material

McGraw-Hill books are available at special quantity discounts to use as premiums and sales promo-
tions, or for use in corporate training programs. For more information, please write to the Director of
Special Sales, Professional Publishing, McGraw-Hill, Two Penn Plaza, New York, NY 10121–2298.
Or contact your local bookstore.

This book is printed on acid-free paper.

CONTENTS

v

Chapter 18

Risk-Managing the Uncertainty in VaR Model Parameters   385

Jason C. Hsu and Vitali Kalesnik

Chapter 19

Structural Credit Modeling and Its Relationship To Market Value at Risk: An Australian Sectoral Perspective   403

David E. Allen and Robert Powell

Chapter 20

Model Risk in VAR Calculations   415

Peter Schaller

Chapter 23

**How Investors Face Financial Risk Loss Aversion and Wealth
Allocation with Two-Dimensional Individual Utility: A VaR
Application   485**

Erick W. Rengifo and Emanuela Trifan

EDITOR

Greg N. Gregoriou is Professor of Finance in the School of Business and Economics at State University of New York (Plattsburgh). He obtained his joint PhD (Finance) from the University of Quebec at Montreal, which pools its resources with Montreal's three other major universities (McGill, Concordia, and HEC). He has published 25 books for John Wiley & Sons, McGraw-Hill, Elsevier-Butterworth-Heinemann, Palgrave-MacMillan, and Risk Books. He is coeditor for the peer-reviewed scientific *Journal of Derivatives and Hedge Funds* and an editorial board member for the *Journal of Wealth Management* and the *Journal of Risk Management in Financial Institutions.* He has authored over 50 articles on hedge funds and managed futures in various U.S. and UK peer-reviewed publications, including the *Journal of Portfolio Management, Journal of Futures Markets, European Journal of Operational Research,* and *Annals of Operations Research.*

CONTRIBUTORS

Zeno Adams is currently a research assistant at the Department of Finance and Banking. Prior to this, he worked as student assistant at the Department of Applied Econometrics. He holds a diploma in economics from the University of Freiburg. His research focuses on alternative investments and risk management.

David E. Allen is Professor of Finance at Edith Cowan University, Perth, Western Australia. He is the author of three monographs and more than 70 refereed publications on a diverse range of topics covering corporate financial policy decisions, asset pricing, business economics, funds management and performance bench-marking, volatility modeling and hedging, and market microstructure and liquidity.

Monica Billio is Professor of Econometrics at the University Ca' Foscari of Venice, where she teaches econometrics and financial econometrics in the undergraduate program and econometrics in the PhD program. She graduated in economics from the University Ca' Foscari of Venice and holds a doctorate in applied mathematics at the University Paris Dauphine in 1999. She was Assistant Professor of Econometrics from 1996 to 2000 at the University Ca' Foscari of Venice and then Associate Professor of Econometrics until 2006. Her main research interests include financial econometrics with applications to risk measurement and management, volatility modeling, financial crisis and hedge funds, business cycle analysis, dynamic latent factor models, and simulation-based inference techniques. She is participating in many research projects financed by the European Commission, Eurostat, and the Italian Ministry of Research (MIUR); she is now the local coordinator for the University Ca' Foscari of Venice of the MIUR project Financial Variables and Business Cycle: Interdependence and Real Effects of Financial Fluctuations. The results of these and other research projects have appeared in peer-refereed journals including *Journal of Econometrics, Journal of Statistical Planning and Inference, European*

Journal of Finance, Journal of Economics and Business, Journal of Empirical Finance, Journal of Financial Econometrics, Applied Financial Economics Letters, and *Journal of Multinational Financial Management.* Moreover, she is a member of the Executive Committee of the Department of Economics of the University Ca' Foscari of Venice and member of the teaching committee for the PhD in quantitative economics at the same University. She advises banks and hedge funds on quantitative modeling.

S. Ilker Birbil is an Associate Professor at Sabanci University, Istanbul, Turkey. He received his PhD degree from North Carolina State University, Raleigh. He worked as a postdoctoral research fellow in Erasmus Research Institute of Management, Rotterdam, Netherlands. His research interests lie mainly in algorithm development for various nonlinear programming and global optimization problems arising in different application areas.

Carlos Blanco is an expert in financial, energy, and commodity risk management and modeling. His expertise ranges from risk and pricing model development to strategic risk management and policy related issues. He lectures extensively on topics related to enterprise-wide risk management, energy derivatives pricing and hedging, and other risk topics. He has published over 75 articles on financial, energy, and commodity risk management and modeling and, more recently, on enterprise risk management (ERM) topics. He is currently a lecturer in the Finance Department at the University of California, Berkeley. Carlos is a former vice president of risk solutions at Financial Engineering Associates (FEA). He worked over six years there as an essential contributor in the development of the energy and risk management models of the firm, providing strategic and tactical leading-edge risk advisory and educational services to over 500 energy and commodity trading firms and financial institutions worldwide. He also managed the development and execution of short-term and long-term market and product strategic plans and created and managed the world-class support and professional services department within the firm. Prior to FEA, Carlos worked for a hedge fund in the Midwest and an asset management firm in Madrid, Spain. He is a regional director of the Professional Risk Managers' International Association (PRMIA).

Bastian Breitenfellner is a PhD candidate in the field of financial econometrics and credit risk at the University of Passau, Germany. He is also research assistant at the DekaBank Chair of Finance and Financial Control at the University of Passau. Bastian holds a MS degree in technology and management of the TUM Business School, which is part of the Munich University of Technology. He also studied at the University of Zurich. He has research interests in the fields of capital markets, credit risk, and applied econometrics.

Kevin Dowd is Professor of Financial Risk Management at Nottingham University Business School, where he works with the Centre for Risk and Insurance Studies. He held previous positions with the University of Sheffield and Sheffield Hallam University. His research interests cover risk management, pensions, insurance, monetary and macroeconomics, financial regulation, and political economy, and he has links with the Cato Institution in Washington, the Institute of Economic Affairs in London, and the Open Republic Institute in Dublin.

Dean Fantazzini is a Lecturer in Econometrics And Finance at the Moscow School of Economics, Moscow State University. He graduated with honors from the Department of Economics at the University of Bologna (Italy) in 1999. He obtained a Master's in Financial and Insurance Investments at the Department of Statistics, University of Bologna (Italy) in 2000 and a PhD in Economics in 2006 at the Department of Economics and Quantitative Methods, University of Pavia (Italy). Before joining the Moscow School of Economics, he was research fellow at the Chair for Economics and Econometrics, University of Konstanz (Germany) and at the Department of Statistics and Applied Economics, University of Pavia (Italy). Dean is a specialist in time series analysis, financial econometrics, and multivariate dependence in finance and economics with more than 20 publications.

Viviana Fernandez holds a PhD in Economics from the University of California at Berkeley. She currently works as an Associate Professor at the Department of Industrial Engineering of the University of Chile. She was a Visiting Scholar at the Economics Department of the University of Chicago (September 1997 to March 1998), and she is currently an External

Research Associate of the INFINITI Group of the IIS at Trinity College Dublin. She has published in the *Review of Economics and Statistics*, the *International Review of Financial Analysis, Studies of Nonlinear Dynamics & Econometrics*, the *Journal of Financial Intermediation*, the *Journal of Futures Markets*, and *Physica A*, among others.

Hanks Frenk is an Associate Professor in Operations Research at the Econometric Institute of the Erasmus University, Rotterdam, Netherlands. His main research interests are stochastic processes, nonlinear programming, and applications of these techniques to problems in engineering and economics.

Roland Füss is Lecturer at the Department of Empirical Research and Econometrics and Assistant Professor at the Department of Finance and Banking at the University of Freiburg, Germany. He holds an MBA from the University of Applied Science in Lörrach, an MA in economics, and a PhD in economics from the University of Freiburg. His research interests are in the field of applied econometrics, risk management, alternative investments, as well as international and real estate finance. Mr. Füss has authored and coauthored several articles in finance journals and book chapters. In addition, he is a member of the Verein für Socialpolitik and of the German Finance Association.

Mila Getmansky is an Assistant Professor of Finance at Isenberg School of Management at the University of Massachusetts, Amherst. Professor Mila Getmansky's research specializes in the empirical asset pricing, hedge funds, performance of investment trading strategies, and system dynamics. She received a BS degree from MIT and a PhD degree in Management from the MIT Sloan School of Management. She was a postdoctoral fellow at the MIT Lab for Financial Engineering before joining the University of Massachusetts, Amherst. Professor Getmansky is an active faculty member of the Center for International Securities and Derivatives Markets (CISDM) at the University of Massachusetts, Amherst, whose goal is to facilitate research in international investment and derivative markets and to promote interactions between the academic and business communities. She published her work in several journals including the *Journal of Financial Economics* and the *Journal of Investment*

Management. Professor Getmansky has participated in numerous conference-organizing committees including the Financial Management Association and the European Financial Association. She has presented her work at several academic and nonacademic conferences including the American Finance Association, Western Finance Association, and Institutional Investor meetings. She is a referee for several journals including the *Journal of Finance, Review of Financial Studies*, and the *Journal of Financial and Quantitative Analysis*. Professor Getmansky is on the editorial board of the *Journal of Alternative Investments*. Before joining the University of Massachusetts, Amherst, Professor Getmansky worked in the quantitative research group at the Deutsche Asset Management in New York. Professor Getmansky is currently teaching corporate finance and financial modeling.

Peter Grundke is at the University of Osnabrück as a professor for finance. He earned degrees in mathematics and business administration at the RWTH Aachen. He completed his PhD thesis on the arbitrage-free pricing of credit risks in 2002 and received his habilitation degree for business administration in 2006, both at the University of Cologne. His academic main interest is currently in the field of banking regulation and credit risk management.

Ulrich Hommel is a Professor of Finance as well as the Director of the Strategic Finance Institute (SFI) at the European Business School (EBS) International University, Germany. He holds a PhD in Economics from the University of Michigan, Ann Arbor, and has completed his habilitation at the WHU-Otto Beisheim School of Management, Germany. He is the coeditor of *Risk Management: Challenge and Opportunity*, 2nd edition, published by Springer. His main research interests are corporate risk management, family business finance, and venture capital contracting.

Jason C. Hsu is a principal at Research Affiliates and is the Managing Director of Research and Investment Management. He oversees the firm's subadvisory and hedge fund businesses, which total 35B USD and conducts research on the asset allocation models and equity strategies. Jason was recognized in 2008 by *Institutional Investor Magazine* as one of the 20 Rising Stars in Hedge Fund. He is also a Professor of Finance at the

Anderson School of Management at UCLA. Jason received his undergraduate degrees from California Institute of Technology and his PhD in finance from the University of California, Los Angeles.

Vitali Kalesnik is a senior researcher and economist at Research Affiliates. He conducts research on commodity futures trading, quantitative equity strategies, and asset allocation. Dr. Vitali received his PhD in economics from UCLA and was a researcher at the Belarus Ministry of Economics.

Gökhan Karaahmet is a research assistant at the Economics Department of Fatih University, Istanbul. He is currently finishing his Master's degree and has BA from the Economics Department of Bosphorus University, Istanbul. His areas of interest are econometrics, stock market returns, and volatility of assets.

Bahar Kaynar graduated from Middle East Technical University in 2004 with an undergraduate degree in mathematics and minor degree in statistics. Following this, she attended graduate program on Industrial Engineering at Sabanci University. After working from 2006 to 2007 as a credit risk analyst in risk management department at Garanti Bank Istanbul, she is currently doing her PhD study at Vrije University, Amsterdam, studying cross entropy and rare event simulation.

Andreas Kemmerer holds a PhD in finance from the Goethe University of Frankfurt, Germany. He published several research articles on the private equity industry. After he completed his master studies of business administration in 2002, he started as an associate in corporate finance at Haarmann & Hemmelrath. Since 2006, he has worked for KfW, Frankfurt, where he writes second opinions as well as deals with risk management for leveraged finance, mezzanine, and venture capital transactions for KfW's investments and portfolio, respectively. KfW is one of the most important and presumably the largest venture capital investor in Germany.

Frederik Kramer studies statistics at the University of Dortmund. Since 2005 he is a student assistant in the faculty of statistics and focuses on modeling rating migrations in credit risk. He completed an internship at an international bank in credit risk management. In 2007 he was awarded with third prize of the Postbank Finance Award 2006/07 for a paper on the optimal combination of rating migrations.

Wilhelm Kross is currently senior vice president at Marsh, Germany. He holds a postgraduate degree in engineering from RWTH Aachen, Germany, and a doctoral degree in finance from the European Business School (EBS) International University, Germany. Wilhelm Kross is a recognized expert in the fields of project and risk management. He is the author of *Organized Opportunities: Risk Management in Financial Services Operations*, published by Wiley.

R. McFall (Mac) Lamm, Jr., PhD is chief strategist for Deutsche Bank's Global Investment Management Group in London. His responsibilities include asset allocation, advising clients, and managing portfolios. He has 20 years of experience in market analysis and investment research, and is well known for his expertise in alternative investments, where in the 1990s he was instrumental in integrating alternative investments with traditional assets. He is especially known for publishing *Why Not 100% Hedge Funds [Journal of Investing* (1999) 8(4):87–97] in advance of the stock market bubble burst in the early 2000s—advice that saved many investors from significant losses. Dr. Lamm is a frequent speaker at conferences and events around the globe. He also writes market commentary that is disseminated worldwide and is often quoted in the news media. In addition, Dr. Lamm is an energetic writer having published numerous book chapters and professional articles in the *Journal of Portfolio Management, Journal of Economic Dynamics and Control, Journal of Alternative Investments, Journal of Financial Transformation, Journal of Investing, Journal of Wealth Management, Alternative Investments Quarterly,* and *Journal of Private Equity,* among others.

Peter Lerner received his undergraduate and graduate education in physics in Moscow Institute for Physics and Technology and Lebedev Institute for Physical Sciences. He conducted research with Los Alamos National Laboratory and Penn State University. During this time, he authored more than 50 papers and book contributions in optics, atomic physics, and materials science. In 1998 Peter graduated from Katz School of Business (University of Pittsburgh) with an MBA and worked two years as a risk quant in energy trading. He received his PhD in finance from Syracuse University in 2006 at the ripe old age of 48.

Claudia Lawrenz joined Westdeutsche Landesbank, Germany, in March 2001, where she is responsible for the team Methods, developing rating systems for credit risks. She received degrees (diploma) in Applied Systems Science and obtained her doctoral degree in Economics University of Osnabrueck (Germany). Her PhD thesis dealt with bounded rationality models in game theory. Her current interests are statistical methods in finance, estimation, and modeling of credit risk-related parameters (i.e., default probability, loss given default, conversion factor, and rating migration matrices). She has been published in several international journals, such as *Empirical Economics*, dealing with bounded rationality models in finance and rating methods.

Germán Navarro holds degrees in engineering and computer science. He is a researcher at the SUN Microsystems Laboratory of Computational Finance. He is also a Professor at the Masters of Financial Engineering at CIFF.

Nilay Noyan received her PhD in operations research from Rutgers University, NJ. Her research interests lie in diverse areas of operations research, including risk measures, probabilistic optimization problems, stochastic optimization with dominance constraints, and statistical inference methods. During her PhD studies, she also worked as a research scientist at the Data Analysis Research Department of AVAYA Labs Research in New Jersey. After her PhD, she joined Sabanci University as a faculty member in September 2006.

Ignacio Olmeda holds a PhD in finance. He is an Associate Professor of Economics and Computer Science at the University of Alcalá. He has been a Fulbright Visiting Scholar at several institutions in the United States and in Asia. He is the Director of the Masters of Finance at CIFF (Bank of Santander-UAH) and the Director of the SUN Microsystems Laboratory of Computational Finance.

Mehmet Orhan is an associate professor at the Economics Department of Fatih University, Istanbul. He is also Director of the Social Sciences Institute that is responsible for the coordination of graduate programs. He has a graduate degree from the Industrial Engineering Department and obtained a scholarship and received his PhD from Bilkent University, Ankara. His main interest is econometrics, both theoretical and applied. He has published articles in *Economics Letters, Applied Economics, International Journal of Business*, and *Journal of Economic and Social Research*. His theoretical research interests include HCCME estimation, robust estimation techniques, and Bayesian inference. He is working on IPO performances in Turkey, optimal control of the Turkish economy, inflation, exchange rate, hedge fund returns, tax revenue estimation, and international economic cooperations as part of his applied research studies.

Loriana Pelizzon is Associate Professor of Economics at the University of Venice. She graduated from the London Business School with a doctorate in Finance. She also holds a degree from the University of Venice (Laurea in business administration). She was Assistant Professor in Economics at the University of Padova from 2000 to 2004. Her research interests are on risk measurement and management, asset allocation and household portfolios, hedge funds, financial institutions, and financial crisis. Her work includes papers published in the *Journal of Financial and Quantitative Analysis, Journal of Banking and Finance, European Journal of Finance, Journal of Economics and Business*, and *Journal of Empirical Finance* and has presented at the Western Finance Association and European Finance Association. Pelizzon has been awarded the EFA 2005–Barclays Global Investor Award for the Best Symposium paper and FMA European Conference, 2005 best conference paper. She is participating to many research projects: NBER, FDIC, RTN, HCM, TACIS, ACE, MURST, and PRIN. She is referee of the following journals: *JMCB, JFI, JEFM, JMFM, JB&F, RoF, JIFMIM, Journal of Macroeconomics, Risk Analysis, Research in Economics, RISEC,* and Elsevier: Finance Publications. Moreover, she is member of the Program Committee: European Finance Association Conferences, Coordinator of the EFA Doctoral Tutorial and Member of the Teaching Committee of the PhD in

Economics, University of Venice. She teaches financial economics and investments at the International Master in Economics and Finance program and economics and financial economics at the undergraduate program. She has been awarded the Best Teacher 2006 at the Ca' Foscari University of Venice. She frequently advises banks and government agencies on risk measurement and risk management strategies.

Robert Powell has 20 years banking experience in South Africa, New Zealand, and Australia. He has been involved in the development and implementation of several credit and financial analysis models in Banks. He has a PhD from Edith Cowan University, where he currently works as a researcher and lecturer in banking and finance, in the School of Accounting, Finance, and Economics at Edith Cowan Univeristy.

François-Éric Racicot is Professor of Finance and graduate program director at the Department of Administrative Sciences of University of Quebec at Outaouais (UQO). Professor Racicot has published numerous books in quantitative finance and has also published several articles in peer-reviewed journals such as *Economics Letters, Journal of Derivatives & Hedge Funds, Journal of Wealth Management,* and *International Advances in Economic Research.*

Jan Rietzschel works as consultant in the Department of Corporate Finance for EM.Sport Media AG. He obtained a first-class Master's in Business Administration with the specialization in finance at Goethe University Frankfurt, Germany, in 2005. After his master studies, he worked for two years as analyst at Landesbank Hessen-Thüringen in the Department of Leveraged Finance. He also had internships at Deutsche Bank, PricewaterhouseCoopers, and BC Brandenburg Capital, a venture capital company. His main interests cover venture capital, portfolio management, and financial modeling.

Erick W. Rengifo has a PhD in Economics from CORE—Université catholique de Louvian, Belgium. My fields of research include financial econometrics, market microstructure, portfolio optimization, and behavioral finance. An Assistant Professor at the department of Economics at Fordham

University, New York, he teaches the graduate courses of financial economics and financial econometrics. His recent publications are in *Journal of Empirical Finance and Computational Statistics* and *Data Analysis*.

Peter Schaller is the leading expert in the strategic risk management division of the largest Austrian bank (Bank Austria–Creditanstalt). He holds a PhD in Theoretical Physics and had worked in research institutes in this field for several years, before he joined Bank Austria. Besides his work in the bank, he gives lectures at the Technical University of Vienna and is a frequent speaker at academic and industry conferences on financial risk management.

Bernd Scherer is global head of Quantitative Structured Products. He joined Morgan Stanley in 2007 and has 13 years of investment experience. Prior to joining the firm, Bernd worked at Deutsche Bank Asset Management as head of the Quantitative Strategies Group's Research Center as well as head of portfolio engineering in New York. Before this, he headed the Investment Solutions and Overlay Management Group in Frankfurt. Bernd has also held various positions at Morgan Stanley, Oppenheim Investment Management, Schroders, and JPMorgan Investment Management. He authored several books on quantitative asset management and more than 40 articles in refereed journals. Bernd received a Masters degrees in economics from the University of Augsburg and the University of London and a PhD from the University of Giessen. He is an Adjunct Professor of Finance at the European Business School and visiting professor at Birkbeck College (University of London).

Henry Schoenball works as consultant in the Department of Asset Planning and Controlling for the ERGO Insurance Group. He obtained his Master diploma in Business Administration with the specialization in finance at the Goethe University Frankfurt, Germany. His main research interests cover portfolio management, venture capital, and financial modeling.

Willi Semmler is Chair and Professor at the Department of Economics at The New School, New York. He holds a PhD from the Free University of Berlin. He is author or coauthor of over 85 refereed articles in international journals and is author or coauthor of 11 books. He has been a visitor of Columbia University and Stanford University and the Cepremap in Paris. He was Fortis-Bank Visiting Professor of the University of Antwerp, Visiting Professor at the University of Marseilles–Aix-en-Provence and has taught financial economics for the European Quantitative Economics Doctorate (QED) Program at universities in Italy, Spain, Portugal, and Germany. He serves on the Board of Directors for the Center for Empirical Macroeconomics, Bielefeld University and has served to evaluate research projects for the National Science Foundations of Austria, Germany, Belgium, and the UK. He has also lectured at the UNAM in Mexico City, the University of Orlean, France; Chuo University, Tokyo; and Bielefeld University, Germany and evaluates research projects for the European Union. He is on the scientific committee of the Society for Nonlinear Dynamics and Econometrics, the Society for Computation in Economics and Finance, and the Workshop on Computational and Financial Econometrics.

Raymond Théoret is Professor of Finance and director of the undergraduate programs in management in the Department of Finance of University of Quebec at Montreal (UQAM). He is also a graduate of this university. He has published many peer-reviewed articles and several books in quantitative finance and banking and has consulted with numerous firms on risk management in financial institutions. Finally, he has written many articles in well-known journals, collective works, and newspapers.

Emanuela Trifan is a PhD student in economics at the Institute of Economics, Darmstadt University of Technology, Germany. His fields of research include behavioral finance, neuroeconomics, market microstructure, and portfolio optimization. As research associate at the Department of Econometrics, J. W. Goethe University Frankfurt and Main, Germany, he teaches undergraduate and graduate courses of statistics, economics, and financial econometrics.

Niklas Wagner is Professor of Finance at Passau University, Germany. Former positions were at Hannover, Munich, and Dresden. After receiving his PhD in finance from Augsburg University in 1998, he held postdoctoral visiting appointments at the Haas School of Business, University of California, Berkeley, and at Stanford GSB. Academic visits also led him to the Center of Mathematical Sciences at Munich University of Technology and to the faculty of Economics and Politics, University of Cambridge. Professor Wagner has coauthored several international contributions, including articles in *Economic Notes, Quantitative Finance*, the *Journal of Banking and Finance*, and the *Journal of Empirical Finance*. He regularly serves as a referee for finance and economics journals. His research interests include empirical asset pricing, applied financial econometrics, market microstructure, as well as banking and risk management. His industry background is in quantitative asset management.

Rafael Weißbach joined the faculty of statistics as Assistant Professor at the University of Dortmund, Germany in 2007 after receiving his degrees from Göttingen University (diploma in mathematics, 1997) and the University of Dortmund (doctorate in statistics, 2001). He was promoted to Assistant Professor for Econometrics in 2007. Rafael Weißbach currently acts as Chair for Econometrics at the faculty of Economics, University of Mannheim, Germany. In the years 2001 to 2004, he worked full time as risk analyst and portfolio manager in the credit risk management division of an international investment bank. His current interest is statistics in finance, especially estimation and modeling of credit-risk-related parameters such as rating migration matrices and default correlations. His master and doctoral students have earned awards in finance, e.g., the diploma award of the DeKa Bank in 2007 (second, €5000) and the Postbank Finance Award 2007–2008 (third, €10000). Rafael Weißbach has published over 20 papers in international journals including the *Journal of the American Statistical Association*.

Martin Wiethuechter is a doctoral research assistant at the European Business School (EBS) International University, Germany. He holds a diploma degree in business administration from the University of Mannheim. His main research interests are risk management and performance measurement for alternative investments.

Karim M. Youssef is a doctoral student in economics at the New School for Social Research. Currently his work is focused on interest rate volatilities and commodity-based structured finance vehicles. Previously, he has worked for the World Economic Forum Financing for Development Project and the Social Science Research Council Global Security Program. He received his MA in economics from the New School for Social Research and his BA in history and international studies from Dickinson College.

PART ONE

VaR Measurement

CHAPTER 1

Calculating VaR for Hedge Funds

M. Billio, M. Getmansky, and L. Pelizzon

ABSTRACT

It is well known that hedge funds implement dynamic strategies; therefore, the exposure of hedge funds to various risk factors is nonlinear. In this chapter, we propose to analyze hedge fund tail event behavior conditional on nonlinearity in factor loadings. In particular, we calculate VaR for different hedge fund strategies conditional on different states of the market risk factor. Specifically, we are concentrating on dynamic risk factors that are switching from a market regime or state that we call *normal* to two other regimes that could be identified as "crisis" and "bubble" and that are usually characterized, respectively, by (1) largely low returns and high volatility and (2) high returns. We are proposing a factor model that allows for regime switching in expected returns and volatilities and compare the VaR determined with this methodology with the other VaR approaches like GARCH(1,1), IGARCH(1,1), and Cornish Fisher.

INTRODUCTION

In recent years, the flow of funds into alternative investments for pension funds, endowments, and foundations has experienced a dramatic increase. Unfortunately, the very fact that hedge funds and commodity trading advisors (managed futures funds) have only lately come into prominence during the last decade, has meant that they generally have only recently been considered as substitutes or as additions to other more "traditional" private-equity-based alternative investment vehicles.

Hedge funds are considered by some to be the epitome of active management. They are lightly unregulated investment vehicles with great trading flexibility, and they often pursue highly sophisticated investment strategies. Hedge funds promise "absolute returns" to their investors, leading to a belief that they hold factor-neutral portfolios. They have grown in size noticeably over the past decade and have been receiving increasing portfolio allocations from institutional investors. According to press reports, a number of hedge fund managers have been enjoying compensation that is well in excess of US$10 million per annum.

It is well known that hedge funds implement dynamic strategies; therefore, the exposure of hedge funds to various risk factors is nonlinear. In this chapter, we propose to analyze hedge fund value at risk (VaR) conditional on nonlinearity in factor loadings. In the current VaR literature there are some papers arguing in favor or against of certain VaR models for hedge funds [see Liang and Park (2007), Bali et al. (2007), and Gupta and Liang (2005), for example]. We add to the literature by proposing a model that takes into consideration the dynamic exposure of hedge funds to market and other risk factors. Moreover, it is important to perform a consistent comparison of major VaR models in order to determine the model with the best performance. The main objective of our work is thus, to propose a model of VaR based on regime switching of hedge fund returns, and to provide a consistent comparison of the VaR estimation based on regime switching and three other major VaR models: GARCH(1,1), IGARCH(1,1), and Cornish–Fisher.

The structure of the chapter is as follows. The first section provides an overview of hedge fund literature and hedge fund strategies. The following section presents models used to calculate VaR and to perform backtesting analyses. The final two sections describe hedge funds datasets and their properties and present results of our analysis. Finally, some concluding remarks are provided.

HEDGE FUNDS

The tremendous increase in the number of hedge funds and availability of hedge fund data has attracted a lot of attention in the academic literature that has been concentrated on analyzing hedge funds styles (Fung and Hsieh, 2001; Mitchell and Pulvino, 2001), performance and risk exposure (Bali et al., 2005; Gupta and Liang, 2005; Agarwal and Naik, 2004; Brealey and Kaplanis, 2001; Edwards and Caglayan, 2001; Schneeweis et al., 2002; and Fung and Hsieh, 1997), liquidity, systemic risk, and contagion issues (Billio et al., 2008; Boyson et al., 2007; Chan et al., 2005; Getmansky et al., 2004). All of the above studies find that risk–return characteristics of hedge fund strategies are nonlinear, that hedge funds implement dynamic strategies and exhibit nonlinear and nonnormal payoffs.

Hedge fund strategies greatly differ from each other and have different risk exposures. Fung and Hsieh (2001) analyzed a trend following strategy and Mitchell and Pulvino (2001) studied a risk arbitrage strategy. Both studies find the risk–return characteristics of the hedge fund strategies to be nonlinear and stress the importance of taking into account optionlike features while analyzing hedge funds. Moreover, Agarwal and Naik (2004) show that the nonlinear optionlike payoffs, also called *asset-based style factors* [ABS-factors introduced by Fung and Hsieh (2002)], are not restricted just to these two strategies but are an integral part of payoffs of various hedge fund strategies.

Hedge funds may exhibit nonnormal payoffs for various reasons such as their use of options, or more generally dynamic trading strategies. Unlike most mutual funds (Koski and Pontiff, 1999), hedge funds frequently trade in derivatives. Furthermore, hedge funds are known for their opportunistic nature of trading and a significant part of their returns arise from taking state contingent bets. For this reason the inclusion of dynamic risk factor exposures is extremely relevant in the VaR calculation. In this work we show the relevance of this issue by introducing a model based on dynamic and state-contingent factor loadings that is able to capture VaR hedge fund risk exposures and compare this model with other models that do not allow for dynamic risk exposures.

VALUE AT RISK

Theoretical Definition

The VaR is considered as a measure of downside risk. It is a measure of the left tail risk of a financial series. Value at risk is the maximum amount of loss that can happen over a given horizon at a certain confidence level. It usually appears in statements like

The maximum loss over one day is about $47 million at the 95 percent confidence level.

If we assume that F is the Cumulative Distribution function of return process we can define VaR as

$$F(\text{VaR}) = \alpha \qquad (1.1)$$

where α is the corresponding probability for the specified confidence level. For instance, for 99 percent confidence level $\alpha = 0.01$. Using a density function f of returns, VaR can also be equivalently defined as

$$\alpha = \int_{-\infty}^{VaR} f(x)dx \qquad (1.2)$$

The main question pertinent to the VaR analysis is thus how to forecast the return distribution f over the specified horizon. This study uses the Markov regime-switching approach to forecast the return distribution and thus to compute the VaR. The results are compared with estimates of VaR obtained by other methods like GARCH(1,1), IGARCH(1,1), and Cornish Fisher. In the next section, a brief discussion of these methods is provided along with relative estimation methods.

Empirical Issues

Estimation Methods

When it comes to applying the theoretical formulae to compute the VaR for a specific data set, there are a number of problems which force us to make strong assumptions. The first problem we are going to face is that it is impossible to know the true probability distribution (density) of returns. A number of parametric and nonparametric methods are suggested to overcome this problem.

The traditional nonparametric way is to take the appropriate percentile of a historical return distribution. This is achieved by sorting the returns in ascending order and taking the $(\alpha N)th$ element of the sorted series, where α is the corresponding probability. If αN is not an integer value, VaR is interpolated. That is, for instance, if $\alpha N = 4.6$, the linear interpolation is obtained as follows:

$$\text{VaR} = 4^{th}\ obs + 0.6\ (5^{th}\ obs - 4^{th}\ obs) \tag{1.3}$$

The simplest case, in parametric models, is where the return series is assumed to be normally distributed with the mean and variance estimated form the available sample data. This assumption of normality of returns seems to be in conflict with the empirical properties of most financial time series. More specifically, hedge fund returns, due to the dynamic nature of the trading strategies, are known to highly deviate from normality. In the next four subsections we will have a brief discussion of other methods that try to relax the strong assumption of normality. The parametric and semiparametric methods discussed below assume a specific distribution of returns. They use estimation methods like maximum likelihood estimation (MLE) to estimate the relevant parameters of the distribution, which are then used to forecast the future return distribution and thus VaR. In all these models, we denote the return of hedge funds at the end of each period t as r_t.

GARCH(1,1) Model

The GARCH(1,1) approach allows the conditional distribution of the return series to have a time-varying variance. In this study we assume that the returns are conditionally normally distributed with conditional mean μ_t and conditional variance h_t. That is,

$$r_t \sim N\ (\mu_t, \sigma_t^2) \tag{1.4}$$

with

$$\mu_t = E[r_t \mid I_{t-1}]$$
$$h_t = Var[r_t \mid I_{t-1}] = E[(r_t - \mu_t)^2 \mid I_{t-1}] \tag{1.5}$$

where I_{t-1} is all the available information at time $t - 1$.

This gives the following model:

$$r_t = \mu_t + \varepsilon_t \sqrt{h_t} \qquad (1.6)$$

where $\varepsilon_t \sim N(0, 1)$.

Regarding the estimation of the conditional mean, given the relevance of factor loadings we consider a factor model where the return dynamics could be represented as

$$r_t = \mu + \sum_{i=1}^{n} \beta_{Fi} F_i + v_t \qquad (1.7)$$

with F_i being certain market risk factors.

The conditional variance h_t is modeled as

$$h_t = \omega + \theta (r_{t-1} - \mu_t)^2 + \beta h_{t-1} \qquad (1.8)$$

where all the parameters ω, θ, and β should be nonnegative to guarantee a positive conditional variance at all times.

The parameters of all the GARCH models are estimated by MLE. Once we have the estimates of the parameters, we can get the forecast of the conditional mean and variance of the return for the next period. This enables us to compute the one-period VaR using the forecasted normal distribution of returns. Therefore, the VaR is given by

$$\text{VaR}_t = (\bar{\mu}_t - \eta \cdot \sqrt{\bar{h}_t}) \qquad (1.9)$$

where $\bar{\mu}_t$ and $\bar{h}_t$ are the forecasted conditional mean and variance, respectively, and η is the appropriate quantile in the $N(0, 1)$ distribution.

RiskMetrics IGARCH(1,1) Model

The JP Morgan RiskMetrics approach uses the GARCH(1,1) framework with specific constraints on the parameters. The conditional mean and the constant term in the conditional variance equation are assumed to be zero and $\theta + \beta = 1$. Thus, we have the model:

$$r_t \sim N(0, h_t) \qquad (1.10)$$

$$h_t = \text{Var}[r_t | I_{t-1}] = E[r_t^2 | I_{t-1}] \qquad (1.11)$$

This gives the return as

$$r_t = \varepsilon_t \sqrt{h_t} \qquad (1.12)$$

where $\varepsilon_t \sim N(0, 1)$. The conditional variance h_t is given by

$$h_t = \theta\, h_{t-1} + (1 - \theta)\, r_{t-1} \qquad (1.13)$$

After estimating the parameter θ by MLE method, we get the VaR as

$$\text{VaR}_t = -\eta \cdot \sqrt{h_t} \qquad (1.14)$$

Cornish–Fisher Method

The traditional and perhaps the most naïve approach to estimate VaR is to assume the returns are normally distributed with mean μ and variance σ^2. The VaR is thus given by $\text{VaR} = (\mu - \eta\sigma)$, with η as the appropriate quantile point in the $N(0,1)$ distribution. Considering the fact that hedge funds use dynamic trading strategies and various empirical studies showed that hedge fund return series strictly deviate from the Gaussian distribution [Bali et al. (2007), Gupta and Liang (2005), Agarwal and Naik (2004), Schneeweis et al. (2002), Brealey and Kaplanis (2001), Edwards and Caglayan (2001), and Fung and Hsieh (1997)), this is a very strong assumption to make.

The Cornish–Fisher (CF) approach tries to adjust for the nonnormality of the returns by correcting the critical value η for excess kurtosis and skewness of the historical time series of returns. This is done by taking

$$\Omega = \eta + \frac{1}{6}(\eta^2 - 1)S + \frac{1}{24}(\eta^3 - 3\eta)K - \frac{1}{36}(2\eta^3 - 5\eta)S^2 \qquad (1.15)$$

where η is the critical value for the standard Gaussian distribution and S and K are the empirical skewness and kurtosis of the return series, respectively. The CF VaR is thus given by

$$\text{VaR} = (\mu - \Omega \cdot \sigma) \qquad (1.16)$$

Markov Regime-Switching Models

Following Billio and Pelizzon (2000), this study considers two different types of regime-switching models.

A. Simple Regime-Switching Models

In simple regime-switching models (SRSM), we consider that the volatility of the return process has different regimes or states. For instance, in a case of two regimes, we can consider high volatility and low volatility regimes. This assumption is consistent with the volatility clustering we observe in financial data series. We can also let returns to have different expectations in different regimes. Then,

$$r_t = \mu_t(S_t) + \sigma_t(S_t)\varepsilon_t \qquad (1.17)$$

where μ_t and σ_t are the mean and standard deviation of the return r_t, respectively, ε_t is a unit variance and zero mean white noise, and S_t is a Markov chain variable with n states and a transition probability matrix Π. Theoretically, it is possible to consider as many states as possible. In practice, however, it is usually sufficient to consider two or three states. Considering only two states, 0 and 1, results in the following:

$$r_t = \begin{cases} \mu_0 + \sigma_0\varepsilon_t & \text{if } S_t = 0 \\ \mu_1 + \sigma_1\varepsilon_t & \text{if } S_t = 1 \end{cases} \qquad (1.18)$$

Since $\varepsilon_t \sim IIN(0, 1)$, we can write the distribution of r_t as:

$$r_t \sim \begin{cases} N(\mu_0, \sigma_0^2) & \text{if } S_t = 0 \\ N(\mu_1, \sigma_1^2) & \text{if } S_t = 1 \end{cases} \qquad (1.19)$$

where P_{ij} is the probability of switching from regime i to j and P_{ii} is the probability that the Markov chain does not switch and stays in the same regime. Since $P_{ij} + P_{ii} = 1$, we can write the transition matrix as

$$\Pi = \begin{pmatrix} P_{00} & 1 - P_{11} \\ 1 - P_{00} & P_{11} \end{pmatrix} \qquad (1.20)$$

As for the GARCH model, we also consider a factor specification, i.e.,

$$r_t = \mu_t(S_t) + \sum_{i=1}^{n} \beta_i F_{it} + \sigma_t(S_t)\varepsilon_t \tag{1.21}$$

The VaR for the next period is analytically defined as

$$\alpha = \sum_{S_{t+h}} P(S_{t+h} \mid I_t) \int_{-\infty}^{\mathrm{VaR}_t} N(x, \mu(S_{t+h}), \sigma^2(S_{t+h}) \mid I_t) dx \tag{1.22}$$

where α is the corresponding probability for the desired confidence level, h is the horizon, and $P(S_{t+h}|I_t)$ is the forecasted probability of the regime S at the end of the horizon, which can be obtained from the Hamilton filter [see Hamilton (1994)].

B. Regime-Switching Beta Models

In regime-switching beta models (RSBM) we capture hedge fund exposure to market and other risk factors based on the state of the market, S_{mt}. In the simplest case, where market (β) and other risk factor (θ) exposures are based on switching of only one market risk factor (r_{mt}), we obtain the following model:

$$\begin{cases} r_{mt} = \mu_m(S_{mt}) + \sigma_m(S_{mt}) \\ r_{it} = \mu_i(S_{it}) + \beta(S_{mt})r_{mt} + \sum_{K-1}^{K} \theta_k(S_{mt})F_{k,t} + \sigma_i(S_{it}) \end{cases} \tag{1.23}$$

where i indicates a hedge fund strategy, m is the market risk factor, ε_t and ε_{it} are both $IIN(0, 1)$ distributed, and S_{mt} and S_{it} are independent Markov chains related to the market risk factor and the hedge fund strategy, respectively.

The VaR in this case is defined as

$$\alpha = \sum_{S_{m,t+h}} \sum_{S_{i,t+h}} P(S_{m,t+h}, S_{i,t+h} \mid I_t) \int_{-\infty}^{\mathrm{VaR}_t} N(x, \mu(S_{m,t+h}, S_{i,t+h} \mid I_t),$$

$$\sigma^2(S_{m,t+h}, S_{i,t+h} \mid I_t))dx \tag{1.24}$$

Evaluation

As discussed in Kupiec (1995) and Lopez (1997) a variety of tests are available to test the null hypothesis that the observed probability of occurrence over a reporting period equals to a. In other words, a measures the number of exceptions observed in the data, i.e., the number of times the observed returns are lower than VaR. In our work two evaluation methods are used in evaluating VaR model accuracy: the proportion of failure (PF) test (Kupiec, 1995) and the time until first failure (TUFF) test (Kupiec, 1995).

The first test is based on the binomial probability distribution of observing x exceptions in the sample size T. In particular,

$$\Pr(x; a, T) = \binom{T}{x} a^x (1 - a)^{(T-x)} \qquad (1.25)$$

Value at risk estimates must exhibit that their unconditional coverage, measured by $\hat{a} = x/T$ equals the desired coverage level a_0 (that corresponds to the VaR confidence level α). Thus the relevant null hypothesis is $H_0 : a = a_0$, and the appropriate likelihood ratio statistic is

$$LR_{PF} = 2\left[\ln\left(a^x (1 - a)^{(T-x)} \right) - \ln\left(a_0^x (1 - a_0)^{(T-x)} \right) \right] \qquad (1.26)$$

which is asymptotically distributed as a $X^2(1)$ distribution.

The TUFF test is based on the number of observations we get before the first exception. The relevant null hypothesis is still $H_0 : a = a_0$ and the likelihood ratio statistic is

$$LR_{TUFF}(\tilde{T}, \hat{a}) = -2\ln\left[\left(\hat{a}(1 - \hat{a})^{(\tilde{T}-1)} \right) + 2\ln\left(\frac{1}{\tilde{T}} \left(1 - \frac{1}{\tilde{T}} \right)^{\tilde{T}-1} \right) \right] \qquad (1.27)$$

Here $\tilde{T}$ is a random variable that indicates the number of observations before an exception. Also the LR_{TUFF} test has an asymptotic $X^2(1)$ distribution.

Unfortunately, as Kupiec (1995) observed, these tests have a limited ability in distinguishing among alternative hypotheses. However, these approaches have been followed by regulators in the analysis of internal models to define the zones into which the different models are categorized in backtesting, i.e, green (safe), yellow (cautious), and red (prone to crisis).

DATA

For the empirical analysis, we use aggregate hedge-fund index returns from the CSFB/Tremont database from January 1994 to January 2008 (a total of 169 observations). The Appendix provides detailed descriptions of all hedge fund strategies considered.

The CSFB/Tremont indices are asset-weighted indices of funds with a minimum of $10 million of assets under management, a minimum one-year track record, and current audited financial statements. An aggregate index is computed from this universe, and 10 subindices based on investment style are also computed using a similar method. Indices are computed and rebalanced on a monthly frequency and the universe of funds is redefined on a quarterly basis. We use net-of-fee monthly returns. This database accounts for survivorship bias in hedge funds (Fung and Hsieh, 2000). Table 1.1 describes the sample size, annualized mean, annualized standard deviation, skewness, excess kurtosis, Sharpe ratio, minimum, and maximum using monthly CSFB/Tremont hedge fund index returns.

We concentrate on directional strategies such as dedicated short bias, long/short equity, and emerging markets as well as nondirectional strategies such as distressed, event-driven multistrategy, equity market neutral, convertible bond, and risk arbitrage (see Appendix for detailed strategy descriptions).

T A B L E   1.1

Statistics for CSFB/Tremont Hedge Fund Index returns

	Ann. Mean	Ann. Std. Dev.	Skewness	Excess Kurtosis	Sharpe Ratio	Min	Max
Convertible bond arbitrage	6.11	4.51	−1.36	0.45	0.39	−5.04	3.10
Dedicated short bias	−3.74	16.79	0.82	−0.92	−0.06	−9.12	22.31
Emerging markets	11.85	15.58	−0.76	2.20	0.22	−23.43	16.04
Equity market neutral	5.91	2.74	0.18	−2.32	0.62	−1.58	2.83
Event-driven MS	8.15	5.57	−3.24	21.21	0.42	−12.17	3.43
Distressed	8.75	6.17	−2.84	16.77	0.41	−12.85	3.81
Risk arbitrage	3.50	4.05	−1.13	3.69	0.25	−6.55	3.38
Long/short equity	7.46	9.83	0.12	1.21	0.22	−11.83	12.58

Categories greatly differ. For example, annualized mean of excess return for the dedicated short seller category is the lowest: -3.74 percent, and the annualized standard deviation is the highest at 16.79 percent per month. Emerging Markets has the highest mean, 11.85 percent. The lowest annualized standard deviation is reported for the equity market neutral strategy at 2.74 percent with an annualized mean of 5.91 percent. Hedge fund strategies also show different third and fourth moments. Specifically, nondirectional funds such as event-driven multistrategy, risk arbitrage, convertible bond arbitrage, and equity market neutral all have negative skewness and high excess kurtosis. Directional strategies such as dedicated short seller, long/short equity have positive skewness and small excess kurtosis. Emerging Markets strategy has a slight negative skewness of -0.76 and a small excess kurtosis.

RESULTS AND DISCUSSION

We split the sample of 169 observations into two samples: (1) 133 observations and (2) remaining 36 observations. The first step in the empirical analysis is the estimation of all models (GARCH, IGARCH, CF, SRSM, and RSBM) presented above using 133 observations of the data set. For the regime-switching models, we assume that Markov chains (S_t and S_{it}) have two states (0, 1), and the Markov chain describing the dynamics of the market risk factor (S_{mt}) has three states, following Billio et al. (2008). For all models, we estimate relevant parameters using a MLE approach (in particular, the Hamilton's filter for the regime-switching models is used).

Since the RSBM model takes into account different risk factors, when results from this model are compared against other models, the same factor specifications are used for all models (except for the CF method). Thus, in the mean of these models, we add the exposure to the market risk factor (represented by the return on the Standard & Poor's 500 index), and for the RSBM we also add other risk factors that have been identified as relevant[1] in modeling hedge fund exposure following Billio et al. (2008). Value at risk for all these models has been computed conditional on the

---

[1] These risk factors are large-small, value growth, USD, Lehman Government Credit, term spread, change in VIX, credit spread, gold, MSCI Emerging Markets Bond Index, MSCI Emerging Markets Stock Index, and momentum.

market risk factor knowledge. In all models, market risk factor and hedge fund strategy returns are in excess of a three-month T-Bill.

For the regime-switching models, in order to determine forecasted return distributions, we need to know actual regimes for the Markov chains S_t, S_{it}, and S_{mt}. The probabilistic inference of being in one regime can be calculated for each date t of the sample using the Hamilton's filter. For an illustrative purpose, the resulting series for the convertible bond arbitrage strategy are shown in Figure 1.1. It is easy to observe how rapidly the probability of switching from one regime (in this case Markov chain S_{it} is considered) to another changes over time. This demonstrates the ability of the regime-switching model to capture the effect of potential changes in the volatility of returns.

The second step in the empirical analysis is the estimation of VaR for different strategies. For this step, the out-of-sample of remaining 36 observations is used. We estimate the next period rolling VaR at 1, 2.5, 5, and 10 percent levels of significance.[2]

F I G U R E   1.1

Smoothed Probabilities of Being in the High Volatility Regime ( ) for the Convertible Bond Arbitrage Strategy

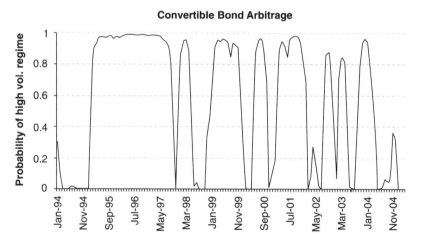

_____

[2] This out-of-sample analysis also includes the recent subprime crisis of August 2007 and the aftermath of the crisis in the fall 2007 and 2008.

To analyze the results of our different models, we perform a back-testing analysis, i.e., we analyze the number of exceptions (the number of times the observed returns are lower than VaR estimated by a model) observed in the 36 months. The goodness-of-fit test is applied to the null hypothesis that the frequency of such exceptions is equal to 1, 2.5, 5, and 10 percent with respect to the different VaR estimations.

Here we present the results for the emerging markets and dedicated short bias strategies.[3] Specifically, in Figure 1.2 we present excess returns and VaR estimates at the 5 percent level for different models (GARCH, IGARCH, CF, SRSM, and RSBM) for these two strategies.

According to Figure 1.2, it is clear that for both strategies, especially the emerging markets, the CF model largely overestimates the true risk of the strategies and is not in line with the dynamics of underlying returns.

Note: The number of failures (exceptions) for each hedge fund strategy is plotted for different degrees of confidence for each model. GARCH, IGARCH, CF, SRSM, and RSBM are considered. Each point on the graphs represents a unique hedge fund strategy. Dedicated short bias, long/short equity, emerging markets, distressed, event-driven multistrategy, equity market neutral, convertible bond arbitrage, and risk arbitrage strategies are considered.

The other four models are more close to the dynamics of the underlying returns and therefore better capture hedge fund return and risk dynamics. The model that captures these dynamics the best is the RSBM approach. The SRSM is not performing quite as well. The intuition behind this result is that it is not enough for a model to capture changes in volatility of hedge fund strategy returns. It is imperative to capture dynamic risk exposures of hedge fund strategy returns to market and other risk factors in order to correctly model hedge fund returns and estimate VaR. The RSBM is able to capture the dynamics of hedge fund returns and, in particular, the impact of the recent subprime crisis (August 2007 and the aftermath stretching into the fall of 2007 and 2008) on the emerging markets strategy.

Furthermore, to provide an analysis of the number of failures or exceptions (where VaR estimated by a model is lower than an observed

---

[3] Results for other strategies are not presented but available upon request.

F I G U R E   1.2

VaR at 95% Level for GARCH, IGARCH, Cornish-Fisher (CF), Simple Regime-Switching Model (SRSM), and Regime-Switching Beta Model (RSBM) for Emerging Markets and Dedicated Short Bias Strategy Returns.

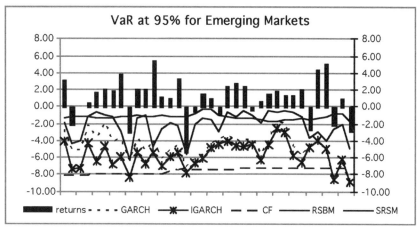

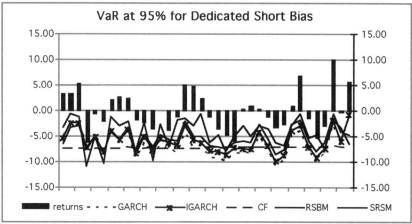

return) in Figure 1.3, we report results for backtesting analysis for all our models and hedge fund strategies at different confidence levels.

Figure 1.3 represents the percentage of failures (where VaR estimated by a model is lower than an observed return) at different confidence levels for GARCH, IGARCH, CF, SRSM, and RSBM. The models that better

FIGURE   1.3

Backtesting Over 36 Observations

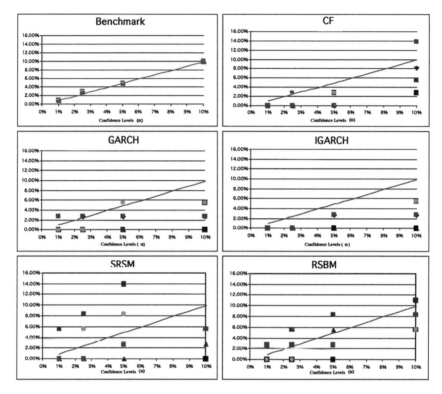

measure the VaR for different hedge fund strategies are the ones that resemble or are close to the benchmark case where the percentage of failures equals to a corresponding confidence level. For example, in the benchmark case, 5 percent failure rate corresponds to the 5 percent confidence level of a model.

As Figure 1.3 shows, the level of dispersion of the percentage of failures for different hedge fund strategies is quite large for the CF model at the 10 percent level. For some strategies the CF model overperforms, i.e., the VaR estimation is larger than the benchmark case and therefore the number of failures is lower than theoretically expected. For some other strategies the CF model underperforms, i.e., the VaR is lower than the benchmark case and the number of failures is larger than the one theoretically expected. For the other confidence levels, the model systematically overestimates the VaR by providing values that do not generate the number of failures in line with the confidence level.

The GARCH and the IGARCH models are performing better compared to the CF model, i.e., the percentages of failures are more in line with the benchmark percentages, but still both models overestimate the VaR. The SRSM, as Figure 1.3 also shows, is not performing very well; however, it is not systematically under- or overestimating the VaR.

The RSBM model performs the best and presents the lowest number of overestimation and is quite in line with the theoretical benchmark case. This result confirms that it is extremely important to consider both the changes in the volatility as well as the dynamic exposures to risk factors in order to capture risk of hedge fund strategies.

We consider different evaluation methods to evaluate our VaR results—the PF test and the TUFF test. As Kupiec (1995) observed, these tests have a limited ability in distinguishing among alternative hypotheses. Unfortunately, the out-of sample period we are considering is very limited due to the monthly frequency of the available sample, and therefore the power of these tests is not so high. In most of the cases, in line with Kupiec (1995), the tests are not able to disentangle among the different models, and in some cases we cannot compute the tests, since there are no failures. However, in some cases these tests are able to disentangle among the different models.[4] We find that the RSBM never fails to accept the null hypothesis that the number of failures is in line with the benchmark case (the PF test). On the contrary, we find rejections for other models. The SRSM is performing poorly, and for almost all strategies it has been rejected at least at the 10 percent level. The GARCH presents failures for three strategies at the 10 percent level: long/short equity, distressed, and convertible bond arbitrage; the IGARCH presents failures for three strategies at the 10 percent level: long/short equity, risk arbitrage, and distressed; and CF presents failures again for three strategies at the 10 percent level: dedicated short bias,

---

[4] Results for the PF and the TUFF tests for each strategy are not reported, but they are available upon request.

emerging markets, and event-driven multistrategies. Regarding the TUFF test, we find that all models have some rejections for equity market neutral, event-driven multistrategies, and distressed. Therefore, for the TUFF we have that the RSBM and the IGARCH perform quite well, and in most of the cases the RSBM presents higher p-values.

CONCLUSION

Risk management for alternative investments is an important issue. In this chapter we have shown that the use of models based on dynamic factor loadings like the regime-switching models are able to capture hedge fund tail risk exposure. Surprisingly, even if hedge fund returns typically exhibit highly nonnormal returns with significant negative skewness and excess kurtosis, the CF approach is performing quite poorly since it is overestimating the risk of different hedge fund strategies. GARCH and IGARCH models that capture both risk exposures and dynamics of return volatility are performing relatively better. The SRSM is performing poorly, and the RSBM is performing very well and does not over or underestimate the risk exposures and never rejects the null hypothesis for the PF test. These results indicate that it is fundamental for the VaR measurement of hedge funds to include dynamic risk exposures to market and other relevant risk factors. This aspect has been almost ignored in the previous literature.

REFERENCES

Agarwal, V. and Naik, N.Y. (2004) Risks and Portfolio Decisions Involving Hedge Funds. *Review of Financial Studies*, 17(1): 63–98.

Bali, T.G., Gokcan, S., and Liang, B. (2007) Value-at-Risk and the Cross-section of Hedge Fund. Returns. *Journal of Banking and Finance*, 31(4): 1135–1166.

Billio, M., Getmansky, M., and Pelizzon, L. (2008) Crises and Hedge Fund Risk. University of Massachusetts, Amherst, MA, Working Paper.

Billio, M. and Pelizzon, L. (2000) Value-at-Risk: A Multivariate Switching Regime Approach. *Journal of Empirical Finance*, 7(5): 531–554.

Boyson, N.M., Stahel, C.W., and Stulz, R.M. (2007) Is There Hedge Fund Contagion? Northeastern University, Working Paper.

Brealey, R. and Kaplanis, E. (2001) Hedge Funds and Financial Stability: An Analysis of Their Factor Exposures. *Journal of International Finance*, 4(2): 161–187.

Chan, N.T., Getmansky, M., Haas, S.M, and Lo, A.W. (2005) Systemic Risk and Hedge Funds. *NBER Book on Risks of Financial Institutions*, Topic: Systemic Risk.

Edwards, F.R. and Caglayan, M.O. (2001) Hedge Fund Performance and Manager Skill. *Journal of Futures Markets*, 21(11): 1003–1028.

Fung, W. and Hsieh, D.A. (1997) Empirical Characteristics of Dynamic Trading Strategies: The Case of Hedge Funds. *Review of Financial Studies*, 10(2): 275–302.

Fung, W. and Hsieh, D.A. (2000) Performance Characteristics of Hedge Funds and Commodity Funds: Natural versus Spurious Biases. *Journal of Financial and Quantitative Analysis*, 35(3): 291–307.

Fung, W. and Hsieh, D.A. (2001) The Risk in Hedge Fund Strategies: Theory and Evidence from Trend Followers. *Review of Financial Studies*, 14(2): 313–341.

Fung, W. and Hsieh, D. A. (2002) Asset-Based Style Factors for Hedge Funds. *Financial Analysts Journal*, 58(5): 16–27.

Getmansky, M., Lo, A.W., and Makarov, I. (2004) An Econometric Analysis of Serial Correlation and Illiquidity in Hedge-Fund Returns. *Journal of Financial Economics,* 74 (3): 529–610.

Gupta, A. and Liang, B. (2005) Do hedge funds have enough capital? A Value-at-Risk Approach. *Journal of Financial Economics*, 77(1): 219–253.

Hamilton, J.D. (1994) *Time Series Analysis*. Princeton, NJ: Princeton University Press.

Koski, J.L. and Pontiff, J. (1999) How Are Derivatives Used? Evidence from the Mutual Fund Industry. *Journal of Finance*, 54(2): 791–816.

Liang, B. and Park, H. (2007) Risk Measures for Hedge Funds: A Cross Sectional Approach. *European Financial Management,* 13(2): 333–370.

Mitchell, M. and Pulvino, T. (2001) Characteristics of Risk and Return in Risk Arbitrage. *Journal of Finance*, 56(6): 2135–2175.

Schneeweis, T., Karavas, V., and Georgiev, G. (2002) Alternative Investments in the Institutional Portfolio. University of Massachusetts, Amherst, MA, Working Paper.

APPENDIX: STRATEGY DESCRIPTIONS

Convertible bond arbitrage managers seek to profit from investments in convertible securities employing both single security and portfolio hedging strategies. Managers typically build long positions of convertible and other equity hybrid securities and then hedge the equity component of the long securities positions by shorting the underlying stock or options of that company. Interest rate, volatility, and credit hedges may also be employed. Hedge ratios need to be adjusted as markets move, and positions are typically designed with the objective of creating profit opportunities irrespective of market moves.

Dedicated short bias managers seek to profit from maintaining overall net short portfolios of long and short equities. Detailed individual company research typically forms the core alpha generation driver of short bias managers, and a focus on companies with weak cash flow generation is common. Risk management consists of offsetting long positions and stop-loss strategies. The fact that money-losing short positions grow in size for a short bias manager makes risk management challenging.

Emerging markets managers seek to profit from investments in currencies, debt instruments, equities, and other instruments of "emerging" markets countries (typically measured by GDP per capita). Emerging markets include countries in Latin America, Eastern Europe, Africa, and Asia. There are a number of subsectors, including arbitrage, credit and event driven, fixed-income bias, and equity bias.

Equity market neutral managers seek to profit from exploiting pricing relationships between different equities or related securities while typically hedging exposure to overall equity market moves. There are a number of subsectors including statistical arbitrage, quantitative long/short, fundamental long/short, and index arbitrage. Managers often apply leverage to enhance returns.

Event-driven multistrategy has an objective to provide an estimate of the rate of return to event-driven multistrategy managers who attempt to seek to capitalize on investment opportunities relating to specific corporate events, such as spin-offs and restructurings, and other potential firm-based actions.

Distressed high-yield securities (also known as *distressed security and opportunities*) fund managers in this nontraditional strategy invest in the debt, equity, or trade claims of companies in financial distress or already in default. The securities of companies in distressed or defaulted situations typically trade at substantial discounts to par value due to difficulties in analyzing a proper value for such securities, lack of street coverage, or simply an inability on behalf of traditional investors to accurately value such claims or direct their legal interests during restructuring proceedings. Various strategies have been developed by which investors may take hedged or outright short positions in such claims, although this asset class is, in general, a long-only strategy.

Risk (merger) arbitrage invests simultaneously long and short in the companies involved in a merger or acquisition. Risk arbitrageurs are typically long the stock of the company being acquired and short the stock of the acquirer. By shorting the stock of the acquirer, the manager hedges out market risk and isolates his or her exposure to the outcome of the announced deal. In cash deals, the manager needs only long the acquired company. The principal risk is deal risk, should the deal fail to close. Risk arbitrageurs also often invest in equity restructurings such as spin-offs or "stub trades."

Long/short equity (also known as *equity hedge*) managers seek to profit from investing on both the long and short sides of equity markets. Managers have the ability to shift from value to growth, from small to medium to large capitalization stocks, and from net long to net short.

Managers can change their exposures from net long to net short or market neutral at times. In addition to equities, long/short managers can trade equity futures and options as well as equity-related securities and debt. Manager focus may be global, regional, or sector specific, such as technology, healthcare, or financials. Managers tend to build portfolios that are more concentrated than traditional long-only equity funds.

CHAPTER 2

Efficient VaR: Using Past Forecast Performance to Generate Improved VaR Forecasts

Kevin Dowd and Carlos Blanco

ABSTRACT

This chapter proposes a method of "improving" future VaR forecasts by making use of the information in the VaR model's past forecast record. The resulting VaR forecasts are efficient in a sense reminiscent of efficient financial markets and provide a natural benchmark against which to assess future VaR forecasts.

INTRODUCTION

Value-at-risk modeling involves three main steps that follow each other in a natural order: we first calibrate the model; we then use the calibrated model to forecast VaR; and we end by evaluating the model's forecasts ex post. The steps involved are shown in Figure 2.1, where we implicitly assume that our VaR model is a parametric one.

At first sight the steps involved and the links between them seem natural enough: forecasting follows calibration, and backtesting follows forecasting. However, when one thinks of these steps in terms of a flow chart, what is striking about the figure is the absence of a feedback loop

F I G U R E   2.1

Steps Involved in VaR Modelling

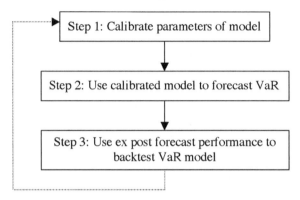

from step 3 back to step 1. If the model performs well at the backtesting stage, then all is well, but what if it performs poorly? The standard advice is that if the model performs poorly in step 3, then we might suspect there is something wrong with it and should start to think again about it. Unfortunately, this is not particularly informative or helpful to the model builder, because it gives him or her little real idea what might be wrong with the model's forecasts.

Moreover, most backtests rely on formal hypothesis tests that give the VaR model the benefit of the doubt: We assume the model is correct to start with and only regard the model as having "failed" once a reasonably sized sample of observations has been accumulated and backtests have suggested that the hypothesis of forecast adequacy is implausible. To put the same point in another context, if we suspect that the horse has gone, we don't rush out to check the stable; instead, we wait and make absolutely sure it has gone before we go out to bolt the stable door.

Yet the advice to "wait and make sure" must be inefficient: it must be possible to use information from backtest results to guide us in re-specifying our model. If a backtest exercise reveals *any* evidence of model inadequacy, whether statistically significant or not, surely that information is valuable and can be used to help improve future VaR forecasts? And why should we wait and accumulate enough evidence for the model to fail a backtest before we decide to act? Can we not apply less demanding standards of evidence and act sooner?

The answers to these questions are self-evidently affirmative, and the present chapter suggests a way in which backtest information might be used to improve model forecasts. The approach suggested is very simple and builds on a well established approach to backtesting; it also leads to some simple rules that can be used to "correct" parameter calibrations so that they take account of evidence of past forecast inadequacies. Using these rules leads to VaR forecasts that are efficient in that they take full account of the information embodied in a model's past forecasting record, i.e., a VaR model's forecasts are efficient if it is not possible to use the information in the model's track record to improve those forecasts. This gives us an implementable criterion for efficient VaR forecasts, analogous to the familiar notion of asset price efficiency (or efficient financial markets): this criterion not only allows us to determine if a model's forecasts are efficient given the information in its past track record, but it also allows us correct its forecasts if they are not efficient.

This chapter is organized as follows. The second section in this chapter sets out a backtesting framework that generates information about possible model inadequacy. The third section shows how we might use this information to improve the calibration of our VaR model, and hence improve future VaR forecasts. This chapter's fourth section gives some examples of the calculations involved, and the final two sections discuss some of the issues raised by efficient VaR forecasts and conclude the chapter.

A BACKTESTING FRAMEWORK

Suppose we have a model that on each day $t-1$ produces forecasts of the day-t distribution function of the losses on a portfolio.[1] Denote the forecasted distribution function (or cumulative density function) of day-t losses as $F_t(.)$. Let us assume to begin with that $F_t(.)$ is normal with

---

[1] For the sake of convenience, we focus on 1-step ahead forecasts in which forecasts are made 1-day ahead and the forecast-observation cycle is complete before the next forecasts are made.

mean μ_t and standard deviation σ_t.[2] The distribution function $F_t(.)$ is defined over a domain that can be regarded as the set of all possible loss quantiles (or VaRs over all possible confidence levels). The day-t VaR forecast at the p confidence level is then given by the quantile q_t in Equation (2.1):

$$p = F_t(q_t) \Rightarrow q_t = F_t^{-1}(p) \tag{2.1}$$

So, for example, if $p = 0.95$, then $q_t = F_t^{-1}(0.95)$.

Now suppose that we have a data set consisting of a set of density forecasts for days $t = t - n, \ldots, t - 1$ and a set of corresponding realized losses X_t for the same days. Positive values of X_t correspond to actual realised losses and negative values correspond to realized profits.

We can now run the realised values X_t through the Probability Integral Transformation (or PIT)

$$p_t = F_t(X_t) \quad t = t - n, \ldots, t - 1 \tag{2.2}$$

to give us a set of n realized values of p_t which are predicted to independent and identically distributed (i.i.d.) U(0,1) under the null hypothesis of model adequacy.[3] If we wished to, we could then test this prediction directly using textbook tests of standard uniformity (e.g., Kolmogorov-Smirnov, Lilliefors, Kuiper, Anderson-Darling, etc.), but testing is often more convenient if we transform p_t so that they become i.i.d N(0,1) under the null. To do so, we put p_t through the following transformation suggested by Berkowitz (2001):

$$z_t = \Phi^{-1}(p_t) \tag{2.3}$$

Under the null, z_t is predicted to be i.i.d N(0,1), so we can test the performance of the model by testing the z_t for i.i.d N(0,1), and we can

---

[2] The distribution function $F_t(.)$ and the parameters have a t subscript because the precise calibration of the model will typically differ from one day to the next as the model parameters are updated on a daily basis.

[3] As explained, e.g., in Diebold et al. (1998), the PIT series p_t are predicted to be i.i.d in the 1-step ahead case; they are not, however, predicted to be i.i.d in multistep ahead cases (e.g., where forecasts are made on a daily basis over horizons of 2 or more days). We prefer to avoid the complications that ensure in the multistep ahead case. For more on these, see, e.g., Dowd (2007).

do this by applying textbook tests of the predictions of N(0,1) (e.g., a *t*-test that z_t has a mean 0, a variance ratio test that z_t has a variance 1, a Jarque-Bera test that z_t is normal, etc.) and textbook tests that z_t is i.i.d (e.g., portmanteau tests, runs tests, BDS tests, etc.).

USING BACKTEST RESULTS TO RECALIBRATE THE PARAMETERS OF THE VaR MODEL

Now let us assume that we have obtained our z_t series and we find that z_t is not standard normal.[4] Let us also suppose that we are satisfied that z_t is normal or approximately so, but we find that at least one of the first two moments – either the mean or the variance – is not equal to its predicted value of 0 or 1.[5] This means that

$$z_t = \Phi^{-1}(p_t) \sim N(m_z, s_{\tilde{z}}^2) \tag{2.4}$$

where $m_z \neq 0$ and/or $s_z \neq 1$. It does not matter what the precise values of m_z and s_z are or we are not especially concerned whether these values are sufficiently different from 0 and 1 to fail statistical tests. What matters to us here is that the mean is not 0 and/or the variance is not 1, and we wish to use this information to improve our VaR forecasts.

We now define a standardized $z_t, \tilde{z}_t = (z_t - m_z)/s_z$, and note that Equation (2.4) implies

$$\tilde{z}_t \sim N(0,1) \tag{2.5}$$

This means that the first and second moments of $\tilde{z}_t$ have been "matched" to have exactly the correct first and second moments.[6] This

---

[4] We are not particularly interested here in the i.i.d. prediction so we do not discuss this any further here.

[5] We therefore restrict ourselves to correcting for first and second moment departures of the distribution of z_t from standard normality. The moment-matching approach suggested here can also be extended (though with some difficulty) to higher moment departures as well.

[6] This moment matching—and the term *moment matching* itself—has an obvious parallel in the moment matching sometimes used in Monte Carlo simulation introduced by Barraquand in 1995. In that context, moment matching involves adjusting the values of simulated random variables so that the simulated sample has exactly the correct first and sometimes second moments. This removes the effect of sampling variation from the simulated sample and, therefore, produces Monte Carlo estimates that are more accurate.

implies, in turn, there is a corresponding $\tilde{p}_t$ series that is distributed as standard uniform, viz.,

$$\tilde{p}_t = \Phi(\tilde{z}_t) \sim U\,(0,1) \tag{2.6}$$

However, it is also the case that

$$\tilde{p}_t = \Phi(\tilde{z}_t) = \Phi\left(\frac{z_t - m_z}{s_z}\right) = \Phi\left(\frac{\Phi^{-1}(p_t) - m_z}{s_z}\right) \tag{2.7}$$

If the original confidence level is p, we can use Equation (2.7) to obtain an "adjusted" confidence level $\tilde{p}$.[7] We do this by replacing p with p and $\tilde{p}_t$ with $\tilde{p}$ as follows:

$$\tilde{p} = \Phi\left(\frac{\Phi^{-1}(p) - m}{s}\right) \tag{2.8}$$

We can now insert $\tilde{p}$ into (1) in place of p to obtain the following adjusted VaR forecast

$$\tilde{p} = F_t(q_t) \Rightarrow q_t = F_t^{-1}\,(\tilde{p}) \tag{2.9}$$

Note that the actual VaR number remains the same, but what alters is the confidence level or cumulative probability on which the VaR is predicated: q_t is the VaR at the $\tilde{p}$ rather than the p confidence level.

To obtain the VaR at other confidence levels, we use the information in m_z and s_z to modify the parameters in our VaR model. Suppose therefore that our day t–1 VaR model postulates that next day losses are normal

---

[7] There are natural analogies here with the risk-neutralization pricing methods routinely used in finance and the distortion functions used in actuarial science applications (see Wang, (1996; ibid., 2000; ibid., 2002), and the transformed series $\tilde{p}$ can in fact be regarded as a form of risk-neutralised or distorted probability. In particular, Equation (2.8) bears a curious partial resemblance to the Wang transform $\tilde{p} = \Phi(\Phi^{-1}(p) - \lambda)$, where λ is the market price of risk. However, whereas risk-neutralised or distorted probabilities are usually used for pricing purposes, Equation (2.8) is used to estimate a risk measure and, where distortion functions are used to obtain the VaR [as in Wang (2002)], his VaR distortion function is a simple binary function instead of the 'smooth' function on the right-hand side of Equation (2.8).

with mean μ_t and variance σ^2_t. Our revised estimates of the mean and standard deviation of the loss distribution function are obtained using the following results derived in the Appendix:

$$\mu_t^* = \mu_t + \sigma_t m_z \tag{2.10a}$$

$$\sigma_t^* = \sigma_t s_z \tag{2.10b}$$

As of day t–1, our forecast of the day-t distribution function is then $N(\mu_t^*, \sigma_t^*)$ and the forecast of the VaR at the p confidence level is

$$\text{VaR} = \mu_t^* + \sigma_t^* \times \Phi^{-1}(p) = \mu_t + \sigma_t m_z + \sigma_t s_z \times \Phi^{-1}(p) \tag{2.11}$$

As an aside, we can also see that the impact of moment-matching depends on the values of m_z and s_z: applying the moment-matching rules Equations (2.10a) and (2.10.b) can increase or decrease our VaR estimates depending on the values of these parameters.[8]

To summarize the implementation: each day, the forecaster makes a "best effort" forecast of the mean and standard deviation of the next day's loss distribution: these give us values for μ_t and σ_t. These forecasts would be based on information set Ω_{t-1}. Let us also suppose that by day t–1, the forecaster has obtained Berkowitz values for the previous n days. The forecaster now calculates m_z and σ_z, and then uses Equations (2.10a) and (2.10b) to obtain the "improved" parameter forecasts μ_t^* and σ_t^*.

SOME EXAMPLES

Example 1

It might help to illustrate this analysis with some examples. Suppose, therefore, that at day $t - 1$, we have a normal VaR model predicated on a mean loss of 0 and a loss standard deviation of 1. Unbeknownst to us, the true distribution is a normal with a mean of 1 and a standard deviation

---

[8] There is also another familiar analogy here. Given the parameters of the VaR model, the first two moments of z_t can also be interpreted as giving us "implied portfolio views" sometimes found in risk management [see Litterman (1999)]. They are also somewhat analogous to the implied volatility and implied correlations often found in derivatives pricing.

of 1. We are interested in the VaR at the 95 percent confidence level and use the model calibrated on a mean of 0 and a standard deviation of 1 to incorrectly estimate the VaR as

$$\text{Estimated VaR} = \mu + \sigma \times \Phi^{-1}(p) = \Phi^{-1}(0.95) = 1.6445 \qquad (2.12)$$

Now note, as an aside, that the unknown to us true VaR is

$$\text{True VaR} = \mu_t + \sigma_t \times \Phi^{-1}(p) = 1 + \Phi^{-1}(0.95) = 2.6445 \qquad (2.13)$$

We now obtain the z_t series, and find that this has a mean and standard deviation both equal to 1, consistent with the true but unknown loss distribution. We now calibrate Equation (2.10) to obtain

$$\tilde{p} = \Phi\left(\frac{\Phi^{-1}(p) - m_z}{s_z}\right) = \Phi\left(\frac{\Phi^{-1}(0.95) - 1}{1}\right) = 0.6449 \qquad (2.14)$$

This tells us that the quantity 1.6449 is the VaR at the 64.49 percent confidence level rather the VaR at the 95 percent confidence level.

We now apply Equation (2.10) to adjust the parameters of our VaR model:

$$m_z^* = \mu_t + \sigma_t m_z = 1 \qquad (2.15a)$$

$$s_z^* = \sigma_t s_z = 1 \qquad (2.15b)$$

and these estimates now match the parameters of the unknown true distribution.[9] Using these parameter values will then give us correct estimates of the VaR. We now input these parameter values into Equation (2.16) to correctly estimate the VaR at the 95 percent confidence level:

$$\text{Revised VaR} = m^* + s^* \Phi^{-1} \times (p) = 1 + \Phi^{-1}(0.95) = 2.6445 \qquad (2.16)$$

---

[9] Under "reasonable" conditions, these estimators should also have the attractive properties of being unbiased, consistent, and statistically efficient.

FIGURE 2.2

Illustrative Moment-Matching (I)

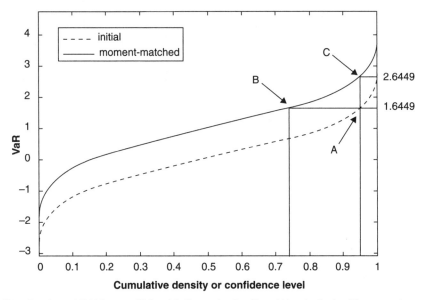

Notes: Based on an initial false normal VaR model with mean loss 0 and loss std 1, and estimates of the mean and standard deviation of both being 1 reflecting an unknown true loss distribution that is normal with both mean and std equal to 1.

The calculations are illustrated in Figure 2.2. We select our initial confidence level (0.95) and then use our VaR model to estimate the VaR as 1.6449: this combination of VaR and confidence level is shown as point A. We then moment-match the confidence level to obtain a revised confidence level of 0.7405, and the VaR at this confidence level is shown as point B. After this, we adjust the parameters of the model and obtain the true VaR at the 95 percent confidence level at point C.

Example 2

We now suppose a slightly more "realistic" example. Suppose we have a normal VaR model predicated on a mean loss of 5/250 and a loss standard deviation of $\sqrt{20/250}$. We are again interested in the VaR at the 95 percent

confidence level and use the model calibrated on these parameter values
to incorrectly estimate the VaR as

$$\text{Estimated VaR} = \mu_t + \sigma_t \times \Phi^{-1}(p) = \frac{5}{250} + \sqrt{\frac{20}{250}}$$
$$\times \Phi^{-1}(0.95) = 0.4852 \qquad (2.17)$$

We now obtain z_t, and find that this series has a mean 0.04 and standard deviation 1.4. We then calibrate (7) to obtain

$$\tilde{p} = \Phi\left(\frac{\Phi^{-1}(p) - m_z}{s_z}\right) = \Phi\left(\frac{\Phi^{-1}(0.95) - 0.04}{1.4}\right) = 0.8742 \qquad (2.18)$$

which tells us that the quantity 0.4852 is the VaR at the 87.42 percent confidence level.

We now apply Equation (2.8) to adjust the parameters of our
VaR model:

$$m_z^* = \frac{5}{250} + \sqrt{\frac{20}{250}} \times 0.04 = 0.0313 \qquad (2.19a)$$

$$s_z^* = \sqrt{\frac{20}{250}} \times 1.4 = 0.3960 \qquad (2.19b)$$

and then use Equation (2.9) to correctly estimate the VaR at the 95 percent
confidence level:

$$\text{Revised VaR} = 0.0313 + 0.3960 \times \Phi^{-1}(0.95)$$
$$= 1 + \Phi^{-1}(0.95) = 0.6826 \qquad (2.20)$$

These calculations are illustrated in Figure 2.3.

Example 3

As a third example, suppose that we wish to forecast the VaR using the
following GARCH model:

F I G U R E   2.3

Illustrative Moment-Matching (II)

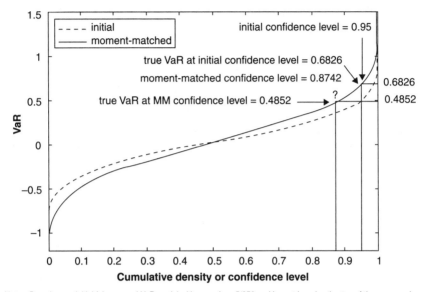

Notes: Based on an initial false normal VaR model with mean loss 5/250 and loss std, and estimates of the mean and
standard deviation of being 0.04 and 1.4 reflecting an unknown true loss distribution that is normal with mean 0.0313
and std equal to 0.3960.

$$r_t = \mu_t + \varepsilon_t \tag{2.21a}$$

$$\sigma_t^2 = \alpha_t \times \varepsilon_{t-1}^2 + \beta_t \times \sigma_{t-1}^2 \tag{2.21b}$$

where the noise process ε_t is normal[10] and the parameters μ_t, α_t, and β_t
take the values $0, 0.05,$ and $0.90,$ respectively. We also have an initial values
$\varepsilon_{t-1} = 0.02$ and $\sigma_{t-1} = 0.02$. Thus, the model postulates that
$\varepsilon_t \sim N(\mu_t, \sigma_t^2)$, where $\mu_t = 0$ and $\sigma_t^2 = 0.05 \times 0.02^2 + 0.90 \times 0.02^2 \approx$
1.95%. Now suppose that we obtain our z_t series and find that this has a mean
0.03 and a standard deviation 1.1. Applying Equation (2.10), we then obtain

$$\mu_t^* = \mu_t + \sigma_t m_z = 0.0195 \times 0.03 = 0.058\% \tag{2.22a}$$

---

[10] The analysis would follow similar lines had we assumed an alternative process such as a t. The
only difference would have been to use the t-VaR formula in Equation (2.24) rather the
normal VaR formula actually used.

$$\sigma^*_t = \sigma_t s_z = 0.0195 \times 1.1 \approx 2.15\% \qquad (2.22b)$$

Putting all this together, our model therefore makes the following forecast

$$r_t \sim N(0.058\%, 2.15\%) \qquad (2.23)$$

and the VaR at the 95 percent confidence level is[11]

$$\text{VaR} = -0.058\% + 2.15\% \times \Phi^{-1}(p) = -0.058\%$$
$$+ 2.15\% \times 1.6449 \approx 3.59\% \qquad (2.24)$$

CONCLUSION

The parameter-improvement procedure proposed here makes use of all the information present in the $z_{t-n}, \ldots, z_{t-1}$ sample. Therefore, given the assumption that the parametric form of the loss function has been correctly identified, we can say that implementing this rule will produce parameter forecasts that lead to efficient VaR forecasts conditional on the information set $\{\Omega_{t-1}, z_{t-n}, \ldots, z_{t-1}\}$. In other words, VaR forecasts can be said to be efficient, conditional on this information set, if they satisfy Equation (2.10), and VaR forecasts that do not satisfy this condition are inefficient.

This notion of efficient VaR forecasts is a natural analogue of the notion of efficient markets that is one of the centrepieces of modern finance: In the latter case, markets are efficient if it is not possible to predict future price changes. In the former case, VaR forecasts are efficient if it is not possible to use available information to improve them.

Efficient VaR forecasts also provide natural default forecasts. Most of the time, a VaR modeler will not have strong views about unusual developments in the market, and in such cases the modeler would be advised to go with the efficient VaR forecasts because he or she does not have any reason to do anything else. However, in those circumstances

---

[11] Note that the mean term in Equation (2.24) enters with a negative return because the model forecasts returns rather than losses.

where the modeler has other information (which might only take the form of a strong hunch), then she or he might decide to depart from the efficient VaR forecasts in an effort to make use of this additional information that is not reflected in the efficient VaR forecasts. Nevertheless, even in this case, the efficient forecasts provide a useful benchmark and help to discipline the modeling process: any departures from the efficient ones would have to be justified by reference to the additional information.[12]

REFERENCES

Barraquand, J. (1995) Numerical Valuation of High Dimensional Multivariate European Securities. *Management Science,* 41(12): 1882–1891.

Berkowitz, J. (2001) Testing Density Forecasts, with Applications to Risk Management. *Journal of Business and Economic Statistics,* 19(4): 465–474.

Dowd, K. (2007) Temporal Dependence in Multi-Step Density Forecasting Models. *Journal of Risk Model Validation,* 1(1): 1–20.

Litterman, R. (1996) Hot Spots and Hedges. *Journal of Portfolio Management,* 22(9): 52–75.

---

[12] The forecasting procedure proposed here also has some curious impacts on backtesting. As time passes after it is first implemented, the feedback loop from the backtests to the model calibration—from step 3 to step 1 in Figure 2.1—will gradually produce samples of z_t observations with nearly perfect means and variances. This means that any backtesting procedure based on the mean and variance of z_t will have nearly perfect scores, depending on the precise periods used. At one level, this is a very good thing as it means that the feedback loop is working. However, there is also a downside, in that it would make the mean and variance of z_t effectively useless for backtesting. If model inadequacy is to be detected, then the onus of detection would fall on other backtests. This raises a curious conundrum: If some other backtesting procedure detects information about model inadequacy that is overlooked by the z_t, then surely we would want to find some way to incorporate *that* information into our model recalibration. However, if we do so, we ensure that our forecasts do well against all backtests that have proved effective in the past, and consequently, we ensure that they will not prove effective in the future.

Wang, S.S. (1996) Premium Calculation by Transforming the Layer
    Premium Density. *ASTIN Bulletin* 26: 71–92.

Wang, S.S. (2000) A Class of Distortion Operators for Pricing Financial
    and Insurance Risks. *Journal of Risk and Insurance* 67: 15–36.

Wang, S.S. (2002) A Risk Measure that Goes Beyond Coherence.
    Mimeo. SCOR Reinsurance Co, Itasca IL.

APPENDIX

Suppose that we have a random loss variable X, which has a true distribution $N(\mu_B, \sigma_B^2)$, the parameters of which are unknown. The VaR modeler falsely believes that X is distributed as $N(\mu_A, \sigma_A^2)$ and regards the parameters μ_A and σ_A as known.

    Under the modeler's false beliefs, the Berkowitz-transformed variable is $z = (X - \mu_A)/\sigma_A$, and the modeler falsely believes z is distributed as $N(0, 1)$. Instead, it is the unobserved variable $z^* = (X - \mu_B)/\sigma_B$ that is distributed as $N(0, 1)$.

    Now note that

$$z = \frac{X - \mu_A}{\sigma_A} = \frac{\mu_B - \mu_A}{\sigma_A} + \frac{X - \mu_B}{\sigma_A} = \frac{\mu_B - \mu_A}{\sigma_A} + \left(\frac{\sigma_B}{\sigma_A}\right)\frac{(X - \mu_B)}{\sigma_B}$$

$$= \frac{\mu_B - \mu_A}{\sigma_A} + \left(\frac{\sigma_B}{\sigma_A}\right)z^* \Rightarrow z \sim \frac{\mu_B - \mu_A}{\sigma_A} \qquad (2A.1)$$

$$+ \left(\frac{\sigma_B}{\sigma_A}\right)N(0,1) \Rightarrow z \sim N\left(\frac{\mu_B - \mu_A}{\sigma_A}, \frac{\sigma_B^2}{\sigma_A^2}\right)$$

If the true mean and variance of z are μ_z and σ_z, it then follows that

$$\mu_z = \frac{\mu_B - \mu_A}{\sigma_A} \Rightarrow \mu_B = \mu_A + \sigma_A\mu_z \qquad (2A.2a)$$

$$\sigma_z^2 = \frac{\sigma_B^2}{\sigma_A^2} \Rightarrow \sigma_B = \sigma_A\sigma_z \qquad (2A.2b)$$

The true values of μ_z and σ_z are unknown, but if we now use m and s to denote estimates of the unknown means and standard deviations in Equation (2A.2), then we can substitute these estimates into Equation (2A.2) to obtain the following estimates of μ_B and σ_B

$$m_B = \mu_A + \sigma_A m_z \tag{2A.3a}$$

$$S_B = \sigma_A S_z \tag{A2.3b}$$

Thus, Equation (2A.3) enables us to use the estimates of m_z and s_z to obtain improved estimates of the parameters of the original VaR model and so improve our VaR forecasts.

Now note that Equations (2A.3a) and (2A.3b) will still hold even if X is not normal; so we can still use these expressions to adjust the mean and variance parameters of our VaR model even if that model is not normal: The only restriction is that the VaR model must have defined (i.e., finite) mean and variance parameters.

CHAPTER 3

Applying VaR to Hedge Fund Trading Strategies: Limitations and Challenges

R. McFall Lamm, Jr.

ABSTRACT

Value at risk (VaR) is often used as a control device for managing portfolio exposure to a predetermined risk budget. Even nontraditional market participants such as hedge funds are increasingly using the technique. This is paradoxical because many hedge fund strategies contain embedded risk-control mechanisms. In such cases, overlaying a VaR control system is duplicative. It can even be detrimental to investment performance when a tight risk budget is imposed. The extent of this effect is illustrated using two common hedge fund strategies—trend following and mean reversion. A major implication is that widely applying VaR control may produce a metamorphosis of the hedge fund industry into something fundamentally different from what it is today.

INTRODUCTION

The vast majority of banks and asset managers have long employed VaR systems to monitor and control market exposure. This makes a great deal of sense because it allows firms to explicitly quantify the risk they face in a single numeric measure that is easily understood. Although VaR is not perfect and has a dark side—most VaR systems employ short history that sometimes leads to unpleasant surprises—its merits are generally perceived to outweigh any intrinsic limitations.

In recent years the near universal acceptance of VaR has extended to new frontiers such as the hedge fund industry, which has experienced enormous growth and expansion. The motivation for adding VaR in the case of hedge funds does not come from individual managers themselves, however. Rather, it is institutional investors and consultants that have provided the impetus—they desire a familiar and well-known metric for appraising risk embedded in various trading strategies. The result is a situation where if hedge fund managers desire to raise new money, they must "tick the boxes" of due diligence reviews that virtually always require VaR.

Many hedge fund managers do not believe VaR is necessary because their trading systems contain built-in risk-control devices. In this regard, they view the addition of VaR for risk management as redundant. Furthermore, many hedge fund managers fear that if VaR is applied rigorously for risk-control purposes—that is, with a tight risk budget—it will mute performance by eviscerating the essence of particular trading strategies. This has led numerous hedge funds to implement "loose" VaR control systems that are little more than cosmetic.

In this chapter I attempt to determine whether applying stringent VaR control impairs hedge fund performance. Two basic hedge fund trading strategies are considered—trend following and mean reversion. I first present a brief topical review and then produce an unadulterated set of daily returns for each trading system over the 2005 to 2007 period. I then create a second series that incorporates a restrictive VaR risk limit, quantify the effects compared with the unconstrained systems, and then explore using varying horizons to set the risk budget. The key conclusion is that VaR control does in fact reduce both absolute and risk-adjusted returns by restricting market exposure precisely at times when the payoff to risk taking is high. This suggests that hedge fund managers may be correct in arguing that widespread application of tight VaR control systems may be deleterious.

BACKGROUND

The use of VaR has become entrenched and is now accepted as a near universal standard for risk measurement and control. This is despite the fact that different methods are sometimes used by system designers and that VaR has various conceptual shortcomings. For example, Jorion (2001) cites the Long Term Capital Management debacle in 1998 and notes that VaR is as much art as it is science. Nonetheless, VaR acceptance is so predominant that any other risk-control methodology is often viewed as heresy.

Even normally independently minded and audacious hedge fund managers are now caught up in a VaR embrace. The reason is that until recently the hedge fund industry was a small cottage industry that primarily served high net worth investors and endowments. However, the sharp equity market sell-off from 2000 to 2002, combined with arguments for investing in hedge funds by Edwards and Liew (1999), Lamm (1999), Swensen (2000), and others, stimulated interest in alternative investments. Once institutional consultants began to bless hedge fund investing, flows into hedge funds surged. By the end of 2007 hedge fund assets under management reached nearly $2.0 trillion according to Hedge Fund Research (2008). This represents a tripling over the past half decade (Figure 3.1).[1]

Institutional investment in hedge funds has not come without strings attached, however. In particular, hedge fund managers have been coerced by consultants to add VaR systems to meet standardized due diligence requirements for proper risk management and control. Traditional risk management techniques such as loss-limit trading, restrictions on sector or geographical market exposure, delta hedging, or other methods often employed by hedge funds are viewed as inadequate — to qualify for institutional investment, VaR has become necessary. In response, many hedge funds have added VaR control systems whether they believe them necessary or not.

---

[1] I take some liberties with the HFR reported totals by subtracting out long-only fixed-income and equity funds. In addition, I add estimates of CTA assets from the Barclay Group.

F I G U R E   3.1

Hedge Fund Assets under Management by Strategy

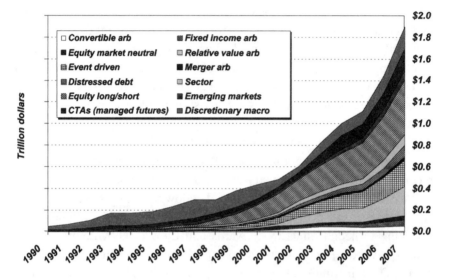

Obviously, simply calculating and reporting VaR is no impediment and may prove beneficial for large and complex hedge funds applying multiple strategies across numerous global markets. Certainly, at a minimum VaR provides useful information.

Furthermore, applying a VaR control system to assure that risk does not exceed a preset limit need not be inhibiting—one just sets the bound inordinately high so there is no influence on trading results whatsoever. Of course, such "loose" VaR control systems are largely impotent and for aesthetic purposes only. Otherwise, if VaR control is applied with a tight limit that forces position reduction at times, it may be that VaR would significantly dilute performance by overriding trading strategy mechanics.

ANALYTICAL APPROACH

To examine the potential effect of imposing tight VaR control on hedge fund trading strategies, I consider two simple rule-based examples that can be easily quantified. The first is the standard Appel (2005) moving average convergence/divergence (MACD) model. This and similar

approaches are most often used by commodity trading advisors (CTAs)—
a sector of the industry often referred to generically as *trend followers*.[2]

Moving average convergence/divergence is very straightforward and
requires only a return series as input. The equiweighted MACD model is
simply $w_{kt} = 1/K$ if $r_{kS} > r_{kL}$ and $w_{kt} = -1/K$ if $r_{kS} < r_{kL}$, where r_{kS} is the
short-term moving average return up to $t - 1$, r_{kL} is the long-term moving
average return to $t - 1$, and w_{kt} represents the kth asset weight in period t
for each of K assets. The maximum or minimum position is 100 percent of
the capital available for investment. In older versions of MACD, prices are
used instead of returns. Also, exponential weighting is often employed as
well as other modifications to improve trading profits. I initially use
MACD to produce an unadulterated return series where the portfolio return
in any period is $r_{pt} = \mathbf{w}_t^T \mathbf{r}_t$, realized risk is $\sigma_t = \sqrt{\mathbf{w}_t^T \mathbf{V}_t \mathbf{w}_t}$, and $\mathbf{V}_t$ is the
trailing covariance matrix through $t - 1$. I then repeat the exercise incor-
porating a VaR risk limit where if expected portfolio risk exceeds an arbitrary risk limit $\hat{s}$, then the portfolio weights are reduced proportionately to
restrict expected risk to no more than target VaR.

In the second example, I examine the impact of imposing a tight VaR
limit on a mean reversion (MR) model. The elementary MR model I select
is described by Lo and MacKinlay (1990) and reexamined by Khandani
and Lo (2007). It takes the form $w_{kt} = -(r_{k, t-1} - r_{p, t-1})/K$ with r_{pt} the
equiweighted K asset portfolio return for period t. This formulation is
even more rudimentary than MACD since it is entirely derivative from
last period's returns. That said, MR is often applied laterally on a very
broad scale such as to the Standard & Poor's (S&P) 500 index, where
every stock is bought or sold short. Managers employing this strategy are
often placed in the statistical arbitrage or quantitative market neutral
hedge fund classification since the net portfolio position is zero.

As with MACD, I produce an initial raw portfolio return series using
MR. I then incorporate a one standard deviation VaR portfolio risk limit
and repeat the exercise. Again, if expected portfolio risk exceeds the

---

[2] For those unfamiliar with CTAs, the term is regulatory in nature and derives from the fact that
decades ago commodity trading was the primary focus. However, today commodities
represent only a small portion of activity that now includes equity and fixed-income futures,
as well as currency futures contracts traded on public exchanges. Commodity trading
advisors are thus also sometimes referred to as *managed futures funds*.

maximum allowable level, then the portfolio weights are reduced proportionately to reach target risk. This leads to a second MR portfolio return series, which reflects the VaR overlay.

I apply both systems to portfolios consisting of four assets—stocks, bonds, commodities, and currencies. For MACD, long positions are established when the 5-day moving average rises above the 20-day average and conversely for short positions. Investments are equiweighted and fully funded such that at any time there are at most four one-way exposures (long or short) with each constituting 25 percent of the portfolio. Clearly, at extremes, MACD can simultaneously be 100 percent long or short all four assets and at this point portfolio risk is usually greatest. In addition, to mimic the way many MACD users manage downside risk, I set loss limits at one standard deviation off trailing 20-day volatility.

For the MR system, I compute an equiweighted return for the four-asset portfolio and then set weights for the next period at the negative of this period's relative return. Again, I employ one-standard deviation loss limits—as many managers do—to protect against extreme shocks.[3]

APPLICATION CONSIDERATIONS

A few comments are appropriate before utilizing these two trading systems for the intended purpose. First, while initially it might appear that they encompass only a small portion of the universe of hedge fund strategies, they nonetheless can be reproduced easily and objectively. For sure, the dominant class of quantitative models applied in the hedge fund world are causal systems of the form $r_{pt} = \alpha + \sum \mathbf{w}^T_{t-j} \mathbf{f}_{t-j} + \xi_t$, where $\mathbf{f}_t$ is a vector of lagged endogenous and exogenous factor values. However, both MACD and MR are special cases of this when $\mathbf{f}_t$ is defined to include past returns and the appropriate weighting scheme is used. The problem with attempting to apply VaR control to factor-based formulations is that virtually all practitioner versions are different. Thus, for investigative purposes, one is left considering simpler specifications driven by purely mechanistic trading rules.[4]

---

[3] Note that from a risk management perspective, loss limits are applied for protection at the asset level. In contrast, VaR risk limits are set for the portfolio as a whole.

[4] The use of factor models to construct trading systems that exploit the predictability in returns is described by Arshanapalli et al. (2004), Solnick (1993), Ferson and Harvey (1994), and Hardy (1990).

Moreover, restricting the analysis to examining the behavior of MACD and MR systems does reflect the activity of a large swath of the hedge fund industry. For example, Barclay estimates that there were $205 billion in CTA assets under management at the end of 2007. This represents approximately a tenth of total industry assets under management. A similar comparison indicates that mean reversion traders account for up to 5 percent of hedge fund industry assets under management. Thus, focusing on MACD and MR is representative.

Second, one major advantage of considering MACD and MR is that these two trading approaches are essentially antithetical from a conceptual perspective. Moving average convergence/divergence posits that recent winning trades repeat, while MR is contrarian and postulates that yesterday's winners lose today. Of course, the reality is a little more complex—MACD evolves over time relative to momentum in the asset's price cycle. Mean reversion looks back only at yesterday but considers large relative price moves as aberrations within a broad cross section of assets or securities. It is a smoothing technique. For both systems, one would imagine that the performance success varies distinctly depending on the market environment.

Finally, it is important to note that specific risk controls are automatically embedded within each trading system. Indeed, the weighting schemes themselves represent a form of risk control. For MACD, weights equal $1/K$. This prevents an unduly concentrated position in any asset or security. Similarly, weights in the MR model are set at last period's relative return. This allows more extreme exposure but still typically produces a well-balanced portfolio. Furthermore, the addition of limit or stop loss orders is a risk-control device that prevents unexpectedly adverse price changes from excessively hurting profitability.[5]

IMPACT OF VaR CONTROL

I generate the unsterilized portfolio return streams by applying MACD and MR to daily data over the 2005 to 2007 period. The four assets traded are the MSCI world equity index, the Lehman aggregate bond index, the CRB

---

[5] Stop or limit loss orders are a type of synthetic option that assures that if positions move significantly against the manager, they are kicked out of the trade. This is one reason why CTAs historically have exhibited positively skewed returns as reported by Lamm (2005).

T A B L E   3.1

Summary statistics for underlying portfolio assets, 2005–2007

Metric	Stocks (MSCI)	Bonds (AGG)	Currency (DXY)	Commodities (CRY)
Geometric price return	14.4%	−0.5%	−1.6%	8.1%
Volatility	10.7%	3.7%	6.8%	15.1%
Skew	−0.34*	−0.19	−0.05	−0.14
Kurtosis	0.90*	0.90*	0.62*	0.42
JB test	40.40*	30.08*	12.30*	7.88*
Sharpe	1.35	−0.12	−0.24	0.54

* Denotes statistical significance with 99 percent confidence.

commodity index, and the DXY index for currency. Table 3.1 displays summary distribution statistics for these series. I then overlay a VaR system on the underlying models, forcing proportionate portfolio trimming when trailing 20-day portfolio volatility exceeds one standard deviation-a relatively tight limit. This is a "moving volatility cap" control device and is designed to replicate proximately the way a VaR control system might affect the performance of these strategies in practice.[6]

The summary results presented in Table 3.2 indicate that MACD is significantly more profitable than the MR system in absolute terms over the sample. Indeed, MACD produces double-digit returns every year while the MR system delivers only mid single-digit performance. That said, MACD also exhibits significantly higher realized volatility so that the return-to-risk ratios for both systems are comparable over the 2005 to 2007 period. This is why MR managers normally use significant leverage to amplify performance.

The second columns in the table under each strategy heading show the impact on returns of overlaying one-standard deviation VaR control on

---

[6] I make no allowance for transaction costs or execution slippage away from daily closing prices, both of which are likely quite small. Nor do I allow leverage or add back yields from margin collateral proceeds. In addition, I adjust the standard deviation by the Cornish Fisher z approximation although this makes little difference in the results. Moving volatility caps are discussed by writers such as Figelman (2004).

T A B L E   3.2

Impact of Overlaying VAR on MACD and Mean Reversion Trading Systems

		MACD		Mean reversion	
Metric	**Year**	**Raw system**	**VaR overlay**	**Raw system**	**VaR overlay**
Return	2005	12.0%	9.9%	1.1%	0.3%
	2006	12.2%	7.4%	2.7%	1.4%
	2007	22.0%	14.3%	9.0%	8.3%

top of the initial systems. Clearly, the VaR overlay significantly reduces returns and risk over the entire sample and for each year. However, the return-to-risk ratios are less affected since lower returns produced by VaR control are offset to a considerable extent by reduced risk. Nonetheless, the VaR overlay clearly compromises performance robustness.

Figure 3.2 illustrates graphically the effects of overlaying VaR control on MACD over the sample. This provides a bit more clarity than simply examining summary statistics. Although it is evident that a relatively tight risk limit waters down performance—while simultaneously reducing volatility—it is also apparent that the impact is gradual and

F I G U R E   3.2

Impact of VAR Control on MACD System Performance

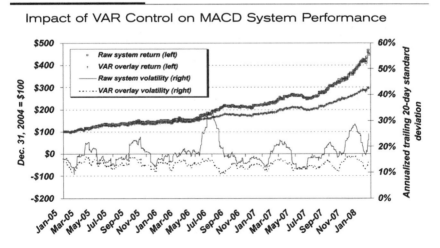

FIGURE 3.3

Impact of VAR Control on Mean-Reversion System
Performance

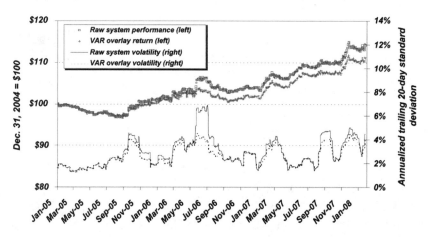

becomes glaring only when cumulative returns are examined. Even so, one can see that raw system performance tends to accrue during periods when underlying asset volatility is high—such as in the summer of 2006. In contrast, VaR control tends to cut exposure at precisely these moments.

As Figure 3.3 illustrates, a very similar pattern emerges for the MR system. Value at risk control trims performance by restricting risk taken in general but especially at moments when the payoff to taking risk is high. Indeed, VaR reduces performance dramatically in October 2005 and June 2006—two periods when most of the raw MR system returns are captured. In this regard, imposing VaR control on MR is somewhat more detrimental than with MACD, which has a propensity to produce steady returns instead of in a lump-sum fashion.

The quick conclusion is that imposing an effective VaR control process reduces both portfolio returns and risk. This is of large magnitude in some periods, especially when underlying asset volatility is high, though of little consequence otherwise. These findings are sample dependent, but it is important to be aware that the study covers a wide range of market experiences in 2005 through 2007 when the prices of the underlying assets both rose and fell significantly. Furthermore, the results are consistent across two fundamentally different but very active trading systems—which

F I G U R E   3.4

Changes in MACD Portfolio Positions

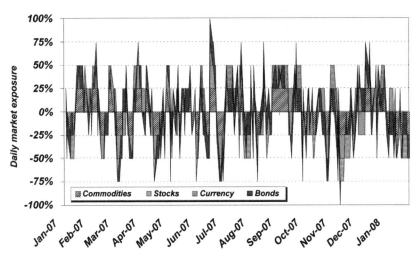

offers a good test. The extent of trading activity is illustrated in Figure 3.4, which shows weight changes for MACD over the 2007 sample period.[7]

SHORT VERSUS LONG HISTORY FOR SETTING VaR RISK LIMITS

The analysis to this point is based on a portfolio risk limit set at trailing 20-day volatility. In reality, most VaR systems use longer-dated history. Also, because market conditions frequently change drastically from month to month, one may desire to set the VaR risk budget off a longer trailing horizon to avoid hyperactive and quickly reversing adjustments in portfolio positions—the dog-chasing-its-tail effect. What difference does it make if more history is used to establish portfolio risk limits?

To answer this question, I replicate the preceding analysis by setting the VaR budget at one standard deviation for the 50,100, and 200 previous trading days. This has a critical influence on the risk limit as demonstrated in Figure 3.5, which displays the time evolution of volatility measured

---

[7] I do not show changes in MR weights since they move extraordinarily from day to day and the results are not easily amenable to graphic display.

F I G U R E   3.5

MACD Portfolio Risk Off Various Trailing Volatility Windows

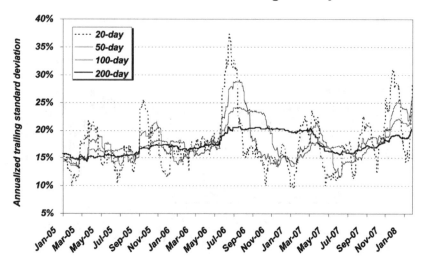

using these trailing horizons for the MACD system. Obviously, short-dated volatility results in a very reactive risk limit that moves up and down around longer-period volatility. Indeed, 20-day trailing portfolio volatility is at times nearly double 200-day trailing volatility. At other times, it approaches half the level. One might presume that this would have a strong influence on system performance because short-history produces a highly variable portfolio risk limit, while the longer-history portfolio risk limit becomes almost a constant.

Interestingly, the results for the MACD trading system (Table 3.3) indicate there is little difference whether one uses short or long history to set volatility caps. Returns, realized volatility, and the return-to-risk ratios are all nearly the same. The reason is that while VaR limits based on longer history curtail performance during high-volatility periods, there is an offset during low-volatility intervals when the trading system operates freely and produces unfettered profits under a more liberal volatility cap. As a result, the horizon used for risk limit setting does not appear to matter.

Although this is enlightening, it does not address whether using a full-cycle approach to set volatility caps would make any difference. For

T A B L E   3.3

Effect of VaR Time Horizon on MACD

Metric	Year	20 days	50 days	100 days	200 days
Return	2005	9.9%	9.9%	10.3%	10.6%
	2006	7.4%	7.0%	7.8%	8.2%
	2007	14.3%	16.0%	17.0%	17.3%

example, equity, fixed income, currency, and commodity cycles typically last many years and the analysis presented here examines a relatively limited and arbitrary time frame. If we included years where there were sharper reversals and more severe price breaks or employed a factor-based cyclical approach, the results might be different. The conclusion then is simply that it does not appear to make much difference whether 20 or 200 days are employed for the two examples examined here.

IMPLICATIONS

The normal application of VaR for controlling exposure for large multifaceted portfolios is sound and has rationale underpinnings. In the case of banks, trading desks are assigned risk limits and these are monitored for compliance by an independent risk officer. When market volatility increases and a trading desk breaches its risk limit, a reduction in exposure is required to bring positions back to within the risk budget—typically by selling riskier assets. This process keeps in check the natural inclination of traders to take large risks due to incentive compensation structures and prevents blowups. In addition, VaR control allows intervention by senior management on occasion when the firm desires to reduce company-wide risk exposure.

Large hedge funds should realize similar benefits from the application of VaR control, particularly when complex strategies covering numerous markets are involved. However, as already demonstrated, VaR does not appear essential for hedge funds that specialize in explicit trading strategies that have embedded risk-control mechanisms. In these situations, investors who insist on tight VaR control as a precondition for committing funds may be inducing a metamorphosis of the hedge fund's strategy into something different from what it was initially. The outcome could be less robust risk and reward payoff characteristics.

A related issue is that VaR risk control forces a sharp delineation between the roles of traders and risk managers. Indeed, the separation of responsibility for return generation versus risk management creates a situation where traders have a tendency to ignore risk—they simply aggressively seek out the highest potential return knowing that the risk officer will force them to scale back when they go too far. As a result, one might argue that VaR control creates traders with a less astute understanding of risk because the ultimate responsibility for risk control has been passed to others.

Similarly, the risk officer may become little more than an accounting technician who has limited knowledge of trade payoffs or market dynamics. This may have been the situation in the recent subprime debt crisis. Traders saw a quick and easy payoff from carrying long positions in high-yielding securities, while the risk officer observed reasonably low trailing volatility. No one was left to ask whether simultaneously extrapolating high returns with low risk really was credible. In this context, there may be a role for asset or security-specific risk control. Indeed, if subprime securities were included in either the MACD or the MR trading systems, the results would not have been as disastrous since both possess their own special risk-control rules.[8]

The VaR-induced "separation of power" doctrine between return-focused traders and risk managers can also be viewed relative to the standard asset allocation approach. For example, a comparison of Jorion versus Campbell and Viciera (2002), Fabozzi, et.al. (2007), or Lamm (2003) indicates a vast conceptual difference between the pure risk management view of the world and that of asset allocators. Jorion says little about return forecasting—as is appropriate because in the very short run expected returns for many assets appear to be near zero. Yet, stocks,

---

[8] For example, MACD managers would likely have gone short subprime debt as 5-day trend returns fell below 20-day averages. Mean reversion might not have fared as well but would have been protected by loss limits on contrarian positions that did not work.

currencies, commodities, and even bonds can produce large returns in a matter of days. These are not entirely random events but contain a predictable component. The asset allocation literature takes this into account, focusing as much attention on methodical return forecasting as on risk control.[9]

From this perspective the implicit return prediction contained in MACD and the MR models are revealed as richer than their simple structures might imply. For example, MACD is entirely consistent with ebbs and flows of asset demand and supply. If for some unknown reason a large market participant or group begins to build positions in an asset over time—stimulating unusual price appreciation—MACD recognizes this and then reverses position when the buying impulse begins to fade. The MR model posits that markets overreact on the upside and downside—perhaps due to lumpy buying and selling by large institutions or even due to VaR-induced trimming by bank trading desks.

CONCLUSION

The bottom line is that although VaR might make sense for complex portfolios, it has deficiencies when applied as an overlay on trading systems that have stringent embedded risk controls. Specifically, the evidence indicates that tight VaR control mutes risk-adjusted returns. This is demonstrated here for trend followers and mean reversion contrarians but may generalize to include other hedge fund strategies as well.

For this reason, institutional demands for hedge funds to employ VaR as a precondition for investment appear misplaced. While most hedge funds do not employ tight VaR control at this time, they may increasingly do so in the future as the industry grows even more. As embedded risk control gives way to VaR overlays, hedge fund managers could eventually lose their effectiveness. This is increasingly likely as more and more funds are forced into an unnatural VaR embrace.

---

[9] Examples of shorter term asset allocation models include Nam and Branch (1994), Larsen and Wozniak (1995), and Bossaerts and Hillion (1999). Kahn et al. (1996) provide an overview.

REFERENCES

Appel, G. (2005) *Power Tools for Active Traders*. New York: FT Prentice Hall.

Arshanapalli, B., Switzer, L., and Hung, L. (2004) Active Versus Passive Strategies for EAFE and the S&P 500. *Journal of Portfolio Management*, 30(3): 51–60.

Hedge, B. (2008) Money under Management in Managed Futures. Alternative Investment Database. Available at http://www.barclayhedge.com.

Bossaerts, P. and Hillion, P. (1999) Implementing Statistical Criteria to Select Return Forecasting Models: What Do We Learn?" *The Review of Financial Studies*, 12(2): 405–428.

Campbell, J. and Viceira, L. (2002) *Strategic Asset Allocation*. New York: Oxford University Press.

Edwards, F. and Liew, J. (1999) Hedge Funds versus Managed Futures as Asset Classes. *Journal of Derivatives*, 6(3): 475–517.

Fabozzi, F., Kolm, P., Pachamanova, D., and Focardi, S. (2007) *Robust Portfolio Optimization and Management*, Hoboken, NJ: John Wiley & Sons.

Ferson, W. and Harvey, C. (1994) An Exploratory Investigation into of the Fundamental Determinants of National Equity Returns. In J.A. Frankel (ed.), The Internationalization of Equity Markets. Chicago: University of Chicago Press.

Figelman, I. (2004) Optimal Active Risk Budgeting Model. *Journal of Portfolio Management*, 30(3) 22–35.

Hardy, D. (1990) Market Timing and International Diversification. *The Journal of Portfolio Management*, 16(4): 23–27.

Hedge Fund Research. (2008) *HFR Industry Report: Year End 2007*. Hedge Fund Research, Inc., Chicago.

Jorion, P. (2001) Value at Risk: The New Benchmark for Managing Financial Risk. New York: McGraw-Hill.

Kahn, R., Roulet, J., and Tajbakhsh, S. (1996) Three Steps to Global Asset Allocation. *The Journal of Portfolio Management*, 23(1): 23–31.

Khandani, A. and Lo, A. (2007) What Happened to Quants in August 2007?, MIT, Cambridge, MA, Working Paper.

Lamm, R. (1999) Why Not 100% Hedge Funds? *The Journal of Investing*, 8(4): 87–97.

Lamm, R. (2003) Asymmetric Returns and Optimal Hedge Fund Portfolios. *Journal of Alternative Investments*, 6(4): 9–21.

Lamm, R. (2005) The Answer to Your Dreams? Investment Implications of Positive Asymmetry in Hedge Fund Returns. *Journal of Alternative Investments*, 8(1): 1–11.

Larsen, G. and Wozniak, G. (1995) Market Timing Can Work in the Real World. *The Journal of Portfolio Management*, 21(3): 23–31.

Lo, A. and MacKinlay, A.C. (1990) When Are Contrarian Profits Due to Stock Market Overreaction? *Review of Financial Studies*, 3(2): 175–206.

Nam, J. and Branch, B. (1994) Tactical Asset Allocation: Can It Work? *Journal of Financial Research*, 17(4): 465–79.

Swensen, D. (2000) Pioneering Portfolio Management: An Unconventional Approach to Institutional Investment. New York: The Free Press.

Solnick, B. (1993) The Performance of International Asset Allocation Using Conditional Information. *Journal of Empirical Finance*, 1(1): 33–55.

CHAPTER 4

Cash Flow at Risk: Linking Strategy and Finance[1]

Ulrich Hommel

ABSTRACT

The chapter builds on the natural linkage between strategic planning, investment valuation, and risk management to explain the relevance and usage of cash flow at risk (CFaR) for the management of corporate risk exposures. There exists a natural connection between CFaR and value-based management, which explains the importance of an integrative approach linking a nonfinancial firm's strategy selection; its governance structures and its financial management. Cash-flow-at-risk-based risk management can serve as the tool for connecting these activities within a corporate organization.

INTRODUCTION

Implementing a firm-wide system of risk management provides a number of important benefits for companies and their stakeholders. It assists firms to meet their cash flow targets and eliminate market-induced financial distress

---

[1] This chapter is a revised and extended version of Hommel (2001, chapters 1 and 4).

and helps to protect operating margins against financial price volatility and forces management to develop an understanding of the potential interdependencies between business and financial price risks.

Corporate governance can play a key role in ensuring the adequacy of the nonfinancial firm's risk management system, and an adequate risk management system will lead to more effective corporate governance by providing a detailed assessment of the company's risk profile. The focus of this chapter is to highlight and substantiate this interdependence. The analysis starts out by characterizing the risk management function in process form. The subsequent discussion emphasizes the task of integrating hedging objectives and exposure mapping to obtain the firm's preferred hedging strategy. It is well known that cash flow at risk (CFaR) represents a risk-control methodology that enables corporate decision makers to measure and manage the firm's aggregate exposure as part of the company's value-based management system.

As explained in Figure 4.1, corporate strategy and risk management are two sides of the same coin. The company's strategy selection within

F I G U R E   4.1

Linking Strategy and Finance with Cash Flow at Risk

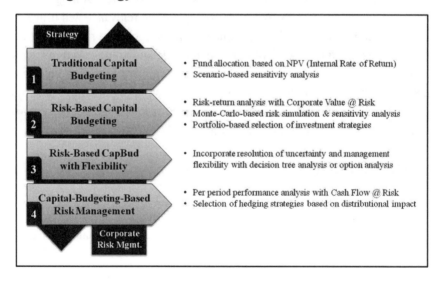

the traditional capital budgeting process is quite naturally extended to include risk and flexibility considerations. CFaR-based risk management activities use these processes as the basis and actually require no add-on tools for the management of corporate risk exposures.

The natural linkage between strategy and finance is exemplified by the various ways of looking at the firm's risk position in the context of CFaR analysis. As depicted in Figure 4.2, CFaR may be used to manage the so-called *cone of uncertainty*, i.e., the expected value and spread of future cash flows. This involves not just financial measures or operational adjustments to the existing investment portfolio but necessarily has to be extended to include the selection of new projects (Figure 4.2, graphs A1. and A2.). In fact, selecting projects without explicitly considering the value spread can lead to highly undesirable outcomes (Figure 4.2, graph B1.). It is also important how project riskiness aggregates up into the risk–return trade-off on the company level (Figure 4.2, graph B2.). The present chapter will consider all of these issues but will place the main emphasis on

FIGURE 4.2

Applications of Cash Flow at Risk Analysis

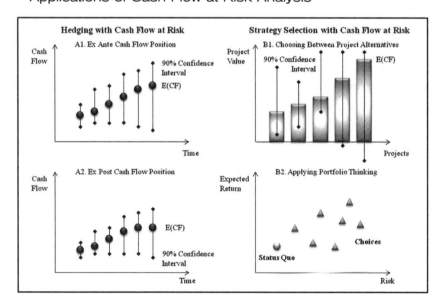

the usage of CFaR analysis, how it needs to be tied into the design of the risk management function and how CFaR can be related to value-based management and corporate governance.

The remainder of this chapter is structured as follows. The next section provides the corporate risk management function. This chapter's third section discusses the various value-based motives for firm-level risk management and explains why the cash flow at risk approach is consistent with the so-called *coordination hypothesis* of risk management. The section after that contains the key arguments why standard VaR cannot directly be applied to risk management activities of nonfinancial firms. CFaR implementation issues are presented in the fifth section of this chapter, and governance implications are covered in the sixth section. The chapter closes with a short summary.

A PROCESS VIEW OF THE CORPORATE RISK MANAGEMENT FUNCTION

Firm-wide risk management must cover the whole spectrum of corporate risks, extending from market and event risks to the various forms of financial risks. Given widespread data availability, financial risks are typically dealt with within a formal risk-control system. In contrast, business and event risks lack this property and are typically dealt with in a much less rigorous fashion using so-called *early risk indicators*.[2]

The design of an enterprise-wide risk management program in a corporate environment requires management to overcome a number of unique challenges which prevent the simple transfer of the risk management methodology employed by financial intermediaries. In particular,

- Product and factor market risks are largely nonhedgeable but may not be fully uncorrelated with financial price risks. Capturing these statistical dependencies can make the

---

[2] Examples include liquidity (1st and 2nd degree), liquidity reserves, inventory, average inventory duration, customer complaints, personnel costs and/or sales, accounts receivable and/or sales, R&D expenditures and/or sales, and employee turnover. These indicators are typically summarized by balanced scorecards. Alternatively, they can be summarized by risk matrices and risk maps that relate likelihood and impact and/or severity. See Chapman (2006) for a discussion of informal risk management tools.

implementation of a firm-wide risk management system a complex analytical challenge that forces management to integrate the measurement of risk exposures into the capital budgeting process.

- Risk management for bank trading activities aims at managing the maximum value loss over the time span needed to wind down the bank's asset holdings. While corporate risk management is also rationalized on the basis of its value-enhancing effect, difficulties associated with modeling long-term exposure effects and a negligible sensitivity to daily fluctuations of financial market rates force companies to focus on longer-term performance data.

On a more practical level, a formal system of risk controls provides a number of benefits for the firm. First and foremost, it helps management to enhance the transparency of the company's risk profile and improve risk awareness within the corporate organization. Second, it serves as a basis for measuring risk exposures, designing a hedging program and fine-tuning the allocation of corporate funds.

The design and implementation of a formal risk management system can be represented in process form, which encompasses five distinct steps. Figure 4.3 provides an overview and, in addition, highlights the link to corporate governance.

The effectiveness of corporate risk management depends on the management's ability to link these five steps using a reiterative process, which ensures that decisions on the microlevel are compatible with the overall objective to maximize shareholder value.

Specification of the Hedging Objective

A large number of behavioral motives may plausibly be used to rationalize the role of risk management as a driver of shareholder value. Corporate decision makers are faced with the challenge to identify which motives should serve as a basis for the formulation of risk management policies, for prioritizing them if necessary, and for aggregating them into a coherent controlling framework that serves as a benchmark for the evaluation of hedging performance. This is clearly not a stand-alone

The 5-Step Risk Management Process

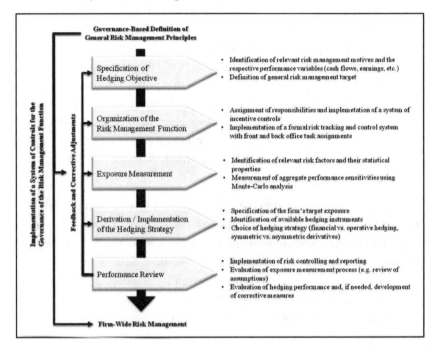

problem that can be resolved without understanding the firm's organizational constraints and without taking into account the firm's risk exposures as well as the effectiveness of the hedging instruments available to management.

Organization of the Risk Management Function

Setting up a risk management system is above all an analytical problem but its performance depends critically on the ability to devise incentives for all levels of management to supply the relevant market data for forecasting risk exposures and to properly integrate hedging strategies with the firm's other financial and operative policies. Of particular importance is the degree of centralization of the risk management function. While full-scale centralization ensures that hedging activities only target aggregate net exposures, too much centralization will distort the incentives of management at the level of the individual business unit.

Exposure Measurement

A firm-wide risk management system can only be functional if management has the ability to quantify exposures at the onset as well as the impact of hedging policies. This requires the identification of all relevant risk factors, the characterization of their statistical attributes and the mapping of the risk factors onto corporate performance variables (e.g., cash flows, before- and/or after-tax earnings).

Derivation and Implementation of the Hedging Strategy

In theory, devising and implementing a corporate hedging strategy appears to be a straightforward problem: The firm simply chooses the mix of hedging instruments that satisfy the hedging objectives at minimal cost. However, a number of complications arise in practice. Hedging activities may not only eliminate exposures, they may also create new ones by subjecting corporate performance to basis, default and/or replacement, agency, and other types of risk. In addition, firms may quite consciously choose to mix hedging with speculation (by for instance leaving contracted exposure positions unprotected). Finally, corporate decision makers need to treat risk management as a dynamic problem and are faced with the added complication that the costs and availability of hedging instruments changes as we extend the planning horizon.

Performance Review

Risk management policies must be subjected to continuous review within an institutionalized system of risk controlling.[3] Corporate planning and forecasting procedures must be appraised in the context of realized data. Hedging objectives and policies may have to be adjusted as market conditions and

---

[3] See, for instance, the discussion in Weber and Liekweg (2005).

the firm's investment strategy change over time. In addition, risk controllers play a critical role in managing the interface between formal risk-control systems dealing with financial price risks and other sources of performance volatility, in particular market (business) and event risks.

The risk management framework, as described above, needs to be embedded in a formal risk architecture which involves company acceptance, monitoring as part of corporate governance, acquisition of human resource competencies, communication and training as well as other forms of sourcing.

VALUE-BASED MOTIVES OF FIRM-LEVEL RISK MANAGEMENT

Overview

The selection of the objective function is probably one of the most neglected aspects of corporate risk management in practice, mainly because of the difficulty to establish a causal link between hedging activities and firm value. In theory, incorporating the selection of the hedging objective into a firm-wide risk management system is a straightforward problem. One simply needs to model how reductions in performance volatility (cash flows, earnings, etc.) affect shareholder value with the hedging motives discussed in the previous chapter acting as value drivers. Ex-ante preventive control must therefore do more than simply ensure the firm's survival and compliance with basic governance regulations (e.g., COSO). Hedging strategies must be evaluated on the basis of their impact on after-tax cash flows as well as the firm's cost of capital. Shareholder value rises with an increase of projected cash flows and a reduction of the cost of capital which requires that the reduction of performance volatility also eliminates systematic risk.

Corporate risk management can create shareholder value in an environment with less than perfect capital markets by eliminating the direct and indirect opportunity costs associated with performance volatility (Hommel 2005). Direct costs come in the form of an increase in the firm's average tax bill, an increase in the transaction costs of hedging and financial distress and the systematic under-compensation

F I G U R E   4.4

Value-Based Motives of Firm-Level Corporate
Risk Management

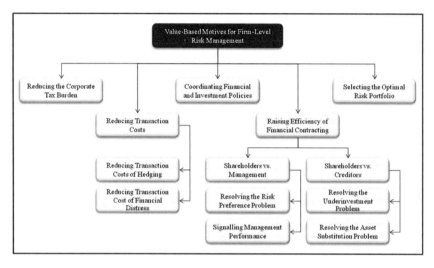

of certain types of risk bearing. Indirect costs are the consequence of less favorable contracting terms with corporate stakeholders who require a premium for seeing their relationship rents being exposed to default risk. Benefits associated with the coordination of financing and investment policies have, in this context, a particular intuitive appeal and represent an economic rationale for modeling risk management behavior using an adaptation of VaR, the so-called *cash-flow-at-risk* approach. Figure 4.4 summarizes the motives discussed in the risk management literature.

If the firm's hedging activities are shaped by multiple motives, then corporate decision makers face the added challenge of integrating them into a single objective function. Benefit additivity will not necessarily prevail given that cash flow based motives for instance generate different strategies than value-based motives. In addition, as Tufano (1998) points out, hedging with the objective of eliminating financial distress risk or meeting a certain cash flow target has the tendency of increasing the agency cost associated with the risk preference problem.

Real-world limitations which already curtail the manager's ability to forecast risk exposures help explain why firms generally fail to implement such a comprehensive approach. Corporate risk management guidelines are often inflexible and fail to provide incentives for decision makers to structure hedging activities in a value-maximizing fashion. In Continental Europe, legislative efforts to establish minimum standards for corporate risk management are focusing on bankruptcy avoidance, i.e., excluding the worst-case scenario (Hommel, 2001). Empirical studies on derivatives usage rationalize corporate hedging activities in ways that appear to be somewhat contrived since companies typically lack the governance mechanisms that trigger agency-cost minimizing, risk-portfolio-optimizing, or tax-minimizing hedging behavior. Hence, employing the coordination hypothesis combined with the CFaR methodology for this study is not much more than a working hypothesis, albeit an intuitively appealing one that seems to match corporate practice.

The Coordination Hypothesis and CFaR

The most convincing rationalization of managing risk on the level of the firm has been developed by Froot et al. (1993; 1994) and Froot (1996). In order to maintain their long-term competitiveness, companies have to keep up a certain investment expenditure flow and, in addition, have to be in a position to take advantage of unexpected investment opportunities that come up irregularly.[4] Take a provider of telecommunication services as an example: The firm needs to make certain investments in each budgeting period in order to maintain and expand its communication network. Failing to do so would necessarily reduce the perceived service quality relative to other providers. The firm must further be able to fund investment spikes, for instance, triggered by the ability to participate in public auctions of new broadcasting frequencies.

Corporate risk management can make an important contribution towards achieving these investment objectives if the firm needs to primarily rely on internally generated funds to finance core investment projects. This

---

[4] See Hommel (2005) for a comprehensive overview of the empirical literature.

will be the case if external finance is significantly more costly to obtain than internal funds and if the marginal cost function for internal financing is less steep.[5] Transaction costs associated with external financing, information acquisition and financial distress as well as other forms of capital market imperfections can help to rationalize these cost differences.[6] A number of general guidelines for the design of corporate hedging policies follow:

- Coordinating financing and investment policies can be accomplished with selective (rather than full-cover) hedging.
- The optimal hedging strategy must also be a function of the rivals' hedging behavior and their ability to exploit investment opportunities in low-tail states of nature (strategic interdependence).
- The benefits from hedging are a negative function of the correlation between internally generated cash flows and funding needs. Corporate hedging is of particular importance if a drop in internal cash flows tends to trigger costly adjustments to the company's asset portfolio.
- Hedging against extreme events can help rationalize the use of asymmetric instruments, in particular, "deep out-of-the-money" options that can be acquired at a low premium and yield a payoff only in lower-tail states of nature (Dufey and Hommel, 1996).

Hedging with the purpose of generating a minimum cash-flow stream simultaneously reduces or even eliminates exposure to financial distress risk. It is in essence equivalent to the liquidity-based financial distress motive, just with a more tightly defined cash-flow constraint.

---

[5] This "pecking order" argument goes back to Myers (1984) and Myers and Majluf (1984). Its existence follows, for instance, from information asymmetries between managers and the providers of external finance (see also Froot 1996). As Gertner et al. (1994) show, the choice between internal and external financing is also influenced by the implications for monitoring, the effects on management's entrepreneurial incentives, and the relative ease to redeploy assets within the corporate organization.

[6] The preference for internal finance may also be the result of an agency problem. Management may simply want to avoid more intense monitoring that may result from tapping into financial markets.

THE INCOMPATIBILITY OF SIMPLE
VALUE AT RISK WITH CORPORATE
RISK MANAGEMENT

Corporate hedging against extreme events seems to display a natural fit
with the standard risk management methodology for the trading operations of banks, value at risk (VaR). Value at risk expresses the firm's risk
exposure as a single measure, the maximum loss at a pre-specified level
of statistical significance (e.g., 99 percent). Hedging aims at reducing the
maximum loss by either employing derivative instruments, by closing out
individual positions, or by liquidating certain assets. Simple VaR is however not an appropriate tool for measuring and managing risk exposures
of nonfinancial firms (with the exception of certain corporate treasury
activities). The specific reasons are as follows:

- The application of VaR requires that assets are liquid and can
  be subjected to marking to market. Both conditions are
  generally not met for real investment portfolios. Financial
  intermediaries employ VaR to manage their day-to-day risk
  exposures, while nonfinancial firms need a much longer time
  frame to restructure or even liquidate individual business units.
  Applying marking to market is further hampered by the
  difficulty to value intangibles such as a firm's research and
  development (R&D) pipeline.
- A universally accepted VaR calculation method does not exist.
  The three standard approaches (variance–covariance, historical
  simulation, Monte Carlo simulation) generate different results
  with the differences becoming more pronounced for longer
  forecast periods.[7]
- The sample size for VaR calculations tends to be much too
  small in a corporate setting. Historical calculations typically
  require more than 100 observations with daily data—a
  condition that is easily met for traded financial instruments
  but not for real assets. Corporate assets are typically valued
  based on quarterly reporting, which would require the use of

---

[7] For an overview of the VaR methodology, see, in particular, Jorion (2007) and Saita (2007).

25+ years of data, which clearly extends beyond the maturity of real investments.

- Value-at-risk approaches based on the delta-normal version of the variance–covariance method require normally distributed investment returns. In contrast, real investment returns are strongly influenced by embedded optionalities and are therefore more consistent with a chi-squared distribution. In addition, long-term cash-flow forecasts tend to have fatter tails than predicted by the normal distribution.

It is, however, possible to adapt the VaR methodology to match the needs of corporate users. The CFaR approach requires the derivation of a detailed period-by-period cash-flow forecast for the planning horizon; Monte Carlo simulations for each individual period capture the exposure to the various risk factors.[8] In this context, identifying the relevant risk factors and determining the variance–covariance matrix as well as the factor-specific cash-flow sensitivities represent the real challenge of operationalizing the CFaR concept. The firm's aforementioned hedging objective is reflected by the minimum probability of meeting a certain cash-flow target. Cash flow at risk therefore represents a tool which allows corporate decision makers to integrate risk management considerations quite naturally into the strategic planning process. Cash flow at risk can be calculated for the entire firm as well as for individual operating units which permits management to express the firm's risk management objective in terms of cash-flow targets for each business unit. In absolute terms, CFaR represents a minimum cash flow to be obtained with a given level of statistical significance (typically set at 95 percent in a corporate setting). It can also be calculated as a relative risk measure with risk being measured as a potential deviation from a target cash flow. Cash-flow targets can be derived from pro forma cash-flow statements, which are constructed as part of regular capital budgeting. Risk factors are represented by forward rates, budget rates or whatever other value management considers appropriate.

---

[8] General discussions can be found in Damodaran (2008), Merna and Al-Thani (2008), and Koller (2005). More formal treatments can be found in Condamin et al. (2006), Mun (2004; 2006; 2008), and Vose (2008).

The advantages of CFaR relative to the standard VaR methodology include

- The focus on cash-flow or earnings forecasts rather than on changes in firm value which is a comparatively less meaningful measure in the context of corporate risk management
- The ability to work with multiyear time horizons, to explicitly capture macroeconomic dynamics and to easily deal with nonnormalities
- The relative ease of implementing the methodology given its reliance on much of the same tools and information that are employed by standard capital budgeting and strategic planning

Cash flow at risk implementations typically rely on simulation and optimization software packages such as Palisade's Decision Tool Suite (including @Risk for conducting Monte Carlo simulations).[9] Corporate risk managers may also use earnings as an alternative metric for quantifying exposures (earnings-at-risk, or EaR). While cash flows represent an attractive target variable due to their consistency with capital budgeting, earnings represent one of the most important variables used by the investor community to value companies, for instance as an input for market benchmark indicators such as price-to-earnings (P/E) ratios or return on equity (ROE). Analogous to CFaR, EaR may also be computed as an absolute or a relative risk measure with the latter quantifying the earnings shortfall relative to a target value derived from the pro forma income statement. Shareholder VaR is obtained by multiplying EaR with the projected P/E ratio. Earnings per share at risk (EPSaR) can be obtained by computing the ratio of EaR and the number of shares outstanding (which is particularly meaningful measure for financial analysts). EPSaR multiplied with the projected P/E ratio yields the share price at risk.

OPERATIONALIZING CFAR

Operationalizing CFaR forces management to initially resolve a number of basic issues, among them the choice of the relevant performance variable (e.g., cash flows, earnings), the hedging horizon (ideally in sync with

---

[9] A detailed introduction into the use of Decision Tool Suite can be found in Clemen and Riley (2001) and Winston (2001; 2006).

FIGURE   4.5

Operationalizing Cash Flow at Risk

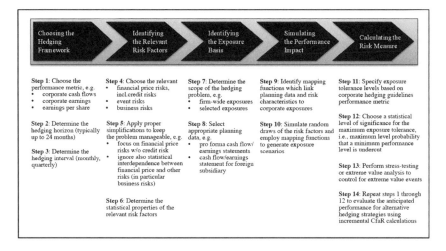

short-term capital budgeting), and the hedging interval (ideally congruent with quarterly reporting). The next steps involve the identification of the relevant risk factors as well as their statistical properties, the linkage of risk factors and corporate performance (also called *exposure mapping*) and the calculation of the CFaR measure. Figure 4.5 provides a comprehensive overview. Hedging performance can be evaluated by calculating incremental CFaR, which expresses the marginal cash-flow impact in absolute or relative terms from adding the hedge portfolio. Performing this calculation in practice will however be quite cumbersome given the difficulty to specify the impact of operational adjustments and financial policy changes on the distribution of cash flows.

Corporate hedging necessarily involves a mixture of financial as well as operative instruments:

- Overemphasizing financial hedging limits the company's risk awareness and acts against the establishment of a firm-wide risk management system. Risk management responsibilities are allocated away from corporate activities, which are ultimately responsible for the creation of risk exposures.
- Financial hedges merely compensate for operative losses; they do not eliminate them. They typically provide only one-time

compensation and therefore fail to hedge flow exposures or permanent shifts (level changes) of financial market rates.

- Financial hedges are not available for all risk factors. They involve substantial transaction costs for long maturities and exotic underlyings. Exchange-traded instruments are only available for a few instruments; over-the-counter (OTC) instruments tend to have large spreads and are generally illiquid. Using short-term instruments to cover long-term risks or to engage in cross hedging do not provide general solutions either. The former may lead to illiquidity and, in extreme cases, bankruptcy. The latter exposes the firm to additional basis risk, which tends to increase with the volatility of the underlying exposure.

- Financial hedges may fail to account for the stochastic nature of operative cash flows.

- Financial hedges may imply a simple exchange of risk exposures rather than an actual exposure reduction. In particular, the elimination of financial price exposures may lead to additional credit, moral hazard, or basis risk.

Financial and operative hedging instruments are strategic substitutes if one only considers reduction of transaction exposures. They represent strategic complements as the focus is shifted to longer-term exposures and flexibility creation.

Linking risk factors to corporate performance clearly constitutes the key challenge of any CFaR implementation. Exposure mapping is a manageable task if the company faces pure financial price risk or financial price risk coupled with a known effect on business variables. Statistical interdependencies between hedgeable and nonhedgeable forms of risk are typically company specific and therefore need to be incorporated by the end-user.

When constructing a consolidated exposure mapping for the entire firm, it is useful to first decompose the pro forma cash-flow statement into individual components, for instance according to the source of activity (operations, investment, financing), and then to generate component exposure maps which can be aggregated into a firm-wide picture. Figure 4.6

F I G U R E   4.6

Cash-Flow–based Implementation of Corporate
Risk Management

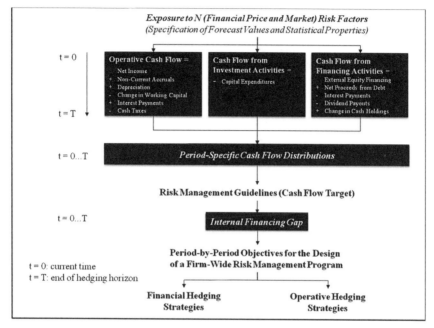

Source: Mello and Parsons (1999)

illustrates this approach for risk management activities motivated by internal financing constraints. Since CFaR manages the firm's exposure on a
period-by-period basis, management needs to predict the timing of cash
flows, which tends to be a notoriously difficult task in practice.

The projected distribution for the financial risk factors can be
obtained in a number of different ways. We may simply use the efficient
market hypothesis as a starting point and assume that risk factors follow
a random walk, possibly with drift. The specifics of the stochastic
process can be specified using forward rates and market-implied volatilities. While this approach is straightforward to implement, we may lack
an adequate data basis for risk factors of the more exotic type. Users may
alternatively employ advanced regression techniques (Oxelheim and
Wihlborg, 1997), specifically vector error correction models, to forecast

financial price distributions. This approach may be better equipped to represent macroeconomic fundamentals and cointegration relationships but tends to overtax the abilities of the average user. Finally, corporate decision makers may always perform their own scenario modeling as a fallback option which ensures consistency with traditional capital budgeting but which exposes the firm to the danger of ad hoc modeling.

Figure 4.7 depicts the @Risk simulation output for a project-level corporate VaR analysis. The output for CFaR is analogous. Particular informative is the regression-based tornado diagram, which highlights the sensitivities of corporate value to the different valuation levers. It provides a clear indication about the effectiveness of different hedging instruments in reducing the value spread.

A clear downside of corporate VaR is the difficulty to pick the appropriate discount factor. While it is nearly impossible to account for all forms of risk, future cash flows are typically discounted with the risk-free

F I G U R E   4.7

Corporate Value-at-Risk Simulation Output with Palisade's Decision Tool Suite

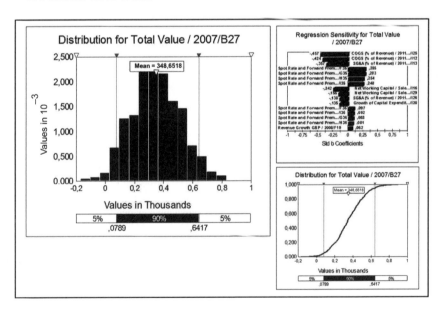

F I G U R E   4.8

Dynamic Cash Flow at Risk Analysis

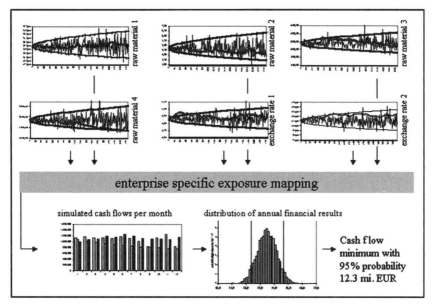

Source: Wiedmann consulting, http://www.approximity.com/risk/Products/cfar.html

rate in order to avoid the double counting of risk. Focusing on per-period cash flows avoids this issue altogether. The simulation output however becomes increasingly less informative for corporate decision makers as the analysis moves into the more distant future. It is reflective of the well-known cone of uncertainty, i.e., volatility of cash flows is a positive (but in a real investment setting not necessarily linear) function of time. Figure 4.8 illustrates this insight.

An added complication is the general need to take into account project-related real options. In practice, the inputs for valuing the different options are directly taken from the simple CFaR analysis (in particular, the value of the underlying asset and volatility). Pricing requires the application of numerical option pricing techniques such as the binomial model or finite differences.[10]

---

[10] See Mun (2002; 2003; 2008) for a detailed discussion of this aspect.

GOVERNANCE IMPLICATIONS

Corporate governance shapes the risk management function by establishing external and internal risk governance structures. External risk governance is directly subject to ex-ante preventive control, for instance via the definition of risk management guidelines coupled with the scheduling of regular performance reviews by the supervisory board. In contrast, the effectiveness of internal risk governance depends largely on the shareholders' ability to provide top management with incentives to minimize the agency costs.

While the design of a corporate risk management policy may formally be described as the maximization of a value function subject to a diverse set of constraints, this representation implies a highly inadequate characterization of the complex set of management tasks associated with the controlling of corporate risk. Most importantly, the problem must, on the one hand, be disaggregated into subresponsibilities and control rights and, on the other hand, be incorporated into the firm's organizational matrix. The key issue is how to ensure coordination within the corporate organization, above all, horizontally between treasury and/or finance department and the operative units as well as vertically between headquarters and strategic business units with a potentially large number of subsidiaries which are typically set up as separate legal entities.

These organizational challenges are difficult to resolve in practice because operating responsibility as the primary source for risk exposure is typically allocated to the operative business units with some constraints imposed on capital budgeting and sourcing while treasury operations and the finance function tend to be much more centralized. Dufey and Hommel (1996) propose "centralized coordination" as a solution that balances the benefits from centralization with the costs of reducing the degrees of freedom for managers of individual operating units. Figure 4.9 provides an illustration of the concept with a focus on currency risk management.

Centralization (in particular of the treasury function) is clearly desirable from a shareholder value perspective, at least to a certain degree. First of all, the management of subsidiaries receives guidance on the firm's overall financial objectives and constraints. Second, it enables the firm to optimize short-term borrowing and lending via the netting of funding needs. It helps to coordinate the interaffiliate transfer of funds

Implementing the "Centralized Coordination" Concept

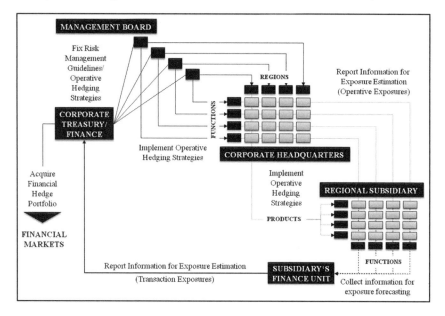

and facilitate the maximization of returns for surplus funds. Finally, centralization enables top management to determine the firm's aggregate risk exposure and to limit the external transfer of exposure to the firm's net exposure.

Excessive centralization can however have a number of pitfalls, especially if the responsibilities of risk management are to a large degree allocated to the corporate treasury. In particular, centralization may exacerbate agency problems between corporate headquarters (as the principal) and subsidiary management (as the agent) if risk management policies lead to a detachment of reward schedules and job competencies. Thus, the design of the risk management program must also actively regulate the vertical incentive structure within the firm.[11]

Treasury departments of multinational companies are often more or less isolated from the corporate planning and capital budgeting process as

---

[11] See Koller (2007) for a managerial discussion of this issue.

well as from operations management, especially to the extent that the management of nontransaction exposures is concerned. They generally have few (if any) direct links with local affiliates and deal mainly with corporate controlling and the management board on matters regarding the formulation and implementation of corporate funding policies. Isolation of the treasury implies the danger that, on the one hand, constraints implicitly defined by funding and hedging policies may lack flexibility and ignore the needs of affiliate operations. On the other hand, if affiliates lack the responsibility for funds management, they will tend to ignore the treasury in their day-to-day decision making. As a consequence, working capital management will be geared toward the maximization of shareholder value, while cash and asset management will suffer.

Applying centralized coordination as an organizing principle for the risk management function also helps to overcome potential divisions between financial and operative hedging activities. The corporate treasury is able to establish an institutionalized link with departments at headquarters overseeing company operations as well as indirectly with operative units at the level of the subsidiary. In fact, information flows necessary for projecting future cash-flow exposures require the same channels of communication as the implementation of a coordinated hedging program.

From a corporate governance point of view, the key issue is how to structure the economic incentives of lower-tier management so as to ensure truthful and complete reporting as well as compliance with risk management guidelines. In particular, one needs to deal with the effort provision and risk preference problem. Nontransaction exposures are likely to be heavily influenced by implicit contracting issues given that subsidiaries will always retain a significant degree of operational discretion with a potentially profound influence on future cash-flow exposures.

CONCLUSION

Implementing a firm-wide risk management system poses two major challenges for nonfinancial firms: (1) modeling the exposure profile and the impact of corporate risk management activities correctly and (2) integrating the risk management function into existing value-based management systems as well as covering the governance dimension properly. It has been

shown that there exists a direct linkage between shareholder value maximization and CFaR analysis. The remainder of the chapter has outlined
how CFaR can be implemented in practice—analytically and as an integral
part of a firm-wide risk management system.

REFERENCES

Chapman, R.J. (2006) *Simple Tools and Techniques for Enterprise Risk
    Management*. Hoboken, NJ: John Wiley & Sons.

Clemen, R.T. and T. Reilly (2001) *Making Hard Decisions with
    Decision Tools*. Pacific Grove, CA: Duxbury Press.

Condamin, L., J.-P. Louisot, and P. Naim (2006) *Risk Quantification:
    Management, Diagnosis and Hedging*. Hoboken, NJ:
    John Wiley & Sons.

Damodaran, A. (2008) *Strategic Risk Taking*. Upper Saddle River, NJ:
    Pearson.

Dufey, G. and U. Hommel (1996) Currency Exposure Management in
    Multinational Companies: "Centralized Coordination" as an
    Alternative to Centralization. In J. Engelhard (ed.), *Strategische
    Führung internationaler Unternehmen: Paradoxien, Strategien und
    Erfahrungen*. Wiesbaden: Gabler-Verlag.

Froot, K. (1996) Incentive Problems in Financial Contracting—Impacts
    on Corporate Financing, Investment, and Risk Management Policies.
    In: D. Crane (ed.), *The Global Financial System: A Functional
    Perspective*, Boston, MA: Harvard Business School Press.

Froot, K., D. Scharfstein, and J. Stein (1993) Risk Management,
    Coordinating Corporate Investment and Financing Policies.
    Journal of Finance, 48(5): 1629–1658.

Froot, K., J. Stein, and D. Scharfstein (1994) A Framework for Risk
    Management. *Harvard Business Review*, 72(6): 91–102.

Gertner, R., D. Scharfstein, and J. Stein (1994) Internal vs. External Capital
    Markets. *Quarterly Journal of Economics*, 109(3): 1211–1230.

Hommel, U. (2001) *Governing the Corporate Risk Management Function*. Vallendar: WHU, Vallendar, Germany (mimeo).

Hommel, U. (2005) Value-Based Motives for Corporate Risk Management. In M. Frenkel, U. Hommel, and M. Rudolf (eds.), *Risk Management: Challenge and Opportunity*, 2nd edition. Heidelberg: Springer.

Jorion, P. (2007) *Value at Risk*, 3rd edition. New York: McGraw Hill.

Koller, G.R. (2005) *Risk Assessment and Decision Making in Business and Industry*, 2nd edition. Boca Raton, FL: Chapman & Hall.

Koller, G.R. (2007) *Modern Corporate Risk Management: A Blueprint for Positive Change and Effectiveness*. Fort Lauderdale, FL: J. Ross.

Mello, A. S. and J. E. Parsons (1999) Strategic Hedging. In *Journal of Applied Corporate Finance*, 12(3): 43–54.

Merna, T. and F. F. Al-Thani (2008) *Corporate Risk Management*, 2nd edition. Hoboken, NJ: John Wiley & Sons.

Mun, J. (2002) *Real Options Analysis: Tools and Techniques for Valuing Strategic Investments*. Hoboken, NJ: John Wiley & Sons.

Mun, J. (2003) *Real Options Analysis Course: Business Cases and Software Applications*. Hoboken, NJ: John Wiley & Sons.

Mun, J. (2004) *Applied Risk Analysis: Moving Beyond Uncertainty in Business*. Hoboken, NJ: John Wiley & Sons.

Mun, J. (2006) *Modelling Risk: Applying Monte Carlo Simulation, Real Options Analysis, Forecasting and Optimization Techniques*. Hoboken, NJ: John Wiley & Sons.

Mun, J. (2008) *Advanced Analytical Models*. Hoboken, NJ: John Wiley & Sons.

Myers, S.C. (1984) The Capital Structure Puzzle, *Journal of Finance*, 39(3); 575–592.

Myers, S. C. and N.S. Majluf (1984) Corporate Financing and Investment Decisions When Firms Have Information That Investors Do Not Have. *Journal of Financial Economics*, 13(13): 187–221.

Oxelheim, L. and C. Wihlborg (1997) *Managing in the Turbulent World Economy—Corporate Performance and Risk Exposure.* Chichester, UK, and New York: John Wiley & Sons.

Saita, F. (2007) *Value at Risk and Bank Capital Management.* New York: Elsevier.

Tufano, P. (1998) Agency Costs of Corporate Risk Management. *Financial Management*, 27(1): 67–77.

Vose, D. (2008) *Risk Analysis—A Quantitative Guide*, 3rd edition. Hoboken, NJ: John Wiley & Sons.

Weber, J. and A. Liekweg (2005) Statutory Regulation of the Risk Management Function in Germany: Implementation Issues for the Non-Financial Sector. In Frenkel, M., U. Hommel, and M. Rudolf (eds.), *Risk Management: Challenge and Opportunity*, 2nd edition. Heidelberg: Springer.

Winston, W. (2001) *Financial Models using Simulation and Optimization II*. Ithaca, NY: Palisade.

Winston, W. (2006) *Financial Models using Simulation and Optimization*, 2nd edition. Ithaca, NY: Palisade.

CHAPTER 5

Plausible Operational Value-at-Risk Calculations for Management Decision Making

Wilhelm Kross, Ulrich Hommel, and Martin Wiethuechter

ABSTRACT

In this chapter the authors present an enhanced framework for the integrated management of operational risk, employing several commonly unused decision analysis techniques and concepts and, in particular, modern real option valuation approaches to capture flexibility and uncertainty. This chapter demonstrates how the value-at-risk concept can be applied and enhanced to more adequately address operational risk; and how the "management" perspective in operational risk management can be integrated into a strategy-enforcing, enterprise-wide, and beyond-enterprise risk and opportunity management framework.

INTRODUCTION

Operational risk management frameworks of financial institutions have in the last decade been dominated by the advantages and the inherent shortfalls of the framework put forward by the Bank for International Settlements

(BIS), commonly referred to as *Basel II*.[1] This chapter provides a discussion of how operational risk frameworks have evolved more recently and what complementary methodological steps are needed to move further along on the path toward a comprehensive and integrated operational risk and opportunity management.

OPERATIONAL RISK UNDER BASEL II

Besides introducing operational risk as a new category and requiring that certain minimum regulatory capital be allocated in lieu of operational risk factors, Basel II intensifies the working relationship between financial institutions and the regulatory agencies on the basis of the so-called *second pillar* (see Figure 5.1).

It is striking that for two of the three permissible approaches to calculate operational risk regulatory capital under the first pillar, it is not

F I G U R E   5.1

The Basel II Capital Accord

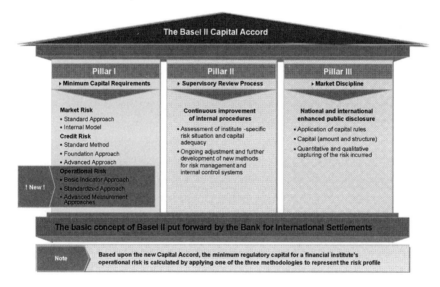

---

[1] For further information on the Basel II framework, please refer to the website of the BIS: www.bis.org.

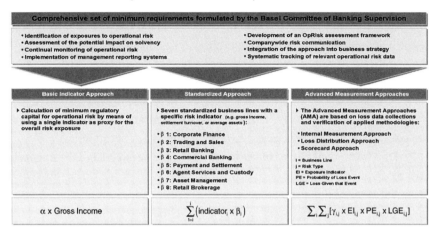

F I G U R E   5.2

Calculation of Operational Risk Capital under Basel II

necessary to develop an appreciation of the true orders of magnitude of operational risk in the respective financial institution (see Figure 5.2). Moreover, the basic indicator and the standard approaches merely use a factor alpha or beta, respectively, determined by the regulatory authority and then multiplied with the gross turnover (per business line) of the financial institution. Under the advanced approaches, in contrast, it is necessary to implement as a prerequisite those qualitative and quantitative requirements, which were published by the BIS in 2003 in their operational risk best practices guide:[2] the identification of exposures to operational risk, the assessment of the potential impact on solvency, continual monitoring of operational risk, the implementation of management reporting systems, the development of an operational risk assessment framework, company-wide risk communication, the integration of the operational risk assessment and management approach into the business strategy, and the systematic tracking of all relevant operational risk data.[3] That in turn is what is needed for second pillar compliance.

---

[2] Please refer to the Website of the Bank for International Settlements: www.bis.org.
[3] For a formal treatment, see Alexander (2005). See also Chernobai et al. (2007).

Transferred into local laws and regulations in several countries using more or less the same wording that was chosen by the BIS, and incorporating several other regulatory features that had evolved in the respective countries over the years, the second pillar of the Basel II framework has reportedly helped[4] to refocus operational risk frameworks away from the traditionally rather selective appreciation of (market and credit) risk factors and their respective implications as well as the predominant focus on the documentation of auditable facts. In particular, modern approaches to operational risk management seem to focus to an increasing extent on the effectiveness and efficiency of risk management at the board level.[5]

However, while it is understood that no one-size-fits-all approach will exist in the near future to cover all types of risk factors in all types financial institutions wherever they are based, it appears that until now there does virtually not exist a practical or theoretical guidance on the implementation do's and don'ts and the best practices in real-life organizations. Practitioners in the field seem to be struggling with some unresolved issues in data consistency and data aggregation, which resemble the modeling paradigm "garbage in–garbage out." Furthermore, a variety of conceptual issues remains, only some of them seem to have been addressed in practice (see also Figure 5.3):[6]

- Operational risk under Basel II is addressed in a structure of seven risk factor categories and eight business lines. Any losses resulting from risk factors are booked to the category in which the initial event incurred. Hence, any observable correlations between the individual silos in the 8×7 matrix are undesired— whether immediately after a risk event, or with some delay. However, real-life facts such as process interdependencies, internal cost accounting procedures and systems, internal transfer pricing arrangements, personnel reward and recognition schemes, and various laws and regulations to be considered in external financial reporting may not be supportive of this logic.

---

[4] Refer to the first chapter in Kross (2006).
[5] See, for example, Kross (2007).
[6] Refer to the second and third chapters in Kross (2006).

F I G U R E   5.3

Inherent Weaknesses of the Basel II Framework

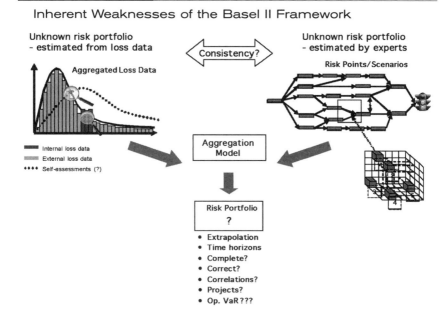

- Losses incurred from risk factors that are not driven by a discrete event, such as those incurred following a pandemic flu breakout, are not systematically tracked. Moreover, it may be effectively impossible to follow the above logic in this case.
- Basel II's business line orientation is not always compatible with the means and ways in which projects and project-related risk factors are managed and accounted for—in particular when these projects are rather large in duration and scope and are interdepartmental. In fact, in early operational risk initiatives, real-life banks seem to have neglected project risk all together. This is particularly critical given that most change initiatives in today's financial services organizations are set up and implemented as projects.
- The way in which Basel II initiatives were implemented in real life appears to have been backward oriented—to some extent

what authors referred to as a tail wagging the dog.[7] Of course, it was and is sensible that operational risk reporting and regulatory capital calculation are managed by the regulatory reporting and risk-controlling departments of a financial institution. However, the question to be addressed is in how far the risk controlling department may be entitled and authorized to tell risk managers or risk owners what to do and how. A risk-controlling department that becomes overly proactive in managing managers actually has the potential to violate the principle of functional segregation, or what is commonly referred to as the *four-eyes-principle*.

- The Basel II framework dictates the use of a technique commonly referred to as *self-assessment* but neglects the inherent challenges in individual and group subjective estimating. The compatibility with other techniques is not discussed, in spite of the fact that rather dubious results may come to surface if, for example, estimations are carried out on the basis of just a few individually assessed point estimates.[8]

- The Basel II framework and the various support documents contain little guidance on how to assess and manage reputational risk factors and how to synthesize loss estimates in that performance dimension with estimates in the other (i.e., financial and time) performance dimensions.[9]

- Only a small number of risk transfer solutions like insurance can currently be used for the reduction of operational risk regulatory capital—the true effects on the risk factors portfolio are only taken into consideration rather fractionally.

- According to the Basel II framework, risk estimates are derived from (anticipated) loss estimates. Opportunity costs or losses resulting from foregone opportunities are not incorporated. Neither are some of the more sophisticated approaches to

[7] See, for example, Kross (2005).
[8] For a more in-depth discussion of the challenges in individual and group subjective quantification efforts, please refer to Keeney and Raiffa (1993), Morgan and Henrion (1990), Von Winterfeldt and Edwards (1986), Keeney (1992), or Roberds (1990).
[9] See, for instance, Jorion (2006, Chapter 20). Saita (2007, Chapter 5) has provided a conceptualization of operational risk measurement.

estimating net value destruction by for example reducing operational flexibility.

- The Basel II framework excludes so-called *strategic risk* factors in the assessment of minimum regulatory capital, which can be considered a major weakness in case the Basel II operational risk approach were used as the basis of an integrated enterprise-wide risk management framework.

It is hence appropriate to conclude that with respect to management decision making, the Basel II framework for the incorporation of operational risk factors leaves a lot to be desired and is in some regards even counterproductive.

DESIRABLE SIDE EFFECTS OF OPERATIONAL RISK INITIATIVES

Financial services organizations have for many years been struggling to keep up with externally driven change. New laws and regulations and industry and accounting standards are not only rather complex and require a significant investment in risk systems, but also product life cycles and the speed of product innovation have changed quite considerably (see Figure 5.4).

Of course significant investments in risk analytics and risk reporting software come at a cost. This is not to say that such investments necessarily have the effect of adding net costs only; moreover, they can add insult to injury when other commercial factors have had rather detrimental effects on the financial institution's bottom line anyway. The question to be answered, in this case, is whether and how an operational risk management initiative can be modified or enhanced to achieve desirable side effects.

A common framework for the evaluation of a financial services organization's return on equity (ROE) is presented in Figure 5.5. Accordingly, the ROE is calculated from the net revenues derived in the period of interest and the proprietary capital ratio. Net revenues are calculated by means of deducting risk provisions from gross revenues. Gross revenues are the result of deducting the gross cost margin from the gross turnover margin. The cost margin is dominated by personnel costs and other (including project) costs,

F I G U R E   5.4

The Dynamics of the Financial Services Sector

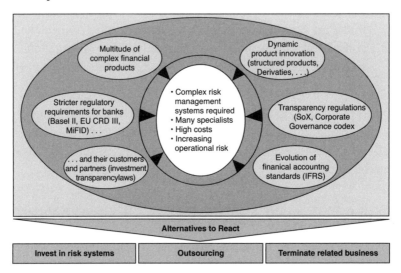

F I G U R E   5.5

The Impact of Operational Risk on the Return of Equity

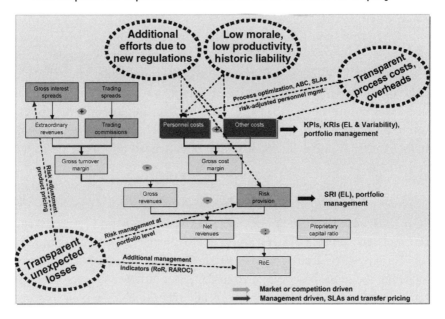

the latter usually being a mixture of variable, fixed, and stepwise variable cost factors. Trading and interest spreads, commissions, and extraordinary revenues dominate the gross turnover margin. Most of these key indicators for turnover are either calculated or market driven; while the personnel and other cost factors can in most cases be manipulated to improve the bottom line over the short to medium term.

Whether a financial institution envisages change and conceives room for improvement, several factors can result in a further deterioration of the ROE. These are in particular any operational cost increases for example due to regulatory compliance and non-business-development initiatives; and costs incurred through decision delays, and low morale while operating in a recessive and cost-cutting-focused environment. So things are bound to get worse.

On the other hand, a variety of factors have been recognized to potentially add net value, or at least render more transparent what has historically gone wrong. In particular, enhanced transparency in unexpected losses (both in the fields of operational risk and in the more traditional credit and market risk) can enable a more appropriate and product-specific risk-adjusted pricing structure, and add to the breadth and depth of risk management approaches at the portfolio level. Even more importantly in the field of operational risk, transparency in process costs and overhead structures, explicitly reflecting the likely impact of individual and combined risk factors, can help to reduce personnel and other costs. Commonly used techniques and methodological approaches in this regard commonly include process optimization approaches, the structuring of dynamic service level agreements, enhanced probabilistic applications of activity-based costing in combination with target and life-cycle costing, and risk-adjusted personnel management and organizational design.[10]

While it would be unrealistic to expect that the introduction of operational risk management techniques automatically pays for itself instantaneously, it is conceivable that some more intensified analyses will ultimately enable an organization to break out of traditional downward spirals in which poorly designed processes prohibit the early recognition of and the appropriate reaction to risk factors—a suboptimal solution that

---

[10] Refer to the second and third chapters in Kross (2006).

Operational Risk Issues of IT Mega-Projects

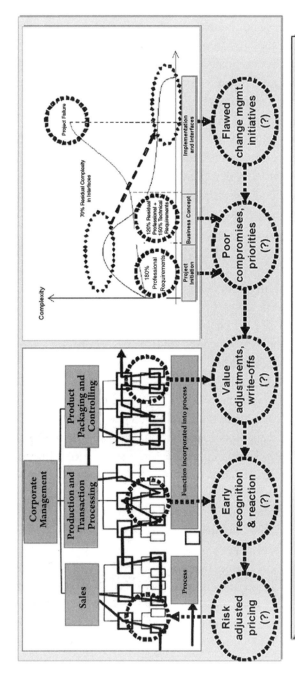

- Poor management of IT architectures and IT projects, poor management of processes, poor organizational designs, over-emphasized controlling (tail wagging with the dog), poor management of (mega-)projects, overly selective and over-constrained approaches to (portfolio-level) risk management
- Scope of change initiatives fundamentally underestimated, increasingly reactive approaches to strategy

is often further augmented through flawed change initiatives, in particular the failure of a so-called *mega-project* and the inherent resulting operational workarounds (see Figure 5.6).[11]

Hence in summary the authors submit that an operational risk initiative that does not simply address the various minimum regulatory capital calculation requirements and the compulsory set of regulatory-driven best practices but rather incorporates an appreciation of desirable and achievable side effects and can be compatible with and supportive of a variety of initiatives that bank management will need to achieve.

TOWARD STRATEGY-ENHANCING OPERATIONAL RISK INITIATIVES

It is therefore no surprise that the methodological toolset and the management paradigms that were employed in the early stages of Basel II compliance initiatives are far from adequate and sufficient; in some regards they are counterproductive to addressing the challenges that board members will be facing in the foreseeable future. So what is actually required to develop an operational risk framework that has the potential to be strategy enforcing and to be compatible with both the enterprise-wide and the beyond-enterprise-boundaries perspectives?

The authors submit that the first step entails conceptual thinking. Regulatory compliance is a threshold, not a substitution of corporate strategy. Hence, if certain calculations and methodological approaches are chosen for regulatory compliance purposes, this does not necessarily imply that an entire organization must be setup and managed following the same logic. To the contrary, it is necessary that corporate managers of financial institutions start to understand "management" as a complementary set of activities to the mandated regulatory capital calculation framework. This in effect implies that a financial institution may be calculating several VaR figures, only one of which addresses regulatory reporting. More practically phrased, financial institutions need to start appreciating the required interaction between management, controlling, and regulatory

---

[11] A few contributions to the literature have addressed this issue so far; see, for instance, Wahler (2003), as well as Döbeli et al. (2003). See also Panjer (2006). Comprehensive overviews have also been provided by Cruz (2004), as well as Davis (2005).

and financial reporting—as opposed to believing that this is all done simultaneously in one shot.

A second conceptual issue relates to the ultimate goal of operational risk initiatives. In particular, it is necessary to understand that a business-as-usual type line organization focus alone will not suffice, and that net value generation frameworks need to be appreciated (see Figure 5.7).[12]

A third set of issues relates to the fact that risk management cannot operate efficiently and effectively if it is conceptualized retroactively—as would be the case if risk management is designed for financial accounting purposes—or if it is setup to address static performance only (see Figure 5.8). History has shown that rather different risk factors need to be dealt with, only part of which are more or less under control in real-life organizations.

FIGURE 5.7

Operational Risk Management and Shareholder Value Creation

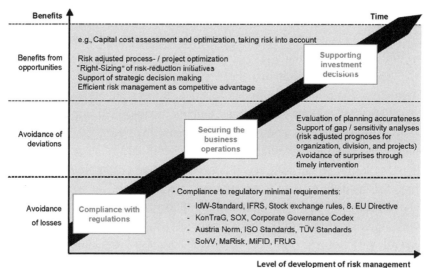

---

[12] It is noted that layout and concept of the representation in Figure 5.7 were adopted from presentations and articles authored by the FutureValue Group and/or its founder Dr. Werner Gleissner.

F I G U R E   5.8

A Forward-Looking Risk Management Framework

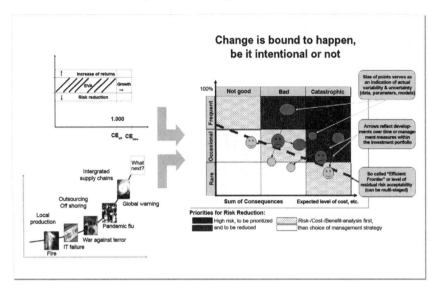

A fourth set of issues relates to the understanding that operational risk management frameworks should not be designed such that the wheel needs to be reinvented. Rather, an in-depth appreciation of current facts should be reflected, including but not limited to the variety of risk management approaches that are already implemented before a more formalized and more focused approach to the management of operational risk is actually designed and implemented. Figure 5.9 reflects a generic approach that real-life organizations may consider useful in this regard.[13]

The fifth set of issues relates to which methodological approaches and techniques actually need to be employed if an operational risk initiative is to become useful as a means of triggering a more intensified opportunity generation and opportunity management framework. In this context it becomes a *must* to appreciate that some of the more intangible factors in management and decisional choices, such as operational flexibility, truly

---

[13] See, for example, Kross (2004).

F I G U R E   5.9

An Exemplary Risk Management Process

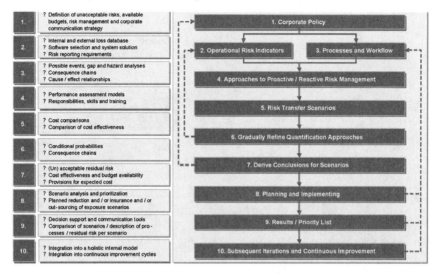

need to be incorporated. Literature research and practitioners' experienced in the field of risk management reflect that both the employment of advanced decision analysis approaches, incorporating uncertainty and variability with the respective cases and consequences in managerial decision making, as well as advanced real option techniques should be considered a prerequisite to successful implementation. The following section elaborates on how real option techniques can enhance the standard toolset, in particular with its contribution toward the appreciation of otherwise intangible factors and toward the "opportunity" side of risk and opportunity management.

Finally, decision makers and managers of operational risk must develop a better understanding of the challenge of reaching enterprise-wide integration, especially with the various "soft" factors that can play an even more predominant role than modeling and risk calculation at the portfolio level.[14] Furthermore, in today's rather complex world, it will be

---

[14] While the formal integration of operational risk considerations into established bank risk management frameworks might be considered helpful, it is likely to miss the softer issues. See, for example, Chapelle et al. (2005).

necessary to expand the horizon of operational risk management initiatives beyond the traditional boundaries of enterprise-wide risk management. Some more recent publications in the field of supply chain risk management reflect that practitioners and researchers are starting to appreciate this "beyond-enterprise" perspective, given that many organizations create only a fraction of the net value generation as perceived by the customers and manage only a portion of the overall value chain, in their in-house operations. Needless to say, neglecting the complexities inherent in the interaction with the outside world has the potential to easily become detrimental for an organization's sustained competitive advantage.

EMPLOYMENT OF REAL OPTION TECHNIQUES IN OPERATIONAL RISK INITIATIVES

In practice, banking organizations have to cope with the negative effects of formalized operational risk management, mostly in the form of excessive bureaucratization and suboptimal specification of business processes and decision-making. Constraints on the managers' degrees of freedom in responding to environmental changes may particularly problematic and are likely to result in value destruction. Hence, the costs of managing operational risk may go well beyond the administrative expenses of setting a functioning control system and may directly impede on the organization's ability to operate on the market side effectively.

The real option concept of investment valuation can be employed to gain further understanding of how the excessive formalization of risk management activities may have detrimental effects on shareholder value creation.[15] Formally speaking, a real option is equivalent to decision-making flexibility in the context of real investments. Managers can alter capital budgeting decisions or the way they run investment projects in response to changes in the economic environment. Behavioral degrees of freedom are equivalent to options in a financial sense if the following three conditions are satisfied: (1) uncertainty over future returns, (2) ability to influence a project decision or how a project is operated, and (3) sunk cost associated with managerial decision making. In contrast, if only conditions (1) and (2)

---

[15] For a general introduction, see Trigeorgis (1996).

are satisfied but there is no sunk cost associated with the investment, then we are faced with a "least cost dealing" opportunity rather than an option right. In the real options world, total investment value is equivalent to the sum of the net present value of future cash flows and the value of embedded option rights. Managerial responses to the resolution of economic uncertainty are treated as a potentially value-creating activity and really represent the core of what it means to manage a company.

Decision-making flexibility may come in many different forms but almost always represents as a fairly standard option right that can be valued with standard contingent claims analysis.[16] Managers may, for instance, delay an investment (call option on the project's cash flows), may terminate a project (put option on the project's cash flows), may scale a project up or down (call and/or put on the cash flow delta), or may switch resources from one project to another (exchange option on the underlying cash flows). Actually, the main challenge of doing real options analysis properly is to identify the different value levers (e.g., volatility of the underlying asset) and to capture interdependencies between different options embedded in the same project.[17]

In the context of long-term value creation, growth options are of particular relevance. Strategic investments typically open up new markets and enable firms to undertake follow-up investments. Formally speaking, such investments represent compound options, i.e., call options on investments which themselves represent call option on follow-up investments. Firms typically hold "long" positions in real options when undertaking or managing projects. In contrast, ignoring them in the valuation process leads to a systematic undervaluation and to the potential rejection of worthwhile investments. When considering risk management activities, however, the logic is often reversed: Formalized risk management systems force organizations to stick to strict risk management guidelines and, in the process, foster the creation of an environment hostile to entrepreneurial thinking.

Operational risk management systems in their real-life implementation have a natural tendency to regulate the behavior rather than outcomes. After all, preventing misbehavior by individuals and the breakdown of

---

[16] See, in particular, Trigeorgis (1995, Chapter 1, Trigeorigs: Introduction).
[17] See Trigeorgis (1996, Chapter 7).

organizational chains of command are at the core of managing operational risk. Doing so seems to dictate a norm-based approach of how to handle standardized tasks as well as an extensive approval process for management responses to unusual and infrequently occurring events, not the least because history books are full of examples where laxer approaches have led to financial disasters for banking institutions. As a consequence, risk managers expropriate decision-making rights from the front office and, due to a structural competency gap, adopt a "safety first" approach, which is equivalent to sacrificing organizational flexibility. Incidentally, it is noted that in real life, the safety first approach is often incorporated into corporate policies and procedures without truly appreciating at what cost this may come.

Asymmetric reward schedules can further exacerbate the problem and foster a culture of excessive operational risk aversion. If bankers are primarily rewarded for managing projects successfully rather than managing successful projects, i.e., strictly fulfilling their obligations as per the project charter within time and budget without even questioning what would be best for the organization's sustainable competitive advantage, then they will more than willingly relinquish degrees of freedom to the risk management function. Risk management rule books may consequently evolve into "iron laws" for process design and project management. Ultimately, banking organizations will concentrate their innovation capabilities on creating value within the existing risk management framework and thereby systematically underchallenge the adequateness of self-imposed constraints derived from operational risk management objectives.

Adopting a real option view of risk management design can help to avoid or can at least alleviate the aforementioned problems. Several layers of risk management guidelines are needed ranging from binding codes of conduct to eliminate management actions completely inconsistent with corporate objectives or ethics, to flexible response roadmaps rewarding front and middle offices for innovations in process design and business execution. A workable system necessarily requires the internalization of the opportunity cost of forgone flexibility and a linkage to the performance measurement system of risk management. In practice, multistage bargaining with binding arbitration can be used to systematically relate the costs of formalized risk management structures to the corresponding organizational benefits in terms of exposure reduction.

How can these real option and enhanced decision analysis techniques be integrated into the operational risk aggregation and regulatory capital calculation model that has become mandatory under the local regulatory regimes' implementation of Basel II and the key indicator systems that were introduced in Figure 5.5 above? The answer is simple, other than one might expect when being involved in the real-life implementation and operation of such initiatives.

Corporate accounting and many facets of corporate controlling are usually backward focused and determine key indicators based on historic data collection and statistical analyses. In contrast, decision analysis techniques and scenario risk analyses are usually forward focused. This latter scope is the environment in which the employment of real option techniques is useful, if not essential. To put it differently, addressing such issues as planning uncertainty and the forecast of corporate performance does need to take into account an appreciation of opportunity generation potential under uncertainty, irrespective of whether the Basel II framework considers strategic risk or opportunity generation potential as relevant factors for operational risk regulatory capital calculation purposes. In this context banks should consider themselves lucky in that in comparison with other industry segments, they already have a tremendous wealth of historic experience in the incorporation of sophisticated option valuation approaches into portfolio valuation and risk estimate aggregation; hence upgrading the corporate framework for investment analysis (including upgrades to the own operational risk management framework) to include real option valuation techniques should be considered a bearable undertaking.

CONCLUSION

It has been recognized that risk management of banking institutions must be set up for specific circumstances, consisting of various interlayered analysis and management levels. The authors demonstrate that significant issues and implementation related challenges are already resolved. There is no reason to strive for a narrow-minded approach, and there is no reason to call for a reinvention of the wheel. It appears that historically, financial institutions overemphasized the controlling and regulatory reporting perspectives, which has the potential to ultimately resemble a tail wagging the dog. Truly significant, the authors submit, is the handling of soft factors as opposed to risk calculations at the portfolio level and the appreciation of what truly constitutes value for an organization.

Other authors have demonstrated that risk management on the systems, processes, projects, portfolio, initiative, enterprise-wide, and supply-chain levels is currently experiencing a fundamental change in mindset. A cultural paradigm change is observable, toward incentive schemes for the delegated responsibility. This article demonstrates how important and how far-reaching the employment of advanced methodological approaches is and can be.

REFERENCES

Alexander, C. (2005) Assessment of Operational Risk Capital. In Frenkel, Hommel, and Rudolf (eds.), *Risk Management: Challenge and Opportunity*. Berlin: Springer.

Chapelle, A., Y. Crama, G. Hübner, and J.-P. Peters (2005) Measuring and Managing Operational Risk in the Financial Sector: An Integrated Framework. HEC Management School, University of Liège, SSRN Working Paper #675186.

Chernobai, A., S.T. Rachev, and F.J. Fabozzi (2007) *Operational Risk: A Guide to Basle II Capital Requirements, Models and Analysis*. Hoboken, NJ: John Wiley & Sons.

Cruz, M. (ed.) (2004) *Operational Risk Modeling and Analysis: Theory and Practice*. London: Risk Books.

Davis, E. (2005) *Operational Risk: Practical Approaches to Implementation*. London: Risk Books.

Döbeli, B., M Leippold., and P. Vanini (2003) From Operational Risks to Operational Excellence. In P. Mestchian (ed.), *Advances in Operational Risk: Firm-Wide Issues for Financial Institutions*, 2nd edition. London: Risk Books.

Jorion, P. (2006) *Value at Risk: The New Benchmark for Managing Financial Risk,* 3rd edition. New York: McGraw-Hill.

Keeney, R.L. (1992) Value-Focused Thinking—A Path to Creative Decisionmaking. Cambridge MA: Harvard University Press.

Keeney, R.L. and H. Raiffa (1993) Decisions with Multiple Objectives: Preferences and Value Tradeoffs. Cambridge, UK: Cambridge University Press (1st edition, NewYork: Wiley, 1976).

Kross, W. (2005) Operational Risk: The Management Perspective. In Frenkel, Hommel, and Rudolf (eds.), *Risk Management: Challenge and Opportunity.* Berlin: Springer.

Kross, W. (2006) *Organized Opportunities: Risk Management in Financial Services Organizations. Weinheim.* Frankfurt, Germany: John Wiley & Sons.

Kross, W. (2007) Kulturwandel durch MARisk (Cultural Change Through MARisk). *Interview, Compliance Manager,* 9(4): 1–5.

Morgan, M.G. and M. Henrion (1990) *Uncertainty: A guide to Dealing with Uncertainty in Quantitative Risk and Policy Analysis.* New York: Cambridge University Press.

Panjer, H. (2006) *Operational Risk: Modelling Analytics.* Wiley-Interscience: Hoboken, NJ.

Roberds, W.J. (1990) Methods for Developing Defensible Subjective Probability Assessments. *Transportation Research Record*, 1288, 183–190.

Saita, F. (2007) *Value at Risk and Bank Capital Management.* Amsterdam: Academic Press.

Trigeorgis, L. (ed) (1995) *Real Options in Capital Investment: Models, Strategies, and Applications.* Westport, CT: Praeger.

Trigeorgis, L. (1996) *Real Options: Managerial Flexibility and Strategy in Resource Allocation.* Cambridge, MA: The MIT Press.

Von Winterfeldt, D. and W. Edwards (1986) Decision Analysis and Behavioral Research. Cambridge, UK: Cambridge University Press.

Wahler, B. (2003) Process-Managing Operational Risk. Hochschule für Bankwirtschaft, Frankfurt/Main, Frankfurt, SSRN Working Paper #674221.

CHAPTER 6

Value-at-Risk Performance Criterion: A Performance Measure for Evaluating Value-at-Risk Models

Zeno Adams and Roland Füss

ABSTRACT

In this chapter we present a new performance measure for evaluating value-at-risk (VaR) models that merges four common risk characteristics of financial return series with the individual preferences of the risk manager. This performance criterion reflects the trade-off between efficient allocation of financial assets and the need to hold adequate levels of capital reserves. In particular, it accounts for (1) the accurate risk precaution, (2) the efficient allocation of financial resources, (3) the flexibility, and (4) the reliability of VaR models. This performance criterion is applicable on a wide range of various VaR models and data sets. Thereby, Monte Carlo simulations show the behavior of the VaR performance criterion (VPC) in response to different return series with respect to the degree of volatility and the shape of the distribution. According to this VPC, flexible VaR models generally outperform the conventional VaR measure but may appear inferior if a period of stable volatility is considered. Therefore, the risk manager should compare various VaR approaches over short as well as long periods in order to find the most adequate VaR model.

INTRODUCTION

Backtesting VaR models is an essential step in model validation. If the model performed well in the past, its quality is confirmed. If, however, the use of the model leads to a poor protection against downside risk, backtesting indicates that the model is not well specified and should be recalibrated.

The most common performance measure, which is also proposed in the Basel (1996) rules on backtesting the internal-model approach, is the number of returns that are more negative than the VaR. This hit ratio or ratio of exceptions, θ, should be as close as possible to its predicted value. Consequently, the θ percent VaR, normally defined as 1 or 5 percent VaR, should exhibit hits or exceptions θ percent of all times. Hit ratios significantly lower than θ indicate an overestimation of risk, while a significantly higher hit ratio indicates systematic underestimation. Confidence intervals to test the significance of deviations have been proposed by Kupiec (1995) for parametric models, by Kendall (1994) and Jorion (2007) for nonparametric models, and by Engle and Manganelli (2004) for semiparametric models. Other backtesting methods for evaluating the performance of VaR models have been proposed. For instance, Bao et al. (2006) measure the performance of VaR models using quantile loss functions by capturing the loss in the case of a hit. However, it also measures the distance from the returns to the predicted value if a hit does not occur. Christoffersen (1998) suggests a measure of conditional coverage, i.e., the number of exceptions conditional on the elapsed time to the last exception. This test is useful since it can point to the fact when a VaR model encounters several consecutive hits, for instance, because the model it is not able to respond adequately to periods of volatility clustering. The limitations of the existing performance measures lie in the focus on only one or two characteristics of a VaR model without considering other important characteristics.

This study presents a new VaR performance criterion (VPC) that measures the quality of a VaR model on four different dimensions and combines those characteristics with the risk preferences of the portfolio manager. This extended performance measure is completely general and can be applied to all kinds of VaR models and underlying return-generating processes.

The next section discusses the four constituents and their relationship in the VPC. The third section shows the behavior of this performance measure over 100 simulated return series with different characteristics. Our simulations also show the robustness of the VPC, i.e., VaR models that, according to the VPC, are expected to be superior to others consistently outperform other models over a wide range of different return distributions. The last section draws some conclusions.

VALUE-AT-RISK PERFORMANCE CRITERION (VPC)

Although hit ratios are standard practice in VaR literature, they have some distinct weaknesses pointed out in Figure 6.1, which uses a return series of the Euro Stoxx 50 index from 01/01/1990 to 31/12/2007 (4,697 Obs.) and the standard VaR models: normal VaR and GARCH VaR.

F I G U R E   6.1

Normal VaR and GARCH VaR on Euro Stoxx 50 Returns

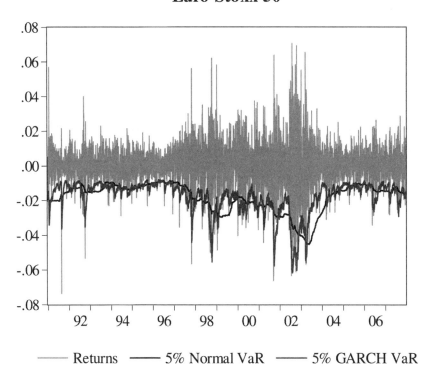

Euro Stoxx 50

—— Returns   —— 5% Normal VaR   —— 5% GARCH VaR

Both VaR models have approximately the same hit ratio (GARCH VaR: 5.1 percent; normal VaR: 4.9 percent). However, it is apparent that the GARCH VaR is able to react better to a changing volatility than the normal VaR. Although both models have approximately the same number of hits, the hit values (measured as the difference between the return and the VaR in the case a hit occurs) of the GARCH VaR are much lower and the portfolio manager is much better prepared in terms of sufficient capital reserves. Thus, relying solely on hit ratios can be misleading. Other factors such as the value of the hits should be considered as well. In particular, we are interested in the following four risk characteristics of a VaR model:

1. If hits occur, how large are they in absolute terms? Obviously, the hit value should be as small as possible.

2. If the return does not penetrate the VaR, what is its distance to the VaR? This question addresses the problem of too conservative capital reserves, which are expensive and involve unnecessary opportunity costs. A good VaR model exhibits small values.

3. How well can the VaR measure adapt to changes in the underlying return process? To answer this question, we measure the correlations between squared returns and the VaR at the same day. A good VaR model should have high negative correlation, i.e., positive or negative changes in returns lead to a decrease in the VaR and an increase in the absolute value of the VaR.

4. How close are the hit ratios to the predicted theoretical values? Hit ratios below or above the theoretical value indicate systematic overestimation and underestimation, respectively.

In short, we are concerned about risk protection (first VPC term), efficient allocation of capital (second VPC term), flexibility (third VPC term), and hit ratios (fourth VPC term). We combine those characteristics in the following VPC:

$$\text{VPC} = w_1 \cdot \frac{1}{n} \sum_{h=1}^{H} \left(hitvalue_h - \text{VaR}_h \right)^2 + w_2 \cdot \sqrt{\left| \frac{1}{n} \sum_{j=1}^{J} \text{VaR}_j - R_j \right|} \cdot I\left(R_j < 0 \right)$$

$$+ \; w_3 \rho + w_4 \left| \theta - ratio \right| \tag{6.1}$$

where n is the number of observations, H is the number of hits, J is the number of negative returns that do not constitute hits, and θ is the theoretical hit ratio (here 5 percent). The first two terms in Equation (6.1) show the trade-off. Since hits are dangerous when they get large, the first term is squared. In contrast, the opportunity costs of reserves are less important as long as risk management is concerned and therefore the second term comes with a square root. The correlation coefficient ρ is calculated as the correlation between the VaR and squared returns. The last term in Equation (6.1) measures the deviation of the hit ratio from its theoretical value. The weights w_1, w_2, w_3, and w_4 sum to unity and are set in such a way that each term contributes a fraction to the VPC measure that reflects the preferences of the risk manager. To compute the weights, the VPC is first calculated for a specific VaR model (benchmark model) using equal weights, i.e., $w_i = 0.25$. According to the preferences of the risk manager, the weights are then set and applied to all VaR models. In consideration of risk protection as the most important term, we set $w_1 = 0.55$, $w_2 = 0.10$, $w_3 = 0.30$, and $w_4 = 0.05$.[1] As will be shown below, the choice of the benchmark does not have a strong effect on the results. As expected, the GARCH VaR dominates the normal VaR in Figure 6.1 (VPC = 0.59 vs. 0.72, respectively).

EFFECTS OF CHANGING VOLATILITY AND RETURN DISTRIBUTION

Figure 6.1 suggests that every flexible model, such as conditional heteroschedasticity models or models from the semiparametric CAViaR family, will dominate any inflexible one, such as the normal VaR or historical simulation. However, the power of those models is only revealed if the return series has changing distributions and periods of high volatility. During tranquil periods, the former models may be dominated by the latter even when high weights for hit values and flexibility are used. Under such situations, the first VPC term generally will be small, and the correlation will be low and insignificant.

---

[1] One may object that the weights could be set so that some preferred model appears superior to the others. However, this often implies setting extreme weights, which would be difficult to justify. In addition, if performance measurement is used for internal purposes, there are no incentives to deliberately misrepresent results.

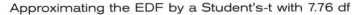

F I G U R E   6.2

Approximating the EDF by a Student's-t with 7.76 df

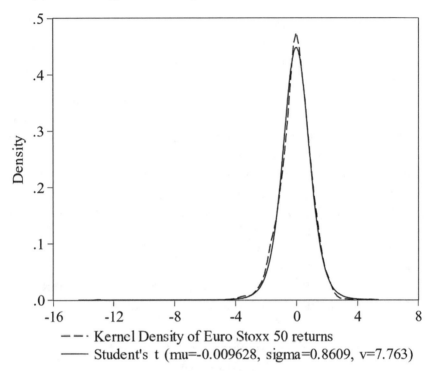

In order to show how the individual VPC terms react to different distributions in returns, we simulate 100 series, which differ in terms of volatility and persistence. The random shocks to the return series are based on the empirical distribution function (EDF) of the standardized residuals from the GARCH model, which we approximate by a parametric distribution that has the same mean and variance as the EDF. Figure 6.2 shows that a Student's-*t* distribution with 7.76 degrees of freedom closely approximates the kernel density of standardized residuals. Our low volatility series have 70 percent of the Euro Stoxx 50 return volatility, but they increase to 110 percent for our high-volatility series.[2] Our

---

[2] We tried larger volatility values but frequently encountered overflow warnings even at volatilities slightly higher than 110 percent.

low persistence series have $\beta = 0.8$ and $\alpha = 0.15$ from a standard GARCH(1,1) model $\sqrt{h_t} = \sqrt{\omega + \sum_{j=1}^{q} \alpha_j \varepsilon_{t-j}^2 + \sum_{i=1}^{p} \beta_i h_{t-i}}$.

The persistence increases to $\beta = 0.92$ and $\alpha = 0.03$ for our high persistence series. The sum $\alpha + \beta$ always stays at representative 0.95. Combining 10 volatility levels with 10 persistence levels results in our 100 simulated series.

Figure 6.3 shows the response surface of the first VPC term, i.e., the hit values for different settings of volatility and persistence. Higher volatility increases the hit values for both VaR models. The GARCH VaR, however, is able to adapt better to changes in volatility than the normal VaR, hence the smaller increase in the VPC from around 100 to 350.[3] Higher levels of persistence, in contrast, do not seem to have a strong effect on the value of the first VPC term. Overall, both VaR models seem to react similarly to the underlying return series, with the GARCH VaR outperforming the normal VaR in terms of hit values.

Figure 6.4 shows the second VPC term. The opportunity costs are generally higher for high-volatility series, but change much less in absolute terms compared to the first VPC term. Both VaR models show similar values, so that this term seems less suited for distinguishing VaR models.

The third VPC term measures the flexibility by calculating the correlation between squared returns and the VaR. We use squared returns because both positive and negative return changes lead to higher volatility in general and, thus, have an influence on the VaR. It also seems to be more important that a VaR model can capture larger return fluctuations, which indicate increased financial or even default risk, than small return changes. Figure 6.5 shows how the correlation becomes stronger (i.e., more negative) with increasing volatility and decreasing persistence.

A higher volatility induces the VaR to decrease, leading to a stronger correlation than during tranquil periods, where the VaR virtually does not change. For the simulated returns, low persistence means high α-values and

---

[3] For comparison reasons, we normalized the hit values to 100 for the lowest volatility and persistence series. Furthermore, we set the series with the lowest persistence and highest volatility to zero because of extremely large values.

F I G U R E   6.3

Hit Values for Different Settings of Volatility and Persistence

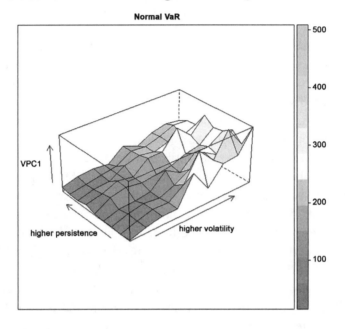

Normal VaR

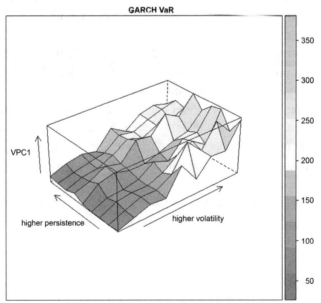

GARCH VaR

F I G U R E   6.4

Opportunity Costs for Different Settings of Volatility and Persistence

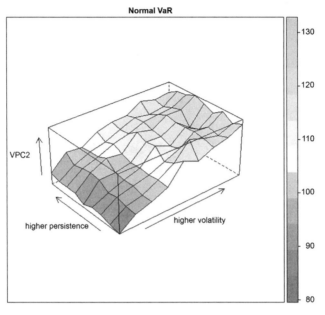

Normal VaR

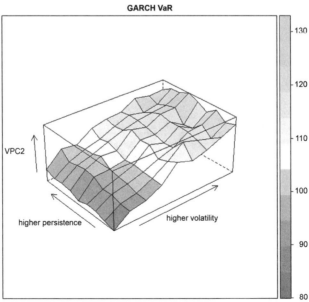

GARCH VaR

F I G U R E   6.5

Flexibility for Different Settings of Volatility and Persistence

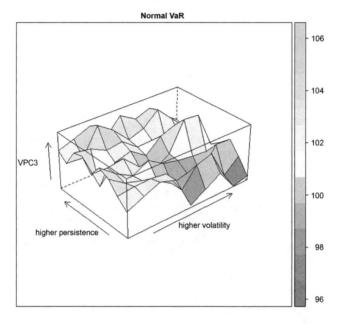

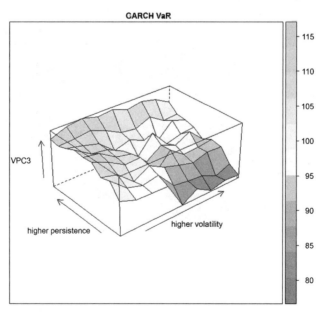

thus large spikes in the return series. Accordingly, the effect on correlation is similar to the case of high volatility. As expected, the effects are more pronounced and generally more negative in the case of the GARCH VaR.

The fourth VPC term measures the absolute deviations of the hit ratios from the theoretically predicted values (here 5 percent). Hit ratios smaller than 5 percent indicate a systematic overestimation of risk, while hit ratios larger then 5 percent indicate that the model systematically underestimates the risk of hits. The hit ratios in Figure 6.6 show no tendency to increase or decrease over different return series. For the GARCH VaR, however, the fluctuations are larger in absolute values. This shows that solely relying on hit ratios can be misleading since the normal VaR is often better with respect to this performance measure.

Finally, Figure 6.7 shows the compounded VPC consisting of all four terms with the weights $w_1 = 0.55$, $w_2 = 0.10$, $w_3 = 0.30$, and $w_4 = 0.05$.

The high weight $w_1 = 0.55$ leads to a dominant effect of the first term on the final VPC measure. The GARCH VaR outperforms the normal VaR in 65 out of 100 times. The 35 cases in which the normal VaR seems to be superior are periods of low volatility and high persistence where the normal VaR offers low values for the hit ratios.

It should be noted that the choice of the benchmark does not have a major influence on the results. This can be seen from Figure 6.8, which shows how the proportions of the VPC vary over the 100 simulated series with the top panel showing the weights of the normal VaR and the GARCH VaR being used as the benchmark.

Figure 6.8 demonstrates that the proportions stay relatively stable over time. Switching the benchmark to the normal VaR in the lower panel shows similar results, although some exceptions do exist. If many VaR models are to be compared, it can be useful to take the mean or median weight over all models instead of relying on one benchmark. This option is also provided in the Eviews program developed for this study.

CONCLUSION

Current VaR performance measures focus only on some risk characteristics, while ignoring others, which can lead to wrong inference concerning the performance of VaR models.

F I G U R E   6.6

Hit Ratios for Different Settings of Volatility and Persistence

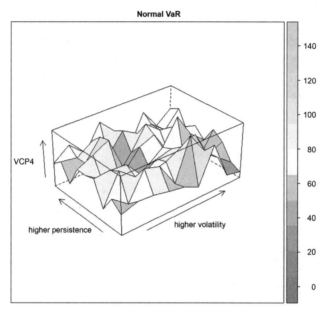

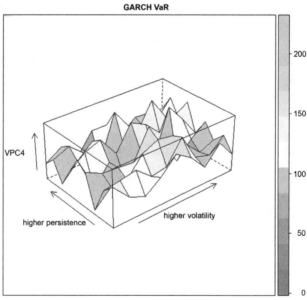

VPC for Different Settings of Volatility and Persistence

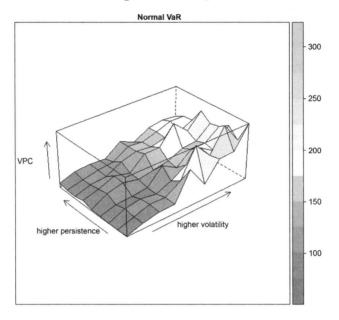

Normal VaR

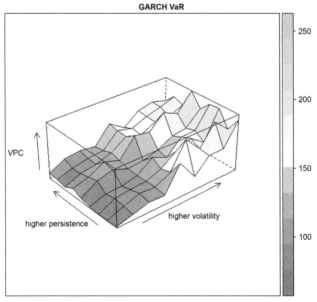

GARCH VaR

F I G U R E   6.8

Variability in VPC Proportions Depending on the Choice of the Benchmark

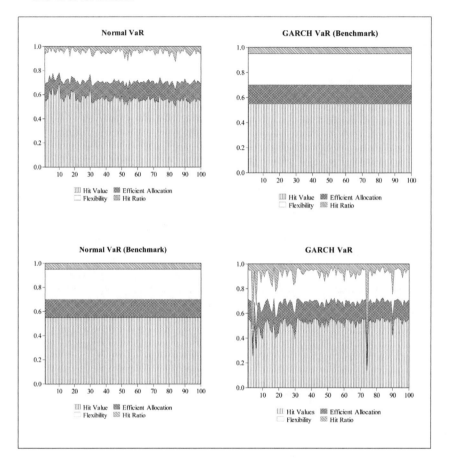

In this chapter, we develop an extensive performance measure in order to evaluate VaR models on a broader basis. The aim of the VPC is to capture all risk characteristics and allow the risk manager to enter his or her individual preferences into the calculation process. Simulated return series show that VaR models, which are able to quickly adapt to changes in the return process, outperform inflexible VaR models, provided that periods of changing volatility can be observed. Value-at-risk models that generally perform better than others can suddenly appear inferior during tranquil periods according to the VPC. Therefore, risk managers should compare various VaR models over short and long time horizons in order to find the most adequate VaR model for their security portfolios.

REFERENCES

Bao, Y., T.-H Lee, and B. Saltoglu (2006) Evaluating Predictive Performance of Value-at-Risk Models in Emerging Markets: A Reality Check. *Journal of Forecasting*, 25(2): 101–128.

Basel Committee on Banking Supervision (1996) *Supervisory Framework for the Use of "Backtesting" in Conjunction with the Internal Models Approach to Market Risk Capital Requirements.* Basel, Switzerland: BIS.

Christoffersen, P. (1998) Evaluating Internal Forecasts. *International Economic Review,* 39(4): 841–862.

Engle, R.F. and S. Manganelli (2004) CAViaR: Conditional Autoregressive Value at Risk by Regression Quantiles. *Journal of Business & Economic Statistics*, 22(4): 367–381.

Jorion, P. (2007) *Value at Risk. The New Benchmark for Managing Financial Risk,* 3rd edition. New York: McGraw-Hill.

Kendall, M. (1994) *Kendall's Advanced Theory of Statistics*. New York: Halsted Press.

Kupiec, P. (1995) Techniques for Verifying the Accuracy of Risk Measurement Models. *Journal of Derivatives,* 2(1): 73–84.

CHAPTER 7

Explaining Cross-Sectional Differences in Credit Default Swap Spreads: An Alternative Approach Using Value at Risk

Bastian Breitenfellner and Niklas Wagner

ABSTRACT

Cross-sectional differences in credit default swap (CDS) spreads for different issuers should be explainable by different levels of issuer specific credit risks. Unfortunately, assessing the credit risk of an issuer typically involves complex risk models, which hampers market participants in determining whether CDS spreads are fairly priced. Via performing a panel regression for different CDS contracts out of the DJ CDX.NA.IG universe, we examine the suitability of the value-at-risk measure of daily CDS spread changes and daily stock returns in explaining the spread level for the respective CDS. We derive the historical value-at-risk measures for different maturities of CDS spread changes and test for their power in explaining cross-sectional differences in spread levels. Our results provide strong evidence that the level of the CDS spread is positively related to the value at risk (VaR) of its past daily spread changes. Furthermore, the explanatory power of VaR is higher than the one of past spread volatility. These results help market participants to judge whether a CDS is over- or underpriced relative to a CDS with equivalent maturity of another issuer.

INTRODUCTION

The market for credit risk is one of the fastest growing segments of the financial services industry. It allows hedgers, as well as speculators and arbitrageurs to actively trade credit exposures in certain reference entities. Probably the most common instrument in the credit risk market is the credit default swap (CDS). A CDS provides insurance against the default of a certain issuer of debt capital, called *reference entity*, at the cost of a periodic fee, called *spread*. In case of an issuer default, the protection buyer is compensated for his or her losses by the protection seller. Therefore, CDS spreads can be regarded as a measure for the credit risk of the reference entity, as they represent the compensation an investor has to be offered in order to be willing to obtain exposure to the default risk of the reference entity. Compared to other credit risky instruments, CDS contracts have at least two exceptional features. First of all, CDS spreads are already quoted as real spreads, so there is no need to worry about which risk-free rate one has to deduct from, e.g., corporate bond yields in order to derive the respective credit spread of the issuer. Secondly, CDS spreads are less related to price drivers other than credit risk, like liquidity or tax effects, which is the case for corporate bonds as already stated by Elton et al. (2001), for example.

The pricing of credit derivatives, like CDS contracts, has gained increasing attention in the literature recently. Currently there are two fundamental approaches available. On the one hand, there are the structural models based on the seminal work of Merton (1974). Expansions to the original structural framework are introduced, for example, by Black and Cox (1976), Longstaff and Schwartz (1995), or Zhou (2001). In structural models the default process is explicitly modeled by assuming that an issuer defaults on its obligations when its firm value falls below a certain threshold. Although seeming perfectly reasonable in the first place, structural models suffer from a considerable drawback. Major input data like the firm value or its volatility cannot be observed directly and have to be approximated, often causing a poor model fit to empirical data. On the other hand, there is the class of reduced form models where an issuer default is an unpredictable event driven by a random jump process. Among the most popular reduced form models are the approaches of Jarrow and Turnbull (1995), Duffie and Singelton (1999), as well as Hull and White (2000). Regardless of their increased flexibility compared with structural models, they suffer from the difficult calibration of the jump process modeling the issuer default. Both approaches have one thing in common. Their output is largely influenced by the quality of the data input.

As the relevant input data are often not available or difficult to calibrate, both pricing approaches are somewhat impractical for a quick assessment of fair CDS spreads. Because of the deficiencies of the aforementioned modeling approaches, an alternative, "relative"[1] approach to the pricing of derivatives appears to be helpful. In this approach the influence of variables, which in theory affect CDS spreads, is tested. This allows market participants to evaluate the influence of changes in certain variables, e.g., the risk-free rate, firm leverage, or the condition of the overall economy on CDS spreads, which makes it possible to judge whether a specific CDS contract is priced fairly relative to another one. Benkert (2004) uses the structural framework to derive theoretical determinants of CDS spreads and uses them as explanatory variables in a panel regression to explain CDS spread levels. This approach was first introduced by Collin-Dufresne et al. (2001), who use the theoretical determinants of credit spreads implied by the structural framework to explain changes in corporate bond spreads. A similar access is also followed by Campbell and Taksler (2003). Benkert (2004) concludes that CDS spreads are largely influenced by the determinants implied by the structural approach, especially by equity volatility. Ericsson et al. (2004) also the test the explanatory power of the explanatory variables implied by the structural framework in explaining CDS spread levels, as well as spread changes. They find strong evidence that firm leverage, volatility, and the risk-free rate are statistically, as well as economically, significant in the

---

[1] In this approach, CDS contracts are priced relative to other CDS contracts. This allows one to judge whether they are priced correctly on a relative value basis. Such approaches do not yield absolute pricing results, as do the models described above.

determination of CDS spreads. A principal component analysis of the residuals suggests that the structural framework explains a significant amount of variation in the data and that there is only weak evidence in favor of missing common explanatory factor.

Hull et al. (2004) analyze the relationship between credit default spreads and bond yields, as well as the influence of credit rating announcement by Moody's on CDS spreads. They find that reviews for downgrades contain significant information, in contrast to downgrades and negative outlooks. Nevertheless, all three types of information are anticipated by CDS markets. The results for positive rating events are much less significant. Another study by Das et al. (2007) examines the importance of accounting data in explaining CDS spreads. They find evidence that issuer default models based on accounting data are not inferior to models based on market data. Furthermore, they find that a model of issuer default, which is based on both accounting data and market data, outperforms models based on either of the two sources of information on a stand-alone basis. Consequently, they conclude that accounting and market data contain complementary rather than substitutional information.

Byström (2005) analyzes the relationship between equity market returns, equity market volatility, and iTraxx spreads. He finds strong evidence that current, as well as lagged stock returns explain much of the variation in CDS index spreads. Furthermore, he discovers significant correlations between stock markets and CDS markets, whereas the stock market seems to lead the CDS market in the transmission of firm specific information. Alexander and Kaeck (2007) introduce a Markov switching model to examine the determinants of iTraxx Europe index spreads in two different regimes. They confirm the statistically significant explanatory power of the variables implied by the structural framework. Additionally, they find that CDS spreads are more sensitive to stock returns than stock volatility in normal market conditions. In times of turbulences, spreads are extremely sensitive to stock volatility.

Given those empirical studies described above, we propose yet another approach in evaluating the CDS spread of a certain reference entity. In the structural framework, the volatility of the firm value has a major influence on credit risk, as the position of a debt investor in a certain firm can be replicated by holding a riskless bond and selling a put option on the firm's assets. As volatility is a major driver of option value, the put option becomes more expensive with rising volatility, at the costs of the debt investor. Anyhow, volatility is a two-sided measure. Not only negative tail events gain probability mass with rising volatility, but also positive tail events, which generally are favorable for debt investors. Therefore, it remains questionable whether volatility is really an appropriate model input. From this point of view, a one-sided measure like value at risk (VaR), which only accounts for one tail of the distribution function, should lead to a better estimation of the credit risk the dept investor is exposed to.[2]

Our empirical research is dedicated to the examination of the relationship between VaR of CDS spread changes and the cross section of CDS spread levels. As an increase of default risk inherent with a certain reference entity is accompanied by positive spread changes, VaR of past spreads, as well as volatility account for an increase of credit risk. Consequently, CDS contracts with high past spread VaR are more credit risky and should trade at higher spread levels. The same is true for CDS contracts with high past spread volatility. Nevertheless, VaR should perform better in explaining CDS spread levels, due to the shape of the actual empirical distribution of spread changes, which is skewed and characterized by excess kurtosis. We use a panel regression to check for the explanatory of VaR of both past CDS spread changes as well as past equity returns of the reference entity in determining CDS spread levels for different confidence levels and estimation periods of VaR. To compare the explanatory power of VaR with past spread volatility, we repeat our regression with the standard deviation of past CDS spread changes. The results of this empirical study are of special interest for traders in the credit risk market, as they allow identifying underpriced CDS contracts on a simple relative value basis.

---

[2] Bali and Cakici (2004) is one of the first studies that examine the explanatory power of VaR in determining asset prices. They find evidence that a model comprising firm size, liquidity, and the VaR of past stock returns can explain the cross-sectional variations in expected returns on NYSE, AMEX, and NASDAQ stocks, as well as portfolios composed of those stocks. In a further study Bali et al. (2007) examine the cross-sectional relationship between VaR and hedge fund returns. They find that high VaR portfolios of hedge funds have significantly higher returns than low VaR portfolios, which they interpret as support for the presence of a relation between downside risk and expected hedge fund returns.

To the best of our knowledge, this is the first study to shed light on the relationship between the VaR of past CDS spread changes and the cross-sectional variations in CDS spread levels. We observe that the VaR of past spread changes has statistically, as well as economically significant explanatory power in determining CDS spread levels. Furthermore, the explanatory power, measured in terms of R^2, of VaR is higher than the one of past spread change volatility.

In order to test the suitability of our results for designing a trading rule for CDS contracts based on VaR, we go one step further. If VaR has significant explanatory power in determining CDS spread levels, CDS contracts with a low past VaR but a relatively high CDS spread level are underpriced. The reverse holds for high VaR CDS contracts with relatively low spread levels. Therefore, we divide our original sample of CDS contracts in portfolios based on past VaR and spread levels. If VaR can be the basis for a trading rule, the high VaR low level portfolio spreads should widen in the near future. The spreads of the low VaR high-level portfolio should show a tendency toward tightening. Our analysis does not provide evidence in favor of a trading rule based on VaR. Mispricing relative to VaR levels seem to be corrected quickly by the market, so there do not exist any persistent trading opportunities.

The remainder of this chapter is structured as follows. The second section introduces the estimation methodology for the panel as well as the portfolio analysis. The third section describes the data set and explanatory variables used in our analysis. The fourth section is dedicated to the empirical investigation of the explanatory power of past spread changes VaR in determining CDS spread levels. The fifth section concludes the chapter.

ESTIMATION METHODOLOGY

Panel Data Analysis

In order to examine the explanatory power of VaR in determining CDS spreads, we perform a panel regression of the form

$$S_t^{(i)} = \beta_0 + \beta_1 \text{VaR}_t^{(i)} + \varepsilon_t^{(i)} \tag{7.1}$$

where $S_t^{(i)}$ represents the spread of entity i at quarter t, $\text{VaR}_t^{(i)}$ is the VaR measure for entity i in quarter t, and ε_t^i is the normally distributed error term for entity i at time t. The regression is repeated for different confidence levels and estimation periods of VaR in order to assess the robustness of our results. To be consistent with theory, the expected sign of the regression coefficient for VaR is positive. This is because positive spread changes represent an increasing default risk; therefore the spread changes we are interested in are located on the right side of the empirical distribution of past spread changes. From this point of view it is intuitively clear that a high VaR represents an increased likelihood of positive spread changes, which increase the credit risk of the respective reference entity. For a comparison of the VaR measure with volatility of past spread changes in terms of their explanatory power, we also perform a panel regression of the form

$$S_t^{(i)} = \beta_0 + \beta_1 \mathrm{VOL}_t^{(i)} + \varepsilon_t^{(i)} \tag{7.2}$$

where $\mathrm{VOL}_t^{(i)}$ represents the standard deviation of past CDS spread changes. The expected sign of the regression coefficient of the volatility measure is positive, since an increased volatility in CDS spread changes represents an increase in the credit risk of the issuer. Therefore, an increase in the spread volatility should be accompanied by an increase in the spread level of the respective CDS contract. From a logical point of view, the VaR of past CDS spread changes should be a better estimator of the credit risk, measured in terms of R^2, inherent with a certain issuer than the volatility, as VaR only considers one side of the empirical distribution. In contrast, volatility considers both sides of the empirical distribution, making it sensitive to movements, which are actually positive in the view of the investor exposed to the credit risk of the reference entity.

Portfolio Analysis

After assessing the explanatory power of VaR in determining CDS spread levels, we investigate the suitability of VaR as a basis for simple trading strategies in the CDS market. For this purpose we need to identify those CDS contracts that are underpriced and overpriced relative to the VaR of their past spread changes. Contracts with low VaR and relatively high spread levels should tighten in the near future, whereas CDS contracts with high VaR and relatively low spread levels should widen. Consequently, we divide our data sample into three sub portfolios based on the VaR of past spread changes. We use a VaR measure with a three-month estimation period in order to have sufficient observations. The high VaR portfolio contains the 17 CDS contracts with the highest VaRs in the estimation period, the medium VaR portfolio contains 18 CDS contracts, and the low VaR portfolio consists of the 17 CDS contracts with the lowest VaR in the estimation period. Next, we take the high VaR portfolio and further subdivide it into three portfolios based on the spread levels of the portfolio members. The high VaR high-level portfolio contains the six CDS contracts with the largest spreads, the high VaR medium-level portfolio has five members, and the high VaR low-level portfolio consists of the remaining six members with the lowest spread levels. The same procedure is repeated for the low VaR portfolio. For our purpose two of the subportfolios are of special interest, namely the high VaR low-level portfolio and the low VaR high-level portfolio. The former contains those CDS contracts with spread levels to low relative to their VaR; the latter is composed out of those CDS contracts whose spread level is to high relative to their VaR. If VaR is suited in constructing a trading rule for the CDS market, the first portfolio should show a tendency toward spread widenings, and the spreads of the second should tighten.[3]

DATA AND EXPLANATORY VARIABLES
The Data Set

For our empirical analysis we use CDS spread data of firms included in the sixth revision of the Dow Jones CDX North America Investment Grade Index (DJ CDX.NA.IG). The DJ CDX.NA.IG index consists of 125 investment grade U.S. companies, for which CDS contracts are actively quoted. The index is further divided into five subsectors. The choice of this index ensures that the single reference entities are widespread among several industries, in order to avoid any biases stemming from the choice of a certain industries. Additionally the CDS contracts of members of the DJ CDX.NA.IG index universe are adequately liquid,

[3] Since market effects are also part of the spread developments, the portfolio spreads could indeed follow a spread development opposite that described above. Nevertheless, the high VaR low-level portfolio should tighten relative to the low VaR high-level portfolio, regardless of the movement of the overall CDS market.

which avoids any biases due to illiquidity of the respective CDS contract. We download daily averages of bid and ask spreads for the most liquid five-year CDS contracts from Open Bloomberg, for the period between 03/31/2004 and 07/01/2006, which represents 528 trading days of spread data. Companies that do not have satisfactory spread data available are removed from the sample. This leaves us with a sample of 52 companies, for which continuous CDS spread data is available.[4]

Explanatory Variables

We derive the VaR measure of the CDS spread changes by looking at their empirical distribution. For every quarter starting from Q2 2004 we use the past three-month CDS spread changes to estimate the VaR with confidence levels of 5, 1, and 0.1 percent of the respective reference entity.[5] After the estimation for the first quarter, we move one quarter further and repeat the aforementioned estimation routine until Q2 2006. Finally, we have nine quarterly VaR estimates for every reference entity and confidence interval, or a total of 1,404 VaR estimates. We repeat the same estimation process for half-year VaR measures as well, ending up with four estimates for every reference entity and confidence level. In order to compare the explanatory power of the VaR measure with the volatility of past spread changes, we estimate the volatility of CDS spreads as well. Therefore, for every quarter, we compute the quarterly empirical standard deviation of CDS spread changes taking into account the last three months for every company of our sample. We begin with Q2 2004 end with Q2 2006, leaving us with a total of nine quarterly measures for past CDS spread change volatility for each of the 52 reference entities. The same procedure is rerun for half-year standard deviations.

---

[4] In fact, there are still companies with missing quotes included in the sample. Nevertheless, the number of missing data points is very small. As we estimate VaR, which is driven by tail events, we do not interpolate to fill gaps in the data, as these interpolated results are very unlikely to have a measurable influence on VaR.

[5] These confidence levels seem somewhat exceptional in the first place, since normal confidence levels of VaR are 95, 99, and 99.9 percent. The reason for this lies in the nature of the CDS spreads. Rising spreads represent an increase in credit risk of the reference entity, which is an unfavorable development for a debt investor. Therefore, the negative events with which a debt investor is concerned lie in the right tail of the distribution of spread changes, which explains the confidence levels for VaR.

Descriptive Statistics

In this section we present some descriptive statistics of our sample of CDS spreads to motivate our further proceeding. Figure 7.1 shows the distribution of spread changes for four reference entities included in our sample. Having a look at the empirical distribution of the CDS spreads for the single reference entities, two things become apparent. First, the distributions of all reference entities show excess kurtosis. The actual values range between 5.78 and 167.85, indicating that the empirical distributions have much fatter tails than implied by the normal distribution. Second, the majority of the distributions (71.15 percent) are skewed to the left. These two facts clearly speak in favor of using VaR rather than volatility as explanatory variable for the determination of CDS spread levels, as VaR emphasizes the role of the tails of the empirical distribution and better accounts for skewed data samples.

F I G U R E   7.1

Empirical Distributions of Spread Changes for Different Reference Entities, Period: April 1, 2004 to June 30, 2006

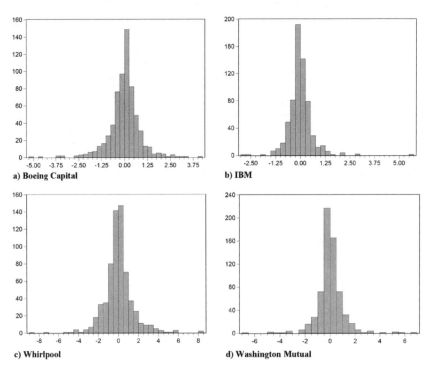

a) Boeing Capital

b) IBM

c) Whirlpool

d) Washington Mutual

This idea also was brought forward by Gupta and Liang (2005), who argue that VaR is a better measure for hedge fund risk due to the negative skewness and excess kurtosis in hedge fund returns.

EMPIRICAL RESULTS

Since our data set has both a time dimension as well as a cross-sectional dimension, we use a panel OLS regression to measure the explanatory power of VaR in the determination of CDS spread levels. Our estimation model is described in a previous section. Table 7.1 provides a summary of the estimation results using VaRs with different confidence levels and estimation windows.

Throughout the estimation results one thing is apparent, namely that the VaR measure of past spread changes has a statistically as well as economically highly significant influence on CDS spread levels. The relationship between the VaR of past spread changes and current CDS spread levels is positive, which makes sense intuitively. All the results are significant with in a 1 percent confidence interval. The explanatory power of VaR differs among different confidence levels and estimation windows. In general, our results indicate that longer estimation windows for VaR have better explanatory power expressed in terms of adjusted R^2.

T A B L E   7.1

Estimation output of the panel analysis for the explanatory power of VaR with t-values in parenthesis, period: April 1, 2004 to June 30, 2006

Variables	VaR 0.05 Quarterly	VaR 0.01 Quarterly	VaR 0.001 Quarterly	VaR 0.05 Half-year	VaR 0.01 Half-year	VaR 0.001 Half-year
Dependent variable spread						
Explanatory variables						
Intercept	22.510	25.038	28.639	15.670	17.319	24.227
	(18.80)	(20.42)	(22.88)	(9.19)	(10.90)	(12.83)
VaR	9.725	4.532	2.735	12.366	5.786	2.545
	(20.67)	(17.99)	(14.47)	(17.41)	(18.04)	(10.93)
Adjusted R^2	0.48	0.41	0.31	0.59	0.61	0.36

For the six-month estimation window, R^2 ranges between 0.36 and 0.61, whereas it ranges between 0.31 and 0.48 for the three-month estimation window for VaR. Hence, it seems as if market participants do take into account longer time periods in order to asses the credit risk inherent with a certain reference entity.

Another conclusion that can be drawn out of the estimation results in Table 7.1 is that lower confidence levels of the VaR measure seem to have a higher explanatory power, throughout both estimation windows. Extreme events in the evolution of CDS spreads for a certain issuer seem to have not such a big impact on the assessment of the credit risk inherent with that issuer. This is kind of contraintuitive in the first place, nevertheless this fact can be explained by the structure of the data. Especially for the three-month estimation window the VaRs with high confidence levels are not market by an actual spread observed but are generated by linear extrapolation. This view is also promoted by the fact that the effected of increasing predictive power with lower confidence levels of VaR is much less pronounced when looking at the six-month estimation window. Here, the explanatory power slightly increases when using 1 percent VaR instead of 5 percent VaR. Overall, VaR explains a significant proportion of cross-sectional and time series differences of CDS spread levels, with R^2 ranging between 0.36 and 0.61. Therefore, VaR seems well suited to judge

T A B L E   7.2

Estimation output of the panel analysis for the explanatory power of volatility with *t*-values in parenthesis

Variables	Volatility Quarterly	Volatility Half-year
Dependent variable spread Explanatory variables		
Intercept	22.790	16.641
	(17.13)	(8.68)
VOL	14.084	16.898
	(17.70)	(14.64)
Adjusted R^2	0.40	0.51

spread levels of different reference entities in terms of a relative value analysis, in order to identify relatively under- and overpriced CDS contracts. Table 7.2 summarizes the estimation results of the panel regression with past spread volatility as explanatory variable.

In line with the results for VaR as explanatory variable, the explanatory power of past spread volatility in determining CDS spread levels is statistically as well as economically significant. The relationship is positive as predicted by theory. The influence is significant both for three-month and six-month volatility at the 1 percent level. Comparable to the results for VaR is the fact that the explanatory power of volatility, expressed in terms of adjusted R^2, is rising with a larger estimation window. R^2 rises to 0.51 when using a six-month estimation window, compared with a R^2 of 0.40 when using a three-month estimation window. Again, these points to the fact that market participants tend to use longer time horizons in order to judge the credit risk inherent with a certain issuer. Just like VaR, volatility explains a significant part of the variance in spread levels, both in a time-series and cross-sectional dimension, which makes it suitable to judge the prices of certain CDS contracts on a relative value basis.

When it comes to the comparison of the explanatory power of VaR and volatility, VaR performs better in terms of adjusted R^2 than volatility. The difference is 0.08 for the three-month estimation window and 0.11 for the six-month estimation window. Therefore, past spread change VaR seems to be better suited than volatility to explain the cross-sectional differences in CDS spreads. The fact that far is only affected by one tail of the empirical distribution is one possible explanation. Another reason for this is the fact that VaR explicitly take into account the extreme values in the empirical distribution of spread changes. Observations left of the significance level are not taken into account by the VaR measure, except when the number of observations in the estimation window is limited. In contrast, to calculate volatility, all observations of past spread changes are accounted for, which somehow dilutes the influence of the extremes. Nevertheless, these extreme values determine the amount of credit risk an investor is exposed to. Taking into account the aforementioned facts, it does not come as a surprise that VaR performs better in explaining CDS spread levels than volatility does.

T A B L E   7.3

Comparison of the portfolio performance for different
investment horizons

	Quarter		10 Trading Days		3 Trading Days	
	Change HL	Change LH	Change HL	Change LH	Change HL	Change LH
Q2 2004	−9.93	−7.86	0.51	1.46	0.55	−0.28
Q3 2004	−8.09	−13.75	−0.98	−2.69	−0.49	−1.44
Q4 2004	5.10	7.12	4.28	3.96	0.30	0.69
Q1 2005	4.73	5.36	0.26	−0.33	−0.79	0.18
Q2 2005	−7.60	−5.26	−2.50	−1.36	−0.09	−0.22
Q3 2005	0.13	−2.13	9.60	2.20	−0.19	0.76
Q4 2005	−6.46	−1.74	−0.61	0.15	−1.01	−0.14
Q1 2006	2.83	2.37	−2.22	−0.10	−0.31	−0.01

Next, we perform a portfolio analysis as described in a previous section to find out more about the suitability of VaR as input for a simple trading rule in the CDS market. The results of our analysis are presented in Table 7.3.

First we investigate the developments of the two portfolios of interest, namely the high VaR low spread level portfolio (HL) and the low VaR high spread level portfolio (LH), with a holding period of one quarter for each portfolio. The results are presented in column 2 of Table 7.3. The spread developments of the two portfolios generally do not show the predicted characteristics when comparing the development over the last three months. Neither does the HL portfolio show a tendency toward wider spreads, nor does the LH portfolio tend toward spread tightening. Even when looking on the relative spread development of the two portfolios, there is no significant trend to be captured. A possible explanation of this behavior might lie in the characteristics of CDS markets. Market participants are aware of the mispricing of certain CDS contracts relative to their past spread VaR, consequently the relative under pricing or overpricing gets corrected quickly. Therefore, a three-month holding period is too long to capture spread movements due to mispricing. Therefore, we repeat our analysis with shorter holding periods of 10 trading days and 3 trading days. The results do not differ largely from the three-month holding period. Again, there does not seem to be a trend in the spread development of the portfolios, neither toward spread widening of the HL portfolio, nor toward spread tightening of the LH portfolio. This suggests that the relative pricing errors based on the VaR of past spread changes are corrected quickly after their occurrence. Even for a holding period of as short as three trading days, a trading strategy based on this mispricing does not generate a significant return. This points to the conclusion that CDS markets quickly react to new information, making them considerably efficient.

CONCLUSION

In this chapter we empirically investigate the influence of the VaR of past spread changes in explaining cross-sectional differences in CDS spread levels. We find evidence that VaR has a significant influence in the determination of CDS spread levels, both statistically and economically. Additionally, we show that past spread VaR performs better, in terms of R^2, than past spread volatility. This can be explained by the empirical distribution of CDS spread changes, which is skewed and shows excess kurtosis throughout or sample. Despite the highly significant explanatory of VaR in determining CDS spread levels, we are not able to exploit this fact by a simple trading rule based on VaR. This failure is likely caused by firm-specific effects concealing the error correction effect triggered by the mispricing in terms of VaR. This problem could be mitigated by the use of a larger sample than the one we had at our disposal.

REFERENCES

Alexander, C. and A. Kaeck (2007) Regimes in CDS Spreads: A Markov Switching Model of iTraxx Europe Indices. Working paper, ICMA Center, Reading, UK.

Bali, T. and N. Cakic (2004) Value at Risk and Expected Stock Returns. *Financial Analysts Journal*, 60(2): 57–73.

Bali, T., S. Gokcan, and B. Liang (2007) Value at Risk and the Cross-section of Hedge Fund Returns. *Journal of Banking & Finance*, 31(4): 1135–1166.

Benkert, C. (2004) Explaining Credit Default Swap Premia. *Journal of Futures Markets*, 24(1): 71–92.

Black F. and J. Cox (1976) Valuing Corporate Securities: Some Effects of Bond Indenture Provisions. *Journal of Finance*, 31(2): 351–67.

Byström, H. (2005) Credit Default Swaps and Equity Prices: The iTraxxCDS Index Market. In Wagner N. (ed.) *Credit Risk—Models, Derivatives and Management*. Boca Raton, FL: Chapman & Hall, pp. 377–390.

Campbell, H. and G. Taksler (2003) Equity Volatility and Corporate Bond Yields. *Journal of Finance*, 58(6): 2321–2350.

Collin-Dufresne, P., R. Goldstein, and S. Martin (2001) The Determinants of Credit Spread Changes. *Journal of Finance*, 56(6): 2177–2207.

Das, S., P. Hanouna, and A. Sarin (2007) Accounting-Based versus Market-Based Cross-sectional Models of CDS Spreads. Working paper, Santa Clara University, Santa Clara, CA.

Duffie D. and K. Singleton (1999) Modeling Term Structures of Defaultable Bonds. *Review of Financial Studies*, 12(4): 687–720.

Elton, E., M., Guber, D. Agrawal, and C. Mann (2001) Explaining the Rate Spread on Corporate Bonds. *Journal of Finance*, 56(1): 247–277.

Ericsson, J., K. Jacobs, and R. Oviedo-Helfenberger (2004) The Determinants of Credit Default Swap Premia. Working paper, Swedish Institute for Financial Research, Stockholm, Sweden.

Gupta, A. B. and Liang (2005) Do Hedge Funds Have Enough Capital? A Value-at-risk Approach. *Journal of Financial Economics*, 77(1): 219–253.

Hull, J., M. Predescu, and A. White (2004) The Relationship between Credit Default Swap Spreads, Bond Yields, and Credit Rating Announcements. *Journal of Banking & Finance*, 28(11): 2789–2811.

Hull, J. and A. White (2000) Valuing Credit Default Swaps I: No Counterparty Default Risk. *Journal of Derivatives*, 8(1): 29–40.

Jarrow, R. and S. Turnbull (1995) Pricing Derivatives on Financial Securities Subject to Credit Risk. *Journal of Finance*, 50(1): 53–85.

Longstaff, F. and E. Schwartz (1995) A Simple Approach to Valuing Risky Fixed and Floating Rate Debt. *Journal of Finance*, 50(3): 789–819.

Merton, R. (1974) On the Pricing of Corporate Debt: The Risk Structure of Interest Rates. *Journal of Finance*, 29(2): 449–70.

Zhou, C. (2001) The Term Structure of Credit Spreads with Jump Risk. *Journal of Banking & Finance*, 25(11): 2015–2040.

C H A P T E R   8

Some Advanced Approaches to VaR Calculation and Measurement

François-Éric Racicot and Raymond Théoret

ABSTRACT

In this chapter, we consider methods that are frequently used in practice and provide useful empirical applications for practitioners. First, we present basic methods, such as historical simulation, bootstrapping, and Monte Carlo simulation. Second, we cover more recent methods involving non-Gaussian returns: the copula method, the Fourier transform, and the GARCH methods. Finally, we briefly discuss new developments oriented toward the use of the UHF-GARCH coupled with historical simulation in order to obtain a better estimation of value at risk.

INTRODUCTION[1]

Risk measures have greatly evolved following Markowitz's (1952) theory of portfolio diversification. The standard deviation was then considered as the risk measure of an efficient portfolio, but for an asset it was deemed not

---

[1] This article is based on: Racicot and Théoret (2006, paper 16).

relevant. In fact, in the case of an individual asset, risk is computed using the covariance between its return and another asset representing a well-diversified portfolio. The standard deviation of an asset's return includes both diversified and nondiversifiable risk. However, only the nondiversifiable risk is priced by the market and is represented by the covariance between the return of an asset and the market portfolio.

The risk theories following Markowitz were concerned by the factors explaining the risk of an asset and also by the equilibrium of financial markets. The capital asset pricing model (CAPM) developed by William F. Sharpe in the 1960s reduced the dimension of the Markowitz covariance matrix. Capital asset pricing model is based on only one factor explaining the risk of an asset, which is the correlation between the return of an asset and the asset portfolio, known as the *systematic risk*. The unsystematic risk, also called the *idiosyncratic risk*, is diversifiable and is thus not priced by the market. In the CAPM, the systematic risk of an asset is measured by its beta, which is a relative measure of risk by comparing the portfolio beta against the market portfolio.

In the mid-1970s, a generalization of the CAPM based on the concept of no arbitrage was developed by Ross (1976) called the *arbitrage pricing theory* (APT). This model documented that the risk of an asset was a multidimensional phenomenon explained by several factors. In the APT framework, the beta of an asset for a given factor is called the *factor loading* and is the relative exposure of the asset's return to this factor. At the start of the 1980s, a new measure of risk called *value at risk* (VaR), similar to an approach developed by Baumol (1963), was initially proposed for the banking sector to compute the maximum loss in a given period (i.e., 10 days for the case of a bank) on the total assets of a given bank at a particular confidence level. In 1997, the Basel Accord imposed banks to regularly compute VaR and in 2007, the Basel Accord II required banks to use more than one VaR measure. The risks as defined by the Accord consisted of three dimensions: (1) market risk, (2) credit risk, and (3) operational risk.

This chapter is organized as follows. First, we consider parametric methods for computing VaR using the Normal distribution and then present the basic methods: (1) historical simulation, (2) bootstrapping, and (3) Monte Carlo simulation. Finally, we cover more recent methods involving non-Gaussian returns such as the copula method, the Fourier transform, and GARCH methods. Future research might be oriented toward the integration of the distribution of returns, the use of the UHF-GARCH to model the return volatility at the higher frequency, the integration of higher moments of returns resorting to tail distributions coupled with nonparametric methods like historical simulation or bootstrapping to obtain a better estimation of VaR.

PARAMETRIC VAR AND THE NORMAL DISTRIBUTION

By definition, VaR is the maximum loss that a portfolio manager may realize within a given period of time and for a predetermined probability. If we assume that this probability is 95 percent, then the corresponding error margin for this maximum loss is 5 percent. We further suppose that the cash flows of this portfolio follow a normal distribution, thus the VaR can be computed as follows, for an α equal to 5 percent:

$$\text{VaR} = \mu - N^{-1}(0.05)\sigma = \mu - 1.655\sigma \qquad (8.1)$$

For example, assume a portfolio of $100, with an expected return of 15 percent and a standard deviation of 30 percent. For the identical alpha, the VaR is $[0.15 - 1.655(0.30)] \times 100 = -0.3435 \times 100 = -\$34.35$. Table 8.1 shows how to implement this method in an Excel spreadsheet.

T A B L E   8.1

Excel spreadsheet

	A	B
1	Expected return	0.15
2	Standard deviation	0.3
3	Initial investment	100
4	Final investment	= NormInv(0.05, 65.6544 (1+B1)*B3, B2*B3)

USING HISTORICAL SIMULATION
TO COMPUTE VAR[2]

The historical simulation method is a simple approach for computing VaR. In what follows, we will show how to compute the VaR using an example. Let us assume we want to compute the VaR of a forward contract that allows us to purchase USD$1 million in three months in exchange for receiving CAD$1.59 million. The value f_t of this contract may be computed as follows:

$$f_t = S_t \frac{1}{1 + r_t^{US}\tau} - K \frac{1}{1 + r_t^{CAN}\tau} \tag{8.2}$$

where S is the spot price of U.S. dollars in Canadian dollars; K, the exchange rate of the American dollar as specified by the contract; r^{US}, the American risk-free rate; r^{CAN}, the Canadian risk-free rate; and τ, the maturity of the contract fixed to three months here. Equation (8.2) is very similar to Black and Scholes formula, the only difference being the absence of the cumulative distribution functions of d_1 and d_2, denoted by $N(d_1)$ and $N(d_2)$. Indeed, a forward contract requires the delivery of the underlying, which gives way to a probability of exercise $N(d_2)$ equal to 1. $N(d_1)$ is therefore also equal to 1.[3]

Using Equation (8.2), we can compute the VaR assuming U.S. and Canadian interest rates of 2.75 percent and 3.31 percent respectively. If the U.S. exchange rate is CAD$1.588, then the price of the forward contract is $206. To implement the historical simulation, we resort to a time series of the most recent 101 days of our three risk factors, which are the U.S. and the Canadian interest rates and the exchange rate of the U.S. dollar.

We first compute the daily variations of the two interest rates, taking into account the historical ordering of the data, and also the daily percentage variation of the exchange rate. This computation is provided in an Excel spreadsheet at Table 8.2.

We are now in position to run the historical simulation. The input of this simulation is constituted by the three factors observed on the day of the simulation and by the daily variations appearing at Table 8.2.

---

[2] For this section, see Jorion (2007). For a useful reference on how to implement historical simulation in practice, see Christoffersen (2003). See also Dowd (2005) for a thorough discussion on the risk measure theory in relation to VaR or ETL (ES or C-VaR).

[3] For instance, let us recall that $N(d_1)$ is the delta of the call. When the call is exercised, the behavior of the call is the same as the underlying. Thus, the angle of the payoff with the abscissa, which represents the price of the underlying, is 45 degrees.

T A B L E   8.2

Daily variations of historical data

	r(CAD)	r(EUR)	S($CAD/ EUR)
1	2.4906	2.0732	1.2594
2	2.5009	2.0765	1.2868
3	2.5011	2.0318	1.3426
4	2.5859	2.0859	1.3469
5	2.4939	2.0703	1.3504
6	2.4902	2.0226	1.3678
7	2.5276	2.0833	1.3548
8	2.4912	2.0542	1.3765
9	2.4127	2.0842	1.3973
10	2.4336	2.0798	1.4131
11	2.4122	2.0748	1.3514
12	2.4109	2.0352	1.3691
13	2.4108	1.9962	1.3436
14	2.4074	2.0199	1.3297
15	2.4138	2.0632	1.2822
16	2.3866	2.0030	1.3103
17	2.4103	1.9642	1.3730
18	2.4504	1.9732	1.3953
19	2.4457	1.9295	1.3843
20	2.4665	1.9449	1.3203
21	2.4858	2.0057	1.3456
22	2.5475	1.9707	1.3217
23	2.5792	2.0323	1.3434
24	2.6175	1.9949	1.3739
25	2.6376	1.8744	1.3706

To obtain the simulated series reported at Table 8.3, we use the variations appearing in Table 8.2, which we add to the observed exchange rate on that day. On that day, the observed Canadian exchange rate is equal to 3.31 percent. On day 1, the simulated rate is thus: $3.31 + 0.0103 = 3.3141$. We repeat the same procedure for the other interest and the exchange rate: $2.75 + 0.0033 = 2.8789$ and $1.588 (1 + 0.0217) = 1.6153$. Inserting these values in Equation (8.2), we obtain the first simulated price for the forward contract:

$$f_t = \left[1.6153 \frac{1}{1 + (0.028789 \times 0.25)} - 1.59 \frac{1}{1 + (0.033141 \times 0.25)} \right]$$
$$\times 10^6 = 26859$$

For day 2, we proceed in the same way in that we apply the variations of day 2 again on the actual values of the three factors, which are: 3.31 percent (Canadian interest rate), 2.75 percent (U.S. interest rate) and 1.5888 (American exchange rate). The simulated values for our contract on the first 25 days are reported at Table 8.3.

Once computed the hundred simulated values of the contract in increasing order, we construct the histogram displayed in Figure 8.1.

TABLE 8.3

Computation of the simulated contract value

	r(1$CAD)	r(1$EUR)	S	PV($1CAD)	PV(1$EUR)	Contract value
1	3.3141	2.8789	1.61533663	0.9917829	0.99285413	26859
2	3.3039	2.8308	1.64949937	0.99180784	0.9929727	60933
3	3.3886	2.9297	1.58592444	0.99159977	0.9927289	−2251
4	3.2117	2.8599	1.58499867	0.99203461	0.99290102	−3588
5	3.3000	2.8279	1.60129081	0.99181742	0.99297978	13060
6	3.3411	2.9362	1.56584591	0.99171643	0.99271293	−22394
7	3.2673	2.8465	1.60628799	0.99189791	0.99293403	17820
8	3.2252	2.9055	1.60477387	0.99200137	0.99278855	15919
9	3.3246	2.8712	1.59881025	0.99175695	0.99287307	10522
10	3.2823	2.8705	1.51183259	0.99186099	0.99287482	−75998
11	3.3025	2.8360	1.60167706	0.99181131	0.99295987	13421
12	3.3036	2.8366	1.55147333	0.99180858	0.9929585	−36427
13	3.3003	2.8992	1.56448372	0.99181683	0.99280406	−23763
14	3.3102	2.9189	1.5244285	0.99179252	0.99275551	−63565
15	3.2765	2.8153	1.61556964	0.9918753	0.99301085	27196
16	3.3275	2.8368	1.65649592	0.99174988	0.99295791	67948
17	3.3438	2.8845	1.6065927	0.99170992	0.99284037	18271
18	3.2991	2.8320	1.56849839	0.9918198	0.99296988	−19522
19	3.3246	2.8909	1.50781173	0.99175711	0.9928245	−79901
20	3.3230	2.9363	1.61116181	0.99176086	0.99271266	22521
21	3.3654	2.8406	1.55287434	0.99165675	0.99294869	−34810
22	3.3355	2.9373	1.60686588	0.99173021	0.99271039	18301
23	3.3420	2.8382	1.61680981	0.99171419	0.99295453	28593
24	3.3239	2.7550	1.57711759	0.99175881	0.9931595	−10567
25	3.2577	2.8705	1.55722124	0.99192152	0.99287491	−31029

Distribution of Contract Prices

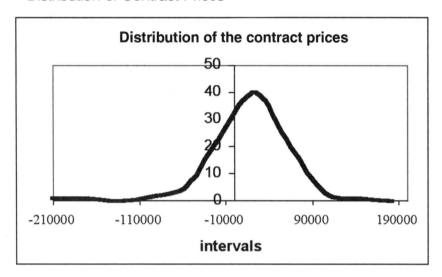

We notice in Figure 8.1 that the distribution of the prices of the contract is not normal. At 7.85, the kurtosis indicates the presence of fat tails. For its part, the skewness is −0.7, which reveals a relative degree of negative asymmetry. The VaR computed using this approach for a confidence level of 95 percent, which is the fifth percentile of the distribution when the data are organized in an increasing order, is equal to $80,107.

THE DELTA METHOD FOR COMPUTING VAR

We rewrite Equation (8.2) in the following manner:

$$f_t = S_t P_t^* - K P_t \qquad (8.3)$$

where P^*_t is the American discount factor and P_t is the corresponding Canadian discount factor. The delta method for computing VaR is based on the following first-degree Taylor expansion of Equation (8.3): $df = \partial f / \partial S \, dS + \partial f / \partial P \, dP + \partial f / \partial P^* \, dP^*$. By computing the total differential of

Equation (8.3), we obtain $df = P^*\,dS + S\,dP^* - K\,dP$, which may be written in terms of percentage rate of growth:

$$df = \left(SP^*\right)\frac{dS}{S} + \left(SP^*\right)\frac{dP^*}{P^*} - \left(KP\right)\frac{dP}{P} \qquad (8.4)$$

The forward contract thus corresponds to a portfolio of the three following elements: (1) a long position of SP^* in the exchange rate; (2) a long position also amounting to SP^* in an American deposit; (3) a short position equal to KP (borrowing) in a Canadian deposit. The exposure of the portfolio to the risk factor S is SP^*; it also applies to the risk factor represented by P^*. Concerning the risk factor P, its risk exposure is negative and equal to KP.

Equation (8.4) may be rewritten as

$$df = \chi_1 dz_1 + \chi_2 dz_2 + \chi_3 dz_3 \qquad (8.5)$$

where the χ_i represent the respective degrees of exposure to the risk factors and dz_i represent the risk factors that are normal random variables. Let Ω be the variance–covariance matrix of the risk factors, and χ is defined as previously. We can compute VaR using the variance of Equation (8.5), which is equal to $\sigma^2\,(df)\,\chi'\Omega\chi$. We then calculate the vector of the degrees of exposure to the risk factors from observed data on S, P, and P^*, which are, respectively, 1.588, 0.9917, and 0.9931.[4] The vector of the risk factor exposures is thus

	(K*P)	S*P*	S*P*
Exposures	−1576803	1577043	1577043

We can compute the variance–covariance matrix from the historical standard errors and correlations from the three risk factors. To do so, we resort to our sample of hundred observations. The vector of standard errors is given by

---

[4] The Canadian and U.S. interest rates are equal to 3.31 and 2.75 percent, respectively. The discount factors P and P^* are computed using these interest rates every three months.

	dP/P	dP*/P*	dS/S
Standard error	1.06370E–05	1.11E–05	0.0323

whereas the correlation matrix of the three risk factors is given by

	dP/P	dP*/P*	dS/S
dP/P1			
dP*/P*	0.092	1	
dS/S	0.038	0.106	1

Since $Cov(X, Y) = \sigma_x \sigma_y \rho_{xy}$, we can deduce the variance–covariance matrix of the risk factors:

	dP/P	dP*/P*	dS/S
dP/P	1.12E–10	1.07E–11	1.30E–08
dP*/P*	1.07E–11	1.22E–10	3.78E–08
dS/S	1.30E–08	3.78E–08	0.001

From these tables, we can compute the standard error of df: $\sigma(df) = \sqrt{\chi' \Omega \chi} = 50695$.

For an a of 5 percent, the critical value corresponding to the normal distribution is 1.645. Using these numbers, the 95 percent VaR is $50,695 $\times$ 1.645 = $83,393. This number is relatively close to the VaR of $80,107[5] using historical simulation.

THE MONTE CARLO SIMULATION

We now compute the VaR of a forward contract that gives the right to buy US$1 million in three months for delivery of CAD$1.59 Million. The Monte Carlo simulation is a method to compute the distribution of the gains and losses of this contract, which in turn will be used to evaluate the VaR of this contract. To run the Monte Carlo simulation in this

---

[5] We should not forget that the exchange rate follows a Student's distribution. The critical value used for computing the VaR that lays on the Student's law is thus only an approximation.

context, we must first specify the stochastic process of the exchange rate of the Canadian dollar and also those of the Canadian and U.S. interest rates. To implement these stochastic processes, we must compute their parameters by using calibration or estimation.[6] Then we must design scenarios of the three variables of the contract. For each of these scenarios, we compute the profits or losses related to the contract. The simulation of an appropriate number of scenarios generates the distribution of profits or losses of the contract necessary for the computation of the VaR.

Assume that the exchange rate of the Canadian dollar follows a geometric Brownian motion (GBM): $dtc = (tc \times 0.5 \times dt) + (tc \times 0.2 \; \varepsilon \sqrt{dt})$ with tc, the exchange rate of the Canadian dollar. The innovation term of the exchange rate follows a Student's distribution with 4 degrees of freedom. This assumption will allow the simulated Canadian exchange rate to jump. The simulation of the scenarios of the Canadian exchange rate is shown in Table 8.4.

As we can see in Table 8.4, each scenario is based on 100 steps. In other terms, the maturity of the contract, which is three months, has been divided in 100 intervals. We can write the result of each scenario in a spreadsheet in order to compute the gains and losses of the contract.

The U.S. and Canadian interest rates follow the same GBM process as described previously, which is given by, $dr = dt + 0.4 \times \varepsilon \sqrt{dt}$, whereby the only difference lays in the seed value. The Canadian and U.S. interest rates are fixed initially at 3.31 percent and 2.75 percent, respectively. The Visual Basic for Applications (VBA) program to implement the Canadian interest rate simulation is given in Table 8.5.

The first ten scenarios of the profits and losses of the forward contract are reproduced at Table 8.6. We generate 1,000 scenarios in the same way. The gains/losses of the contract are computed using a seed value of $206 for the contract.

The histogram of the gains and/or losses is shown in Figure 8.2.

---

[6] For estimation and calibration methods, see Racicot and Théoret (2006, section 5). See also Rouah and Vainberg (2007) for an excellent presentation of the subject.

T A B L E   8.4

VBA program for simulating scenarios of the Canadian exchange rate

```
Sub CAN()
T = 0.25
N = 100
dt = T / N
mu = 0.5
sigma = 0.2
For j = 1 To 1000
tc = 1.588
For i = 1 To N
Randomize
eps = Application.WorksheetFunction.TInv(Rnd, 4)
If Rnd < = 0.5 Then
eps = −eps
Else
eps = eps
End If
tc = tc + (tc * mu * dt) + (tc * sigma * eps * Sqr(dt))
Next i
Range("tc").Offset(j, 0) = tc
Next j
End Sub
```

THE BOOTSTRAPPING METHOD

In this section, we discuss the method of bootstrapping developed by Efron (1979).[7] The concept of bootstrapping assumes a sample of observations, such as a time series of stock prices over a given period. Then, we randomly sample those observations with or without replacement. When using the method with replacement to generate a new sample of observations can be repeated numerous times in the same sample. By repeating this process

---

[7] For a more recent article by this author, see Efron (1994).

T A B L E   8.5

VBA program for simulating the Canadian
interest rate

```
Sub rcan()
a = 1
sigma = 0.4
T = 0.25
N = 100
dt = T / N
For j = 1 To 1000
rc = 3.31
For i = 1 To N
Randomize
eps = Application.WorksheetFunction.NormSInv(Rnd)
rc = rc + (a * dt) + (sigma * eps * Sqr(dt))
Range("tauxc").Offset(j, 0) = rc
Next i
Range("tauxc").Offset(j, 0) = rc
Next j
End Sub
```

T A B L E   8.6

Gains and/or losses scenarios of the contract

	Exchange Rate	rcan	reu	PV(1$CAD)	PV(1$USD)	Contract Value	Gains/ Losses
1	1.648	3.231	3.233	0.992	0.992	57742.908	57536.908
2	1.781	3.412	3.222	0.992	0.992	190138.703	189932.703
3	1.884	3.483	2.821	0.991	0.993	294367.532	294161.532
4	2.288	3.585	3.086	0.991	0.992	694828.614	694622.614
5	1.513	3.674	2.916	0.991	0.993	−73848.890	−74054.890
6	1.313	3.247	3.069	0.992	0.992	−274031.730	−274237.730
7	1.787	3.612	3.243	0.991	0.992	197179.455	196973.455
8	1.690	3.448	3.141	0.991	0.992	100180.991	99974.991
9	2.422	3.448	2.736	0.991	0.993	829345.305	829139.305
10	1.547	3.640	2.896	0.991	0.993	−39368.138	−39574.138

F I G U R E   8.2

Distribution of Gains/Losses of the Forward Contract

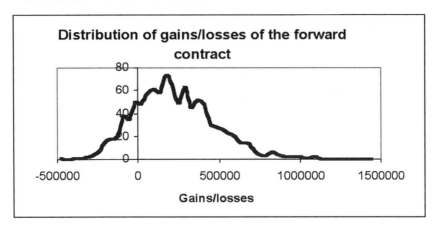

several times, the method of bootstrapping converges to the theoretical distribution when the number of observations becomes important.[8]

Bootstrapping of One Stock

As an example, assume the following hypothetical situation. We invest in the S&P/TSX and compute the VaR of our investment for a given period. In this case, we could assume that the distribution of the stock returns is normal and compute the VaR using equation (1). However, looking at Figure 8.3, we observe that the TSX index has a nonnormal distribution using the p-value of the Jarque-Bera statistic, which is less than 0.01.

Benninga (2000) suggests the following simulation, where the input is a daily time series of returns of the TSX starting in 2001. First, we generate a random number for each observation. This number follows a uniform distribution so the results are not biased and we obtain a re-sampled series of the TSX. We associate a return to this series, which is the spread between the final and the beginning indices of this series expressed in

---

[8] When the observations are not independent, the method seems to perform poorly. On this subject, see Stuart et al. (1999, Vol. 1, p. 7).

F I G U R E   8.3

Return Distribution of the S&P/TSX 1992-2001

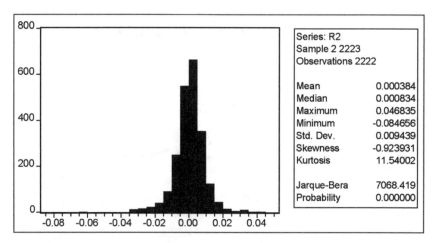

Series: R2	
Sample 2 2223	
Observations 2222	
Mean	0.000384
Median	0.000834
Maximum	0.046835
Minimum	-0.084656
Std. Dev.	0.009439
Skewness	-0.923931
Kurtosis	11.54002
Jarque-Bera	7068.419
Probability	0.000000

Source: EViews, version 6.0.

percentage of the initial value of the index,[9] constituting a first element in computing the VaR. We repeat this procedure several times to generate the empirical distribution of the TSX returns. We then compute the VaR of the portfolio by finding the return associated to the required critical value (α). As an example, Benninga (2000) provides a VBA program that resorts to the Excel SORT command. This command ranks the components of a series. The corresponding VBA program to bootstrap the TSX is reported in Table 8.7.

The results of the bootstrapping are given in Table 8.8.

From Table 8.8, we can see that the bootstrapped returns deviate strongly from the normal distribution. It would be quite hazardous to compute the VaR of the TSX using the normal distribution. Since this distribution is bimodal, the null returns are the most frequent.

To compute the VaR of the TSX, we interpolate the numbers in column S of the spreadsheet. For an α of 1 percent, the return that is associated with

---

[9] We could also compute the return with the following formula: $\ln(P_t / P_{t-1})$, where P_{t-1} is the initial index and P_t is the final one.

T A B L E   8.7

VBA procedure to bootstrap the TSX

```
Sub Varin()
Range("starttime") = Time
Range("O1:O15000").ClearContents
Application.ScreenUpdating = False
For Iteration = 1 To Range("iiterations")
For Row = 1 To 2223
Range("TSE").Cells(Row, 1) = Rnd
Next Row
Range("B2:C2224").Select
Selection.Sort Key1:=Range("C2"), Order1:=xlAscending, Header:=xlNo, _
    OrderCustom:=1, MatchCase:=False, Orientation:=xlTopToBottom
Range("returndata").Cells(Iteration, 1) = Range("rmoyen")
Next Iteration
Range("pelapsed") = Time − Range("pstarttime")
End Sub
```

the cumulative frequency would be -63.20 percent and for an α of 5 percent, the interpolated number would be -51.83 percent. This result is obtained over a period comprising 2223 days. For α given a of 1 percent, the return associated to the VaR would be equal to 0.0284 percent for one day and for an α of 5 percent, the corresponding return is 0.0233 percent. Over the ten day standard period used in practice to compute the VaR, the loss would be \$2,840, for an α of 1 percent, on a portfolio of \$1 million.

Another Way to Compute the VaR of a Portfolio of Assets

Assume a portfolio composed of two assets, say 1 and 2. We have an estimation of the respective VaR of the assets denoted by VaR_1 and VaR_2. Assume also that we have the correlation matrix of these two assets given by

$$\begin{bmatrix} 1 & p_{12} \\ p_{21} & 1 \end{bmatrix}$$

TABLE 8.8

Distribution of the TSX over the period 1992 to 2001

	O	P	Q	R	S	T	U	V	W	X	Y
1			Bins	Freq.	Cumul.						
2	-0.300	1	-69.43%	1	0.10%						
3	0.679	2	-63.62%	8	0.90%						
4	0.207	3	-57.81%	14	2.30%						
5	0.068	4	-51.99%	26	4.90%						
6	-0.093	5	-46.18%	38	8.70%						
7	0.534	6	-40.37%	42	12.90%						
8	1.460	7	-34.55%	47	17.60%						
9	0.722	8	-28.74%	58	23.40%						
10	-0.264	9	-22.93%	45	27.90%						
11	0.871	10	-17.12%	46	32.50%						
12	0.913	11	-11.30%	62	38.70%						
13	-0.347	12	-5.49%	59	44.60%						
14	-0.460	13	0.32%	77	52.30%						
15	0.259	14	6.14%	58	58.10%						
16	1.37218	15	11.95%	43	62.40%						

The VaR of the portfolio of these two assets, denoted by VaR$_p$, is given by

$$\text{VaR}_p = \sqrt{\begin{bmatrix} \text{VaR}_1 & \text{VaR}_2 \end{bmatrix} \begin{bmatrix} 1 & \rho_{12} \\ \rho_{21} & 1 \end{bmatrix} \begin{bmatrix} \text{VaR}_1 \\ \text{VaR}_2 \end{bmatrix}} \tag{8.6}$$

We can analyze Equation (8.6) by considering three cases. The first case is when the correlation between the two asset returns is 1. Then Equation (8.6) reduces to Var$_P$ = VaR$_1$ + VaR$_2$. The VaR of the portfolio is then equal to the sum of the VaRs of each asset. Recall the diversification principle of Markowitz, when diversification of the portfolio does not exist when the correlation between the pooled returns in a portfolio is equal to 1. Therefore, there is no advantage in diversifying the portfolio.

The second case corresponds to the correlation between the returns of the two assets, which is equal to −1. In this case, Equation (8.6) reduces to VaR$_P$ = |VaR$_1$ − VaR$_2$|. According to Markowitz, this is the ideal case for diversification. We can obtain a perfect hedge if VaR$_1$ = VaR$_2$, which gives a null VaR$_p$. The last case is where the correlation is 0, which is known as risk pooling. In this case, Equation (8.6) is written VaR$_p$ = $\sqrt{\text{VaR}^2_1 + \text{VaR}^2_2}$.

CORNISH-FISHER EXPANSION AND VaR

Value at risk is only an approximation, and using several methods such as the Cornish-Fisher expansion is better than resorting to only one computational method. This method is an approximate relation between the percentiles of a distribution and its moments. Stuart et al. (1999, Vol. 2A) mention that a large number of distributions converge (to the normal) when the number of observations tends to infinity. However, when the number of observations is small, the normal law is not a very good approximation for these distributions. Therefore, we have to use the Cornish-Fisher (1937) expansion to get a better approximation of the percentiles of a distribution. This approximation is based on a Taylor series expansion using higher moments of a distribution that deviates from the normal distribution to compute percentiles. Hull (2006) provides only this approximation to the third moment of a distribution, which can be written as

$$w_\alpha \cong z_\alpha + \frac{1}{6}\left(z_\alpha^2 - 1\right) AS \qquad (8.7)$$

In this approximation, w_α is the adjusted percentile of the distribution for a level of significance denoted by α; z_α is the percentile corresponding to a N(0,1) and AS is the asymmetry coefficient. Some authors suggest that the approximation should increase to the fourth moment, which may be written as[10]

$$w_\alpha \cong z_\alpha + \frac{1}{6}\left(z_\alpha^2 - 1\right) AS + \frac{1}{24}\left(z_\alpha^3 - 3z_\alpha\right) EKUR - \frac{1}{36}\left(2z_\alpha^3 - 5z_\alpha\right) AS^2 \quad (8.8)$$

where EKUR is the excess of kurtosis. We now offer an example to compare Equations (8.7) and (8.8). It is often the case in finance that EKUR is substantially greater than 0 while AS is low. Assume therefore that EKUR = 4 and AS = 0. We assume that the expected return of the portfolio is 0.15 and its standard error is 0.30. α is fixed to 0.05. In this case, the VaR is equal to 0.15 − 1.583(0.30) = −0.3249, while in the previous

---

[10] Stuart et al. (1999, p. 238) present a Cornish–Fisher expansion up to the sixth moment.

simplest case, which does not take into account kurtosis, the VaR is *Loss* $= \mu - 1.655\sigma = 0.15 - 1.655(0.30) = -0.3435$. On the other hand, with AS $= -0.05$ and EKUR $= 0$, we get $0.15 - 1.80(0.30) = -0.3900$. The excess kurtosis has the effect of reducing the VaR for an α of 5 percent. However, the excess kurtosis does not have a one-way effect on the VaR, but its effect depends on the desired margin error.[11]

VALUE AT RISK FOR A DISTRIBUTION OTHER THAN THE NORMAL BUT USING A NORMAL COEFFICIENT

The approach based on the Cornish-Fisher expansion for computing the VaR aims to change the coefficients associated with the normal law by integrating the higher moments. Assume we prefer a better approximation for the volatility appearing in the following equation:

$$\mu_{r,t+1} + st_{\alpha,v}\sigma_{r,t+1} \tag{8.9}$$

where $\sigma_{r,t+1}$ is now estimated by a GARCH(1,1) process: $\sigma_{t+1} = E(h_{t+1})$ $= \beta_0 + \beta_1 h_t + \beta_2 \mu_t^2$. In this equation is the coefficient st, which is a Student's t critical value to account for the nonlinearity present in financial time series, which is also accounted for by the GARCH model. The usual underlying model for the returns is given by $r_t = c + \mu_t$, where $\mu_t = \varepsilon_t \sqrt{h_t}$ and $\mathrm{VaR}(\mu_t) = h_t$. ε_t also follows a standardized Student distribution.

Other models developed by Giot and Laurent (2003) suggest using the model APARCH[12](1,1) that is a Box–Cox transformation of the GARCH model. However, it should be noted that we could have used the Cornish–Fisher expansion in conjunction with the GARCH model to improve the estimation of the VaR.

Recently, Racicot et al. (2007; 2008) proposed using ultra-high frequency data to improve the VaR estimation in conjunction with historical simulation. This approach may be implemented as follows. First, the

---

[11] In fact, the breakeven point, which is where the excess kurtosis begins to have a negative effect on the VaR, is at $z_\alpha = -1.73$.

[12] That is, the Asymmetric-Power ARCH.

volatility of the observed data either using a UHF-GARCH one-step ahead forecast or a one-step ahead realized volatility forecast has to be estimated. Then, we use these estimated models in conjunction with the historical simulation formula proposed by Hull (2007) or Hull and White (1998):

$$v_n \frac{v_{i-1} + \left(v_i - v_{i-1}\right)\sigma_{n+1} / \sigma_i}{v_{i-1}} \qquad (8.10)$$

This formula used with available UHF data should generate better estimates for VaR. In this formula, σ_{n+1} and σ_i are updated using UHF GARCH forecast or realized volatility and v_i and v_n are defined respectively, as usual in historical simulation, as the value of the market variable on day i and its value on today, say n.

COPULAS, FOURIER'S TRANSFORM, AND THE VaR

The Copula method is another means to measure the dependence between two random variables similar to the Spearman's coefficient.[13] However, its advantage over the Pearson's coefficient is that it can measure nonlinear relations between two random variables. In this section, we will explain the relation between copulas and credit VaR and present a practical application using an Excel spreadsheet. We further show how to use Fourier's transform to estimate an option price and present other financial applications to show how to implement this procedure in Excel and MATLAB.

An Application of Copulas to the Estimation of Credit VaR[14]

The credit VaR can be defined in a similar way as the market VaR. The credit VaR using a copula correlation is the credit loss that will not be

---

[13] On that subject, see Zivot and Wang (2006, paper 19).
[14] For this section, we follow Hull (2006; 2007).

exceeded at the confidence level of 99.9 percent over a one-year period. Thus, the VaR defined in term of copulas may be written as

$$\text{VaR} = L\,(1 - R)\,V\,(X, T) \tag{8.11}$$

where L is the value of the loan portfolio; R is the debt recovery rate;

$$V(X,T) = N\left(\frac{N^{-1}\left(Q(T)\right) + \sqrt{\rho}N^{-1}(X)}{\sqrt{1-\rho}}\right)$$

defines the probability at X percent that the loss percentage over T years for a large portfolio will be lower than this value V(X,T);[15] Q(T) is the cumulative probability of default at time T; ρ is the correlation in terms of Gaussian copulas; N(.) is the cumulative normal distribution and the inverse of this distribution at the level of 5 percent, say, is N (1.645) = 5% $\Rightarrow 1.645 = N^{-1}$ (0,05).

Before giving a practical application of the credit VaR, we will clarify some basic concepts. Note that the default probability, or sometimes referred to as the *intensity of default*, is related to the hazard function[16] (hazard rate) often used in financial econometrics. Consider a short period of time noted Δt. The default intensity, designed by $\lambda(t)$, is the conditional probability of default and is defined such as that $\lambda(t)\Delta t$ is the probability of default for the interval between t and $t + \Delta t$, conditional no default over this time interval.

Define $V(t)$ as the cumulative probability that a firm will survive up to time t, that is there was no default until time t. Thus the relation between $V(t)$ and $\lambda(t)$ is given by $V(t + \Delta t) - V(t) = -\lambda(t)V(t)V(t)\Delta t$.

Taking the limit of this expression for $\Delta t \to 0$, we obtain

$$\lim_{\Delta t \to 0}\left(V(t + \Delta t) - V(t)\right) = \lim_{\Delta t \to 0}\left(-\lambda(t)V(t)\Delta t\right)$$

$$\Rightarrow dV(t) = -\lambda(t)V(t)dt \tag{8.12}$$

$$\Rightarrow \frac{dV(t)}{dt} = -\lambda(t)V(t)$$

---

[15] This result is due to Vasicek (1987).
[16] For more financial applications and EViews programs, see Racicot (2003, Chap. 2) or Racicot and Théoret (2004, Chap. 14).

This equation is nothing but a simple differential one for which the solution for $V(t)$ is given by

$$V(t) = e^{-\int_0^t \lambda(\tau)d\tau} \tag{8.13}$$

By defining Q(t) as the cumulative default probability up to time t and knowing that the total surface under the probability distribution from $-\infty$ to ∞ is 1, then Q(t) is given by $Q(t) = 1 - V(t) = 1 - e^{\int_0^t \lambda(\tau)d\tau}$.

If a definite integral is a sum of small rectangles, then we can redefine $\int_0^t \lambda(\tau)d\tau$ as the mean of $\lambda(t)$ multiplied by t $t\,\overline{\lambda}(t)$. We thus obtain that Q(t) can be defined in terms of average intensity of default between 0 and t (or conditional probability of default), that is

$$Q(t) = 1 - e^{\overline{\lambda}(t)t} \tag{8.14}$$

Thus to find $Q(t)$, we only need an average conditional probability of default. For instance, Moody's computes the average intensity of default for different ratings on corporate bonds. A four-year corporate bond rated at Aaa has a cumulative default probability of $Q(4) = 1 - e^{\overline{\lambda}(4)4} = 0.04\%$. Thus the average default intensity over a four-year period is

$$\overline{\lambda}(4) = -\frac{1}{4}\ln(1 - Q(4)) = -\frac{1}{4}\ln(1 - 0.00004) = 0.0010\%$$

It is important to note that these default probabilities are not risk neutral. Indeed, these are physical probabilities defined in a real world and calculated from historical data, and are generally much lower than risk neutral probabilities. We compute risk neutral probabilities from corporate bonds applying the formula $h = s/(1 - R)$, where h is the conditional probability (per year) of no previous default's, the spread between the return of a corporate bond and the risk-free rate and R, the expected rate of debt recovery. We observe that the real probability converges to the risk neutral one while the corporate bond rating decreases. We can thus ask ourselves what the best procedure is to compute risk-neutral probability. The answer depends on the analysis performed when we are trying to evaluate the impact of default risk on the pricing of credit

derivative products making it preferable to resort to risk-neutral probabilities. When this type of analysis is performed, we must deal with computations requiring the discounting of the expected cash flows, what
implies, implicitly or explicitly, the use of risk-neutral evaluation.
However, it is advisable to use objective probabilities in the case where
we must perform scenario analysis of potential future losses caused by
payment defaults.

We proceed to the calculation of the Gaussian copula for the credit
VaR. If we assume that a bank has loans totaling $L = \$150$ million, then
the average default probability for one year is equal to 2 percent, the average recovery rate is 61 percent and the copula correlation is estimated at
15 percent. By doing the calculations in Excel, we obtain Table 8.9 where
the VaR is equal to $10.31 million.

Note that Basel II agreement proposed changes to credit VaR calculations. Indeed, the new changes imply resorting to copula to compute
VaR, which is associated to take into account the nonlinear structure
of dependence. The theory of copula proposes new robust methods to

T A B L E   8.9

Computation of the credit VaR using the Gaussian copula

	A	B	
3	Inverse normal at the level of 5%:	−1.64485	= NormInv(0.05, 0, 1)
4	Inverse normal at the level of 2%:	−2.05375	= NormInv(0.02, 0, 1)
5	Inverse normal at the level of 99.9%:	3.0923	= NormInv(0.999, 0, 1)
6	L =	150	
7	R =	61%	
8	Copula correlation =	0.15	
9	Q(T) =	2%	
10	$N^{-1}(0.02) =$	−2.05375	
11	$N^{-1}(0.999) =$	3.09023	
12	V(0.099, 1) =	0.17633	= NormSDist([B8 + Sqrt(B6)*B9]/ Sqrt(1−B6))
13	VaR=	10.31	= B6*(1−B7)*B12

calculate the correlation, since the copula correlation is similar to the Spearman correlation.

The Fourier's Transform[17]

Let f(t) be a continuous nonperiodic time series. Its Fourier transform is equal to $\Im(\alpha) = \dfrac{1}{\sqrt{2\pi}} \displaystyle\int_{t=-\infty}^{\infty} f(t)e^{-i\alpha t}\,dt$, where $\Im(\alpha)$ is also called the *spectral density function* of f(t). The inverse Fourier transform can be written as $\Im^{-1} f(x) = \dfrac{1}{\sqrt{2\pi}} \displaystyle\int_{-\pi}^{\pi} \Im(\alpha)e^{i\alpha x}\,d\alpha$, where $i = \sqrt{-1}$. The Fourier transform[18] may be used to accelerate the computation in the context of a binomial tree when valuing a European call. The formula used to make this calculation is given by

$$C_0 = \Im\left\{ \Im^{-1}\left(C_T\right) \times \left[\Im(b) \right]^N \right\} \tag{8.15}$$

where C_0 is the price of the European call; $\Im(.)$, is the Fourier transform operator; $\Im^{-1}(.)$ is the inverse Fourier transform operator and $\mathbf{C_T}$, the payoff vector at maturity of the option whose dimension is $(N + 1)$, where N is the number of steps in the binomial tree. The vector b has dimension $(N + 1)$. The first entry of this vector is the ratio of the two following terms: (1) the probability of an upward movement in the binomial tree; (2) $(1 + r_f)$, r_f being the risk-free rate. The second entry contains the same calculation but for the downward probability. The other elements of the vector are null.[19]

We are now able to show how to compute Equation (8.15) using the MATLAB software. In this software, the function fftn is used to compute the Fourier transform of a vector of dimension n. For instance, the fftn(c) serves to compute the transform of vector c. The ifftn function computes the inverse Fourier transform of a vector.

---

[17] For an excellent presentation of this subject, see Piskounov (1976, paper 17).

[18] For the Fourier transform an its applications in Finance, see Cerny (2004, paper 7).

[19] For an excellent Excel application of the Fourier transform transposed to finance, see Racicot and Théoret (2006, Chap. 16).

To implement this in MATLAB, we first write the vector c:

```
>> c = [9.04 2.92 0 0]
c = 9.0400 2.9200 0 0
```

then the vector b:

```
>> b = [.4927 .5073 0 0]
b = 0.4927 0.5073 0 0
```

Then we write Equation (8.15) in the MATLAB language:

```
>> pro=fftn(ifftn(c).*((1)*fftn(b)).^3)
pro =
2.1600 1.5295 3.8200 4.4505
```

MATLAB estimate of the European call price is equal to 2.16 when adopting the Fourier transform using three steps. When increasing the number of steps up to 10, we obtain

```
>> pro=fftn(ifftn(c).*((1)*fftn(b)).^10)
pro =
Columns 1 through 7
1.9429   0.7586   0.3955   0.9752   2.8055   5.7268   8.5574
Columns 8 through 11
9.7798   8.8565   6.5265   3.9553
```

The price of the call is $1.94, which is close to the theoretical value of $1.99. As we know, VaR lays in the distribution of returns. The inverse Fourier transform might be used to facilitate the computation of any inverse cumulative distribution.

CONCLUSION

Risk is a multidimensional concept, which is very difficult to measure. These last few years, the theory of risk has consolidated its positive knowledge to the one of stochastic dominance, which seems a promising avenue for an eventual approach encompassing an integrated approach of risk theory. By giving a large weight to the cumulative distribution, the new theories of risk look further at the shape of the return distribution since at the early stage in the traditional theory of risk they assumed normality for the return distribution. However, the returns are not normally distributed and this stylized fact has been known to exist for a long time.[20]

The modern theory of risk is embedding progressively the teachings of the option theories. For instance, the payoffs produced by negative events are similar to those of a short position in a put option. Risk management practices use payoff options to measure risk. For instance, the omega indicator[21] uses the price of a short-term put to measure the risk of a portfolio, whereby this measures the cost of protection for the portfolio. This cost might be considered as the risk of a portfolio, and the price of the put is thus the insurance cost of the portfolio. The perspective that option theory opens new avenues for risk measures is very promising. The approach of risk theory using the cumulants of the distribution is another way for future research.

REFERENCES

Benninga, S. (2000) *Financial Modeling.* Cambridge, MA: The MIT Press.

Cerny, A. (2004) *Mathematical Techniques in Finance: Tools for Incomplete Markets.* Princeton: Princeton University Press.

Christoffersen, P.F. (2003) *Elements of Financial Risk Management.* Santiago: Academic Press.

Cornish, E.A. and R.A. Fisher (1937) Moments and Cumulants in the Specification of Distributions. *Revue de l'Institute International de Statistique,* 4(2): 1–14.

---

[20] In fact, this had been known since about 100 years ago with the study of the cotton price by the first researchers in this field. For more information on this subject and for an application to derivatives, see Haug (2007, Chap. 1). Furthermore, new models for computing VaR have emerged, which are based on extreme value theory. A popular distribution in this area of research is the GED (GEV) one, for which the researchers found an analytical formula where the parameters may be estimated by maximum likelihood. Computing VaR in this way has the advantage of taking into account the high kurtosis of the distribution, and it is also very easy to apply. For more details on this subject, see Zivot and Wang (2006, Chap. 5).

[21] On omega, see Kazemi et al. (2003).

Dowd, K. (2005). *Measuring Market Risk,* 2nd edition. Chichester, UK: John Wiley & Sons.

Efron, B. (1994) Missing Data, Imputation and the Bootstrap. *Journal of the American Statistical Association*, 89(427): 463–475.

Efron, B. (1979) Bootstrap Methods: Another Look at the Jackknife. *Annals of Statistics,* 7(1): 1–26.

Giot, P. and S. Laurent (2003) Value-at-Risk for Long and Short Trading Positions. *Journal of Applied Econometrics*, 18(6): 641–664.

Haug, E.G. (2007) *Derivatives: Models on Models*. Chichester, UK: John Wiley & Sons.

Hull, J.C. (2007) *Risk Management and Financial Institutions*. Upper Saddle River, NJ: Prentice Hall.

Hull, J.C. (2006) *Options, Futures and Other Derivatives*. Upper Saddle River, NJ: Prentice Hall.

Hull, J.C. and A. White (1998) Incorporating Volatility Updating into Historical Simulation Method for Value-at-Risk. *Journal of Risk*, 1(1): 5–19.

Jorion, P. (2007) *Financial Risk Manager Handbook*. Hoboken, NJ: Wiley.

Kazemi, H., T. Schneeweis, and R. Gupta (2003) Omega as a Performance Measure. Working paper, University of Massachusetts, Amherst.

Markowitz, H. (1952) Portfolio Selection. *Journal of Finance,* 7(1): 77–91.

Piskounov, N. (1976) *Calcul différential et intégral, Tome 2,* 7th edition. Moscou: MIR.

Racicot, F.E. (2003) Les modèles de Durée Classiques et Modernes Avec Applications Aux Données Économiques et Financières. In *Trois Essais sur L'analyse Des Données Économiques et Financières*, Ph.D. thesis. Montreal: ESG-UQAM.

Racicot, F.-É., R. Théoret, and A. Coën (2008) Forecasting Irregularly Spaced UHF Financial Data: Realized Volatility vs UHF-GARCH Models. *International Advances in Economic Research* 14(1): 112–124.

Racicot, F.-É., R. Théoret, and A. Coën (2007) Forecasting UHF Financial Data: Realized Volatility vs UHF-GARCH Models. Research Notes. *International Advances in Economic Research*, 13(2): 243–244.

Racicot, F.-É. and Théoret, R. (2006) *Finance Computationnelle et Gestion des Risques: Ingénierie Financière avec Applications Excel (Visual Basic) et Matlab*. Quebec: University of Quebec Press.

Racicot, F.-É. and R. Théoret (2004) *Le Calcul Numérique en Finance Empirique et Quantitative: Ingénierie Financière et Excel (Visual Basic)*, 2nd edition. Quebec: University of Quebec Press.

Rouah, F.D. and Vainberg, G. (2007) *Option Pricing Models & Volatility Using Excel-VBA*. New Jersey: Wiley.

Stuart, A., J.K. Ord, and S. Arnold (1999) *Kendall's Advanced Theory of Statistics. Volume 1: Distribution Theory*. London: Arnold.

Stuart, A., J.K. Ord, and S. Arnold (1999) *Kendall's Advanced Theory of Statistics. Vol. 2A*, 6th edition. London: Arnold.

Vasicek, O. (1987) Probability of Loss on a Loan Portfolio. Working paper, KMV.

Zivot, E. and J. Wang (2006) *Modelling Financial Time Series with S-plus*, 2nd edition. New York: Springer.

CHAPTER 9

Computational Aspects of Value at Risk

By Germán Navarro and Ignacio Olmeda

ABSTRACT

It is well known that the calculation of value at risk involves extremely computationally intensive simulations that must be done using high-performance machines. Even for problems of moderate size and employing quite expensive machines, this approach has important drawbacks due to the intrinsic parallel structure of conventional computers. Nowadays, personal computers are equipped with graphics processing units (GPUs) that can be employed to execute complex algorithms in a parallel fashion. This new approach allows obtaining, in some cases, implementations that are hundreds of times faster that the standard ones. This chapter introduces such technology and discusses one example, in the context of VaR, that illustrates the usefulness of this approach. Our results, on a synthetic problem, indicate that the GPU approach is two orders of magnitude faster than Monte Carlo run on standard computers.

INTRODUCTION

Generally, as the adage goes, when risk managers are asked to provide a fast, accurate, and understandable estimate of risk, they have to choose one with only two of these characteristics. When facing this dilemma, risk managers prefer value at risk (VaR), due both to its formal simplicity and to its clear economic interpretation. Value at risk provides risk managers, and investors, a measure of risk concentrated in just a single figure, which also has a straightforward economic interpretation. This preference for VaR is also quite clear in the financial industry just by taking a look at the systems that employ it as the basic risk measure: JP Morgan's *Riskmetrics*, Credit Swiss First of Boston's *PrimeClear,* or Chase Manhattan's *Charism*, to cite a few.

Regulators and advising committees have also a preference for VaR and both the Capital Adequacy Accord of 1988 as well as the New Revised Framework on International Convergence of Capital Measurement and Capital Standards (*Basel II*) consider VaR as the standard measure to calculate risks in financial institutions. Nevertheless, VaR is not a "perfect" risk measure and has been severely criticized because of its many technical as well as epistemological problems [see, e.g., Taleb and Pilpel (2007)]. Even so, VaR is demonstrating a quite strong position in the rude world of performance measures.

As it is well known, VaR can be computed under three different approaches: parametric, historical, and Monte Carlo. It is widely recognized that, out of the three, Monte Carlo simulation is by far the most flexible, since it allows considering arbitrarily complex models and/or portfolio instruments. Unfortunately, Monte Carlo simulation is extremely computationally intensive because it is based on the iteration of a particular, generally simple, procedure. The importance and ubiquity of VaR justify the amount of work that is dedicated to reduce its computational load by simplifying the analytics (delta approaches) or by proposing more efficient ways to generate the simulation paths (e.g., variance reduction techniques).

In this chapter we will focus on a less studied aspect which, in our view, it is also important. At the end, simulations are run on computers so that it seems also relevant to analyze the alternatives that the computer industry offers in the solution of this problem. Specifically, we argue that

Monte Carlo simulation has a special characteristic (it is inherently parallel) that badly fits with the standard Von Neumann (sequential) architecture but that makes specially attractive other approaches. We suggest that graphical processing units (GPUs) computing provides a more interesting approach to the calculation of VaR when problems are of some magnitude (e.g., portfolios with thousands of assets) as to require important efficiency gains in the computations.

The rest of the chapter is organized as follows: In the next section we provide a brief introduction to the alternatives that the computer industry offers on problems that require a huge amount of computation, specifically we describe the three main approaches to supercomputing: mainframes or "supercomputers," grid computing, and GPU computing. In the third section, we provide a nonspecialist introduction to GPU computing, highlighting the main differences against standard computing. The fourth section gives an example of the GPU approach by computing VaR stress test on synthetic portfolios of different sizes; we show that under this implementation it is possible to obtain quite significant efficiency gains. The fifth section presents our conclusions.

SUPERCOMPUTING TECHNOLOGIES

As we have mentioned, the main problems of Monte Carlo VaR is that it generally requires a formidable amount of computing power, making it difficult to be applied in portfolio's problems that take into account a high number of instruments or of considerable complexity. For this motive, the usual approach consists in constraining the real problem by consider a fewer number of instruments, assuming linearity in the payoff functions and/or reducing the number of scenarios and simulations. Obviously this clearly reduces the potential power of the Monte Carlo approach, which, in principle, it is design to deal with those situations that make the other two approaches (parametric and historical) less realistic.

Nevertheless, the formidable speed at which computing power is progressing shows, particularly in the financial world, that problems which were considered intractable in the near past become feasible in the near future; this is due to advances in supercomputing, whose objective is to provide as much as processing power as possible. *Supercomputing* was a term restricted until quite recently to the government and research units, but due to the incredible development of personal computers, it is now accepted that supercomputing is accessible to the general public.

The term *supercomputing* is ill-defined, since it can not be measured in absolute terms: what was "supercomputing" some years ago has become "personal computing" today. For that reason we employ the term *supercomputing* to refer to the computing power needed in situations where actual personal computers are useless. Today we can basically distinguish among three approaches to supercomputing: mainframes or "supercomputers," grid computing, and GPU computing.

- **Mainframes or "supercomputers":** This is the traditional approach to supercomputing. Supercomputers are last generation computers that implement front-edge technologies. The main drawback is that the cost of these systems is so high that they can be employed only in large corporations, universities or government agencies.

- **Grid computing:** Under this approach, a number of independent processors are arranged in a grid to support the execution of large-scale, resource-intensive, and distributed applications (Berman et al., 2003). The basic idea consists in a communication network that connects each of the systems, as well as on specific software that allows them to work in a coordinated way. Under this approach when one has a large number of smaller computers it is possible to obtain a processing power similar to that of a supercomputer. Apart from its modularity, this approach is also appealing because the systems employed need not be homogeneous and may be connected through the Internet.[1]

- **Graphics processing unit (GPU) computation:** Graphics processing units are devices present in every personal computer, which handle the processing of the monitor's graphics. They are

---

[1] Perhaps the most popular application of this approach is the Search of Extraterrestrial Intelligence project (SETI@home); in the context of VaR calculation, an example of Grid computing is found in Fusai et al. (2006).

specially prepared for 3D graphics, and so they are particularly interesting in art and graphic design. With the tremendous expansion of the videogames industry, these devices have tripled their power in the last few years and have become, in some sense, much more powerful than microprocessors (Owens, 2005). Moreover, the parallel structure of GPU makes them suitable for general-purpose processing in problems that are inherently parallel.

Both supercomputers and grids have previously been employed in VaR calculations; so we only focus on the GPU approach. In the following section we provide a brief introduction to GPU computing and motivate its usefulness in VaR calculations.

GRAPHICS PROCESSING UNIT COMPUTING

As we previously mentioned, GPUs have evolved at an incredible speed in the past few years. To give an idea of the power and sophistication of these devices it is suffice to say that the one tested here employs over 680 million transistors. Graphics processing unit computing offers a particularly interesting alternative to the standard approach when calculations can be run in a parallel fashion such as in Monte Carlo. The problem is that it is not straightforward to implement a particular solution under this technology, and specifically designed programming interfaces and programs are needed. Nvidia, one of the most important providers of graphical units, recently released an interface that allows executing specifically built programs on their GPU (Nvidia, 2007). This interface is the *compute unified device architecture* (CUDA), and it is the one employed in this chapter.

The architecture of a GPU is known as *single instruction multiple data* (SIMD); from a technical point of view this means that these devices can not process threads that are completely independent (as in a system with several processors) but they are capable of executing a single program on a set of different data. Figure 9.1 gives an intuition of this idea.

For example, assume a trivial example that consists in multiplying a set of numbers by another fixed one. Under the central processing unit (CPU) architecture, we multiply them sequentially (first, second, …) in the processor, while with a GPU we apply the same operation to the 10

F I G U R E   9.1

Execution models

Single Processor   Multiple Processor   GPU: SIMD

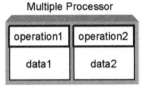
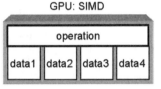

numbers simultaneously. A single graphic device can process up to 128 data at the same time. The main drawback of the GPU approach is that when a particular problem needs to be implemented, the developer has to take into account specific details of the architecture. This means that one needs to rewrite the code to fit with the architecture at a deeper level [see, e.g., Harris (2005)]. In Figure 9.2 we provide the code for the example under both approaches.

F I G U R E   9.2

CPU and GPU Codes

CPU Code

```
void mul_by_cpu(float* v, int sizev, float n) {
        for (int i=0; i<sizev; i++) {
                v[i] *= n;

                }

}
mul_by_cpu(v, sizev, n);
```

GPU Code

```
__global__void mul_by_gpu(float* v, float n) {
int i = blockIdx.x * blockDim.x + threadIdx.x;
                v[i] *= n;

        }
mul_by_gpu<<<sizev, 1>>>(v, n);
```

The main advantage of graphical devices is that their cost is much lower than standard processors, when taking into account the computational power they offer. This is a consequence of the amplitude of the GPU market, which is much wider than that of standard processors and which allows reducing costs. Other advantages of graphical devices are their low energy consumption and the much faster speed of innovation than of standard processors. This, together with the strong demand in the market, permits companies to release new high performance products at a faster rate.

In terms of computing power, the last generation GPUs such as HD 3870 X2 (ATI) or 9800 GX2 (Nvidia) provide over 1 teraflop (one trillion floating operations per second). To give an idea of this power one can take a look at Figure 9.3 [based on Dongarra (2007)], which shows the evolution that supercomputers has experienced in the last decade. Note that, in practical terms, a single GPU device provides the same computing power than the most powerful supercomputer in the world 10 years ago.

Moreover, this technology is also modular in the sense that it is possible to build supercomputers employing simple GPU devices together with standard microprocessors. An example is the *Bull NovaScale*, under development by Grand Equipement National de Calcul Intensif, which will be under exportation in 2009 and which will become the second most powerful computer in the world.

F I G U R E   9.3

Power of World's Most Powerful Supercomputer

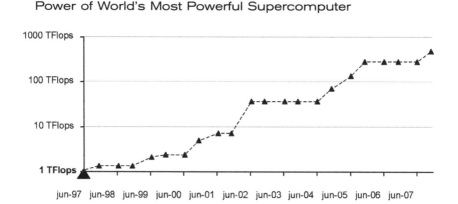

AN EXAMPLE

In this section we will provide an example that gives a clear intuition on the power, in the VaR context, of the GPU technology discussed earlier. Our example consists in a simple VaR stress test using Monte Carlo for a portfolio of synthetic assets. The procedure is quite simple: first we generate one replication of a number of assets, which are assumed to follow continuous random walks. Then, we build an equally weighted portfolio using these prices, which are taken as the "real" evolution of the portfolio, and compute the VaR at the 1 percent confidence level. After this "estimation" of VaR is obtained, we perform a stress test by simulating alternative paths and computing the number of times that the value of the portfolio along each path exceeds the estimated VaR.[2]

Each one of the simulations consists in daily data of five years (that is, each simulation has 1,250 points), and we consider several sets of examples by increasing the number of assets in the portfolio as well as the number of simulations. We also consider two different situations. In the first one, assets are assumed to be uncorrelated, so that the simulation of the path of a particular asset is completely independent on the others. In the second case, we assume correlated assets so that, at each step, we need to employ the corresponding covariance matrix; note that in this case the simulation of a particular path depends on the others, which constrains the possibilities of a full parallelization of the process.

The process described above is implemented in exactly the same manner under the two mentioned approaches, that is, using a conventional computer (CPU) and a GPU. All the programs were written in C. Using the "classical approach," all the simulations must be executed sequentially, so that a particular path has to be finished before the other one begins and a particular simulation has to finish before another one is initiated. Figure 9.4 gives an intuition of the process.

Under the second approach, we exploit the power of the GPU approach that comes from the fact that it is possible to conduct a huge number of operations in a parallel fashion. As we mentioned, the main

---

[2] Note that this problem is equivalent to compute the number of times that a down-and-in barrier option activates; this suggests that this approach can be used for exotic option valuation quite straightforwardly.

F I G U R E   9.4

Sequential Execution

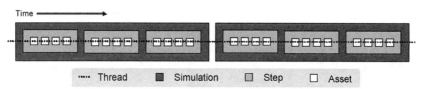

drawback is that one needs to fully redesign the program to specify, explicitly, which calculations that should be executed simultaneously and which ones in a parallel fashion. Moreover, the implementation of parallelization can be done in two different ways since one can consider parallelizing simulations or assets. Here we implement both approaches with the purpose of analyzing the advantages of each one of them.

In the first case, we chose to parallelize simulations. Internally, each simulation is completely executed after another simulation of another asset is begun. This method would provide more advantages when the number of simulations is high. In the case that few simulations are executed, a number of threads would not be used losing computing power of the GPU. Figure 9.5 shows the flow of the process.

The second approach consists in a parallelization at a deeper level. For each step of the simulations, the evolution of each one of the assets is calculated simultaneously. This approach should be more efficient when the number of assets, in relation with the number of simulations, is high,

F I G U R E   9.5

Parallelization of Simulations

Time ⟶

⸱⸱⸱⸱ Thread

■ Simulation

☐ Step

☐ Asset

F I G U R E   9.6

Parallelization by Assets

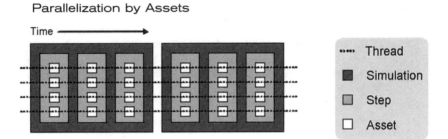

since all the available resources would be used at each step. Figure 9.6 shows how this approach is implemented

As we mentioned, assets are generated synthetically as continuous random walks of the form

$$S_{t+\delta t} = S_t e^{(\mu - 1/2\sigma^2)\delta t + \sigma\sqrt{\delta t}\varepsilon_t}, \quad \varepsilon_t \approx N(0,1)$$

First, we assume that assets are independent, so that it is possible to generate each on the series assets in the portfolio without taking into account the evolution of the others. We consider equally weighted portfolios of different sizes with 10, 100, 1,000, 10,000, 100,000, and 1,000,000 assets. Note that the last magnitudes are far beyond the usual size of banks' portfolios and are just employed to demonstrate the power of our approach. Since the accuracy of Monte Carlo calculation of VaR critically depends on the number of simulations, it is important to see how computational load scales with this parameter, here we consider 1, 10, 100, 1,000, and 10,000 simulations.

In Table 9.1 we show the number of seconds that it takes to perform the stress test for each one of the combinations of assets and simulations. To give a clear view of the potential gains of the GPU approach, we provide, for each of these combinations, the number of seconds that it takes to perform the same experiment on a conventional computer.[3] First (upper panel), note that 10,000 simulations of the stress test on a portfolio of 10,000 assets takes

---

[3] All the simulations were run on a Sun Ultra 40 workstation with two Dual Core AMD Opteron 280 processors and 8 GB of memory. The GPU computations were performed on a GeForce 8800 Ultra using the same computer.

T A B L E   9.1

Uncorrelated assets

		CPU				
		Simulations				
		1	10	100	1k	10k
	10	0.00	0.03	0.31	3.12	31.72
	100	0.02	0.29	3.30	29.62	297.26
Assets	**1k**	0.30	2.96	29.48	298.43	2,991.15
	10k	3.05	30.67	300.30	2,936.37	29,351.02
	100k	30.42	297.82	2,926.51	29,558.70	309,631.63
	1M	296.34	2,997.51	29,922.35	297,344.25	*n.a.*

		GPU				
		Simulations				
		1	10	100	1k	10k
	10	0.34	0.94	6.86	66.21	658.57
	100	0.35	0.94	6.93	66.35	669.86
Assets	**1k**	0.35	0.97	6.89	66.47	663.95
	10k	0.35	1.16	8.15	79.29	805.52
	100k	0.46	2.23	19.75	195.03	1,942.84
	1M	1.61	13.69	134.64	1,365.09	13,419.88

		Ratio				
		Simulations				
		1	10	100	1k	10k
	10	0.00	0.03	0.05	0.05	0.05
	100	0.06	0.31	0.48	0.45	0.44
Assets	**1k**	0.86	3.05	4.28	4.49	4.51
	10k	8.71	26.44	36.85	37.03	36.44
	100k	66.13	133.55	148.18	151.56	159.37
	1M	184.06	218.96	222.24	217.82	n.a.*

* n.a., not available.

2,951 s or about 8.2 h in a conventional computer. Note that even though this figure seems "reasonable," it would make extremely difficult to develop alternative models or sceneries which require a significant number of modifications of the parameters of the model. Moreover, if we increase the number of assets, the implementation of this approach makes the problem infeasible: it would take about 35 days to execute a single set of simulations of portfolios with 1M assets. Finally, note that, as expected, the computational load using a conventional computer increases linearly with the complexity of the problem (number of assets) and the number of simulations.

When using the GPU approach, the results change in a radical manner. For portfolios of usual sizes and using a considerable number of simulations (10,000 assets and 10,000 simulations) it takes just about 13 min to perform the test; moreover, using a huge number of assets it takes only about 3.5 h. Note also that the execution time for portfolios or number of simulations of moderate sizes is, more or less, constant. Essentially this means that the computing power of the GPU is not fully exploited. Note that only when the complexity of the problem increases substantially does the computing time increase at a quadratic rate. This means that the computing bounds of GPU units are well beyond the sizes here presented.

Finally, to give a clearer idea of the efficiency gain of the GPU approach, we compute a ratio by dividing the execution time of the conventional CPU computer against the one of the GPU; the results are shown in the lower panel of the table. Note that, as expected, for less than 1,000 assets the efficiency of the conventional computer is higher than the GPU but that the efficiency of the former increases quite rapidly making the GPU between 150 and 220 times faster than the conventional computer for the biggest portfolio, and about 35 times faster for portfolios of usual sizes.

In our second set of experiments we perform similar computations but considering, in this case, correlated assets. Note that this approach is extremely computationally intensive because the evolution of one of the assets depends on the other. Due to the computational complexity of the problem, as well as the unreality of the situation of computing a covariance matrix of 1,000,000 assets we restrict our simulations to the case of, at most, 10,000 assets (a quite implausible situation, anyways).[4] To compute the covariance matrix of the returns the Cholesky factorization is used.

---

[4] A number of alternatives to simplify the computation of the covariance matrix have been proposed; see, e.g., Ledoit and Wolf (2003).

Our results are shown in Table 9.2. They suggest that, even for moderate sizes of the portfolio (1,000 assets), the problem becomes too difficult for a conventional computer. The calculation of the test for 10,000 simulations and 1,000 assets takes about 12 h and for 10,000 assets takes about 170 days. When the same problem is implemented in the GPU version, the problem becomes feasible even for portfolios with a high number of assets. It would require between 3 h and 4.5 days to perform the test in portfolios of the same sizes.

T A B L E   9.2

Correlated assets

		CPU				
		Simulations				
		1	**10**	**100**	**1k**	**10k**
Assets	**10**	0.01	0.07	0.75	3.49	31.61
	100	0.10	0.68	4.67	38.93	387.80
	1k	4.35	40.27	406.72	4,023.51	43,375.99
	10k	1,472.11	14,534.05	146,379.23	*n.a.*	*n.a.*
		GPU				
		Simulations				
		1	**10**	**100**	**1k**	**10k**
Assets	**10**	0.47	1.41	10.26	97.66	969.99
	100	0.52	1.84	14.97	146.61	1,476.12
	1k	1.36	10.90	105.98	1,056.64	10,584.61
	10k	39.32	389.64	3,891.40	38,916.67	389,178.50
		Ratio				
		Simulations				
		1	**10**	**100**	**1k**	**10k**
Assets	**10**	0.02	0.05	0.07	0.04	0.03
	100	0.19	0.37	0.31	0.27	0.26
	1k	3.20	3.69	3.84	3.81	4.10
	10k	37.44	37.30	37.62	n.a.	n.a.

* n.a., not available.

The efficiency ratio is also low in this case for a small number of simulations or assets (about one hundred), but, again, it increases quite rapidly
reaching a ratio of about 35 times for portfolios of 10,000 assets. However,
the differences for portfolio of small sizes are minimal since computing
times in these cases are measured in seconds or minutes. This suggests that,
from a practitioner's point of view, it would be useless to implement both
approaches instead of just choosing the GPU implementation.

Finally, we analyze a rather technical question that we mentioned
before, i.e., is parallelizing by simulations or parallelizing by assets the
most profitable strategy to obtain the best results in terms of speed? To do
this, we compare the computing speed for different portfolio sizes and
number of simulations. In Figures 9.7 and 9.8 we plot the computing
times of each of the approaches, while in Table 9.3 we present the computing time ratios. From the figures is quite clear that when we parallelize
simulations instead of assets, the computing time increases at a much
faster rate. Note, however, that as the number of assets in the portfolio
increases, the efficiency of the second approach is higher, in particular
when the number of simulations is low. Obviously, this trade-off between
simulations and assets reflects the fact that the computing power of the
GPU is fixed, so that when we choose the wrong parameter to be paral-
lelized, we lose such power.

F I G U R E   9.7

Parallelizing Assets

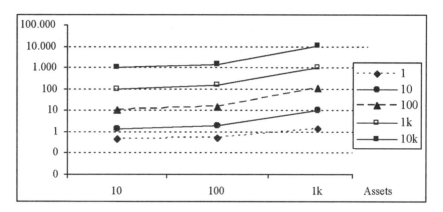

F I G U R E   9.8

Parallelizing Simulations

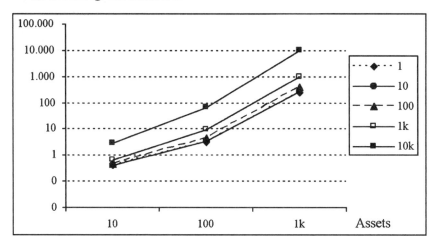

T A B L E   9.3

Ratio

		Assets vs. Simulations				
		Simulations				
		1	**10**	**100**	**1k**	**10k**
	10	1.12	3.36	22.80	152.59	346.43
Assets	**100**	0.16	0.56	3.19	15.68	21.40
	1k	0.01	0.04	0.27	1.07	1.08

Finally, considering just the costs in hardware, the GPU approach described here is tens or even hundreds of times cheaper than the other two supercomputing approaches (mainframes and grid computing). For example, the calculations of our example were run on a single device that costs less than US$500.[5]

---

[5] NVIDIA has announced that a new, more powerful device will be released in the next months, priced at a similar amount and about 50 percent faster.

CONCLUSION

Value at risk is an important performance measure widely used in the industry. Its main flaw is that estimates are either too simplistic (under the delta and historic approaches) or extremely computationally demanding (under the Monte Carlo approach). When Monte Carlo simulation is used to compute VaR, the computational complexity makes it often impossible to value portfolios with a high number of assets or which include instruments with complicated payoffs. For this reason, an important number of firms adopt simplifying approaches that degrade the accuracy of estimations.

In these situations, the availability of computer power becomes a critical factor. Since high quality of computer power comes at a cost, it is essential to explore alternative approaches that make it more affordable. One such approach is the use of Graphical Processing Units, present in personal computers, which due to their intrinsic parallelism and low cost make them particularly suitable on for problem.

In this chapter we have provided a simple example of the computation of VaR using such approach. We found that GPU computing makes it feasible to calculate VaR measures for portfolios with a huge number of assets since they provide computing speeds that are two orders of magnitude faster than usual systems. Note that our example gives just an intuition on how GPU computing can be employed to a number of other problems related to VaR. One such example is the computation of the "greeks" of the portfolio, a problem that is known to be computationally demanding.

A final point should be taken into account: the GPU approach requires a substantial effort on implementations, which are problem dependent and so less portable. To the extent that speed is not critical or that upgrades and/or modifications are common, standard or even mixed approaches would be preferred.

REFERENCES

Berman, F., G. Fox, and T. Hey (2003) *Grid Computing: Making the Global Infrastructure a Reality.* Chichester: John Wiley & Sons.

Dongarra, J. (2007) *TOP500 Supercomputer Sites.* Available at http://www.top500.org/lists/2007/11.

Fusai, G., R. Chinelli, D. De Martini, G. Longo, M. Marena, L. Mariano, R. Cappuccio, R. Sgherri, L. Regini, W. Chierici, and E. Cocca (2006) Grid Based Full Portfolio Revaluation for VaR Computation. *VaR GRID*. Available at http://www2.units.it/~amases06/ cd/abstracts /155.pdf.

Harris, M. (2005) Mapping Computational Concepts to GPUs. In M. Pharr (ed.), *GPU Gems 2*. Cambridge, MA: Addison-Wesley.

Ledoit, O. and M. Wolf (2003) Improved Estimation of the Covariance Matrix of Stock Returns with an Application to Portfolio Selection. *Journal of Empirical Finance*, 10(5): 603–621.

Nvidia Corporation (2007) *NVIDIA CUDA Compute Unified Device Architecture Programming Guide*. Available at http://developer.nvidia.com/cuda.

Owens, J. (2005) Streaming Architectures and Technology Trends. In M. Pharr (ed.), *GPU Gems 2*. Cambridge, MA: Addison-Wesley.

Taleb, N. and A. Pilpel (2007) Epistemology and Risk Management. *LSE*. Available at http://www.fooledbyrandomness.com/LSE-Taleb-Pilpel.pdf.

PART TWO

Risk and Asset Management

CHAPTER 10

Value-at-Risk–Based Stop-Loss Trading

By Bernd Scherer

ABSTRACT

Recent events in active quantitative management have seen large losses in July and August 2007. Given these sudden losses came as a surprise to the whole industry, this caused many quantitative managers to review the case for and against automated risk management practices like stop-loss trading rules or volatility cut outs. It is well known that a stop-loss policy in a market without downside momentum operates very much like a random market timing strategy, which Samuelson has famously shown to destroy value. However, this result relies on the notion of the absence of serial correlation in asset returns. Given recent evidence on the success of momentum strategies, we will review the case against stop-loss rules and see whether it still holds. Can the returns from avoiding downside momentum offset the opportunity costs of remaining not invested after a stop out occurs? In particular, this chapter will investigate whether extreme returns from popular currency trading strategies create conditional positive (negative) autocorrelation that makes stop loss profitable (value destroying).

INTRODUCTION

Recent events in active quantitative management have seen large and sudden losses in July and August 2007. While the likely reasons for this performance drawdown have been discussed in Lo and Khandani (2007), much debate on the appropriate risk management for quantitatively managed funds remain. Consequentially buy side risk managers (and sometimes client guidelines) lobby for the application of a stop-loss discipline (cut exposures to market risk after a given cumulative loss) as an automated risk management strategy for an automated investment process. This warm embracement by practitioners contrasts with the academic treatment of stop-loss rules. With the exception of Dybvig (1988), Acar (1998), and Taleb (2000), references are extremely difficult to find. The reason for this has been the popularity of the random walk hypothesis in academic finance. After all, a stop loss is just a version of a momentum rule (stay invested if markets are rising and sell if markets have fallen by a given cumulative amount).

Should markets follow a random walk, this strategy would not add value, and at the minimum an investor suffers from the obvious transaction cost drag. A stop-loss policy in a market without downside momentum effectively operates as a random market timing strategy. We know from Samuelson (1994) that a random market timing strategy underperforms a buy and hold strategy, where asset proportions are given by timing probabilities.[1] However, all the above results rely on the notion of the absence of serial correlation in asset returns. Given recent evidence on the success of momentum strategies we will review the case for stop-loss rules and see whether it still holds. In particular we will investigate whether extreme returns create conditional positive autocorrelation in return series that make stop-loss trading a valuable risk management device. The second section in this chapter presents closed-form solutions for the expected opportunity gain (loss) of a stop-loss trading strategy. The expressions relate to commonly known risk measures and will be easy to calculate. In this chapter's third section we introduce some real-world trading strategies commonly

---

[1] See also Kritzman (2000) for a detailed analysis of random market timing and a survey of related topics.

used in active currency management. The application of the derived closed form cost estimates is disappointing. We therefore review the linearity assumption in the fourth section estimating so-called threshold autoregressive processes. These processes fit the data better and allow us to closely replicate the gains and losses of a stop-loss strategy. Contrary to supporters of stop-loss strategies we find negative conditional autocorrelation (strategy losses are more likely to be followed by strategy gains than further losses).

STOP-LOSS RULES FOR ALTERNATIVE RETURN PROCESSES

We assume time t log returns of an asset or an active quant strategy, r_t, are drawn from an AR(1) model without drift. This is a specification that would not attach opportunity costs to a stop-loss strategy while still offering an opportunity gain for a de facto strategy timing strategy. We assume

$$r_t = a_1 r_{t-1} + \varepsilon_t, \varepsilon_t \sim N(0, \sigma_\varepsilon^2) \tag{10.1}$$

where $\mathrm{Var}(r) = \sigma^2 = \dfrac{1}{1-a_1^2}\,\sigma_e^2$ and $E(r) = \mu = 0$. Suppose we start with a stop-loss strategy that will stop out a strategy for any $r_{t-1} < 0$, i.e., as soon as the previous day ended with a loss. What we need to do is calculate the expected profit for such a strategy. The gain for a stop loss is an opportunity gain (losses not occurred) of not having invested in a strategy for the next day. To evaluate it, we need to calculate the next days expected return, i.e., the average returns that would follow for Equation (10.1). If next days return is on average negative temporarily shutting down a strategy is on average worthwhile. We calculate

$$E\left(r_t \,\middle|\, r_{t-1} < 0\right) = a_1 E\left(r_{t-1} \,\middle|\, r_{t-1} < 0\right)$$
$$= a_1 \cdot \left(\int_{-\infty}^{0} f(r)\cdot dr\right)^{-1} \left(\int_{-\infty}^{0} r\cdot f(r)\cdot dr\right) \tag{10.2}$$

where $f(r) = \dfrac{1}{\sigma\sqrt{2\pi}} e^{-\frac{1}{2}\frac{(r-u)^2}{\sigma\sqrt{2x}}}$ with denotes the unconditional density of r.

Note that we need to calculate the average negative return if a negative return occurs, i.e., $E(r_{t-1}|r_{t-1} < 0)$ in order to see how next days return is on average affected.

Using calculus, this particular case simplifies to

$$E\left(r_t \,|\, r_{t-1} < 0\right) = -\frac{a_1 \cdot \sigma \cdot \sqrt{\dfrac{1}{2\pi}}}{\dfrac{1}{2}} = -a_1 \cdot \sigma \cdot \sqrt{\dfrac{2}{\pi}} \qquad (10.3)$$

where the first integral is used for conditioning on the left hand side of a symmetric distribution around zero, i.e., $\int_{-\infty}^{0} f(r)\, dr = 1/2$. The second integral $\int_{-\infty}^{0} rf(r)\, dr = -\sigma\, 1/\sqrt{2\pi}$, i.e., the average realization to the left of the distribution mean. For example, if a process exhibits a daily volatility of 10 bps, we should expect to loose about $\sigma \cdot \sqrt{\dfrac{2}{\pi}} = 7.97bps$ on an average down day. Given a value for the autoregressive coefficient, $a_1 = 0.1$, this would lead to an expected gain of 0.79 bps each time a stop loss occurred. The expected next days return (average opportunity gain and/or loss of a stop-loss strategy) is positive for $a_1 > 0$, i.e., if r_t exhibits positive momentum. Also note that as long as Equation (10.1) shows positive momentum, we would always stop out when $r_{t-1} < 0$ as the return expectation is always negative (and the opportunity gain positive). Conditioning on large drawdowns would make no sense, as it would remove the breadth of the strategy.

Needless to mention, there are better ways to exploit the regularity in Equation (10.1). For example, we would rather go short than only stop out in the presence of this information. From this it should be clear that a stop loss looked at this way is just a clumsy momentum strategy. Given that practitioners use stop outs usually after extreme market movements, they must suspect some nonlinearity in the real return generating process that is not present in a linear process. We revert back to this when we look at threshold autoregressive models (TAR) in later sections. In this section however, we will extend Equation (10.1) by adding a constant drift term to more realistically introduce the opportunity costs that usually come with a stop-loss strategy.

We assume

$$r_t = a_0 + a_1 r_{t-1} + \varepsilon_t, \, \varepsilon_t \sim N(0, \sigma_\varepsilon^2) \qquad (10.4)$$

where now $E(r) = \mu = \dfrac{a_0}{1-a_1}$ and $\text{Var}(r) = \sigma^2 = \dfrac{1}{1-a_t^2}\sigma_\varepsilon^2$. We assume a stop-loss rule that closes a strategy after a value at risk threshold at the $1 - \alpha\%$ confidence has been passed. Following our approach in Equation (10.2) the expected return from a stop-loss rule can now be formulated as

$$E\left(r_t\big|r_{t-1} \leq \text{VaR}_{1-\alpha}\right) = a_0 + a_1 \cdot E\left(r_{t-1}\big|r_{t-1} \leq \text{VaR}_{1-\alpha}\right)$$

$$= a_0 + a_1 \cdot \left(\int_{-\infty}^{\text{VaR}_{1-\alpha}} f(r)\cdot dr\right)^{-1}\left(\int_{-\infty}^{\text{VaR}_{1-\alpha}} r\cdot f(r)\cdot dr\right) \quad (10.5)$$

$$= a_0 - a_1 \cdot CVaR_{1-\alpha}$$

i.e., a stop loss will only lead to an opportunity gain, if Equation (10.5) becomes negative. This will only happen if a_1 is sufficiently positive such that the combined negative effect of $a_1 \cdot CVaR_{1-\alpha}$ significantly overcompensates a positive value for a_0.[2] We used the fact that

$$CVaR_{1-\alpha} = -\left(\int_{-\infty}^{\text{VaR}_{1-\alpha}} f(r)\cdot dr\right)^{-1}\left(\int_{-\infty}^{\text{VaR}_{1-\alpha}} r\cdot f(r)\cdot dr\right) \quad (10.6)$$

for the usage in Equation (10.5).[3] This allows us to merry readily available calculations from risk reports into our stop-loss analysis. In order to evaluate $CVaR_{1-\alpha}$, we can either evaluate Equation (10.6) for any assumed distribution or calculate it nonparametrically from observed data. Under normality, we get

$$CVaR_{1-\alpha} = \mu - \frac{n\left(\dfrac{-\text{VaR}_{1-\alpha} + \mu}{\sigma}\right)}{N\left(\dfrac{-\text{VaR}_{1-\alpha} + \mu}{\sigma}\right)}\sigma \quad (10.7)$$

where n denotes the *pdf* and N the *cdf* for a standard normal. Suppose for example $\mu = 1bp$, $\sigma = 7bp$ and $\alpha = 1\%$ (daily return and risk for a

---

[2] Nobody would invest in a strategy if $\alpha_0 \leq 0$.
[3] In the above example we used $\alpha = 50\%$ and $\text{VaR}_{50\%} = 0$ for a random walk without drift.

strategy with 111-bps annual risk and an information ratio of 2.27). In this case, $VaR_{99\%} = 15.27bp$, $CVaR_{99\%} = 17.65\,bp$. Assume $\mu = 1$ has been generated by a linear AR(1) process with $a_0 = 0.95$, $a_1 = 0.05$. A stop-loss policy even at the extreme would on average give you a very noisy 0.88-bps opportunity gain against a 0.95-bps opportunity loss. We are now equipped to calculate the opportunity costs/gains of a stop loss for alternative strategies.

SOME WELL-KNOWN STRATEGIES

The framework derived above is now applied to four popular currency strategies, commonly used in quantitative funds. The implicit assumption here is that stop outs occur at the strategy and not at the individual currency level. The reasons for this are twofold. First we want to control losses where it matters most, i.e., on the strategy level. Otherwise stop-loss rules become a hidden (downward) momentum strategy. It is not clear that individual stop outs always reduce risks as a portfolio might become unbalanced once a correlated asset has been removed. For comparison we will also report all tests on a naive strategy (NAIVE), that is long the New Zealand dollar (NZD) and short the Japanese Yen (JPY). We first define the strategies.

Carry Strategy (CARRY)

The strategy is created by using implied interest rate differentials versus the U.S. dollar (USD) from one week forward rates on a large universe of 28 currencies (including emerging market currencies) and as expected returns μ_{carry} (assuming an on average zero move in the exchange rate) and then by calculating $w = \Omega^{-1} \mu_{carry}$ every week, where Ω is the variance covariance matrix of currency returns in USD. This will create a new long and/or short portfolio every week. The covariance matrix is constructed using a multivariate GARCH model. We use the full currency universe as provided in the Appendix. Note that this is not a simple "carry" strategy, but rather it tries to exploit risk-adjusted "carry." It will not simply go long the highest interest rate differentials, but rather it will invest in those with the highest marginal contribution to return relative to its marginal contribution of risk.

Equity Flow (EFLOW)

Every month the AUD, NZD, CAD, CHF, EUR, JPY, NOK, SEK, and GBP are ranked by the relative performance of their stock markets versus the U.S. stock market. Strong stock markets are used as instruments for future currency returns (induced by flows into the currencies of the best performing markets); we build equally weighted long and/or short portfolios of relative winners versus relative losers.

Bond Flows (BFLOW)

Every month we rank the AUD, NZD, CAD, CHF, EUR, JPY, NOK, SEK, and GBP dependent on the slope of their yield curves (2 year –10 year) and again build equally weighted long and/or short portfolios. The idea here is that an attractive bond market should attract bond flows that in turn would lift the currency.

Emerging Market Momentum (EMOM)

Every week we rank the emerging market currencies (in our universe in Appendix A) dependent on their one-month momentum and build equal weighted long and/or short portfolios. In doing this we attribute a ± 1 score to each currency that gets rescaled by the currencies respective volatility to adjust for risk. We can think of this as a Markowitz optimization with a diagonal covariance matrix (zero correlations between currencies) and a return forecast that equals score times volatility.

None of the strategy portfolios is dollar neutral, i.e., the residual position (the position that will guarantee that the sum of active weights adds to zero) will be USD cash. A performance summary is given in Table 10.1. Given that we know these have been popular (surviving) strategies, the highly significant information ratios are not surprising, particularly for the NAIVE strategy that has been going long NZD versus JPY. Data summaries are given in the Appendix (see Tables 10A.1 and 10A.2).

In Table 10.2 we see that autocorrelation coefficients are hardly significant for weekly and monthly data. At the daily horizon the evidence is mixed. It seems that daily returns for a naive carry strategy are

T A B L E   10.1

Performance summary for popular foreign exchange strategies

	CARRY	BFLOW	EQFLOW	EMOM	NAIVE
μ	1.22	0.31	0.41	0.54	0.4
σ	7.21	5.88	6.52	5.94	6.29
1R	2.68	0.84	1.01	1.45	1.01
t-value	7.10	2.21	2.68	3.84	2.61

T A B L E   10.2

Autocorrelation of typical currency strategies

	Daily Data				
	CARRY	BFLOW	EQFLOW	EMMOM	NAÏVE
a_1	−0.016	0.037	0.048	−0.042	0.068
t-value	−0.683	1.542	2.006	−1.764	2.88
LB_1	0.494	0.123	0.045	0.078	0.00
	Weekly Data				
	CARRY	BFLOW	EQFLOW	EMMOM	NAIVE
a_1	−0.012	0.028	−0.037	0.023	0.021
t-value	−0.192	0.440	−0.593	0.364	0.34
LB_1	0.847	0.659	0.551	0.716	0.73
	Monthly Data				
	CARRY	BFLOW	EQFLOW	EMMOM	NAIVE
a_1	0.054	−0.240	−0.073	0.075	−0.17
t-value	0.417	−1.842	−0.558	0.573	−1.31
LB_1	0.670	0.069	0.575	0.561	0.18

significantly autocorrelated. A similarly significant result is only observed for EFLOW. All other coefficients remain statistically indistinguishable from zero. We can now apply Equation (10.5) to the return series of NAÏVE as an example. The expected opportunity gain (avoided loss) from a stop loss (based on the 99% VaR) on NAIVE is given by. $a_0 - a_1 CVaR_{1-1\%} = -0.45$.

Average daily returns and risks (in basis points, such that 1.22 means 1.22 basis points or 0.01%) are given by μ and σ. The sampling period for these strategies is January 2003 to 30. November 2007 (about five years of daily data). All strategies have been ex ante targeting a 100 basis points risk per annum.

For the period tested (daily data from January 2003 to December 2007) we find modest evidence on the strategy level for significantly positive autocorrelation (return momentum). While CARRY even exhibits (insignificant) negative autocorrelation, EFLOW and predominantly NAIVE show significantly positive autocorrelation. Note that returns are aggregated to lower frequency by adding higher frequency log returns.

This again is not a huge benefit. More importantly it is worthwhile to check how well this approximation works. After all it relies on the linearity assumption in Equation (10.4). When we calculate the average return of all days after a stop out (at the $VaR_{99\%}$ level) has occurred, we are somewhat disheartened. Instead of a small opportunity gain of 0.45 bps as indicated above we detect on average an opportunity loss of 0.92 bps.[4] This reminds us of an important caveat with the above analysis: we have been so far looking at unconditional (average) correlations. In fact we have been looking at a linear model. However, what we need to know is not the average autocorrelation but the crisis autocorrelation. If positive autocorrelation comes from low-volatility regimes (in other words, if momentum works better in low-volatility regimes) but conditional autocorrelation is negative (spiking volatility leads to underperforming strategy that bounces back the following day), we might still observe positive average autocorrelation while stop losses might be deeply destructive. Of course, the contrary could also be true. A positive crisis (downward) autocorrelation could be masked behind a low positive or even slightly negative average autocorrelation. We therefore move

---

[4] However, it must be said that the distribution of returns on the "day after" ranges from a further fall of 28 bps (a negative 4.5 sigma event) and a mere 14 bps reversal. The return distribution on the day after a stop out looks asymmetric.

away from linear time series models to nonlinear models to capture reversals after extreme events.

CONDITIONAL AUTOCORRELATION: THRESHOLD AUTOREGRESSIVE MODELS

In practice stop outs do not occur if a strategy makes a small loss, but only at highly unusual, i.e., extreme losses. Do these extreme scenarios come with different correlation patterns, i.e., do extreme losses create positive conditional autocorrelation? Can we find the type of nonlinearity that the use of these strategies implies? To test for this, we can rewrite Equation (10.4) as a self-inflicting threshold autoregressive model (SETAR)

$$r_t = I_t(a_0 + a_1 r_{t-1}) + (1 - I_t)(b_0 + b_1 r_{t-1}) + \varepsilon_t$$

$$I_t = \begin{cases} 1 & r_{t-1} \le \mathrm{VaR}_{1-\alpha} \\ 0 & r_{t-1} > \mathrm{VaR}_{1-\alpha} \end{cases} \qquad (10.8)$$

for $\mathrm{VaR}_{1-\alpha} = z_{1-\alpha}\,\sigma$ with $\alpha = 0.1, 0.05, 0.01$. In effect there are two regimes separated by an indicator function that depends on a chose threshold (stop loss) level. Once a strategy hits a particular value at risk limit, it is stopped out. Conditional autocorrelation is a_1 for $r_{t-1} \le \mathrm{VaR}_{1-\alpha}$ and b_1 otherwise. This allows us to estimate the autocorrelations conditional on being stopped out after $1.282, 1.645, 2.326$ times σ move, where σ denotes the unconditional standard deviation of our strategy. It also enables us to include changes in the expected return in our evaluation of a stop-loss strategy. In fact, if a_0 should become significantly negative, a stop loss would still add value even if a_1 should not exhibit positive autocorrelation, as it would help to avoid days with negative expected returns. The results for Equation (10.8) are shown in Table 10.3.[5] We realize that t-values for the stressed regime are not significant which is an indication of either limited nonlinearity or the wrong specification of thresholds.

---

[5] For a known threshold the estimation of Equation (10.8) can be performed using simple OLS (with dummy variables).

However the litmus test is to calculate performance, i.e., average returns for all days that follow a stop out day.[6] The conditional return after a stop out day in our SETAR model is shown in Table 10.3.

Conditional autocorrelations show different signs in up (black dots) and down markets (orange dots).

$$E\left(r_t \middle| r_{t-1} \leq VaR_{1-\alpha}\right) = \left(\sum I_t\right)^{-1} \cdot \sum I_t \cdot (a_0 + a_1 \cdot r_{t-1}) \qquad (10.9)$$

where again the indicator is defined as previously, i.e., $l_t = 1$ for $r_{t-1} \leq$ $VaR_{1-\alpha}$ and 0 otherwise. Please note that a_0 and a_1 are dependent on the threshold level as seen in Table 10.3. Hence, we can not use Equation (10.9) for different stop-out levels without estimating a new TAR model. The results are summarized in Table 10.4.

For almost all strategies and stop-out levels a day of extreme negative returns is followed by a day of on average positive returns. An example of this is shown in Figure 10.1. Conditional forecasts are given by the orange (stop out) and black line (no stop out); the corresponding data points are also marked black and gray. There is little that suggests that stop outs are followed by falling strategy returns. The opposite seems to be true. However these relationships are mostly insignificant at even the modest confidence requirement. This is mixed news for followers of stop-loss policies. On the one hand a stop loss will not bring superior returns.

---

[6] Note that without the knowledge of daily data, we cannot assume that we would have stopped out at any given day due to the path dependency of an intraday stop out. While one certainly would have stopped out at a −20 bps stop-out level if the strategy returned −40 bps a day (we still would not know at what exact level and slippage that occurred), the same could not be said if the strategy was up 10 bps at the end of the day. We simply do not now whether the return path during that day would have passed the −20 bps stop-out level. Investors should take great care when looking at backtested stop-out rules. First, stop outs create path dependency. We can therefore find many calendar-based rules (always re-enter the market on Tuesdays) or real-time-based rules (always re-enter after 2 business days that work for one particular path, but not for others). The trouble is, we have only one historical path. Second, many claim to have backtested intraday stop outs. Given the amount of high-frequency data needed and their availability for a large currency universe, this is unlikely. Often intraday stop outs are guessed using high-low-close data. However this is not useful for strategy stop outs as highs and lows might have occurred at different times during a day. For our investigation this means that we look at daily stop outs at WMR market closes not at intraday stop-out rules.

T A B L E   10.3

Estimation results from SETAR model

$\alpha = 10\%$	CARRY	EFLOW	BFLOW	EMMOM	NAIVE
a_0	−2.530342	−1.621611	0.978865	2.298800	−1.354720
	(2.220193)	(1.803660)	(1.763866)	(2.069790)	(1.749691)
a_1	−0.197242	−0.150478	0.147862	0.119576	−0.141737
	(0.180448)	(0.144295)	(0.168481)	(0.206701)	(0.145188)
b_0	1.497580	0.373966	0.432137	0.597309	0.325811
	(0.195183)*	(0.161219)*	(0.146451)*	(0.154125)*	(0.151918)*
b_1	−0.043226	0.066992	−0.002362	−0.033949	0.095134
	(0.042605)	(0.033494)†	(0.031922)	(0.031921)	(0.034011)*
$\alpha = 5\%$	CARRY	EFLOW	BFLOW	EMMOM	NAIVE
a_0	−4.995526	−1.795796	4.130019	7.835002	−3.216425
	(4.230564)	(2.641682)	(2.881830)	(4.407489)†	(2.498420)
a_1	−0.316530	−0.166780	0.366235	0.496078	−0.254786
	(0.237131)	(0.178204)	(0.233470)	(0.343078)	(0.174410)
b_0	1.381346	0.362553	0.370141	0.589098	0.367290
	(0.181641)*	(0.156877)*	(0.141404)	(0.147429)*	(0.146769)*
b_1	−0.020102	0.070692	0.014860	−0.032224	0.083426
	(0.039627)	(0.031927)†	(0.029890)	(0.029211)	(0.032051)*
$\alpha = 1\%$	CARRY	EFLOW	BFLOW	EMMOM	NAIVE
a_0	12.369312	−7.737212	−1.480977	0.750484	−5.634611
	(20.198445)	(4.155944)†	(9.254461)	(7.336787)	(4.565604)
a_1	0.362714	−0.489374	0.037071	0.088794	−0.360678
	(0.753539)	(0.219331)*	(0.540254)	(0.417884)	(0.211121)†
b_0	1.249465	0.383352	0.370927	0.634552	0.392059
	(0.17795)*	(0.15238)*	(0.13770)*	(0.148044)*	(0.144199)*
b_0	0.009321	0.066734	0.015051	−0.044053	0.073522
	(0.038289)	(0.029768)	(0.027626)	(0.029239)	(0.030904)*

Note: Robust (autocorrelation and heteroskedasticity consistent) standard errors for the regression coefficients are given in parentheses. Significance at the 10, 5, and 2.5 percent level is marked with a *, †, and ‡, respectively.

T A B L E   10.4

Conditional expected returns after stop out

α = 10%	CARRY	EFLOW	BFLOW	EMMOM	NAÏVE
AR(1) Model	1.42	−0.02	−0.05	0.96	−0.15
SETAR Model	0.26	−0.38	0.10	1.09	0.25
Actual	0.25	−0.34	0.18	1.00	0.39
Standard Error	(1.08)	(0.55)	(0.66)	(0.63)**	(0.69)
α = 5%	CARRY	EFLOW	BFLOW	EMMOM	NAÏVE
AR(1) Model	1.45	−0.09	−0.16	1.04	−0.23
SETAR Model	0.36	−0.55	0.42	1.72	0.15
Actual	0.33	−0.49	0.56	1.53	0.26
Standard Error	(1.65)	(0.72)	(0.87)	(1.12)	(0.88)
α − 1%	CARRY	EFLOW	BFLOW	EMMOM	NAÏVE
AR(1) Model	1.49	−0.22	−0.32	1.19	−0.45
SETAR Model	4.05	−2.09	1.33	−1.85	0.78
Actual	3.84	−1.85	1.66	−2.4	0.92

Note: The table shows average projected returns from the AR(1) model (10.4), the SETAR model (12), as well as actual average returns on the day following a stop-out day. While the SETAR model seems to fit the data well, judgments on the ability of a stop loss to generate an opportunity gain should not be based on the AR(1) model. Estimates are many magnitudes off relative to realized returns. Despite fewer data, standard errors become smaller relative to estimated means, which suggests that at the very extremes next days performance is more likely to be down in the case of EFLOW or up as in BFLOW. Significance at the 2.5, 5, and 10 percent level is marked with *, †, and ‡, respectively.

On the other hand given that all four unconditional strategy returns are highly significant on average (see Table 10.1), days that follow stressed days might be affordable to pass on. At the minimum the risk of a given strategy is reduced with no significant expected return penalty. How much did the SETAR model improve? Are the forecasts any better than those of a simple AR(1) model? The answer to this question is shown in Table 10.4. We see what we already suspected in the previous section. The AR(1) model is not able to make realistic forecasts for days following large losses. A nonlinear alternative is needed. Our SETAR specification does

F I G U R E   10.1

SETAR Model for a Long NZD / Short YEN position
(scaled to 100 bps volatility) with $\alpha = 10\%$. Conditional
autocorrelations show different signs in up (black dots)
and down markets (orange dots).

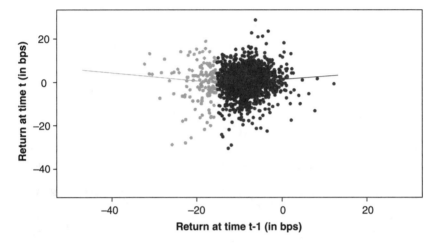

much better. It seems to fit the data well, while estimates from the AR(1)
model are many magnitudes off relative to realized returns. We also see
that the further we go into the tails the more significant do average returns
after a stop out day become. This is a clear indication of nonlinearity and
might be an artefact of us assuming to know the threshold rather than
making it a free parameter in our estimation process.

Again, so far we assumed thresholds to be known. This is appropriate if we want to ask ourselves if a given stop loss (defined by the stop-
loss level) is appropriate. However, we can also turn the question around:
At what level does the conditional correlation change, i.e., where do we
set the breakpoint in Equation (10.8) and what is the nature of the change?
If we would find that the optimal (best fitting) breakpoint is at -20 bps
and it is associated with trend following behavior, we would have identified a profitable stop-loss policy. If, however, the breakpoint is at $+5$ bps
and comes with conflicting coefficient signs, a stop-loss policies should
be dismissed. Also getting the correct threshold might improve on the
above results that showed little support for a stop-loss strategy. In order to

T A B L E   10.5

Estimation of SETAR model

	CARRY	EFLOW	BFLOW	EMMOM	NAIVE
b_0	5.41	3.65	0.32	0.57	**0.86**
	(0.96)*	(1.16)*	(0.17)†	(0.14)*	**(0.28)***
b_1	−0.33	−0.23	0.01	−0.02	**0.08**
# obs	(0.081)*	(0.119)†	(0.037)	(0.02)	**(0.053)†**
a_0	1.21	029	2.26	6.10	−0.28
	(0.19)*	(0.16)†	(0.77)*	(3.51)†	**(0.31)**
a_1	0.003	0.012	0.26	0.38	−0.05
	(0.03)	(0.036)	(0.09)*	(0.28)	**0.05**
#obs	1358	1420	335	84	**757**
z	7.35	6.101	−3.19	−8.92	**0.28**
p − value	0.008	0.21	0.42	0.77	**0.09**
AIC_{SETAR}	3.82	3.50	3.39	3.51	**3.29**
$AIC_{AR}(1)$	3.91	3.51	3.42	3.55	**3.47**
F_{TSAY}	1.21	2.61‡	1.94	0.26	**3.58***
p-value	**0.28**	**0.07**	**0.14**	**0.76**	**0.02**

Note: We calculate p-values for estimated thresholds using the method by Hansen (1996) with 1,000 draws each. The rows titled AIC exhibit values for the Akaike criterion for both the SETAR model and a simple AR(1) alternative. In all cases a simple AR(1) model compares well, i.e., the Akaike criterion is only marginally higher. Finally, we report the value of TSAYS F-Test (F_{TSAY}) for the presence of an autoregressive threshold model. The respective p-values are given in the row below, but none of these suggests significance at the 5 percent level. Significance at the 2.5, 5, and 10 percent level is marked with *, †, and ‡, respectively.

investigate this question we run Equation (10.8) again, but this time the threshold level z is unknown (i.e., a variable that needs to be estimated by the data). The results are summarized in Table 10.5. First we realize, that threshold levels z are either insignificant (EFLOW, BFLOW, EMMOM) or have the wrong sign. The threshold value for CARRY is at 7.35 bps and as such incompatible with a stop-loss strategy. However, the AKAIKE criterion (used to compare alternative models) marginally favours our threshold regression versus a simple AR(1) alternative. Second, there seems to be no statistical evidence for the presence of a threshold autoregressive effect on a strategy level if judged by the F-Test suggested by Tsay (1989). However, this is not true for NAIVE, i.e., a long NZD short

JPY position where the F-test is highly significant. There might be significant nonlinearity going on the individual currency (cross-rate) level. We realize that a two regime might be too restrictive. Therefore, we finally estimate a so-called LSTAR model. Contrary to the previous section we model, we allow for varying degrees of autoregressive behaviour dependent on the previous days move:

$$r_t = \alpha_0 + \alpha_1 r_{t-1} + \left(\frac{1}{1 + e^{-\gamma\, r_{t-1}}} \right) \cdot \left(\beta_0 + \beta_1 r_{t-1} \right) + \varepsilon_t \qquad (10.10)$$

For $\gamma \rightarrow 0$, Equation (10.10) resembles a simple $AR(1)$ model as $\left(\dfrac{1}{1 + e^{-\gamma r_{t-1}}} \right)$ becomesa constant. The same applies for $\gamma_{\rightarrow\infty}$. For all values in between the degree of autoregressive behavior is a function of r_{t-1}. The autoregressive coefficient is given by $\alpha_1 + \left(\dfrac{1}{1 + e^{-\gamma r_{t-1}}} \right) \cdot \beta$, and as it is a direct function of r_{t-1}, we can look at the conditional autocorrelation as a function of lasts days returns. The results are summarized in Table 10.6. There is no evidence for the presence of an LSTAR model in the data. In fact we would always prefer the SETAR model on the basis of the Akaike criterion. Also the hypothesis that $\gamma = 0$ can not be overthrown for four of the five models in which case we are back to an AR(1) model.

CONCLUSION

Recent turmoil in financial markets renewed interest in automated risk management strategies that attempt at cutting the "tail risk" of a given strategy. The implicit assumption behind this notion is the idea that today's large loses tend to be followed on average by next days losses rather than next days gains. For this to be true we would expect positive conditional autocorrelation where the conditioning takes place on past returns. Empirically, we have found very limited evidence. In fact, the contrary seems to be true. Using threshold autoregressive models we find that conditional autocorrelation becomes actually negative, indicating reversals rather than continuation. This is not supportive for stop-loss policies.

T A B L E   10.6

Results for LSTAR model

	CARRY	EFLOW	BFLOW	EMMOM	NAIVE
α_0	1.82	0.52	0.68	0.42	**−0.32**
	(0.41)*	(0.32)‡	(0.2)*	(0.25)	**(0.24)**
α_1	0.09	0.13	0.11	−0.05	**−0.05**
	(0.03)*	(0.08)‡	(0.03)*	(0.04)	**(0.03)‡**
β_0	−0.05	0.05	−0.12	0.34	**1.07**
	(0.05)	(0.31)	(0.3)	(0.36)	**(0.34)***
β_1	−0.17	0.09	−0.13	0.00	**0.08**
	(0.06)*	(−0.11)	(0.05)	(0.05)	**(0.06)**
γ	69.23	15.61	12.1	4.37	**4.88**
	(1.39)*	(112)	(57)	(12.32)	**(4.76)**
AIC_{LSTAR}	3.91	3.52	3.43	3.55	**3.46**
$\min\left(\alpha_1 + \beta_1 \dfrac{1}{1 + e^{-\gamma\, r_{i-1}}}\right)$	−0.08	−0.04	−0.02	−0.06	**−0.05**
$\max\left(\alpha_1 + \beta_1 \dfrac{1}{1 + e^{-\gamma\, r_{i-1}}}\right)$	**0.09**	**0.13**	**0.10**	−0.05	**0.03**

Note: The LSTAR model is estimated using nonlinear least squares, which will be equal to maximum likelihood if residuals are normally distributed. As the LSTAR model switches continuously between regimes, we report the range of autocorrelations from $\min(\alpha_1 + \beta_1\ 1/1 - e - \gamma r_{t-1})$ to $\max(\alpha_1 + \beta_1\ 1/1 - e - \gamma r_{t-1})$. Significance at the 2.5, 5, and 10 percent level is marked with *, †, and ‡, respectively.

REFERENCES

Acar, E. (1998) Expected Returns of Directional Forecasters. In E. Acar and S. Satchel (eds.), *Advanced Trading Rules*. Londo, UK: Elsevier.

Bohl, M. and P.L. Siklos (2008) Empirical Evidence on Feedback Trading in Mature and Emerging Stock Markets. *Applied Financial Economics* (forthcoming).

Dybvig, P. (1988) Inefficient Dynamic Portfolio Strategies or How to Throw Away a Million Dollars in the Stock Market. *Review of Financial Studies*, 1(1): 67–88.

Hansen, B. (1996) Inference When a Nuisance Parameter Is Not Identified under the Null Hypothesis. *Econometrica*, 64(2): 413–430.

Kritzman, M. (2000) *Puzzles of Finance*. Hoboken, NJ: John Wiley & Sons.

Lo, A. and A. Khandani (2007) *What Happened to the Quants in August 2007?* Available at http://papers.ssrn.com/sol3/papers.cfm?abstract_id=1015987.

Samuelson, P. (1994) The Long-Term Case for Equities: And How It Can Be Oversold. *Journal of Portfolio Management*, 21(1): 15–24.

Taleb, N. (2000) Trading with a Stop. Lecture Notes 11. Available at http://www.fooledbyrandomness.com/stop.pdf

Tsay, R.S. (1989) Testing and Modeling Threshold Autoregressive Processes. *Journal of the American Statistical Association*, 84(5): 231–240.

APPENDIX: CURRENCY UNIVERSE AND DATA AVAILABILITY

T A B L E   10A.1

Currency universe for strategy definition

Currency	Example Quote	Convention
AUD: Australia ($)	0.7571	AUD/USD
CAD: Canada ($)	1.1115	USD/CAD
CHF: Switzerland (Franc)	1.244	USD/CHF
EUR: Europe (Euro)	1.2712	EUR/USD
GBP: Britain (Pound)	1.8726	GBP/USD
JPY: Japan (Yen)	116.22	USD/JPY
NOK: Norway (Krone)	6.4833	USD/NOK
NZD: New Zealand ($)	0.6398	NZD/USD
SEK: Sweden (Krona)	7.356	USD/SEK
ARS:* Argentina (Peso)	3.099	USD/ARS
BRL:* Brazil (Real)	2.1514	USD/BRL
CLP:* Chile (Peso)	593.25	USD/CLP
COP:*Columbia (Peso)	2,384.55	USD/COP
MXN: Mexico (Peso)	11.0138	USD/MXN
CZK: Czech Republic (Koruna)	22.2685	USD/CZK
HUF: Hungary (Forint)	216.54	USD/HUF
ILS: Israel (Shekel)	4.389	USD/ILS
PLN: Poland (Zloty)	3.133	USD/PLN
RUB:* Russia (Ruble)	26.76	USD/RUB
SKK: Slovakia (Koruna)	29.587	USD/SKK
TRY: Turkey (Lira)	1.4725	USD/TRY
ZAR: South Africa (Rand)	7.3666	USD/ZAR
IDR:* Indonesia (Rupiah)	9,125.00	USD/IDR
KRW:* Korea (Won)	956.35	USD/KRW
PHP:* Philippines (Peso)	50.49	USD/PHP
SGD: Singapore ($)	1.5701	USD/SGD
THB: Thailand (Baht)	37.39	USD/THB
TWD:* Taiwan ($)	32.876	USD/TWD

*These currencies are traded via non-deliverable forwards (NDFs).

T A B L E   10A.2

Data availability

Currency	Start Date of Floating	Regime Prior to Floating	WMR Start Date Forward Data
ARS	06-Jan-02	Peso fxed to 1.4 USD	29-Mar–04
BRL	14-Jan-99	Managed foat	29-Mar-04
CLP	02-Sep-99	Floating band with various margins since 1995	29-Mar-04
COP	25-Sep-99	Managed float within intervention band	29-Mar-04
MXN	22-Dec-94	Crawling peg regime	02-Jan-97
CZK	27-May-97	Crawling peg against currency basket, widening band	02-Jan-97
HUF	01-Oct-01	Crawling peg against currency basket, then euro +/− 15% band	24-Oct-97
ILS	17-Dec-91	Effectively free float within a very wide band	29-Mar-04
PLN	12-Apr-00	Crawling peg against currency basket, widening band	11-Feb-02
RUB	—	Heavily managed floating—crisis in 1998	29-Mar-04
SKK	01-Oct-98	Crawling peg against currency basket, widening band	11-Feb-02
TRL	22-Feb-01	Crawling peg against the USD	02-Jan-97
ZAR	—	Has been floating for the past 20 years	02-Jan-97
IDR	14-Aug-97	Managed floating with widening band	02-Jan-97
KRW	16-Dec-97	KRW/USD within +/− 2.5% range	11-Feb-02
PHP	—	Managed floating with no fluctuation between mid-95 and mid-97	02-Jan-97
SGD	—	Has been floating for the past 20 years	02-Jan-97
THB	02-Jul-97	—	02-Jan-97
TWD	03-Apr-89	Managed floating	02-Jan-97

Note: Currencies are added to the respective strategies once they become available.

CHAPTER 11

Modeling Portfolio Risks with Time-Dependent Default Rates in Venture Capital

Andreas Kemmerer, Jan Rietzschel, and Henry Schoenball

ABSTRACT

Previous risk management in the venture capital industry has focused mainly on qualitative risk management, such as team selection and due diligence. As investment volume has increased during the past decade, and as venture capital becomes more important as an asset class for institutional investors, rules of thumb do not apply any more and high-risk management standards are demanded for this asset class. In his study, Kemmerer (2005) introduced a risk model by adjusting the CreditRisk$^+$ model to fit the characteristics of venture capital. Based on the initial idea of this approach, the current study's aim is to develop a risk model that considers time-dependent default rates as input parameters, which are adjusted yearly. The empirical results strongly support the assumption that the introduced model measures risks more accurately than the original model.

INTRODUCTION

Previous risk management in the venture capital industry has focused mainly on qualitative risk management, such as team selection and due diligence. As investment volume has increased during the past decade, and as venture capital becomes more important as an asset class for institutional investors, rules of thumb do not apply any more. Furthermore, high-risk management standards, which are common and established for other assets, are demanded for this asset class.

In his study, Kemmerer (2005) introduced a risk model for venture capital portfolios by adjusting the CreditRisk$^+$ model to fit the characteristics of venture capital. The input parameter, "default rate," is entered as the calculated long-term average of the companies' sector. Based on the initial idea of this approach, the current study's aim is to develop a risk model that considers time-dependent default rates as input parameters, which are adjusted yearly.

By using time-dependent default rates, instead of long-term average default rates, it is expected that the predictability of the model will increase. This assumption is plausible because historical regression results, with the default rate as the dependent variable, are highly significant and demonstrate an outstanding explanation of the coefficient of determination. The empirical results strongly support the assumption that the introduced model measures risks more accurately than the original model. By using time-dependent default rates, instead of long-term average default rates, the predictability of losses increases significantly.

INITIAL MODEL
Idea

The following describes the principles of the risk model developed by Kemmerer (2005), which is used as a template to incorporate time-dependent default rates. The initial model adjusts the CreditRisk$^+$ model to the needs of venture capital portfolios. CreditRisk$^+$ is chosen because compared with other standard approaches, such as CreditMetrics™, CreditPortfolioView™, and PortfolioManager™, it is most appropriate for application to venture capital portfolios.[1] CreditMetrics and PortfolioManager are not appropriate vehicles with which to model venture capital portfolios' risk because they need continuous pricing of the investments, which are typically observable for listed companies but not for venture-capital-backed companies.[2] Furthermore, both these models, as well as the CreditPortfolioView approach, need long time series to calculate migration matrices. As the venture capital market is both young and illiquid, no long track records are available. In summary, CreditMetrics, CreditPortfolioView, and PortfolioManager are not appropriate vehicles for modeling venture capital portfolios' risks. In comparison to these models, the Credit-Risk⁺ approach has the lowest data requirements. Rating and migration matrices are not needed as correlations are incorporated indirectly by jointly shared risk factors.

In CreditRisk⁺, each obligor has one of two possible states at the end of the period: default or nondefault. Rating determines a company's unconditional default probability $\overline{P}_\zeta$ for a rated ζ company. Risk factors are introduced to model correlation and diversification effects. The conditional default probability $p_i(x)$ is a function of the realization of K risk factors x, the vector of factor loadings w_{ik} $(k = 1, \ldots, K)$, and the rating class $\zeta(i)$ of company i:[3]

$$p_i(x) = \overline{P}_{\zeta(i)} \left(\sum_{k=1}^{K} w_{ik} x_k \right) \qquad (11.1)$$

---

[1] The tool with which to estimate portfolio risks with CreditRisk⁺ in practice is a publicly provided VBA program from Credit Suisse Financial Products. See http://www.csfb.com/institutional/research/credit_risk.shtml.

[2] Risk models can be classified into asset-value models and models based on default rates. CreditMetrics and PortfolioManager are asset-value models because they need continuous pricing. CreditPortfolioView and CreditRisk⁺ are based on default rates. These models assume that default rates are exogenous and derived from historical data. See Wahrenburg and Niethen (2000, pp. 237ff).

[3] In the CreditRisk⁺—Technical Document is the conditional probabilities given by

$p_i(x) = \overline{P}_{\zeta(i)}(\sum_{k=1}^{K} w_{ik}(x_k / \mu_k))$ and the risk factor x_k has mean μ_k and variance σ^2. Here, the

constants $1/\mu_k$ are incorporated into the normalized x_k without any loss of generality. See Credit Suisse Financial Products (1997).

The risk factors x_k are positive and have a mean of one. The weights w_{ik} quantify how sensitive company i's default rate is to each risk factor. The factor loadings for each obligor total one to guarantee that

$$E\left[p_i(x)\right] = \bar{p}_{\zeta(i)} \qquad (11.2)$$

CreditRisk$^+$ introduces three sector approaches to calculate loss distributions. Each approach incorporates correlation and diversification effects differently.

The first approach, namely the single-sector model, has only one sector, and all companies belong to this single sector. Besides the rating classification, this sector analysis does not require classification into several sectors. A default correlation of 1 is assumed among the obligors; changes in default rates of all obligors are parallel and have the same direction. Diversification effects are not considered.

The second sector analysis, namely the one-sector model, classifies each company to one sector. So, the sector classification equals the rating of the company, and the number of sectors equals the number of rating classifications. All companies of one sector are explained by one factor, i.e., its sector. Therefore, segmentation into industrial sectors assumes uncorrelated sector default rates and the approach considers diversification effects.

The third approach, namely the multisector model, assigns each company to different sectors. It is assumed that a number of independent systematic factors and one idiosyncratic factor influence the company's fortunes.[4] The risk factors are independent among each other. Default correlations among obligors are incorporated by jointly shared systematic factors. The idiosyncratic risk can be diversified in the portfolio because this factor is attributed a standard deviation of zero.

The problem is that CreditRisk does not provide a convincing solution on how to rate companies and how to identify appropriate sector

---

[4] The idiosyncratic risk factor measures the company-specific risks, which are independent from the business development of other obligors. The standard deviation of the idiosyncratic risk factor is zero, whereas the proportionate values of the standard deviation of the idiosyncratic risk factors sum up to the entire standard deviation.

classifications and sector weightings that are necessary for sector analysis. Therefore, Kemmerer (2005) determined in his model that these were not specified factors.

CreditRisk$^+$ models default risk, not by calculating the default distribution directly, but by using the probability-generating function (pgf) to calculate the defaults.[5] As this procedure is well defined in the CreditRisk$^+$ framework, no modifications or assumptions are necessary.

The following describes the adjustments and assumptions made by Kemmerer (2005) in order to use CreditRisk$^+$ to model portfolio risks for venture capital investments.

Specifications to Model Risks in Venture Capital

The input parameters of the CreditRisk$^+$ model are default probability, the default rate's standard deviation, sector classification, net-exposure, and recovery rates. A default for a venture-capital-financed company is defined if all or part of the company is sold at a loss, or if the whole investment is a total loss with no sales revenues (total write-off). A loss occurs if the sales price is lower than the corresponding investment amount.[6] The model uses default rates as an estimator for default rate volatility because the relatively short database history makes an adequate calculation unfeasible.[7] The recovery rate is the share of the exposure the investor obtains in the case of a default. The recovery rate is calculated as the average over the entire period for each rating class. As venture-capital-backed entrepreneurs typically do not have any, or at best very low, collaterals, and as investors' claims are typically subordinated to other investors in the case of a default, the total investment amount in the company is considered as the exposure. Net-exposure is the possible amount of loss in the case of a default, and it equals the company's exposure reduced by the recovery rate of the

---

[5] For more information see CreditRisk$^+$ — Technical Document (Credit Suisse Financial Products, 1997).

[6] If a company has more than one exit during the period for which the default rate distribution is calculated, the single results are added up. The final sum decides if it is a default or not.

[7] Defaults are assumed to be binomially distributed. If default rates are very small and if the number of observations is relatively large, they can be used as a proxy for default rates' volatility.

company's rating class.[8] As CreditRisk$^+$ calculates loss distributions for a single period, the incorporated parameters are determined for yearly observation periods, which equal a calendar year.

As financial statements of venture-capital-financed companies are usually not available or have low explanatory power,[9] typical credit sector rating models, like scoring, discriminant analysis, logistic regression, or artificial neural networks, cannot be used. Therefore, the introduced model uses a simple approach to rate companies, namely its industrial sector.[10] The underlying assumption is companies that are in the same industrial sector are influenced by similar risk factors and, therefore, have similar unconditional default probabilities.[11]

Numerous studies have analysed the predictability of macroeconomic factors on the default rate.[12] Highly significant regression results, as well as extremely well-established coefficients of determination, show that macroeconomic factors have a high explanatory power to project default rates. Therefore, this approach uses macroeconomic variables as risk factors, which represent the systematic influence on the sector-specific default rate. Sector default rates are estimated by regression of macroeconomic factors as independent variables.

---

[8] The exposure to calculate the default distribution for year t refers to the exposure of December 31 at year $t - 1$. If a fund invests in a company in the year of the final exit, losses are lowered by approximately the investment amount that is made in the exit year, because this investment is not incorporated into the exposure that is used to calculate the default distribution.

[9] Venture-capital-backed companies are typically very young, unprofitable companies that operate in innovative markets with high, but uncertain, growth prospects.

[10] Other possible variables are stage or country. Stage can be used as an indicator for the company's size and age. Jones and Rhodes-Kropf (2003) found a significant correlation between stage and idiosyncratic risk in the venture capital industry. Ong (2000) identified a correlation between company size and idiosyncratic risk for credit-financed companies. To our knowledge, no study in the venture capital industry examined the factors that influence the correlation between default probabilities and stage. Because no explanatory variables are known, the stage is not used as a classification variable in this chapter. A classification into sector-stage samples or sector-country samples is not applicable because the number of each sample is too small due to the limited number of observations in the database. As all companies are located in the European Union, it can be assumed that the resulting error of a missing sector-country sample classification is relatively low.

[11] Regression results of previous studies have shown that industrial sector-specific default probabilities can be successfully estimated by macroeconomic variables. See Knapp and Hamerle (1999) and Wilson (1997c).

[12] See Hamerle et al. (2002).

The model uses a logistic forward entry regression to extract systematic factors.[13] At each step, the entry statistic is computed for each eligible value for entry in the model. The variable with the largest increase of R^2 is used as the entry statistic.[14] Stepping is terminated if the increase of the coefficient of determination is lower than 5 percent points or if the maximum of three factors is reached.[15] Assuming that macroeconomic factors are independent, the improvement of the R^2 of each forward entry can be interpreted as the proportion of the entered factor to explain the sector default rate. Hence, the increase of each entered factor is used in this approach as the weight w_{ik} of a ζ rated company i. The sum of all weights of the systematic factors equals R^2. As this approach assumes that all relevant systematic risk factors are incorporated in the model, the systematic risk is explained entirely by the selected variables. The remaining not explained sample variance, $(1 - R^2)$, is considered as the idiosyncratic risk of the rating class.[16] As the sum of the weights of the idiosyncratic risk factor and the systematic risk factors is one, the sector default rate is unbiased.[17]

Sector correlations are modeled if the regression results for different sectors include the same independent variable(s).[18] The regression results from Knapp and Hamerle (1999) have shown that sector default rates can be explained very well by few macroeconomic factors.[19] Hence, the nine

---

[13] A logistic regression is used because the dependent variable is a default rate. All independent variables are transformed into growth rates, which mean that they show the relative change in comparison to the previous period. Especially as the input variables are time-series variables, autocorrelation, which is a typical source of error in regression analysis, can be reduced by using growth rates.

[14] The coefficient of determination R^2 is the proportion of a sample variance of the dependent variable that is explained by independent variables when a linear regression is done.

[15] This is based on the results of Wilson (1997c), who analyzed a multifactor model to explain logit-transformed default rates and showed that three macroeconomic factors explain more than 90 percent of the variation of the default rate.

[16] The idiosyncratic risk of each company is assigned an additional sector in CreditRisk$^+$, which is called *sector* 0.

[17] A company's expected default rate equals the average default rate of its sector.

[18] Another possibility would be to abandon the independent assumption between the sectors by integrating correlation effects into the model. Bürgisser et al. (1999, pp. 2ff.) described such a method, which is neither easy nor feasible to implement.

[19] Knapp (2002) determined that all macroeconomic variables affect the default rate with a lag of one to two years. Thus, the necessary variables are known ex ante and do not need to be estimated separately, which avoids an additional source of error.

macroeconomic factors with the highest significance build all the macro-economic variables used in this model.[20]

Empirical Evidence

The empirical analysis uses a database from a large, private equity fund investor with investments in more than 200 European private equity funds. The analysis only considers venture capital investments. The final sample consists of nearly 200 funds with more than 2,000 companies and more than 8,000 observations for the period from 1997 to 2004.

The regression results to estimate sectors' default rates, and to estimate the weight of each factor are highly significant. The high predictability and reliability of the introduced model is confirmed as default rates diverge on average only about 0.8 percentage points from the empirically observed default rate, with a maximum difference of only 3.1 percentage points. The final sector regression results have coefficients of determination ranging between 0.75 and 0.95. Thus, the weight of the systematic risk of the single sectors varies between 5.1 and 25.2 percent. The average R^2 is smaller than for the regression results of larger companies used in previous studies.[21] This supports the assumption that venture-capital-financed companies, which are typically small, young, and growth-oriented, have higher idiosyncratic risks compared to large, established companies.

The results of the loss distribution are in line with expectation. The single-sector model overestimates portfolio risks due the assumed perfect correlation among all companies. The other two approaches are less risky, whereas the multisector model has lower probabilities for extreme low and high losses. This can be explained with the more sophisticated modeling of diversification and correlation effects. The comparison of realized losses and forecasted losses for 1999 to 2003 shows that the realized losses are always below the forecasted 95 percent value at risk-confidence

---

[20] The included variables are producer price index, gross domestic product, value of retail sales, three-month Euribor interest rate, industrial production, Dow Jones Euro Stoxx 50, euro-dollar exchange rate, oil price, and unemployment rate.
[21] See Wilson (1997a; 1997b; 1997c; 1997d).

level losses. A drawback of the analysis is that the introduced risk model is empirically tested using a portfolio of venture-capital-financed companies. As the model does not take into account that venture-capital-backed companies' returns are, theoretically, unlimited, the results can be considered as the lower bound for loss distributions for loans of venture-capital-financed companies.

RISK MODELING WITH TIME-DEPENDENT DEFAULT RATES

Intention

The following introduces a model to calculate loss distributions for venture capital portfolios. Based on the approach described above, the extended model considers time-dependent default rates in the estimation procedure. The initial model used a regression analysis with industrial sectors' default rates as dependent variables and macroeconomic variables as explanatory variables to extract and weight systematic risk factors. This approach uses a time-dependent regression estimate of the sector default rate, instead of the long-term average of past sector default rates, as input variable. Therefore, it should be expected that losses could be estimated more accurately.[22] This assumption is supported by the very good regression estimates by Kemmerer (2005) as well as by empirical results from other authors. In addition, most selected variables are lagged factors that reduce the estimation error because these variables are known ex ante and do not have to be estimated.[23] CreditRisk$^+$ considers one idiosyncratic risk factor and several systematic risk factors to incorporate correlation and diversification effects between companies in its loss distribution estimates. This approach aims to ensure that the estimate of the time-dependent default rate also considers both kinds of risks.

Systematic risks are incorporated through the selected macroeconomic variables of the regression as they express the economic situation.

---

[22] See Ott (2001, p.108).

[23] It can be assumed that the forecast error is lower in comparison to the model proposed by Wilson (1997a; 1997b; 1997c; 1997d), who uses only actual values as input variables.

Therefore, the default rate estimated by regression is considered to incorporate systematic risks. Using sectors' regressions, default rates can be estimated for each period. Hence, the systematic risk component is time dependent.

Company-specific risks are not considered in the regression estimates because the estimates are based on the average pooled sector default rate.[24] To specify the idiosyncratic risk component, a company's financing stage is chosen. Jones and Rhodes-Kropf (2003) and Ong (2000) found in their studies a significant negative correlation between idiosyncratic risk and stage of financing of the investment.[25] Companies of a more mature stage are typically older and larger than companies from a younger stage. It can be assumed that larger and older companies are less risky, and therefore, on average, have a lower probability to default than younger, smaller companies. Idiosyncratic risks are calculated as stages' long- term average default rate. Therefore, the estimation of the idiosyncratic risk component is time independent.

Finally, the company's total default rate consists of a time-dependent systematic risk component and a time-independent idiosyncratic component. As both parts are modeled separately, the total default rate is made up of both components. The implementation is described in the next section.

Calculation of Time-Dependent Default Rates

The following introduces a framework to calculate time-dependent default rates for venture capital investments that consist of a time-dependent systematic risk component and a time-independent idiosyncratic risk component.

The idiosyncratic risk component is considered through a relative adjustment of regression's calculated default rate $\hat{p}_{\zeta(A),\,t}$ for company A's

---

[24] See Pesaranet al. (2005, p.3).

[25] Jones and Rhodes-Kropf (2003) found a negative relationship between stage and idiosyncratic risks for venture capital investments. Ong (2000) examined a negative relationship between company size and idiosyncratic risks for credit-financed companies.

sector ζ at time t. The relative increase or decrease is considered through the ratio λ_c of the average default rate $\bar{p}_c$ of stage c to the average default rate of companies form all stages $\bar{p}$:

$$\lambda_c = \frac{\bar{p}_c}{\bar{p}} \tag{11.3}$$

with

λ_c = multiple for stage c

$\bar{p}_c$ = average default rate for stage c

$\bar{p}$ = average default rate for companies form all stages

Assuming that the number of investments of each sector is comparable regarding the split-up into single stages, the time-dependent default rate of each company $\tilde{p}_{A,c,t}$ can be calculated as follows:

$$\tilde{p}_{A,t} = \hat{p}_{\zeta(A),t} \lambda_{c(A)} \tag{11.4}$$

with

$\tilde{p}_{A,\hat{t}}$ = default rate for company A at time t

$\hat{p}_{\zeta(A),t}$ = regression-estimated default rate for industrial sector ζ at time t

$\lambda_{c(A)}$ = multiple for company A with stage c

The introduced model has many advantages. As the original model, this approach also enables an unbiased modeling of the company's default rate, in which the systematic risks are incorporated separately to the idiosyncratic risk. Because the break-up between time-dependent and time-independent components remains, the initial idea of a separate modeling of both risks is obtained. The adjustment of regression-estimated default rates by using a multiple guarantees that the relative change of the estimated time-dependent default rate equals the relative change of the calculated regression default-rate in the case of a changed macroeconomic environment. The sensitivity regarding changed macroeconomic variables is achieved, which means that a change of a company's default rate, conditional on a changed macroeconomic environment, is independent of the company's stage. However, this holds conversely, since a change of company's default rate conditional on stages' changes is independent of the macroeconomic environment. Furthermore, as this approach does not need the coefficient of determination to calculate a company's time-dependent default rate, R^2 can be used to model correlation and diversification effects, as used by Kemmerer (2005) in his sector analysis. In addition, as explained in the following, the assumption that all systematic risk factors are included in the regression can be omitted.

The model assumptions of the initial risk model need to be reviewed and adjusted if necessary to model portfolio risks based on time-dependent default rates. The implementation of the sector analysis in the CreditRisk$^+$ framework, with which correlation and diversification effects are modeled, is explained in the following section.

Implementation in Sector Analysis

Correlations between defaults are explained in CreditRisk$^+$ by jointly shared systematic risk factors that influence investments' default rate uncertainty. The initial model uses the selected macroeconomic factors indirectly as systematic risk factors, which explain correlations between companies' default rates. Whereas the approach introduced in this study considers systematic factors explicitly to calculate a sector's time-dependent default rate, which are part of a company's default rates. The macroeconomic variables of the regression explain to a large extent default rates' variance.[26] Therefore, the time-dependent default rate used should be more accurate on average than the time-independent default rate because the difference between the realized and expected default rate is lower compared to the formerly time-independent, long-term sectors' average default rate. However, as the macroeconomic variables are already used to calculate a company's time-dependent default rate, they cannot explain default correlations. Hence, the risk factors of the initial model cannot be employed any more.

---

[26] This is in line with other empirical results. For example, Wilson (1998) shows that the bulk of the systematic or nondiversifiable risk of any portfolio can be explained by the economic cycle.

To model portfolio risks with the new approach in CreditRisk$^+$, unconsidered correlation effects need to be identified. Remaining default correlations can result through forecasting error of the regression analysis. The prediction error is measured as the regression's not- explained sample variance $(1 - R^2)$. The forecasting error depends on the factors to estimate default rates, and the lower the error is, the better the time-dependent regression model is calibrated.[27] The forecasting error can be explained by idiosyncratic risks and not considered systematic risk factors of the regression.

The idiosyncratic risks are already considered through an adjustment of the regression's estimated default rate. Therefore, they cannot be used as an explanation for the remaining not explained sample variance. Hence, apart from the assumption that all systematic risk factors are included in the regression, default correlations can be explained by not considered systematic risks. Assuming that the prediction uncertainty is the same for companies of the same sector, correlation effects can also be modeled on the time-dependent approach. Nevertheless, as the correlations are just included to a large extent in the estimated time-dependent default rate, the remaining correlations that can be considered are lower than in the initial model.

Sectors' definition as introduced by CreditRisk$^+$ must be redefined because default rates' uncertainty of the time-dependent model is restricted to the not explained sample variance. In this approach, the original idiosyncratic risk sector is labeled as a general sector, and the systematic risk sectors are labeled as residual sectors.

The general sector does not model correlation effects. As just explained, correlation effects are included in the regression's default rate through its macroeconomic variables. In CreditRisk$^+$, the general sector is attributed a variance of zero to model diversification effects. In this approach, default rates' uncertainty exists up to the not explained sample variance, $(1 - R^2)$. Therefore, the weight of the general sector equals sectors' coefficient of determination, R^2, of the regression. Only the not explained sample variance can be used to consider correlations in the sector analysis. As each regression estimates the default rate for companies

---

[27] See Hamerle, Liebig and Scheule (2004), p. 27.

that belong to the same sector, each company belongs to one residual sector, which is equal to its sector classification. Hence, the number of residual factors is equal to the number of sectors. The weight of this sector is equal to the not explained sample variance of the sector's regression. This assumes that companies that belong to the same sector are influenced by the same not considered systematic risk factors.

EMPIRICAL EVIDENCE

Database

We are grateful to have had access to the database of a private equity fund investor who invests in venture capital funds in several European countries. The database includes information about the funds' portfolio companies, like investment and divestment amounts, write-offs, and sales revenues. Other information known about each fund includes stage, sector, and geographical region. The used database and input variables for the analysis are the same as those used in the study by Kemmerer (2005).

Our last data update is from the end of April 2005. As there is a time gap between the report's closing date and delivery, only data with a closing key date until December 31, 2004, is considered. Furthermore, funds that do not have the typical fund structure—like mezzanine funds and buyout funds—and all funds that have not yet had a drawdown are excluded from the analysis. The final sample consists of nearly 200 funds. They were invested in more than 2,000 companies. The average net exposure of each company investment is EUR 2,339,715 and the median is EUR 1,283,041. The calendar year is the basis from which to calculate the one-year default rate. The number of observations per company in the analysis equals the number of calendar years the company is held by a fund. In the end, the analysis contained more than 8,000 observations.

The strength of the database comes from the fact that all of its funds have to report, which is very different from the databases of a data provider like Venture Economics. Moreover, by using an investor's database, this study had access to all information available to the fund investor, unlike the database of Venture Economics, where only anonymous and aggregated data is available. Hence, the bias of the sample is limited to that of atypical investment behavior of the fund investor with respect to the general market.

Generally, we believe that the fund investor's investment behavior is a good representation of the European private equity industry.[28]

A point of contention might be that the average fund age of the portfolio is about four years and nine months and that most funds are still active. A longer time series would improve the predictability of the developed risk model. However, we are aware that the sample largely captures the period 1998 to 2004, during which the industry showed a dramatic increase, followed by considerable consolidation.

Analysis

Stages' long-term average default rates were used to model time-dependent default rates. Table 11.1 shows the stage-specific default rates $\bar{p}_c$ and the multiples λ_c for each stage c. The average default rates decrease as the financing stage matures. The seed and start-up stages have a risk premium and the stages' expansion, replacement capital and buyout have a risk discount. The results confirm the assumption of a negative correlation between stage and default rate. Furthermore, the results are in line with previous empirical studies that examined the impact between stage and risk of venture capital investments.[29]

T A B L E   11.1

Stage default rates and stage multiples. The average default rate and the ratio of stage's average default rate to average default rate of companies from all stages

Stage	$\bar{p}_c$	λ_c
Seed	10.5%	1.37
Start-up	8.3%	1.08
Expansion	5.9%	0.77
Replacement capital	5.7%	0.75
Buyout	4.7%	0.62

---

[28] The fund-of-fund investment behavior is compared with the accumulated data for the European venture capital market, as provided by EVCA.

[29] See Jones and Rhodes-Kropf (2003) and Ong (2000).

We compare the results of the model developed in this study (the New Model) with the Original Model (Kemmerer, 2005), to assess whether the New Model leads to more accurate loss estimates.

Table 11.2 shows the results by models for 1999 to 2003. In respect of our data provider, the numbers in the table are shown as ratios, and not as absolute values. The ratio of standard deviation to expected loss is higher for the New Model than for the Original Model, which shows that the former attributes higher risks to venture capital than the Original Model does.

The direction of the estimation bias is the same for both models, which means either they overestimate or underestimate losses.[30] Both models show that realized losses were increasingly underestimated with variation in time.[31]

T A B L E   11.2

Expected versus realized losses by models and years

Year (t)	Standard Deviation (t) to Expected Loss (t)		[Expected Loss (t) – Realized Loss(t)]/ Realized Loss(t)		Position of Realized Loss (t) in VaR	
	Original Model	New Model	Original Model	New Model	Original Model	New Model
1999	0.57	1.03	298%	134%	5%	37%
2000	0.49	0.93	133%	46%	8%	48%
2001	0.48	0.91	188%	72%	14%	41%
2002	0.47	0.91	−23%	2%	78%	62%
2003	0.46	0.91	−45%	−33%	94%	78%
2004	0.46	0.91	−30%	−22%	84%	73%
(Absolute) max	0.57	1.03	298%	134%	94%	78%
(Absolute) average	0.49	0.93	119%	52%		

This table shows the different ratios and the position of realized loss in the Value at Risk (VaR) of the Original Model developed by Kemmerer (2005) and the New Model introduced in this study.

---

[30] An exception is year 2002, in which all models show the best results; whereas the Original Model underestimates the losses, the New Model overestimates the losses.

[31] A potential bias occurs as our data provider began investing in 1997; the database is relatively young and nearly no fund is liquidated. Because fund managers generally hold their investments between five and eight years, the losses are underestimated, especially in the first years. The older the fund gets, the more realistic are the estimations.

For the New Model the difference between expected and realized loss is always lower, and the position of the VaR confidence level is always nearer to the 50 percent VaR than for the Original Model. The position of the realized loss in the value-at-risk confidence level shows that the maximum decreases from 94 to 78 percent. In summary, the New Model can be seen as an improvement over the Original Model. This confirms the previously made assumption that time-dependent default rates are capable of measuring risks more accurately.[32]

Figure 11.1 shows the loss distribution for 2005 by models. With respect to our data provider the loss is shown as a ratio of loss amount to exposure. It can be seen that the probability of having very low as well as very high losses is higher for the time-dependent model than for the

F I G U R E   11.1

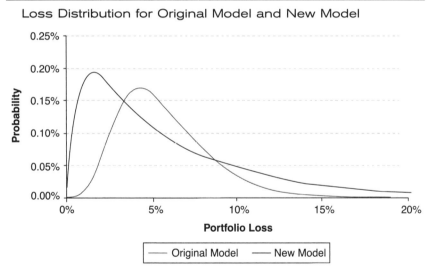

Loss Distribution for Original Model and New Model

This graph shows the expected default distribution for 2005 by models. The loss is shown as a ratio of loss amount to exposure as of December 31, 2004.

---

[32] Backtesting models test ex post how often actual losses exceed forecasted losses; they are used to verify risk models in the credit sector. They cannot be used for venture capital portfolios because they need long track records with a large number of observations, which are not available for the relatively young and opaque venture capital industry. For more information about backtesting see Frerichs and Löffler (2003) and Lopez and Saidenberg (2000).

Original Model. Therefore, the New Model considers the higher risks of venture capital investments more accurately than the Original Model does.

Table 11.3 shows the descriptive statistics and the value at risk for 2005 by models. The time-dependent model assumes that the default rates for 2005 are lower on average than the longer-term average default rate, which can be explained by the fact that the average expected loss in 2005 for the New Model is lower than for the Original Model. The standard deviation for the New Model is higher than for the Original Model, because the New Model assumes a higher variation of the loss distribution. The VaR estimates the likelihood that a given portfolio's losses will exceed a certain amount. The confidence levels show that the probability of very high losses

T A B L E   11.3

Descriptive statistics and the forecasted value at risk for 2005 for the Original Model and the New Model by different portfolios

	Original Model			New Model		
	Unadjusted Portfolio	Adjusted Portfolio	Change of Absolute Values	Unadjusted Portfolio	Adjusted Portfolio	Change of Absolute Values
Expected loss	5.9%	5.8%	−6.44%	5.0%	4.7%	−9.40%
Standard deviation	2.7%	2.6%	−7.61%	4.5%	4.3%	−9.34%
VaR Quartile	**Portfolio Loss**					
50.00%	5.40%	5.40%	−6.22%	3.62%	3.45%	−9.39%
75.00%	7.30%	7.20%	−6.56%	6.69%	6.38%	−9.38%
90.00%	9.50%	9.30%	−6.87%	10.75%	10.26%	−9.37%
92.50%	10.10%	9.90%	−6.95%	12.03%	11.48%	−9.37%
95.00%	11.00%	10.80%	−7.05%	13.83%	13.19%	−9.37%
97.50%	12.50%	12.20%	−7.20%	16.90%	16.13%	−9.37%
99.00%	14.40%	14.10%	−7.37%	20.97%	20.00%	−9.37%

The original portfolio contains all companies. In the adjusted portfolio, total exposure is reduced by about 5 percent for all investments that have the largest ratio of marginal risk to net exposure. The data for the original portfolio and the adjusted portfolio are shown as the ratios of actual value to exposure. The change of absolute values is calculated with the actual values and not on the ratios of actual value to exposure.

is higher for the New Model than for the Original Model. Hence, the New Model assumes that venture capital portfolios are more risky.

Diversification effects can be shown by using marginal risk. The marginal risk capital is obtained in Merton and Perold (1993) by calculating the risk capital required for the portfolio without a new business, and subtracting it from the risk capital required for the entire venture capital portfolio. It enables an optimization of venture capital portfolios because it is used to make investment and divestment decisions. To get a picture of the degree of the marginal risk, the total exposure is reduced by about 5 percent on all investments that have the largest ratio of marginal risk to net-exposure.[33]

Figure 11.2 shows the loss distributions for the unadjusted and adjusted portfolios of the New Model. It can be seen that the loss distribution for the adjusted portfolio has a higher probability of having smaller losses and a lower probability of having relatively high losses.

F I G U R E   11.2

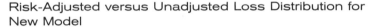

Risk-Adjusted versus Unadjusted Loss Distribution for New Model

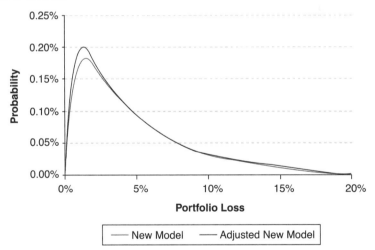

This graph shows the expected default distribution for 2005 by different portfolios for the New Model. In the risk adjusted portfolio, the total exposure is reduced about 5% on all investments that have the largest ratio of marginal risk-to-risk exposue. In respect to the data provider, the loss is shown as a ratio of loss amount to exposure as of December 31, 2004.

---

[33] The marginal risks are calculated for the 95th percentile.

Table 11.3 shows the descriptive statistic of the unadjusted portfolio and the adjusted portfolio for the New Model and the Original Model. It can be seen for both models that the decrease of expected loss, standard deviation, and value at risk is greater than the 5 percent decrease of the net-exposure. The decrease is larger for the New Model than for the Original Model. Therefore, the marginal risk can be used to optimize venture capital portfolios, whereas the New Model offers a higher optimisation potential.[34]

CONCLUSION

This study introduces a risk model for venture capital portfolios that uses time-dependent default rates. The results are compared with the initial model developed by Kemmerer (2005), who uses time-independent default rates. Both models use the CreditRisk$^+$ tool to estimate the probability distribution for losses. The sector analysis is adjusted to fit the assumptions of the time-dependent default rate modeling. In doing so, some restricting assumptions of the initial model can be omitted. The empirical results confirm the assumption that a model with time-dependent default rates enables a more accurate estimation of portfolios' default losses in comparison to the model that uses long-term average default rates as an input variable.

REFERENCES

Bürgisser, P., A., Kurth, A. Wagner, and M. Wolf (1999) Integrating Correlations. *Risk Magazine*, 12(7): 1–7.

Credit Suisse Financial Products (1997) *CreditRisk$^+$—Technical Document.* Available at http://www.csfb.com/creditrisk.

Frerichs, H. and G. Löffler (2003) Evaluating Credit Risk Models Using Loss Density Forecasts. *Journal of Risk*, 5(4): 1–23.

---

[34] In this context it should be considered that this analysis considers only risks. An exclusive examination of potential losses is unsuitable for optimizing venture capital portfolios. An advanced portfolio management should consider not only losses but also returns for portfolio optimization.

Hamerle, A., T. Liebig, and D. Rösch (2002) Assetkorrelationen der Schlüsselbranchen in Deutschland. *Die Bank,* 42(7): 470–473.

Jones, C.M. and M. Rhodes-Kropf (2003) The Price of Diversifiable Risk in Private Equity and Venture Capital. Working paper, Columbia Business School, New York.

J.P.Morgan (1997) *CreditMetrics™ — Technical Document.* Available at http://www.riskmetrics.com.

Kemmerer. (2005) A Model to Measure Portfolio Risks in Venture Capital. Working paper University of Frankfurt, Frankfurt am Main.

Knapp, M. (2002) *Zeitabhängige Kreditportfoliomodelle.* Wiesbaden. Deutscher Universitäts-Verlag.

Knapp M. and A. Hamerle (1999) Multi-Faktor-Modelle zur Bestimmung Segmentspezifischer Ausfallwahrscheinlichkeiten für die Kredit-Portfolio-Steuerung. *Wirtschaftsinformatik,* 41(2): 138–144.

Lopez, J. and M. Saidenberg (2000) Evaluating Credit Risk Models. *Journal of Banking and Finance,* 24(1–2): 151–165.

Merton, R. and A.F. Perold (1993) Theory of Risk Capital in Financial Firms. *Journal of Applied Corporate Finance,* 5(1): 16–32.

Moody's Corporation (2005). *Moody's KMV PortfolioManager™.* Available at http://www.moodyskmv.com/products/Portfolio_Manager.html.

Ong, M.K. (2000) *Internal Credit Risk Models: Capital Allocation and Performance Measurement.* London: Risk Books.

Ott, B. (2001). Interne Kreditrisikomodelle. In B. Rudolph (ed.), Risikomanagement und Finanzcontrolling. Uhlenbruch Verlag: Bad Soden/Ts.

Pesaran, M.H., T. Schuermann, B.-J Treutler, and S.M. Weiner (2006) Macroeconomic Dynamics and Credit Risk: A Global Perspective. *Journal of Money Credit and Banking,* 38(5): 1211–1262.

Wahrenburg, M. and S. Niethen (2000) Vergleichende Analyse alternativer Kreditrisikomodelle. *Kredit und Kapital,* 33(2): 235–257.

Wilson, T.C. (1997a) Measuring and Managing Credit Portfolio Risk: Part I of II: Modelling Systematic Default Risk. *Journal of Lending & Credit Risk Management,* 79(11): 61–72.

Wilson, T.C. (1997b) Measuring and Managing Credit Portfolio Risk: Part II of II: Portfolio Loss Distribution. *Journal of Lending & Credit Risk Management,* 79(12): 67–68.

Wilson, T.C. (1997c) Portfolio Credit Risk (I). *Risk Magazine,* 10(9): 111–117.

Wilson, T.C. (1997d) Portfolio Credit Risk (II). *Risk Magazine,* 10(10): 56–61.

Wilson, T.C. (1998) Portfolio Credit Risk. *FRBNY Economic Policy Review,* 4(3): 71–82.

CHAPTER 12

Risk Aggregation and Computation of Total Economic Capital

Peter Grundke

ABSTRACT

Banks and other financial institutions face the necessity to merge the economic capital for credit risk, market risk, operational risk, and other types of risk to one overall economic capital number in order to assess their capital adequacy in relation to their risk profile. In this chapter, different approaches for solving this task are reviewed, and their pros and cons are evaluated. In particular, two sophisticated risk management approaches, the top-down and the bottom-up approach, are discussed.

INTRODUCTION

Banks and other financial institutions, such as insurance companies, are exposed to many different risk types due to their business activities. Among these are credit risk, market risk, and operational risk. All these different risk types have to be measured and aggregated in order to determine the total economic capital (TEC). For a correct aggregation of losses resulting from different risk types, existing stochastic dependencies between these risk-specific losses have to be considered. This is also a prerequisite for fulfilling the requirements of the second pillar of the New Basel Accord [see Basel Committee on Banking Supervision (2005)]. The second pillar requires that banks have a process for assessing their overall capital adequacy in relation to their risk profile. During the capital assessment process, all material risks faced by the bank should be addressed, including, for example, interest rate risk in the banking book. However, for identifying the bank's risk profile, it is important to correctly consider the interplay between the various risk types.

If economic capital is understood as a value-at-risk number, it is the deviation of the total loss from its mean that is not exceeded until the risk horizon with a very high probability α (see Figure 12.1).[1] This is the difference between the α-percentile q_α (L) of the total loss distribution and its mean. If a bank holds economic capital equal to this figure and given that the loss models are correct, no default of the bank due to unexpected portfolio losses is possible, at least with the high probability α of the value at risk (VaR), which is also called its *confidence level*.

The length of the risk horizon and the confidence level usually depend on the risk type that is measured. For example, for measuring the

F I G U R E   12.1

Economic Capital

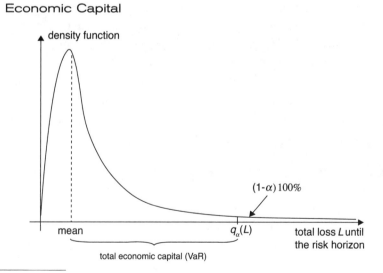

---

[1] The usage of other risk measures (e.g., the expected shortfall) is, of course, also possible.

market risk in banks' trading books, short risk horizons (1 to 10 days) and a relatively low confidence level (99%) are chosen, whereas in a credit risk context, these values are much larger. The confidence level is usually larger than 99.9% and depends on the desired rating of the bank. The risk horizon is usually chosen as one year.

Predominantly, the economic capital (EC) is determined for each risk type separately and later these various amounts of capital are aggregated to one overall capital number. Beside just adding the single EC numbers or merging them using strong assumptions with respect to the multivariate distribution of the risk-specific loss distributions, there exist two more sophisticated approaches: top-down and bottom-up, respectively.

Within the top-down approach, the separately determined marginal distributions of losses resulting from different risk types are linked by copula functions. The difficulty is to choose the correct copula function, especially given limited access to adequate data. Furthermore, there are complex interactions between various risk types in bank portfolios. For example, changes in market risk variables, such as risk-free interest rates, can have an influence on the default probabilities of obligors or on the exposure at default of OTC derivatives with counterparty risk. It is not obvious at all whether copula functions can sufficiently represent this complex interaction because all interaction is pressed into some parameters of the (parametrically parsimoniously chosen) copula and the functional form of the copula itself.

In contrast, bottom-up approaches model the complex interactions described above already on the level of the individual instruments and risk factors. These approaches allow determining simultaneously, in one common framework, the EC needed for different risk types (typically credit and market risk), whereby possible stochastic dependencies between different risk factors can directly be taken into account. Thus, there is no need for a later aggregation of risk-specific loss distributions by copulas.

In this chapter, these different approaches for aggregating risks and computing total EC are reviewed and their pros and cons are evaluated. The chapter is structured as follows: In the second section of this chapter, the additive approach is shortly sketched and, in the following section, the main idea of the correlation-based square-root formula, frequently applied in practice, is described. Afterwards, in the fourth and fifth sections of this chapter, the top-down and the bottom-up approach are reviewed. In this chapter's final section, the main conclusions are summarized.

ADDITIVE APPROACH

The simplest solution for aggregating different risk-specific EC numbers to the total EC is just adding them. This procedure corresponds to the so-called building-block approach stipulated by the regulatory authorities. However, this is a quite conservative approach because it ignores diversification effects between the risk types. Implicitly, it is assumed that losses resulting from different risk types always occur simultaneously. Consequently, in general, the true total EC that is needed is overestimated.[2]

CORRELATION-BASED SQUARE-ROOT FORMULA

Considering diversification effects between losses resulting from different risk types requires modeling the multivariate dependence between them. In practice, some kind of heuristics, based on strong assumptions, are often used to merge the EC numbers for the various risk types into one overall capital number.[3] Frequently, in practice, the following correlation-based aggregation formula is employed, which resembles the formula for computing the standard deviation of the return of a portfolio of financial instruments [see Saita (2007, p. 150)]:

$$\text{TEC} = \sqrt{\sum_{i=1}^{R} EC_i^2 + \sum_{i=1}^{R} \sum_{\substack{j=1 \\ j \neq i}}^{R} EC_i EC_j \rho_{ij}} \qquad (12.1)$$

where $EC_1, \ldots, EC_R$ are the separately determined EC figures for the 1 to R risk types, and ρ_{ij} ($i, j \in \{1, \ldots, R\}$) are the correlation coefficients between loss returns resulting from different risk types.[4]

---

[2] The term in general is used because of the well-known non-subadditivity of the risk measure VaR.

[3] For an overview on risk aggregation methods used in practice, see Joint Forum (2003), Bank of Japan (2005), and Rosenberg and Schuermann (2006).

[4] A recent survey of the IFRI foundation and the CRO Forum concerning the economic capital practices of 17 banks and 16 insurers in Europe, North America, Australia, and Singapore shows that more than 80 percent of the banks apply this risk aggregation approach [see IFRI (2006)].

Problems

As Rosenberg and Schuermann (2006) show, computing total EC with Equation (12.1) is theoretically justified when the loss returns resulting from the different risk types are elliptically (e.g., multivariate normally) distributed. In this case, the percentiles of the standardized marginal loss return distributions are identical to the percentiles of the standardized distribution of the total loss return. Only if this identity is given, the total EC figures produced by Equation (12.1) are exact. However, the assumption of elliptically distributed loss returns is certainly no adequate assumption for losses resulting from credit risks or operational risks due to the asymmetric shape of the loss return distributions. In spite of its theoretical deficiency, Rosenberg and Schuermann (2006) find that this approach is surprisingly close to the results of their more sophisticated top-down approach.

Further problems arise from the fact that confidence levels and risk horizons are differently chosen for EC computations for different risk types. Thus, the risk-specific EC figures $EC_1, \ldots, EC_R$ are not directly comparable, but have to be scaled in order to reach an identical risk horizon (usually one year) and an identical confidence level (usually larger than 99.9%) for all risk types. However, for this scaling procedure, again simplifying assumptions are needed (see, e.g., *Saita* (2007, Ch. 6.1)).

TOP-DOWN APPROACH
Literature Review

Examples of applications of the top-down approach have been presented, for example, by Ward and Lee (2002), Dimakos and Aas (2004), and Rosenberg and Schuermann (2006). Dimakos and Aas (2004) apply the copula approach together with some specific (in)dependence assumptions for the aggregation of market, credit and operational risk.[5] Rosenberg and Schuermann (2006) deal with the aggregation of market, credit and operational risk of a typical large, internationally active bank. They analyze the sensitivity of the aggregate VaR and expected shortfall estimates with respect to the chosen inter-risk correlations and copula functions as well as the given business mix. Furthermore, they compare the aggregate risk estimates resulting from an

---

[5] Later, this work was significantly extended by Aas et al. (2007), where ideas of top-down and bottom-up approaches are mixed.

application of the copula approach with those computed with heuristics used in practice. Kuritzkes et al. (2003) discuss and empirically examine risk diversification issues resulting from risk aggregation within financial conglomerates, whereby they also consider the regulator's point of view. Finally, using a normal copula, Ward and Lee (2002) apply the copula approach for risk aggregation in an insurance company.

An approach, which does not fit entirely neither into the top-down approach nor into the bottom-up approach (as understood in this chapter), is from Alexander and Pezier (2003). They suggest explaining the profit and loss distribution of each business unit by a linear regression model where changes in various risk factors (e.g., risk-free interest rates, credit spreads, equity indices, or implied volatilities) until the desired risk horizon are the explaining factors. From these linear regression models, the standard deviation of the aggregate profit and loss is computed and finally multiplied with a scaling factor to transform this standard deviation into a total EC estimate. However, this scaling factor has to be determined by Monte Carlo simulations.

Basics of Copulas

The essential part of the top-down approach is the choice of the copula function that links the different risk-specific marginal loss distributions. According to Sklar's Theorem, any joint distribution function $F_{X,Y}(x, y)$ can be written in terms of a copula function $C(u, v)$ and the marginal distribution functions $F_X(x)$ and $F_Y(y)$:[6]

$$F_{X,Y}(x,y) = C(F_X(x), F_Y(y)) \tag{12.2}$$

The corresponding density representation is

$$f_{X,Y}(x,y) = f_X(x)\, f_Y(y)\, c\,(F_X(x), F_Y(y)) \tag{12.3}$$

where $c(u, v) = (\partial^2/\partial u \partial v)\, C(u, v)$ is the copula density function and $f_X(x)$ and $f_Y(y)$ are the marginal density functions. For recovering the copula function of a multivariate distribution $F_{X,Y}(x, y)$, the method of inversion can be applied:

---

[6] Standard references for copulas are Joe (1997) and Nelsen (2006). For a discussion of financial applications of copulas, see, e.g., Cherubini et al. (2004).

$$C(u,v) = F_{X,Y}(F_X^{-1}(u), F_Y^{-1}(v)) \qquad (12.4)$$

where $F_X^{-1}(x)$ and $F_Y^{-1}(y)$ are the inverse marginal distribution functions. In the context of the top-down approach, $F_X(x)$ and $F_Y(y)$ are the marginal distributions of risk-specific losses until the risk horizon (e.g., market and credit risk losses), measured on a stand-alone basis. Two copula functions frequently used for risk management and valuation purposes are the normal copula and the t-copula. The bivariate normal copula is given by

$$C(u,v;\rho) = \int_{-\infty}^{\Phi^{-1}(u)} \int_{-\infty}^{\Phi^{-1}(v)} \frac{1}{2\pi\sqrt{1-\rho^2}} \exp\left(-\frac{s^2 - 2\rho st + t^2}{2(1-\rho^2)}\right) ds\, dt \qquad (12.5)$$

where $\Phi^{-1}(\cdot)$ denotes the inverse of the cumulative density function of the standard normal distribution. The only parameter of the bivariate normal copula is the correlation parameter ρ. In contrast, the bivariate t-copula needs two parameters, the number of degrees of freedom n and the correlation parameter ρ:

$$C(u,v;n,\rho) = \int_{-\infty}^{T_n^{-1}(u)} \int_{-\infty}^{T_n^{-1}(v)} \frac{1}{2\pi\sqrt{1-\rho^2}} \left(1 + \frac{s^2 - 2\rho st + t^2}{n(1-\rho^2)}\right)^{-(n+2)/2} ds\, dt \qquad (12.6)$$

where $T_n^{-1}(\cdot)$ denotes the inverse of the cumulative density function of the t-distribution with n degrees of freedom. In contrast to the normal copula, the t-copula exhibits a (symmetric) positive upper and lower tail dependence for $\rho > -1$. Intuitively, the coefficient of tail dependence makes a statement about the presence of joint extreme events.[7]

Estimation Issues

The parameters of a parametric family of copulas can, for example, be estimated by maximum likelihood.[8] Basically, the parameters of the marginal

---

[7] For a formal definition see, e.g., Schönbucher (2003, p. 332).

[8] Alternatively, the parameter ρ of the bivariate normal copula can be computed based on the estimated value $\hat{\rho}_{sp}$ of Spearman's coefficient of correlation and the relationship $\rho = 2 \sin(\pi\rho_{sp}/6)$ [see McNeil et al. (2005, p. 230)]. When a t-copula is employed, ρ can be estimated by $\rho = \sin(\pi\hat{\tau}/2)$, where $\hat{\tau}$ is the estimated value of Kendall's τ [see McNeil et al. (2005, p. 231)], and afterward, only the degree of freedom n is estimated by maximum likelihood.

distributions and the parameters of the copula, combined in the parameter vector θ, can be estimated simultaneously by the maximum likelihood method. Taking into account the density representation in Equation (12.3), the log-likelihood function is:

$$
\begin{aligned}
l(\theta) &= \ln\left(\prod_{t=1}^{T} f_{X,Y}(x_t, y_t; \theta)\right) \\
&= \sum_{t=1}^{T}\left(\ln\left(\left.\frac{\partial^2 C(u,v;\theta)}{\partial u \partial v}\right|_{(u,v)=(F_X(x_t;\theta),F_Y(y_t;\theta))}\right) + \ln\left(f_X(x_t;\theta)f_Y(y_t;\theta)\right)\right)
\end{aligned} \tag{12.7}
$$

As usual, the maximum likelihood estimator (MLE) can be obtained by maximizing the log-likelihood function:

$$
\theta_{\mathrm{MLE}} = \arg\max_{\theta \in \Theta} l(\theta) \tag{12.8}
$$

where Θ is the parameter space. Of course, to apply Equations (12.7) and (12.8), an a priori choice of the type of the marginal distribution and the parametric family of copulas is necessary. To reduce the computational costs for solving the optimization problem in Equation (12.8), which results from the necessity to estimate jointly the parameters of the marginal distributions and the copula, the method of inference functions for margins (IFM) can be applied [see Joe (1997, pp. 299), Cherubini et al. (2004, pp. 156)]. The IFM method is a two-step-method where, first, the parameters θ_1 of the marginal distributions are estimated and, second, given the parameters of the marginal distributions, the parameters θ_2 of the copula are determined. A further possibility for estimating the copula function is the canonical maximum likelihood (CML) estimation. For this method, there is no need to specify the parametric form of the marginal distributions because these are replaced by the empirical marginal distributions (for example, resulting from single-risk-type portfolio models, such as RiskMetrics (market risk) or CreditMetrics (credit risk). Thus, only the parameters of the copula function have to be estimated by maximum likelihood [see Cherubini et al. (2004, p. 160)].

Simulation

Having estimated the risk-specific marginal distributions of losses and the parameters of the copula function, the total EC can simply be computed by Monte Carlo simulation. For example, generating realizations $\{(x_1, y_1), \ldots, (x_D, y_D)\}$ of two random variables X and Y from a bivariate normal and t-copula, respectively, with given marginal distributions $F_X(x)$ and $F_Y(y)$ can be easily done by the following algorithms [see, e.g., Cherubini et al. (2004, p. 181)]:

Normal Copula

1. Draw a realization (a, b) of two standard normally distributed random variables A and B with $Corr(A, B) = \rho$, where ρ is the correlation parameter of the normal copula.

2. Transform the realizations (a, b) into the realizations $(\tilde{a}, \tilde{b})$ of two random variables $\tilde{A}$ and $\tilde{B}$, which are uniformly distributed on the interval [0, 1], by computing $\tilde{a} = \Phi(a)$ and $\tilde{b} = \Phi(b)$, where $\Phi(\cdot)$ is the cumulative distribution function of a standard normal distribution.

3. Finally, to ensure the correct marginal distributions, compute $x = F_X^{-1}(\tilde{a})$ and $y = F_Y^{-1}(\tilde{b})$.

t-Copula with n Degrees of Freedom

1. Draw a realization (a, b) of two standard normally distributed random variables A and B with $Corr(A, B) = \rho$, where ρ is the correlation parameter of the t-copula.

2. Transform the realizations (a, b) into the realizations $(\tilde{a}, \tilde{b})$ of two random variables $\tilde{A}$ and $\tilde{B}$, which are t-distributed with n degrees of freedom, by computing $\tilde{a} = a\sqrt{n/s}$ and $\tilde{b} = b\sqrt{n/s}$, where s is a realization of $S \sim \chi^2(n)$ independent of A and B.

3. Transform the realizations $(\tilde{a}, \tilde{b})$ into the realizations $(\hat{a}, \hat{b})$ of two random variables $\hat{A}$ and $\hat{B}$, which are uniformly distributed on the interval [0, 1], by computing $\hat{a} = T_n(\tilde{a})$ and $\hat{b} = T_n(\tilde{b})$,

where $T_n(\cdot)$ is the cumulative distribution function of a t-distribution n with degrees of freedom.

4. Finally, to ensure the correct marginal distributions, compute $x = F_X^{-1}(\hat{a})$ and $y = F_Y^{-1}(\hat{b})$.

Having generated sufficient realizations of the dependent risk-specific losses $\{(x_1, y_1), \ldots, (x_D, y_D)\}$, the empirical distribution function of the total losses $\{(x_1 + y_1), \ldots, (x_D + y_D)\}$ can be determined. Based on this empirical distribution function, the total EC can be computed.

Problems

An obvious advantage of the copula-based top-down approach is its flexibility because arbitrary, very different marginal loss distributions can be linked to a total loss distribution by means of a copula function. However, one major problem of the top-down approach is the correct identification of the right copula function. In practical applications, the copula function itself is often just *assumed* to be the correct one, and often even the parameters of this assumed copula function are not estimated on time series data but are based on expert judgements. However, doing this, nearly any desired risk measure and hence EC figure can be produced. Thus, an important question is whether it is possible to infer from given time series data of loss returns the correct copula function or, at least, to reject the null hypothesis of specific parametric copula assumptions. The appropriate tool for answering this kind of question is goodness-of-fit (GoF) tests for copula functions.[9] Unfortunately, preliminary results of Grundke (2007b) indicate that, given limited access to time series data of loss returns, it is rather difficult to decide which copula function is an adequate modeling approach. Within a simulation study, Grundke (2007b) employs a GoF test based on the Rosenblatt transformation to test whether the null hypothesis of a normal copula and a t-copula, respectively, can be rejected as an adequate

---

[9] GoF tests were not extensively discussed in the literature in the past, but lately, more and more contributions have emerged [see, e.g., Malevergne and Sornette (2003), Breymann et al. (2003), Mashal et al. (2003), Chen et al. (2004), Dobrić and Schmid (2005; 2007), Fermanian (2005), Genest et al. (2006), and Kole et al. (2007)].

model for describing the stochastic dependence between market and credit risk loss returns. However, based on time series with 60 data points, which corresponds to quarterly data of 15 years, it cannot be differentiated between a normal and a *t*-copula. As a consequence, nonverifiable *assumptions* on the adequate copula function of the top-down approach are unavoidable, and a considerable amount of model risk remains.

Saita (2007, pp. 154–156) points at a further problem of the parameter estimation procedure for the top-down approach. Loss time series on which the top-down approach has to be calibrated are not only short in practice, but there might also exist a serial cross-autocorrelation between different risk-specific loss time series. Consequently, the stochastic dependence (e.g., measured by simple correlation coefficients) between different risk-specific losses might be underestimated. Serial cross-autocorrelation between different risk-specific loss time series could be caused by different accounting practices for different risk types or by a different reaction of losses to the same event. As an example for the latter reason, consider the case of interest rate and credit risk. An increase in risk-free interest rates leads directly to a market risk loss in a bond portfolio or a credit portfolio that is marked to market. However, credit risk losses due to an increased number of defaults that are at least partially caused by the previous increase in risk-free interest rates will only occur with some delay.

A further critical detail of the top-down approach is the bank's choice of the loss definitions for the various risk types. For some financial instruments, such as market risk derivatives with counterparty risk, it might be difficult to differentiate clearly between losses due to market risks and those that are due to credit risks. In any case, loss definitions have to be used that ensure that the sum of the risk-specific losses equals the total loss. Otherwise, the top-down approach is, at least, incorrect as a consequence of misspecified marginal distributions. Furthermore, these loss definitions have to be consistently employed throughout the whole financial institution so that reasonable time series of loss data can be gathered on which the top-down approach can be calibrated.

Finally, not much is known about the overall accuracy of the top-down approach. Grundke (2007b) deals with the question how large the difference between total EC computations based on a top-down and a bottom-up approach is for the market and credit risk of banking book instruments. To focus on the differences caused by the different methodological approaches, market and credit loss data are generated with a simple example of a bottom-up approach for market and credit risk [see the section Bottom-Up Approach in this chapter]. Afterward, the top-down approach is estimated and implemented based on the generated data and the resulting integrated loss distribution is compared with that one of the bottom-up approach. Thus, it is assumed that the bottom-up approach represents the real-world data generating process and the performance of the top-down approach is evaluated relative to the bottom-up approach. Grundke (2007b) observes that in specific situations, for example, for portfolios with lower credit qualities or when high confidence levels are needed, the total EC can be underestimated by the top-down approach.

BOTTOM-UP APPROACH
Literature Review

Bottom-up approaches described in the literature exclusively deal with a combined treatment of the two risk types *market risk* and *credit risk*. Thus, these approaches could also be termed *integrated market* and *credit portfolio* models. Kiesel et al. (2003) analyze the consequences from adding rating-specific credit spread risk to the standard CreditMetrics model. The rating transitions and the credit spreads are assumed to be independent. Furthermore, the risk-free interest rates are nonstochastic as in the original CreditMetrics model. However, Kijima and Muromachi (2000) integrate interest rate risk into an intensity-based credit portfolio model. Grundke (2005) presents an extended CreditMetrics model with correlated interest rate and credit spread risk. He also analyzes to which extent the influence of additionally integrated market risk factors depends on the model's parameterization and specification. Jobst and Zenios (2001) employ a similar model as Kijima and Muromachi (2000), but additionally introduce independent rating migrations. Beside the computation of the future distribution of the credit portfolio value, Jobst and Zenios (2001) study the intertemporal price sensitivity of coupon bonds to changes in interest rates, default probabilities and so on, and they deal with the tracking of corporate bond indices. This latter aspect is also the main focus of Jobst and Zenios (2003). Dynamic asset and liability management modeling under credit risk is studied by Jobst et al. (2006). Barth (2000) computes by Monte Carlo simulations various worst-case risk measures for a portfolio of interest rate swaps with counterparty risk. Arvanitis et al. (1998) and Rosen and Sidelnikova (2002) also account for stochastic exposures when computing the EC of a swap portfolio with counterparty risk.

An extensive study with regard to the number of simulated risk factors is from Barnhill and Maxwell (2002). They simulate the term structure of risk-free interest rates, credit spreads, a foreign exchange rate, and equity market indices, which are all assumed to be correlated. Another extensive study with respect to the modeling of the bank's whole balance sheet (assets, liabilities, and off-balance sheet items) has been presented by Drehmann et al. (2006). They assess the impact of credit and interest rate risk and their combined effect on the bank's economic value as well on its future earnings and their capital adequacy.

There are also attempts to build integrated market and credit risk portfolio models for commercial applications, such as the software Algo Credit developed and sold by the risk management firm Algorithmics [see Iscoe et al. (1999)].

Simple Example of a Bottom-Up Approach

In the following, a simple example of a bottom-up approach for the measurement of the credit and market risk of banking book instruments is sketched. Basically, it is JP Morgan's standard CreditMetrics model extended by correlated interest rate and credit spread risk. A similar model has also been used by Grundke (2005; 2007a; 2007b; 2009).

The risk horizon of the model is denoted by H. P denotes the real-world probability measure. The number of possible credit qualities at the risk horizon, measured by the obligor's rating, is K: one denotes the best rating (e.g., AAA) and K the worst rating, the default state. The conditional probability of migrating from rating $i \in \{1, \ldots, K-1\}$ to $k \in \{1, \ldots, K\}$ within the risk horizon H is assumed to be

$$P\left(\eta_H^n = k \mid \eta_0^n = i, Z = z, X_r = x_r\right)$$

$$= \Phi\left(\frac{R_k^i - \sqrt{\rho_R - \rho_{X_r,R}^2}\, z - \rho_{X_r,R} x_r}{\sqrt{1 - \rho_R}}\right) - \Phi\left(\frac{R_{k+1}^i - \sqrt{\rho_R - \rho_{X_r,R}^2}\, z - \rho_{X_r,R} x_r}{\sqrt{1 - \rho_R}}\right) \quad (12.9)$$

where η_0^n and η_H^n, respectively, denotes the rating of obligor $n \in \{1, \ldots, N\}$ in $t = 0$ and at the risk horizon $t = H$, respectively, and $\Phi(\cdot)$ is the cumulative density function of the standard normal distribution. Given an initial rating i, the conditional migration probabilities are not assumed to be obligor-specific. The thresholds R_k^i are derived from a transition matrix $Q = (q_{ik})_{1 \le i \le K-1, 1 \le k \le K}$, whose elements q_{ik} specify the (unconditional) probability that an obligor migrates from the rating grade i to the rating grade k within the risk horizon.[10] The above specification of the conditional migration probabilities corresponds to defining a two-factor model for explaining the return R_n on firm n's assets in the CreditMetrics model:

$$R_n = \sqrt{\rho_R - \rho_{X_r,R}^2}\, Z + \rho_{X_r,R} X_r + \sqrt{1 - \rho_R}\, \varepsilon_n \quad (n \in \{1, \ldots, N\}) \quad (12.10)$$

where Z, X_r, and $\varepsilon_1, \ldots, \varepsilon_N$ are mutually independent, standard normally distributed stochastic variables. The stochastic variables Z and X_r represent systematic credit risk, by which all firms are affected, whereas ε_n stands for idiosyncratic credit risk. An obligor n with current rating i is assumed to have a rating k at the risk horizon when the realization of R_n lies between the two thresholds R_{k+1}^i and R_k^i with $R_{k+1}^i < R_k^i$. The specification in Equation (12.10) ensures that the correlation $Corr(R_n, R_m)$ ($n \ne m$) between the asset returns of two different obligors is equal to ρ_R. The correlation $Corr(R_n, X_r)$ between the asset returns and the factor X_r is $\rho_{X_r,R}$. As X_r is also the random variable that drives the term structure of

---

[10] For details concerning this procedure, see Gupton et al. (1997, p. 85).

risk-free interest rates [see Equation (12.12)], $\rho_{X_r,R}$ is the correlation between the asset returns and the risk-free interest rates. A natural extension of the modeling approach in Equation (12.10) is to introduce more market risk factors explaining the obligors' asset returns and/or to introduce sector-specific systematic credit risk factors $Z_1, \ldots, Z_s$ so that different inter- and intrasector asset return correlations could be modeled.

For simplicity, the stochastic evolution of the term structure of risk-free interest rates can be described by the approach of Vasicek (1977).[11] Thus, the risk-free short rate is modeled as a mean-reverting Ornstein–Uhlenbeck process:

$$dr(t) = \kappa(\theta - r(t))dt + \sigma_r dW_r(t) \qquad (12.11)$$

where $\kappa, \theta, \sigma_r \in \mathbb{R}_+$ are constants and $W_r(t)$ is a standard Brownian motion under P. The process $(r(t))_{t \in \mathbb{R}_+}$ always tends back to the mean level θ; the higher the value κ is, the more unlikely are deviations from this level. The solution of the stochastic differential Equation (12.11) is

$$r(t) = \underbrace{\theta + (r(t-1) - \theta)e^{-\kappa}}_{= E^P[r(t)]} + \sqrt{\frac{\sigma_r^2}{2\kappa}\left(1 - e^{-2\kappa}\right)}X_r \qquad (12.12)$$

where $X_r \sim N(0, 1)$. As the random variable X_r also enters the definition of the conditional transition probabilities [see Equation (12.9)], transition risk and interest rate risk are dependent in this model. The degree of dependence is determined by the parameter $\rho_{X_r,R}$: the larger this value is, the higher is the influence of the risk-free interest rates on the asset returns and hence on the conditional transition and default probabilities.

Within this approach, market risk factors do not only influence credit quality changes of the obligors until the risk horizon, but they also determine the value of the financial instruments at the risk horizon. For example,

---

[11] It is well known that the Vasicek model can produce negative interest rates. However, for empirically estimated parameters, the probability for negative interest rates is usually very small. Unfortunately, this is not the only drawback of the Vasicek model: it is not possible to adapt the model perfectly to a given current term structure of risk-free interest rates. Actually, the CreditMetrics model could also be combined with any other term structure model.

the price of a defaultable zero coupon bond with maturity date T and nominal value one at the risk horizon H, whose issuer n has not already defaulted until H and exhibits the rating $\eta_H^n \in \{1, \ldots, K-1\}$, is given by

$$p(X_r, S_{\eta_H^n}, H, T) = \exp\left(-\left(R(X_r, H, T) + S_{\eta_H^n}(H, T)\right)\cdot(T - H)\right) \quad (12.13)$$

Here, $R(X_r, H, T)$ denotes the stochastic risk-free spot yield for the time interval $[H, T]$ calculated from the Vasicek (1977) model [see de Munnik (1996, p. 71) and Vasicek (1977, p. 185)]. In the Vasicek model, the stochastic risk-free spot yields are linear functions of the single risk factor X_r, which drives the evolution of the whole term structure of risk-free interest rates. $S_{\eta_H^n}(H, T)$ ($\eta_H^n \in \{1, \ldots, K-1\}$) is the stochastic credit spread of rating grade η_H^n for the time interval $[H, T]$.[12] The rating-specific credit spreads are assumed to be multivariate normally distributed random variables.[13] This is what Kiesel et al. (2003) found for the joint distribution of credit spread changes, at least for longer time horizons such as one year, which are usually employed in the context of total EC computations. Furthermore, it is assumed that the interest rate factor X_r is correlated with the credit spreads. In reality, this correlation depends on the rating grade and the remaining time to maturity. However, for the sake of simplicity, this correlation parameter could be set equal to a constant $\rho_{X_r,S}$.[14] Besides, it is assumed that the idiosyncratic credit risk factors ε_n ($n \in \{1, \ldots, N\}$) are independent of the rating-specific credit spreads $S\eta_H^n(H, T)$ ($\eta_H^n \in \{1, \ldots, K-1\}$). The price of a default risk-free zero coupon bond

---

[12] Actually, $S_{\eta_H^n}(H, T)$ is the stochastic *average* credit spread of all obligors in the rating grade η_H^n. The gaps between the firm-specific credit spreads and the average credit spread of obligors with the same rating are not modeled, but all issuers are treated as if the credit spread appropriate for them equals the average credit spread of the respective rating grade.

[13] Several reasons why average credit spreads for different rating grades can exhibit volatility are mentioned by Kiesel et al. (2003, p. 4): "sticky" ratings, which means that ratings are changed too slowly so that they do not always represent the current credit quality of an obligor; changes in the risk premiums demanded by the investors for bearing credit risk; the "rating-through-the-cycle" methodology employed by rating agencies, and liquidity effects.

[14] As $R(X_r, H, T)$ is a linear function of X_r, $\rho_{X_r,S}$ is also the correlation parameter between the risk-free spot yields $R(X_r, H, T)$ and the credit spreads $S_{\eta_H^n}(H, T)$.

is computed by discounting the standardized nominal value only with the stochastic risk-free spot yield $R(X_r, H, T)$. If the issuer n of a zero coupon bond has already defaulted (i.e., $\eta_H^n = K$) until the risk horizon H, a recovery payment has to be defined. For example, a "recovery-of-treasury" assumption, frequently employed in credit risk pricing models, can be used. In this case, the recovery payment is defined as a fraction δ_n of the value of a risk-free, but otherwise identical, zero coupon bond. The parameters of the recovery rate's distribution (typically a beta distribution) can vary with the seniority of a claim and the value of individual collaterals. Usually, the recovery rate is assumed to be independent across issuers and independent from all other stochastic variables of the model. However, systematic recovery rate risk can also be considered [see, e.g., Frye (2000) or Pykhtin (2003)].

In standard credit portfolio models, such as CreditMetrics or Credit Portfolio View, both interest rate terms in Equation (12.13) are assumed to be known in advance because risk-adjusted forward rates that are observable in $t = 0$ (instead of risk-adjusted spot rates in $t = H$) are used for discounting future cash flows beyond the risk horizon. Thus, given the simulated credit quality of an obligor, no stochastic fluctuations of the value of the financial instruments are allowed for any more.

Problems

One disadvantage of the bottom-up approach compared to the top-down approach is that the latter one can aggregate basically all risk types, whereas the former one usually only deals with market risk (interest rate and credit spread risk) and credit risk (transition and default risk). Obviously, it would be preferable to consider further risk types, such as operational risk. However, it would be rather difficult to integrate operational risk into a bottom-up approach. Thus, only a combined approach is imaginable: first, the profit and loss distribution of the banking book could be computed by a bottom-up approach, which, then, could enter into a top-down approach that aggregates all bank risks.

Furthermore, it would be preferable to extend the bottom-up model described above in such a way that also trading book instruments could be considered. However, measuring different risk types of banking book and trading book instruments simultaneously in a bottom-up approach, would make it necessary to employ a dynamic version of a bottom-up approach because only in a dynamic version, changes in the trading book composition, as a bank's reaction to adverse market movements, could be considered for measuring the total risk of both books at the common risk horizon. Such a dynamic version would also be necessary when active portfolio strategies in the banking book (e.g., for hedging interest rate risk) shall be considered. While it is theoretically possible to construct dynamic portfolio models, however, not much is known about model and estimation risk of these kinds of extended models.

An additional problem of the bottom-up approach is the increasing computational costs compared with single-risk-type portfolio models. Adding market risk factors to a standard credit portfolio model, the computational burden of calculating risk measures increases because the revaluation of the instruments at the risk horizon gets more complex. The computational burden is especially high when the portfolio is large and inhomogeneous, when risk measures with a high confidence level have to be computed or when the pricing functions of the financial instruments are complex or even no closed-form solutions exist for them. The question arises whether it is technically possible to apply computational efficiency enhancing methods originally developed either for standard credit portfolio models or for standard market risk portfolio models also to integrated market and credit portfolio models. Even if it is technically possible, it is by no means obvious that these techniques are still superior to brute force Monte Carlo simulations for these extended models. The results of Grundke (2007a; 2009) indicate that both questions might not always be answered with yes.[15]

Finally, analogously to the problem of finding an adequate copula function for the top-down approach, more research about the true stochastic dependence between market and credit risk factors is necessary to implement integrated market and credit portfolio models. Furthermore, as with standard credit portfolio models, backtesting these extended models is an important issue.

---

[15] For more encouraging results concerning computational efficiency enhancing methods for bottom-up approaches, see De Prisco et al. (2007).

CONCLUSION

The aggregation of stochastically dependent losses resulting from different risk types and the computation of total EC needed as a buffer to absorb unexpected losses in banks are challenging and up to now not satisfactorily solved tasks in risk management. These questions have not been dealt with as detailed as individual risk modeling and measuring issues. Research and practice on these topics are still in an early stage. Beside conceptual problems, the lack of adequate data available for estimating stochastic dependencies between risk-specific losses is certainly one main reason for this fact.

In this chapter, four differently sophisticated approaches to risk aggregation have been described, and the respective problems of each approach have been sketched. In particular, the top-down and the bottom-up approach, which are the most sophisticated methods currently discussed, have been analyzed in more detail. While the top-down approach has a broader scope of application than the bottom-up approach, it is not clear how accurate the top-down approach is and whether its sensitivity to model and estimation risk is comparable to that one of the bottom-up approach.

In any case, much research work has to be done until risk aggregation and total EC results are as reliable as, for example, EC estimates for market risk portfolios.

REFERENCES

Aas, K., X.K. Dimakos, and A. Øksendal (2007) Risk Capital Aggregation. *Risk Management*, 9(2): 82–107.

Alexander, C. and J. Pezier (2003) On the Aggregation of Market and Credit Risks. ISMA Centre Discussion Papers in Finance No. 2003–13, University of Reading.

Arvanitis, A., C. Browne, J. Gregory, and R. Martin (1998) A Credit Risk Toolbox. *Risk*, 11(12): 50–55.

Bank of Japan (2005) Advancing Integrated Risk Management. Tokyo.

Barnhill Jr., T.M. and W.F. Maxwell (2002) Modeling Correlated Market and Credit Risk in Fixed Income Portfolios. *Journal of Banking and Finance*, 26(2–3): 347–374.

Barth, J. (2000) *Worst-Case Analysis of the Default Risk of Financial Derivatives Considering Market Factors* (in German). Dr. Kovač: Hamburg.

Basel Committee on Banking Supervision (2005) International Convergence of Capital Measurement and Capital Standards. A Revised Framework. Bank for International Settlements, Basel.

Breymann, W., A. Dias, and P. Embrechts (2003) Dependence Structures for Multivariate High-Frequency Data in Finance. *Quantitative Finance*, 3(1): 1–14.

Chen, X., Y. Fan, and A. Patton (2004) Simple Tests for Models of Dependence between Multiple Financial Time Series, with Applications to U.S. Equity Returns and Exchange Rates. Working paper, New York University, Vanderbilt University, and London School of Economics.

Cherubini, U., E. Luciano, and W. Vecchiato (2004) *Copula Methods in Finance*. Chichester: Wiley.

De Munnik, J.F.J. (1996) *The Valuation of Interest Rate Derivative Securities*. London: Routledge.

De Prisco, B., I., Iscoe, Y. Jiang, and H. Mausser (2007) Compound Scenarios: An Efficient Framework for Integrated Market-Credit Risk. Working paper, Algorithmics Software LLC, Toronto.

Dimakos, X.K. and K. Aas (2004) Integrated Risk Modelling. *Statistical Modelling*, 4(4): 265–277.

Dobrić, J. and F. Schmid (2005) Testing Goodness of Fit for Parametric Families of Copulas—Application to Financial Data. *Communications in Statistics—Simulation and Computation*, 34(4): 1053–1068.

Dobrić, J. and F. Schmid (2007) A Goodness of Fit Test for Copulas Based on Rosenblatt's Transformation. *Computational Statistics & Data Analysis*, 51(9): 4633–4642.

Drehmann, M., S. Sorensen, and M. Stringa (2006) Integrating Credit and Interest Rate Risk: A Theoretical Framework and an Application to Banks' Balance Sheets. Working paper, Bank of England.

Fermanian, J.-D. (2005) Goodness of Fit Tests for Copulas. *Journal of Multivariate Analysis*, 95(1): 119–152.

Frye, J. (2000) Collateral Damage. *Risk*, 13(4): 91–94.

Genest, C., J.F. Quessy, and B. Rémillard (2006) Goodness-of-Fit Procedures for Copula Models Based on the Probability Integral Transformation. *Scandinavian Journal of Statistics*, 33(2): 337–366.

Grundke, P. (2005) Risk Measurement with Integrated Market and Credit Portfolio Models. *Journal of Risk*, 7(3): 63–94.

Grundke, P. (2007a) Computational Aspects of Integrated Market and Credit Portfolio Models. *OR Spectrum*, 29(2): 259–294.

Grundke, P. (2007b) Integrated Risk Management: Top-Down or Bottom-Up? Working paper, University of Osnabrück.

Grundke, P. (2009) Importance Sampling for Integrated Market and Credit Portfolio Models. *European Journal of Operational Research*, 194(1): 206–226.

Gupton, G.M., C.C. Finger, and M. Bhatia (1997) *CreditMetrics— Technical Document.* New York: JP Morgan.

IFRI Foundation and Chief Risk Officer Forum (2006) Insights from the Joint IFRI/CRO Forum Survey on Economic Capital Practice and Applications.

Iscoe, I., A. Kreinin, and D. Rosen (1999) An Integrated Market and Credit Risk Portfolio Model. *Algo Research Quarterly*, 2(3): 21–38.

Jobst, N.J., G. Mitra, and S.A. Zenios (2006) Integrating Market and Credit Risk: A Simulation and Optimisation Perspective. *Journal of Banking and Finance*, 30(2): 717–742.

Jobst, N.J. and S.A. Zenios (2001) Extending Credit Risk (Pricing) Models for the Simulation of Portfolios of Interest Rate and Credit Risk Sensitive Securities. Working paper 01–25, Wharton School, Center for Financial Institutions.

Jobst, N.J. and S.A. Zenios (2003) Tracking Bond Indices in an Integrated Market and Credit Risk Environment. *Quantitative Finance*, 3(2): 117–135.

Joe, H. (1997) *Multivariate Models and Dependence Concepts*. Monographs on Statistics and Applied Probability 73. London, New York: Chapman & Hall.

Joint Forum. (2003) *Trends in Risk Integration and Aggregation*. Bank for International Settlements, Basel.

Kiesel, R., W. Perraudin, and A. Taylor (2003) The Structure of Credit Risk: Spread Volatility and Ratings Transitions. *Journal of Risk*, 6(1): 1–27.

Kijima, M. and Y. Muromachi (2000) Evaluation of Credit Risk of a Portfolio with Stochastic Interest Rate and Default Processes. *Journal of Risk*, 3(1): 5–36.

Kole, E., K. Koedijk, and M. Verbeek (2007) Selecting Copulas for Risk Management. *Journal of Banking and Finance*, 31(8): 2405–2423.

Kuritzkes, A., T. Schuermann, and S.M. Weiner (2003) Risk Measurement, Risk Management and Capital Adequacy of Financial Conglomerates. In R. Herring and R. Litan (eds.), *Brookings-Wharton Papers in Financial Services*. Philadelphia, PA: Wharton.

Malevergne, Y. and D. Sornette (2003) Testing the Gaussian Copula Hypothesis for Financial Assets Dependences. *Quantitative Finance*, 3(4): 231–250.

Mashal, R., M. Naldi, and A. Zeevi (2003) On the Dependence of Equity and Asset Returns. *Risk*, 16(10): 83–87.

McNeil, A.J., R. Frey, and P. Embrechts (2005) *Quantitative Risk Management, Concepts, Techniques, Tools*. Princeton, Oxford: Princeton University Press.

Nelsen, R.B. (2006) *An Introduction to Copulas*. Second edition, Springer Series in Statistics. Berlin: Springer.

Pykhtin, M. (2003) Unexpected Recovery Risk. *Risk*, 16(8): 74–78.

Rosen, D. and M. Sidelnikova (2002) Understanding Stochastic Exposures and LGDs in Portfolio Credit Risk. *Algo Research Quarterly*, 5(1): 43–56.

Rosenberg, J.V. and T. Schuermann (2006) A General Approach to Integrated Risk Management with Skewed, Fat-Tailed Risks. *Journal of Financial Economics*, 79(3): 569–614.

Saita, F. (2007) *Value at Risk and Bank Capital Management, Risk Adjusted Performances, Capital Management and Capital Decision Making*. Amsterdam: Elsevier.

Schönbucher, P.J. (2003) *Credit Derivatives Pricing Models*. Chichester: Wiley.

Vasicek, O.A. (1977) An Equilibrium Characterization of the Term Structure. *Journal of Financial Economics*, 5(2): 177–188.

Ward, L.S. and D.H. Lee (2002) Practical Application of the Risk-Adjusted Return on Capital Framework. Working paper, Berkeley, CA.

CHAPTER 13

Value at Risk for High-Dimensional Portfolios: A Dynamic Grouped t-Copula Approach

Dean Fantazzini

ABSTRACT

Daul et al. (2003), Demarta and McNeil (2005), and McNeil et al. (2005) underlined the ability of the grouped t-copula to take the tail dependence present in a large set of financial assets into account, particularly when the assumption of one global parameter for the degrees of freedom (as for the standard t-copula) may be oversimplistic. We extend their methodology by allowing the copula dependence structure to be time varying, and we show how to estimate its parameters. Furthermore, we examine the small samples properties of this estimator via simulations. We apply this methodology for the estimation of the value at risk of a portfolio composed of 30 assets, and we show that the new model outperforms both the constant grouped t-copula and the dynamic Student's t-copula when long positions are of concern. As for short positions, a dynamic multivariate normal model is already a proper choice, instead.

INTRODUCTION

The theory of copulas dates back to Sklar (1959), but its application in financial modeling is far more recent and dates back to the late 1990s, instead. Examples include Rosenberg (1998; 2003), Bouy'e et al. (2001), Embrechts et al. (2003), Patton (2004; 2006a; 2006b), Fantazzini (2008), and Dalla Valle et al. (2008). A copula is a function that embodies all the information about the dependence structure between the components of a random vector. When it is applied to marginal distributions that do not necessarily belong to the same distribution family, it results in a proper multivariate distribution. As Daul et al. (2003, p. 1) state ". . . it has become popular to model vectors of risk factor log returns with so-called meta-t distributions, i.e., distributions with a t-copula and arbitrary marginal distributions." For more details about copulas in finance, we refer the interested reader to the recent methodological overviews by Cherubini et al. (2004) and McNeil et al. (2005).

The grouped t-copula is an extension of the Student's t-copula suggested by Daul et al. (2003). The basic idea is to construct a copula closely related to the Students t-copula and where different subvectors of random variables may present quite different levels of tail dependence. This copula allows us to model more accurately the tail dependence present in financial asset returns because it is very rich in parameters. According to Daul et al. (2003, p. 5) ". . . setting the degrees of freedom parameters to be equal yields the usual Student t-copula, and letting this, common degrees of freedom parameter tend to infinity yields the Gaussian copula." While time variation in the first and second conditional moments of the marginals has been widely investigated [see Tsay (2002), for example, and references therein], conditional dependence has been dealt with only by a smaller and more recent literature: empirical works that deal with this issue are those of Patton (2004; 2006a; 2006b), Jondeau and Rockinger (2006), Granger et al. (2006), and Fantazzini (2008). Besides, no application has considered a time varying grouped t-copula so far. Therefore, allowing for the time variation in the conditional dependence of such a copula seems to be natural.

What we do in this work is to allow for possible time variation in the conditional correlation matrix of the grouped t-copula by employing the dynamic conditional correlation (DCC) model of Engle (2002). Chen et al. (2004, p.16) state ". . . . this model allows the conditional correlation matrix of a collection of assets to be time varying, and does so in a manner that easily extends to large collections of assets. This is important, as we wish to consider collections of up to 30 assets." Furthermore, we quote the following passage from Pancenko (2005)

> Chen et al. (2004) show that the Gaussian DCC model provided a good fit to the data in the context of the unconditional copula. Relying on these results, we suggest using the DCC model to specify the time evolution of the correlation matrix of the grouped t-copula. It is important to notice that there are other, possibly better, ways to model the time evolution of correlation matrixes. Recent work of Hafner (2005) and Pelletier (2006) suggest new promising semi-parametric and nonlinear techniques for modeling the correlation dynamics.

We adopt the DCC of Engle (2002) for simplicity and plan a future extension of this chapter to include other correlation dynamics. We perform Monte Carlo simulations to study the small-sample properties of the estimator under different data generating processes, and we investigate its behavior when dealing with conditional quantile estimation, given the increasing importance of the value at risk (VaR) as risk measure; see, for example, the Basel Committee on Banking Supervision (2005). We find that the error in the approximation of the quantile can range between 0 and 3 percent. Particularly, the simulation studies highlighted that in up to medium-sized datasets consisting of $n = 1,000$ observations, the effects of the biases in the degrees of freedom, and the biases in the correlations tend to offset each other, and the error in approximating the quantile is almost zero. We also find that the error is much smaller (1 percent or less) for extreme quantiles, like for the 99 percent quantile required by the Basel committee for market risk management.

Given this evidence, we analyzed a portfolio composed of 30 assets from the Dow Jones Industrial Index. By using a rolling window estimation scheme, we compare different multivariate models by looking at their VaR forecasts with different tests and statistical techniques: Kupiec's unconditional coverage test (1995), Christoffersen's conditional coverage test (1998), Giacomini and Komunjer (2005) asymmetric loss function, and Hansen's superior predictive ability (SPA) test (2005). When long positions are of concern, we found that the dynamic grouped t-copula (together with skewed-t marginals) outperforms both the constant grouped t-copula and the dynamic student's t copula as well as the dynamic multivariate normal model proposed in Engle (2002). As for short positions, we found out that a multivariate normal model with dynamic normal marginals and constant normal copula is already a proper choice. This last result confirms previous evidence in Junker and May (2005) and Fantazzini (2008) for bivariate portfolios, who show that the "normal model . . . leads to a significant underestimation of the loss tail, whereas the win tail is adapted quite well" (Junker and May, p. 451). The rest of the chapter is organized as follows. In the second section of this chapter we define the dynamic grouped t-copula, and we propose a multistep estimation procedure. The third section presents the results of a Monte Carlo study of the finite-sample properties of this estimator with different data generating processes (DGPs) and discusses the effects on conditional quantile estimation. This chapter's fourth section shows an empirical application with a high-dimensional portfolio composed of 30 assets, and conclusions are drawn in the final section of this chapter.

DYNAMIC GROUPED T-COPULA MODELING: DEFINITION AND ESTIMATION

The grouped t-copula is a model that is no more difficult to calibrate than the t-copula but allows for subgroups with different dependence structures. We extend the original contribution by Daul et al. (2003) by considering a dynamic structure for the correlation matrix.

Let $\mathbf{Z} \mid F_{t-1} \sim \mathbf{N_n}(0, \mathbf{R_t}), t = 1, \ldots, T$, given the conditioning set F_{t-1}, where $\mathbf{R_t}$ is the $n \times n$ conditional linear correlation matrix with a dynamic structure and $\bar{\mathbf{R}}$ is the unconditional correlation matrix. Furthermore let $U \sim$ Uniform$(0, 1)$ be independent of $\mathbf{Z}$. Let G_v denote the distribution function of $\sqrt{v/\chi_v}$, where χ_v is a chi square distribution with v degrees of freedom, and partition $1, \ldots, n$ into m subsets of sizes $s_l, \ldots, s_m$. Set $W_k = G_{v_k}^{-1}(U)$ for $k = 1, \ldots, m$ and then $\mathbf{Y} \mid F_{t-1} = (W_1 Z_1, \ldots, W_1 Z_{s1}, W_2 Z_{s1+1}, \ldots, W_2 Z_{s1+s2}, \ldots, W_m Z_n)$, so that $\mathbf{Y}$ has a so-called grouped t distribution. Finally, define

$$\mathbf{U}\big|F_{t-1} = \left(t_{v1}(Y_1),\ldots,t_{v1}(Y_{s1}),\ t_{v2}(Y_{s1+1}),\ldots,t_{v2}(Y_{s1+s2}),\ldots,t_{vm}(Y_n)\right) \quad (13.1)$$

$\mathbf{U}$ has a distribution on $[0, 1]^n$ with components uniformly distributed on $[0, 1]$. We call its distribution function the dynamic grouped t-copula. Note that $(Y_1, \ldots, Y_s)$ has a t distribution with υ_1 degrees of freedom, and in general for $k = 1, \ldots, m-1, (Y_{s1 + \ldots + sk+1}, \ldots, Y_{s1+ \ldots + sk+1})$ has a t distribution with υ_{k+1} degrees of freedom. Similarly, subvectors of $\mathbf{U}$ have a t-copula with υ_{k+1} degrees of freedom, for $k = 0, \ldots, m-1$. In this case no elementary density has been given. However, there is a very useful correlation approximation, obtained by Daul et al. (2003) for the constant correlation case:

$$\rho_{i,j}\left(z_i, z_j\right) \approx \sin(\pi \tau_{ij}(u_i, u_j) / 2 \qquad (13.2)$$

where i and j belong to different groups and τ_{ij} is the pairwise Kendall's tau. This approximation then allows for maximum likelihood estimation for each subgroup separately. The generalization of the previous estimation procedure for the case of dynamic correlation is the following:

Definition 13.1 *Dynamic Grouped t-Copula Estimation*

1. Transform the standardized residuals $(\hat{\eta}_{1,t}, \hat{\eta}_{2,t}, \ldots, \hat{\eta}_{n,t})$ obtained from a univariate GARCH estimation, for example, into uniform variates $(\hat{u}_{1,t}, \hat{u}_{2,t}, \ldots, \hat{u}_{n,t}$ using either a parametric cumulative distribution function (CDF) or an empirical CDF

2. Collect all pairwise estimates of the unconditional sample Kendall's tau given by

3. $$\hat{\tau}_{i,j}\left(\hat{u}_j, \hat{u}_k\right) = \left(\frac{T}{2}\right)^{-1} \sum_{1 \leq t < s < T} sign\left(\left(\hat{u}_{i,t} - \bar{\hat{u}}_{i,s}\right)\left(\hat{u}_{j,t} - \bar{\hat{u}}_{j,s}\right)\right) \qquad (13.3)$$

   in an empirical Kendall's tau matrix $\sum^{\tau}$ defined by $\hat{\sum}_{jk}^{\tau} = \hat{\tau}(\hat{u}_j, \hat{u}_k)$, and then construct the unconditional correlation matrix using this relationship $\hat{\bar{\mathbf{R}}}_{j,k} = \sin\left(\pi / 2 \cdot \hat{\mathbf{O}}_{jk}^{\tau}\right)$ where the estimated parameters are the $q = n\,(n-1)/2$ unconditional correlations $[\bar{\rho}_1, \ldots, \bar{\rho}_q]'$. According to DeMarta and McNeil (2004, p. 9) "... since there is no guarantee that this component wise transformation of the empirical Kendall's tau matrix is positive definite, when needed, $\mathbf{R}$ can be adjusted to obtain a positive definite matrix using a procedure such as the eigenvalue method of Rousseeuw and Molenberghs (1993) ..." or other methods.

4. Look for the ML estimator of the degrees of freedom υ_{k+1} by maximizing the log-likelihood function of the T-copula density for each subvector of $\mathbf{U}$, for $\mathrm{k} = 0, \dots, \mathrm{m}-1$

$$\hat{v}_1 = \arg\max \sum_{t=1}^{T} \log c_{t\text{-}copula}\left(\hat{u}_{1,t}, \dots, \hat{u}_{s_1,t}; \hat{\bar{\mathbf{R}}}, v_1\right)$$

$$\hat{v}_{k+1} = \arg\max \sum_{t=1}^{T} \log c_{t\text{-}copula}\left(\hat{u}_{s_1,s_k+1,t}, \dots, \hat{u}_{s_1+\dots+s_{k+1},t}; \hat{\bar{\mathbf{R}}}, v_1\right),$$

$$k = 1, \dots, m-1$$

5. Estimate a DCC(1,1) model for the conditional correlation matrix $\hat{\mathbf{R}}_t$, by using QML estimation with the normal copula density:

$$\alpha, \beta = \arg\max \sum_{t=1}^{T} \log c_{normal}\left(\hat{u}_{1,t}, \dots, \hat{u}_{s_1,t}; \hat{\bar{\mathbf{R}}}, \mathbf{R}_t\right) =$$

$$= \arg\max \sum_{t=1}^{T} \frac{1}{|\mathbf{R}_t|^{1/2}} \exp\left(-\frac{1}{2}\varsigma'\left(\mathbf{R}_t^{-1} - I\right)\varsigma\right) \qquad (13.4)$$

where $\varsigma = (\Phi^{-1}(\hat{u}_{1,t}), \dots, \Phi^{-1}(\hat{u}_{n,t}))'$ is the vector of univariate normal inverse distribution functions, and where we assume the following DCC(1,1) model for the correlation matrix $\hat{\mathbf{R}}_t$

$$\mathbf{R}_t = (diag\ \mathbf{Q}_t)^{-1/2}\ \mathbf{Q}_t\ (diag\ \mathbf{Q}_t)^{-1/2} = \qquad (13.5)$$

$$\mathbf{Q}_t = \left(1 - \sum_{l=1}^{L}\alpha_l - \sum_{l=1}^{s}\beta_s\right)\bar{\mathbf{Q}} + \sum_{l=1}^{L}\alpha_l\mathbf{u}_{t-1}\mathbf{u}_{t-1}' + \sum_{l=1}^{s}\beta_s\mathbf{Q}_{t-s} \qquad (13.6)$$

where $\bar{\mathbf{Q}}$ is the $n \times n$ unconditional correlation matrix of $\hat{\mathbf{u}}_t$, α_l ($\geqslant 0$) and β_s ($\geqslant 0$) are scalar parameters satisfying $\Sigma_{l=1}^{L}\ \alpha_l + \Sigma_{s=1}^{S}\ \beta_s < 1$.

Note that the second step corresponds to a method-of-moments estimation based on q moments and Kendall tau rank correlation, as first pointed out

by McNeil et al. (2005) and McNeil and S. Demarta (2005). If we define
a moment function of the type

$$E[\psi \ (F_i(\eta_i), F_j(\eta_j); \bar{\rho}_{ij})] = E[\bar{\rho} \ (z_i, z_j) - \sin \ (\pi\tau(F_i(\eta_i),$$
$$F_j(\eta_j))/2) = 0 \tag{13.7}$$

where the marginal CDFs F_i, $i = 1, \dots, n$ can be estimated either parametrically or nonparametrically, we can easily define a $q \times 1$ moments
vector for the parameter vector $\theta_0 = [\bar{p}_1, \dots, \bar{p}_q]'$ as reported below:

$$\psi\big(F_1(\eta_1), \dots, F_n(\eta_n); \theta_0\big) = \begin{pmatrix} E\big[\psi_1\big(F_1(\eta_1), F_2(\eta_2); \bar{\rho}_1\big)\big] \\ \vdots \\ E\big[\psi_q\big(F_{n-1}(\eta_{n-1}), F_n(\eta_{n-1}); \bar{\rho}_q\big)\big] \end{pmatrix} = 0 \tag{13.8}$$

By using this moment vector, it is possible to show that the estimator
presented in Definition 13.1 is consistent and asymptotic normal under
particular restrictions for the correlation matrix $\mathbf{R}_t$. For more details we
refer to Daul et al. (2003), Fantazzini (2007), and the discussions therein.

SIMULATION STUDIES

The asymptotic properties shown in Daul et al. (2003) and Fantazzini
(2007) hold only under the very special cases when $\mathbf{R}$ is the identity
matrix and when z_i and z_j are asymptotically uncorrelated, respectively.
When these restrictions do not hold, the estimation procedure described
in the section previous may not deliver consistent estimates. Daul et al.
(2003) performed a Monte Carlo study with a grouped t-copula with constant $\mathbf{R}$ employing an estimation procedure equal to the first three steps
of Definition 13.1. They showed that the correlations parameters present
a bias that increases nonlinearly in $\mathbf{R}_{j,k,}$ but the magnitude of the error is
rather low. Instead, they did not report any evidence for the degrees of
freedom.

We generalize the work of Daul et al. (2003), and we present here the
results of a Monte Carlo study of the estimator discussed in the section

previous for a representative collection of DGPs with dynamic $\mathbf{R}_t$. We consider the following possible DGPs:

1. We examine the case that four variables have a grouped t-copula with $m = 2$ groups, with unconditional correlation matrix $\bar{\mathbf{R}}$ of the underlying multivariate normal random vector $\mathbf{Z}$ equal to

1	0.3	−0.2	0.5
0.3	1	−0.25	0.4
−0.2	−0.25	1	0.1
0.5	0.4	0.1	1

2. We examine different values for the DCC(1,1) model parameters, equal to $[\alpha = 0.10, \beta = 0.60]$ and $[\alpha = 0.01, \beta = 0.95]$. The former corresponds to a case of low persistence in the correlations, while the latter implies strong persistence in the correlation structure, instead.

3. We examine two cases for the degrees of freedom υ_k for the $m = 2$ groups:
   - $\upsilon_1 = 3$ and $\upsilon_2 = 4$;
   - $\upsilon_1 = 6$ and $\upsilon_2 = 15$;

   The first case corresponds to a situation of strong tail dependence, i.e., there is a high probability to observe an extremely large observation on one variable, given that the other variable has yielded an extremely large observation. The last exhibit low tail dependence, instead.

4. We consider three possible data situations: $n = 500, n = 1,000$ and $n = 10,000$.

Tables 13.1 to 13.4 report the true values of the parameters, the mean across simulations, the bias in percent, the root mean square error (RMSE), and the relative root mean square error, i.e the RMSE with respect to the true value.

The simulation studies show some interesting results:

- *Unconditional correlation parameters* $\bar{\mathbf{R}}_{j,k}$: There is a general negative bias that stabilize after $n = 1,000$. However, this bias is quite high when there is strong tail dependence among variables

TABLE 13.1

Monte Carlo results for $\alpha = 0.10$, $\beta = 0.60$, $\nu_1 = 3$, $\nu_2 = 4$

	0	n = 500				n = 1,000				n = 10,000			
		$\hat{\theta}$	BIAS (%)	RMSE	RRMSE	$\hat{\theta}$	BIAS (%)	RMSE	RRMSE	$\hat{\theta}$	BIAS (%)	RMSE	RRMSE
$\rho_{2,1}$	0.300	0.296	-1.482	0.077	0.256	0.298	-0.782	0.054	0.181	0.295	-1.796	0.018	0.061
$\rho_{3,1}$	-0.200	-0.161	-19.530	0.072	-0.361	-0.165	-17.642	0.057	-0.284	-0.168	-16.157	0.035	-0.177
$\rho_{3,2}$	-0.250	-0.203	-18.612	0.076	-0.305	-0.208	-16.883	0.060	-0.241	-0.210	-15.835	0.042	-0.168
$\rho_{4,1}$	0.500	0.426	-14.823	0.091	0.181	0.427	-14.553	0.082	0.163	0.424	-15.292	0.077	0.155
$\rho_{4,2}$	0.400	0.343	-14.293	0.082	0.205	0.340	-15.028	0.072	0.180	0.338	-15.384	0.063	0.157
$\rho_{4,3}$	0.100	0.107	6.520	0.072	0.723	0.100	0.364	0.053	0.530	0.100	-0.251	0.017	0.166
α	0.100	0.132	32.186	0.040	0.402	0.132	31.560	0.036	0.358	0.133	32.660	0.033	0.331
β	0.600	0.608	1.343	0.077	0.128	0.623	3.855	0.055	0.092	0.631	5.148	0.035	0.058
θ_1	3.000	2.695	-10.167	0.650	0.217	2.754	-8.200	0.531	0.177	2.965	-1.167	0.187	0.062
θ_2	4.000	3.543	-11.425	0.876	0.219	3.531	-11.725	0.771	0.193	3.666	-8.350	0.578	0.144

TABLE 13.2

Monte Carlo results for $[\alpha = 0.01, \beta = 0.95, \upsilon_1 = 3 \; \upsilon_2 = 4]$

	0	$n = 500$				$n = 1{,}000$				$n = 10{,}000$			
		$\hat{\theta}$	BIAS (%)	RMSE	RRMSE	$\hat{\theta}$	BIAS (%)	RMSE	RRMSE	$\hat{\theta}$	BIAS (%)	RMSE	RRMSE
$\rho_{2,1}$	0.300	0.296	−1.482	0.077	0.256	0.298	−0.782	0.054	0.181	0.295	−1.796	0.018	0.061
$\rho_{2,1}$	0.300	0.298	−0.565	0.090	0.301	0.298	−0.513	0.064	0.214	0.299	−0.490	0.022	0.072
$\rho_{3,1}$	−0.200	−0.161	−19.266	0.072	−0.358	−0.161	−19.280	0.057	−0.287	−0.163	−18.365	0.039	−0.196
$\rho_{3,2}$	−0.250	−0.203	−18.954	0.078	−0.312	−0.202	−19.099	0.065	−0.259	−0.205	−18.072	0.047	−0.189
$\rho_{4,1}$	0.500	0.414	−17.169	0.101	0.202	0.414	−17.279	0.094	0.188	0.411	−17.891	0.090	0.180
$\rho_{4,2}$	0.400	0.335	−16.264	0.086	0.215	0.330	−17.390	0.080	0.201	0.329	−17.835	0.072	0.181
$\rho_{4,3}$	0.100	0.103	3.415	0.077	0.772	0.102	2.269	0.056	0.559	0.100	0.003	0.018	0.183
α	0.010	0.019	94.229	0.014	1.447	0.019	90.643	0.011	1.125	0.019	86.190	0.009	0.882
β	0.950	0.900	−5.223	0.124	0.130	0.933	−1.774	0.038	0.040	0.950	−0.032	0.006	0.007
θ_1	3.000	3.010	0.333	0.585	0.195	3.008	0.267	0.412	0.137	3.000	0.000	0.000	0.000
θ_2	4.000	3.894	−2.650	0.817	0.204	3.938	−1.550	0.662	0.165	4.000	0.000	0.077	0.019

T A B L E 13.3

Monte Carlo results for $\alpha = 0.10$, $\beta = 0.60$, $\nu_1 = 6$, $\nu_2 = 15$

		n = 500				n = 1,000				n = 10,000		
	θ	$\hat{\theta}$	BIAS (%)	RMSE	RRMSE	$\hat{\theta}$	BIAS (%)	RMSE	RRMSE	$\hat{\theta}$	BIAS (%)	RMSE	RRMSE
$\rho_{2,1}$	0.300	0.301	0.264	0.064	0.212	0.302	0.654	0.045	0.151	0.297	−0.852	0.015	0.049
$\rho_{3,1}$	−0.200	−0.181	−9.433	0.061	−0.305	−0.187	−6.579	0.044	−0.220	−0.187	−6.356	0.018	−0.092
$\rho_{3,2}$	−0.250	−0.231	−7.536	0.062	−0.246	−0.235	−6.013	0.043	−0.171	−0.235	−5.923	0.020	−0.079
$\rho_{4,1}$	0.500	0.472	−5.609	0.055	0.109	0.474	−5.151	0.042	0.084	0.472	−5.554	0.030	0.059
$\rho_{4,2}$	0.400	0.381	−4.657	0.056	0.140	0.379	−5.370	0.045	0.112	0.377	−5.671	0.026	0.064
$\rho_{4,3}$	0.100	0.107	6.893	0.059	0.586	0.103	2.757	0.044	0.437	0.100	0.066	0.014	0.145
α	0.100	0.110	10.496	0.026	0.259	0.110	10.460	0.019	0.195	0.111	11.232	0.012	0.123
β	0.600	0.580	−3.282	0.098	0.163	0.599	−0.142	0.067	0.111	0.608	1.389	0.021	0.035
θ_1	6.000	5.001	−16.650	1.542	0.257	5.114	−14.767	1.336	0.223	5.190	−13.500	0.908	0.151
θ_2	15.000	7.417	−50.553	7.768	0.518	8.704	−41.973	6.565	0.438	11.362	−24.253	3.900	0.260

TABLE 13.4

Monte Carlo results for $\alpha = 0.01$, $\beta = 0.95$, $\nu_1 = 6$, $\nu_2 = 15$

		$n = 500$				$n = 1{,}000$				$n = 10{,}000$			
	θ	$\hat{\theta}$	BIAS (%)	RMSE	RRMSE	$\hat{\theta}$	BIAS (%)	RMSE	RRMSE	$\hat{\theta}$	BIAS (%)	RMSE	RRMSE
$\rho_{2,1}$	0.300	0.303	1.058	0.060	0.200	0.301	0.495	0.045	0.149	0.300	0.125	0.014	0.048
$\rho_{3,1}$	-0.200	-0.184	-8.060	0.060	-0.299	-0.184	-7.889	0.044	-0.220	-0.190	-5.213	0.017	-0.084
$\rho_{3,2}$	-0.250	-0.230	-7.968	0.060	-0.239	-0.234	-6.597	0.043	-0.172	-0.237	-5.140	0.018	-0.073
$\rho_{4,1}$	0.500	0.475	-4.975	0.051	0.103	0.477	-4.503	0.040	0.080	0.473	-5.434	0.029	0.058
$\rho_{4,2}$	0.400	0.381	-4.719	0.052	0.130	0.381	-4.863	0.041	0.102	0.378	-5.429	0.024	0.061
$\rho_{4,3}$	0.100	0.105	5.411	0.060	0.602	0.103	2.725	0.042	0.416	0.101	0.553	0.014	0.137
α	0.010	0.014	35.109	0.012	1.240	0.013	30.382	0.008	0.821	0.012	21.134	0.003	0.272
β	0.950	0.881	-7.248	0.166	0.175	0.909	-4.329	0.122	0.128	0.948	-0.222	0.010	0.011
θ_1	6.000	5.458	-9.033	1.468	0.245	5.766	-3.900	1.220	0.203	5.931	-1.150	0.493	0.082
θ_2	15.000	8.055	-46.300	7.171	0.478	9.410	-37.267	5.919	0.395	13.541	-9.727	2.334	0.156

(v_k are low), while it is much lower when the tail dependence is rather weak (v_k are high). Besides, it almost disappears when correlations are lower than 0.10, thus confirming the previous asymptotic results. The effects of different dynamic structure in the correlations are negligible, instead.

- *DCC(1,1) parameters α, β* : The higher is the persistence in the correlations structure (high β), the quicker the estimates converges to the true values. In general, the effects of different DGPs on β are almost negligible. The parameter α describing the effect of past shocks shows positive biases, instead, that are higher in magnitude when high tail dependence and high persistence in the correlations are considered.

- *Degrees of freedom v_k*: The speed of convergence towards the true values is, in general, very low and changes substantially according to the magnitude of v_k and the dynamic structure in the correlations. Particularly, when there is high tail dependence (v_k are low), the convergence is much quicker than when there is low tail dependence (v_k are high). Furthermore, the convergence is quicker when there is strong persistence in the correlation structure (β is high), rather than the persistence is weak (β is low). This is good news since financial assets usually show high tail dependence and high persistence in the correlations [see Cherubini et al. (2004), McNeil et al. (2005), and references therein]. Besides, it is interesting to note that the biases are negative for all the considered DGPs, i.e., the estimated $\hat{v}_k$ are lower than the true values v_k.

Therefore, the previous simulation evidence highlights that our multi-step estimation procedure usually results in lower correlations than the true ones, as well as lower degrees of freedom. If the aim of the empirical analysis is conditional quantile estimation, which is the usual case for financial risk management, then these two biases will probably offset each other.

Implications for Conditional Quantile Estimation

Due to the large growth of trading activity and the well-known trading loss of financial institutions, the regulators and supervisory committee of banks have developed and supported quantitative techniques in order to evaluate the possible losses that these institutions can incur. The most well-known risk measure is the value at risk (VaR), which is defined as the maximum loss which can be incurred by a portfolio, at a given time horizon and at a given confidence level $(1 - p)$. If the cumulative distribution function (CDF) of the joint distribution is known, then the VaR is simply its pth quantile times the value of the financial position; however, the CDF is not known in practice and must be estimated.

Jorion (2000) provides an introduction to VaR as well as discussing its estimation, while the www.gloriamundi.org Web site comprehensively cites the VaR literature as well as providing other VaR resources. While we remark that VaR as a risk measure is criticized for not being subadditive and hence may fail to stimulate diversification [see Embrechts (2000) for an overview of the criticism], still, the final Basel Capital Accord that has come in force since 2007 focuses on VaR only. Therefore, we explore here the consequences of our multistep estimation procedure of the dynamic grouped t-copula on VaR estimation, by using the same DGPs discussed at the beginning of this chapter's third section. As we want to study only the effects of the estimated dependence structure, we consider the same marginals for all DGPs, as well as the same past shocks $\hat{u}_{t-1}$. For sake of simplicity, we suppose to invest an amount $Mi = 1, i = 1, \ldots, n = 4$ in every asset.

We consider eight different quantiles to better highlight the overall effects of the estimated copula parameters on the joint distribution of the losses: 0.25, 0.50, 1.00, 5.00, 95.00, 99.00, 99.50, and 99.75 percent; that is, we consider both the "loss tail" and the "win tail." Tables 13.5 to 13.8 report the true VaR, the mean across simulations, the bias in percent, the RMSE, and the relative root mean square error, i.e., the RMSE with respect to the true value.

In general, the estimated quantiles show a very small underestimation, which can range between 0 and 3 percent. Particularly, we can observe that

- *The lower the tail dependence between assets is, the lower the error in the approximation of the quantiles is, i.e., when $\hat{v}_k$ are high, ceteris paribus.* Looking at Tables 13.1 and 13.2, we see that in such a case the estimated degrees of freedom are much lower than the true values. Consequently, when estimating the quantile they tend to offset the effect of lower correlations, which would decrease the computed quantile, instead.

T A B L E   13.5

VaR estimation: Monte Carlo results for $\alpha = 0.10$, $\beta = 0.60$, $\nu_1 = 3$, $\nu_2 = 4$

		n = 500				n = 1,000				n = 10,000			
	VaR	VaR	BIAS (%)	RMSE	RRMSE	VaR	BIAS (%)	RMSE	RRMSE	VaR	BIAS (%)	RMSE	RRMSE
0.25%	0.068	0.067	−1.427	0.003	0.045	0.067	−1.561	0.003	0.044	0.066	−1.898	0.003	0.042
0.50%	0.062	0.061	−1.593	0.003	0.047	0.061	−1.750	0.003	0.046	0.060	−2.033	0.003	0.045
1.00%	0.055	0.054	−1.868	0.003	0.051	0.054	−2.037	0.003	0.049	0.054	−2.291	0.003	0.048
5.00%	0.039	0.037	−3.002	0.002	0.061	0.037	−3.108	0.002	0.059	0.037	−3.240	0.002	0.057
99.75%	−0.069	−0.068	−1.392	0.003	0.045	−0.068	−1.459	0.003	0.043	−0.068	−1.890	0.003	0.043
99.50%	−0.063	−0.062	−1.576	0.003	0.047	−0.062	−1.689	0.003	0.046	−0.062	−2.054	0.003	0.045
99.00%	−0.056	−0.055	−1.872	0.003	0.051	−0.055	−1.993	0.003	0.049	−0.055	−2.336	0.003	0.048
95.00%	−0.039	−0.038	−2.939	0.002	0.060	−0.038	−3.007	0.002	0.059	−0.038	−3.227	0.002	0.057

TABLE 13.6

VaR estimation: Monte Carlo results for $\alpha = 0.01$, $\beta = 0.95$, $\upsilon_1 = 3$, $\upsilon_2 = 4$

	VaR	n = 500				n = 1,000				n = 10,000			
		VaR	BIAS (%)	RMSE	RRMSE	VaR	BIAS (%)	RMSE	RRMSE	VaR	BIAS (%)	RMSE	RRMSE
0.25%	0.068	0.067	−0.505	0.002	0.028	0.067	−0.543	0.001	0.022	0.067	−0.679	0.001	0.014
0.50%	0.062	0.061	−0.643	0.002	0.029	0.061	−0.687	0.001	0.023	0.061	−0.837	0.001	0.014
1.00%	0.055	0.055	−0.806	0.002	0.031	0.055	−0.862	0.001	0.024	0.055	−0.975	0.001	0.015
5.00%	0.038	0.038	−1.254	0.001	0.035	0.038	−1.290	0.001	0.028	0.038	−1.425	0.001	0.018
99.75%	−0.069	−0.069	−0.775	0.002	0.028	−0.069	−0.849	0.002	0.023	−0.069	−0.972	0.001	0.015
99.50%	−0.063	−0.063	−0.838	0.002	0.029	−0.062	−0.946	0.001	0.024	−0.062	−1.050	0.001	0.016
99.00%	−0.056	−0.056	−0.800	0.002	0.030	−0.056	−0.897	0.001	0.024	−0.056	−0.994	0.001	0.015
95.00%	−0.039	−0.039	−1.335	0.001	0.035	−0.039	−1.403	0.001	0.029	−0.039	−1.531	0.001	0.019

TABLE 13.7

VaR estimation: Monte Carlo results for $\alpha = 0.10$, $\beta = 0.60$, $v_1 = 6$, $v2 = 15$

	VaR	n = 500 VaR	BIAS (%)	RMSE	RRMSE	n = 1,000 VaR	BIAS (%)	RMSE	RRMSE	n = 10,000 VaR	BIAS (%)	RMSE	RRMSE
0.25%	0.067	0.066	-1.471	0.003	0.045	0.066	-1.771	0.003	0.044	0.066	-2.023	0.003	0.043
0.50%	0.062	0.060	-1.689	0.003	0.047	0.060	-1.937	0.003	0.045	0.060	-2.152	0.003	0.044
1.00%	0.055	0.054	-1.856	0.003	0.049	0.054	-2.084	0.003	0.047	0.054	-2.270	0.003	0.045
5.00%	0.039	0.038	-2.318	0.002	0.055	0.038	-2.472	0.002	0.051	0.038	-2.583	0.002	0.049
99.75%	-0.068	-0.068	-1.090	0.003	0.045	-0.068	-1.388	0.003	0.043	-0.067	-1.672	0.003	0.042
99.50%	-0.063	-0.062	-1.178	0.003	0.046	-0.062	-1.411	0.003	0.044	-0.061	-1.662	0.003	0.042
99.00%	-0.056	-0.055	-1.657	0.003	0.049	-0.055	-1.879	0.003	0.046	-0.055	-2.083	0.003	0.045
95.00%	-0.040	-0.039	-2.289	0.002	0.054	-0.039	-2.446	0.002	0.050	-0.039	-2.565	0.002	0.049

TABLE 13.8

VaR estimation: Monte Carlo results for $\alpha = 0.01$, $\beta = 0.95$, $\upsilon_1 = 6$, $\upsilon_2 = 15$

	VaR	n = 500				n = 1,000				n = 10,000		
		VaR	BIAS (%)	RMSE	RRMSE	VaR	BIAS (%)	RMSE	RRMSE	VaR	BIAS (%)	RMSE	RRMSE
0.25%	0.067	0.066	−1.471	0.003	0.045	0.066	−1.771	0.003	0.044	0.066	−2.023	0.003	0.043
0.25%	0.067	0.067	−0.259	0.002	0.027	0.067	−0.421	0.001	0.020	0.067	−0.806	0.001	0.013
0.50%	0.061	0.061	−0.256	0.002	0.027	0.061	−0.381	0.001	0.019	0.061	−0.693	0.001	0.012
1.00%	0.055	0.055	−0.260	0.002	0.028	0.055	−0.354	0.001	0.020	0.055	−0.620	0.001	0.011
5.00%	0.039	0.039	−0.428	0.001	0.029	0.039	−0.423	0.001	0.021	0.038	−0.594	0.000	0.011
99.75%	−0.068	−0.068	0.093	0.002	0.027	−0.068	−0.122	0.001	0.019	−0.068	−0.455	0.001	0.011
99.50%	−0.063	−0.062	−0.145	0.002	0.027	−0.062	−0.296	0.001	0.019	−0.062	−0.573	0.001	0.011
99.00%	−0.056	−0.056	−0.317	0.002	0.027	−0.056	−0.402	0.001	0.020	−0.056	−0.664	0.001	0.011
95.00%	−0.039	−0.039	−0.482	0.001	0.029	−0.039	−0.491	0.001	0.021	−0.039	−0.675	0.000	0.011
0.25%	0.067	0.067	−0.259	0.002	0.027	0.067	−0.421	0.001	0.020	0.067	−0.806	0.001	0.013

- *The higher the persistence in the correlations is, the lower the error in the approximation of the quantiles is, ceteris paribus.* Looking at Tables 13.1 and 13.2, this result is due to the much smaller biases of the parameters α, β when the true DGPs are characterized by high persistence in the correlations.

- *The error in the approximation of the quantiles tend to slightly increase as long as the sample dimension increases.* Such a result can be explained by using again the previous Monte Carlo (MC) evidence in Tables 13.1 and 13.2, which shows that the computed degrees of freedom $\hat{\upsilon}_k$ slowly converge to the true values when the dimension of the dataset increases, while the negative biases in the correlations tend to stabilize. Consequently, the computed $\hat{\upsilon}_k$ do not offset any more the effect of lower correlations, and therefore the underestimation in the VaR increases.

- *The approximations of the extreme quantiles are much better than those of the central quantiles*, while the analysis reveals no major difference between left tail and right tail. This is good news, since the Basel Capital Accord is interested in the extreme losses, which cause the major damages to financial portfolios. It is interesting to note that up to medium-sized datasets consisting of $n = 1,000$ observations, the effects of the biases in the degrees of freedom and the biases in the correlations tend to offset each other and the error in approximating the quantile is close to zero.

The previous MC evidence highlights that using a dataset of 1,000 observations or lower, where the assets show low tail dependence and high persistence in the correlations, should provide the best conditions to have precise VaR estimates. However, it also highlights that the multistep estimation procedure described in Definition 13.1 is able to produce a good approximation of the VaR in a wide variety of DGPs.

EMPIRICAL ANALYSIS

In order to compare our approach with previous multivariate models proposed in the literature, we measured the VaR of a high-dimensional portfolio by performing simulations from different conditional multivariate

T A B L E   13.9

Multivariate distribution specifications

Marginal Distribution	Moment Specification	Copula	Copula Parameters. Specification.
Normal	AR(1) T-GARCH(1,1)	**Normal**	Const. Corr.
Normal	AR(1) T-GARCH(1,1)	**Normal**	DCC(1,1)
Skew-T	AR(1) T-GARCH(1,1), Constant Skewness Constant D.o.F.	**T-Copula**	Const. Corr. Const. D.o.F.
Skew-T	AR(1) T-GARCH(1,1), constant skewness constant D.o.F.	**T-Copula**	DCC(1,1) Const. DoF.
Skew-T	AR(1) T-GARCH(1,1), constant skewness constant D.o.F.	**Grouped T**	Const. Corr. Const. D.o.F.s
Skew-T	AR(1) T-GARCH(1,1), constant skewness constant D.o.F.	**Grouped T**	DCC(1,1). Const. DoFs

distributions. Particularly, we considered six possible conditional models whose details are reported below in Table 13.9.

The first model corresponds to the Constant Conditional Correlation by Bollerslev (1990), the second one to the Dynamic Conditional Correlation by Engle (2002), the third model was proposed in Patton (2006) and Fantazzini (2008) for bivariate portfolios, the fourth model is new in the literature, the fifth model is a particular extension of the constant grouped t-copula proposed in Daul et al. (2003), while the sixth one was described in Section 2. As for the grouped t-copula, we classify the assets in five groups according to their credit rating: (1) AAA; (2) AA (AA+,AA,AA−); (3) A (A+,A,A−); (4) BBB (BBB+,BBB,BBB-); (5) BB (BB+,BB,BB-). We use this grouping methodology given its widespread use in financial practice; see, e.g., Cherubini et al (2004), McNeil et al. (2005), and references therein.

We analyzed a portfolio composed of 30 assets from the Dow Jones Industrial Index, with daily data taking into consideration the very volatile period between March 1996 and November 2003.[1] Following Giacomini and Komunjer (2005) and Gonzalez-Rivera et al. (2006), we use a rolling forecasting scheme of 1,000 observations, because it may be more robust to a possible parameter variation. We chose this time dimension because the previous simulation studies presented in the section Implications for Conditional Quantile Estimation highlighted that up to medium-sized datasets consisting of $n = 1,000$ observations, the effects of the biases in the grouped t-copula parameters tend to offset each other and the error in approximating the quantile is close to zero.

Christoffersen and Diebold (2000) and Giot and Laurent (2003) showed that volatility forecastability decays quickly with the time horizon of the forecasts. An immediate consequence is that volatility forecastability is relevant for short time horizons (such as daily trading) but not for long time horizons. Therefore, we focused on daily returns and VaR performances for daily trading portfolios, only.

A general algorithm for estimating the 0.25, 0.5, 1, 5, 95, 99, 99.5, and 99.75 percent VaR over a one-day holding period for a portfolio P of n assets with invested positions equal to M_i, $i = 1, \ldots, n$ is the following:

1. Simulate $j = 100,000$ scenarios for each asset log returns, $\{y_{1,t}, \ldots, y_{n,t}\}$, over the time horizon $[t-1, t]$, using a general multivariate distribution as in Table 13.5, by using this procedure:

   - Firstly, generate a random variate $(u_{1,t}, \ldots, u_{n,t})$ from the copula $\hat{C}_{t-1}$ forecast at time t, which can be normal, Student's t, or grouped t.

   - Secondly, get a vector $n \times 1(T_t)$ of standardized asset log returns $\eta_{i,t}$ by using the inverse functions of the forecast marginals at time t, which can be normal or skewed-t :
   $T_t = (\eta_{1,t}, \ldots, \eta_{n,t} = (F_1^{-1}(u_{1,t}; \hat{\alpha}_1), \ldots, F_n^{-1}(u_{n,t}; \hat{\alpha}_n))$.

   - Thirdly, rescale the standardized assets log-returns by using the forecast means and variances, estimated with AR-GARCH models:

$$\left\{ y_{1,t}, \ldots, y_{n,t} \right\} = \left(\hat{\mu}_{1,t} + \eta_{1,t} \cdot \sqrt{\hat{h}_{1,t}}, \ldots, \hat{\mu}_{n,t} + \eta_{n,t} \cdot \sqrt{\hat{h}_{n,t}} \right) \quad (13.9)$$

   - Finally, repeat this procedure for j = 100, 000 times.

---

[1] The complete list of stocks for the two portfolios is reported in the Appendix.

2. By using these 100,000 scenarios, the portfolio P is re-evaluated at time t, that is,

$$P_t^j = M_{1,t-1} \cdot \exp\left(y_{1,t}\right) + \ldots + M_{n,t-1} \cdot \exp\left(y_{n,t}\right), j = 1 \ldots 100{,}000 \quad (13.10)$$

3. Portfolio losses in each scenario j are then computed[2]:

$$\mathrm{Loss}_j = P_{t-1} - P_t^j, j = 1 \ldots 100{,}000 \qquad (13.11)$$

4. The calculus of the 0.25, 0.5, 1, 5, 95, 99, 99.5, and 99.75 percent VaR is now straightforward:
   - Order the 100,000 $Loss_j$ in increasing order.
   - The pth VaR is the $(1 - p)\,100{,}000$th ordered scenario, where $p = \{0.25\%, 0.5\%, 1\%, 5\%, 95\%, 99\%, 99.5\%, 99.75\%\}$. For example, the 0.25 percent VaR is the 99,750th ordered scenario.

Value at Risk Evaluation

We compare the different multivariate models by looking at their VaR forecasts by using the Hansen's superior predictive ability (SPA) test (2005) together with Giacomini and Komunjer (2005) asymmetric loss function. The Hansen's (2005) SPA test compares the performances of two or more forecasting models, by evaluating the forecasts with a pre-specified loss function, e.g., the one described below in Equation (13.12). The best forecast model is the model that produces the smallest expected loss. The SPA tests for the best standardized forecasting performance with respect to a benchmark model, and the null hypothesis is that none of the competing models is better than the benchmark one. As suggested by Hansen et al. (2003) ". . . testing multiple inequalities is more complicated than testing equalities (or a single inequality) because the distribution is not unique under the null hypothesis. Nevertheless, a consistent estimate of the p-value can be obtained by using a bootstrap procedure, as well as an upper and a lower bound." Lopez (1998, p. 8) further states, ". . . as noted by the Basel Committee on Banking Supervision (1996), the

---

[2] Possible profits are considered as negative losses.

magnitude as well as the number of exceptions are a matter of regulatory concern. This concern can be readily incorporated into a so called 'loss function' by introducing a magnitude term."

Since the object of interest is the conditional quantile of the portfolio loss distribution, we use the asymmetric linear loss function proposed in Gonzalez-Rivera et al. (2006) and Giacomini and Komunjer (2005), and defined as

$$T_\alpha(e_{t+1}) \equiv (\alpha - \mathbf{1}(e_{t+1} < 0)) \, e_{t+1} \qquad (13.12)$$

where $e_{t+1} = L_{t+1} - \widehat{\text{VaR}}_{t+1|t}$, L_{t+1} is the realized loss, while $\widehat{\text{VaR}}_{t+1|t}$ is the VaR forecast at time $t + 1$ on information available at time t. We also employ the Kupiec's unconditional coverage test (1995) and the Christoffersen's conditional coverage test (1998), given their importance in the empirical literature. However, we remark that their power can be very low.

Value at Risk Out-of-Sample Results

Table 13.10 reports the p-values of the SPA test for all the quantiles and both for long and short positions, while Table 13.11 the asymmetric loss functions (13.12). Finally, Tables 13.12 and 13.13 report the actual VaR exceedances N/T, the p-values p_{UC} of Kupiec's unconditional coverage test, and the p-values p_{CC} of Christoffersen's conditional coverage test, for the VaR forecasts at all probability levels.

The following tables show that we have a different picture according to whether we are dealing with long or short positions: In the former case, the dynamic grouped t-copula results to be the best choice according to the asymmetric loss functions Equation (13.12) and Kupiec's and Christoffersen's tests. However, the Hansen's SPA test highlights that the less parameterized dynamic t-copula (i.e., model 4), is not statistically different and cannot be outperformed by the dynamic grouped t-copula. Instead, the empirical results clearly highlight that the sample being analysed does yield strong evidence against the constant grouped t-copula as well as the multivariate normal models. As for short positions, except for the extreme quantile 0.25 percent, in all other cases the simple multivariate normal models perform rather well and cannot be

T A B L E   13.10

Hansen's SPA test for the portfolio consisting of 30 Dow Jones stocks

	Long Position				Short Position			
Benchmark	0.25%	0.50%	1%	5%	0.25%	0.50%	1%	5%
Model 1)	**0.012**	**0.003**	**0.013**	0.115	0.113	0.133	0.113	0.113
Model 2)	**0.009**	**0.015**	0.132	0.780	0.299	0.300	0.279	0.248
Model 3)	0.380	0.165	**0.093**	**0.005**	0.999	0.951	0.999	0.994
Model 4)	0.239	0.221	0.239	0.171	0.276	0.300	0.297	0.591
Model 5)	**0.096**	**0.091**	**0.093**	**0.016**	0.875	0.990	0.735	0.866
Model 6)	0.979	0.970	0.967	0.917	0.832	0.155	0.800	0.959

p-values smaller than 0.10 are reported in bold font.

T A B L E   13.11

Asymmetric loss functions (5.4)

	Long Position				Short Position			
Models	0.25%	0.50%	1%	5%	0.25%	0.50%	1%	5%
Model 1)	5.275	8.963	14.512	47.131	5.722	8.855	13.987	44.517
Model 2)	4.843	8.281	13.967	45.584	7.598	11.006	16.521	47.243
Model 3)	3.610	7.603	13.929	46.574	**4.777**	8.118	**13.508**	44.314
Model 4)	4.462	8.354	14.381	46.386	4.974	8.265	13.644	**44.138**
Model 5)	3.880	7.942	14.304	47.101	4.870	**8.082**	13.797	44.432
Model 6)	**3.374**	**7.143**	**13.448**	**45.553**	4.901	8.447	13.661	44.329

The smallest value is reported in bold font.

outperformed by more flexible models, such as Student's t and grouped t-copula models. This evidence confirms previous evidence in Junker and May (2005) and Fantazzini (2008) for bivariate portfolios, who show that the "normal model . . . leads to a significant underestimation of the loss tail, whereas the win tail is adapted quite well" (Junker and May, 2005, p. 451).

T A B L E   13.12

Actual VaR exceedances N/T, Kupiec's, and Christoffersen's tests (long positions)

| Models | Long Position | | | | | | | | | | | |
| | 0.25% | | | 0.50% | | | 1% | | | 5% | | |
	N/T	puc	pcc	N/T	puc	pcc	N/T	puc	pcc	N/T	puc	pcc
Model 1)	1.40%	**0.00**	**0.00**	1.90%	**0.00**	**0.00**	2.30%	**0.00**	**0.00**	6.30%	0.07	0.19
Model 2)	1.30%	**0.00**	**0.00**	1.60%	**0.00**	**0.00**	1.90%	**0.01**	**0.03**	5.80%	0.26	0.49
Model 3)	0.90%	**0.00**	**0.01**	1.40%	**0.00**	**0.00**	2.00%	**0.01**	**0.01**	6.60%	**0.03**	0.08
Model 4)	0.60%	0.06	0.17	1.40%	**0.00**	**0.00**	1.90%	**0.01**	**0.03**	6.20%	0.09	0.24
Model 5)	0.80%	**0.01**	0.02	1.30%	**0.00**	**0.00**	1.90%	**0.01**	**0.03**	6.10%	0.12	0.18
Model 6)	0.50%	0.16	0.37	1.10%	**0.02**	**0.02**	1.80%	**0.02**	0.05	6.00%	0.16	0.35

T A B L E   13.13

Actual VaR exceedances N/T, Kupiec's, and Christoffersen's tests (short positions)

| Models | Short Position | | | | | | | | | | | |
| | 0.25% | | | 0.50% | | | 1% | | | 5% | | |
	N/T	puc	pcc	N/T	puc	pcc	N/T	puc	pcc	N/T	puc	pcc
Model 1)	0.80%	**0.01**	**0.02**	1.00%	0.05	0.06	1.50%	0.14	0.16	5.30%	0.67	0.71
Model 2)	0.70%	**0.02**	**0.06**	0.90%	0.11	0.06	1.30%	0.36	0.56	5.00%	1.00	0.95
Model 3)	0.20%	0.74	0.94	0.70%	0.40	0.07	0.90%	0.75	0.87	5.90%	0.20	0.43
Model 4)	0.30%	0.76	0.95	0.70%	0.40	0.06	0.90%	0.75	0.87	5.50%	0.47	0.77
Model 5)	0.30%	0.76	0.95	0.80%	0.22	0.06	0.90%	0.75	0.87	4.80%	0.77	0.54
Model 6)	0.30%	0.76	0.95	0.70%	0.40	0.35	0.90%	0.75	0.87	5.20%	0.77	0.94

CONCLUSION

This chapter proposed a dynamic grouped t-copula approach for the joint modeling of high-dimensional portfolios, where we use the DCC model to specify the time evolution of the correlation matrix of the grouped t-copula. We performed Monte Carlo simulations to study the small-sample properties of the estimator under different data generating processes, and we found that our multistep estimation procedure usually results in lower correlations than the true ones. However, the biases change substantially according to the magnitude of the degrees of freedom and the dynamic structure in the correlations. Besides, they almost disappear when correlations are lower than 0.10 in absolute value, thus confirming previous asymptotic results in Daul et al. (2003) and Fantazzini (2007). As for the DCC (1,1) parameters, we find that the effects of different DGPs on the persistence parameter β are almost negligible. Instead, the parameter α describing the effect of past shocks shows positive biases that are higher in magnitude when high tail dependence and high persistence in the correlations are considered. Furthermore, our Monte Carlo evidence showed that the estimated degrees of freedom are lower than the true values and such a bias disappears as the sample dimension increases. However, the convergence to the true values is much quicker when there is high tail dependence and strong persistence in the correlations structure: in this case, the bias is smaller than 1 percent already with a dataset composed of n = 1,000 observations.

We investigated the effects of such biases and finite sample properties on conditional quantile estimation, given the increasing importance of the VaR as risk measure. We found that the error in the approximation of the quantile can range between 0 and 3 percent. Particularly, the error is lower when the time-varying correlations are highly persistent and when the degrees of freedom are higher in magnitude. In such a case, the simulation studies highlighted that up to medium-sized datasets consisting of $n = 1,000$ observations, the effects of the negative biases in the degrees of freedom and the negative biases in the correlations tend to offset each other and the error in approximating the quantile is almost zero. We also found that the error is much smaller (1 percent or less) for extreme quantiles, like the 99 percent quantile required by the Basel committee for market risk management.

We analyzed a high-dimensional portfolio composed of 30 assets from the Dow Jones Industrial Index. By using a rolling window estimation scheme, we compared different multivariate models by looking at their VaR forecasts with different tests and statistical techniques. When long positions were of concern, we found that the dynamic grouped t-copula (together with skewed-t marginals) outperformed the constant grouped t-copula and the dynamic student's T copula as well as the dynamic multivariate normal model proposed in Engle (2002). As for short positions, we found out that a multivariate normal model with dynamic normal marginals and constant normal copula was already a proper choice. This last result confirms previous evidence in Junker and May (2005) and Fantazzini (2008) for bivariate portfolios.

An avenue for future research is in more sophisticated methods to separate the assets into homogenous groups when using the grouped t-copula, for example, using the cluster analysis. Finally, an alternative to DCC modeling for high-dimensional portfolios could be the semiparametric and nonlinear techniques proposed in Hafner (2005) and Pelletier (2006).

REFERENCES

Basel Committee on Banking Supervision (1996) Supervisory Framework for the Use of Backtesting in Conjunction with the Internal Models Approach to Market Risk Capital Requirements. Basel.

Basel Committee on Banking Supervision (2005) Amendment to the Capital Accord to Incorporate Market Risks Bank for International Settlements. Basel.

Bollerslev, T. (1990) Modelling the Coherence in Short-run Nominal Exchange Rates: A Multivariate Generalized ARCH Model. *Review of Economics and Statistics*, 72(3): 498–505.

Bouye', E., V. Durrleman, A. Nikeghbali, G. Riboulet, and T. Roncalli (2001) Copulas for Finance a Reading Guide and Some Applications. Groupe de Recherche Operationnelle, Credit Lyonnais, Paris, France.

Chen, X., Y. Fan, and A. Patton (2004) Simple Tests for Models of Dependence between Multiple Financial Time Series with Applications to U.S. Equity Returns and Exchange Rates. FMG technical report n.483, London, UK: London Stock Exchange (LSE).

Cherubini, U., E. Luciano, and W. Vecchiato (2004) Copula Methods in Finance. Hoboken, NJ: John Wiley & Sons.

Christoffersen, P. (1998) Evaluating Interval Forecasts. International Economic Review, 39(4): 841–862.

Christoffersen, P. and F.X. Diebold (2000) How Relevant Is Volatility Forecasting for Financial Risk Management? *Review of Economics and Statistics*, 82(1): 12–22.

Dalla Valle, L., D. Fantazzini, and P. Giudici (2008) Copulae and Operational Risks. *International Journal of Risk Assessment and Management* 9(3): 238–257.

Daul, S., E. De Giorgi, F. Lindskog, and A. McNeil (2003) The Grouped T-copula with an Application to Credit Risk. *Risk*, 16(11): 73–76.

Demarta, S. and A. McNeil (2005) The t Copula and Related Copulas. *International Statistical Review*, 73(1): 111–129.

Embrechts, P. (2000) Extreme Value Theory: Potential and Limitations as an Integrated Risk Management Tool. *Derivatives Use, Trading and Regulation*, 6(1): 449–456.

Embrechts, P., F. Lindskog, and A.J. McNeil (2003) Modelling Dependence with Copulas and Applications to Risk Management. In S. Rachev (ed.), *Handbook of Heavy Tailed Distributions in Finance*. London, UK: Elsevier/North-Holland.

Engle, R.F. (2002) Dynamic Conditional Correlation—A Simple Class of Multivariate GARCH Models. Journal of Business and Economic Statistics, 20(3): 339–350.

Fantazzini, D. (2007) A dynamic grouped t-copula approach for high-dimensional portfolios. Proceedings of the International workshop on Computational and Financial Econometrics, Geneva, Switzerland, April 20–22, 2007.

Fantazzini, D. (2008) Dynamic Copula Modelling for Value at Risk. *Frontiers in Finance and Economics* 5(2): 72–108.

Giacomini, R. and I. Komunjer (2005) Evaluation and Combination of Conditional Quantile Forecasts. *Journal of Business and Economic Statistics*, 23(4): 416–431.

Giot, P. and S. Laurent (2003) VaR for Long and Short Positions. *Journal of Applied Econometrics*, 18(6): 641–664.

Gonzalez-Rivera, G., T. Lee, and M. Santosh (2006) Forecasting Volatility: A Reality Check Based on Option Pricing, Utility

Function, Value-at-Risk, and Predictive Likelihood. *International Journal of Forecasting*, 20(4): 629–645.

Granger, C., A. Patton, and T. Terasvirta (2006) Common Factors in Conditional Distributions for Bivariate Time Series. *Journal of Econometrics*, 132(4): 43–57.

Hafner, C., D. Van Dijk, and P. Franses (2005) Semi-parametric Modelling of Correlation Dynamics. Econometric Institute Research Report 2005–26, Erasmus University Rotterdam.

Hansen, P. (2005) A Test for Superior Predictive Ability. *Journal of Business and Economic Statistics*, 23(4): 365–380.

Kupiec, P. (1995) Techniques for Verifying the Accuracy of Risk Measurement Models. *Journal of Derivatives*, 2(3): 173–184.

Jondeau, E. and M. Rockinger (2006) The Copula-GARCH Model of Conditional Dependencies: An International Stock-Market Application. *Journal of International Money and Finance*, 25(5): 827–853.

Jorion, P. (2000). *Value at Risk: The New Benchmark for Managing Financial Risk*, 2nd edition. New York: McGraw-Hill.

Junker, M. and A. May (2005) Measurement of Aggregate Risk with Copulas. *Econometrics Journal*, 8(3): 428–454.

Lopez, A. (1998) Methods for Evaluating Value-at-Risk Estimates. *Economic Review, Federal Reserve Bank of San Francisco*, 3(2):3–17.

McNeil, A., R. Frey, and P. Embrechts (2005) *Quantitative Risk Management: Concepts, Techniques and Tools*. Princeton, NJ: Princeton University Press.

McNeil, A. and S. Demarta (2005) The t Copula and Related Copulas. *International Statistical Review*, 73(1): 111–129.

Panchenko, V. (2005) Estimating and Evaluating the Predictive Abilities of Semiparametric Multivariate Models with Application to Risk Management. Working paper, CeNDEF University of Amsterdam, Netherlands.

Patton, A. (2004) On the Out-of-Sample Importance of Skewness and Asymmetric Dependence for Asset Allocation. *Journal of Financial Econometrics*, 2(1): 130–168.

Patton, A. (2006a) Estimation of Copula Models for Time Series of Possibly Different Lengths. *Journal of Applied Econometrics*, 21(2): 147–173.

Patton, A. (2006b) Modelling Asymmetric Exchange Rate Dependence. *International Economic Review*, 47(2): 527–556

Pelletier, D. (2006) Regime Switching for Dynamic Correlations. *Journal of Econometrics*, 127(1–2): 445–473.

Rosenberg, J.V. (1998) Pricing Multivariate Contingent Claims Using Estimated Risk-Neutral Density Functions. *Journal of International Money and Finance*, 17(2): 229–247.

Rosenberg, J.V. (2003) Nonparametric Pricing of Multivariate Contingent Claims. *Journal of Derivatives*, 10(3): 926.

Rousseeuw, P. and Molenberghs, G. (1993) Transformation of Non Positive Semidefinite Correlation Matrices. *Comm. Statist. Theory Methods*, 22(4): 965–984.

Sklar, A. (1959) Fonetiens de Répartition àn Dimensions et Leurs Marges. Publications de l'Institut de Statistique de l'Université de Paris, 8: 229–231.

Tsay, R. (2002) *Analysis of Financial Time Series* Hoboken, NJ: Wiley.

APPENDIX: LIST OF ANALYZED STOCKS

3M, AT&T, Alcoa & Altria, American Express, Boeing, Caterpillar, Citigroup, Coca Cola, Du Pont, Eastman Kodak, Exxon Mobil, General Electric, General Motors, Hewlett-Packard, Home Depot, Honeywell Intl., Intel, IBM, Intl. Paper, JP Morgan Chase, Johnson & Johnson, McDonald's, Merck, Microsoft, Procter & Gamble, SBC Communications, United Technologies, Wal Mart Stores, Walt Disney

CHAPTER 14

A Model to Measure Portfolio Risks in Venture Capital

Andreas Kemmerer

ABSTRACT

This study constructs and evaluates a risk model for the venture capital industry in which the CreditRisk$^+$ model is adjusted to calculate loss distributions for venture capital portfolios. A forward entry regression with macroeconomic factors as independent variables is used as the procedure to extract systematic factors for the sector analysis. The coefficient of determination R^2 divides the risk into one idiosyncratic risk factor and several systematic risk factors. Under the assumption that macroeconomic factors are independent, the improvement of the R^2 of each forward entry is considered as the weight of the entered factor. Further, under the assumption that all relevant systematic risk factors are incorporated in the model, the systematic risk is entirely explained. The remaining unexplained sample variance is considered the idiosyncratic risk.

The introduced risk model is empirically tested using a portfolio of venture-capital-financed companies. The database contains more than 2,000 European venture-capital-backed companies over the period 1998 to 2004. The results are highly significant and show that the model is applicable to modeling portfolio risks for venture capital portfolios.

INTRODUCTION

The dynamics of the relatively young venture capital market are not yet well understood, so risk assessment and objective performance measurements are difficult to employ. Convincing and generally accepted portfolio models for venture capital investments do not exist in theory or in practice. Broad implementation of a widely accepted risk model would enhance venture capital investments' transparency.

The aim of this study is to develop a practical portfolio model to measure the risks and diversification capabilities of venture capital portfolios. This chapter analyzes which of the most common credit risk models can be adjusted to meet the needs of venture capital portfolios and shows that the CreditRisk$^+$ model best fits the needs to quantify risks. CreditRisk$^+$'s data requirements are lower than those for other risk models, the assumptions and parameters are most applicable to the special features in the venture capital market, and the model is easy to implement. The chapter analyzes the required adjustments on a theoretical as well as on a practical level and quantifies the effects of correlation and diversification.

The model can be used to calculate the loss distribution for credits to venture-capital-backed companies. If the model is used to calculate loss distributions for portfolios of venture capital investments, the results can be only considered as the worst-case scenario because they do not take into account earnings. To make reasonable investment decisions, it is necessary to estimate both. Due to the lack of accessibility to a representative database of credits to venture-capital-backed companies, the model is empirically tested using a portfolio of venture-capital-financed companies. This chapter's second section presents some general aspects of the risk profile of venture capital investments and explains which of the most common credit risk models are most appropriate to be adjusted to quantify venture capital portfolios' risk. The third section describes the adjustments of the CreditRisk$^+$ model necessary to meet the needs of venture capital portfolios. How to calculate the input parameters is explained, and the sector model is presented. This chapter's fourth section describes the database, while its fifth section contains the main results from the empirical analysis. The fifth section also implements the constructed sector analysis model—the results are highly significant and show the predictability of the model—and evaluates the risk profile of venture capital portfolios. Four different default distributions based on different assumptions are calculated.

TOWARD A RISK MODEL IN VENTURE CAPITAL

Risk Profile of Venture Capital

Venture capital funds have a higher risk than other more common investments, like shares or bonds, but this risk is compensated for through higher returns on average. They typically invest in young, innovative companies with high growth prospects but also with a relatively high probability to default. Because of these characteristics are common company valuation methods like the discounted cash-flow valuation are not very meaningful.

In addition, unlike other investment types, venture-capital-backed entrepreneurs do not have any—or, at best, relatively small—collateral. To compensate, venture capital managers have control rights and rights of determination in the companies in which they invest. The deep involvement of venture capital managers and their manifold contacts is very helpful and increases the probability of successfully breaking into a new market.

Despite the high risks, however, there is no convincing risk model for private equity in theory or in practice. As venture capital's risks cannot be sufficiently quantified, investors are not able to optimize their investment decisions. An analysis of the portfolio risks enables a quantification of the correlations among the investments and, hence, an evaluation of their diversification capabilities. Probability distributions of potential losses enable a risk structure analysis and a calculation of maximal losses. Investment and divestment decisions can be optimized as they are made on a more objective basis.

Company-specific risks can be eliminated in a portfolio through diversification. If idiosyncratic risk can be priced, the price the entrepreneur receives decreases with the amount of idiosyncratic risk. As a result, if venture capital funds are able to diversify their portfolios more effectively, they should be willing to support riskier projects.[1]

Jones and Rhodes-Kropf (2003) found that idiosyncratic risk premiums are independent from fund investors' individual diversification capabilities. Venture capital funds can decrease idiosyncratic risks through diversification without decreasing received risk premiums. The resulting additional returns can be used to increase venture capital firms' and venture capital investors' profits or to reduce demanded risk premiums. Hence, a better diversification facilitates more competitive fund proposals, which increase the ability to issue funds.

Jones and Rhodes-Kropf (2003) also determined that a more diversified venture capital investor can price more competitively because he or she does not need to be compensated as highly for the idiosyncratic risk. The early, successful funds should be able to continue to win the good deals, which would lead to a strong persistence in returns (Kaplan and Schoar, 2003). This also suggests that, over time, there should be pressure for the industry to become more concentrated in spite of the principal agent problem. Early success would allow the funds to get larger as investors update their expectations of the venture capitalist's skill. Investors should be willing to trade-off a greater principal-agent problem for a greater certainty that they have found a good venture capitalist and be willing to invest more. Larger funds will be more diversified and will, therefore, be able acquire good projects because they hold less idiosyncratic risk.

The fund management typically shares in funds' profits, which are called *carried interests*. A better risk–return structure through diversification increases funds' as well as fund managers' profits. Further, fund managers' communication of portfolio risks to their investors increases transparency, reduces asymmetrical information distribution, and, hence, increases the venture capital firms' reputation. This makes the venture capital firm more attractive and increases its ability to raise money in a following financing round, as well as to issue a follow-on fund.

The more developed a venture capital industries' portfolio management in a country, the larger the amounts of idiosyncratic risks borne by

---

[1] Jones and Rhodes-Kropf (2003, pp.13, 26, 27).

the market,[2] the more attractive venture capital investments become for investors, and the more investments are made. Overall, countries that want to develop a venture capital industry may find that significant time and wealth is required before its venture capitalists become able to bear large amounts of idiosyncratic risks. Therefore, many governments support investments in venture capital through legislation or subsidized capital because they consider venture-capital-backed companies, which are typically highly innovative, as growth factors in their economies.[3]

Analysis of Risk Models

The following section illustrates which of the common credit risk models is most appropriate for application to venture capital portfolios. The models are analyzed in terms of how their assumptions and data requirements fit the characteristics of venture capital in order to quantify venture capital portfolios' risks as realistically as possible. The standard approaches that are analyzed are CreditMetrics, CreditRisk[+], CreditPortfolioView, and PortfolioManager.[4] These models can be classified into asset value models and models based on default rates.[5]

The asset value models are developed from the 1974 Merton (1974) model, which regards credits as a put option on the company value. The value is calculated with the Black-Scholes formula. A default arises if the company value is lower than the liabilities at the end of the holding period. The most important models are CreditMetrics[6] and PortfolioManager.[7] An important aspect of these models is that they need continuous pricing and long time series of the investments to calculate migration matrices. Because the venture capital market is both young and illiquid, neither

---

[2] See Jones and Rhodes-Kropf (2003, pp. 26, 27).

[3] In Europe, this development is backed by government programs like tax-driven vehicles, subsidization, and financial institutions that act like market players.

[4] As these models are widely described in literature, and as the focus of this chapter is the modification and implementation of a portfolio model for venture capital, a comprehensive description of the models that do not fit the requirements is not undertaken. To get more general information about the models, see e.g., Caouett et al. (1998), Ong (2000), Crouhy and Mark-Galai (2000), Jarrow andTurnbull (2000), and Gordy (1998).

[5] See Wahrenburg and Niethen (2000, pp. 237ff).

[6] See J.P.Morgan (1997).

[7] See Moody's (2005).

continuous pricing nor long track records are available. Finally, asset value models are not appropriate vehicles with which to model venture capital portfolios' risks.

Default rate-based models calculate credit defaults directly. Unlike asset value models, default rates are assumed to be exogenous and are derived from historical data. Correlations among default rates are incorporated by jointly shared systematic factors. The most important models are CreditPortfolioView[8] and CreditRisk[+9] CreditPortfolioView estimates default rates through a regression model with macroeconomic factors as independent variables. The disadvantage of this approach is that migration matrices need to be calculated. Because the available data for venture capital funds is insufficient to calculate migration matrices, the model cannot be applied to determine risks for venture capital portfolios.

In comparison to other risk models, CreditRisk[+] considers only events of default, not rating-grade changes. The general approach is designed to calculate a one-year default distribution, and correlations are incorporated indirectly, so a complex direct estimation is not required. The primary advantage of this model is its relatively low data requirements and the absence of the requirement to estimate migration matrices. Only default probability, default rate's standard deviation, sector classification, exposure, and recovery rates are needed to analyze the portfolio risks. The risk assessment takes place in a closed analytical form without complex simulations. The model is appropriate for illiquid portfolios, which are typical in the venture capital industry. In summary, the CreditRisk[+] model has the capability to be adjusted for venture capital portfolios and is, therefore, chosen to be adjusted to analyze the risk profile of venture capital portfolios.

CreditRisk[+]

In CreditRisk[+] each obligor has one of two possible states at the end of the period: default or non-default. Default correlations are incorporated by K risk factors x. Conditional on x, it is assumed that defaults of individual obligors are independently distributed Bernoulli random variables. The conditional default probability $p_A(x)$ is a function of the realization of risk

---

[8] See Wilson (1997c; 1997d; 1998).
[9] See Credit Suisse Financial Products (1997).

factors x, the vector of factor loadings w_{Ak} $(k=1,\ldots,K)$, and the rating class $\zeta(A)$ of obligor A:[10]

$$p_A(x) = \overline{p}_{\zeta(A)}(\sum_{k=1}^{K} w_{Ak} x_k) \cdot \overline{p}_{\zeta}$$

is the unconditional default probability for a rated ζ obligor. The risk factors are positive and have a mean of 1. The weights w_{Ak} quantify how sensitive obligor A is to each risk factor. The factor loadings for each obligor total 1 to guarantee that $E[p_A(x)] = \overline{p}_{\zeta(A)}$.

CreditRisk$^+$ introduces three different approaches to model sector analysis.[11] It models default risk, not by calculating the default distribution directly, but by using the probability-generating function (pgf) to calculate the defaults.

The probability generating function (pgf)$F_M(z)$ of a discrete random variable M is a function of an auxiliary variable z in such a way that the probability that M = n is given by the coefficient on the z^n in the polynomial expansion of $F_M(z)$. The pgf is essentially a discrete random variable analogue to the moment-generating function. If $F_M(z|x)$ is the pgf of M conditional on x, and x has distribution function H(x), then the unconditional pgf is simply $F_M(z) = \int_x F_M(z|x)dH(x)$. If M_1 and M_2 are independent random variables, then the pgf of the sum $M_1 + M_2$ is equal to the product of the two pgfs.

For a single obligor A with a Bernoulli random variable, the conditional pgf is:

$F_A(z|x) = (1 + p_A(x))(z - 1)) = (1 + p_A(x)(z - 1))$. If one supposes that the individual default probabilities are generally small, the logarithm can be replayed using a Taylor series expansion:

$F_A(z|x) = (1 + p_A(x))(z - 1)) = \exp(\log(1 + p_A(x))(z - 1))) \approx \exp$ $(p_A(x)(z - 1))$ *for* $p_A \approx 0, z \approx 0)$. This is called the Poisson approximation because the pgf on the right-hand side is the pgf for a Poisson $(p_A(x))$ distributed random variable.

Conditional on x, as default events are independent across obligors, the pgf of the sum of obligor defaults is the product of the individual pgfs:

---

[10] In CreditRisk$^+$ — Technical Document, the conditional probabilities are given by

$p_i(x) = \overline{p}_{\zeta(i)}(\sum_{k=1}^{K} w_{ik}(x_k / \mu_k))$, and the risk factor x_k has mean μ_k and variance σ^2. Here, the constants $1/\mu_k$ are incorporated into the normalized x_k. without any loss of generality. See Credit Suisse Financial Products (1997).

[11] The sector models are described in the section Sector Analysis.

$$F(z|x) = \prod_A F_A(z|x) \approx \prod_A \exp\left(p_A(x)(z-1)\right) = \exp\left(\mu(x)(z-1)\right) \ with$$

$\mu(x) = \sum_A p_A(x)$. The risk factors are assumed to be independent gamma-distributed random variables with mean μ_k and variance σ_k^2. By integrating out the x, the unconditional probability-generating function $F(z)$ is:

$$F(z) = \prod_{k=1}^{K}(1 - \delta_k/1 - \delta_k z)^{1/\sigma_k^2} \ with \ \delta_k = \sigma_k^2 \mu_k/1 + \sigma_k^2 \mu_k \ and$$

$\mu_k = \sum_A w_{AK} \ \bar{p}_{\zeta(A)}$. The loan size for obligor A is denoted as L_A. In the case of a default, the loss has a fixed size and is called exposure. In CreditRisk$^+$, a loss, given default, is modelled as a constant fraction λ of loan size. The loss exposure amounts λL_i are expressed as integer multiples of a fixed base unit of loss v_0 (e.g., €1 million). The integer multiple v_A, which is equal to $\lambda L_A/v_0$ rounded to the nearest integer, is called the *standardized exposure* for obligor A. The adjusted exposure is exogenous to the model and independent of market and downgrade risks.

The probability-generating function (pgf) for losses on obligor A is denoted as G_A. The conditional independence of defaults is used to obtain the conditional pgf for losses in the portfolio:

$$G(z|x) = \prod_A G_A(z|x) = \prod_A F_A(z^{v(a)}|x)$$

$$= \exp\left(\sum_{k=1}^{K} x_k \sum_A \bar{p}_{\zeta(A)} w_{Ak}(z^{v(A)} - 1)\right)$$

Integrating out x and rearranging yields:

$$G(z) = \prod_{k=1}^{K}\left(\frac{1-\delta_k}{1-\delta_k P_k(z)}\right)^{1/\sigma_k^2} \quad with \quad P_k(z) = \frac{1}{\mu_k}\sum_i w_{Ak} p_{\zeta(A)} z^{v(A)}$$

The unconditional probability that there will be n units of v_0 loss in the entire portfolio is given by the coefficient on z^n in the Taylor series expansion of $G(z)$.

A RISK MODEL FOR VENTURE CAPITAL

Input Parameters

The tool with which to estimate portfolio risks with CreditRisk$^+$ in practice is a publicly provided Visual Basic for Applications (VBA) program from Credit Suisse Financial Products.[12] The program requires the following input parameters for each creditor in order to calculate portfolio risk: net exposure, expected default rate, default-rate volatility, and the segmentation of the creditor's total risk in company-specific and systematic risk factors. Because CreditRisk$^+$ calculates default rates for a single period, the incorporated parameters are determined for yearly observation periods, which equal the calendar year.

The expected default rate is calculated as the long-term average default rate $\bar{P}_k$ for all K sectors: $\bar{P}_k = 1/N\Sigma_{A=1}^{N} I_{A,k}$ *with* $I_A = \{1,$ *default* $0,$ *else.* A default is defined if all or part of the company is sold at loss or if the whole investment is a total loss with no sales revenues (total write-off). A loss occurs if the sales price is lower than the corresponding investment amount. If a company has more than one exit during the period for which the default rate distribution is calculated, the single results are added up. The final sum decides if it is a default or not.

The default probability equals the expectation of I, and the variance can be calculated as $Var(I_A) = E[(I_A - E(I_A))^2] = p_A(1-p_A)$ *with* $p_A = P(I_A = 1)$. Because of the relatively short history of our database, the calculation of the default rate volatility is based on a seven-year period, which is not an adequate time frame with which to calculate the default rate volatility. If the default rates are very small, they can be used as a proxy for the volatility: $Var(I_A) = p_A$. Therefore, this model uses default rates as an estimator for default rate volatility.[13]

Net exposure $E_{A,t}^{net}$ is the possible amount of loss in the case of a default. It is calculated as the exposure $E_{A,t}$ reduced at the average recovery rate $\overline{RR}_k$ of sector k:[14] $E_{A,t}^{net} = (1 - \overline{RR}_k)\, E_{A,t}$.

The exposure for venture capital is defined in this chapter as the invested amount in company A at time t. The total investment amount is considered because, due to very low or missing securities, the total sum is at risk in the case of a default. The exposure is re-determined in each period and equals the exposure of the previous period $E_{A,t-1}$, plus follow-on investments $F_{A,t}$, minus discharges $D_{A,t}$ of proportionate investment amounts from

---

[12] See http://www.csfb.com/institutional/research/credit_risk.shtml.

[13] See Credit Suisse Financial Products (1997, p. 44).

[14] The term $(1 - RR)$ is also called *loss given default* (LGD).

partial sales, full exits or total write-downs: $E_{A,t} = E_{A,t-1} + F_{A,t} - D_{A,t}$. If it is a full exit or total write-down, $D_{A,t}$ equals $E_{A,t-1} + F_{A,t}$. The discharged investment amount $D_{A,t}$ is the sum of sales $S_{A,t}$ plus write-offs or less write-ups. In the case of a write-off, it is a default; otherwise, it is not.

The recovery rate is the share of the exposure that the investor obtains in the case of a default. It is calculated as the average over the entire period for each rating class ζ, and is in the interval (0, 1). The recovery rate of company A equals the ratio of sales revenue to the corresponding investment amount: If $I_A = 1$, then $RR_A = S_A/D_A$ with $S_A =$ sales revenue, $E_A =$ exposure, and $D_A =$ discharge.

Sector Analysis

A sector model for venture capital investments is presented in this section. A concretion is necessary, as CreditRisk$^+$ does not provide a convincing model with which to identify appropriate sector classifications.

A rating model is necessary to adjust CreditRisk$^+$ to venture-capital-financed companies. The rating determines a company's unconditional default probability for one period. Company-specific data, which is not usually available for venture-capital-backed companies, is needed to make a rating. Further, the explanatory power of the balance sheet is low because of the inherent characteristics of venture-capital-financed companies.[15] Therefore, typical credit sector rating models, like scoring, discriminant analysis, logistic regression, or artificial neural networks, are not used in this framework.

The transfer of publicly available rating grades from external rating agencies onto venture-capital-backed companies is not recommended because the companies which are used to evaluate the rating model are not comparable to the venture-capital-financed companies to be rated. The available rating grades typically refer to large or medium-sized companies with publicly available information, not to venture-capital-backed companies.

The simple rating approach uses the average default probability of all portfolio companies as an estimator for the unconditional default probability.

---

[15] Venture-capital-backed companies are typically very young, unprofitable companies that operate in innovative markets with high, but uncertain, growth prospects.

This chapter extends this approach by using company-specific variables to classify companies in risk classes. The risk class determines the rating of the company. The unconditional expected default rate of a company equals the average default probability of its risk class.

In this approach, the company's industrial sector is used as rating variable.[16] It is assumed that companies that are in the same industrial sector are influenced by similar risk factors and, therefore, have similar unconditional default probabilities. Regression results of previous studies have shown that industrial sector-specific default probabilities can be successfully estimated by macroeconomic variables.[17] It is also possible that the macroeconomic environment influences companies' default rates.

CreditRisk$^+$ introduces three different approaches to model sector analysis, and this section adjusts all three approaches to venture capital investments. The first approach assumes that all companies are assigned to a single sector, so besides the rating classification, this sector analysis does not require classification into several sectors. A default correlation of 1 is assumed among the obligors; changes in default rates of all obligors are parallel and have the same direction.

The second sector analysis classifies each company to one sector, so the sector classification equals the rating of the company, and the number of sectors equals the number of rating classifications. Segmentation into industrial sectors assumes uncorrelated sector default rates because all companies of one sector are explained by one factor, i.e., its sector.

The third approach assigns each company to different sectors, following the assumption that a number of independent systematic factors

---

[16] Other possible variables are stage or country. Stage can be used as an indicator for the company size and company age. Jones and Rhodes-Kropf (2003) found a significant correlation between stage and idiosyncratic risk in the venture capital industry. Ong (2000, p.145) identified a correlation between company size and idiosyncratic risk for credit-financed companies. To our knowledge, no study in the venture capital industry examined the factors that influence the correlation between default probabilities and stage. Because no explanatory variables are known, the stage is not used as a classification variable in this chapter. A classification into sector-stage-samples or sector-country-samples is not applicable because the number of each sample is too small due to the limited number of observations in the database. As all companies are located in the European Union, it can be assumed that the resulting error of a missing sector-country-sample classification is relatively low.

[17] See Knapp and Hamerle (1999) and Wilson (1997c).

and one idiosyncratic factor influence the company's fortunes. Numerous studies analyzed the predictability of macroeconomic factors on the default rate.[18] Highly significant regression results, as well as extremely well established coefficients of determination, show that macroeconomic factors have a high explanatory power to project default rates. Therefore, this approach uses macroeconomic variables as risk factors, which represent the systematic influence on the sector-specific default rate. Sector default rates are estimated by regression of macroeconomic factors as independent variables.

Multivariate regressions assume metric-scaled dependent variables. As default rates $P\zeta_t$ are in the interval of $[0, 1]$, the following transformation of the default probability is used to create a dependent variable $Z\zeta_t$, which is metric scaled and in the interval $[-\infty, +\infty]$: $P\zeta_{,t} = 1/(1+\exp(Z\zeta_{,t})$ transformation leads to $Z\zeta_{,t} = \ln(1/P\zeta_{,t} - 1)$ with

$P\zeta_{,t}$ = default probability for companies with rating ζ in time t.

$Z\zeta_{,t}$ = transformed default probability for companies with rating ζ in time t.

The regression model is $Z_{\zeta,t} = \beta_{\zeta,0} + \Sigma^z_{\zeta=1} \beta_{\zeta,k} x_{k,t} + \varepsilon_{\zeta,t}$ with

$\beta_{\zeta,0}$ = absolute term for companies with rating ζ.

$\beta_{\zeta,k}$ = regression coefficient of risk factor k for companies with rating ζ.

$x_{k,t}$ = risk factor k in time t.

$\varepsilon_{\zeta,t}$ = interfering variable for companies with rating ζ in time t.

A forward entry regression is used as the procedure to extract systematic factors. At each step after step 0, the entry statistic is computed for each eligible value for entry in the model. If no effect has a value on the entry statistic that exceeds the specified critical value for model entry, then stepping is terminated; otherwise, the effect with the largest value on the entry statistic is entered into the model. The variable with the largest increase of R^2 is used as the entry statistic. An increase of 5 percentage points of the R^2 is used as the specified critical value for model entry. Stepping is also terminated if the maximum number of steps is reached. Wilson (1997c) analyzed a multifactor model to explain logit-transformed default rates and showed that three macroeconomic factors explain more

---

[18] See Hamerle et al. (2002).

than 90 percent of the variation of the default rate. Therefore, stepping of the forward entry regression is terminated if three variables are entered in the regression.

The coefficient of determination R^2 is used to divide the risk into one idiosyncratic risk factor and several systematic risk factors. The coefficient of determination R^2 is the proportion of a sample variance of the dependent variable that is explained by independent variables when a linear regression is done. If macroeconomic factors are independent, the improvement of the R^2 of each forward entry can be interpreted as the proportion of the entered factor to explain the sector default rate. The increase of each entered factor k is used in this approach as the weight w_{Ak} of a ζ rated company A. The sum of all weights of the systematic factors equals R^2.

We assume that all relevant systematic risk factors are incorporated in the model, and the systematic risk is entirely explained under this assumption. The remaining not-explained sample variance, $1 - R^2$, is considered as the idiosyncratic risk of the rating class.[19] The sum of the weights of the idiosyncratic risk factor and the systematic risk factors is 1; the sector default rate is, therefore, unbiased.[20]

Single-sector default rates are not independent of one another. Correlations are incorporated in this approach as the forward entry regression for each sector uses the same macroeconomic factors as independent variables' population, from which the regression selects a maximum of three variables.[21]

The regression results from Knapp and Hamerle (1999) are used to choose macroeconomic factors.[22] This study performed regression analyses for different sectors to select among several macroeconomic factors those with the highest significance. It can be shown that the sector default rates can be explained very well by few, mostly for all sectors identical macroeconomic factors.[23] Because Knapp and Hamerle (1999) analyzed a

---

[19] The idiosyncratic risk of each company is assigned an additional sector in CreditRisk$^+$, which is called the *sector* 0.

[20] The expected sector default rate of the model equals the actual default rate.

[21] Another possibility would be to abandon the independent assumption between the sectors by integrating correlation effects into the model. Bürgisser et al. (1999, pp. 2ff.) described such a method, which is neither easy nor feasible to implement.

[22] Dr. Knapp kindly provided us the variables.

[23] See Knapp and Hamerle (1999, p.140).

very large set of macroeconomic variables and because the regression results of this study are highly significant, it is assumed that all relevant factors are included in this approach. The included variables are Producer Price Index (PPI), Gross Domestic Product (GDP), Value of Retail Sales (Ret_Sal), 3 Month Euribor Interest Rate (Euribor), Industrial Production (Ind_Prod), Dow Jones Euro Stoxx 50 (Stoxx), Euro-Dollar-Exchange-Rate (EUR_USD), Oil Price (Oil), and Unemployment Rate (UnEmR). Except for Unemployment Rate (UnEmR), Euro-Dollar-Exchange-Rate (EUR_USD), Oil Price (Oil), and 3-Month Euribor Interest (Euribor), all are index-based variables in our sample and show relative changes. The non-index-based variables have to be transformed into growth rates as follows:

$$x_{k,t} = \frac{F_{k,t}}{F_{k,t-1}} - 1$$

with

$x_{k,t}$ = growth rate of macroeconomic variable k in time t.

$F_{k,t}$ = stationary value of macroeconomic variable k in time t.

One assumption in regression analysis is that residuals are uncorrelated. This assumption is often violated in time series because time-dependent variables are often highly correlated. Because this approach transforms the time series in growth rates, this source of error can be reduced.

Knapp (2002) determined that all macroeconomic variables affect the default rate with a lag of one to two years. Thus, the necessary variables are known ex-ante and do not need to be estimated separately, which avoids an additional source of error. The lagged impact is also empirically and theoretically supported by other authors.[24] In this approach, time lags of $t = 0, -1, -2$ of all macroeconomic factors are separately incorporated to consider the impact of the sector-specific time lag.[25]

---

[24] Hamerle et al. (1998, p. 429) empirically analyzed the predictability of risk factors and made a sector–risk sensitivity analysis. Their study discovered that macroeconomic factors have a lagged impact. Bär (2002) theoretically analyzed the necessity for integrating lagged macroeconomic variables by using yearly lags.

[25] The selection in the forward entry regression of the lagged macroeconomic variables follows the coefficient-of-determination selection criteria, which were previously described.

DATA SAMPLE

We are grateful to have had access to the database of a private equity fund investor who invests in venture capital funds in several European countries. The database includes information about the funds' portfolio companies, like investment and divestment amounts, write-offs, and sales revenues. Other information known about each fund includes sector, stage, and geographical region.

Our last data update is from the end of April 2005. Because there is a time gap between reports' closing date and delivery, only data collected before December 31, 2004, is considered. In addition, those funds that do not have the typical fund structure—like mezzanine funds, and atypical buyout funds—are eliminated, as are all funds that have not yet had a drawdown. The final sample of nearly 200 funds was invested in more than 2,000 companies. The average net exposure is €2,339,715 and the median is €1,283,041.

The basis from which to calculate the one-year default rate distribution is the calendar year. The number of observations per company in the analysis equals the number of calendar years the company is held by a fund. In the end, the analysis contained more than 8,000 observations. The strength of the sample comes from the fact that all of its funds have to report, which is very different from the databases of a data provider like Venture Economics. Moreover, by using the investor's database, this study had access to all information available to the fund investor, unlike the database of Venture Economics, where only anonymous and aggregated data is available. Thus, the bias of the sample is limited to that of atypical investment behavior of the fund investor with respect to the general market. Generally, we believe that the fund investor's investment behavior is a good representation of the European private equity industry.[26]

A point of contention might be that the average fund age of the portfolio is about four years and nine months and that most funds are still active. A longer time series would improve the predictability of the developed risk model; however, we are aware that the sample largely captures the period 1998 to 2004, during which the industry showed a dramatic

---

[26] The fund-of-fund investment behavior is compared with the cumulated data for the European venture capital market, as provided by EVCA.

increase, followed by a considerable consolidation. With fewer than 100 observations, the number of exits before 1998 is relatively low. Another database from a large European investor is included to increase the number of observations in order to make reasonably meaningful regressions.[27] The second database is comparable with the first database regarding the sector- and regional investment focus, and the databases are combined to calculate the sector default rates for the period 1993 to 2004. It is possible that the merged database contains some observations twice because the second database is anonymous, and a removal of double observations is not feasible. The resulting bias is relatively low because the overlapping observations are random and will not meaningfully distort the ratio of defaults and nondefaults on average.

As shown in Table 14.1, the default rates for years with more than 70 observations are between 2 and 14 percent and show a relatively high fluctuation.[28] The sectors with the highest default rates are communications

T A B L E   14.1

Default rate by industrial sector. This table presents the default rate by industrial sector for European venture-capital-financed companies for the period between 1993 and 2004. The default rates are calculated on the basis of the merged database of two large European venture capital investors. The bold numbers used fewer than 70 companies to calculate the default rate. The average is the average of all observations during the period 1993 to 2004.

Default rate	1993	1994	1995	1996	1997	1998	1999	2000	2001	2002	2003	2004	Average
Biotechnology	1%	0%		0%	7%	2%	4%	2%	2%	3%	4%	6%	7%
Communications	4%	3%	1%	3%	5%	4%	4%	5%	9%	13%	11%	14%	8%
Computer	13%	2%	6%	2%	4%	3%	2%	4%	7%	11%	13%	11%	7%
Consumer	0%	8%	11%	3%	6%	6%	3%	3%	4%	8%	6%	6%	5%
Industrial Production	3%	2%	3%	3%	4%	5%	5%	6%	4%	4%	2%	7%	4%

---

[27] The two databases are merged only to calculate default rates. The other analyses are based only on the initial database.

[28] Default rates' standard deviations are not shown because the number of observations is too low to calculate meaningful standard deviations. The model uses the average sector default rate as an estimator for the standard deviation. See the section Input Parameter.

and computer. Thus, the default rates since 2000 are on a higher level than they were previously.

The recovery rates are shown in Table 14.2. Since 2000, the recovery rates decreased significantly and fluctuated around 14 percent, possibly because of the booming capital markets in 1998 and 1999. As the capital markets were doing very well in 1998 and 1999, it can be assumed that it was easier to sell bad investments for a better price during this time.

Multicollinearity exists if variables are linearly intercorrelated among each other. Such data redundancy can cause overfitting in regression analysis models. The coefficients of correlation are examined to determine multicollinearity. The largest correlation between two independent variables has a value of |0.74|. The average correlation between the included macroeconomic variables is |0.31|. It can be assumed that the regression results are not distorted by multicollinearity because only values of about |0.9| indicate high correlation.[29]

EMPIRICAL EVIDENCE
Sector Analysis

This section shows the results of implementing the sector-analysis model described above. Table 14.3 shows the regression results and the weights. F tests and t tests confirm that the regression results are highly significant.[30]

T A B L E   14.2

Recovery rates by years and by industrial sectors

Year	1998	1999	2000	2001	2002	2003	2004	Average by Number
Recovery Rate	30%	25%	13%	15%	14%	13%	15%	15%

[29] See Kennedy (2003, p. 209).

[30] The forward entry regression uses nine independent variables, but in the final sector regression results, only seven variables are selected from the forward entry regression model, deleting the macroeconomic variables EUR_USD and oil. Therefore, the sector analysis includes only seven systematic risk factors and one idiosyncratic risk factor. The regression results for the consumer sector includes only two independent variables because the third selected variable does not improve the R^2 in the required increase of 5 percentage points.

TABLE 14.3

Sector analysis. The results of the stepwise entry regression by industrial sectors. Lag indicates the lag of the selected variable. The weights for the variables equals the improvement of the R2 of each forward entry. The weight of the constant, which equals the remaining unexplained sample variance, is the weight of the idiosyncratic risk factor. The bold numbers are significant at the 5 percent level

Industrial Sector	Variable	Lag	Coefficient	t-test	p-value	Weight	R^2	Adj. R^2	dw-test	F-test	p-value
Bio-technology	Constant		−1.45	−18.5	1.6×10^{-06}	6.2%	94%	91%	2.28	30.20	5.1×10^{-04}
	GDP	1	−12.75	−7.0	4.3×10^{-04}	62.2%					
	Euribor	2	4.82	4.6	3.9×10^{-03}	25.3%					
	Ind_Prod	0	2.23	2.5	0.049	6.3%					
Communications	Constant		1.08	4.9	1.2×10^{-03}	5.1%	95%	93%	2.75	49.91	1.6×10^{-05}
	UnEmR	0	−23.99	−10.3	6.8×10^{-06}	57.9%					
	Stoxx	1	−0.69	−6.2	2.7×10^{-04}	29.8%					
	PPI	2	4.77	3.4	9.7×10^{-03}	7.2%					
Computer	Constant		1.02	2.2	0.056	11.4%	89%	84%	1.53	20.78	3.9×10^{-04}
	GDP	0	−16.88	−4.2	3.1×10^{-03}	63.5%					
	UnEmR	1	−19.19	−4.0	4.1×10^{-03}	10.1%					
	Ret_Sal	2	−9.82	−3.2	0.012	15.0%					
Consumer	Constant		−1.09	−24.6	8.0×10^{-09}	21.2%	0.79	73%	1.70	14.87	2.0×10^{-03}
	Ret_Sal	2	−10.88	−5.0	1.1×10^{-03}	45.3%					
	Stoxx	0	−0.52	−3.6	7.5×10^{-03}	33.5%					
Industrial Production	Constant		−0.55	−1.5	0.160	25.2%	75%	65%	3.11	7.94	8.8×10^{-03}
	Euribor	2	−4.64	−3.2	0.013	40.9%					
	Stoxx	0	0.60	3.3	0.011	25.0%					
	UnEmR	1	−6.73	−1.7	0.129	9.0%					

The weight of the systematic risk of the single sectors varies between 5.1 and 25.2 percent. As venture-capital-financed companies are typically small, young, and growth-oriented, it could be assumed that they have higher idiosyncratic risks in comparison to the large, established companies.[31] As the average R^2 is smaller than for the regression results of larger companies used in previous studies,[32] the results confirm the assumption that venture-capital-financed companies have higher idiosyncratic risks in comparison to large, established companies.

The Durbin–Watson test is used to test the regressions for autocorrelation. The Durbin–Watson values (dw) are in the range of dw = 1.5 for the computer sector and dw = 3.1 for the Industrial sector.[33] Hence, the values are either in an interval in which no autocorrelation can be suggested or they are in the statistical indeterminacy interval, in which case no conclusions can be made.[34] As the time series is relatively short, a reliable testing of the regression on linearity and heteroschedasticity is not feasible.

Table 13.4 shows the comparative empirically observed default rates and estimated default rates for each sector.

The numbers show clearly the predictability of the model. Default rates diverge on average only about 0.8 percentage points from the empirically observed default rate, with a maximum difference of only 3.1 percentage points. Therefore, based on these outcomes, the developed regression model can be considered reliable. However, the capacity of the results remains restricted, as the number of observations is relatively low.

Venture Capital Risk

The publicly available CreditRisk$^+$ tool is used to evaluate the default distribution.[35] Graph 1 shows the analyzed models, which are based on different

---

[31] See Knapp and Hamerle (1999).

[32] See Wilson (1997a; 1997b; 1997c; 1997d).

[33] A value close to zero indicates positive autocorrelation; a value close to 4 indicates negative autocorrelation. Values close to 2 indicate nonautocorrelation of the residuals.

[34] The critical value, i.e., the limit of the critical band, depends not only on the number of observations and the number of independent variables but also on the calculated values of the regression coefficient. Thus, the critical band of the typically used tables for this test does not reach a decision if the value is in this band.

[35] CreditRisk$^+$ is developed from Credit Swiss First Boston (CSFB) and is a Microsoft Visual Basic for Applications (VBA) tool available for download. See http://www.csfb.com/institutional/research/credit_risk.shtml.

TABLE 14.4

The actual default rates and forecasted default rates by industrial sector. The bold numbers show a difference between actual default rate and forecasted default rate of more than 1 percentage point.

Industrial Sector	Biotechnology		Communications		Computer		Consumer		Industrial Production	
Year	Actual	Estimate	Actual	Estimate	Actual	Estimate	Actual	Estimate	Actual	Estimate
1993	9.8%	10.4%	3.8%	4.1%	**13.0%**	**14.7%**	—	8.0%	2.6%	2.6%
1994	—	12.9%	3.4%	3.7%	1.8%	2.3%	**7.6%**	**5.6%**	1.9%	2.0%
1995	3.7%	3.3%	1.5%	1.6%	**5.6%**	**8.2%**	10.8%	11.2%	2.8%	2.4%
1996	—	4.4%	3.2%	2.7%	1.8%	1.9%	**2.8%**	**4.2%**	2.8%	2.8%
1997	**6.7%**	**5.6%**	**4.7%**	4.7%	**3.8%**	**2.3%**	6.1%	7.0%	3.6%	3.7%
1998	2.0%	2.3%	4.2%	3.9%	3.3%	4.0%	**5.5%**	**4.1%**	5.2%	5.0%
1999	3.6%	4.0%	4.1%	5.0%	2.0%	2.3%	3.4%	3.1%	5.0%	5.3%
2000	2.4%	2.5%	5.1%	5.7%	3.8%	3.5%	2.6%	3.0%	5.6%	6.3%
2001	2.0%	1.8%	**9.4%**	**7.2%**	6.6%	7.5%	4.4%	4.6%	3.8%	3.8%
2002	3.5%	4.4%	**12.9%**	**16.0%**	**10.7%**	**8.8%**	7.8%	7.2%	**4.3%**	**3.1%**
2003	4.4%	4.0%	11.1%	9.8%	**13.0%**	**11.3%**	5.5%	6.3%	**1.9%**	**3.2%**
2004	5.6%	5.1%	14.1%	12.6%	**11.1%**	**7.9%**	5.6%	5.1%	**7.1%**	**5.6%**
Maximum Difference	1.1%		3.1%		3.2%		2.0%		1.5%	
Average Absolute Difference	0.4%		0.9%		1.3%		0.7%		0.5%	

302

assumptions. The portfolio loss is shown as the ratio of loss to exposure as of December 31, 2004.[36] The risk model is empirically tested using a portfolio of venture-capital-financed companies. As the model does not take into account that venture-capital-backed companies' returns are, in theory, unlimited, the results can be considered as the lower bound for loss distributions for loans of venture-capital-financed companies.

The model with constant default rates considers no default rate uncertainties. As shown in Figure 14.1, the probability for very small and very large portfolio losses is underestimated because correlations among companies are not considered in this approach. This leads to an underestimation of the portfolio risk.

The single-sector model has only one sector. This approach implies that changes in default rates among companies within an industrial sector have the same direction and are parallel and that the assumed high default

F I G U R E   14.1

Default Distribution

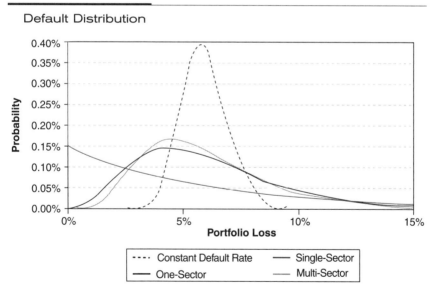

This graph shows the expected default distribution for 2005 by sector models. In respect to the data provider, the loss is shown as a ratio of loss amount to exposure as of December 31, 2004.

---

[36] The portfolio losses, as well as further results, are shown at the rate of the exposure to ensure anonymity of our data provider.

rate correlations among companies within a sector lead to an overestimation of portfolio risk and portfolio loss. The probability of extreme losses—very high as well as very low losses—is relatively high.

Company correlations are more sophisticated when incorporated in the one-sector model and the multisector model. The portfolio risk of these models lies between the nonvarying default rate model and the single-sector model. This allows a more realistic portfolio risk estimation. The one-sector model classifies each company in one risk sector, which equals its industrial sector, and the default rate is determined by classification into that industrial sector. This requires the assumption that companies within an industry have a default rate correlation of 1, whereas companies that are not in the same industry have a correlation of 0. Diversification effects between companies of different industries are incorporated, but the effect is overestimated because a correlation of 0 is understated. Diversification effects of companies within an industrial sector are not considered because changes in default rates among these companies have the same direction and magnitude. In summary, the effects compensate one another, but it is not clear which effect dominates.

The multisector model uses the results of the sector analysis' regression model to weight each factor. It classifies each company into one idiosyncratic risk factor and seven systematic risk factors, following the assumption that a number of independent systematic factors and one idiosyncratic factor influence the company's default rate. Because this model takes company-specific risks into account, the diversification effect is larger in comparison to the one-sector approach. Further, the sources of risk of the idiosyncratic sector are company-specific and, therefore, independent from each other. The resulting default correlation of this idiosyncratic risk factor is zero.[37] In comparison with the first multifactor model, probability for small and very large portfolio losses is lower because the diversification and correlation effects are more realistically considered.

Table 14.5 shows the descriptive statistics and the value at risk for 2005 by sector models. The expected loss of all models is identical,

---

[37] See Credit Suisse Financial Products (1997, pp. 20ff).

T A B L E   14.5

Value at risk. The descriptive statistics and the VaR for 2005 by sector models. The data are shown as the ratios of actual value to exposure.

	Constant Default Rate	Single Sector	One Sector	Multisector
Expected Loss	5.91%	5.91%	5.91%	5.91%
Standard Deviation	0.97%	3.34%	3.04%	2.70%
VaR Quartile	**Portfolio Loss**			
50.0%	5.9%	4.1%	5.4%	5.4%
75.0%	6.5%	8.2%	7.5%	7.3%
90.0%	7.2%	13.7%	9.9%	9.5%
92.5%	7.4%	15.4%	10.6%	10.1%
95.0%	7.6%	17.9%	11.6%	11.0%
97.5%	8.0%	22.0%	13.3%	12.5%
99.0%	8.4%	27.5%	15.4%	14.4%

whereas the default rate distribution differs.[38] As expected, the 95 percent value at risk (VaR)[39] confidence level shows that the expected loss for the one-sector and multisector models lies between the model with nonvarying default rates and the single-sector model. Backtesting[40] of the introduced venture capital risk model is not feasible because the venture capital industry is a relatively young industry and the time series of this study is relatively short.

Table 14.6 shows a comparison of forecasted losses and realized losses for 1999 to 2003. The results show that the realized losses are below the forecasted 95 percent confidence level losses and an increasing trend in

---

[38] If a fund invests in a company in the year of the final exit, losses are lowered by approximately the investment amount, which is made in the exit year, because this investment is not incorporated into the exposure that is used to calculate the default distribution. The exposure to calculate the default distribution for year t refers to the exposure of December 31 at year $t - 1$.

[39] The VaR estimates the likelihood that a given portfolio's losses will exceed a certain amount.

[40] These models test ex post how often actual losses exceed forecasted losses. Long time series are necessary to make this kind of model validation.

T A B L E   14.6

Expected loss versus realized loss. The expected loss and realized loss as a ratio of portfolio exposure by year. The exposure refers to the closing date of December 31 of the former year because the portfolio loss refers to the composition of the portfolio at this date. In respect to the data provider, the numbers are shown as ratios to the exposure.

Year (t)	Expected Loss (t) to Exposure (t − 1)	Realized Loss (t) to Exposure (t − 1)	Realized Loss (t) to Expected Loss (t)	VaR 95% (t) to Exposure (t)	Position of Realized Loss (t) in VaR
1999	6.5%	1.6%	25.2%	13.5%	5%
2000	6.6%	2.8%	42.9%	12.7%	8%
2001	6.6%	3.5%	53.2%	12.4%	14%
2002	6.5%	8.3%	129.3%	12.2%	78%
2003	6.2%	11.4%	182.1%	11.7%	94%
2004	6.0%	8.6%	142.6%	11.3%	84%
2005	5.9%	—	—	11.0%	—

the ratio of realized loss to expected loss. A potential bias occurs as our data provider began investing in 1997; the database is relatively young and no fund is liquidated. Because fund managers generally hold their investments between five and eight years, the losses are underestimated, especially in the first years. The older the fund gets, the more realistic the estimations.

Diversification effects can be shown by using marginal risk. The marginal risk capital is obtained in Merton and Perold (1993) by calculating the risk capital required for the portfolio without a new business and subtracting it from the risk capital required for the full venture capital portfolio. It enables an optimization of venture capital portfolios because it is used to make investment and divestment decisions. To get a picture of the degree of the marginal risk, the total exposure is reduced about 5 percent on all investments that have the largest ratio of marginal risk to net exposure.[41] Both default distributions are shown in Figure 14.2.

As shown in Table 14.7, the decrease of expected loss, standard deviation, and value at risk is greater than the 5 percent decrease of the net

---

[41] The marginal risks are calculated for the 95th percentile.

F I G U R E   14.2

Caption

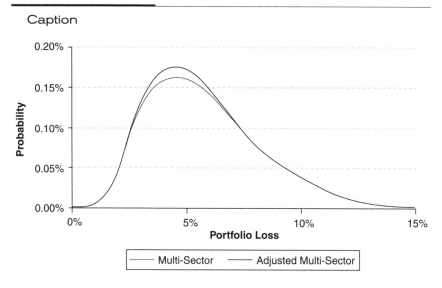

---- Multi-Sector   ---- Adjusted Multi-Sector

T A B L E   14.7

Risk-adjusted portfolio. The descriptive statistics and the forecasted value at risk for 2005 for the multisector model by different portfolios. The original portfolio contains all companies. In the adjusted portfolio, the total exposure is reduced about 5 percent for all investments that have the largest ratio of marginal risk to net exposure. The data for the original portfolio and the adjusted portfolio are shown as the ratios of actual value to exposure.

	Original Portfolio	Adjusted Portfolio	Change of the Absolute Values
Expected Loss	5.91%	5.84%	−6.44%
Standard Deviation	2.70%	2.63%	−7.61%
VaR Quartile		**Portfolio Loss**	
50.0%	5.4%	5.4%	−6.22%
75.0%	7.3%	7.2%	−6.56%
90.0%	9.5%	9.3%	−6.87%
92.5%	10.1%	9.9%	−6.95%
95.0%	11.0%	10.8%	−7.05%
97.5%	12.5%	12.2%	−7.20%
99.0%	14.4%	14.1%	−7.37%

exposure. Therefore, the marginal risk can be used to optimize venture capital portfolios. However, an exclusive examination of potential losses is unsuitable to optimizing venture capital portfolios because this analysis considers only risks and does not consider returns. An advanced portfolio management should include both risks and rewards, i.e., potential losses as well as potential returns.

CONCLUSION

Convincing and generally accepted portfolio models for venture capital investments do not exist in theory or in practice. Broad implementation of a widely accepted risk model would enhance venture capital investments' transparency. A better risk assessment allows a more accurate loss estimate of the venture capital fund investments making the decision less difficult.

This study constructs and evaluates a risk model for the venture capital industry based on the CreditRisk$^+$ model. The practicability of the model is successfully tested through an empirical analysis with data from one of the largest European venture capital investors. As relatively little effort is required to implement the model, it can be a practical tool in enhancing active portfolio management.

REFERENCES

Bär, T. (2002) Predicting and Hedging Credit Portfolio Risk with Macroeconomic Factors. Hamburg, Germany: Kovac Verlag.

Bürgisser, P., A. Kurth, A. Wagner, and M. Wolf (1999) Integrating Correlations. *Risk Magazine*, 12(7): 1–7.

Caouette, J.B., E.I. Altman, and P. Narayanan (1998) Managing Credit Risk. Hoboken, NJ: John Wiley & Sons.

J.P.Morgan (1997) CreditMetrics—Technical Document. Available at http://www.riskmetrics.com.

Credit Suisse Financial Products (1997) CreditRisk$^+$—Technical Document. Available at http://www.csfb.com/creditrisk.

Crouhy, M. and D.R. Mark-Galai (2000) A Comparative Analysis of
Current Credit Risk Models. *Journal of Banking and Finance*,
24(1): 59–117.

Gordy, M.B. (1998) A Comparative Anatomy of Credit Risk Models.
Journal of Banking and Finance, 24(1–2): 119–149.

Hamerle, A., M. Knapp, B. Ott, and G. Schacht (1998) Prognose und
Sensitivitätsanalyse von Branchenrisiken – ein neuer Ansatz. Die
Bank, 38(7): 428–430.

Hamerle, A., T. Liebig, and D. Rösch (2002) Assetkorrelationen der
Schlüsselbranchen in Deutschland. Die Bank, 42(7): 470–473.

Jarrow, R.A. and S.M. Tumbull (2000) The Intersection of Market and
CreditRisk. *Journal of Banking and Finance*, 24: 271–299.

Jones, C.M., and M. Rhodes-Kropf (2003) The Price of Diversifiable
Risk in Private Equity and Venture Capital. Working paper,
Columbia Business School, New York.

Kaplan, S. and A. Schoar (2003) Private Equity Performance: Returns,
Persistence and Capital. NBER Working Paper Series, No. 9807,
Cambridge, MA.

Kennedy, P. (2003) *A Guide to Econometrics*. Cambridge, MA: MIT Press.

Knapp M. and A. Hamerle (1999) Multi-Faktor-Modelle zur Bestimmung
Segmentspezifischer Ausfallwahrscheinlichkeiten für die Kredit-
Portfolio-Steuerung. Wirtschaftsinformatik, 41(2): 138–144.

Knapp, M. (2002) Zeitabhängige Kreditportfoliomodelle. Deutscher
Universitäts-Verlag: Wiesbaden.

Merton, R. (1974) On the Pricing of Corporate Debt: The Risk Structure
of Interest Rates. *Journal of Finance*, 29(2): 449–470.

Merton, R. and A.F. Perold (1993) Theory of Risk Capital in Financial
Firms. *Journal of Applied Corporate Finance*, 5(1): 16–32.

Moody's Corporation (2005). Moody's KMV PortfolioManager™.
Available at http://www.moodyskmv.com/products/Portfolio_
Manager.html.

Ong, M.K. (2000) *Internal Credit Risk Models: Capital Allocation and Performance Measurement*. London: Risk Books.

Wahrenburg, M. and S. Niethen (2000) Vergleichende Analyse Alternativer Kreditrisikomodelle. Kredit und Kapital, 33(2): 235–257.

Wilson, T.C. (1997a) Measuring and Managing Credit Portfolio Risk: Part I of II: Modelling Systematic Default Risk. *Journal of Lending & Credit Risk Management*, 79(11): 61–72.

Wilson, T.C. (1997b) Measuring and Managing Credit Portfolio Risk: Part II of II: Portfolio Loss Distribution. *Journal of Lending & Credit Risk Management*, 79(12): 67–68.

Wilson, T.C. (1997c) Portfolio Credit Risk (I). *Risk Magazine* 10(9): 111–117.

Wilson, T.C. (1997d) Portfolio Credit Risk (II). *Risk Magazine*, 10(10): 56–61.

Wilson, T.C. (1998) Portfolio Credit Risk. *FRBNY Economic Policy Review*, 4(3): 71–82.

CHAPTER 15

Risk Measures and Their Applications in Asset Management

S. Ilker Birbil, Hans Frenk, Bahar Kaynar, and Nilay Noyan

ABSTRACT

Several approaches exist to model decision making under risk, where risk can be broadly defined as the effect of variability of random outcomes. One of the main approaches in the practice of decision making under risk uses mean-risk models; one such well-known model is the classical Markowitz model, where variance is used as risk measure. Along this line, we consider a portfolio selection problem, where the asset returns have an elliptical distribution. We mainly focus on portfolio optimization models constructing portfolios with minimal risk, provided that a prescribed expected return level is attained. In particular, we model the risk by using value at risk (VaR) and conditional value at risk (CVaR). After reviewing the main properties of VaR and CVaR, we present short proofs to some of the well-known results. Finally, we describe a computationally efficient solution algorithm and present numerical results.

INTRODUCTION

In recent years, off-balance sheet activities, such as trading financial
instruments and generating income from loan sales, have begun to be
profitable for banks in the competitive environment of the financial world.
One of the main goals of such banks trading in these markets is to reduce
the risk associated with their activities; however, with the taken positions
trading may even be riskier. In particular, after the insolvency of some
banks, the collapse of Barings in February 1995, risk management became
quite significant in terms of internal control measures. One of these internal controls is recognition of the maximum loss that a portfolio can attain
over a given time interval, termed *value at risk* (VaR). With VaR methodology, not only is exposed risk identified but VaR can also be used as a
decision tool to take positions in the market so as to reduce the risk and,
if possible, minimize it. The importance of VaR also stems from its status
as universal risk measure employed in banking regulations, like Basel II,
to evaluate capital requirements for banks' trading activities. Technically
speaking, VaR at the confidence level α of a portfolio is the α-quantile of
the distribution function of total random loss associated with the portfolio
at a specified probability level. A closely related recent risk measure,
Conditional value at risk (CVaR), on the other hand, is the expectation of
loss values exceeding the VaR value with the corresponding probability
level (Rockafellar and Uryasev, 2000).

Comparing random outcomes is one of the main interests of decision
theory in the presence of uncertainty. Several decision models have been
developed to formulate optimization problems in which uncertain quantities
are represented by random variables. One method of comparing random
variables is via the expected values. For the basic limitations of optimization models considering the expected value see, e.g., Ruszczyński and
Shapiro (2006). In cases where the same decisions under similar conditions
are repeatedly made, one can justify the optimization of the expected value
by the law of large numbers. However, the average of a few results may be
misleading due to the variability of the outcomes. Therefore, sound decision
models in the presence of uncertainty should take into account the effect
of inherent variability, which in turn leads to the concept of risk. The preference relations among random variables can be specified using a risk

measure. There are two main approaches for quantifying risk; it can be identified as a function of the deviation from an expected value or as a function of the absolute loss. The former approach is the main idea of the Markowitz mean-variance model. The latter approach involves the two recent risk measures mentioned above, VaR and CVaR.

The challenge of managing a portfolio that includes finitely many assets has been a mainstay in finance literature. The simplest, most widely used approach for modeling changes in the portfolio value is the variance–covariance method popularized by RiskMetrics Group (1997). Two main assumptions of this model are as follows (Glasserman et al., 2002): (1) The risk factors are conditionally multivariate normal over a specified short horizon. (2) The change in the portfolio value, mainly profit–loss function, is a linear function of the changes in the risk factors. In this setting, the term conditionally means that conditioned on the information available at the beginning of the short horizon—such as the prices of the instruments or the value of the portfolio—the changes in the risk factors become multivariate normal.

The central problem is to estimate the profit–loss function and its relation with the underlying risk factors of a portfolio over a specified horizon. Since VaR deals with the extreme losses, estimating the tail of the loss distribution is crucial for portfolio management. For example, although two different possible distributions for the price changes have the same mean, the probability of facing very large changes may be much greater for one than it is for the other. Starting from this model, we may relax either the linearity assumption or the normality assumption. Methods such as delta-gamma, interpolation, or low variance Monte Carlo simulation relax the linearity assumption. Monte Carlo simulation is universally adaptable; however, since it is common in risk management to deal with rare events, Monte Carlo simulation works much slower (Glasserman et al., 2002; Sadefo-Kamdem, 2005). The other option is to relax the normality assumption and use another family of distributions to model the returns of the underlying risk factors. The latter option, in fact, is the main focus of our work.

In this chapter, we analyze a general risk management model applied to portfolio problems with VaR and CVaR risk measures. We assume that our portfolio is linear and the risk factor changes have an elliptical distribution. A similar approach was initiated by Rockafellar and Uryasev (2000) for the special case of multivariate normally distributed returns. The class of elliptical distributions is a general class of distributions, which contains the normal and the Student's t-distributions. Contrary to Rockafellar and Uryasev (2000); we do not explicitly talk about applications of financial concepts (such as hedging), which actually lead to similar models. In the literature, it is observed that market returns have heavier tails compared to normal distributions; many studies moreover discuss the comparisons of portfolios among families of distributions on returns (Fama, 1965; Praetz, 1972; Blattberg and Gonedes, 1974; Embrechts et al., 2002). In particular Blattberg and Gonedes (1974) illustrate that the student model has greater descriptive validity than do the other models. Although most of the works are restricted to t-distribution, Sadefo-Kamdem generalizes VaR and Expected Shortfall to the family of elliptical distributions. Embrechts et al. (2002) also analyze the class of elliptical distributions within the context of risk management. On one hand, these papers concentrate on measuring VaR and CVaR measures. On the other hand, these do not include a discussion on portfolio optimization. In this chapter, we explicitly focus on constructing optimal portfolios.

We first concentrate on general risk measures and then concentrate on VaR and CVaR. We also briefly review the theory of coherent risk measures, thoroughly studied in Arztner et. al. (1999). We then discuss the behavior of VaR and CVaR in terms of coherency. By converting the ideas used for rewards (Ogryczak and Ruszczyński, 2002), a different definition of CVaR is given. Following risk measures, we define general portfolio optimization problems. Additionally, we draw attention to the effect of adding a riskless asset. After a condensed introduction on elliptical distributions, we give short proofs on properties of VaR, CVaR, and linear loss functions. We note that the important risk measure CVaR is also discussed by Embrechts et. al. (2002) under the term *expected shortfall* or *mean excess loss* together with properties of elliptical distributions. Using the well-known equivalence between the mean-risk approach employing VaR and CVaR as risk measures and the famous mean-variance approach of Markowitz, we adapt an algorithm for special quadratic programming problems originally proposed by Michelot in 1986. In this algorithm, the number of steps to find the optimal allocation of the assets is finite and equals at most the number of the considered assets. Our computational results suggest that the adapted algorithm is a faster alternative to the standard solver used in the financial toolbox of MATLAB. We also present some numerical results to emphasize the fact that we can construct optimal portfolios for returns having distributions different than normal; in particular we provide results for multivariate t-distributions.

RISK MEASURES

Consider an optimization problem in which the decision vector **x** affects an uncertain outcome represented by a random variable $Z(\mathbf{x})$. Thus, for a decision vector **x** belonging to a certain feasible set $\chi \subseteq R^n$, we obtain a realization of the real-valued random variable $Z(\mathbf{x})$, which may be interpreted as some reward or loss of the decision **x**. In our work $Z(\mathbf{x})$ and $-Z(\mathbf{x})$ represent the loss and the reward of the decision **x**, respectively. Therefore, smaller values of $Z(\mathbf{x})$ are preferred to larger ones. To find the 'best' values of the decision vector **x**, we need to compare the random variables $Z(\mathbf{x})$ according to a preference relation. While comparing random variables, sound decision models should take into account the effect of inherent variability, which leads to the concept of risk. The preference relations among random variables can be specified using a risk measure. One of the main approaches in practice uses mean-risk models. In these models one uses a specified risk measure ρ : $B \rightarrow [-\infty, +\infty]$, where ρ is a functional and B is a linear space of F-measurable functions on a probability space (Ω, F, P). Notice that for a given vector **x**, the argument of the function ρ is a real-valued random variable denoted here by $Z(\mathbf{x})$ with the cumulative distribution function (cdf)

$$F_{Z(\mathbf{x})}(a) : = P\{Z(\mathbf{x}) \leqslant a\} \tag{15.1}$$

Clearly $\rho(Z(\mathbf{x}_1)) = \rho(Z(\mathbf{x}_2))$ for $Z(\mathbf{x}_1)$ and $Z(\mathbf{x}_2)$ having the same cdf [denoted by $Z(\mathbf{x}_1) = {}^d Z(\mathbf{x}_2)$].

In the mean-risk approach for a given risk measure ρ one solves the problem

$$\max_{\mathbf{x} \in X} \left\{ E[-Z(\mathbf{x})] - \lambda \rho(Z(\mathbf{x})) \right\} \tag{15.2}$$

where $\lambda \geq 0$ is the trade-off coefficient representing our desirable exchange rate of mean reward for risk. We say that the decision vector **x** is efficient (in the mean-risk sense) if and only if for a given level of minimum expected reward, **x** has the lowest possible risk, and for a given level of risk, **x** has the highest possible expected reward. In many applications, especially in portfolio selection problems, the mean risk efficient frontier is identified by finding the efficient solutions for different trade-off coefficients.

The classical Markowitz (1952) model discussed in Steinbach (2001) uses variance as a risk measure. One of the problems associated with the Markowitz's mean-variance formulation, however, is that it penalizes over-performance (positive deviation from the mean) and underperformance (negative deviation from the mean) equally. When typical dispersion statistics such as variance are used as risk measures, the mean-risk models may lead to inferior solutions. That is, there may exist other feasible solutions which would be preferred by any risk-averse decision maker to the efficient solution obtained by the mean-risk model.

Example 15.1. Consider two decision vectors $\mathbf{x}_1$ and $\mathbf{x}_2$ for which the probability mass functions of the random outcomes (losses) are given as follows:

$$P\{Z(\mathbf{x}_1) = a_1\} = \begin{cases} 1/2 & a_1 = 2 \\ 1/2 & a_1 = 4 \\ 0 & \text{otherwise} \end{cases} \quad \text{and} \quad P\{Z(\mathbf{x}_2) = a_2\} = \begin{cases} 1 & a_2 = 10 \\ 0 & \text{otherwise} \end{cases}$$

Any rational decision maker would prefer the decision vector $\mathbf{x}_1$ with the random loss $Z(\mathbf{x}_1)$. However, when a dispersion type risk measure $\rho(Z(\mathbf{x}))$ is used, then both decision vectors lie in the efficient frontier of the corresponding mean-risk model, since for each such a risk measure $\rho(Z(\mathbf{x}_1)) > 0$ and $\rho(Z(\mathbf{x}_2)) = 0$.

To overcome the preceding disadvantage, alternative asymmetric risk measures, such as downside risk, have been proposed and significant effort has been devoted to the development of downside risk models (see, e.g., Ogryczak and Ruszczyński, 2002). We refer to Ruszczyński and Shapiro (2006) as well as Rockafellar et al. (2006), and the references therein for other stochastic optimization models involving general risk functionals. Value at risk and CVaR are also among the popular downside risk measures.

Definition 15.1. The *first quantile function* $F_X^{-1} :(0, 1] \to \mathrm{R}$ corresponding to a random variable X is the left-continuous inverse of the cumulative distribution function F_X:

$$F_X^{-1}(\alpha) = \inf\{\eta \in \mathrm{R} : F_X(\eta) \ge \alpha\}$$

In the finance literature, the α-quantile $F_X^{-1}(\alpha)$ is called the *Value at Risk* at the confidence level α and denoted by $\mathrm{VaR}_\alpha(X)$. Using Definition 15.1 and relation (15.1), we can state that the realizations of the random variable X larger than $\mathrm{VaR}_\alpha(X)$ occur with probability less than $1 - \alpha$.

A closely related and recently popular risk measure is the CVaR, also called *Mean Excess Loss or Tail* VaR. Conditional VaR at level α is defined as follows (Rockafellar and Uryasev, 2000; ibid. 2002; Pflug, 2000):

$$\mathrm{CVaR}_\alpha(X) = \inf_{\eta \in \mathrm{R}} \left\{ \eta + \frac{1}{1-\alpha} E\big[\max\{X - \eta, 0\}\big] \right\} \qquad (15.3)$$

The correspondence between the concepts of CVaR and VaR and the fact that CVaR is also based on a quantile approach can be seen from the following result. Employing a similar argument, a closely related statement has been proven in Ogryczak and Ruszczyński (2002), where the random variable X represents rewards (returns) instead of losses. As in Rockafellar (1972), the set $\partial f(y)$ denotes the subgradient set of a finite convex function $f : \mathrm{R} \to \mathrm{R}$ at y.

Lemma 15.1. *For any real valued random variable X having a finite first absolute moment*

$$\mathrm{CVaR}_\alpha(X) = \frac{1}{1-\alpha} \int_\alpha^1 \mathrm{VaR}_u(X)\,du$$

for all $0 < \alpha < 1$.

Proof. Introducing the convex and continuous function $f : \mathrm{R} \to \mathrm{R}$ given by

$$f(y) := E[\max\{X - y, 0\}] \qquad (15.4)$$

it follows by relation (15.3) that

$$\text{CVaR}_\alpha (X) = (1-\alpha)^{-1} v(Q) \tag{15.5}$$

where $v(Q) := \inf_{y \in R} \{(1-\alpha) y + f(y)\}$. Since

$$f(y) = \int_y^\infty (x-y)dF_X (x) = \int_y^\infty (1 - F_X (x))dx$$

we obtain that y^* is an optimal solution of the convex optimization problem

$$\inf_{y \in R} \{(1 - \alpha)y + f(y)\}$$

if and only if $1-\alpha$ belongs to $-\partial f (y^*)$. It is now easy to verify by the definition of the subgradient set and relation (15.4) that $1-\alpha$ belongs to $-f (\partial F_X^{-1}(\alpha))$. This result shows that $F_X^{-1}(\alpha)$ is an optimal solution of the optimization problem $\inf_{y \in R} \{(1-\alpha) y + f (y)\}$ and so

$$v(Q) = (1-\alpha) F_X^{-1} (\alpha) + E[\max \{X - F_X^{-1} (\alpha), 0\}] \tag{15.6}$$

Since $X =\, ^d F_X^{-1} (U)$, where U is a uniform distributed random variable on $(0, 1)$, we obtain

$$E\left[\max\{X - F_X^{-1}(\alpha), 0\}\right] = E\left[\max\{F_X^{-1}(U) - F_X^{-1}(\alpha), 0\}\right]$$
$$= \int_\alpha^1 \text{VaR}_u (X)du - (1-\alpha)F_X^{-1}(\alpha)$$

and by relation Equations (15.5) and (15.6) the assertion holds true.

It is easy to see that the function $\alpha \mapsto \text{VaR}_\alpha (X)$ is increasing; therefore, an immediate consequence of Lemma 15.1 is given by

$$\text{CVaR}_\alpha (X) \geq \text{VaR}_\alpha (X)$$

Moreover, when F_X is continuous on $(-\infty, \infty)$, we know that $\text{VaR}_\alpha (X)$ is not an atom of the distribution of X; therefore, $1-\alpha = P\{X \geq \text{VaR}_\alpha(X)\}$. Then we have

$$\int_{\alpha}^{1}\text{VaR}_u\,(X)du = E\left[F_X^{-1}\,(U)1_{\{U\geq\alpha\}}\right] = E\left[F_X^{-1}\,(U)1_{\{F_X^{-1}(U)\geq F_X^{-1}(\alpha)\}}\right]$$

$$= E\left[X1_{\{X\geq VaR_\alpha(X)\}}\right]$$

It follows from the last equation that

$$\text{CVaR}_\alpha(X)\,!\,E[X\,|\,X\,!\,\text{VaR}_\alpha(X)] \tag{15.7}$$

which has been also shown in Rockafellar and Uryasev (2000) by using another approach.

This definition provides a clear understanding of the concept of CVaR, i.e., the conditional expectation of values above the VaR at the confidence level α. For example, in the portfolio optimization context, VaR_α is the α-quantile (a high quantile) of the distribution of losses (negative returns), which provides an upper bound for a loss that is exceeded only with a small probability $1 - \alpha$. On the other hand, CVaR_α is a measure of severity of loss if we lose more than VaR_α.

An axiomatic approach to construct risk measures has been proposed by Artzner et al. (1999). It is now widely accepted that risk measures should satisfy the following set of axiomatic properties:

1. Monotonicity: $\rho(X_1) \geqslant \rho(X_2)$ for any $X_1, X_2 \in B$ such that $X_1 \geqslant X_2$ (where the inequality $X_1 \geqslant X_2$ is assumed to hold almost surely).
2. Subadditivity: $\rho(X_1 + X_2) \leqslant \rho(X_1) + \rho(X_2)$ for $X_1, X_2 \in B$.
3. Positive homogeneity: $\rho(\lambda X) = \lambda\rho(X)$ for any $\lambda > 0$ and $X \in B$.
4. Translation invariant: $\rho(X + a) = \rho(X) + a$ for any $a \in R$ and $X \in B$.

A risk measure satisfying the above properties is called a coherent risk measure. It is well known that CVaR is a coherent risk measure, but due to the lack of subadditivity, VaR fails to be a coherent risk measure in general (Pflug, 2000).

Optimization models involving VaR are technically and methodologically difficult; for details see Rockafellar and Uryasev (2002). As also observed by Crouhy et al. (2001), using VaR as a risk measure has been criticized mainly for not being subadditive; hence, not being convex. In some applications, nonconvexity is a significant objection since it does not reward diversification. For example, in the portfolio selection theory, lack of conversity implies that portfolio diversification may increase the risk and considering the advantages of a portfolio diversification strategy, this objection cannot be ignored. However, as discussed by Embrechts et al. (2002), VaR is convex in the elliptical world (see the section Elliptical World), and so, within this framework VaR is a coherent risk measure. Therefore, we can use VaR in our portfolio selection problems. In the next section, we present single period portfolio optimization models.

A SINGLE-PERIOD PORTFOLIO OPTIMIZATION PROBLEM

In this section, we consider a single-period (short-term) portfolio selection problem with a set of n risky assets. At the beginning of the period, the length of which is specified, the investor decides on the amount of capital to be allocated on each available asset. At the end of the investment period, each asset generates a return, which is uncertain at the beginning of the period since the future price of an asset is unknown. We represent these uncertain returns with random variables and denote the vector of random returns of assets $1, 2, \ldots, n$ by $\mathbf{Y}^{\mathrm{T}} = (Y_1, Y_2, \ldots, Y_n)$. In finance, the ratio of money gained or lost on an investment relative to the money invested is called the *rate of return* or *percentage return*, which throughout the chapter we just refer to as simply *return*.

We denote the fractions of the initial capital and the amounts of the initial capital invested in assets $j = 1, \ldots, n$ by $\mathbf{x}^{\mathrm{T}} = (x_1, \ldots, x_n)$ and $\widetilde{\mathbf{x}}^{\mathrm{T}} = (\widetilde{x}_1, \ldots, \widetilde{x}_n)$, respectively. Thus, if $\widetilde{x}_j$ is the amount of the capital invested in asset j and C is the total amount of capital to be invested, we have $x_j = \widetilde{x}_j / C$ for $j = 1, \ldots, n$. The constructed portfolio may be represented by either of these two decision vectors. We assume that short selling is not allowed, which means that investors can not sell assets they do not own presently in the hope of repurchasing them later at a lower price. Therefore, the portfolio decision variables are nonnegative. If short selling is allowed, however, the decision variables would be unrestricted. As mentioned in Steinbach (2001), the classical Markowitz model to be introduced next has in this case an analytical solution. Clearly, the set of possible asset allocations is

$$\{\tilde{\mathbf{x}} \in R^n : \tilde{x}_1 + \ldots + \tilde{x}_n = C,\ x_j \geq 0,\ j = 1,\ldots,n\}$$

or equivalently,

$$\{\mathbf{x} \in R^n : x_1 + \cdots + x_n = 1,\ x_j \geq 0,\ j = 1,\ldots,n\}$$

Then, at the end of the investment period, the total value of the portfolio is $C + \tilde{\mathbf{x}}^T\,\mathbf{Y}$; therefore, the loss of the portfolio for the period under consideration is

$$Z(\tilde{\mathbf{x}}) = C - (C + \tilde{\mathbf{x}}^T\,\mathbf{Y}) = -\tilde{\mathbf{x}}^T\mathbf{Y}$$

Let $\boldsymbol{\mu}^T = (\mu_1,\ldots,\mu_n)$, where μ_i denotes the expected return of asset i, i.e., $\mu_i = E[Y_i]$ for $i = 1,\ldots,n$. Then the expected total return (reward) of the portfolio $\tilde{\mathbf{x}}$ is $\tilde{\mathbf{x}}^T\,\boldsymbol{\mu}$.

The problem of choosing between portfolios becomes the problem of choosing between random losses according to a preference relation, which is specified using a risk measure. The mean-risk models have been widely used for portfolio optimization under risk. In these models one uses two criteria: the mean, representing the expected total return or loss of a portfolio, and the risk, which is a scalar measure of the variability of the random total return or loss of the portfolio. Markowitz's mean-variance model (1952, 1959), which uses variance of return as the risk measure, has been one of the most widely used mean-risk models for the portfolio selection problem. However, as mentioned in the previous section, the model has several disadvantages such as equally treating overperformance as underperformance. Markowitz (1959) also recommends using semivariance rather than variance as risk measure, but even in this case significant deficiencies remain as mentioned in, e.g., Ogryczak and Ruszczyński (2002). In particular, here we use VaR and CVaR as risk measures.

There are alternative approaches to implement a mean-risk model. For example, one approach is based on the model constructing a portfolio with minimum risk, provided that a desired level of expected return of the portfolio is attained (by enforcing a lower bound on the expected total return of the portfolio). Another approach is based on the problem formulated in the form of Equation (15.2), in which the preference relation is defined using a trade-off between the mean (reward) and risk, where a larger value of mean (reward) and a smaller value of risk are preferable. In many applications, the trade-off coefficient does not provide a clear understanding of the decision makers' preferences. The commonly accepted approach to implement a mean-risk model is to minimize the risk of the random outcome while enforcing a specified lower bound on the total expected return [see, e.g., Mansini et al. (2003)]. We also prefer to use this widely accepted bounding approach. Thus, among alternative formulations of the mean-variance Markowitz model, we consider the formulation constructing a portfolio with minimal risk provided that a prescribed expected return level w is attained:

$$\min\left\{\rho(-\tilde{\mathbf{x}}^T \mathbf{Y}) : \mathbf{e}^T \tilde{\mathbf{x}} = C, \tilde{\mathbf{x}}^T \boldsymbol{\mu} = w, \tilde{\mathbf{x}} \geq \mathbf{0}\right\}$$

Notice that $\rho(-\tilde{\mathbf{x}}^T \mathbf{Y})$ is the risk of the portfolio represented by $\tilde{\mathbf{x}}$.

With the use of the decision vector $\mathbf{x}$ representing the fractions of the capital invested in each asset, we obtain an equivalent optimization problem:

$$\min\{\rho(-C\mathbf{x}^T \mathbf{Y}) : \mathbf{e}^T \mathbf{x} = 1, \mathbf{x}^T \boldsymbol{\mu} = wC^{-1}, \mathbf{x} \geq \mathbf{0}\} \qquad (15.8)$$

Suppose that $C + w = (1 + r)C$ where r is the desired rate of the return of the portfolio. When the specified risk measure is positive homogeneous, Equation (15.8) takes the form of

$$\min\{\rho(-\mathbf{x}^T \mathbf{Y}) : \mathbf{e}^T \mathbf{x} = 1, \mathbf{x}^T \boldsymbol{\mu} = r, \mathbf{x} \geq \mathbf{0}\} \qquad (Q)$$

If we also consider a nonrisky asset characterized by a known return r_0 that usually reflects the interest rate on the money market, this asset would generate a return of $r_0 x_0$ at the end of the period, where x_0 denotes the fraction of the capital invested in the nonrisky asset and C the total capital available. In this case, we obtain the following optimization problem:

$$\min\{\rho(-\mathbf{x}^T \mathbf{Y}) : \mathbf{e}^T \mathbf{x} + x_0 = 1, \mathbf{x}^T \boldsymbol{\mu} + r_0 x_0 = r, \mathbf{x} \geq \mathbf{0}, x_0 \geq 0\}$$

In the above portfolio selection problems, no transaction costs are involved. Nonetheless, if the transaction costs are linear functions in terms of the decision vectors, we have similar formulations and our subsequent discussion still applies.

In our work, we use the class of multivariate elliptical distributions to model the random returns. This general class of multivariate distributions contains both (multivariate) normal and t-distributions. The most popular approach for modeling (short term) changes in portfolio value is the analytical variance–covariance approach popularized by RiskMetrics Group (1997). This method assumes that the vector of rate of returns is multivariate normal. However, there is a considerable amount of evidence that empirical rate of returns over a short horizon have heavier tails than given by the multivariate normal distribution. For example, Fama (1965) and Mandelbrot (1963) show through empirical studies on real stock portfolios that the distribution of returns can be distinguished from the normal distribution. Recent studies by Embrechts et al. (2002), Glasserman et al. (2002) and Huisman et al. (1998) also support this theory. Heavy tails imply that extreme losses are more likely to occur. Thus, if a risk measure based on the tail of the loss distribution, such as VaR, is used to optimize the portfolio, we underestimate the actual risk under a normality assumption. To overcome the problem of heavy tails, several alternative distributions for rates of returns are offered. One of the strongest is the multivariate t-distribution which belongs to the class of elliptical distributions. Empirical support on modeling univariate rate of returns with a t-distribution can be found in Huisman et al. (1998), Praetz (1972), Glasserman et al. (2002), and Blattberg and Gonedes (1974). The multivariate t-distribution is fully characterized by the mean μ, the covariance matrix Σ and an additional parameter called the degree of freedom v to control the heaviness of the tail. As v goes to infinity, the multivariate t-distribution approaches the multivariate normal distribution. According to Crouhy et al. (2001) and Glasserman et al. (2002), the values of parameter v for most of the rate of returns are between 3 and 8 — in fact, usually around 4. However, a shortcoming of the multivariate t-distribution is that all the risk factors in the portfolio have the same degrees of freedom. As suggested by Glasserman et al. (2002) to overcome this shortcoming, copulas can be used with different v values for each rate of return. The other candidate for a multivariate distribution of the rates of returns is the family of multivariate stable distributions [see Feller (1971)] for a discussion of univariate stable distributions). The comparison of stable distributions with a t-distribution and the normal distribution can be found in Blattberg and Gonedes (1974) and Praetz (1972).

The class of elliptical distributions within the context of risk management has been studied by Embrechts et al. (2002) and Sadefo-Kamdem (2005). On one hand, both papers concentrate on measuring VaR and CVaR measures. On the other hand, they do not include a discussion on portfolio optimization. In this chapter, we explicitly focus on constructing the optimal portfolios. We next briefly discuss the properties of elliptical distributions.

ELLIPTICAL WORLD

To analyze our general risk model for portfolio management, we first introduce the following class of multivariate distributions [see also Embrechts et al. (2002) and Fang et al. (1990)]. Recall a linear mapping is called *orthogonal* if $U^{\mathrm{T}} U = U U^{\mathrm{T}} = I$. We also use the notation $\mathbf{X} : F$, meaning the random vector $\mathbf{X}$ has the joint distribution function F.

Definition 15.2. A random vector $\mathbf{X} = (X_1, \ldots, X_n)^{\mathrm{T}}$ has a *spherical distribution* if for any orthogonal mapping $U : \mathrm{R}^n \rightarrow \mathrm{R}^n$, it holds that

$$U\mathbf{X} =^d \mathbf{X}$$

It is well known that $\mathbf{X} \sim N(\mathbf{0}, I)$ has a spherical distribution, where $N(\mu, \Sigma)$ denotes the multivariate normal distribution with mean μ and covariance matrix Σ. Since $U = -I$ is an orthogonal mapping we obtain for $\mathbf{X}$ having a spherical distribution that

$$-\mathbf{X} =^d \mathbf{X} \tag{15.9}$$

Hence, if a spherically distributed random vector $\mathbf{X}$ has a finite expectation, its expected value equals 0. It can be easily shown using the above definition [see Fang et al. (1990)] that the random vector $\mathbf{X} = (X_1, \ldots, X_n)^{\mathrm{T}}$ has a spherical distribution if and only if there exists some real-valued function $\phi : \mathrm{R}_+ \rightarrow \mathrm{R}$ such that the characteristic function $\psi(\mathbf{t}) := E[\exp(i\mathbf{t}^{\mathrm{T}} \mathbf{X})]$ is given by

$$\psi(\mathbf{t}) = \phi(\|\mathbf{t}\|^2) \tag{15.10}$$

This representation, based on the characteristic function, provides us with an alternative definition of a spherically distribution random vector. It is easy to show [see Fang et al. (1990)] for any spherically distributed random vector $\mathbf{X}$, there exists some nonnegative random variable R such that

$$\mathbf{X} = {}^d R \mathbf{U}^{(n)} \tag{15.11}$$

where R is independent of the random vector $\mathbf{U}^{(n)}$ that is uniformly distributed on the unit sphere surface $S_n = \{\mathbf{x} \in R^n : \mathbf{x}^T \mathbf{x} = 1\}$. The alternative representation Equation (15.12) will be useful for the computation of the covariance matrix for an elliptically distributed random variable. As mentioned before, an important member of the class of spherical distributions is the standard multivariate normal distribution $N(\mathbf{0}, \mathbf{I})$ with mean $\mathbf{0}$ and covariance matrix I. For this distribution, the generating random variable R in Equation (15.11) has a chi distribution χ_n with n degrees of freedom. Another important member is the standard multivariate t-distribution with v degrees of freedom. In this case $R^2 n^{-1}$ has a $F(n,v)$ t-distribution with n and v degrees of freedom. As stated by Fang et al. (1990) an important proper subclass of the elliptical distributions is the so-called class of scale mixtures of multivariate normal distributions. The random vector associated with such a scale mixture is given by $\mathbf{X} = S\mathbf{V}$, where $\mathbf{V} \sim N(\mathbf{0}, \mathbf{I})$ and S is a real-valued random variable, which is independent of $\mathbf{V}$. The already introduced standard multivariate t-distribution with v degrees of freedom belongs to this class. For this distribution, the random variable $v^{1/2} S$ has a chi distribution χ_v with v degrees of freedom. This representation will be useful in our computational section. From the representation of the characteristic function we immediately obtain for all $t \in R$ and $1 \le j \le n$ that

$$E[\exp(itX_j)] = \phi(t^2) \tag{15.12}$$

This confirms [see also relation (15.9)] that $-X_1 = {}^d X_1$.

Using the characteristic function representation of a spherical distribution, another useful description can also be derived. For completeness, here a short proof is presented [see also Fang et al. (1990)].

Lemma 15.2. *The random vector* $\mathbf{X} = (X_1, \ldots, X_n)^T$ *has a spherical distribution if and only if* $\mathbf{a}^T \mathbf{X} = {}^d\|\mathbf{a}\| X_1$ *for all* $\mathbf{a} \in \mathbb{R}^n$.

Proof: If the random vector $\mathbf{X}$ has a spherical distribution, then by Equation (15.10) there exists some function $\phi : \mathbb{R}_+ \to \mathbb{R}$ such that $E[\exp(i\mathbf{a}^T \mathbf{X})] = \phi(\|\mathbf{a}\|^2)$ for all $\mathbf{a} \in \mathbb{R}^n$. Hence, for all $t \in \mathbb{R}$ and $\mathbf{a} \in \mathbb{R}^n$ it follows by (15.12) that

$$E[\exp(it\mathbf{a}^T \mathbf{X})] = \varphi(\|t\mathbf{a}\|^2) = E[\exp(it\|\mathbf{a}\| X_1)]$$

By using the one to one correspondence between the characteristic function and the cumulative distribution function of the associated random variable [see Feller, (1971)], we obtain $\mathbf{a}^T \mathbf{X} = {}^d\|\mathbf{a}\| X_1$. To prove the reverse implication we observe that

$$E[\exp(it\mathbf{a}^T \mathbf{X})] = E[exp(i\|\mathbf{a}\|X_1)] \qquad (15.13)$$

This implies for all $\mathbf{a} \in \mathbb{R}^n$ that $E[\exp(-i\mathbf{a}^T \mathbf{X})] = E[\exp(i\mathbf{a}^T \mathbf{X})]$, and so the function $\mathbf{a} \mapsto E[\exp(i\mathbf{a}^T \mathbf{X})]$ is real-valued. Hence, by Equation (15.13), the function $\mathbf{a} \mapsto E[\exp(i\|\mathbf{a}\|X_1)]$ is also real-valued. Introducing $\phi : \mathbb{R}_+ \mapsto \mathbb{R}$ given by $\phi(t) := E[\exp(i\sqrt{t}\, X_1)]$, it follows again by Equation (15.13) that $E[\exp(i\mathbf{a}^T \mathbf{X})] = \phi(\|\mathbf{a}\|^2)$. It follows from the representation Equation (15.11) that $\mathbf{X}$ has a spherical distribution.

A class of distributions related to spherical distributions is given by the following definition (Embrechts et al., 2002; Fang et al., 1990).

Definition 15.3. A random vector $\mathbf{Y} = (Y_1, \ldots, Y_n)^T$ has an *elliptical distribution* if there exists an affine mapping $\mathbf{x} \mapsto A\mathbf{x} + \mu$ and a random vector $\mathbf{X} = (X_1, \ldots, X_n)^T$ having a spherical distribution such that $\mathbf{Y} = A\mathbf{X} + \mu$.

For convenience, an elliptical distributed n-dimensional random vector $\mathbf{Y}$ is denoted by $(A, \mu, \mathbf{X})$, where $\mathbf{X} = (X_1, \ldots, X_n)^T$. It is now possible to show the following result.

Lemma 15.3. *If the random vector* $\mathbf{Y}$ *has an elliptical distribution with representation* $(A, \mu, \mathbf{X})$ *then* $\mathbf{x}^T \mathbf{Y} = {}^d\|A^T \mathbf{x}\|X_1 + \mathbf{x}^T \mu$ *for all portfolio vectors* $\mathbf{x} \in \mathbb{R}^n$. *Moreover, the parameters of the spherical (marginal) distribution of the random variable* X_1 *are independent of* $\mathbf{x}$.

Proof: Since the elliptical distributed random vector $\mathbf{Y}$ has representation $(A, \mu, \mathbf{X})$ and $\mathbf{X}$ has a spherical distribution, it follows that $\mathbf{x}^T \mathbf{Y} = \mathbf{x}^T A\mathbf{X} + \mathbf{x}^T \mu$. Applying Lemma 15.2 with $\mathbf{a} = A^T \mathbf{x}$ yields the desired result.

To compute the covariance matrix Σ of the random vector $\mathbf{Y}$ having an elliptical distribution with representation $(A, \mu, \mathbf{X})$ we first observe that $\Sigma = Cov\,(\mathbf{Y}, \mathbf{Y}) = Cov\,(A\mathbf{X} + \mu, A\mathbf{X} + \mu) = ACov\,(\mathbf{X}, \mathbf{X})\, A^T$. Moreover, since $\mathbf{X}$ has a spherical distribution it follows by Equation (15.11) that there exists some nonnegative random variable R satisfying $\mathbf{X} = {}^d R\mathbf{U}^{(n)}$ and independent of $\mathbf{U}^{(n)}$. This implies that $Cov(\mathbf{X}, \mathbf{X}) = n^{-1} E[R^2]\mathbf{I}$ and hence with $c = E[\mathbf{R}^2]/n > 0$ we obtain that

$$\Sigma = cAA^T \tag{15.14}$$

Recall that for the vector of one period (short term) returns, $\mathbf{Y}$, the loss of the constructed portfolio is given by $- C\mathbf{x}^T\mathbf{Y}$. Therefore, we need to specify and evaluate a risk measure associated with this random loss. One can now show the following important result for a random vector $\mathbf{Y}$ having an elliptical distribution.

Lemma 15.4. *If $\mathbf{Y}$ has an elliptical distribution with covariance matrix Σ and representation $(A, \mu, \mathbf{X})$ and the considered risk measure ρ is positive homogeneous, translation invariant and $\rho(X_1) > 0$, then for any two nonzero portfolio vectors $\mathbf{x}_1$ and $\mathbf{x}_2$ satisfying, $\mathbf{x}_1^T \mu = \mathbf{x}_2^T\mu$, we have $\rho(-\mathbf{x}_1^T \mathbf{Y}) \leqslant \rho(-\mathbf{x}_2^T\mathbf{Y}) \Leftrightarrow \mathbf{x}_1^T \Sigma\mathbf{x}_1 \leqslant \mathbf{x}_2^T \Sigma\mathbf{x}_2.$*

Proof: Since ρ is translation invariant and $\mathbf{x}_1^T \mu = \mathbf{x}_2^T\mu$, we obtain by Lemma 15.3 that

$$\rho(-\mathbf{x}_1^T \mathbf{Y}) \leqslant \rho(- \mathbf{x}_2^T \mathbf{Y}) \Leftrightarrow \rho(\|A^T \mathbf{x}_1\|X_1) \leqslant \rho(\|A^T \mathbf{x}_2\|X_1) \tag{15.15}$$

Then by the positive homogeneity of ρ and $\rho(X_1) > 0$, we have

$$\rho(\|A^T \mathbf{x}_1\|X_1) \leqslant \rho(\|A^T \mathbf{x}_2\|X_1) \Leftrightarrow \|A^T \mathbf{x}_1\| \leqslant \|A^T \mathbf{x}_2\|$$

$$\Leftrightarrow \mathbf{x}_1^T AA^T\mathbf{x}_1 \leqslant \mathbf{x}_2{}^T AA^T \mathbf{x}_2 \tag{15.16}$$

Relations (15.14) to (15.16) and $c = E[\mathbf{R}^2]/n > 0$ yield the desired result.

As mentioned before, both CVaR and VaR satisfy the assumptions of Lemma 15.4. Therefore, for these important risk measures the portfolio optimization problem (Q) reduces to a mean-variance Markowitz model

$$\min \{\mathbf{x}^T \Sigma \mathbf{x} \mid \mathbf{e}^T \mathbf{x} = 1, \mu^T \mathbf{x} = r, \mathbf{x} \geq \mathbf{0}\} \qquad \text{(MP-Q)}$$

Both problems construct the same optimal portfolio. When $\alpha > 1/2$ implying $\text{VaR}_\alpha (X_1) > 0$, it follows from Lemma 15.4 that for the portfolio loss $-C\mathbf{x}^T \mathbf{Y}$, we obtain

$$\text{VaR}_\alpha (-C\mathbf{x}^T \mathbf{Y}) = C(\text{VaR}_\alpha (-\mathbf{x}^T \mathbf{Y})) = C(\| A^T \mathbf{x} \| \text{VaR}_\alpha (X_1) - \mathbf{x}^T \mu) \quad (15.17)$$

and

$$\text{CVaR}_\alpha (-C\mathbf{x}^T \mathbf{Y}) = C(\| A^T \mathbf{x} \| \text{CVaR}_a (X_1) - \mathbf{x}^T \mu) \qquad (15.18)$$

MODIFIED MICHELOT ALGORITHM

The algorithm introduced by Michelot in 1986 finds in finite steps the projection of a given vector onto a special polytope. The main idea of this algorithm is to use the analytic solutions of a sequence of projections onto canonical simplices and elementary cones. The discussion in Michelot's paper is applicable when the objective function in problem (MP-Q) is perfect quadratic; that is, the covariance matrix Σ is the identity matrix. Unfortunately, the algorithm in Michelot's paper is not clear and difficult to follow. Our next step is to follow the main steps in Michelot's paper and apply necessary modification to solve

$$\min \{\mathbf{x}^T \Sigma \mathbf{x} \mid \mathbf{e}^T \mathbf{x} = 1, \mu^T \mathbf{x} = r, \mathbf{x} \geq \mathbf{0}\} \qquad (15.19)$$

To modify Michelot's algorithm according to our problem, we need to introduce several sets. Let $D = \{\mathbf{x} \in \mathbb{R}^n \mid \mathbf{e}^T \mathbf{x} = 1, \mu^T \mathbf{x} = r\}, \chi_I = \{\mathbf{x} \in \mathbb{R}^n \mid x_i = 0, i \in I\}$, and $D_I = D \cap \chi_I$, where $I \subseteq \{1, 2, ..., n\}$ denotes an index set. Algorithm 15.1 gives the steps of the Modified Michelot Algorithm. The algorithm starts with obtaining the optimal solution of the following quadratic programming problem:

$$P_D := \text{argmin} \{\mathbf{x}^T \Sigma \mathbf{x} : \mathbf{x} \in v\} \qquad (15.20)$$

Naturally, some of the components x_i may be negative; otherwise, the solution is optimal. After identifying the most negative component and initializing the index set I, the algorithm iterates between projections of the incumbent solution $\bar{\mathbf{x}}$ onto subspace χ_I, and then onto subspace D_I until none of the components are negative; i.e., the solution is optimal. The first projection is denoted by

$$P_{x_I}(\bar{\mathbf{x}}) := \operatorname{argmin}\{(\bar{\mathbf{x}}-\mathbf{x})^T \Sigma(\bar{\mathbf{x}}-\mathbf{x}): \mathbf{x} \in \chi_I\} \qquad (15.21)$$

Similarly, the second projection is given by

$$P_{D_I}(\bar{\mathbf{x}}) := \operatorname{argmin}\{(\bar{\mathbf{x}}-\mathbf{x})^T \Sigma(\bar{\mathbf{x}}-\mathbf{x}): \mathbf{x} \in D_I\} \qquad (15.22)$$

At every iteration one index is added to set I. Since we have a finite number of assets, the modified algorithm terminates within at most n iterations [see also Michelot (1986)].

Notice that all three problems (15.20) to (15.22), are equality constrained quadratic programming (QP) problems. Therefore, we consider a general equality constrained QP problem given by

$$\min \{(\bar{\mathbf{x}} - \mathbf{x})^T \Sigma(\bar{\mathbf{x}} - \mathbf{x}): T\mathbf{x} = \mathbf{b}\}$$

where T is an $m \times n$ matrix and $\mathbf{b} \in R^m$. It is easy to show (Bertsekas, 1999) that this general problem has the optimal solution

$$\bar{\mathbf{x}} - \Sigma^{-1} T^{\mathrm{T}} (T\Sigma^{-1} T^{\mathrm{T}})^{-1} (T\bar{\mathbf{x}}-b) \qquad (15.23)$$

A L G O R I T H M   15.1

Modified Michelot algorithm

```
 1: Input Σ, μ, r, I = ∅.
 2: Set x̄ ← P_D.
 3: if x̄ ⩾ 0 then
 4:    Stop; x̄ is optimal.
 5: else
 6:    Select i with most negative x̄ᵢ.
 7:    Set I ← i.
 8:    while x̄ < 0 do
 9:       Set x̄ ← P_{χ_I}(x̄).
10:       Set x̄ ← P_{D_I}(x̄).
11:       if x̄ ⩾ 0 then
12:          Stop; x̄ is optimal.
13:       else
14:          Select i with most negative x̄ᵢ.
15:          Set I ← I ∪ i.
```

The matrix inversions in Equation (15.23) constitute the main computational burden of Algorithm 15.1, since these inversions are required at every iteration. In line 2 of Algorithm 15.1, we need to find P_D. To use relation (15.23), we set $T = [\mathbf{e}\ \mu]^T$ and $\mathbf{b} = [1\ r]^T$. These relations imply that we should compute the inverse of $n \times n$ matrix Σ as well as the inverse of 2×2 symmetric matrix

$$K := \begin{bmatrix} \mathbf{e}^T \Sigma^{-1} \mathbf{e} & \mathbf{e}^T \Sigma^{-1} \mu \\ \mu^T \Sigma^{-1} \mathbf{e} & \mu^T \Sigma^{-1} \mu \end{bmatrix}$$

Luckily, the blockwise inverse method (Lancaster, 1985) allows us to complete Algorithm 15.1 by only these two matrix inversions because at every subsequent iteration, only one index is added to set I. For example, if we denote the ith unit vector by $\mathbf{u}_i$, the first time the algorithm reaches line 10, we set $T = [\mathbf{e}\ \mu\ \mathbf{u}_i]^T$ and $\mathbf{b} = [1\ r\ 0]^T$ in relation (15.23). Therefore, we need to compute the inverse of a 3×3 symmetric matrix given by

$$\begin{bmatrix} K & \mathbf{v} \\ \mathbf{v}^T & c_0 \end{bmatrix} := \begin{bmatrix} \mathbf{e}^T \Sigma^{-1} \mathbf{e} & \mathbf{e}^T \Sigma^{-1} \mu & \mathbf{e}^T \Sigma^{-1} \mathbf{u}_i \\ \mu^T \Sigma^{-1} \mathbf{e} & \mu^T \Sigma^{-1} \mu & \mu^T \Sigma^{-1} \mathbf{u}_i \\ \mathbf{e}^T \Sigma^{-1} \mathbf{u}_i & \mu^T \Sigma^{-1} \mathbf{u}_i & \mathbf{u}_i^T \Sigma^{-1} \mathbf{u}_i \end{bmatrix}$$

Now using the blockwise inverse method yields

$$\begin{bmatrix} K & \mathbf{v} \\ \mathbf{v}^T & c_0 \end{bmatrix}^{-1} = \begin{bmatrix} K^{-1} + c_1 K^{-1} \mathbf{v} \mathbf{v}^T K^{-1} & -c_1 K^{-1} \mathbf{v} \\ -c_1 \mathbf{v}^T K^{-1} & c_1 \end{bmatrix}$$

where $c_1 := 1/(c_0 - \mathbf{v}^T K^{-1} \mathbf{v})$. Since we already computed K^{-1}, the new inverse can be obtained without any matrix inversion. Moreover, the vector $\mathbf{v}$ and the scalar c_0 can be computed fast without any matrix multiplications, since the unit vector $\mathbf{u}$, is involved in their computations (for example, c_0 is simply the ith diagonal component of Σ^{-1}). One can derive similar results for the projection in line 9 of Algorithm 15.1, since T grows again by one unit vector at each iteration and $\mathbf{b}$ is simply the zero vector.

COMPUTATIONAL RESULTS

To analyze the performance of Algorithm 15.1, MATLAB has been our testing environment. All the computational experiments are conducted on an Intel Core 2, 2.00 GHz personal computer running Windows. First, we have randomly generated a set of test problems for different numbers of assets (n) as follows:

- The components of $n \times n$ matrix $\Sigma^{-1/2}$ are sampled uniformly from interval $(-2.5, 5)$.
- The components of vector μ are sampled uniformly from interval $(0.01, 0.50)$, and the first two components are sorted in ascending order; i.e., $\mu_1 \leq \mu_2$.
- To ensure feasibility, the value r is then sampled uniformly from interval (μ_1, μ_2).
- For each value of n, 10 replications are generated.

Clearly, problem (MP-Q) can be solved by any quadratic programming solver. In MATLAB, the procedure that solves these types of problems is called *quadprog*, which is also used in the financial toolbox. Therefore, to compare the proposed algorithm, we also solved the set of problems with *quadprog*. Table 15.1 shows the statistics of the computation times out of 10 replications. The second and third columns in Table 15.1 indicate averages and standard deviations of the computation times obtained by Algorithm 15.1, respectively. Similarly, columns four and five give the average and the standard deviation of the computation times found by *quadprog*, respectively.

The average computational times in Table 15.1 demonstrate that Modified Michelot Algorithm is several times faster than is the MATLAB procedure *quadprog*. However, it is important to note that the MATLAB procedure *quadprog* involves many error checks that may also be the cause of higher computation times. The standard deviation figures in Table 15.1 do not yield a clear conclusion when we compare Algorithm 15.1 and *quadprog*. Nevertheless, Algorithm 15.1 still performs better than does *quadprog* in most of the problems. Overall, these results allow us to claim that Modified Michelot Algorithm is a fast and finite step alternative for solving (MP-Q).

T A B L E   15.1

Computation time statistics of *quadprog* and Algorithm 15.1
in seconds

	Algorithm 15.1		Quadprog	
n	Average	Std. Dev.	Average	Std. Dev.
25	0.0030	0.0063	0.0173	0.0048
50	0.0111	0.0077	0.0451	0.0139
100	0.0548	0.0341	0.2783	0.0829
200	0.5672	0.4480	2.0345	0.5530
400	7.7626	6.4093	32.6268	10.6788
500	19.4047	10.3963	87.0015	23.8663
750	126.8378	92.6268	353.1186	71.8344
1000	378.5811	319.0916	1129.4000	251.4301

As we presented in this chapter's fifth section, the Modified
Michelot Algorithm takes at most n steps. In Table 15.2, we report some
summary statistics regarding the number of iterations required to solve the
problem instances. These figures show that the number of iterations to
solve a problem takes, on average, half of the problem dimension (n).

T A B L E   15.2

Number of iterations statistics of *quadprog* and
Algorithm 15.1

n	Average	Std. Dev.
25	12.1000	3.1429
50	24.0000	8.4853
100	47.4400	17.1995
200	95.4000	39.5058
400	189.5000	65.8707
500	247.8000	63.6375
750	413.1000	159.4926
1000	534.4000	236.9844

An illustrative example explains the intuitive idea behind the optimal objective function values in Equations (15.17) and (15.18). We use the same portfolio optimization example given in Rockafellar and Uryasev (2000) that involves three instruments. The rates of returns on these instruments have multivariate normal distribution, which simplifies the procedure to calculate the optimal objective function values. The mean return vector (in percentage terms) and the covariance matrix are given as $\mu^T = (0.01001110, 0.0043532, 0.0137058)$ and

$$\Sigma = \begin{bmatrix} 0.00324625 & 0.00022983 & 0.00420395 \\ 0.00022983 & 0.00049937 & 0.00019247 \\ 0.00420395 & 0.00019247 & 0.00764097 \end{bmatrix}$$

respectively. The expected return r is equal to 0.011. Assume that our budget C is 1,000 at the beginning of the investment period. We first solve the portfolio problem (15.19) with Algorithm 15.1. We then use Equations (15.17) and (15.18) to obtain the optimal VaR and CVaR values, respectively. Figure 15.1 shows these values against varying α. As expected, CVaR values are always greater than VaR values.

As mentioned in a previous section, the standard multivariate t-distribution with v degrees of freedom (d.f.) belongs to the class of spherical distributions. Therefore, a random vector $\mathbf{X}$ having a standard multivariate t-distribution with v degrees can be represented by $\mathbf{X} = S\mathbf{V}$, where $\mathbf{V} : N(\mathbf{0}, \mathbf{I})$ and S is a real-valued random variable, independent of $\mathbf{V}$. For standard multivariate t-distribution with v degrees of freedom, the random variable $v^{1/2}S$ has a chi distribution χ_v with v degrees of freedom. According to Definition 15.3, we can obtain a (elliptically distributed) random vector Y with a (nonstandard) multivariate t-distribution by applying an affine mapping $\mathbf{x} \rightarrow A\mathbf{x} + \mu$ on the (spherically distributed) random vector X with the standard multivariate t-distribution. Recall Equation 15–18 and 15–19, where in our setup the random variable X_1 has a univariate t-distribution with v degrees of freedom. We have used the MATLAB function *tinv* to calculate $\text{VaR}_\alpha(X_1)$. Using Equation (15.7) and the probability density function of X_1 we obtain

$$\text{CVaR}_\alpha(X_1) = 1/1 - \alpha \, \Gamma(V+1/2)/\sqrt{v\pi} \, \Gamma(v/2) \, v/1 - v$$
$$(-(1+ \text{VaR}_\alpha(X_1)^2/v)^{1-v/2})$$

F I G U R E   15.1

VaR and CVaR Values for the Elementary Example

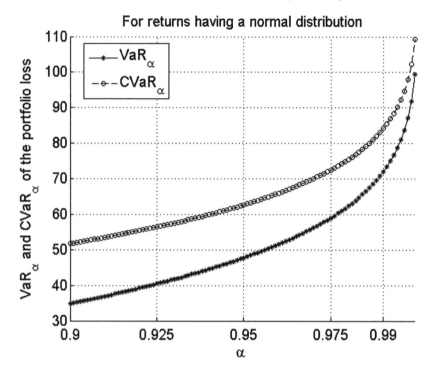

We also consider the same example given in Rockafellar and Uryasev (2000) and provide the optimal VaR and CVaR values of the total portfolio loss for a normal distribution and t-distributions with different degrees of freedom parameters. As mentioned at the end of this chapter's third section, the widely accepted values of degrees of freedom parameter according to the literature are between 3 and 8.

Figure 15.2 shows VaR and CVaR values for different distributions. Clearly, as the degress of freedom parameter v increases, the tail of t-distribution becomes less heavy and hence, approaches to the normal distribution. Therefore, we observe that the differences in VaR [Figure 15.2(a)] and CVaR [Figure 15.2(b)] values between t and the normal distributions diminish.

Figure 15.3 illustrates the difference between VaR and CVaR values for a normal distribution and a particular t-distribution ($v = 4$). As it can

F I G U R E   15.2

Risk Values for Returns having Normal Distribution and
t-Distribution with Different Degrees of Freedom

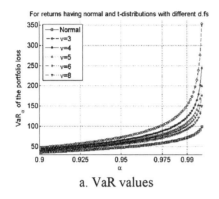

a. VaR values

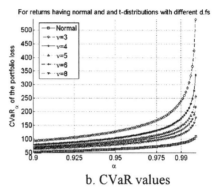

b. CVaR values

F I G U R E   15.3

Comparison of VaR and CVaR values for Different Distributions

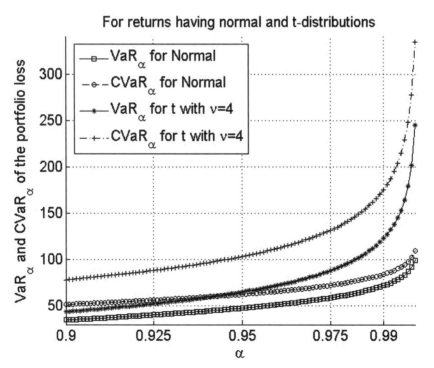

be seen from the figure, VaR and CVaR values are closer to each other for the normal distribution than the t-distribution. This is an expected observation, since a t-distribution has a heavier tail than a normal distribution.

CONCLUSION

In this chapter we first discuss general risk measures and then concentrate on two recent ones, VaR and CVaR. Then we shift our focus to efficiently construct optimal portfolios, where the returns have elliptical distributions and either VaR or CVaR can be used as the risk measure. It is well known that optimization problems, which are in the form of (Q) with VaR or CVaR as the risk measure, are equivalent to the mean-variance Markowitz model in the form of (MP-Q). In fact we discuss this equivalence holds for a larger class of positive homogeneous and translation invariant risk measures. To solve the resulting special quadratic programming problem, we modify a finite step algorithm from the literature and provide some computational results. To the best of our knowledge, portfolio management literature lacks numerical examples where the returns have distributions other than the normal distribution. Therefore, in addition to the numerical results for normal returns, we also provide results for returns that have multivariate t-distributions.

REFERENCES

Artzner, P., F. Delbaen, J.M. Eber, and D. Heath (1999) Coherent Measures of Risk. *Mathematical Finance*, 9(3): 203–228.

Bertsekas, D.P. (1999) *Nonlinear Programming,* 2nd edition. Belmont, CA: Athena Scientific.

Blattberg, R.C. and N.J. Gonedes (1974) A Comparison of the Stable and Student-t-distributions as Statistical Models for Stock Prices. *Journal of Business*, 47(2): 244–280.

Crouhy, M., D. Galai, and R. Mark (2001) *Risk Management*: New York: McGraw-Hill.

Embrechts, P., A. McNeil, and D. Straumann (2002) Correlation and Dependence in Risk Management: Properties and Pittfals.

In M.A.H. Dempster (ed.), *Risk Value Managemant at Risk and Beyond*. Cambridge: Cambridge University Press.

Fama, E.F. (1965) The Behavior of Stock Market Prices. *Journal of Business*, 38(1): 34–105.

Fang, K.T, S. Kotz, and K.W. Ng (1990) *Symmetric Multivariate and Related Distributions*. New York: Chapman & Hall.

Feller, W. (1971) *An Introduction to Probability Theory and Its Applications,* 2nd edition. New York: Wiley.

Glasserman, P., P. Heidelberger, and P. Shahabuddin (2002) Portfolio Value-at-Risk with Heavy Tailed Risk Factors. *Mathematical Finance*, 12(3): 239–269.

Huisman, R., K.G. Koedijk, and R.A.G. Pownall (1998) VaR-x: Fat Tails in Financial Risk Management. *Journal of Risk*, 1(1): 47–62.

Lancaster P. and M. Tismenetsky (1985) *The Theory of Matrices.* San Francisco, CA: Academic Press.

Mandelbrot, B. (1963) The Variations of Certain Speculative Prices. *Journal of Business*, 36(4): 394–419.

Mansini, R., W. Ogryczak, and M.G. Speranza (2003) LP Solvable Models for Portfolio Optimization: A Classification and Computational Comparison. *IMA Journal of Management Mathematics*, 14(3): 187–220.

Markowitz, H. (1952) Portfolio Selection. *Journal of Finance*, 7(1): 77–91.

Markowitz, H.M. (1959) *Portfolio Selection*. New York: John Wiley & Sons.

Michelot, C. (1986) A Finite Algorithm for Finding the Projection of a Point onto the Canonical Simplex of R^n. *Journal of Optimization Theory and Applications,* 50(1): 195–200.

Ogryczak, W. and A. Ruszczyński (2002) Dual Stochastic Dominance and Related Mean-Risks Models. *SIAM Journal of Optimization*, 13(2): 60–78.

Pflug, G. (2000) Some Remarks on the Value-at-Risk and the Conditional Value-at-Risk. In S. Uryasev (ed.), *Probabilistic Constrained Optimization: Methodology and Applications*. Dordrecht: Kluwer Academic Publishers.

Praetz, J. (1972) The Distribution of Share Price Changes. *Journal of Business*, 45(1): 49–55.

RiskMetrics Group (1997) *CreditMetrics Technical Document*. J. P. Morgan Inc., New York. Available at http://www.riskmetrics.com/research.

Rockafellar, R.T. (1972) *Convex Analysis*. Princeton, NJ: Princeton University Press.

Rockafellar, R.T and S. Uryasev (2002) Conditional Value-at-Risk for General Loss Distributions. *Journal of Banking and Finance*, 26(7): 1443–1471.

Rockafellar, R.T, S. Uryasev, and M. Zabarankin (2006) Master Funds in Portfolio Analysis with General Deviation Measures. *Journal of Banking and Finance*, 30(2): 743–778.

Rockafellar, R.T and S. Uryasev (2000) Optimization of Conditional Value-at-Risk. *The Journal of Risk*, 2(3): 21–41.

Ruszczyński, A. and A. Shapiro (2006) Probabilistic and Randomized Methods for Design under Uncertainty. In G. Calafiore and F. Dabbene (ed.), *Optimization of Risk Measures*. London: Springer-Verlag.

Sadefo-Kamdem, J. (2005) Value-at-Risk and Expected Shortfall for Linear Portfolios with Elliptically Distributed Risk Factors. *International Journal of Theoretical and Applied Finance*, 8(5): 537–551.

Steinbach, M.C. (2001) Markowitz Revisited: Mean-Variance Models in Financial Portfolio Analysis. *SIAM Review*, 43(1): 31–85.

CHAPTER 16

Risk Evaluation of Sectors Traded at the ISE with VaR Analysis

Mehmet Orhan and Gökhan Karaahmet

ABSTRACT

In this chapter, we calculate the risks of all sectors traded at the Istanbul Stock Exchange (ISE) with the help of the value at risk (VaR). Our dataset includes daily sector returns from the beginning of 1997 to August 7, 2007. We prefer the historical method of VaR since the Shapiro–Wilk tests revealed that about half of the returns do not follow the normal distribution. We use three major financial crises hitting the Turkish economy in the last decade as benchmark to evaluate the VaR in assessing risk. Furthermore, we make use of VaR to figure out sectors that are most and least risky, particularly at times of economic crises. We use confidence levels of 90, 95, and 99 percent that are most common in the VaR literature.

INTRODUCTION

Value at risk (VaR) is a concept devised to express the market risk faced by investors in a simple and understandable logic. The idea is to state the maximum possible loss over prespecified time interval at certain level of confidence. The time interval, called the holding period, is generally one day, although longer periods such as 10 days are possible. The confidence level is usually 95 or 99 percent. The concept of VaR can be interpreted as the lower quantile of a probability distribution used to represent the loss of a portfolio from the theoretical perspective. One advantage of VaR is expressing risk in terms of a percentage loss, which makes it a unit free measure. Because of its simplicity, VaR has broad applications and it has become one of the standard measures that quantify market risk. While volatility, as a measure of risk, does not distinguish between upward or downward movements, VaR measure always reports the maximum loss. Value-at-risk-based risks are practically used for the purposes of risk management and regulation. For instance, the Basel Committee on Banking Supervision requires financial institutions to determine their capital reserve requirements based on VaR. However, even an insignificant mistake in VaR estimation may lead to erroneous allocation of capital, which in turn can undermine the profitability of financial institutions.

The use of VaR became popular after J.P. Morgan made their Risk Metrics software available to everyone in 1994. Value at risk helps decision makers chose the best risky alternative and figure out the amount of capital required. The main shortcoming of VaR is its ignorance to seldom events that never show up over the time period of the analysis. These rare events should somehow be attributed to the model [see Simons (1996)]. The other shortcoming is the calculation of the net loss boundary once the VaR is exceeded.

There are basically four methods to calculate the VaR with their own assumptions to model the reality or to ease the mathematical derivations:

1. Parametric VaR: In this method, the risk factor returns are assumed to be jointly normally distributed. The VaR of the portfolio can be directly calculated from the volatility and the correlations of risk factors. The data set in hand can easily be used to estimate the parameters of the distribution. For example, the expected value of the return can be measured by the mean of the distribution. The assumption of normality helps convert the time horizons of VaR with the help of the following

formula: $VaR(n) = VaR(1)\sqrt{n}$, where $VaR(n)$ and $VaR(1)$ are the VaR belonging to n-days and one-day horizons, respectively. The conversion over the confidence levels is achieved in a similar fashion as $VaR\{100(1 - \alpha_1)\%\} = VaR\{100(1 - \alpha_2)\%\}$ $F^{-1}(a_2)/F^{-1}(\alpha_1)$, where we convert the confidence level given in $(1 - \alpha_2)$ to $(1 - \alpha_1)$. In this formulation $F^{-1}(\alpha)$ is the critical value of the normal distribution with right tail area α. Indeed, in this method, VaR can be interpreted as the estimation of the quantiles from a statistical point of view.

2. Monte Carlo VaR: As the name implies, this method depends on Monte Carlo simulation. Therefore, it requires effort to code the program and run time to return the VaR. In this method, each scenario first must be modeled to imitate the moves of the market. Then, the losses of the scenarios are computed and sorted out. In the last step, quantiles are stated as the VaRs of the portfolios. Given the effort cost, it is not surprising to see that the Monte Carlo method is preferred for cases with nonlinear returns.

3. Historical VaR: This method makes use of the return data generated in the history of the portfolio and it assumes that the history will regenerate itself. Therefore, histograms of returns are prepared and future returns are directly estimated from these histograms. Historical VaR is a simpler version of the Monte Carlo VaR. There are no assumptions on the distribution and the parameters of the distribution. That is why this method is relatively simpler and more transparent. Historical VaR entails the use of event windows that somehow repeat themselves and periods of six months to two years are common practice (Manganelli and Engle, 2001). The repetition of history in this kind of VaR calculation means that the empirical distribution will be prevailing in coming period windows. This assumption is not realistic and this is the main shortcoming of historical VaR.

4. Delta Gamma VaR: The linearity assumption of the parametric models is sometimes not realistic, and this can be problematic in applications. Linear functions must be replaced with quadratic

ones in this case. As a consequence, the χ^2 distribution must be used instead of the normal distribution.

The selection of the VaR technique to calculate risk is very crucial since different methods lead to different risk figures. For example, Beder (1995) has calculated very different VaR figures when he applied different VaR methodologies to three hypothetical portfolios. One international application of the VaR is the principle announced by the Basel committee that is auditing and controlling the activities of banks in some countries. The committee advises the banks to calculate the amount of capital stock they have to keep in their reserves calculated with the assistance of VaR. The authors suggest tripling the volume of capital calculated by the banks and sometimes more depending on the specific conditions of the countries.

There are numerous applications of VaR in the literature. For example, Jackson et al. (1998) compared the parametric and simulation VaRs. They concluded that the simulation method returned better figures than the parametric VaR. Vlaar (2000) calculated VaR using historical, variance–covariance, and Monte Carlo methods. Jorion (2000) used VaR to estimate the necessary amount of capital in order to support the risk profile. Gencay and Selcuk (2004) examined the relative performances of the VaR models with daily stock markets of nine emerging markets. Similarly, Bao and Saltoglu (2006) investigated the predictive performance of various classes of VaR models in several dimensions. Though not current, a review of VaR literature is provided by Jorion (2000) and Duffie and Pan (1997).

This chapter is original in that it is the first attempt to evaluate the performance of VaR in Turkey, a typical emerging market. We have the losses of sectors that are traded at the ISE at the times of the financial crises. These losses are used as a benchmark to assess VaR in evaluating risk in Turkey. Furthermore, we compare the risks of the sectors with the help of the VaR. The chapter is organized into four main sections, where the first one is devoted to the Introduction. The second section of this chapter compares risks of sectors traded at the ISE after presenting brief information about the ISE. In this chapter's third section, a summary of the recent crises hitting the Turkish economy is provided. The evaluation of the performance of VaR in estimating risk at these crises is also left for this section. Finally, we present concluding remarks in this chapter's final section.

VALUE-AT-RISK COMPARISON OF SECTORS TRADED AT THE ISTANBUL STOCK EXCHANGE (ISE)

Turkey has been experiencing many economic conditions including high and persistent inflation, stagflation, high growth rates, high unemployment rates, and financial crises over the last decade. Thus, one can use the Turkish economy just like an open lab for applied research. Interested readers can utilize the references addressed in the third section, a summary of the recent crises hitting the Turkish economy, if they would like to find out more about the Turkish economy.

Overview of the ISE

The Istanbul Stock Exchange (ISE) became a typical emerging equity market after its inception on January 2, 1986, and it has been growing ever since its inauguration. According to Harris and Kucukozmen (2002), ISE achieved to be the 12th largest emerging market in the world. In 1993, U.S. Securities and Exchange Commission (SEC) made the announcement that the ISE is recognized as a designated offshore securities market. Similarly, the Japan Securities Dealers Association (JSDA) approved the ISE as a convenient foreign investment market for Japanese investors in 1995. The ISE is currently a member of the World Federation of Exchanges (WFE), International Securities Services Association (ISSA), and the European Capital Markets Institute (ECMI).

In Turkey, all kinds of security exchanges must go through the ISE since it is the unique legal market established for such trade. The ISE has the latest hi-tech electronic software and hardware for all kinds of transactions since November 1994. Operations carried at the ISE are transparent to all parties, and the data belonging to these operations are made available through the official website of the ISE (www.ise.org). Foreign traders are enabled to participate in the ISE by a decree passed in 1989. However, the interest of foreign traders in the ISE oscillates due to macroeconomic fluctuations and political instability in Turkey. The index is very sensitive to shocks like economic crises, political instability, and wars in neighboring countries as well as early election decisions.

The Stock Market, Bonds and Bills Market, the International Market, and the Derivatives Market are the four markets of the ISE. There are two sessions for transactions in five days of the week. Trading operations are between 09:30 and 12:00 in the first session and between 14:00 and 16:30 in the second session. Currently, the National Market has about 320 papers belonging to national companies being traded, although the number of firms was 80 at the inauguration of the ISE in 1986. The Istanbul Stock Exchange indexes are updated continuously throughout the transactions, and the return indexes are announced daily at the end of the day. The ISE National–100 Index is the most widely used as the main indicator of the ISE. The other prominent indexes are ISE National–30, ISE National–50, ISE National–100, and the ISE Second National Market Index. The number of firms joining the ISE is much greater than those leaving. The maximum number of initial public offerings (IPOs) in a year was 36 in 2000. The highest returns are from the firms operating under the category of Education, Health, and other Social Service followed by Transportation and Telecommunication.

Value at Risks of the ISE Sectors

In this section we calculate VaRs of the sectors at different points of time. Three of these points belong to the crises experienced by the Turkish economy, and the fourth is when the Turkish economy is functioning well. Very specifically these dates are: 26 August 1998 (1998 crisis), 27 November 2000 (2000 crisis), 16 February 2001 (2001 crisis), and 31 August 2005. We call these dates Cases 1, 2, 3, and 4, respectively. Case 4 is chosen randomly without loss of generality. A few sectors could not be included due to lack of sufficient data. Sectors and the number of firms for each sector are listed in Table 16.1.

We first test for the normality of the sector returns for all cases with the Statistical Package for the Social Sciences (SPSS). Normality is a very crucial assumption since the type of VaR to use depends on the distribution of the returns. We prefer the Shapiro–Wilk test to the Kolmogorov-Smirnov test of normality in SPSS because the sample size we are using is 50. We adopt 5 percent significance level, but returns with p-values close to this level are tolerated as normally distributed. We use the superscript of N* to mean that we

T A B L E   16.1

Sectors included in the VaR analysis

ISE National—Industrials	Abbreviation	No. of Firms
Food, beverage	FOBE	6
Textile, leather	TEXL	17
Wood, paper, printing	WOPP	8
Chemical, petroleum, plastic	CHPP	14
Nonmetal mineral products	NMMP	18
Basic metal	BAME	11
Metal products, machinery	MEPR	14
ISE National—Services		
Electricity	ELEC	3
Transportation	TRAN	2
Tourism	TOUR	1
Wholesale and retail trade	WHRT	5
Telecommunications	TELE	1
ISE National—Financials		
Banking	BANK	14
Insurance	INSU	5
Leasing, factoring	LEFA	5
Holding and investment	HOIN	9
ISE National—Technology		
Information technology	INFO	4

fail to reject the null of normality very strongly and use N to denote that the return data are over the borderline of normality. We could not include TELE and INFO in the normality tests for Cases 1 and 4 due to insufficiency of data over the specified periods. Table 16.2 presents the test results of normality.

We reject the null hypothesis of normality for returns of six sectors for Case 1. Two sectors stand around the borderline since they have p-values between 5 and 10 percent. This means that almost half of the

T A B L E   16.2

Test results of normality

	Case 1		Case 2		Case 3		Case 4	
	SW st	p-value	SW st	p-value	SW st	p-value	SW st	p-value
FOBE	0.91	0.01	0.98	0.73^{N*}	0.92	0.01	0.98	0.74^{N*}
TEXL	0.86	0.01	0.96	0.31^{N*}	0.90	0.01	0.99	0.99^{N*}
WOPP	0.97	0.32^{N*}	0.96	0.27^{N*}	0.92	0.01	0.92	0.01
CHPP	0.94	0.03	0.96	0.15^{N*}	0.94	0.02	0.96	0.30^{N*}
NMPP	0.91	0.01	0.95	0.05^{N}	0.96	0.14^{N*}	0.97	0.31^{N*}
BAME	0.96	0.24^{N*}	0.96	0.14^{N*}	0.87	0.01	0.98	0.62^{N*}
MEPR	0.98	0.67^{N*}	0.95	0.09^{N}	0.88	0.01	0.96	0.25^{N*}
ELEC	0.90	0.01	0.97	0.49^{N*}	0.88	0.01	0.99	0.94^{N*}
TRAN	0.97	0.49^{N*}	0.98	0.70^{N*}	0.92	0.01	0.98	0.67^{N*}
TOUR	0.94	0.02	0.97	0.42^{N*}	0.91	0.01	0.97	0.36^{N*}
WHRT	0.98	0.68^{N}	0.97	0.42^{N*}	0.90	0.01	0.99	0.96^{N*}
TELE	NA	NA	0.95	0.09^{N}	0.91	0.01	0.96	0.20^{N*}
BANK	0.98	0.77^{N*}	0.95	0.04	0.91	0.01	0.97	0.49^{N*}
INSU	0.95	0.06^{N}	0.92	0.01	0.96	0.11^{N*}	0.98	0.58^{N*}
LEFA	0.95	0.08^{N}	0.95	0.08^{N}	0.95	0.08^{N*}	0.88	0.01
HOIN	0.97	0.36^{N*}	0.97	0.36^{N*}	0.97	0.36^{N*}	0.97	0.39^{N*}
INFO	0.96	0.18^{N*}	0.96	0.18^{N*}	0.96	0.18^{N*}	NA	NA

sectors have normally distributed returns and that the remaining half have their own empirical distributions. We fail to reject the normality hypothesis with highest powers for banking (with p-value 77 percent), wholesale and retail trade (with p-value 68 percent), and metal products and machinery (with p-value 67 percent) sectors.

For Case 2, we fail to reject the null hypothesis of normality for 15 out of 17 sectors. The two sectors with nonnormal return distributions are banking and insurance. The decision of normality for NMPP, MEPR, TELE, and LEFA are somehow debatable since the choice of the significance level changes the conclusions of the tests. In general, almost all returns for Case 2 follow the normal distribution.

Twelve out of seventeen sectors for Case 3 have nonnormal distributions. We concluded in the normality of insurance, and leasing and factoring sectors with p-values around 10 percent. We fail to reject the normality of the holding and investment sector with the highest p-value, 36 percent.

Finally, we observe that almost all sector returns for Case 4 are normal. The two exceptions are the wood, paper, and printing and the leasing and factoring sectors. Besides, there are no p-values close to even 10 percent. Indeed, this is expected since returns are normally distributed when economies and financial markets are functioning well.

All in all, normality of sector returns is rejected in 6 out of 16 tests for Case 1, 2 out of 17 tests for Case 2, 12 out of 17 tests for Case 3, and 2 out of 16 tests for Case 4. The histograms for the stock returns of TEXL and WOPP for Case 4 are displayed in Figure 16.1 in order to demonstrate the closeness or otherwise of data to normality. The curves placed over the histograms by SPSS are the best normal curves possible. Apparently, TEXL returns are close to normal, and the null hypothesis of normality is accepted with the very high p-value of 0.99. On the other hand, the histogram for WOPP reveals that the empirical distribution is apparently skewed to the left and the distribution is far from normal. The null hypothesis claiming normality is rejected safely with the p-value of 1 percent.

Overall, results reveal that we cannot assume normality of the return data for all sectors at all periods. Therefore, the use of parametric VaR is not convenient for our study, and we prefer to use the historical VaR,

F I G U R E   16.1

Histograms of Stock Returns

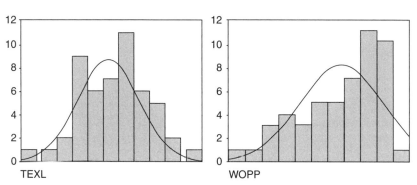

which is relatively easy to compute and interpret. We present the VaR figures of sector returns for 1998 and 2000 crisis in Table 16.3. The confidence levels are 90, 95, and 99 percent.

According to Case 1 VaR figures, ELEC and INSU are the most risky sectors followed by BAME, TOUR, INFO, TEXL, and CHPP. All sectors of industry, service, finance, and technology have high risks, and the daily risk is not below 7 percent even for the least risky sectors of NMMP and WHRT. These comments are for 99 percent confidence level, which means almost certain of return losses. Similar comments apply for lower confidence levels with lower VaRs.

For Case 2, TELE is the far more risky sector than the others. ELEC, TOUR, INSU, and TEXL constitute the next risky group. The least

T A B L E   16.3

Value at risk figures of sector returns at 1998 and 2000 crises

	Case 1			Case 2		
	99%	95%	90%	99%	95%	90%
FOBE	−8.45	−7.34	−3.62	−6.10	−4.33	−3.21
TEXL	−10.66	−8.09	−3.69	−7.33	−4.80	−3.84
WOPP	−7.68	−6.56	−5.75	−6.15	−4.34	−3.70
CHPP	−10.41	−7.17	−5.12	−4.62	−3.91	−3.67
NMMP	−7.12	−6.14	−4.75	−5.24	−3.85	−2.82
BAME	−11.09	−8.20	−6.33	−5.24	−4.03	−3.55
MEPR	−8.44	−5.40	−4.93	−4.48	−3.99	−2.86
ELEC	−14.33	−9.56	−5.72	−10.25	−5.83	−4.96
TRAN	−8.50	−6.66	−4.61	−6.23	−4.37	−3.34
TOUR	−10.92	−9.61	−6.81	−9.11	−6.07	−4.25
WHRT	−7.04	−5.63	−4.45	−5.07	−4.51	−3.41
TELE	NA	NA	NA	−12.12	−7.83	−6.67
BANK	−8.20	−7.46	−4.91	−5.54	−4.34	−3.91
INSU	−12.75	−7.21	−4.75	−7.56	−4.28	−3.12
LEFA	−9.83	−8.84	−5.68	−6.36	−5.51	−3.26
HOIN	−9.40	−7.34	−6.22	−6.34	−4.88	−3.92
INFO	−10.87	−9.21	−3.94	−2.97	−2.83	−2.50

risky sectors are INFO, CHPP, and MEPR. INFO is substantially less risky than other sectors, with daily risk of 2.97 percent at the 99 percent confidence level.

In Table 16.4, we present our findings for Cases 3 and 4. For 99 percent confidence level, 10 sectors have risks higher than 10 percent, and three sectors have risks close to 10 percent, the greatest being TELE with a daily risk greater than 14 percent. TELE and MEPR are the two most risky sectors for 95 percent confidence level. It is interesting to note that the most risky sectors change when confidence level is taken as 90 percent. INSU, TOUR, and HOIN are the most risky sectors for 90 percent

T A B L E   16.4

Value-at-risk figures of sector returns over the 2001 crisis and 2005

	Case 3			Case 4		
	99%	95%	90%	99%	95%	90%
FOBE	−13.66	−8.59	−4.03	−2.56	−2.01	−1.51
TEXL	−11.55	−7.35	−5.48	−2.45	−1.69	−1.15
WOPP	−12.75	−8.62	−6.39	−2.57	−2.17	−1.69
CHPP	−10.69	−6.87	−6.16	−2.26	−1.56	−1.11
NMMP	−10.76	−7.62	−5.64	−1.39	−1.04	−0.74
BAME	−12.04	−7.40	−5.23	−2.68	−2.03	−1.24
MEPR	−12.03	−10.09	−5.56	−2.32	−1.63	−1.13
ELEC	−5.78	−4.58	−3.76	−3.29	−2.12	−1.70
TRAN	−8.63	−6.64	−5.59	−3.40	−2.35	−1.98
TOUR	−10.86	−8.42	−7.25	−6.00	−4.52	−2.52
WHRT	−8.56	−7.12	−5.10	−2.52	−1.82	−1.20
TELE	−14.04	−10.23	−5.10	−2.71	−2.17	−1.47
BANK	−9.27	−6.60	−5.07	−3.54	−2.05	−1.63
INSU	−9.70	−8.38	−7.40	−2.60	−1.98	−1.48
LEFA	−12.28	−9.13	−5.26	−3.62	−2.63	−1.79
HOIN	−9.11	−8.71	−7.09	−2.06	−1.83	−1.15
INFO	−4.03	−3.72	−3.47	NA	NA	NA

NA = not available

confidence level. VaR ordering of sectors is very sensitive to the choice of confidence level. For example, FOBE is one of the most risky sectors at 99 percent confidence level. However, it is one of the least risky sectors when confidence level is 90 percent. All sectors report losses greater than 3 percent even for 90 percent confidence level.

We have much lower VaR values for Case 4. Many of the losses are about 2 to 3 percent with the exception of tourism. The most risky sectors are tourism (6.00 percent VaR), and leasing and factoring (3.62 percent loss) for 99 percent confidence level. The least risky sectors are nonmetal mineral products (1.39 percent loss), and holding and investment (2.06 percent loss) sectors for the same confidence level. Tourism is the most risky sector for all confidence levels.

PERFORMANCE OF VAR IN EVALUATING RISK

In this section, we evaluate how much VaR is able to measure the risks of sectors. Our basic idea is to compare the VaR figures of risks to the actual losses incurred. The selection of crisis periods as well as the stable period is intentional. We start with a brief summary of crises hitting the Turkish economy in the last decade.

Recent Crisis Hitting the Turkish Economy

The Turkish economy was hit by three crises in the last decade, one of which was the greatest of all after World War II. The first crisis we take into account was in 1998. This crisis led to the outflow of $4.5 billion from Turkey (Alper (2001)). The ISE index decreased from 3253 on August 25th to 2603 on August 27th, a decline of almost 20 percent. The U.S. dollar reserve of the Central Bank of Turkey decreased at about $4.3 billion in August. The crisis was accompanied by the Russian and Asian crisis as a result of which Turkish exports to Russia and Asian countries decreased by 45.7 and 34.5 percent, respectively. We choose August 26, 1998 as the day that triggered the crisis hitting the Turkish economy for Case 1.

Turkey had initiated the disinflation program in 2000 with the help of the World Bank and IMF to tame the high inflation rates of three digits. The main objectives of the program were stated as the budget surplus and reorganization of exchange rate and monetary policies in the letter of intention presented to the International Monetary Fund (IMF). These measures were toward controlling the budget deficit due to government expenditures and transfer payments. In 1999, inflation by consumer price index (CPI) was 65 percent, and the growth rate was −6 percent. Domestic debt stock was approximately 30 percent of the gross national product (GNP). The program was somehow promising in that the interest rate declined from 103 percent in 1999 to 40 percent in 2000. This decline in interest rates, in turn, boosted the use of consumer credit and overappreciated Turkish Lira led to the deterioration in net exports. The event triggering the crisis was the withdrawal of foreign investors from Turkey. This amounted to the outflow of $4.8 billion, and the Turkish Banks (many of which belonged to the holding companies that had transferred credits to their corporations with high risks) had difficulty in finding debt in shortage of liquidity. They were caught in open positions. The expropriation of one of the leading banks had started the crisis. Overnight interest rate jumped to 110.8 percent and hit the maximum of 210 percent. The ISE–100 Index had fallen from 13256 on November 15th to 7329 on December 4th, a decline of 45 percent. The U.S. dollar reserves of the Turkish Central Bank shrank from $24.3 billion on November 17th to $18.9 billion on December 1st, a 22.2 percent decline in a 15-day period. Although the additional $7.5 billion IMF credit helped so much in alleviating the negative effects of the crisis, its cost was high because of the short due date. We select December 27, 2000 as the day of the second crisis for Case 2.

The Turkish economy started to recover at the beginning of 2001. The overnight interbank interest rate declined from 199 percent (at the end of December 2000) to 42 percent in January 2001. The Central Bank CB reserves exceeded $25 billion. This time the shock to the economy came from the politicians. An argument between the Prime Minister and the President of Turkey triggered the greatest crisis of the country in the last 50 years. The CB had to intervene immediately, and its reserves declined by more than $5 billion in one day. The most critical decision was the shift from the pegged exchange rate policy to the floating one. This was inevitable since the CB was not capable of offering U.S. Dollars at the announced rates. The TL/USD rate jumped from 688,000 to 962,000 in one night (40 percent increase), and the overnight interbank interest rate jumped from 50 to 6200 percent. The ISE index declined from 10,169 to 8,683 between February 16th and 19th. The interested reader should consult Ertugrul and Selcuk (2001) for an overview of the Turkish economy and the details of the 2001 crises.

We display the daily returns of sectors for the 50 days before the crisis (in Figure 16.2) to demonstrate the large oscillations. Many of the sectors have systematic movements due to the behavior of the markets. The ELEC has a somewhat different behavior because of regulations in the energy resource use and distribution markets. The other interesting point is the relatively milder variance of the returns toward the date of the crisis.

We believe that the dates of the crises are good opportunities to evaluate the measures devised to account for risk. One might think that the circumstances experienced by the Turkish economy are exceptional and could not be taken as an example, but this is the reality lived by the whole country, and similar experiences had hit other economies.

We use the results shown in Tables 16.5 and 16.6, which include the actual losses of the sectors, for the evaluation of VaR in expressing risk. The rightmost column for all cases lists the actual losses (our benchmarks) that we use to evaluate the daily risk estimated by VaR. The reported numbers are the losses recorded at the day of the crisis.

Regarding the 1998 crisis, as reported in Table 16.5, all VaR figures for 99 percent confidence level are below the losses incurred when the crisis hit the economy with the only exception of INFO. The gap gets larger if 95 percent confidence level is taken as the basis to predict expectations for risk. The greatest losses came with the sectors of INSU (almost 18 percent) and ELEC (15.53 percent). All sectors but INFO suffered from losses in excess of 10 percent. As a result, the VaR estimation does not appear to be a good way to express risk, at least for the 1998 crisis period.

Value-at-risk estimates are somewhat better in the 2000 crisis but are still below our expectations. Actual losses are greater than the VaRs for 14 of the 17 sector returns for 99 percent confidence levels. The TOUR sector records the greatest loss of all (almost 15 percent). The sectors TEXL, INSU, WHRT, HOIN, TELE, LEFA, and BAME all have daily losses of more than 10 percent. The largest discrepancies between VaR and actual losses are in WHRT (5.71 percent), TOUR (5.59 percent), TEXL (4.85

F I G U R E   16.2

Behaviors of Sector Returns before the 2001 Crisis

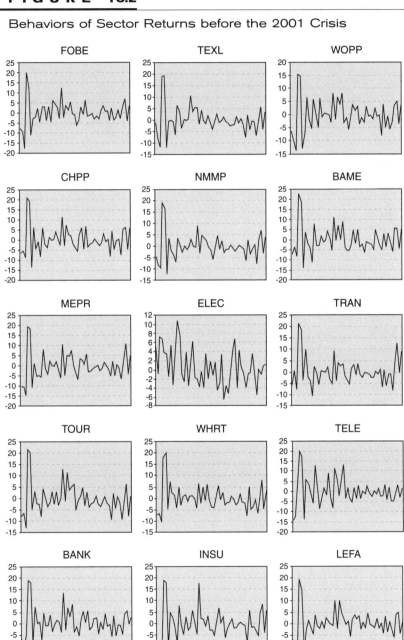

T A B L E   16.5

Value at risk figures compared to actual returns during the 1998 and 2000 crises

	Case 1			Case 2		
	99%	95%	Act. Ret.	99%	95%	Act. Ret.
FOBE	−8.45	−7.34	−12.04	−6.10	−4.33	−4.66
TEXL	−10.66	−8.09	−13.56	−7.33	−4.80	−12.18
WOPP	−7.68	−6.56	−13.30	−6.15	−4.34	−9.83
CHPP	−10.41	−7.17	−10.95	−4.62	−3.91	−7.46
NMMP	−7.12	−6.14	−10.02	−5.24	−3.85	−9.98
BAME	−11.09	−8.20	−12.23	−5.24	−4.03	−10.09
MEPR	−8.44	−5.40	−13.28	−4.48	−3.99	−9.13
ELEC	−14.33	−9.56	−15.53	−10.25	−5.83	2.68
TRAN	−8.50	−6.66	−11.60	−6.23	−4.37	−9.09
TOUR	−10.92	−9.61	−12.87	−9.11	−6.07	−14.70
WHRT	−7.04	−5.63	−13.32	−5.07	−4.51	−10.88
TELE	NA	NA	NA	−12.12	−7.83	−10.78
BANK	−8.20	−7.46	−13.46	−5.54	−4.34	−7.84
INSU	−12.75	−7.21	−17.91	−7.56	−4.28	−11.74
LEFA	−9.83	−8.84	−12.66	−6.36	−5.51	−10.76
HOIN	−9.40	−7.34	−12.89	−6.34	−4.88	−10.82
INFO	−10.87	−9.21	−1.00	−2.97	−2.83	2.09

percent), BAME (4.85 percent), and NMMP (4.74 percent) sectors. The discrepancy gets even larger if the portfolio managers use the 95 percent confidence level.

The largest actual losses are recorded in the 2001 crisis. Many of the sector losses are around 14 percent. The largest losses are from WHRT and TELE sectors, both with losses over 17 percent. INFO and ELEC sectors are the two exceptions with daily losses around 2.5 percent. The 95 percent VaR figures are almost always less than the actual losses. However, the VaRs of 99 percent are sometimes close to the actual losses. The largest differences between expected losses expressed by VaR and the actual losses are from WHRT (8.81 percent), HOIN (5.61 percent), TRAN

T A B L E   16.6

Value at risk figures compared to actual returns during the 2001 and 2005 crises

	Case 3			Case 4		
	99%	95%	Act. Ret.	99%	95%	Act. Ret.
FOBE	−13.66	−8.59	−13.93	−2.56	−2.01	−4.59
TEXL	−11.55	−7.35	−14.98	−2.45	−1.69	−2.24
WOPP	−12.75	−8.62	−11.96	−2.57	−2.17	−3.63
CHPP	−10.69	−6.87	−13.90	−2.26	−1.56	−3.80
NMMP	−10.76	−7.62	−12.30	−1.39	−1.04	−5.06
BAME	−12.04	−7.40	−16.30	−2.68	−2.03	−9.20
MEPR	−12.03	−10.09	−14.18	−2.32	−1.63	−2.89
ELEC	−5.78	−4.58	−2.64	−3.29	−2.12	−9.09
TRAN	−8.63	−6.64	−14.14	−3.40	−2.35	−3.32
TOUR	−10.86	−8.42	−14.83	−6.00	−4.52	−7.44
WHRT	−8.56	−7.12	−17.37	−2.52	−1.82	−2.49
TELE	−14.04	−10.23	−17.11	−2.71	−2.17	−5.52
BANK	−9.27	−6.60	−14.11	−3.54	−2.05	−4.36
INSU	−9.70	−8.38	−14.29	−2.60	−1.98	−6.70
LEFA	−12.28	−9.13	−12.71	−3.62	−2.63	−3.46
HOIN	−9.11	−8.71	−14.72	−2.06	−1.83	−4.20
INFO	−4.03	−3.72	−2.52	NA	NA	NA

NA = not available

(5.51 percent), BANK (4.81 percent), and INSU (4.59 percent). These are the sectors with about 5 percent difference between VaR estimated loss and actual loss. Again, the difference gets larger for the 95 percent confidence level. For instance, the portfolio manager using 95 percent confidence level in calculating the historical VaR will face 10.25 percent difference for WHRT followed by 7.63 percent difference for TEXL and 7.51 percent difference for BANK. These are huge percentages to bear when the manager is almost sure (95 percent confidence level) about the maximum risk he is taking with the VaR method. Eleven out of 17 sectors have more than 5 percent discrepancies between VaR estimates and actual losses.

We change our method of analysis for Case 4. This time the actual losses do not belong to the immediate following day, but rather these losses are the maxima of the following 50 days.

This time VaR figures are much more successful in estimating risk. Again, there are differences between VaR estimates and actual losses, but these differences are much lower this time. The largest differences are from BAME and ELEC, both of which are around 6 percent. The differences are around 1 to 2 percent for the majority of the sectors.

CONCLUSION

We have used VaR estimates that are calculated from the historical data of the sector returns to compare the sectors traded at the ISE, especially at the times of the crises. TELE appears to be the most risky sector followed by ELEC for Cases 1 and 2. TOUR takes place at the top of the risk tables for all cases. Moreover, TEXL is well above the average of the risky sectors. Turkey has made huge amounts of investment in textiles, and this sector is very critical especially after the rise of China and India in the global markets. BAME is also associated with high risk for almost all cases. Turkey has a high capacity of "basic metal" production. This means the real side of the economy suffers from the financial crises immediately. One other observation is that the risk does not discriminate among the sectors much. The exposure of corporations to risk from all sectors of industry, service, technology, and finance are similar.

Value at risk appears to be a good measure to evaluate risk when the economy is functioning smoothly, but starts failing at the times of stress. The three cases of crises we included in our analysis reveal that risks computed by VaR are not good estimates of true losses incurred. If portfolio managers had taken positions according to the risk calculations by VaR in Turkey at the times of the crises, even with 99 percent confidence levels, they could have incurred additional daily losses around 5 percent for many of the sectors. This is due to the main shortcoming of VaR in expressing risk as stated earlier: "The main shortcoming of VaR is its ignorance to seldom events that never show up over the time period of the analysis." Our findings confirm Longin's (2000), which show that VaR measures based on traditional parametric approaches with even normal distribution fail at times of crisis.

In this study, our intention is not to argue that VaR method is unsuccessful. In addition, it is not our intention to suggest a better method especially for stressful economic times. Hence, this leaves the door open for further research. An addition to our analysis could be the use of different starting points of financial crisis. This change may affect the performance of the VaR and hence the conclusions of this study in evaluating risk.

REFERENCES

Alper, C.E. (2001) The Turkish Liquidity Crisis of 2000: What Went Wrong? *Russian and East European Finance and Trade*, 37(6): 51–71.

Bao, Y, T-H. Lee, and B. Saltoglu (2006) Evaluating Predictive Performance of Value-at-Risk Models in Emerging Markets: A Reality Check. *Journal of Forecasting*, 25(2): 101–128.

Beder, T.S. (1995) VaR: Seductive but Dangerous. *Financial Analyst Journal*, 51(5): 12–24.

Duffie, D. and J. Pan (1997) An Overview of Value at Risk. *Journal of Derivatives*, 4(3): 7–49.

Ertugrul, A. and F. Selcuk (2001) A Brief Account of the Turkish Economy: 1980–2000. *Russian and East European Finance and Trade*, 37(6): 6–28.

Gencay, R, and F. Selcuk (2004) Extreme Value Theory and Value-at-Risk: Relative Performance in Emerging Markets. *International Journal of Forecasting*, 20(2): 287–303.

Harris, R.D.F. and C.C. Kucukozmen (2002) Linear and Nonlinear Dependence in Turkish Equity Returns and its Consequences for Financial Risk Management. *European Journal of Operational Research*, 134(3): 481–492.

Jackson, P., D.J. Maude, and W. Perraudin (1998) Bank Capital and Value at Risk. Working Paper Series No 79, Bank of England.

Jorion, P. (2000) Risk Management Lessons from Long Term Capital Management. *European Financial Management*, 6(3): 277–300.

Jorion, P. (2000) *Value-at-Risk: The New Benchmark for Controlling Market Risk.* Chicago: McGraw-Hill.

Longin, F.M. (2000) From Value at Risk to Stress Testing: The Extreme Value Approach. *Journal of Banking and Finance*, 24(7): 1097–1130.

Manganelli, S. and R.F. Engle (2001) Value at Risk Models in Finance. Working Paper Series No 75, European Central Bank.

Simons, K. (1996) Value at Risk-New Approaches to Risk Management. *New England Economic Review*, 2(4): 34–67.

Vlaar, P.J.G. (2000) Value at Risk Models for Dutch Bond Portfolios. *Journal of Banking and Finance*, 24(7): 1131–1154.

PART THREE

Modeling

CHAPTER 17

Aggregating and Combining Ratings

Rafael Weißbach, Frederik Kramer, and Claudia Lawrenz

ABSTRACT

Credit ratings are a key parameter in banking where they influence credit costs and calibrate credit portfolio models. Usually, several ratings for one issue or counterpart are available, e.g., external ratings, internal ratings, and market-implied probability of defaults. Combining these ratings is hindered by different granularities and class definitions. Within the framework of a time-continuous homogeneous Markov process model, we prove a rule on aggregating ratings onto a master scale. The result uses the process generator. Three implications are studied with a real-life portfolio of corporate credit: (1) how the result may be used to estimate a migration matrix based on different individual rating histories, (2) how migration matrices estimated from different sources may be optimally combined, and (3) how the aggregation impacts economic capital.

INTRODUCTION

In the 1990s, large banks started to rate their customers systematically by means of internal rating systems. They use statistical methods (e.g., logistic regression) to find key data for the respective customer segment, which show the highest discriminatory power concerning credit default risk. These internal rating systems provide regularly assessments of credit risks for several debtors. Predominantly the rating of a debtor is linked to the probability of default (PD). Figure 17.1 shows an exemplary credit history. The debtor is solvent until default and insolvent afterwards.

Unbiased estimation of default risks for individual credit obligations and portfolios is an indispensable requirement for appropriate pricing by credit institutions and therefore at the same time a determining competition factor for profitable competitive credit business. Within global bank risk management, time series of rating studies provide an important basis for extensive and statistically established assessment of risk. Basel II allows banks to determine regulatory capital requirements for credits based on internal customer ratings as long as they let bank regulation verify their rating systems within the internal rating approach. In this approach, risk values are determined as a function of the probability of default related to the rating. Alternatively, banks can determine capital requirements using

F I G U R E   17.1

Typical Rating History

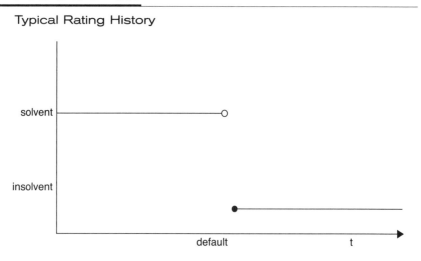

external ratings by using the standardized approach of Basel II, in which risk values are linked directly to external ratings. As most large international banks use the internal rating approach, they have their own internal ratings for many debtors as well as external ratings.

External ratings are only issued by few and therefore very influential independent rating agencies like Standard & Poor's (S&P), Moody's, or Fitch, which are usually paid for their rating service. Banks price their expenses for the debtor analysis within the interest rate, while rating agencies charge the expenses to the rated companies. For this reason, mainly large, financially strong, capital market oriented companies order to be rated by external rating agencies. In contrast to internal ratings, which can be assumed as company secrets, rating agencies usually make their ratings for traded bonds available to market participants free of charge. Therefore, the character of external ratings as public information has a direct effect on the PDs and the market price for these bonds [cf Hand et al. (1992)].

How should a bank deal with debtors for which internal as well as external ratings exist? Whom should they believe "more"? Who is able to rate the debtors better, the bank or the external agencies? Intuitively it is obvious that a combination of two ratings is always better than considering only one rating, because the variance of the prediction and therefore the risk of a wrong prediction decrease. Hence, a smaller use of economical capital is necessary, which shall cover the losses of credit transactions. Furthermore, external ratings present an ideal supplement for internal ratings, because external ratings present a long term "through-the-cycle" rating, while internal ratings are usually designed as "point-in-time" ratings and, therefore, are also applied to short term rating changes. For that reason, changes in short- and long-term ratings can be identified as soon as possible and appropriate counteractive measures like hedging can be taken.

The second section of this chapter reviews the models needed for analyzing rating migration histories. In the third section, we describe the idea of combining two independent ratings with an aggregate class system. In the fourth section, using a simulation we show that the true probabilities of defaults can be estimated more accurate with a combination of internal and external ratings. We also show the connection between generator estimation and economic capital and impacts on the amount of economic capital. The fifth section of this chapter concludes the chapter.

MATHEMATICAL BACKGROUND

Ratings of debtors can migrate between R rating classes during a business relationship. We model the resulting migration histories with continuous-time Markov processes. Rating migration matrices describe the probability of rating migrations over a specific period. All possible migrations between each rating class and the default risk are modeled. The last column of the migration matrix represents the probability of default of debtors for each rating class.

Besides commonly used one-year migration matrices, in practice two- or three-year migration matrices are also available. These matrices describe migration probabilities and the probability of default within two or three years. It is important to note that a time-differentiated setup of the matrices can only be replaced by the definition of one matrix, in case the rating process is homogeneous and the migration probabilities are constant over time.

In the homogeneous case, rating migration matrices can be calculated with the generator Q, a matrix with the same dimensions as the migration matrix. The generator entries λ_{ij} describe the intensities with which the rating process migrates from rating i to rating j. The following relation exists between migration matrices over any time t and the generator Q:

$$P(t) = e^{tQ} = \sum_{n=0}^{\infty} \frac{(tQ)^n}{n!} \qquad (17.1)$$

Migration matrices can easily be calculated with a given generator.[1]

According to Bluhm et al. (2003, p. 197), a reliable estimation of migration matrices with a period shorter than one year is not possible using migration matrices, which consider exactly one year $[P(1)]$. If a study, containing the complete rating histories of n debtors is available, the data contains all migrations between all possible rating classes from the beginning of the observation 0 until the end T. We want to present a generator estimation, which is based on the rating migration histories of n debtors. In Albert (1962), the maximum likelihood estimator for the entries of the generator Q is described as

---

[1] For example, the statistical program R offers a function within the package Matrix.

$$\hat{\lambda}_{ij} = \frac{N_{ij}(T)}{\int_0^T Y_i(s)ds} \tag{17.2}$$

Here, the counting process $N_{ij}(T)$ is the total number of transitions from rating classes i to j over the complete observation period, and $Y_i(s)$ is the number of firms in rating class i at time s. The denominator describes the number of years firms have spent in rating class i. With the estimated generator $\hat{Q}$ with entries $\hat{q}_{ij}$, it is now easily possible to calculate estimated migration matrices $\hat{P}(t)$ with Equation (17.1) as

$$\hat{P}(t) = e^{(t\hat{Q})} \tag{17.3}$$

AGGREGATING RATINGS

For the combination of two ratings, it is often necessary to assure their comparability. Quite often it is possible to define a rougher rating system, which "fits" for both systems. Therefore, at least for one system, rating classes have to be merged. However, how can the migration intensities of the rougher system be determined from the finer system? Again, the use of generators turns out to be helpful. For example, if you try to aggregate migration matrices by averaging probabilities, the matrices lose the attribute of a stochastic matrix. Furthermore, such an aggregation does not maintain the homogeneity property. The aggregation idea of the generator is based on the observation that generators imply slowly decreasing intensities over rows and columns. Hence, one can show that the following process is again approximately homogeneous. The theoretical fundament shows the following theorem.

Theorem 17.1. *Let Q be the generator of a homogeneous rating process* $\mathbf{X} = \{X_t, t \in [0, T]\}$ *with the class system ℓ with cardinality $L = \#\ell$. Let further ℓ' be a sub partition of ℓ with cardinality $L' = 1 < L$. For neighboring classes of the process $\mathbf{X}$ it is assumed to hold that* $\lambda_{(h-1)j} \approx \lambda_{hj} \; \forall \; h-1, \; h \in A \subset \ell' \; and \; \forall \; j \in A' \subset \{\ell' \setminus A\}.$

Denote h the respective state of $\mathbf{X}'$ for the set $A^h \in \ell'$, i.e., the process $\mathbf{X}$ restricted to the state space ℓ'. Then for the entries λ'_{hj} of the generator Q' holds

$$\lambda_{hj}^{'} \approx \frac{\sum_{h \in A^h} \sum_{j \in A^j} \lambda_{hj}}{\# A^h} \tag{17.4}$$

Before we come to the general proof, a special case shall point out the idea of the proof. We consider the case of a rating system with two nondefault states, i.e., $L = 3$. Then we can write $\ell = \{1,2,3\}$. Now we consider the aggregation of the first two rating classes, i.e., $\ell' = \{\{1,2\},3\}$; thus $L' = 2$. We make an empirical detour and consider the observation of n samples from $\mathbf{X}$ and therewith from $\mathbf{X'}$. Again, let the samples be described as counting processes as in the second section. The only open parameter of the process $\mathbf{X'}$ is the intensity from an active firm to an insolvent firm, λ'_{12}. The intensity is estimated by the samples [cf., Equation (17.2)] using the ratio of the number of all defaults over the observation period $[0, T]$ [i.e., $N'12(T)$] and the accumulated observation years (i.e., $\int_0^T Y'_1 (s) \, ds$). However, $N'_{12}(t) = N_{13}(t) + N_{23}(t)$ and $Y'_1(t) = Y_1(t) + Y_2(t)$ hold, so that

$$\hat{\lambda}_{12}' = \frac{N_{12}'(T)}{\int_0^T Y_1'(s)ds}$$

$$= \frac{N_{13}(T) + N_{23}(T)}{\int_0^T Y_1(s)ds + \int_0^T Y_2(s)ds}$$

$$= \frac{\int_0^T Y_1(s)ds \dfrac{N_{13}(T)}{\int_0^T Y_1(s)ds} + \int_0^T Y_2(s)ds \dfrac{N_{23}(T)}{\int_0^T Y_2(s)ds}}{\int_0^T Y_1(s)ds + \int_0^T Y_2(s)ds}$$

Now $N_{h3}(T)/\int_0^T Y_h(s)ds$, $h = 1,2$ is a consistent estimator for $\hat{\lambda}_{h3}$ (cf Albert, 1962). According to the assumptions for large n that $\hat{\lambda}_{13} \approx \hat{\lambda}_{23}$ $(1,2 \in \{1,2\})$, we have

$$\hat{\lambda}_{12} = \frac{\int_0^T Y_1(s)ds\hat{\lambda}_{13} + \int_0^T Y_2(s)ds\hat{\lambda}_{23}}{\int_0^T Y_1(s)ds + \int_0^T Y_2(s)ds}$$

$$\approx \frac{\hat{\lambda}_{13} + \hat{\lambda}_{23}}{2}.$$

The limit $n \to \infty$ concludes the proof. In this case the denominator can also be written as #{1,2}.

Proof: We consider again n samples from $\mathbf{X}$ with the class system ℓ and therewith from $\mathbf{X}'$ and the class system ℓ'. For $h \in A^h \in \ell', h \in \{1, \ldots, \ell'-1\}$ and $j \in \{1, \ldots, \ell'\}$, $j \neq h$, we have $N'_{hj}(t) = \Sigma_{h\in A^h} \Sigma_{j\in A^j} N_{hj}(t)$ and $Y'_h(t) = \Sigma_{h\in A^h} Y_h(t)$, so that

$$\hat{\lambda}_{hj} = \frac{N'_{hj}(T)}{\int_0^T Y'_h(s)ds}$$

$$= \frac{\sum_{h\in A^h} \sum_{j\in A^j} N_{hj}(T)}{\int_0^T \sum_{h\in A^h} Y_h(s)ds}$$

$$= \frac{\sum_{h\in A^h} \int_0^T Y_h(s)ds \sum_{j\in A^j} \dfrac{N_{hj}(T)}{\int_0^T Y_h(s)ds}}{\int_0^T \sum_{h\in A^h} Y_h(s)ds} \quad \text{for large } n.$$

$$\approx \frac{\sum_{h\in A^h} \int_0^T Y_h(s)ds \sum_{j\in A^j} \lambda_{hj}}{\int_0^T \sum_{h\in A^h} Y_h(s)ds}$$

$$\approx \frac{\sum_{h\in A^h} \sum_{j\in A^j} \hat{\lambda}_{hj}}{\# A^h}$$

IMPACT STUDIES

Combining Ratings

For attaining the goal to model a combined Markov process Z_t with internal and external ratings, the challenge is to estimate the associated generator with rating data. We consider the internal rating process X_t defined by the generator Q^x and the external rating process Y_t defined by the generator to Q^y. On the basis of an aggregation as described in this chapter's third section, we can now define the mixed process Z_t:
$Z_t = 1_{\{W=0\}} X_t + 1_{\{W=1\}} Y_t$.

The indicator functions $1_{\{W=0\}}$ and $1_{\{W=1\}}$ can only have the values 0 and 1. Furthermore, $W \sim B(p)$ is a Bernoulli distributed random variable, so that Z_t is based on a random experiment. In addition, if X_t, Y_t, and W are independent, the mixed process Z_t is the external process Y_t with probability p and the internal process X_t with counter probability $1-p$. Between the generators of the initial processes and the generator Q^z exists the following relation: $Q^z = (1-p)Q^X + pQ^Y$.

We want to illustrate why this relation holds. The following relation between intensities and migration probabilities is used:

$$\lambda_{ij}^z = \lim_{t \to 0^+} \frac{P(Z_t = j \mid Z_0 = i)}{t}, i,j \in \Re, i \neq j$$

where t denotes the migration time and $\Re$ the set of all possible states of the processes, in this case rating classes. The following operations use the independency of, X_t, Y_t, and W:

$$\lambda_{ij}^z = \lim_{t \to 0^+} \frac{P(1_{\{W=0\}} X_t + 1_{\{W=1\}} Y_t = j \mid 1_{\{W=0\}} X_0 + 1_{\{W=1\}} Y_0 = i)}{t}$$

$$= \lim_{t \to 0^+} \frac{P(W = 0)P(X_t = j \mid X_0 = i) + P(W = 1)P(Y_t = j \mid Y_0 = i)}{t}$$

$$= \lim_{t \to 0^+} \frac{(1-p)\lambda_{ij}^X(t) + p\lambda_{ij}^Y(t)}{t} = (1-p)\lambda_{ij}^X + p\lambda_{ij}^Y, i,j \in \Re, i \neq j$$

For the generator Q^z and its estimator $\hat{Q}^z$ the following equations hold because of $\lambda_{ii}^Z = -\sum_{j \neq i} \lambda_{ij}^Z$:

$$Q^z = (1-p)Q^X + pQ^Y \qquad\qquad \hat{Q}^z = (1-p)\hat{Q}^X + p\hat{Q}^Y \qquad (17.5)$$

It is obvious that there is a high probability for both processes X_t and Y_t being in nearby states, and therefore the operations do not hold for all $t \in [0, T]$ because of necessary independence. However, we need independence only between X_0 and Y_t, as well as X_t and Y_0. Yet, for sufficient large t independence is plausible; hence, the operations above can be performed.

Our main objective is to find an appropriate proportionality factor $p \in [0, 1]$. The choice of p decides how the behavior of the external and internal processes affect the mixed process. The more p deviates from $1/2$, the more is the mixed process affected by one initial process, which is therefore more important for the identification of rating migrations and equity capital.

In a simplified case in which all nondefault firms are in one rating class, i.e., $R = 2$, the estimation for the entries of the generator λ_{ij} is equivalent to the parameter estimation of the exponential distribution for default times. For combining two generators, the ideal combined generator corresponds to the combined maximum likelihood estimator of two samples of exponential distributed default times $X_1, \ldots, X_n$ and $Y_1, \ldots, Y_m$. Hence, the maximum likelihood estimators $\hat{\lambda}_x$ and $\hat{\lambda}_y$ of the individual samples is the ratio of the number of migrations and the cumulated sum of default times of each sample:

$$\hat{\lambda}_X = \frac{n}{\sum_{i=0}^{n} X_i} \qquad\qquad \hat{\lambda}_Y = \frac{m}{\sum_{j=0}^{m} Y_j}$$

The combined maximum likelihood estimator has the following form:

$$\hat{\lambda}_{XY} = \frac{n + m}{\sum_{i=0}^{n} X_i + \sum_{j=0}^{m} Y_j}$$

which can also be described as a linear combination, so that $\hat{\lambda}_{XY} = (1-p)$ $\hat{\lambda}_X + p\hat{\lambda}_Y$.

However, the optimal combination can only be achieved in special cases. For example, the maximum likelihood estimator can be expressed analytically with one rating class and additional knowledge of the number of migrations n and m in both generator estimations.

In general, however, a number of influence factors can hinder the achievement of optimality. For example, in practice, pairwise unknown numbers of migrations can appear or interactions between the length of the study and the sample size can occur. This problem occurs because not every rating exists over the complete period $[0, T]$, as firms can drop out of the portfolio at earlier times. Hence, you have to refrain from optimality in terms of maximum likelihood. In general, in econometrics the term of optimality is used with "minimum-variance estimation," which we will be using in the simulation example.

In the next step we want to study the mixture of generators from Equation (17.5) with the aim to find an "optimal" proportionality factor p for the relation of Q^X and Q^Y. As calculations with many rating classes distract from the main problem, we consider only two rating classes: investment grade (A) and subinvestment grade (B), as well as the absorbing default state (D). An exemplary credit history for one firm is displayed in Figure 17.2. The results determined in this section can easily be adapted to more rating classes.

In Casjens et al. (2007) this approach was used for real data of a rating agency and a bank. The results are repeated here for discussion. For the simulations to be as realistic as possible we use two generators estimated from real data sets. At first we use a generator from Israel et al. (2001) based on S&P data. The generator was calculated from a migration matrix. We want to use a model with two rating classes, so we aggregate the rating classes AAA-BBB (investment grade) and BB-CCC (subinvestment grade) with Equation (17.4). For consistent notation we would have to write $\hat{Q}^{S\&P'}$ to point out the attribute of the matrix as an estimator of an

F I G U R E   17.2

Exemplary Rating History

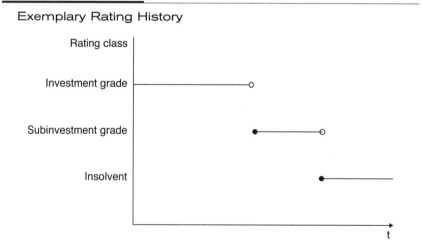

T A B L E   17.1

Generator Q^{S&P} for Standard & Poor's rating

$\lambda_{ij}^{S\&P}$	A	B	D
A	−0.030	0.029	0.001
B	0.045	−0.168	0.123
D	0	0	0

aggregated system. To simplify matters, we will just use $Q^{S\&P}$. The generator in Table 17.1 was estimated from 11,605 rating histories between 1981 and 1991. The intensity for migrations from A to B is $\lambda_{AB}^{S\&P} = 0.029$. The intensity for defaulting from subinvestment grade is $\lambda_{BD}^{S\&P} = 0.123$.

In addition, an estimated generator for internal ratings from Weißbach et al. (2008b) was used. The estimations are based on 3,700 internal ratings of a large German bank over a time period of seven years. Once again we have to aggregate rating classes for our model. The classes 1 to 4 are aggregated as investment grade, and the classes 5 to 8, as subinvestment grade. We assume that this classification is equivalent to the approach of the S&P ratings. Table 17.2 shows the resulting generator based on the internal ratings.

Therefore we have two generators for the following simulations, one based on internal and one based on external ratings. At first, we want to show that the combination of generators from internal and external ratings is a better estimation of the "true" generator. For this reason, we simulate 100 and 200 seven-year rating histories. With the assumptions of a homogeneous

T A B L E   17.2

Generator Q^{Bank} for internal ratings from a large German bank

λ_{ij}^{Bank}	A	B	D
A	−0.036	0.029	0.007
B	0.070	−0.130	0.060
D	0	0	0

process and independency of each rating history we estimate two generators. The first generator presents the smaller sample for internal ratings, and the second generator presents the larger sample for external ratings. Then we use both estimations for a combined rating process from the previous section to get a combined generator. The three estimators are now compared with the original generator from which the rating histories were simulated, and we check for improvements of the combined estimator.

For the simulation of the rating histories we use the generator $Q^{S\&P}$ from Israel et al. (2001). At the start 50 percent of the 100 processes are divided in the investment grade class, and the other 50 percent are divided in the subinvestment grade class. The time of a migration from rating class i into another class is exponentially distributed with parameter $\lambda_i = \lambda_{ij}^{S\&P} + \lambda_{iD}^{S\&P}, i, j = A, B, i \neq j$.

Based on these distributions random numbers are generated as the time for a rating migration for the processes for the first and second rating class. Afterwards, a Bernoulli distributed random number with probability

$$p_i = \frac{\lambda_{ij}^{S\&P}}{\lambda_{ij}^{S\&P} + \lambda_{iD}^{S\&P}}, i = A, B, i \neq j,$$

decides in which rating class the firm migrates. This procedure is repeated for every history until either the firm defaults or seven years have passed. With the same procedure the 200 external rating histories are simulated.

From these simulated processes we will then estimate a generator $\hat{Q}^x$ based on the first 100 histories and a generator $\hat{Q}^Y$ based on the second 200 histories with Equation (17.2). These will be combined as described in Equation (17.5) to $\hat{Q}^{S\&P} = (1-p)\hat{Q}^X + p\hat{Q}^Y$. Here, we choose $p=200/300=2/3$, so that we weight according to the data used for the estimators. Afterwards the three estimators are compared to the original generator. As a measure for the estimation error we use the sum of the absolute deviations $\sum\limits_{i=A, B, D} \sum\limits_{v=A, B, D} |\hat{\lambda}_{ij}^k - \hat{\lambda}_{ij}^{S\&P}|, k=X, Y, S\&P$. Repeating this process 10,000 times, we have the following results:

- In 81 percent of the cases, the combined estimator $\hat{Q}^{S\&P}$ deviates less from $Q^{S\&P}$ than the estimator $\hat{Q}^X$, which is based on 100 observations.

- In 69 percent of the cases, the combined estimator $\hat{Q}^{S\&P}$ deviates less from $Q^{S\&P}$ than the estimator $\hat{Q}^{Y}$, which is based on 200 observations.

In four out of five cases the combined estimator is superior to the internal generator, and in two out of three cases the combined estimator is superior to the external generator. These differences were expected as larger samples usually implicate more accurate estimations. Therefore, we see that a combined generator mostly provides better estimations of the true generator Q than a single estimator.

In addition, we compute the standard deviation of the intensities. In Table 17.3 we can see that the standard deviations based on the larger sample $\hat{\lambda}_{ij}^{Y}$ is smaller than the $\hat{\lambda}_{ij}^{X}$ based on 100 observations.

We can also see, that the combined estimators have smaller standard deviations than the others. Hence, the simulation study shows that a combination of different generators for internal and external ratings is useful.

We repeat the simulation for different values of p. Furthermore, parameters for the rating histories of the estimators $\hat{Q}^{X}$ and $\hat{Q}^{Y}$ are changed. Simulations are performed for periods $T_x = 7,10,21$ and for sample sizes $n_X = 100,200,300$ and $n_Y = 100,200$. The period for the estimator $\hat{Q}^{Y}$ stays constant at $T_Y = 7$. These values are aligned to the conditions of the above described generators $Q^{S\&P}$ and Q^{Bank}.

In Table 17.4, we show again the relative frequencies, how often the combined generator deviates less from the initial generator $Q^{S\&P}$ than the estimators $\hat{Q}^{X}$ and $\hat{Q}^{Y}$, as well as the average of both estimators. On the basis of the average, we can see that for our original model ($T_x = 7, n_x = 100$) the best result is achieved with $p = 0.8$.

TABLE 17.3

Standard deviation of the intensities $\hat{\lambda}_{ij}^{k}$

K	$\hat{\lambda}_{AB}^{k}$	$\hat{\lambda}_{AD}^{k}$	$\hat{\lambda}_{BA}^{k}$	$\hat{\lambda}_{BD}^{k}$
X	0.009	0.002	0.014	0.024
Y	0.007	0.001	0.010	0.017
S&P	0.005	0.001	0.008	0.014

TABLE 17.4

Improvement of the combined estimator for different p and rating histories

p	$T_x = 7, n_x = 100$	$T_y = 7, n_y = 200$	Average	$T_x = 7, n_x = 200$	$T_y = 7, n_y = 200$	Average	$T_x = 21, n_x = 100$	$T_y = 7, n_y = 200$	Average	$T_x = 10, n_x = 100$	$T_y = 7, n_y = 200$	Average	$T_x = 10, n_x = 300$	$T_y = 7, n_y = 100$	Average
0.1	0.92	0.36	0.64	0.86	0.56	0.71	0.86	0.56	0.71	0.91	0.43	0.67	0.70	0.86	0.78
0.2	0.91	0.43	0.67	0.84	0.62	0.73	0.84	0.60	0.72	0.89	0.49	0.70	0.65	0.88	0.76
0.3	0.90	0.47	0.69	0.81	0.66	0.74	0.80	0.66	0.73	0.87	0.54	0.70	0.57	0.91	0.74
0.4	0.88	0.54	0.71	0.79	0.71	0.75	0.77	0.70	0.74	0.84	0.61	0.73	0.51	0.92	0.72
0.5	0.86	0.60	0.73	0.75	0.75	0.75	0.74	0.74	0.74	0.83	0.64	0.74	0.44	0.93	0.69
0.6	0.83	0.65	0.74	0.71	0.78	0.74	0.70	0.78	0.74	0.79	0.70	0.75	0.37	0.94	0.66
0.7	0.81	0.70	0.76	0.66	0.81	0.74	0.65	0.80	0.73	0.77	0.74	0.76	0.30	0.95	0.62
0.8	0.78	0.74	0.76	0.62	0.83	0.73	0.61	0.83	0.72	0.73	0.77	0.75	0.26	0.96	0.60
0.9	0.73	0.78	0.76	0.56	0.86	0.71	0.56	0.85	0.71	0.68	0.81	0.74	0.22	0.96	0.59

By doubling the sample size of the first estimator, the best result for the balanced model (same time period, same sample size) is at $p = 0.5$. To achieve the same result though, the considered time period has to be tripled ($T_x = 21$). This implies, that an increase of the sample size has more impact on the choice of p than the time period. Hence, a model for the calculation of an optimal p in the following form is conceivable:

$$p = \frac{n_Y (T_y)^b}{n_X (T_X)^b + n_Y (T_Y)^b}, \quad 0 < b < 1$$

If the estimators have the same time period, it would have no impact on the choice of p. The same holds for the sample size. By means of the simulations we get an empirical value of $b = 0.5$. Hence, we introduce as an optimal p:

$$p = \frac{n_Y \sqrt{T_Y}}{n_X \sqrt{T_X} + n_Y \sqrt{T_Y}} \tag{17.6}$$

The linear dependence of the optimal proportional factor could be expected a priori; however, the dependence of the root of the observation period is surprising.

Economic Capital Implications

CreditMetrics from J.P.Morgan is one of the most common credit portfolio models considering credit ratings. *CreditMetrics* allows to value credit portfolios based on changes in values due to rating changes of firms in the portfolio. The value at risk concept mainly used in combination with market risks is adjusted to needs in credit risk management, and eventually for the calculation of economic capital.

Within the framework of *CreditMetrics* the measurement of the risk of a credit portfolio is based on the distribution of the market values of the portfolio within the risk horizon H. Changes in market values result, on the one hand, from possible defaults of debtors in the portfolio but, on the other hand, because of migrations of firms between different rating classes. Obviously the market value of a credit transaction increases when a firm migrates into a better rating class [cf., J.P.Morgan (1997, p. 100)].

Now the procedure of *CreditMetrics* is the following: As a first step, a probability distribution of the states of each firm at point H is calculated with the help of a generator and a simulation. In the second step, forward values of each credit and finally also the market value distribution of the portfolio can be calculated. The recovery rate has to be considered for defaulted credits. In the final step the volatility of the portfolio value and therefore the loss can be calculated, in case the market value of the portfolio drops below today's market value. The economic capital can then be calculated as the difference between the expected market value and the α-quantile (respectively, the value at risk). The quantile indicates the bound, under which the portfolio value falls with probability α at time H.

Based on *CreditMetrics*, we investigate with the help of a simulation whether and how the choice of different generators has an effect on the economic capital. For this purpose, we make the following assumptions:

Again, firms can only be in three states, rating class A (investment grade), rating class B (subinvestment grade) and the default state (rating class D). In case of defaulting, the recovery rate is 0, independently of the state the firm has been in before. It would also be possible to choose a deterministic recovery rate, which is not 0. If, however, we assume the recovery rate to be stochastic, it would have to be simulated as well. In this case we would have to question the independency of the recovery rate of the Markov process. For this reason we neglect this assumption. At time 0, the portfolio consists of 10 zero bonds, each with a maturity of two years. Of the 10 zero bonds, five debtors each are in rating classes A and B, and the agreed repayment sum at time 2 is $10 million each.

Using a simulation, we now want to determine with the help of a generator the distribution of the states of each firm at time $H = 1$ and finally the distribution of the market value of the portfolio. For reasons of simplification, we assume that the migrations of each firm are independent. However, in the framework of *CreditMetrics* usually the correlation between the asset value processes of the debtors in the portfolio is included, because the history of debtors depends to a more or less degree on the economic cycle or other macroeconomic values. Of course, these dependencies are very important, but they shall not be topic of this chapter.

The forward value of a zero bond at time H can be calculated as an expected discounted cash flow with the *fundamental formula*

$$V_i^1 = 10 \; million \cdot e^{-\int^2 (0+\lambda_{iD})du} = 10 \; million \cdot e^{-\lambda_{iD}}, \quad i = A,B$$

[cf., Bielecki and Rutkowski, (2002, pp. 221ff)]. Here, τ is the time of default, H the time at which the value shall be calculated, S the maturity of the credit, r_u the interest rate, λ_u the relevant credit spread, X_S the repayment sum, and F_H a given filtration. For the forward value V_i^1 of a credit transaction with a firm, which is in state i at time $H = 1$, and the assumption that the state of a firm does not change after time $H=1$, and with the fact that the credit spread λ_u is identical with the generator entry λ_{iD}, and neglecting the interest rate ($r_u = 0$), we get the following formula: $V_i^1 = 10$ million. $e^{-f_1^2(0 + \lambda iD)}du = 10 \; million. \; e^{-\lambda_{iD}}$, $i = A$, B, and $V_D^i = 0$. To analyze how a wrong specification of the generator affects the economic capital, the above-described simulation will be performed for the generators $Q^{S\&P}$ and Q^{Bank} (see Tables 17.1 and 17.2) introduced in this chapter's third section. For both generators a Monte Carlo simulation is performed with 100,000 iterations each. The resulting expected market values EMV of the portfolio at $H = 1$, the values at risk VaR_α at the level $\alpha = 1\%$ and $\alpha = 0.1\%$, and the economic capital EC_α are shown in Table 17.5. In addition, for $Q^{S\&P}$ the results are illustrated in Figure 17.3, with the market values on the x coordinate and relative frequencies on the y coordinate. Furthermore, the density of a normal distribution is plotted in the graph, where expected value and variance match the values of the market value distribution.

T A B L E   17.5

Results from the simulation in US$ million

	EMV	$VaR_{0.01}$	$EC_{0.01}$	$VaR_{0.001}$	$EC_{0.001}$
$Q^{S\&P}$	89	68	21	60	29
Q^{Bank}	94	77	16	68	26

F I G U R E   17.3

Generator Q$^{S\&P}$

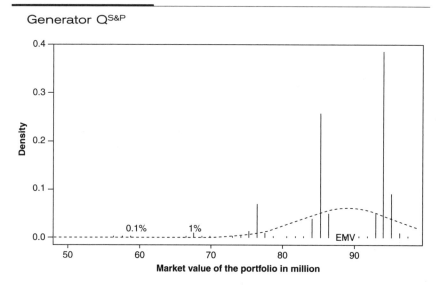

Hence, if we choose the generator Q^{Bank} instead of $Q^{S\&P}$, we have a smaller amount for the economic capital of about 25 and 10 percent, respectively, at the same confidence levels and therefore a considerable saving potential for the bank. We want to point out that these results are not representative, as the estimation of the generators is based on a non-representative subportfolio, and also the portfolio model is using idealized assumptions. In Figure 17.3, we can also see that at time $H = 1$, the market values are basically located in four fields. In the area on the entire right no firm defaulted, to the left one firm defaulted, in the next area two defaulted, and on the entire left three firms defaulted.

As a combination of two generators has better qualities than each generator alone, we ask the question how the combination of both generators $Q^{S\&P}$ and Q^{Bank} affects the economic capital. Using the same approach as in this chapter's fourth section, both generators have to be weight and afterwards added to a new generator Q^{opt}: $Q^{opt} = (1 - p)Q^{Bank} + pQ^{S\&P}$. We have a weight factor of $p = 0.79$ for the two available generators. Using the above-described simulation with the new generator $Q^{opt} = 0.21Q^{Bank} + 0.79Q^{S\&P}$, the results for the expected market value of the portfolio, the 1 and 0.1 percent quantiles, as well as the economic capital, are shown in Table 17.6.

T A B L E   17.6

Results for Q^opt in US$ million

	EMV	$VaR_{0.01}$	$EC_{0.01}$	$VaR_{0.001}$	$EC_{0.001}$
Q^{opt}	90	69	21	67	23

A comparison of Table 17.6 and Table 17.5 shows that the calculated economic capital of the combined generator Q^{opt} does not have to be necessarily, as one might assume, between the calculated values of the generators $Q^{S\&P}$ and Q^{Bank}. The value for $\alpha = 1\%$ is indeed between the calculated values for the economic capital of the generators $Q^{S\&P}$ and Q^{Bank}; however, for $\alpha = 0.1\%$, the economic capital for the combined generator is smaller than the values, which where calculated with individual generators.

CONCLUSION

We have shown that the aggregation of rating classes for a homogeneous Markov model is possible. Consequently, combination of internal and external ratings is possible, however the question how to aggregate the classes to a master scale remains open; potentially, the PD is a sensible indication. On basis of a master scale, combining estimators for unknown histories is possible and has been shown to be more accurate; the variance is smaller, and it has better qualities than each individual estimator. Besides the sample size on which the estimator is based, the time for each generator has to be considered as well for the weight factor p, while the effect of the sample size is bigger than the time. Overall, a proportional factor with the size of the rating frame being linear and using a root for the time turns out to be optimal.

Furthermore, different generator estimations have substantial effects on the amount of the economic capital. In practice, one is interested in a model for the risks as realistic as possible, to reach a most efficient allocation of tight equity resources for different business units. The approach introduced here to model rating migrations provides a contribution to measure changes in credit ratings more precisely with the combination of internal and external ratings and therewith provides better modeling of the economic capital. While combining the generators, it turns out that the economic capital calculated with the combined generator is not necessarily, as one might expect, between the calculated economic capital of the individual generators. For two real rating systems, again, the calculated economic capital of the optimal generator is not always between the economic capital of the individual generators. Here, a problem is how to model the distribution tails of the market value distribution, because often there are only very small probabilities on large portfolio losses. This is important for calculating α-quantiles with a very small α. This issue, however, is a general problem in statistics.

For the derivation of these results, we assumed homogeneous Markov processes for credit histories. For external rating data Kiefer and Larson (2007) and for internal rating data Weißbach et al. (2008b) have detected that homogeneity has to be declined in general. However, these studies are based on very large data sets, so that even small inhomogeneities can lead to significant test results. Kiefer and Larson (2007) find homogeneity for external ratings in small systems; Weißbach and Dette (2007) point out that for internal ratings inhomogeneity can often be referred to few rating class combinations. Furthermore, the process can be adapted to cumulative intensities in the case of inhomogeneity with the Aalen–Johansen estimator [cf., Andersen et al. (1993, pp.288ff)]. An even more exact estimation of the cumulative intensities can be obtained by designing them on the intensity estimations [see, e.g., Weißbach (2006) and Weißbach et al. (2008a)]. Here, one has to consider that there is a very large advantage of homogeneity because of the small amount of parameters, and one should only move away from homogeneity if there are strong violations of this assumption. A formal analysis about "nearly-homogeneity," e.g., in the meaning of equivalence testing [see, e.g., Munk and Pflüger (1999)] is still outstanding.

Furthermore, in our model we did not consider covariates (as, e.g., economic cycle). However, these effects can be integrated in the model with a Cox regression [cf., Cox (1972)], which models the effects on the intensities. In this respect, the question about independent rating histories can be approached.

In this context, it would also be interesting to explore the correlation between internal and external ratings. In this way potential information edges of external rating agencies over banks (and vice versa) can be detected. A big challenge while combining ratings is the different scaling of internal and external rating classes. For example, the data used in our models, the large German bank uses eight, respectively 20, rating classes, and S&P uses seven, respectively 19, rating classes. As a solution for this problem, a combined rougher classification can be used. For the mapping of the parameters of the finer in the rougher model, we would suggest an analytical solution. We have to note, however, that by now also banks work on integrative systems. A further problem while combining internal and external ratings is the determination of the amount of data on which the estimations are based. Especially with external ratings this information is not always available. If only presumptions about the sample sizes are available, they can also be weight, as small deviations are not very important.

Finally, we want to note that concerning our goal to underlay credit transactions with equity, the so-called regulatory capital after Basel II could also be used [cf., Basel Committee on Banking Supervision (2004)]. To point out the effects of the different estimators and therefore to underline the practical relevance of the obtained results, we focused upon the calculation of the economic capital. The assumptions, e.g., the choice of a very simple credit portfolio, the negligence of interest rates, or the choice of a recovery rate of 0, were only taken for reasons of simplifying the model. The obtained results can probably also be transferred to more complicated models.

REFERENCES

Albert, A. (1962) Estimating the Infinitesimal Generator of a Continuous Time, Finite State Markov Process. *Annals of Mathematical Statistics*, 33(2): 727–753.

Andersen, P.K., Ø. Borgan, R.D. Gill, and N. Keiding (1993) *Statistical Models based on Counting Processes*. New York: Springer.

Basel Committee on Banking Supervision. (2004) *International convergence of capital measurement and capital standards*. Technical report, Bank for International Settlements, Basel, Switzerland.

Bielecki, T.R. and M. Rutkowski (2002) *Credit Risk: Modeling, Valuation and Hedging.* New York: Springer.

Bluhm, C., L. Overbeck, and C. Wagner (2003) *Credit Risk Modelling.* Boca Raton, FL: Chapman & Hall/CRC.

Casjens, S., F. Kramer, T. Mollenhauer, and R. Walter (2007) Die Optimale Kombination Interner und Externer Ratings. In W. von Schimmelmann and G. Franke (eds.), Interne und Externe Ratings. Frankfurter Allgemeine Buch.: Frankfurt, Germany.

Cox, D. (1972) Regression Models and Life Tables. *Journal of the Royal Statistical Society,* 34(2): 187–220.

Hand, J.R.M., R.W. Holthausen, and R.W. Leftwich (1992) The Effect of Bond Rating Agency Announcements on Bond and Stock Prices. *Journal of Finance,* 47(2): 733–752.

Israel, R.R., J.S. Rosenthal, and J.Z. Wei (2001) Finding Generators for Markov Chains via Empirical Transition Matrices with Applications to Credit Ratings. *Mathematical Finance,* 11(2): 245–265.

Kiefer, N.M. and C.E. Larson (2007) A Simulation Estimator for Testing the Time Homogeneity of Credit Rating Transitions. *Journal of Empirical Finance,* 14(5): 818–835.

J.P.Morgan. (1997) *CreditMetrics.* Technical Report, New York.

Munk, A. and R. Pflüger (1999) $1 - \alpha$ Equivariant Confidence Rules for Convex Alternatives Are $\alpha/2$-Level Tests with Applications to the Multivariate Assessment of Bioequivalence. *Journal of the American Statistical Association,* 94(448): 1311–1319.

Weißbach R. (2006) A General Kernel Functional Estimator with General Bandwidth—Strong Consistency and Applications. *Journal of Nonparametric Statistics,* 18(1): 1–12.

Weißbach, R. and H. Dette (2007) Kolmogorov–Smirnov-type Testing for the Partial Homogeneity of Markov Processes with Application to Credit Risk. *Applied Stochastic Models in Business and Industry,* 23(3): 223–234.

Weißbach, R., A. Pfahlberg, and O. Gefeller (2008a) Double-Smoothing in Kernel Hazard Rate Estimation. *Methods of Information in Medicine,* 47(2): 167–173.

Weißbach, R., P. Tschiersch, and C. Lawrenz (2008b) Testing Homogeneity of Rating Transitions after Origination of Debt. *Empirical Economics*, forthcoming.

Risk-Managing the Uncertainty in VaR Model Parameters[1]

Jason C. Hsu and Vitali Kalesnik

ABSTRACT

Managing risk successfully requires a detailed understanding of the distributions from which random shocks to asset prices are drawn. However, there is uncertainty in both the actual distribution of returns and the parameters characterizing the distribution. In this chapter, we focus on the uncertainty in estimating the distributional parameters and how this uncertainty impacts value at risk calculations. We illustrate some traditional (but naïve) methods for handling parameter uncertainty and show that these methods could often lead to poor risk management results. We then provide techniques for quantifying risk more accurately when distribution parameters are estimated with low precision or when there are disagreements over the parameter estimates.

---

[1] The authors would like to acknowledge Bryce Little, Vivek Vishwanathan, and Feifei Li for their assistance in completing this chapter.

THE SUBPRIME CRISIS OF 2008

The most familiar risk measure used by practitioners has been the standard deviation of portfolio returns, introduced by Harry Markowitz (1959) in his seminal work on portfolio selection. However, this measure has a considerable drawback: it treats extremely favorable realizations in the same way as the extremely adverse ones. To overcome this shortcoming, several downside risk measures have been introduced and adopted. Most notably, value at risk (VaR), which was popularized in the mid-1990s by J.P. Morgan's RiskMetrics, has become a universal risk management tool in the finance industry. For financial institutions complying with the European Capital Adequacy Directive (CAD) and Basel II Accords or funds seeking qualification under UCIT-III, VaR modeling and computation are not just best practices—they are required. However, like other financial innovations such as mean-variance portfolio optimization and option pricing, successful application of VaR depends on the quality of one's model parameter inputs.

In 2008, 10 years after the 1998 Russian–Asian financial crisis that triggered the collapse of Long-Term Capital Management (LTCM), the world again witnessed a global crisis that threatens to destabilize our capital markets and financial institutions. This new crisis was triggered by the U.S. subprime mortgage debacle and has already brought the collapse of Bear Stearns, the world's fifth largest investment bank. Other investment banks have been forced to recapitalize by issuing mixtures of debt and equity to sovereign wealth funds at distressed prices. The Abu Dhabi Investment Authority (ADIA) acquired a $7.5 billion stake in Citigroup. Singapore's Government Investment Corporation (GIC) invested $9.75 billion and $6.88 billion into UBS and Citigroup, respectively. The GIC's sister entity, Temasek, along with Korean Investment Corporation (KIC), infused a combined $11 billion into Merrill Lynch. Chinese Investment Corporation invested $5 billion in Morgan Stanley. Before the dust settles, poor management of subprime exposure may very well lay claim to more victims.

In the face of mounting subprime losses and the ensuing financial markets crisis, it appears that the finance industry's application of VaR is still far from adequate. At the writing of this chapter, global subprime related losses have surpassed $215 billion according to Japan's Financial Services Agency (FSA). J.P. Morgan Chase and Deutsche Bank estimate that global losses could ultimately reach between $300 billion and $400 billion. This estimate dwarfs the loss posted by the LTCM collapse, which resulted in a wealth destruction of $4.6 billion to investors and financial counterparties.

Additionally, the amplification of asset class correlations has prompted a liquidity crunch throughout credit markets. Unfavorable lending conditions spurred an unprecedented series of liquidity injections and policy interventions from both the European Central Bank and U.S. Federal Reserve banks. It is estimated that the European Central Bank provided $500 billion in liquidity since late 2007. The Federal Reserve, in addition to offering $200 billion in bailout loans and guaranteeing Bear Stearns' balance sheet, embarked on a series of interest rate cuts in an attempt to thaw frozen credit markets. It appears that extreme (tail) events continue to catch our financial institutions by surprise. Noted risk author Nassim Taleb's Black Swans seem, somehow, more frequent than data or conventional wisdom would indicate. However, we argue later in this chapter that the problem might not be due to inadequate modeling of unexpected events but rather might be due to the inappropriate treatment of disagreements in investment beliefs.

Why have things gone so very wrong again? Banks are required to perform VaR calculations to ensure capital adequacy as well as to manage balance sheet risk. However, VaR did not seem to help financial institutions manage their subprime exposure adequately. Many argue that banks may have been using incorrect probability distributions to model asset price risk. Particularly, the distributions used for computing VaR may not sufficiently capture the frequency of extreme shocks to asset prices (kurtosis) as well as the size of the extreme shocks (negative skew). In this chapter, we contend that financial institutions have become sufficiently sophisticated and educated about fat tail distributions in risk modeling. Advanced applications of VaR often involve discussions of fat tail distributions such as Levy or Cauchy distributions.

The progress made in VaR research with respect to extreme event risk modeling has been tremendous since the days of LTCM. There are numerous articles in practitioner journals [see Lucas (2000)] addressing the issue of fat tail distribution and their modeling with respect to VaR. Nassim Taleb, whose Black Swan analogy poetically illustrates our natural tendency to underestimate randomness—or rather, overestimate knowledge—has continued to alert the finance industry to tail event risk. We, as an industry have invested significant resources in applying non-normal and leptokurtotic distributions to model extreme loss events. So, what went awry?

In this chapter, we argue that the poor risk management is caused in large part by the failure to properly recognize and account for disagreements in investment beliefs. In the academic literature, this is known as uncertainty in asset return distribution parameters. A number of financial pundits, including Bill Gross of PIMCO, have warned us of the risk of the aggressive mortgage lending practices and the ensuing real estate speculation that prevailed from 2002 through 2007. The subprime problem is not a Black Swan in that regard. Some investors expected the aggressive subprime lending to lead to problems, while others did not. Certainly, ex ante, neither is 100 percent correct; how do we account for these diverging market views? In the VaR language, we need to adjust for the reality that we do not have perfect information regarding the mean and other moments of the asset return distribution.

The uncertainty regarding distribution parameters can often be very substantial when there is significant disagreement on return assumptions. For example, suppose members of an investment committee disagree about the forward-looking state of the stock market. Two members on the committee believe that a bear market is forthcoming and expect the market to yield a –20 percent return. The remaining three members believe a bull market will continue and expect a 20 percent return. How do we model this difference in investment beliefs? If we do not correctly model this parameter disagreement, but instead naïvely accept the estimate as determined by the majority rule or by some blended averaging, we would mismanage ex ante portfolio risk. Fine tuning the fat tail characteristics would not redress the problem sufficiently.

In this chapter we present a method that appropriately accounts for distributional uncertainty. We illustrate the technique with examples of mean, variance, and correlation uncertainty. Specifically, we compare VaR statistics generated from this approach against other standard (and more naïve) approaches. We show that properly quantifying mean and variance uncertainty leads to significant improvement in ex ante risk characterization of an investment portfolio.

PARAMETER UNCERTAINTY

In traditional VaR analysis, we assume that the parameters, such as the mean and variance, characterizing the probability distribution are known with perfect accuracy. This seems rather counterintuitive since we readily admit our inability to determine the exact probability distribution to model shocks to asset prices. Probability distributions like the Levy distribution, the Cauchy distribution, and other fat tail stable Paretian distributions have been considered for modeling asset returns, in addition to the classic lognormal distribution. Academics and practitioners have argued over the merit of these different modeling choices but have generally conceded that uncertainty exists in identifying the right distribution model. We argue that the uncertainty regarding the mean and covariance is likely far greater in most investment decision process.

What makes estimating the mean and covariance of the return distribution challenging for VaR applications is the short time horizon over which the parameter estimates must hold true. While investing is a long horizon endeavor, risk management is a necessarily a short horizon activity. One simply cannot ignore capital adequacy violations and margin calls because of the assumed effect of time diversification or a belief in long-term price mean reversion after substantial price decline. From a modeling perspective, this means we cannot rely on estimates derived from long horizon sample averages in the same way we use them to design a 10-year horizon strategic investment portfolio.

Given the empirical evidence supporting time-varying equity risk premium and stochastic market volatility, we need to take into account these shifting distributional parameters as well as our inability to accurately estimate them. Additionally, within an investment organization diverging but valid beliefs on the forward-looking state of the economy often coexist. This disagreement in investment beliefs, which represents uncertainty in the true distributional parameters, needs to be treated appropriately in VaR calculations. Lastly, it is important to note that parameter uncertainty is very different from uncertainty in the ex-post asset returns. Realized stock returns can differ substantially from its mean return, even if we are 100 percent certain about the equity mean return. This is the nature of stock return volatility—it is not related to the uncertainty over the mean of the stock return distribution. The classic VaR application addresses the risk arising from return volatility and handles it very successfully. Where it falls short is in accounting for the uncertainty in the mean estimate. We make this point clear in the example that follows, where we illustrate the effect of parameter uncertainty on risk management.

AN ILLUSTRATIVE EXAMPLE
WITH MEAN UNCERTAINTY

We revisit the previous example where a five-member investment committee is split 3 to 2 on the outlook for U.S. financial sector return over the next 12 months. We rewind the clock back to July 2007 when two Bear Stearns hedge funds collapsed from subprime investment losses. Three members on the committee believe that the subprime problem would be isolated to a few banks and that the market has largely priced in the full impact from the subprime problem (this surprisingly was the conventional Street wisdom at the time). Two members on the committee believe that the collapse of the Bear hedge funds was the beginning of a system-wide financial crisis. The bullish camp believes that after the sharp price correction, the forward-looking return for the financial sector would be very positive and would average 20 percent. The bearish camp believes that the financial sector return would be substantially negative at −20 percent. For simplicity, both sides assume a volatility of 15 percent; we will examine the effect of volatility uncertainty in the next section. Note that we use exaggerated numbers in our example to create a more stark illustration.

In this example, we consider four different risk assessment scenarios. Traditionally, the risk manager would take as inputs the assumptions provided by the investment committee; however there can be various ways to interpret the committee's outlooks when characterizing the distribution.

1. By majority balloting, the process would produce an expected return of 20 percent (in this case the parameters are mode estimates).
2. Perhaps the committee members would compromise and take averages of their views on mean and standard deviation, which would lead to an expected return of 4 percent.

3. Perhaps the risk manager would like to manage against the worst-case scenario and assume an expected return of –20 percent.
4. Finally, the risk manager might consider modeling the uncertainty in the expected mean return explicitly.

For the sake of simplicity, we only consider lognormal assumptions in this example. The analysis can be extended to fat tail distributions with similar results. We first write down the return distribution under the four different scenarios.

1. Majority rule estimate: $\ln r_1 \sim N\,(20\%, 15\%)$
2. Blended average estimate: $\ln r_2 \sim N\,(4\%, 15\%$
3. Worst-case estimate: $\ln r_3 \sim N\,(-20\%, 15\%)$
4. Parameter uncertainty:

$$\ln r_4 \sim \begin{cases} prob = \dfrac{3}{5}, N(20\%,15\%) \\[2ex] prob = \dfrac{2}{5}, N(-20\%,15\%) \end{cases}$$

where $N\,(\mu,\sigma)$ is a normal distribution with mean and standard deviation (μ,σ) and where the probability density function is

$$f(x;\mu,\sigma) = \frac{1}{\sqrt{2\pi}\sigma} \exp\left(\frac{-(x-\mu)^2}{2\sigma^2}\right),\ \text{for}\ -\infty < x < \infty$$

The density function for scenario 4 is therefore

$$g(x) = \frac{3}{5}f(x;20\%,15\%) + \frac{2}{5}f(x;-20\%,15\%),\ \text{for}\ -\infty < x < \infty$$

We plot the four ex ante density functions in Figure 18.1. We also compute some basic risk statistics in Table 18.1. In the first four columns, we compute the first four moments for the different ex ante distributions for $\ln x$. We then report, in column five, the VaR at 5 percent confidence assuming a portfolio that is 100 percent invested in the financial sector stocks. In

F I G U R E   18.1

Probability Density Function of Investment with
Mean Uncertainty

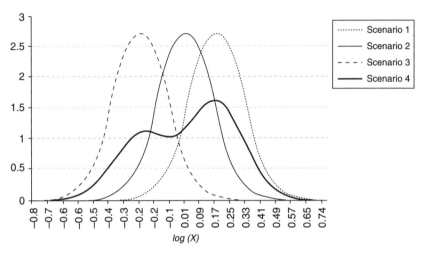

column six we report the expected percentage loss for this portfolio for outcomes in the negative 5 percent tail of the distribution. Finally, in column
seven, we compute the maximum allowable portfolio allocation to financial stocks, in a stock-versus-cash portfolio, assuming a loss tolerance of
–25 percent with 5 percent probability. This last statistic allows readers to
compare portfolio allocations given identical loss tolerance assumptions.
For example, a higher allocation to stocks in scenario 1 versus scenario 4
would suggest that the risk management assumptions in scenario 1 are less
conservative.

Comparing scenario 1 versus scenario 2, we note that the driver of the
disparity in VaR and associated risk statistics is the difference in the distribution mean assumption. Using the committee's blended view on the mean
return estimate instead of the mode estimate (arrived from majority rule)
leads to a more conservative risk estimation in this example. This suggests
that a compromise in the committee's investment beliefs can have beneficial risk management properties relative to a majority rule approach for
determining investment belief, when there is disagreement. However, the
blended mean approach illustrated in scenario 2, while it represents an
improvement over the majority rule approach, remains naïve and does not

produce the correct risk management calculation. Observe that the density function in scenarios 2 and 4 have the identical distribution means at 4 percent. However, the standard deviation in scenario 4 becomes significantly larger when we correctly account for the uncertainty in the mean.

The uncertainty-adjusted model leads to a more accurate and more conservative risk assessment than the naïve model with a simple blended mean. Note that the uncertainty-adjusted distribution is no longer normal, which means parameter uncertainty can lead to a non-lognormal ex ante distribution assumption even when the underlying asset return process is lognormal.

Naturally, the worst-case scenario parameter assumed in scenario 3 leads to the most conservative risk management. However, this risk management approach is also not desirable, because it results in insufficient risk taking, which would hurt investment results. Note that the equity allocation, corresponding to a 5 percent chance of 25 percent loss, under the worst-case scenario, is 69 percent compared to 80 percent for the uncertainty-adjusted model. This represents a significant under-investment where as the majority rule and the blended estimates approaches lead to significant over-investment at 100 percent.

Observe that the log distribution with parameter uncertainty has a significantly higher variance and negative skewness which results in a starkly more conservative risk management guideline resulting from the VaR and expected shortfall calculation. Interestingly, we also observe a negative excess kurtosis in the distribution with uncertain mean. However, the negative excess kurtosis is entirely dominated by the

T A B L E   18.1

Risk characteristics of investment with mean uncertainty

	Mean	Volatility	Skewness	Kurtosis	VaR 5%	Expected Shortfall	Max % Invested (5% Chance of 25% Loss)
Scenario 1	20.00%	15.00%	0.00%	0.00%	4.59%	10.42%	100.00%
Scenario 2	4.00%	15.00%	0.00%	0.00%	18.70%	23.70%	100.00%
Scenario 3	−20.00%	15.00%	0.00%	0.00%	36.05%	39.95%	69.36%
Scenario 4	4.00%	24.68%	−20.44%	−72.89%	31.13%	36.11%	80.30%
Scale	ln x	ln x	ln x	ln x	x	x	x

increase in the variance relative to the normal model with blended mean estimate. This suggests that capturing fat tails (or higher probability for extreme outcomes) may not be as important in risk management as capturing parameter uncertainty correctly.

AN ILLUSTRATIVE EXAMPLE WITH VARIANCE UNCERTAINTY

We now extend the previous example and consider a situation where there is uncertainty over the variance of the distribution. Suppose that the members on the investment committee agree on the forward-looking mean return for the financial sector. They expect return to be 10 percent but disagree on the volatility. Three members expect a forward environment with relatively modest volatility at 12 percent. The remaining two members expect a choppier market with volatility near the historical high of 25 percent.

Again, we consider four different risk assessment scenarios.

1. The majority rule process would produce a volatility assumption of 12 percent.
2. Blending the opinion of the committee would result in an estimated volatility of 17.2 percent.
3. The worst-case scenario assumes a volatility of 25 percent.
4. We apply the parameter uncertainty approach. The return distributions are

   a. Majority rule estimate: $\ln r_1 \sim N(10\%, 12\%)$
   b. Blended average estimate: $\ln r_2 \sim N(10\%, 17.2\%)$
   c. Worst case estimate: $\ln r_3 \sim N(10\%, 25\%)$
   d. Parameter uncertainty: $\ln r_4 \sim \begin{cases} prob = \dfrac{3}{5}, N(10\%,12\%) \\ prob = \dfrac{2}{5}, N(10\%,25\%) \end{cases}$

where again $N(\mu, \sigma)$ is a normal distribution with mean and standard deviation (μ, σ) and where the probability density function is

$$f(x;\mu,\sigma) = \frac{1}{\sqrt{2\pi}\sigma} \exp\left(\frac{-(x-\mu)^2}{2\sigma^2}\right), \text{ for } -\infty < x < \infty$$

The density function for scenario 4 is

$$g(x) = \frac{3}{5} f(x;10\%,12\%) + \frac{2}{5} f(x;-10\%,25\%), \text{ for } -\infty < x < \infty$$

We plot the ex ante density functions in Figure 18.2 and the basic risk statistics in Table 18.2.

Using the committee's blended view on the volatility instead of using the majority rule approach leads again to a more conservative risk assessment. For the density function in scenarios 2 and 4, again, the standard deviation in scenario 4 becomes larger when we correctly account for the uncertainty in variance. Note, however, that the increase in standard deviation was not as pronounced as the situation when there is uncertainty in the distribution mean. Note also that in scenario 4 where we adjust for variance uncertainty, kurtosis becomes positive. The increase in volatility and the increase in kurtosis both contribute to a more conservative risk assessment than the naïve model with a simple blended standard deviation.

Observe that when we adjust for variance uncertainty appropriately, the resulting ex ante log distribution has a slightly higher variance and does not show a negative skew as was seen in the ex ante distribution with

F I G U R E   18.2

Probability Density Function of Investment with Variance Uncertainty

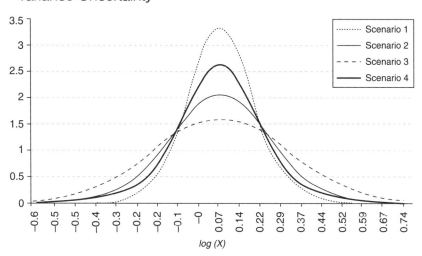

log (X)

T A B L E   18.2

Risk characteristics of investment with variance uncertainty

	Mean	Volatility	Skewness	Kurtosis	VaR 5%	Expected Shortfall	Max % Invested (5% Chance of 25% Loss)
Scenario 1	10.00%	12.00%	0.00%	0.00%	9.31%	13.93%	100.00%
Scenario 2	10.00%	17.20%	0.00%	0.00%	16.74%	22.40%	100.00%
Scenario 3	10.00%	25.00%	0.00%	0.00%	26.77%	33.87%	93.38%
Scenario 4	10.00%	18.34%	0.00%	147.20%	18.09%	26.68%	100.00%
Scale	ln x	ln x	ln x	ln x	x	x	x

mean uncertainty. However, we do pick up positive kurtosis in the face of variance uncertainty. The uncertainty in the variance estimate transforms the lognormal distribution into a fat tail distribution. It is this increase in kurtosis that drives much of the disparity in risk assessment between the blended average approach and the uncertainty approach. Note that when there is uncertainty in the variance estimate, the uncertainty approach can lead to similar risk assessment outcome as an approach that assumes a fat tail distribution.

AN ILLUSTRATIVE EXAMPLE WITH CORRELATION UNCERTAINTY

We extend the above example to study the effect of correlation uncertainty in a too risky asset environment. We consider investments in U.S financial stocks and in commodities. For simplicity, suppose the two asset classes will have equal weights in the portfolio, and the aforementioned committee members agree on both the mean and the variance of the bivariate distribution and disagree only on the correlation. For simplicity, we assume the vector of means and standard deviations are $\mu = (10\%, 10\%)$ and $\sigma = (12\%, 12\%)$. Suppose three members have a view that stocks and commodities would have a negative correlation of –30 percent; they assume that commodities exposure is a good hedge against equity risk. Suppose the remaining two members believe that the forthcoming

U.S. recession would suggest temporary lower demand for commodities, which suggest that equity prices and commodity prices would become correlated on the downside, making the commodity investment a poor hedge; they assume a 90 percent short-term correlation.

In this example we compare only the blended average approach represented in scenario 1 with the parameter uncertainty approach in scenario 2. We write down the joint distribution density function of the form N (μ_x, μ_y; σ_x, σ_y; ρ). Again, for simplicity and with no loss of generality, the log returns for scenario 1 are assumed to be bivariate normal.

1. Blended average: $(\ln r_1, \ln r_2) \sim N$ (10%, 10%; 25%, 25% 18%), where the joint density function is

$$f(x,y;\mu_x,\mu_y,\sigma_x,\sigma_y,\rho)$$

$$= \frac{1}{2\pi\sigma_x\sigma_y\sqrt{1-\rho^2}}\exp\left(\frac{-1}{2(1-\rho^2)}\left(\frac{x^2}{\sigma_x^2}+\frac{y^2}{\sigma_y^2}-\frac{2\rho xy}{\sigma_x\sigma_y}\right)\right), \text{ for } -\infty < x,y < \infty$$

The density function for parameter uncertainty is then

2. Correlation uncertainty:

$$g(x,y) = \frac{3}{5}f(x,y;10\%,10\%;25\%,25\%,-30\%)$$

$$+\frac{2}{5}f(x,y;10\%,10\%;25\%,25\%;90\%), \text{ for } -\infty < x,y < \infty$$

Since the allocations to equities and commodities are fixed at 50 percent each, we can derive the density function for the portfolio log return from the joint density function by integrating over x and y with the constraint that the portfolio return $r = 0.5x + 0.5y$. Using the portfolio return density function we can compute the portfolio VaR. We plot the two portfolio return density functions in Figure 18.3 and present the risk statistics in Table 18.3. In both scenarios, portfolios have identical mean return and volatility. Properly accounting for the correlation uncertainty, results in a significantly fatter tail, as seen by the large excess kurtosis. The excess kurtosis means that the portfolio risk appetite falls dramatically, even with similar mean and variance.

F I G U R E   18.3

Probability Density Function of Investment with
Correlation Uncertainty

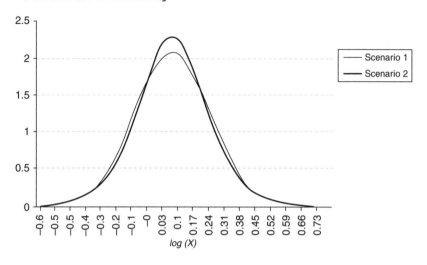

T A B L E   18.3

Risk characteristics of investment with correlation uncertainty

	Mean	Volatility	Skewness	Kurtosis	VaR 5%	Expected Shortfall	Max % Invested (5% Chance of 25% Loss)
Scenario 1	10.00%	19.20%	0.00%	0.00%	29.31%	33.69%	85.29%
Scenario 2	10.00%	19.20%	0.00%	74.46%	31.73%	37.58%	78.79%
Scale	ln x	ln x	ln x	ln x	ln x	ln x	ln x

CONCLUSION

In this chapter, we present a technique that appropriately handles disagreements in investment belief or uncertainty in return distribution parameters. Disagreements in investment belief are common in a diverse and healthy investment organization. People with different experiences and perspectives will often have different investment outlooks. Members on the investment committee will disagree on the outlook for asset class returns, on the forward-looking volatility as well as correlations across the asset classes. From a modeling standpoint, diverse investment outlooks can be characterized as uncertainty about the parameters that govern the joint distribution of asset returns. This is a far stronger statement regarding our inability to forecast the future than what is assumed in standard models. Not only are we unable to forecast the random shocks to the economy that result in volatility in asset returns, we are actually unable to characterize the random distribution which governs the asset returns with certainty. In other words, we are uncertain about the parameters of the probability distribution from which the random returns are drawn.

However, existing standard risk management approaches do not properly handle parameter uncertainty. This, we believe has led to inadequate risk management, which we believe has led to some systemic crises in the financial industry, despite the widespread application of VaR systems. The U.S. subprime crisis, which, according to Street estimates, will ultimately create more than $300 billion in losses for global financial institutions, has again brought to focus the failure of our current risk management practices. It may be convenient to argue that the subprime crisis was a six-sigma event or a Black Swan event that could only be modeled with the most sophisticated fat tail distributions. We posit, however, that the problem may occur with the inappropriate modeling of parameter uncertainty. We illustrate, with a few simplified examples, where the traditional methods for estimating distribution parameters lead to suboptimal risk management when parameters are uncertain. The resulting risk statistics often understate the true risk. Specifically, if beliefs regarding mean and covariance were created through a majority rule process, where the most popular estimates were selected, we would find suboptimal risk taking relative to the proper ex ante belief distribution. The resulting risk characteristics would either wildly under- or overestimate the true risk. If we use a blended average approach to reach a compromise estimate on the mean and covariance, the resulting risk characteristics would always underestimate the true risk and often quite substantially. We show additionally, that using a fat tail distribution to account for potential extreme events does not produce the same risk management effect as accounting for parameter uncertainty and often still results in understating the true risk.

In conclusion, while rare extreme events may contribute to the crises in our financial markets, it is more likely that our risk management approach has simply not accounted for parameter uncertainty appropriately. The effect will be particularly severe in situations where the investment beliefs are very diverse, reflecting large uncertainty in the return distribution parameters. Imagine the debates that went on at the major investment banks as executives argued over the wisdom of holding subprime mortgage papers as triple-A collaterals. There was likely a minority group of executives who forecasted a decline in real estate prices, which would suggest a significantly negative expected return on the subprime mortgage papers. Ultimately, this view was not supported by the majority opinion or had led to only a small revision downward in return assumptions on the subprime papers; this meant that the resulting VaR statistics would understate the ex ante risk. We suspect that had the uncertainty been appropriately modeled, the VaR calculations would have produced very different risk statistics, which might have led the banks to reduce their exposure to subprime related instruments.

ACKNOWLEDGMENT

The authors would like to acknowledge Bryce Little, Vivek Vishwanathan, and Feifei Li for their assistance in completing this chapter.

REFERENCES

Beder, T.S. (1995) VaR: Seductive but Dangerous. *Financial Analysts Journal*, 51(5): 12–23.

Froot, K.A. and S.E. Posner (2002) The Pricing of Event Risks with Parameter Uncertainty. *The Geneva Papers on Risk and Insurance*, 27(2): 153–165.

Hendricks, D. (1996) Evaluation of Value at Risk Models Using Historical Data. *Federal Reserve Bank New York Economic Policy Review*, 2(1): 49–69.

Guldimann, T. (1995) *RiskMetrics—Technical Document*. Morgan Guaranty Trust Company: New York.

Jorion P. (2000) *Value at Risk—The New Benchmark for Managing Financial Risk*. New York: McGraw-Hill.

Lawrence, C. and G. Robinson (1995) How safe Is RiskMetrics? *Risk*, 8(1): 26–29.

Lucas, A. (2000) A Note on Optimal Estimation from a Risk-Management Perspective Under Possibly Misspecified Tail Behavior. *Journal of Business and Economic Statistics*, 18(1): 31–39.

Marshall, C. and M. Siegel (1997) Value at Risk: Implementing a Risk Measurement Standard. *Journal of Derivatives*, 4(3): 91–111.

Markowitz, H.M. (1959) *Portfolio Selection: Efficient Diversification of Investments*. Hoboken, NJ: John Wiley & Sons.

Taleb, N.N. (2007) *The Black Swan: The Impact of the highly improbable*. New York: Random House.

Xiongwei J. and N. Pearson (1999) Using Value-at-Risk to Control Risk Taking: How Wrong Can You Be? *The Journal of Risk*, 1(2): 5–36.

CHAPTER 19

Structural Credit Modeling and Its Relationship to Market Value at Risk: An Australian Sectoral Perspective

David E. Allen and Robert Powell

ABSTRACT

The Basel II accord permits banks to use internal models for credit modeling to calculate capital requirements. Over concentration of credit exposure to particular industry sectors can be a significant contributor to bank risk. The use of conditional value at risk (CVaR) is gaining popularity as a measurement of credit risk; high lending losses are often impacted by a small number of extreme events. This chapter examines the sectoral probability of default (PD) in an Australian context using the structural approach of Merton (1974). A novel feature is the introduction of a CVaR component into structural modeling, which we term the *conditional probability of default* (CPD). We also examine the interaction between sectoral credit and market (equity) risk using VaR and CVaR models for market risk and PD and CPD models for credit risk. Significant correlation is found between all of the approaches implying that sectors that are risky from a credit perspective are not significantly differently risky when viewed from a market perspective.

INTRODUCTION

The Basel II accord (Bank for International Settlements, 2004) has placed a huge focus within the banking industry on risk modeling. Banks are required to set aside capital, calculated as a percentage of their risk weighted assets. There is a significant cost to banks in holding capital, as opposed to being able to get a market return on these funds. Under the Basel II accord, banks that meet certain credit modeling criteria are able to use internal models to help determine risk weighted capital. This could significantly benefit banks that are able to demonstrate a reduced capital requirement.

The importance of credit modeling and of the understanding and management of credit risk is highlighted by the statement by the then Deputy Reserve Bank Governor, G. J. Thompson (1997): "All of the major periods of stress in Australian Banking have been caused by credit losses." This view is supported by the then Group General Manager, Financial and Risk Management of one of the largest Australian banks the Commonwealth Bank, Michael Ullmer (1997), who notes that "... there is overwhelming evidence for the potency of credit related losses on the banking system."

Management of sectoral risk is a key component of credit risk management. Jackson (1996) notes sectoral or regional over concentration as one of the key reasons for 22 banks in the United Kingdom failing or experiencing severe difficulty. Knowledge of relative industry risk is important to banks for risk management purposes such as setting sector concentration limits and allocating discretionary lending authorities. While industry risk can be measured using macroeconomic analysis, for example, the CreditPortfolioView model (Wilson, 1998), macroeconomic approaches to measurement of industry risk are not popular in Australia as noted by the Australian Prudential Regulation Authority (APRA) (1999, p. 4) in their statement:

> Currently none of the Australian banks favours a credit risk modeling approach conditioned on the state of the economy. Apart from the additional modeling complexity involved, the banks express concern that errors in forecasting economic turning points could lead, in particular, to a shortfall in desired capital coverage just as the economy turns sharply downwards.

Based on the premise that all industry information is captured in equity prices, if there is a strong correlation between those industries that are risky from an equities perspective and those that are risky from a market perspective (which we find that there is), then we propose that industry risk can be measured and incorporated into credit modeling using a VaR approach, without the need for the macroeconomic analysis that banks do not favor. Indeed, the equities VaR approach to measuring industry risk is incorporated into transitional matrix modeling of credit risk in a subsequent paper by the same authors (Allen and Powell, 2008b).

Some of the more popular approaches to credit risk measurement have included KMV Credit Monitor (Crosbie and Bohn, 2003), CreditMetrics (Gupton et al., 1997), CreditPortfolioView (Wilson, 1998), CreditRisk$^+$ (Credit Suisse First Boston International, 1997), and reduced form models [e.g., Jarrow et al. (1997)].

This study focuses on the structural approach to credit risk, based on methodology used by Merton and KMV, as discussed in the section Structural Model of this chapter. We also introduce a conditional approach to probability of default (CPD), in a similar manner as CVaR is used as an alternative to VaR. Conditional value at risk considers extreme events, based on losses exceeding VaR. Conditional value at risk studies have traditionally been used in the insurance industry, but are gaining popularity as a credit risk measure, with the increasing recognition that infrequent large losses are an important feature of credit risk measurement. Conditional value at risk has also gained popularity as it does not demonstrate some of the undesirable properties of VaR such as lack of subadditivity; see Artzner et al. (1997; 1999). Conditional value at risk has been used in credit risk studies, for example, Bucay and Rosen (1999) and Uryasev et al. (2000). These studies have centered around the Creditmetrics transition matrix approach. The Uryasev et al. (2000) study focuses on the optimization of portfolios.

This study obtains relative credit risk rankings for Australian industries, based on PD and CPD. We also explore whether there is a link between market (equity) risk and credit risk in these industries, i.e., whether the same industries that are risky from a market perspective are also risky from a credit perspective. Numerous studies have been undertaken using structural methodology on various aspects of credit risk, such as asset correlation (Cespedes, 2002; Kealhofer and Bohn, 1993; Lopez, 2002; Vasicek, 1987; Zeng and Zhang, 2001), predictive value and validation (Bharath and Shumway, 2004; Stein, 2002), the effect of default risk on equity returns (Vassalou and Xing, 2002), and fixed-income modeling (D'Vari et al., 2003). However, we have not identified any studies that use a structural approach to ranking industries in Australia or that apply a CPD approach to structural modeling.

The section Structural Model provides background to the structural approach, with detailed methodology provided in the section Methodology. Results and Conclusions are presented in the forth and fifth sections.

STRUCTURAL MODEL

KMV Credit Monitor (Crosbie and Bohn, 2003) provides an estimated default frequency (EDF) for individual assets, using market information. It is based on a modification of Merton's asset value model (1974).

The Merton–KMV approach as described in Crosbie and Bohn (2003) is based on the option pricing work of Black and Scholes in 1973. In summary, the firm defaults if the debt obligation exceeds the asset value of the firm at a selected time period.

Under the KMV model, probability of default PD is a function of the distance to default (DD) (number of standard deviations between the value of the firm and the debt).

Using Merton's model, probability of default (PD) can be determined from DD using the normal distribution. KMV find that the normal distribution approach followed by Merton results in PD values much smaller than defaults observed in practice. KMV has a large worldwide database from which to provide empirically based EDFs. For example, KMV finds that historical data shows that firms with a DD of 4 have an average default rate of approximately 1% and therefore assign an EDF of 1 percent to firms with this DD.

Thus the KMV model consists of 3 steps which are estimating the market value and volatility of the firm's assets, calculating the distance to default, and matching the distance to default to an empirically obtained EDF. Detailed methodology is discussed in the following section.

METHODOLOGY

Summary of Our Market VaR Methodology

Our market VaR methodology is described in our market risk paper by Allen and Powell (2008a). In summary we use the Australian All Ords index and obtain a VaR measurement for each industry based on the universal GICS industry codes. A parametric approach is used for calculating VaR at the 95 percent level (after considering survivorship bias and adjusting for thin trading) on an undiversified and correlated basis. Market CVaR is calculated as the average of those returns beyond VaR. We used 15 years of data, and calculated VaR using a 7 year rolling window approach (for comparative purposes we also calculated VaR based on 12 month data tranches).

Credit Models Methodology

In the Merton approach, equity and the market value of the firm' assets are related as follows:

$$E = VN(d_1) - e^{-rT} FN(d_2) \tag{19.1}$$

where
- E = market value of firms equity
- F = face value of firm's debt
- r = risk free rate
- N = cumulative standard normal distribution function

$$d_1 = \frac{\ln(V/F) + (r + 0.5\sigma_v^2)T}{\sigma v \sqrt{T}} \tag{19.2}$$
$$d_2 = d_1 - \sigma_v \sqrt{T}$$

Volatility and equity are related under the Merton model as follows:

$$\sigma_E = \left(\frac{V}{E}\right) N(d_1)\sigma_V \tag{19.3}$$

For our credit model, we use the same equity data and industry codes as used in our VaR calculations. In line with KMV, debt is taken as the value of all current liabilities plus half the book value of all long-term debt outstanding. All this information is obtained from Datastream. T is set using common practice of one year. The risk free rate is based on a 12-month-average Australian Government Bond one-year rate. We follow the approach outlined by KMV (Crosbie and Bohn, 2003) and Bharath and Shumway (2004).

Initial asset returns are estimated from our historical equity data using the following formula:

$$\sigma_V = \sigma_E \left(\frac{E}{E + F} \right) \tag{19.4}$$

Equity returns and their standard deviation are calculated exactly the same as for our market approach, using seven-year rolling windows. These asset returns derived above are applied to Equation (19.5) to estimate the market value of assets every day. The daily log return is calculated and new asset values estimated. Following KMV, this process is repeated until asset returns converge (repeated until the difference in adjacent σ's is less than 10^{-3}). These figures are used to calculate DD and PD:

$$DD = \frac{\ln(V / F) + (\mu - 0.5_v^2)T}{\sigma_V \sqrt{T}} \tag{19.5}$$

$$PD = N(- DD) \tag{19.6}$$

As mentioned in the second section, KMV has a large worldwide database from which to provide empirically based EDFs. As also noted, EDFs are much larger than the PDs used by Merton (which yield very small values). This is not an issue for our study as we are interested in rankings rather than absolute values. Distance to default, PD, and EDF will all yield the same rankings because PD and EDF are all calculated from DD. Although we do not have access to the KMV database, there are studies which provide mapping of EDF values to S&P and/or Moody's rating categories [e.g., Lopez (2002) and Risk Management Association (2007)] with EDFs ranging from 0.02 percent for AAA ratings up to 20 percent for D ratings. Such maps can assist in the calibration of calculated DDs to EDF values, thereby obtaining more meaningful values than the very small values normally provided by PD, without disturbing the ranking.

Structural Correlation

Correlation can be calculated through calculating a time series analysis for each firm and then calculating a correlation between each pair of assets. KMV have instead adopted a factor modeling approach to their correlation calculation. KMV produce country and industry returns from their database of publicly traded firms, and their correlation model uses these indexes to create a composite factor index for each firm depending on the industry and country (D'Vari et al., 2003; Kealhofer and Bohn, 1993). We do not have access to the KMV database or factors and, hence, use the former approach to derive a diversified standard deviation. The undiversified standard deviation that was used in the calculation of the undiversified DD and PD is substituted with the diversified asset standard deviation when calculating the diversified DD and PD.

Conditional Approach to Probability of Default Calculation

For the purposes of this study we define CPD as being PD on the condition that standard deviation of asset returns exceeds standard deviation at the 95 percent confidence level, i.e., the worst 5 percent of asset returns. We calculate CPD using nonparametric and parametric methods. Conditional probability of default values can also be calibrated to EDF values as described in the section Credit Model Methodology.

Nonparametric CPD

We calculate the standard deviation of the worst 5 percent of daily asset returns for each rolling seven-year period to obtain a conditional standard deviation (CStdev). We then substitute CStdev into the formula used to calculate DD and obtain a conditional DD (CDD). Conditional probability of default is calculated by substituting DD with CDD into the CPD formula:

$$CDD = \frac{\ln(V/F) + (\mu - 0.5_v^2)T}{\text{CStdev}_V \sqrt{T}} \qquad (19.7)$$

and

$$CPD = N(- CDD) \qquad (19.8)$$

Parametric CPD

Conditional standard deviation is calculated as being the tail 5 percent of a normal distribution using the formula

$$\text{CStdev}_\alpha = \frac{\exp(-q_\alpha^2 / 2)}{\alpha \sqrt{2\pi}} \sigma \qquad (19.9)$$

where q_α is the tail 100α percentile of a standard normal distribution (e.g., 1.645 as obtained from standard distribution tables for 95 percent confidence).

RESULTS

Table 19.1 is a results summary for the structural model. This table provides industry ranking, with 1 being the highest risk and 25 the lowest risk. The market model calculates VaR at the 95 percent confidence level, and CVaR is the average losses beyond VaR. The credit model PD is based on the Merton–KMV structural approach, with CPD based on the worst 5 percent of asset returns.

Technology (hardware and software) ranks high on the risk front for both models. Some noticeable differences are banks and insurance, which rank as higher risk on the credit scale than the market scale due to balance sheet structure (lower equity percentage).

Using a Spearman rank correlation test (99 and 95 percent confidence levels), we find no significant difference in rankings between VaR and PD, VaR and CVaR, PD and CPD, or CVaR and CPD. When substituting diversified VaR (PD) for undiversified VaR (PD) in the above tests, we obtained the same outcomes (no significant difference in rankings).

T A B L E   19.1

Structural Model—Results Summary

	Market Model		Credit Model	
	Annual Undiversified 95% VaR	Non-parametric CVaR	Un-diversified PD	Non-parametric CPD
Automobiles & components	7	7	5	3
Banks	25	25	9	15
Capital goods	15	15	11	9
Chemicals	18	17	13	12
Commercial services & supplies	8	8	8	8
Construction materials	17	19	22	23
Consumer durables & apparel	10	10	15	13
Diversified financials	19	18	24	22
Energy	5	6	19	19
Food & staples retailing	23	24	21	21
Food beverage & tobacco	20	21	18	17
Healthcare equipment & services	11	11	14	10
Hotels restaurants & leisure	12	9	16	16
Insurance	9	5	1	1
Media	16	16	20	20
Metals & mining	6	12	12	18
Paper & forest products	4	4	4	5
Pharmaceuticals & biotechnology	3	3	7	6
Real estate	21	20	23	24
Retailing	13	13	6	7
Software & services	2	2	3	4
Technology hardware & equipment	1	1	2	2
Telecommunication services	24	23	17	14
Transportation	14	14	10	11
Utilities	22	22	25	25

Both the credit model and the market model show significant association in rankings over time using the seven-year rolling window approach but do not when using one-year data tranches.

CONCLUSION

There is significant similarity between industry risk rankings obtained using market VaR methodology and credit PD methodology. This shows that the same industries that are risky from a market perspective are also risky from a credit perspective. This relationship is further supported by the ranking correlation evidenced between CVaR and CPD and the consistency over time between the market and credit models. Our new CPD model produces results consistent with all the modeling techniques used in this study and is deemed a viable alternative for calculating industry risk ranking. The fact that all these modeling techniques (VaR, CVaR, PD, CPD, undiversified, diversified, parametric, and nonparametric) all yield a significantly similar result, highlights the robustness and consistency of these methods in measuring relative industry risk, a critical component of credit and market risk measurement and management.

Because one-year data tranches yield different results to seven-year rolling windows, it is deemed important to use both long- and short-time frames in measuring market or credit risk in order to capture varying cycles as well as focus on current trends.

REFERENCES

Allen, D.E. and R. Powell (2008a) Industry Market VaR in Australia. Working paper, Edith Cowan University, No 0801.

Allen, D.E. and R. Powell (2008b) Transitional Credit and Modeling and Its Relationship to Market Value at Risk. Working Paper, Edith Cowan University, No 0802.

Australian Prudential Regulation Authority (1999) Submission to the Basel Committee on Banking Supervision—Credit Risk Modelling: Current Practices and Applications. Available at http://www.apra.gov.au/RePEc/RePEcDocs/Archive/discussion_papers/creditrisk.pdf

Artzner, P., F.Delbaen, J. Eber, and D. Heath (1999) Coherent Measures of Risk. *Mathematical Finance*, 9(3): 203–228.

Artzner, P., Delbaen, F., Eber, J.M. and Heath, D. (1997) Thinking Coherently. Risk, 10(issue): 68–71.

Bank for International Settlements (2004) Basel II: International Convergence of Capital Measurement and Capital Standards: A Revised Framework. Available at www.bis.org/publ/bcbs107.htm.

Bharath, S.T. and T. Shumway (2004) Forecasting Default with the KMV–Merton Model. Available at http://w4.stern.nyu.edu/salomon/docs/Credit2006/shumway_Kmvmerton1.pdf

Bucay, N. and D. Rosen (1999) Case Study. *ALGO Research Quarterly*, 2(1): 9–29.

Cespedes, J.C.G. (2002) Credit Risk Modelling and Basel II. *ALGO Research Quarterly*, 5(1): 23–56.

Credit Suisse First Boston International (1997) *CreditRisk+* A Credit Risk Management Framework. Boston, MA.

Crosbie, P. and J. Bohn (2003) Modelling Default Risk. Available at http://www.moodyskmv.com/research/files/wp/Modeling DefaultRisk.pdf.

D'Vari, R., K. Yalamanchili, and D. Bai (2003) Application of Quantitative Credit Risk Models in Fixed Income Portfolio Management. Available at http://www.rondvari.com/CIEF%202003_Final.pdf.

Gupton, G.M., C.C. Finger, and M. Bhatia (1997) CreditMetrics Technical Document. Available at http://www.riskmetrics.com/cmtdovv.html.

Jackson, P. (1996) Deposit Protection and Bank Failures in the United Kingdom. *Financial Stability Review*, 2(1): 38–43.

Jarrow, R.A., D. Lando, and S. Turnbull (1997) A Markov Model for the Term Structure of Credit Spreads. *Review of Financial Studies*, 10(2): 481–523.

Kealhofer, S. and J.R. Bohn (1993) Portfolio Management of Default Risk. Available at http://www.moodyskmv.com/research/files/wp/Portfolio_Management_of_Default_Risk.pdf.

Lopez, J.A. (2002) The Empirical Relationship between Average Asset Correlation, Firm Probability of Default and Asset Size. Available at www.frbsf.org/publications/economics/papers/2002/wp02–05bk.pdf.

Merton, R. (1974) On the Pricing of Corporate Debt: The Risk Structure of Interest Rates. *Journal of Finance*, 29(2): 449–470.

Stein, R.M. (2002) Benchmarking Default Prediction Models: Pitfalls and Remedies in Model Validation. Available at http://www.moodyskmv.com/research/files/wp/BenchmarkingDefaultPredictionModels_TR030124.pdf.

The Risk Management Association (2007) Annual Statement Studies: Industry Default Probabilities and Cash Flow Measures 2006 2007. Available at http://www.rmahq.org/NR/rdonlyres/2DD95731-BABA–4771–966C–0225C1313061/0/DefinitionofRatios_IDP_web.pdf.

Thompson, G.J. (1997) Mr. Thompson Discusses the Many Faces of Risk in Banking in Australia. Paper presented at the Australian Institute of Banking and Finance, Canberra.

Ullmer, M. (1997) Managing Credit Risk—An Overview. In B. Gray and C. Cassidy (eds.), *Credit Risk in Banking*. Reserve Bank of Australia, Sydney.

Uryasev, S., F. Andersson, H. Mausser, and D. Rosen (2000) Credit Risk Optimization with Conditional Value at Risk Criterion. Available at http://www.ise.ufl.edu/uryasev/Credit_risk_optimization.pdf.

Vasicek, O.A. (1987) Probability of Loss on Loan Portfolio. Available at http://www.moodyskmv.com/research/files/wp/Probability_of_Loss_on_Loan_Portfolio.pdf.

Vassalou, M. and Y. Xing (2002) Default Risk in Equity Returns. Available at http://papers.ssrn.com/sol3/papers.cfm?abstract_id=297319.

Wilson, T.C. (1998) Portfolio Credit Risk. Available at http://www.newyorkfed.org/research/epr/98v04n3/9810wils.pdf.

Zeng, B. and J. Zhang (2001) An Empirical Assessment of Asset Correlation Models. Available at http://www.moodyskmv.com/research/files/wp/emp_assesment.pdf.

Model Risk in VaR Calculations

Peter Schaller

INTRODUCTION

Risk always expresses some lack of information. This simple fact has a consequence that—while theoretically well understood—is often neglected in the practice of risk management. The risk inherent in a portfolio will not only depend on the structure of the portfolio and the dynamics of the markets but will also depend on the information available to the observer as well. The less information we have, the higher is the risk.

It is interesting to note that the practice of risk management often works the other way round: As long as no information on some risk factor is available, the risk stemming from it is ignored in the risk measurement. As soon as more information is available and the dynamics of the risk factor is understood, the risk resulting from it is taken into account. Therefore, the additional information leads to an increase in the estimate of the risk measure rather than to a decrease. This increase clearly indicates the underestimation of the risk in the previous estimate.

Value-at-Risk (VaR) calculations frequently rely on the choice of statistical models and the estimation of their parameters. Uncertainties induced by this step of the VaR calculation are often seen as part of what is called *model risk*. They obviously reflect some lack of information. In the light of the principles outlined above, such a lack of information should have an increasing effect on the VaR figures. Commonly, this is not the case. Rather, these uncertainties are ignored in the VaR calculation and treated separately as a component of model risk.

The question of how the uncertainties induced by the statistical modeling can be incorporated into VaR estimates in a consistent way is the main topic of this chapter. However, the notion of model risk has a much broader meaning and the question of uncertainties in statistical estimates is intimately related to other aspects of the subject. Acknowledging this fact, we will try to give a brief overview over the entire subject in the second section of this chapter, outlining the relations between its different aspects.

In this chapter's third section we will try to assess the effects of statistical uncertainties on back testing results. Examples from the market risk as well as from the operational risk sector will be provided in the fourth section, and in the fifth section we will set up the theoretical framework for the consistent inclusion of these uncertainties into the VaR estimate. The sixth section of this chapter will use the examples from the fourth section to demonstrate the practical application of this theoretical framework.

The consistent inclusion of model risks into the VaR estimates was—to the best of our knowledge—first discussed in Schaller (2002) in the context of market risks. Its application to operational risks was first suggested in Pflug and Schaller (2008), where also the notion of pivotal quantile estimates was introduced for the underlying mathematical structure.

SOURCES OF MODEL RISK

Choice of VaR as a Risk Measure

Value-at-risk calculations are based on statistical analysis. This may be seen as a strength as well as a weakness. It is a strength since the idea that portfolios with the same loss probabilities exhibit the same risk is most intuitive. It is a weakness as it relies on the assumption that market dynamics can be reasonably described in terms of probabilities and that probabilities can be estimated from historical observations. While the first assumption—though far from being obvious—is widely accepted, the second assumption is most critical.

The estimation of the distribution from historical observations assumes some stationarity in the process underlying the dynamics of the risk factors. This assumption is most problematic, when analyzing long time series: Some of the historical returns seen in such a time series date far back into the past. However, restricting the analysis to most recent returns will reduce the size of the available sample and increase the uncertainty in the statistical analysis. This interplay between two different types of model risk—the assumption of some stationarity as a basic ingredient of VaR calculations on the one hand and the uncertainties implied by the statistical modeling on the other hand—will be further analysed in the fourth section of this chapter.

Eventually the VaR calculation reduces the information about the risk to a single real-valued number. This may also be seen as a strength as well as a weakness. It can be seen as a strength since eventually risk management has to decide whether the portfolio of some company is acceptable in view of the capital available to cover potential losses. Consequently, risk must be compared to capital. As the latter is always a real-valued number, a risk measure sharing this property is ultimately needed. The reduction of the risk to a single number is a weakness as well, as possibly valuable information is lost in this process. In particular, losses higher than the VaR may be encountered with a probability depending on the confidence level of the calculation. The VaR gives no hint as to the size of such potential losses. One might think of overcoming this drawback by choosing an extremely high confidence level. In this case, however, a larger sample size is needed for the estimation, and the problem of estimations based on historical observations considered above becomes increasingly important.

From the theoretical point of view, VaR lacks a property that is widely seen as being most desirable for a risk measure, particularly in the context of capital allocation: It is not subadditive, i.e., the sum of the VARs of two subportfolios may be smaller than the VaR of the composite portfolio (Artzner et al., 1999). This has led to the development of alternative risk measures, e.g., expected shortfall. Expected shortfall was also advertised as a measure to cure the above-mentioned blindness of VaR to losses above the chosen quantile.

Value at risk is still considered as the most favorable risk measure by most risk managers and its use is encouraged by the banking authorities. There is a good theoretical reason for that: Its calculation gives a finite result under any assumptions on the distribution. The fact that with a reasonable choice of the confidence level, the result of the VaR calculation does not depend on assumptions on the tails of the distribution, which are far out of the scope of empirical verification, may be seen as a consequence of that.

The situation is different for risk measures based, e.g., on the standard deviation or on expected shortfall: Extremely large events with extremely small probability that will usually not be encountered even in a large sample may have a large impact on their value. From a mathematical point of view the calculation of such risk measures needs the evaluation of an integral over an infinite range of integration. Thus, the result may become infinite. Even if it does not, it will depend on assumptions on the asymptotic behavior of the distribution density at infinity. This behavior cannot be observed in finite samples, even if they are extremely large. Therefore, the calculation crucially depends on assumptions that can never be tested empirically.

While, despite its weaknesses, the merits of VaR as a risk measure are without controversy in the industry, there is agreement that the risk of using VaR as a risk measure should be mitigated by complementing VaR figures with additional information on potential losses from the portfolio under consideration. Such information may be provided, e.g., in the form of sensitivity analysis, stress testing results, or expected shortfall calculations.

Pricing Models

At the basis of any VaR estimate is the calculation of the price of some portfolio in different states of the market. This calculation often relies on pricing models subject to calibration to market data. Such pricing models might reflect the dynamics of instruments in the portfolio improperly. Two measures may be taken to solve the problem.

One approach would be to include the uncertainty inherent in the choice of the pricing models into the VaR calculation by introducing stochastic elements into the pricing functions. For example, in a Monte Carlo simulation of the VaR, different pricing models or differently calibrated models could be randomly chosen in different scenarios. Usually this choice will not be restricted to a discrete set of models. Rather a parameterized family of models will be used. In practice, this would mean that the pricing function depends on some random variables not directly related to market factors. Effectively, these stochastic elements in the pricing functions will increase the result of the VaR calculation. This is in the spirit of the principle that lack of information should be reflected in higher risk estimates. The drawback of the method is the ambiguity in the choice of the distribution for such stochastic elements.

Possibly for this reason, another approach has become more popular recently and is favored by the banking authorities: the prudent valuation (Basel Committee on Banking Supervision, 2006). It is based on the idea to build inner reserves in order to cover losses from mispricing. Also this solution has a drawback: Valuation is always performed on a trade by trade basis, and a systematic inclusion of netting and diversification effects into the calculation of prudent valuation reserves is difficult. In practice, a more or less arbitrary set of netting rules is often used to get a grip on that problem.

Statistical Modeling

The calculation of some quantile of the profit and loss distribution is straightforward if there are a large number of identically distributed historical changes of market states. However, in practice, the sample may be small if, e.g., the portfolio under consideration contains recently issued instruments and historical market data are not available. Even if a long history is available, returns from the far past possibly can not be assumed to reflect the current distribution of returns due to changes in the dynamics of the markets.

Therefore, the VaR calculation depends on additional assumptions. These assumptions enter the VaR calculation via statistical modeling techniques. Such assumptions are, of course, a source of ambiguity. Two types of ambiguities are commonly distinguished in the literature on statistical modeling: the ambiguity introduced by the choice of a model and the uncertainty in the estimation of the parameters of the chosen model. However, to some extent, the borderline between these two types of ambiguities is artificial: In practice, the choice is often not between a set of distinct models. This will become clearer in the examples provided in the fourth section of this chapter. The choice is rather between a simple model characterized by a small number of parameters and a more complex model characterized by a larger number of parameters, where usually the simple model is a special case of the more complex model, realized by fixing some of the parameters of the latter.

Even in cases, where the choice is between distinct models, it might be reasonable to see these models as special cases of a more complex model such that the models originally considered are obtained by fixing some of the parameters of the more complex model. So, eventually, the problem of the correct specification of the model is traced back to the problem of parameter estimation for some sufficiently complex model.

Consequently, there is a trade-off: A simple model will not cover all features of the distribution, like time-dependent volatility or fat tails, and will result in a biased, possibly too small VaR estimate. A more sophisticated model will have a large uncertainty in the estimation of its parameters. As we will see in the next section, this will have a similar effect on the quality of the VaR results as a biased estimate. To better understand this point, we will start the next section by briefly reviewing the main tool for the assessment of the quality of VaR predictions.

BACKTESTING

The dependence of the risk on the information available to the observer gives risk calculations a subjective component: On the same day for the same portfolio different estimates of the same risk measure (e.g., the VaR) may be correct. Accordingly, tests of some risk estimate must always be based on a series of forecasts rather than on a single forecast.

In the case of VaR calculations the most straightforward method for testing the accuracy of the forecast is given by empirically measuring the probability of the realized loss to exceed the VaR estimate. Eventually, this amounts to counting the number of such excesses. (More strictly speaking, the number of excesses is to be tested against the according binomial distribution.)

More sophisticated methods, e.g., a test of the uniform distribution of the excesses over time, are available [e.g., Haerdle and Stahl (1999)]. Generally, such tests are particularly important, if the VaR exhibits some explicit time dependence, as the following example may illustrate: Assume a daily 99 percent VaR estimate for some portfolio is extremely large compared to the size of the portfolio on 98 percent of the days, while it is extremely small on the remaining 2 percent of the days. Further assume that the distribution of realized profits and losses is symmetric. The loss will exceed the VaR estimate on 1 percent of the days. Therefore, it will pass backtesting based on pure counting of the excesses, while hardly anyone will consider such a VaR estimate as sensible.

If a VaR estimate fails backtesting by simple counting of excesses already, application of more advanced backtesting methods becomes superfluous. Moreover, examples like the one constructed above will be excluded in the following by restricting the considerations to VaR estimates without explicit time dependence. The VaR estimate even for a constant portfolio will still depend on time, due to changing market dynamics entering the VaR estimate implicitly through the changing history of the risk factors.

Now assume the VaR is calculated from a (correctly specified) statistical model; however, some uncertainty is involved in the estimation of the parameters. The estimate for the parameters will fluctuate around the true value rather than reproducing it precisely. Due to these fluctuations, we will underestimate the quantile with some probability. So with some probability we will have a larger probability of excess than the confidence level of the VaR calculation would suggest. However, with some probability, we will overestimate the quantile, and the probability of excess is smaller than the confidence level of the VaR would suggest. Naively, one could hope that the effects would cancel out and overall the excesses would have the correct probability. Unfortunately, this is not the case. The uncertainties in the VaR calculation will lead to a higher probability of excess in the backtesting than the chosen confidence level would suggest, which is best illustrated by the examples in the next section.

BIAS VERSUS UNCERTAINTY

Market Risk: Time-Dependent Volatility

Let us assume the daily returns of some portfolio are normally distributed with a time-dependent volatility. Let us further assume that the variance s^2 of the returns depends on time t via $s^2 = 1 + 0.7 \sin(2\pi t)$. This will lead to a volatility, expressed in terms of s, varying between 0.55 and 1.3, with an average of 1 (measured in some appropriate unit; we are interested here in the effect of the variation of the volatility rather than on its level) (cf. Figure 20.1).

With the assumption of a normal distribution and a long-term average of the volatility, we get a VaR of 2.33 for a 99 percent confidence level of the VaR calculation. Of course, in the periods of low volatility this will effectively overestimate the 0.99 quantile, while in the periods of high volatility, it will underestimate the risk. However, the effects will not cancel out in the backtesting. On the average we will have 1.4 percent of

F I G U R E   20.1

Four Years of a Simulated Time Series of Daily Returns with Varying Volatility

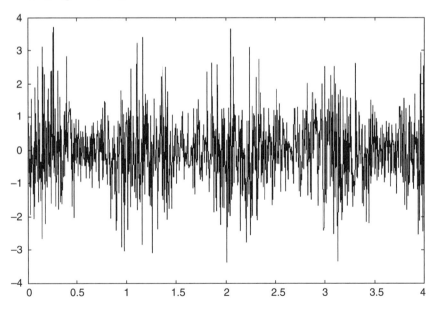

F I G U R E   20.2

Long-term Average for the Volatility and Volatility
Estimate Calculated from a 25-Day Time Window as
Compared with the True Volatility. The Returns from
Figure 20.1 Have Been Used for the Estimate

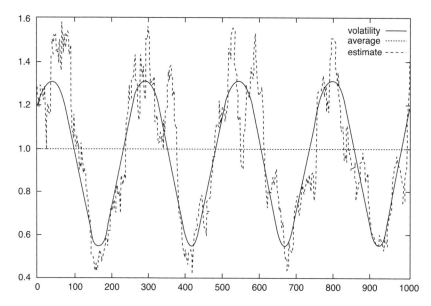

excesses, as can be shown, e.g., by a simple simulation exercise. It is
worthwhile to mention that excesses will not be distributed uniformly
over time: They will, of course, be concentrated in the periods of high
volatility (cf., Figure 20.2).

We could try to improve our estimate by calculating the volatility
from the most recent 25 returns in order to get a more correct time-
dependent estimate for the volatility. Again, a simulation will show that
we will have 1.4 percent of excesses, however, distributed uniformly over
time. The explanation of the result is simple: While the time dependence
of the volatility is now reflected correctly, the estimate is, due to the small
sample size, subject to statistical uncertainties and thus to random fluctuations. So again, we will overestimate the volatility on some days and
underestimate it on some other days. Again, the effects do not average out,
as the average number of excesses of 1.4 percent shows.

Eventually, when estimating time-dependent volatilities, we have the choice between a long look-back period, leading to a systematic error in the volatility estimate, as the latter will not reflect the time dependence of the volatility. A short look-back period will eliminate this systematic error on the price of introducing a stochastic error into the estimate. The effect on the backtesting result will be the same.

In the fifth and sixth sections of this chapter, we will see how the effect of the uncertainty in the volatility estimate on the backtesting results can be treated systematically and how the analysis can be transferred to more sophisticated methods for the estimation of time-dependent volatility like, e.g., weighted averages or GARCH models (Bollerslev, 1986).

Market Risk: Fat-Tailed Distribution

Assume the return distribution is fat tailed: There are more small and more large events than in the normal distribution, while medium sized returns are less frequent. As an example, let us assume that returns have the same distribution as the function $x = a \, \text{sgn}(y)|y|^b$ of a normally distributed variable y. The value of b will determine the tail behaviour for the distribution of x: The latter is normal for $b = 1$ and fat tailed for $b > 1$. For given b, the volatility of x is determined by a.

Assume the distribution has moderate fat tails with $b = 1.25$. If the VaR calculation assumes normally distributed returns, the VaR estimate will be biased, and 1.5 percent of excesses rather than 1 percent will be found when backtesting the 99 percent VaR.

If the fat-tailed distribution is modeled, then two parameters have to be estimated. The distribution of the data can be fitted much better. However, estimating two parameters will result in a higher uncertainty in the estimates. Using the estimation method for a and b described in the sixth section, Applications, applying it to a look-back period of 50 days, and using the quantile of the estimated distribution as VaR estimate, we will obtain 1.5 percent of excesses again. Note, that the result does not depend on the actual value of b, as will be shown in the fifth section of this chapter: Even if data are normally distributed (i.e., $b = 1$), but the risk manager does not have this information and models the fat-tailed distribution described above, he will find 1.5 percent of excesses, while a risk manager, who—for whatever reason—knows that the data are normally distributed and thus uses the normal distribution to fit the data, will have a lower uncertainty in the parameter estimate and find 1.2 percent of excesses only.

Hence, with the complexity of the model, the uncertainty of the parameter estimates increases. Again, we have a trade-off between a possibly biased estimate in a simple model, not able to fit the data, and an uncertain estimate in the complex model. The bias and the uncertainty will affect the backtesting results in a similar way.

Operational Risk: Conservative Estimate

In the operational risk sector the calculation of the VaR proceeds in two steps: In a first step distributions for the frequency of losses and the loss sizes (severities) are estimated separately, and in the second step the distribution of annual losses is deduced from these two distributions by convolution. In other words, the distribution of annual losses is calculated as the distribution of a sum of a random number f of independent and identically distributed (i.i.d.) random variables x_i, where f has the distribution of the loss frequency and the x_i have the distribution of the loss severity.

Severity distributions are usually heavy tailed. As shown in Embrechts et al. (2003), e.g., the loss in a year with large aggregate loss is usually determined by a single loss event. Therefore, a good approximation of the tails of the aggregate loss distribution is given by the distribution of annual loss maxima (single loss approximation).

For a given severity distribution function F and an average loss frequency f the distribution of the annual maxima is given by $F_{max} = F^f$, and thus the quantile for a cumulated probability q is in good approximation given by the quantile of the severity distribution for probability $q^{1/f}$, which in good approximation can be identified with $1 - (1 - q)/f$ for q close to one. So, heuristically speaking, the VaR for the annual loss distribution can be identified with a quantile of the severity distribution for a cumulated probability much closer to one than the confidence level of the VaR calculation. This results in huge uncertainties for the VaR estimate, even in cases where a large sample of severities is available.

Let us illustrate this with a numerical example: Assume that sampling of losses is subject to some lower threshold (i.e., only losses with a severity exceeding this threshold are sampled, while smaller losses are ignored; this is always the case in operational risk data). We may measure severities x in terms of multiples of this threshold. Further assume, that the severity distribution is Pareto, i.e., $F = 1 - x^{1/u}$. Assume that on average we observe 200 losses per year above the threshold. (Note that the number of losses depends on the sampling threshold. We will come back to this point later.) With an observation period of five years we have to estimate the value of u from a sample of size $N = 1000$. The maximum likelihood estimator, identifying u with the sample average of log x, has a standard deviation of $u/\text{sqrt}(N)$.

We have chosen the Pareto distribution to keep the calculation simple. Other distributions may provide a better fit to severities of operational risk losses. However, the Pareto distribution replicates the main features practitioners have found in the analysis of operational risk losses (Moscadelli, 2004) and may thus serve as a toy model to assess the effect of statistical uncertainties on the VaR calculation.

For u = 1 [a value close to values obtained by practitioners, e.g., Moscadelli (2004)] the single loss approximation gives us a result of 202,000 for the VaR (in units of the lower threshold). Assuming an error of 2 standard deviations in the estimate for u, the result will fluctuate between 92,400 and 432,600. (A convolution using Fast Fourier transformation would give a result of 202,500. So, in view of the large uncertainty in the estimate the error in the single loss approximation is negligible.)

We might increase the sample size for the estimation of u by lowering the sampling threshold. In view of the ratio between the value of the VaR and the sampling threshold, this seems to be problematic, however. From the point of view of economical interpretation it is difficult to believe that the distribution of losses more than 200,000 times smaller than the quantile could provide us with relevant information about the quantile. Indeed, practitioners tend to go in the opposite direction: Commonly, a threshold higher than the actual sampling threshold is used for the estimation of the severity distribution (peak over threshold method, see, e.g., Moscadelli, 2004).

Another strategy—mandatory in the calculation of capital requirements—is the use of external data, relying on the assumption that different banks have similar severity distributions. Assume that with this method a company can increase the sample size by a factor of 10. With a sample size of N = 10,000 the VaR estimate in the example above would still fluctuate between 156,600 and 255,100.

Regulators may not be satisfied with an estimate of the quantile that—due to the uncertainties involved in the estimation—possibly underestimates the risk. They ask banks to follow the principle of conservatism in the case of capital calculations: If a precise estimation of the risk is not possible, underestimation of the risk has to be avoided, possibly at the price of the final result overestimating the risk. To comply with this requirement, banks could choose a value on the upper bound of a reasonably chosen error interval as a basis for the capital calculation. As the numbers in our numerical example show, this strategy could be costly.

In the following section we will outline a different strategy and consider the uncertainty in the VaR estimate as an additional source of risk and try to incorporate it into the VaR calculation in a consistent way. To understand what consistency means, let us look at the probability that the VaR estimate is exceeded in our numerical example. Via the following simulation, we calculated this probability empirically: In each simulation run we generated a sample form the severity distribution of size N. We then calculated a best estimate for the 99.9 percent VaR form the maximum likelihood estimator of u. In addition, we calculated a conservative estimate for the VaR with a value of u, which was given by adding to the maximum likelihood estimator two standard deviations of the latter. The resulting VaR estimate was compared to the maximal yearly loss calculated as the maximum of a simulated sample of size f = 200. We found that the best estimate for the 0.999 quantile was exceeded in 1,756 out of 1.6 million simulation runs. This is significantly more than 0.1 percent. The conservative estimate was exceeded in 1,200 runs. This is significantly less than 0.1 percent.

The question arises: Given some historical sample, how can we calculate an estimate for the 99.9 percent VaR such, that the probability for the aggregate loss of the next year to exceed the VaR is precisely 0.1 percent? From the above examples we conclude that such a figure will be higher than the best estimate.

PIVOTAL QUANTILE ESTIMATES

Abstract Formulation of the Problem

Estimation of a quantile of some distribution from a large sample can proceed directly in a purely empirical way. If, however, the sample is not large enough, additional assumptions are necessary. Such assumptions are commonly expressed in terms of a model: A family of distributions is chosen. The members of the family are characterized by a set of parameters. The sample is then used to estimate the values of these parameters corresponding to the member of the family underlying the sample [see, e.g., Fisher, (1956)].

The question arises: Is it possible, to perform the estimation in such a way, that eventually the probability for the next draw from the distribution to be smaller than the quantile coincides with the given probability level? As we have seen above, this is not the case, if we simply use some standard estimator for the parameters and then calculate the quantile of the distribution characterized by the estimated parameter values. To get a better insight into the problem, before moving to the general theory, let us consider a special case.

Guiding Case

Consider a sample $x_1, \ldots, x_n$ from the normal distribution with zero mean and unknown standard deviation. We might proceed as follows to estimate the q quantile of the distribution: We might calculate the empirical standard deviation of the sample as $s = \mathrm{sqrt}((x_1{}^2 + \ldots + x_n{}^2)/n)$ and then derive the quantile estimate by multiplying the q quantile of the standard normal distribution with the estimate s for the standard deviation.

This procedure implies the following model for the next draw x_{n+1} from the distribution: $x_{n+1} = s(x_1, \ldots, x_n)y$, where y follows the standard normal distribution. To see why this is problematic, slightly reformulate the above equation by applying the factor 1/s to both sides to obtain $y = x_{n+1}/s$. Now, the estimate s is a function of the sample $x_1, \ldots, x_n$ and thus a random variable. It is well known in the statistical literature that the sum of squared normals follows a chi-squared distribution and that the ratio between a normally distributed variable and the square of an independent chi-squared distributed variable follows a Student's t distribution (with n degrees of freedom). We conclude that y should be assumed to be

Student's t distributed rather than normally distributed. So, while we assume that x_{n+1} is normally distributed, it is suggestive to estimate its quantile by multiplying the estimate of the standard deviation with the quantile of the Student's t distribution in order to include the uncertainty in the estimate of s into the calculation.

Indeed, it is obvious that the estimate for the q quantile obtained that way will be exceeded with a probability of $1 - q$. This is a direct consequence of the 1:1 relation between x_{n+1} and y, once s is given. The skeptical reader may check this statement by a simple simulation experiment.

It is interesting to note, that the distribution of the variable x_{n+1}/s does not depend on the actual standard deviation of the variable x. This is obvious from a simple scaling argument: Given a normally distributed variable with some standard deviation, a normally distributed variable with a different standard deviation is obtained by scaling the original variable with the ratios of the standard deviations. From the definition of s it is clear that y is not affected by such a scaling.

We see that the inclusion of parameter uncertainties into the VaR calculation is closely related to the existence of pivotal functions, i.e., of functions, whose distributions do not depend on the values of the parameters characterizing the distribution. This idea is suggestive, as the statistics of such functions do not depend on the parameter estimates and are thus not subject to the uncertainties of these estimates. It leads to the following generalization.

General Definition

Let P_a be a family of distributions characterized by some set of parameters α and denote by $x_1, \ldots, x_{n+1}$ a sequence of i.i.d. random variables from some member of P_a. We denote as pivotal quantile estimate an estimate $Q_q(x_1, \ldots, x_n)$ such that the probability $\text{Prob}(x_{n+1} < Q_q(x_1, \ldots, x_n)) = q$.

This definition is related to the quantity y in the above example by the following equivalence:

Lemma 15.1. *The following statements are equivalent:*

1. A family of distributions allows for a pivotal quantile estimate
   $Qq(x_1, \ldots, x_n)$ for all q in the interval $(0, \ldots, 1)$ such that Q_q
   is monotonic in q.

> 2. *A pivotal function V(x₁, . . . , xₙ₊₁) (i.e., a function whose*
>   *distribution does not depend on a exists, such that V is strictly*
>   *monotonic in xₙ₊₁.*

Proof: Part 1 implies part 2 as the solution of the equation $Q_q(x_1, \ldots, x_n)$ = x_{n+1} with resptect to (w.r.t) q provides a uniformly distributed variable. Given V as in part 1, denote by Q^V the quantile function of the distribution of V. Then the solution of the equation $V(x_1, \ldots, x_{n+1})) = Q^V(q)$ w.r.t to x_{n+1} provides a pivotal quantile estimate. So part 2 implies part 1. This completes the proof.

Concerning the definition one should be aware of the fact, that a pivotal quantile estimate is not unique: Different functions $Q_q(x_1, \ldots, x_n)$ may be correct pivotal quantile estimates in the sense of the above definition. From the economical point of view this may be seen as reflecting the dependence of the risk on the observer and the information available to him, as outlined in the introduction. It would, of course be interesting to have a method allowing the systematic construction of pivotal quantile estimates. Indeed, such a method can be found in a straightforward way for the following class of models.

Structural Models

Denote by G a group of monotone and bijective transformations of the real line. Let P_0 be some probability measure on the real line. Then we may denote by P_g the measure defined via $P_g(A) = P_0(g^{-1}A)$, where g is some member of the group G. The family P_g is denoted as structural model (Eaton, 1989).

This abstract definition may become clearer using the following example: A location-scale transformation is given by $g_{a,b}x = a*x + b$, a>0. Given some distribution P_0, the location-scale transformations will generate a two-parameter family of distributions. The family of normally distributed variables, e.g., is generated by applying location-scale transformations to a standard normally distributed variable. Restriction to the subgroup with b = 0 generates the family of normal distributions with zero mean, which has been considered above.

In the group, multiplication between group elements is defined by the composition of transformations. It allows for the notion of equivariant functions: A function g mapping $x_1, \ldots, x_n$ to the group is called *equivariant*, if $g(g(x_1, \ldots, x_n)) = g*g(x_1, \ldots, x_n)$, i.e., there is no difference, whether we apply the function g to the transformed sample or we apply g to the untransformed sample and then multiply the resulting group element (from the left) with the group element generating the transformation. Note, that the action of g on $x_1, \ldots, x_n$ is given by transforming each of the x_i separately.

The property of equivariance is particularly interesting in the context of estimating the parameters of the distribution: An estimator maps the sample that the estimate is based on to G. Now assume that the sample is from P_{g1}. Then we would intuitively expect that the estimator for g is close to g1. Transformation of the sample with g2 generates a sample from the distribution P_{g2*g1}. Thus, we would expect that the estimator for g gives a result close to g2*g1 for the g2 transformed sample. Therefore, equivariance is a natural property in the context of estimators.

Given an equivariant estimator for g, it is straightforward to construct a pivotal quantile estimate by virtue of the following lemma.

Lemma 15.2. *Denote by g an equivariant estimator for some structural model P_g. Then the function $V(x_1, \ldots, x_{n+1}) = g(x_1, \ldots, x_n)^{-1}x_{n+1}$ is pivotal.*

Proof: Assume that $x = gz$. Then $V(x_1, \ldots, x_{n+1}) = g(g(z_1, \ldots, z_n))^{-1}gz_{n+1}$ $= g(z_1, \ldots, z_n)^{-1}*g^{-1}gz_{n+1} = g(z_1, \ldots, z_n)^{-1}z_{n+1} = V(z_1, \ldots, z_{n+1})$. So V does not depend on g. Note that the inverse of a product of group elements is the product of the inverse elements in reverse order. As an immediate consequence of lemma 1 we now have the following corollary:

Corollary. *If V in Lemma 15.2 has a continuous distribution function F, then a pivotal quantile estimate is given by $Q_q(x_1, \ldots, x_n) = g(x_1, \ldots, x_n)$ $(F^{-1}(q))$.*

As outlined above, it is natural to demand equivariance as a property for estimators of structural models. Still, the question arises, how to construct such estimators in order to exploit the above corollary. The following construction will help us.

With each sample $x_1, \ldots, x_n$ we may associate an orbit $O(x_1, \ldots, x_n)$ consisting of all samples that can be generated by applying some group elelment to $x_1, \ldots, x_n$, i.e., $O(x_1, \ldots, x_n) = \{y_1, \ldots, y_n \mid$ there is a g in G with $y_1, \ldots, y_n = g(x_1, \ldots, x_n)\}$

Orbits have two important properties: They are disjoint and they are invariant under group transformations. Now, assume, a set of conditions on the samples selecting those samples that presumably are from the basic distribution P_0 is given. (If, e.g., the basic distribution is the standard normal distribution and the group is formed by location-scale transformations, we might select samples with zero mean and a standard deviation of 1 as presumably belonging to the basic distribution.) With an appropriate choice of the conditions, each orbit will have a unique intersection with the set r of samples selected by the conditions. Given some sample we may now choose the estimator $g(x_1, \ldots, x_n)$ such that $g(x_1, \ldots, x_n)^{-1} (x_1, \ldots, x_n)$ is in the selection r. The equivariance of this estimator follows directly form the invariance of the orbits under group transformations.

It is interesting to note that the maximum likelihood estimator is equivariant. It fits into the scheme outlined above by choosing r to consist of the maxima of the Likelihood function corresponding to P_0 on each orbit.

APPLICATIONS

In the following we will show how to apply the theory outlined in the fifth section to the examples set up in the fourth section of this chapter.

Time-dependent Volatility

The simplest way of handling time-dependent volatility has—to some extent—already been examined in this chapter's fourth section: A short history may be used to estimate the time-dependent volatility. In this case a pivotal function is provided by the ratio between x_{n+1} and the estimate $s = \mathrm{sqrt}((x_1^2 + \ldots + x_n^2)/n)$ for the volatility.

From the point of view of structural models the family of normal distributions with zero mean is generated by the group of scale transformations acting by multiplication and s is an equivariant estimator for the scale parameter: Applying a scale factor to the sample has the same effect as applying the scale factor directly to s, i.e., $s(ax_1, \ldots, ax_n) = as(x_1, \ldots, x_n)$. The distribution of the pivotal function is Student's t with n degrees of freedom, so the pivotal quantile estimate is given by the product of the volatility estimate and the quantile of the Student's t distribution.

In the literature [e.g., RiskMetrics group (1997)] it has been suggested, to deal with time-dependent volatilities by applying a nonuniform weighting to past returns, when calculating the standard deviation rather than restricting the sample to the most recent n returns: Low weights should be used for returns from the far past, while higher weights should be used for more recent returns. In this way, the estimate would reflect the current volatility, even for a large sample size.

It is rather obvious that the estimator of the standard deviation would still be equivariant and thus $x_{n+1}/s(x_1, \ldots, x_n)$ would still provide a pivotal function. Therefore, application of the theory outlined above would still be straightforward. Depending on the choice of the weights, analytical calculation for the statistics of the pivotal function could be difficult. A (possibly expensive) simulation could be necessary to calculate this statistics. One should note, however, that the statistics of the pivotal function by definition does not depend on the standard deviation. So, in the case of daily VaR calculation, the calculation of this statistics has to proceed once only, not daily. The standard normal distribution may be used for this calculation. The quantile obtained is then to be multiplied with the time-dependent volatility. Only the latter has to be calculated form the historical sample on a daily basis.

We have performed the calculation for the 99 percent VaR with an exponentially weighted moving average characterized by a decay factor of 0.94 (i.e., the weight of the return k days ago is by a factor 0.94 lower than the weight of the return $k-1$ days ago). This type of weighting has been suggested, e.g., in RiskMetrics Group (1997) and has been widely used in practice. We found that the pivotal quantile estimate is at 2.44 standard deviations. Commonly, 2.33 standard deviations are used, as the 0.99 quantile of the standard normal distribution is 2.33. The value of 2.33 corresponds to the 0.987 quantile of the pivotal function; so using this value in the VaR calculation will lead to 1.3 percent of excesses in the backtesting, even if the normal distribution assumption behind the model is valid.

Therefore, consistent inclusion of the model risk has a small yet still measurable effect on the result.

Frequently, GARCH processes (Bollerslev, 1986) are used to model time-dependent volatilities. In such models, the parameters of the GARCH process are estimated from a long time series. As soon as these parameters are given, the standard deviation is effectively calculated from a weighted average and the pivotal quantile estimate can be calculated in the way described above. To see this, let us consider the example of a GARCH(1,1) process: The time-dependent standard deviations $s(t)$ of the past returns $r(t)$ is modeled via $s(t)^2 = a + b*s(t-1)^2 + c*r(t-1)^2$. It is straightforward to show, that for given values of a, b, and c, this can be rewritten as $s(t)^2 = p*s_{l.t.}^2 + (1-p)*s_{EMWA}(b)^2$ with p depending on a, b, and c via $p = 1 - c/(1-b)$ and $s_{l.t.} = sqrt(a/(1-b-c))$, respectively. So, for given parameters a, b, and c, the volatility estimate in the GARCH(1,1) process can be considered as a weighted average of the long-term volatility $s_{l.t}$ and the EMWA volatility s_{EMWA} calculated with decay factor b. Due to the scaling behavior of $s_{l.t}$ and s_{EMWA} it is an equi-variant estimator and the scheme outlined above for the calculation of a pivotal quantile estimate can be applied. Note, however, that in the case of a GARCH estimate, the statistics of the pivotal function must be re-calculated after each change of the GARCH parameters a, b, and c. Furthermore, the method does not capture the uncertainties in the estimate of the parameters a, b, and c.

Fat Tails

The model introduced in the fourth section of this chapter was based on transforming a standard normally distributed variable y according to $x = a*sgn(y)*|y|^b$. This is basically equivalent to applying a scale-shift trans-formation to the logarithm of $|y|$. As scale-shift transformations form a group, the model falls into the class of structural models, and the theory outlined in the fifth section, Pivotal Quantile Estimates, can be applied.

We may characterize the standard normal distribution by its vari-ance and kurtosis. This leads to the conditions $y_1^2 + \ldots + y_n^2 = n$ and $y_1^4 + \ldots + y_n^4 = 3*n$ for samples belonging to the selection r in the notion of the fifth section. With this choice the parameters a and b in our model have to be determined such that the inverse of the transformation generating the group, given by $y = \text{sgn}(x)*(|x|/a)^{1/b}$, applied to the historical returns $x_1, \ldots, x_n$ fulfills the above conditions regarding variance and kurtosis. A transformation with these estimated parameters applied to x_{n+1} then provides a pivotal function. The statistics for this function can be calculated by simulation, and the desired quantile can be deduced from it. Given some historical sample, a transformation with the corresponding estimates for a and b may then be applied to the quantile of the pivotal function.

We do not claim that the procedure described here for the estimation of a and b is the most efficient one. We have chosen it mainly for illustrative reasons. Other estimators for a and b may be used, as long as they are equivariant. In particular, as proven in the fifth section of this chapter, the maximum likelihood estimator can be used instead. However, the numerical results given in this chapter's third section were calculated with the estimation method described above.

Operational Risk

The model considered in this chapter's third section for the severities of operational risk losses is structural: Choose $1 - 1/y$ as distribution function of some variable y. Application of the transformation $x = y^u$ will generate the family of Pareto distributions.

The distribution of aggregate annual losses in the single loss approximation is given by the distribution of the maximum x_{max} of f independently draws from the severity distribution, where f denotes the average annual loss frequency. The above transformation, applied to a collection of losses, will imply the same transformation for the maximum x_{max} of the collection. Therefore, in the single loss approximation also, the distribution of the aggregate annual losses is subject to a structural model. Using the most likelihood estimator identifying u with the average of log x, where the average is taken over some historical sample $(x1, \ldots, xN)$ of size N from the severity distribution, the distribution of $F = x_{max}^{1/u(x1, \ldots, xN)}$ is pivotal.

This leads to the following algorithm for the calculation of a pivotal estimate for the 99.9 percent VaR: As a first step determine the 0.999 quantile Q_F of F. This could be done by simulation. The result will depend on the sample size N and the loss frequency f, however, not on the actual value of u. So any value of u can be used in this simulation. In the second step calculate the estimate for u from the historical severities. The VaR is then given by VaR $= (Q_F)^u$. Provided, the distributional assumptions are correct, it will be exceeded in 0.1 percent of the years. So, it may be seen as a conservative estimate, including the uncertainties in the parameter estimates. A (small) add-on may be applied to cover the error induced by the single loss approximation. With the numerical values assumed in the fourth section of this chapter (sample size 10,000; 200 losses per year) we obtain a result of $Q_F = 219,000$.

CONCLUSION

Value at risk forecasts disregarding the uncertainties in the estimate of the profit-and-loss (P/L) distribution may underestimate the risk in the sense that the probability of the actual loss to exceed the VaR forecast is higher than the confidence level of the VaR calculation would suggest.

The obvious strategy to choose conservative estimates for the parameters characterizing the P/L distribution could be costly. The consistent inclusion of the risk, to misestimate the parameters of the P/L distribution into the VaR calculation provides a beneficial alternative.

REFERENCES

Artzner, P., F. Delbaen, J.-M. Eber, and D. Heath (1999) Coherent Risk Measures. *Mathematical Finance*, 9(3): 203–228.

Basel Committee on Banking Supervision (2006) *International Convergence of Capital Measurement and Capital Standards*. Bank for International Settlements, Basel.

Bollerslev, T. (1986) Generalized Autoregressive Conditional Heteroskedasticity. *Journal of Econometrics*, 31(3): 307–327.

Eaton, M.L. (1989) *Group Invariance Applications in Statistics*. Alexandria, VA: Institute of Mathematical Statistics and American Statistical Association.

Embrechts, P., C. Klueppelberg, and T. Mikosch (2003) *Modelling Extremal Events for Insurance and Finance*. New York: Springer-Verlag.

Fisher, C. (1956) *Statistical Methods and Scientific Inference*. New York: Hafner.

Haerdle, W. and G. Stahl (1999) Backtesting beyond VaR. SFB 373 papers, Humboldt Universitaet, Berlin.

Moscadelli, M. (2004) The Modelling of Operational Risk: Experience with the Analysis of the Data Collected by the Basel Committee. Termi di discussione, Bank of Italy.

Pflug, G. and P. Schaller (2008) Pivotal Quantile Estimates in VaR Calculations. Working paper, Bank Austria, Vienna.

RiskMetrics Group (1997) Risk-Metrics Technical Document. Available from http://www.riskmetric.com.

Schaller, P. (2002) Uncertainty of Parameter Estimates in VaR Calculations. Working paper, Bank Austria, Vienna.

CHAPTER 21

Option Pricing with Constant and Time-Varying Volatility

Willi Semmler and Karim M. Youssef

ABSTRACT

Much academic effort has been spent to understand risk transfer and to model and assess credit risk. In this chapter, we first discuss some well-known instruments for transferring credit risk and then study a firm value-based model on evaluating credit risk. We take into consideration that the Black–Scholes and Merton framework is deficient in the sense that it is not well calibrated to prices. As such, we extend the above approach by looking at the impact of time-varying stochastic volatility of the underlying asset on the contingent claim. We will pay particular attention to contrasting the volatility structures arising out of the various models.

INTRODUCTION

In March of 1900 Louis Bachelier's defense of his dissertation entitled Théorie de la Spéculation was perhaps the pivotal moment in the inception of a cornerstone in the modern theory of financial economics. Borrowing from nineteenth century botanist Robert Brown, Bachelier ventured to put together a theoretical foundation for a phenomenon he witnessed on the streets of Paris. Bachelier, observed that street corner traders were in effect placing a present value on probabilistic future events. Sadly Bachelier's achievement received a mixed reaction in the mathematical community, and he was relegated to a life of mediocre academic standing amongst his peers.

More than a half a century passed when the mathematician Edward Thorpe picked up on Balchelier's work and applied it to a mathematical analysis of wagering. Following that, various attempts by Sprenkle, Bonness, and Samuelson were made to revive the ideas that Bachelier began working on. However, it was not until the early 1970s that Fisher Black and Myron Scholes expounded upon Bachelier's theory to produce the Black–Scholes model for option pricing. Even then, their work was not received with due praise or understanding. During that time, Robert Merton, then a professor at M.I.T continuously lobbied the academic journals on behalf of Black and Scholes (1973). The result was the publication of their work in the *Journal of Finance* in 1972 and again with a modified title and content in the *Journal of Political Economy* in 1973.

It is safe to say that Merton's support of Black and Scholes' work allowed the discipline of economics to take the lead in shedding light upon one of the most applicable pieces of theoretical work found today. The importance of this theoretical work is equally related to the motivations behind its inception as it is to the way it has transformed our thinking about financial markets.

In regards to its inception, there is no doubt that Bachelier's motivation was to examine the reality of randomness and probabilistic events which are rooted in our lives as social beings. Perhaps that was done in an effort to allow us to peel away the layers of deterministic thinking to which we have grown accustomed. As for the impact of the result as rendered by the Black–Scholes work. We find ourselves today far from our goal of a firmly grasped understanding of the probabilistic nature of prices and markets, yet far away from our point of departure. As such significant advances have been made on the Black–Scholes model.

With that in mind, the following sections will present a derivation of the Black–Scholes partial differential equation (PDE), a solution for the PDE to arrive at the Black–Scholes formula, and a critique of the weaker underlying assumptions. Following that a presentation of the Heston model based on time-varying volatility will highlight how some of the well-observed financial facts can be comprehended and incorporated in the probabilistic framework that continues to emerge from the pre-Bachelierian era until our present time.

The Black–Scholes PDE

Before deriving the Black–Scholes PDE, we begin by explaining some of the earlier work described above, it's faults, and the reasons the Black–Scholes model is different. The Bachelier work gave rise to a normal distribution for asset prices and hence an arithmetic Brownian motion process of the form, $dS_t = \sigma dW_t$, where S is the underlying asset price at time $t \geq 0$; σ is the volatility; and dW_t is a Wiener process. The Problem with Bachelier's process is that it has a normal distribution that allows for negative values, which is inconsistent with asset prices observed in the market. Subsequently, Sprenkle, Bonness, and Samuelson all added features in their revision of Bachelier's model. Sprenkle began by switching to a geometric Brownian motion process for asset prices through the assumption of a lognormal distribution. Bonness and Samuelson followed suit and respectively added elements that allowed for increases in the rate of return of the underlying asset as well as of the option itself.[1] Based upon this foundation, Black and Scholes imagined a riskless portfolio constructed from a number of stocks and options upon the stock, with the condition that the portfolio position returns to the investor the risk-free interest rate and the caveat that the options are fairly priced. Our imaginary portfolio will contain a single option, and a variable quantity of stocks such that it remains risk-neutral regardless of the movement in the underlying stock's price. This in turn will lead to a distinct relationship between the option price and the stock price (which we know up to the purchase of the option but not afterward), as well as to the volatility of the stock price.[2]

Black and Scholes made the assumptions that the risk-free interest rate and the volatility of the underlying stock price are constants through

---

[1] For a brief overview of the works mentioned, see Haug (2007, p. 14).
[2] We will address these relationships at a later point.

the experiation of the option. Transaction costs, taxes, dividends, and the possibility of arbitrage are all assumed away. Trading is assumed to be continuous and happens with no time delay.[3]

The underlying asset can be described by a stochastic differential equation of the geometric Brownian motion form $dS_t = \mu(S_t, t)dt + \sigma(S_t, t)dW_t$. Here, to the right-hand side of the equality, we have a drift term and a diffusion term, respectively, from left to right, with μ being the annual expected mean return on the stock and σ the annual volatility of the stock price. Both terms are functions of changes in the stock price and in time, and hence they are random. However, the mere fact that a market participant observes them at time t allows them to become constants,[4] and as such we have a geometric Brownian motion process of the form

$$dS_t = \mu S_t dt + \sigma S_t dW_t \qquad (21.1)$$

A pause is necessary here to raise one of the central issues in the Black–Scholes model. The kernel of the idea is that we are trying to model asset prices in such a way so as to isolate the risk feature in the process. As such, a discerning look at Equation (21.1) tells us that dW_t is the source of the risk. Following this view, the task then would be to construct a portfolio that shields us against the risk expressed in dW_t. Let us assume that an ideal portfolio would contain a short position in the options market, and a specific number of shares of the underlying so as to eliminate any risk of losses in the portfolio. Our position can then be expressed as

$$\Pi = \Delta S_t - \phi(S_t, t) \qquad (21.2)$$

whereby Π is the overall portfolio position, Δ is the number of underlying shares we hold at time t, and φ is the current value or price of the option. It is clear here that the movement in our postion as a whole depends on the process expressed in Equation (21.1). It becomes imperative then, to calculate

$$d\Pi = \Delta dS_t - d\phi(S_t, t) \qquad (21.3)$$

[3] See Hull (2006, p.236).
[4] See Neftci (2000, pp. 217 and 218).

in order to ascertain the value for delta which allows us to hold a risk-neutral portfolio free of the risky effects of dW_t.

As we know the process for S_t from Equation (21.1), we simply apply Ito's lemma to $\phi(S_t, t)$ in order to obtain

$$
d\phi(S_t, t) = \left(\frac{\partial \phi(S_t, t)}{\partial S} \mu S_t + \frac{\partial \phi(S_t, t)}{\partial t} + \frac{1}{2} \frac{\partial^2 \phi(S_t, t)}{\partial S^2} \sigma^2 S_t^2 \right)
$$
$$
dt + \frac{\partial \phi(S_t, t)}{\partial S} \sigma S_t dW_t
$$

(21.4)

Substituting the results from Equations (21.1) and (21.4) into the right-hand side of Equation (21.3), we get

$$
d\Pi = \Delta_t \left(\mu S_t dt + \sigma S_t W_t \right)
$$
$$
- \left(\frac{\partial \phi(S_t, t)}{\partial S} \mu S_t + \frac{\partial \phi(S_t, t)}{\partial t} + \frac{1}{2} \frac{\partial^2 \phi(S_t, t)}{\partial S^2} \sigma^2 S_t^2 \right) dt - \frac{\partial \phi(S_t, t)}{\partial S} \sigma S_t dW_t
$$
$$
= \left(\Delta_t \mu S_t - \frac{\partial \phi(S_t, t)}{\partial S} \mu S_t - \frac{\partial \phi(S_t, t)}{\partial t} - \frac{1}{2} \frac{\partial^2 \phi(S_t, t)}{\partial S^2} \sigma^2 S_t^2 \right)
$$
$$
dt + \left(\Delta_t \sigma S_t - \frac{\partial \phi(S_t, t)}{\partial S} \sigma S_t \right) dW_t
$$

Mathematically speaking, if we set $\Delta_t = -\partial \phi(S_t, t)/\partial S$, we have obtained two things. First we have uncovered a value for the hedge ratio or the option delta, which we shall address in further detail later; more importantly in the process we have achieved a portfolio position solution that is entirely risk neutral as it does not include dW_t.

Having done this we now have a solution for $d\Pi$:

$$
d\Pi = \left(-\frac{\partial \phi(S_t, t)}{\partial t} - \frac{1}{2} \frac{\partial^2 \phi(S_t, t)}{\partial S^2} \sigma^2 S_t^2 \right)
$$

(21.5)

Also, let us not forget that a riskless portfolio with a no-arbitrage condition in effect would necessarily grow at the risk-free interest rate, and thus

$$d\Pi = r\Pi dt = r\left(-\frac{\partial\phi(S_t,t)}{\partial S}S_t - \phi(S_t,t)\right)dt \qquad (21.6)$$

Upon equalizing the results of Equations (21.5) and (21.6) and with a little simplification, we have now derived the Black–Scholes PDE:

$$r\phi(S_t,t) = \frac{\partial\phi(S_t,t)}{\partial t} + rS_t\frac{\partial\phi(S_t,t)}{\partial S} + \frac{1}{2}\sigma^2\S_t^2\frac{\partial^2\phi(S_t,t)}{\partial S^2} \qquad (21.7)$$

SOLUTION METHODS

One can reach a solution to Equation (21.7) in one of two well-known ways. First, we can solve the PDE with an appropriate boundary condition $\phi(S_t, T) = max(S_t - k,0)$ for a European style call option or $\phi(S_t,T) = max(k - S_t,0)$ for a European style put option.[5] Second, we can take one of these boundary conditions and use them to calculate an explicit expectation for the payoff by way of probabilities. Considering that the second method is less complicated and provides us with a more intuitive way of reaching the Black–Scholes solution, we will use that.

Recalling our assumption in Equation (21.1) of the geometric Brownian motion process undertaken by stock prices, and replacing μ with r to reflect the risk-free rate of return enjoyed by this risk-neutral measure, we can solve Equation (21.1) for S_T to get

$$S_T = S_0 e^{\left(r-\frac{1}{2}\sigma^2\right)}T + \sigma W_T \qquad (21.8)$$

with $W_T \sim N(0,T)$.

As such calculating the expected value of Equation (21.9) below will give us the solution for a price of a European style call option as the

[5] Note that T is the tenor of the option contract and k is the strike price agreed upon in the contract.

expected value of a the payoff of the option discounted back over $t_n - t_0$ as per the Black–Scholes result.

$$CallOptionPrice = e^{-rt}E\left[\max\left(S_T - k, 0\right)\right] \tag{21.9}$$

It is important to keep a few points in mind here. First, $max(S_T - k, 0)$ $= (S_T - k)\ |_{(S_T \geq k)}$, which means that by integrating $(S_T - k)$ over all the values of S_T, we can effectively figure out the expectation of $max\ (S_T - k, 0)$. Second, by way of the central limit theorem, we can safely replace W_T with $\sqrt{T}W$ within the expectation, and again $W \sim (0,1)$, and thus we will simplify the expectation in terms of W, which is the only randomness involved, and that way the expectation has a standard normal distribution.

Hence,

$$e^{-rt}E\left[\max\left(S_T - k, 0\right)\right] = e^{-rt}E\left[\max\left(S_0 e^{\left(r - \sigma^2/2\right)T + \sigma W_T} - k, 0\right)\right]$$

$$= e^{-rt}E\left[\max\left(S_0 e^{\left(r - \sigma^2/2\right)T + \sigma\sqrt{T}W} - k, 0\right)\right]$$

$$= e^{-rt}\int_{S_0 e^{\left(r - \sigma^2/2\right)T + \sigma\sqrt{T}W \geq k}}\left(S_0 e^{\left(r - \sigma^2/2\right)T + \sigma\sqrt{T}W} - k\right)$$

$$\frac{1}{\sqrt{2\pi}}e^{-W^2/2}dW$$

integrating this against a random variable with density

$$N \sim \left(0,1\right) = e^{-rT}\int_{W \geq \frac{\log(k/S_0) - \left(r - \sigma^2/2\right)T}{\sigma\sqrt{T}}}\left(S_0 e^{\left(r - \sigma^2/2\right)T + \sigma\sqrt{T}W} - k\right)\frac{1}{\sqrt{2\pi}}e^{-W^2/2}dW$$

$$= e^{-rT}\int_{\frac{\log(k/S_0) - \left(r - \sigma^2/2\right)T}{\sigma\sqrt{T}}}^{\infty}S_0 e^{\left(r - \sigma^2/2\right)T + \sigma\sqrt{T}W}\frac{1}{\sqrt{2\pi}}e^{-W^2/2}dW$$

$$- ke^{-rT}\int_{\frac{\log k/S_0 - \left(r - \sigma^2/2\right)T}{\sigma\sqrt{T}}}^{\infty}\frac{1}{\sqrt{2\pi}}e^{-W^2/2}dW$$

Here we bring some elements out of the integration and discover the bounds

$$= S_0 e^{-\sigma^2/2T} \int_{-\infty}^{\frac{\log S_0/k+\left(r-\sigma^2/2\right)T}{\sigma\sqrt{T}}} \frac{1}{\sqrt{2\pi}} e^{-W^2/2+\sigma\sqrt{T}W} dW - ke^{-rT}$$

$$\int_{-\infty}^{\frac{\log S_0/k+\left(r-\sigma^2/2\right)T}{\sigma\sqrt{T}}} \frac{1}{\sqrt{2\pi}} e^{-W^2/2} dW$$

Using the properties of normal densities we change the limits and simplify to get

$$= S_0 \int_{-\infty}^{\frac{\log S_0/k+\left(r-\sigma^2/2\right)T}{\sigma\sqrt{T}}} \frac{1}{\sqrt{2\pi}} e^{-\left(W-\sigma\sqrt{T}\right)^2/2} dW - ke^{-rT}$$

$$\int_{-\infty}^{\frac{\log S_0/k+\left(r-\sigma^2/2\right)T}{\sigma\sqrt{T}}} \frac{1}{\sqrt{2\pi}} e^{-W^2/2} dW$$

setting $\chi = W - \sigma\sqrt{T}$ and simplifying further, we finally have

$$= S_0 \int_{-\infty}^{\frac{\log S_0/k+\left(r+\sigma^2/2\right)T}{\sigma\sqrt{T}}} \frac{1}{\sqrt{2\pi}} e^{-\chi^2/2} d\chi - ke^{-rT} \int_{-\infty}^{\frac{\log S_0/k+\left(r-\sigma^2/2\right)T}{\sigma\sqrt{T}}} \frac{1}{\sqrt{2\pi}} e^{-W^2/2} dW$$

Changing the limits once again, we have now derived the Black–Scholes price of a European call option in the form,

$$= S_0 N(d_1) - ke^{-rT} N(d_2) \tag{21.10}$$

with

$$d_1 = \frac{\log S_0/k + \left(r+\sigma^2/2\right)T}{\sigma\sqrt{T}}$$

It is important to note here that for at-the-money options $d_1 = \Delta$ or the hedge ratio of our position, and

$$d_2 = \frac{\log S_0/k + \left(r - \sigma^2/2\right)T}{\sigma\sqrt{T}} = d_2 = d_1 - \sigma\sqrt{T-t}$$

N represents the cumulative distribution function of a standard normal random variable.

WHAT WE GET AND WHAT WE DO NOT GET FROM BLACK–SCHOLES

The Black–Scholes model gives us some very important information. Given the following inputs: S, the stock price; k, the strike price; r, the risk-free interest rate; T, the time to expiration in years; and σ, the volatility of the relative price change of the underlying stock; we can with near perfect accuracy derive the price of an option contract. However, that is not all, we can also obtain a series of relationships implicit in the Black–Scholes model, which have come to be known as *greeks*, Δ, Γ, Θ, ρ, and v (vega). Respectively, they allow us to measure the option prices' sensitivity to movements in the underlying stock price (in the case of Δ and Γ), time (in the case of Θ), the risk-free rate (in the case of ρ), and the volatility (in the case of v).

Let us for the moment discuss what can arguably be considered the most important of the greeks for the Black–Scholes framework, namely, Δ, Γ, and v. The reasoning here is that they allow us to accuarately hedge our position and maintain a risk-neutral portfolio. Δ is defined as the rate of change of the option price with respect to a change in the price of the underlying asset. In a short at-the-money (ATM)[6] call Δ will always be negative, and it will be approximately -0.5 (or -50 in market terms). The

---

[6] *At the money* refers to when the underlying price observed at time t_0 and the option strike price are the same. When the strike price is greater or smaller than the underlying price observed at time t_0, the position is referred to as *in the money* (ITM) or *out of the money* (OTM), respectively.

mechanics of Δ hedging are as follows: If at some time between buying the option and it's exercise date Δ goes to −0.75, one would have to buy 0.25 of the underlying asset in order to maintain ATM Δ neutrality. A short Δ position means a gain if the underlying price decreases and a loss if the underlying increases. A long Δ position is the inverse.

While (vega) ν is an entirely fictional greek letter, it plays a somewhat important role, as it gives us the change in the price of the option if given a change in volatility. ν is the partial derivative of the price of the option with respect to σ. This may seem trivial; however, in the real world it helps market professionals to assess the impact of their Γ positions.

We explained Δ and ν in order to fully explain Γ. Γ is the rate of change of Δ with respect to changes in the price of the underlying asset. That is to say, it is the second partial derivative of the option price with respect to the underlying. A high positive value for Γ denotes being in a long ATM position, while lower positive Γ values denote deep ITM or OTM long positions, and hence Γ is generally viewed as a good indicator of the need to adjust the Δ position. A high Γ value says that we need to maintain a frequent regime of Δ adjustments, and a low Γ means that Δ changes may occur at a less rapid pace and thus the frequency of portfolio adjustment need not be high. A long Γ position, also known as *long convexity* or *volatility*, is when we buy a call or put and hedge our Δ with opposite postions in the underlying assets. This allows us to bcncfit from an increase in volatility.

As one can see Black and Scholes have given us very important results, and they have all stood the test of time. There is, however, one very weak component in the Black–Scholes model, namely volatility. From the brief description of, Δ, ν, and Γ above we begin to see a picture emerging in which the market participants need to continuously estimate σ the volatility of the underlying asset. Hence this particular topic will exhaust the remainder of the coming pages.

SEEKING SIGMA

In essence the volatility σ we are seeking to understand is a statistical risk measure that allows us to guage the extent to which the underlying asset price may probabalistically move within a given period of time δ.

For example if S_t is the price of the underlying asset at t_0,[7] then or $S_{t+\delta} = S_t + \sigma\sqrt{\delta}$ or $S_{t+\delta} = S_t - \sigma\sqrt{\delta}$.

As such the Black–Scholes framework assumes σ to be some intrinsic property of the underlying asset whereby it does not change insofar as any of the other model inputs are concerned. Luckily we can derive what is refered to as the implied volatility structure from out of the money calls and puts, if the constant volatility assumption were true the implied volatility structure would display a straight line. However, in reality the volatility structure displays either a "smile" or a "smirk."[8] The implied volatility we can derive from market quoted calls and puts will in a sense give us an interpretation as to whether market participants are expecting higher or lower volatility. The question then arises how can we empirically estimate and forecast volatility without market quoted call and put prices, in order to price new options.

Luckily, there are two traditional methods through which we can answer this question, namely historical volaility estimation and GARCH(1,1).

HISTORICAL VOLATILITY[9]

Going back to Equation (21.1), if by Ito's lemma we can say that $\delta S/S \sim N(\mu\delta t, \sigma\sqrt{\delta t})$ implies that

$$\ln\frac{S_T}{S_0} \sim N\left[\left(\mu - \frac{\sigma^2}{2}\right)T, \sigma\sqrt{T}\right] \tag{21.11}$$

and

$$\ln S_T \sim N\left[S_0 + \left(\mu - \frac{\sigma^2}{2}\right)T, \sigma\sqrt{T}\right]$$

that is to say that the stock price follows a lognormal distribution. Then we can use this property to extract information regarding the distribution

---

[7] See Neftci (2000, p.27).
[8] See Hull (2006, Chapter 16)
[9] See Hull (2006, p. 286)

of returns of the stock between time t_0 and time T. Let ξ be the annualized continuously compounded rate of return that will have the distribution

$$\xi_i \sim \left(\mu - \frac{\sigma^2}{2}, \frac{\sigma}{\sqrt{T}} \right) \tag{21.12}$$

From Equation (21.12) we can ascertain that by expressing the return as continuously compounded, we are able to derive the stock price volatility from the standard deviation of the return. As such, if we have n number of observations, the observations being closing prices on a particular stock we can calculate the return as $\xi_i = \ln(S_i/S_{i-1})$ for $i = 1, 2, 3, \ldots, n$; and its mean being $\bar{\xi} = 1/n \ \Sigma \xi_i$.

Then the standard deviation of ξ can be estimated as $v = \sqrt{1/n-1 \sum_{i=1}^{n} (\xi - \bar{\xi})^2}$. Taking into consideration from Equation (21.11) that we know the standard deviation of ξ as $\sigma\sqrt{T}$, then we can estimate historical volatility as $\sigma_{historical} = v/\sqrt{T}$ (Table 21.1).

GARCH(1,1)

Extending Engle's work (1982), in 1986 Bollerslev developed the generalized autoregressive conditional heteroscedasticity, or GARCH, model. In short, GARCH explains the behavior of variance of a time series by way of two lags. The first lag captures high-frequency effects in squared past residuals, and the second shows any longer term characteristics of the

T A B L E   21.1

Historical volatility estimates

Horizon	Volatility
Daily	0.0108
Weekly	0.0241
Monthly	0.0495
Quarterly	0.0852
Yearly	0.1716

variances themselves. Through this relatively simple statistical analysis, we are able to register two things. First, we discover the existence of any clustering behavior in volatility, and second, we can observe any leptokurtosis effects in the distribution of returns.

The GARCH (1,1) framework is the simplest and most popular of the models available through Bollerslev's work. The ones between the parenthesies signify a single autoregressive lag in the equation and a single lag in the discovery of a moving average. Within this framework we can define the conditional mean and variance as $X_t = \mu + \sigma_t \varepsilon_t$ and $\sigma_t^2 = \omega + \beta \sigma_{t-1}^2 + \gamma \sigma_{t-1}^2 \varepsilon_{t-1}^2$ with $\omega > 0$, $\beta \geq 0$, $\gamma > 0$, and $\beta + \gamma < 1$.

As one can see above, the conditional variance σ_t^2 will be variable throughout the time series; as such if we take the unconditional expectation of all elements in the the equation for the conditional variance and assume stationarity, we are able to solve for the unconditional variance as, $\overline{\sigma^2} = \omega/1 - \beta - \gamma$. Thus we see the parameteric nature of the GARCH(1,1) framework. The next step naturally would be to estimate the parameters. As the literature suggests, maximum likelihood estimation is the appropriate method. Maximizing the following log-likelihood function $L = -T/2 \log(2\pi) - 1/2 \sum_{t=1}^{T} \log(\sigma_t^2) - 1/2 \sum_{t=1}^{T} (X_t - \mu)^2/2\sigma_t^2)$ under an assumption of normality will give us the most approriate parameter estimates. Using these estimates, we can then model the volatility structure of our time series to obtain an estimate for volatility (Table 21.2).

T A B L E   21.2

GARCH(1,1) estimates

Parameter	Estimate	Errors
ω	0.0070	(0.0009)
β	0.8707	(0.0128)
γ	0.1089	(0.0101)
Σ_annual	0.1865	
σ_semiannual	0.1319	
σ_quarterly	0.0932	
σ_monthly	0.0538	

HESTON'S VOLATILITY

Despite the elegance of the Black–Scholes model, we see clearly that it leaves much to be desired. The assumption of constant volatility sends us into territory where it becomes necessary to estimate and forecast volatilities in order to deal with the reality that volatility is in fact time varying. In 1993 Steven Heston devised a significant improvement upon the Black–Scholes model. Heston did not begin directly from where Black and Scholes left off. The work of Scott (1987), Hull and White (1987), and Wiggins (1987) provided for a conception of volatility as time varying through a stochastic proces. However, this body of work did not produce a generalized solution for the modeling of option prices (Table 21.3). Heston did just that. The treatment of volatility as time varying through a stochastic process is attractive; however, most importantly, it allows the theory to match the facts in certain fundemental respects. Firstly, the Heston model provides us with the beginnings of a scientific understanding of the volatility structure across maturities and by extension the put–call parity. Secondly, mean reversion, which is a parametric component of the model, allows us to interpret the phenomenon of volatility clustering, which is a well-observed feature of financial markets.

Recalling Equation (21.1), Heston modified the underlying asset process to the form

$$dS_t = \mu S_t dt + \sqrt{V_t}\, S_t dW_t^1 \qquad (21.13)$$

Needless to say, this follows the Black–Scholes framework in that the dependence of the change in the underlying asset remains a function

T A B L E   21.3

Option prices on DJIA at 12993 with strike 13000

Maturity	Market Value	Model Price	Monte Carlo Price
June 2008	2.22	2.27	2.23
September 2008	5.15	5.08	5.15
December 2008	7.10	7.04	7.09

of the Wiener process expressed in dW_t^1. However, the novelty arises as the the variation over time expressed in the volatility V_t is of the form

$$dV_t = \kappa(\theta - V_t)\,dt + \sigma\sqrt{V_t}\,S_t\,dW_t^2 \qquad (21.14)$$

For $V_t, t \geq 0$ we see a Cox et al. (1985) type of mean reverting process with κ being the parameter dictating the speed of mean reversion, θ the long run mean volatility, and σ being the volatility of volatility. Here, the term dW_t^2 is an additional Wiener process that correlates with dW_t^1 in Equation (21.13) through $dW_t^1 dW_t^2 = \rho\,dt$. In this fashion Heston has prescribed a probabilistic market price for the underlying asset as well as its volatility risk. This model provides us with the luxury of fitting the parameters κ, θ, σ, ρ, and V_0 the initial volatility, as well as the challenge of discovering their values that calibrate our model to market realities, as suggested in the seventh section of this chapter.

THE HESTON VALUATION EQUATION

Recalling the necessity for a a riskless portfolio from Equation (21.2) and the compounded necessity to evelute its movement, we can reformulate Equation (21.3) to incorporate the general contingent claim expressed as $\phi(S_t, V\,t)$ paying $max(S_T - k, 0)$ at time T. Again the contingent claim is to be replictaed using a self-financing or riskless portfolio. Such a portfolio will necessarily allow for trading in the underlying asset, the money market, and another derivative security, which we shall define as X. Changes in the riskless portfolio can be expressed as

$$d\Pi = d\phi(S_t, V, t) - \Delta_S\,dS_t - \Delta_X\,dX \qquad (21.15)$$

Here

$$
\begin{aligned}
d\Pi = {}& \left(\frac{\partial\phi(S_t, V, t)}{\partial S} - \Delta_S - \Delta_X\frac{\partial X}{\partial S}\right)dS + \left(\frac{\partial\phi(S_t, V, t)}{\partial V} - \Delta_X\frac{\partial X}{\partial V}\right)dV \\
& + \left(\left(\frac{\partial\phi(S_t, V, t)}{\partial t} + \frac{1}{2}S^2V\frac{\partial^2\phi(S_t, V, t)}{\partial S^2} + \rho S\sigma V^{\gamma+1/2}\frac{\partial^2\phi(S_t, V, t)}{\partial S\partial V}\right. \right. \\
& \left. + \frac{1}{2}\sigma^2 V^{2\gamma}\frac{\partial^2\phi(S_t, V, t)}{\partial V^2}\right) \\
& \left. - \Delta_X\left(\frac{\partial X}{\partial t} + \frac{1}{2}S^2V\frac{\partial^2 X}{\partial S^2} + \rho S\sigma V^{\gamma+1/2}\frac{\partial^2 X}{\partial S\partial V} + \frac{1}{2}\sigma^2 V^{2\gamma}\frac{\partial^2 X}{\partial V^2}\right)dt\right)
\end{aligned}
\qquad (21.16)
$$

setting the first and second terms of the above equation equal to zero we can now solve for

$$\Delta_S = \frac{\partial \phi(S_t, V, t)}{\partial S} - \Delta_X \frac{\partial X}{\partial S}$$

being the number of units to be invested in the underlying at time t, and

$$\Delta_X = \frac{\dfrac{\partial \phi(S_t, V, t)}{\partial V}}{\dfrac{\partial X}{\partial V}}$$

being the number of units to be invested in the secondary derivative security at time t.

Through this portfolio allocation we have eliminated any risk arising from the terms dS and dV in the portfolio. Given an appropriate selection of Δ_s and Δ_x, we can express our risk-free portfolio as

$$d\Pi = r\Pi dt = r(\phi(S_t, V, t) - \Delta_S S - \Delta_X X) dt \qquad (21.17)$$

returning to Equation (21.16) and combining it with the result in Equation (21.17), we can now collect the elements of the terms pertaining to $\phi(S_t, V, t)$ and X, respectively, as follows:

$$\frac{\left(\begin{array}{l} \dfrac{\partial \phi(S_t, V, t)}{\partial t} + \dfrac{1}{2} S^2 V \dfrac{\partial^2 \phi(S_t, V, t)}{\partial S^2} + \rho S \sigma V^{\gamma + 1/2} \dfrac{\partial^2 \phi(S_t, V, t)}{\partial S \partial V} \\[2mm] + \dfrac{1}{2} \sigma^2 V^{2\gamma} \dfrac{\partial^2 \phi(S_t, V, t)}{\partial V^2} + rS \dfrac{\partial \phi(S_t, V, t)}{\partial S} - r\phi(S_t, V, t) \end{array} \right)}{\dfrac{\partial \phi(S_t, V, t)}{\partial V}}$$

$$= \frac{\dfrac{\partial X}{\partial t} + \dfrac{1}{2} S^2 V \dfrac{\partial^2 X}{\partial S^2} + \rho S \sigma V^{\gamma + 1/2} \dfrac{\partial^2 X}{\partial S \partial V} + \dfrac{1}{2} \sigma^2 V^{2\gamma} \dfrac{\partial^2 X}{\partial V^2} + rS \dfrac{\partial X}{\partial S} - rX)}{\dfrac{\partial X}{\partial V}}$$

In order for the above equality to hold we must assume further that both terms equalize to some function $f(S,V,t) = \kappa(\theta - V_t) - \lambda V_t$. Here our arbitrary function equalized the PDEs for ϕ and X to the drift term less the product of the market price for volatility risk λ[10] and V_t. As such and by further assigning a value to $\gamma = 1/2$, we arive at the Heston stochastic volatility valuation equation expressed as

$$\frac{\partial \phi}{\partial t} + \frac{1}{2}S^2 V \frac{\partial^2 \phi}{\partial S^2} + \rho S \sigma V \frac{\partial^2 \phi}{\partial S \partial V} + \frac{1}{2}\sigma^2 V \frac{\partial^2 \phi}{\partial V^2} + rS \frac{\partial \phi}{\partial S}$$
$$+ (\kappa(\theta - V_t) - \lambda V_t)\frac{\partial \phi}{\partial V} = r\phi \qquad (21.18)$$

Following Duffie et al. (2000) and Gatheral (2006), we arrive at a solution for the valuation equation very similar to the Black–Scholes solution, that is to say,

$$\phi(S_t, V_t, t, T) = S_t P_0 - K e^{-r(T-t)}P_1 \qquad (21.19)$$

where $P_j(j = 0, 1)$ are the risk-adjusted probabilities of the log of the underlying price $x = ln(S_t)$ being higher than the log strike price $ln(K)$ at expiration, and that of exercise respectively, conditional on $x(t) = x(0)$ and $V(t) = V(0)$. Plugging the solution expressed in Equation (21.19) into the Heston valuation PDE and solving using a Fourier transform technique and deriving the characteristic function as is done in Hakala and Wystup (2002) and Gatheral (2006) we arrive at

$$P_j(x, V_t, T) = \frac{1}{2\pi}\int_0^\infty Re\left(\frac{exp(C_j(\eta, \tau)\theta + D_j(\eta, \tau)V + i\eta x)}{i\eta}\right)d\eta \qquad (21.20)$$

as the risk-neutral probabilities with the characteristic function being given by $\Phi_T(\eta) = exp(C_j(\eta, \tau)\theta + D_j(\eta, \tau)V)$ with $C_j(\eta, \tau) = \kappa(h\tau - 2/\sigma^2$

---

[10] It is of importance here to note that the existence of a closed form solution for the Heston model renders the estimation of this parameter irrelevant for our purpose of solving the model.

$\log(1 - le - d\tau/1 - l))$ and $D_j(\eta,\tau) = h\ (1 - e - d\tau/1 - le - d\tau)$ for $\tau = T - t$, $j = 0,1$ and

$$a_j = -\frac{\eta^2}{2} - \frac{i\eta}{2} + ij\eta \quad b_j = \kappa - \rho\sigma j - \rho\sigma i\eta \quad c = \frac{\sigma^2}{2}$$

$$d = \sqrt{b_j - 4a_j c} \qquad\qquad g = \frac{b+d}{\sigma^2} \qquad h = \frac{b-d}{\sigma^2}$$

$$l = \frac{h}{g}$$

Equations (21.20) and (21.19) are the Heston integral and the closed form Heston solution for the price of a European style call option, respectively. The integral in Equation (21.19) is a relatively complex one, which may only be approximated not calculated precisely.[11] Nonetheless, here we see the evolution of the Heston stochastic volatility model from the conception of time-varying volatility, through to a coherent model with a closed form solution.

An alternative to the approximation routine described in the footnote is to build a Monte Carlo engine and probabilistically define the value of the option under the Heston model. For this it becomes necessary to reach an appropriate simulation for the Heston processes described in Equations (21.13) and (21.14). As described in van Haastrecht and Plesser (2008), the exact solution for the Heston price dynamic is given by the process

$$S_{t+1} = S_t e^{(-r1/2\ V_t)} dt + \sqrt{V_t dt} W_t^1 \tag{21.21}$$

and following Gatherall (2006), we can use a Milstein discretization of the Heston volatility proces given by

$$V_{t+1} = V_t + \kappa(\theta - V_t)\, dt + \sigma\sqrt{V_t dt} W_t^2 + \sigma^2 dt \frac{W_t^2 - 1}{4} \tag{21.22}$$

---

[11] Cheney and Kincaid (1999) explain that using the basic Simpson's rule, we could numerically integrate a function (.) over two subintervals with three partition points. We use the recursive adaptive Simpson's quadrature function quadv in MATLAB, which allows us to employ this integration technique over as many subintervals as necessary to obtain a trusted level of accuracy.

It is important to note here that we will define W_t^1 and W_t^2, the sources of randomness for the price and volatility processes, respectively, as $W_t^1 \sim N(0,1)$ and $W_t^2 = \rho W_t^1 + \sqrt{1-\rho^2}\,\zeta$ with $\zeta \sim N(0,1)$. Taking into consideration that Heston's volatility process may produce negative values for V_t, we will incorporate a lower bound in the Monte Carlo engine where by the value of V_t will be $Max(V_t,0)$.

Running the truncated and discretized Heston processes in Equations (21.21) and (21.22) through our Monte Carlo engine an adequate number of times should allow us to produce a purely probabilistic mean value for a plain vanilla call option.

CALIBRATING THE HESTON PARAMETERS AND RESULTS

It is clear that the Heston model responds adequately to the shortcomings of the Black–Scholes model. The Heston framework, however, still leaves us with a further task. We are left with the necessity of estimating the model parameters so as to obtain meaningful prices (Table 21.4). To reiterate, we need to estimate values for the mean reversion parameter κ, long run mean volatility θ, initial volatility V_0, the volatility of volatility σ, and ρ the correlation between the two-dimentional Wiener processes.

Bakshi et al. (1997) show that empirical time series estimates of these parameters are very fragile in the face of real-world market prices for contingent claims. In essence, once again we face an inverse problem where we are forced to rely on observed prices to obtain state parameters.

T A B L E   21.4

Heston calibration results

Parameter	Value
κ	15.4682
θ	0.0271
σ	0.5118
ρ	-0.9492
V_0	0.0093

As such the calibration process should adhere to the following steps. First, we obtain a vector of liquid option prices. Using these prices and the price of the underlying security, we attempt to evaluate a first estimation as to what the initial parameters we will use in the calibration process ought to be. Second, we evaluate the model prices using the inital parameters. Third, let χ be a vector of the model parameters we minimize the weighted price difference between the returned model prices and observed market prices as follows:

$$min_\chi \sum_{i=1}^N w_i(Model\ Price_i - Market\ Price_i)^2 \qquad (21.23)$$

Cont (2005) suggested using implied volatilities as weights; however, we follow Moodley (2005) in setting w_i as $1/|bid_i - ask_i|$. The intuition here is that we allow lesser weights for returned model prices that gravitate towards the observed mid market price. More importantly, Moodley's weighting scheme allows us to circumvent the fact that our minimization routine may be returning a local minimum as oposed to a global one, in such a case we can accept the minimization results if the squared sum of the differences in Equation (21.23) is less than or equal to the squared sum of the weighted differences between the bid and the offer ends of the market.[12]

We used three data sets. The first data set is a time series of the Dow Jones Industrial Average daily closing prices from November 20, 1998 through May 15, 2008. This data set was used to obtain an estimate of the DJIA historical volatility during that period. We also used a time series of DJIA monthly closing prices from June 30, 1924 through April 30 2008 to obtain parameter estimates and a voltility estimate using the GARCH(1,1) method. Second, a spectrum of call option prices with varied strikes and three maturities (June 21, 2008, September 20, 2008, and December 20, 2008) written on the DJIA index were used to obtain close to ATM implied volatilities, as well as to calibrate the Heston model parameters. Figure 21.1 displays the calibrated option prices versus observed market prices.

---

[12] See Moodley (2005, pp. 21 and 22).

F I G U R E   21.1

Calibrated Option Prices versus Observed Market Prices

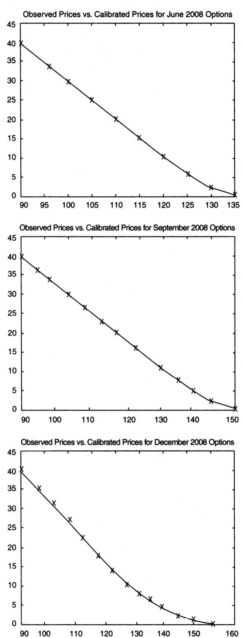

CONCLUSION

It is clear from the above that the framework initiated in Bachelier's work has evolved into an elegant and unique scienctific methodology. We have presented an intuitive derivation of the Black–Scholes and the Heston valuation equations and a popular solution methods using both models to value call style contingent claims. The inadequate assumption of constant volatility in the Black–Scholes model was overcome in the Heston framework through the use of a mean reverting stochastic process for the volatility term. Nonetheless, the inverse problem necessitating the calibration of the Black–Scholes model to real-world price remains intact with the Heston model. Albeit, the Heston model allows for several salient features of the real world, such as the existence of a volatility smile, and volatility clustering. Going forward, we would like to exert some effort into an exposition of forward volatility structures as well as the inclusion of jump processes into the Heston framework. Nonetheless, we have offered an overview and a discussion of two key pieces of literature related to the pricing of contingent claims, without which, much of today's financial realities would remain unrealized.

REFERENCES

Bakshi, G., C. Cao, and Z. Chen (1997) Empirical Performance of Alternative Option Pricing Models. *Journal of Finance*, 52(5): 2003–2050.

Black, F. and M. Scholes (1973) The Pricing of Options and Corporate Liabilities. *Journal of Political Economy*, 81(3): 637–654.

Bollerslev, T. (1986) Generalized Autoregressive Conditional Heteroscedasticity. *Journal of Econometrics*, 31(3): 307–327.

Cheney, W. and D. Kincaid (1999) *Numerical Mathematics and Computing*. Boston: Brooks Cole Publishing.

Cont, R. (2005) Recovering Volatility from Option Prices by Evolutionary Optimization. *Journal of Computational Finance*, 8(4): 43–76.

Cox, J.C., J.E. Ingersoll, and S.A. Ross (1985) A Theory of the Term Structure of Interest Rates. *Econometrica*, 53(2): 385–407.

Engle, R.F. (1982) Autoregressive Conditional Heteroscedasticity with Estimates of the Variance of United Kingdom Inflation. *Econometrica* 50(4): 987–1007.

Gatheral, J. (2006) *The Volatility Surface. A Practitioner's Guide.* Hoboken, NJ: John Wiley & Sons.

Hakala, J. and U. Wystup (2002) *Foreign Exchange Risk, Models, Instruments and Strategies.* London: Risk Books.

Haug, E.G. (2007) *The Complete Guide to Option Pricing Formulas.* New York: McGraw-Hill.

Hull, J. (2006) *Options, Futures and Other Derivatives.* Upper Saddle River, NJ: Pearson Prentice Hall.

Hull, J. and A. White (1987) The Pricing of Options on Assets with Stochastic Volatilities. *Journal of Finance,* 42(2): 281–300.

Moodley, N. (2005) *The Heston Model: A Practical Approach.* University of Witwatersrand: Witwatersrand, Johannesburg.

Neftci, S. (2000) *Introduction to the Mathematics of Financial Derivatives.* Burlington, MA: Academic Press.

Scott, L. (1987. Option Pricing When the Variance Changes Randomly: Theory, Estimation, and an Application. *Journal of Financial and Quantitative Analysis*, 22(4): 419–438.

van Haastrecht, A. and A. Pelsser (2008) Efficient, Almost Exact Simulation of the Heston Stochastic Volatility Model. Available at http://www.ssrn.com.

Wiggins, J. (1987) Option Values under Stochastic Volatilities. *Journal of Financial Economics*, 19(2): 351–372.

CHAPTER 22

Value at Risk under Heterogeneous Investment Horizons and Spatial Relations

Viviana Fernandez

ABSTRACT

The existence of heterogeneous investors and its incidence in gauging value at risk (VaR) have been previously dealt with in the literature in the context of the capital asset pricing model (CAPM), e.g., Fernandez (2005; 2006). In this chapter, in addition to the heterogeneity of investment horizons, we take account of spatial interrelations in financial markets by means of a spatial version of the CAPM (S-CAPM). This way, we can accommodate for firms characteristics in terms of a metric distance, which allows us to quantify systematic and nonsystematic risks under financial linkages across firms. A measure of VaR is formulated from the S-CAPM, which also takes into consideration investors' heterogeneity. We illustrate the use of our methodology by means of a panel of Latin American firms. In addition, we complement the discussion with Monte Carlo simulations aimed at quantifying the benefit of diversification in terms of VaR reduction.

* Funded in part by Fondecyt Grant No. 1070762.

INTRODUCTION

Value at risk (VaR) is a well-known measure of market risk [see, for example, Jorion (2007)], whose origin dates back to the late 1980s at J.P. Morgan. Value at risk answers the question of how much we can lose, with a given probability over a certain time horizon. It became a key measure of market risk after the Basel committee established in 1996 that commercial banks should cover losses on their trading portfolios over a 10-day horizon, 99 percent of the time. Ever since, VaR has become a popular tool for internal-risk control purposes at financial firms.

Mathematically, VaR measures the quantile of the projected distribution of gains and losses over a given time horizon. If α is the selected confidence level, VaR is the $1 - \alpha$ lower-tail level. In practical applications, the computation of VaR involves choosing α, the time horizon, the frequency of the data, the cumulative distribution function of the price change of a financial position over the time horizon under consideration, and the amount of the financial position.

In this chapter, we assume that asset returns can be explained by the CAPM and derive an expression for the portfolio VaR based on such an assumption. However, we add a twist and consider the possibility of spatial interactions among firm returns. That is to say, instead of simply including firms characteristics as additional risk factors, as has been the standard procedure in the finance literature since the seminal article by Fama and French (1992) [see Kothari and Shanken (1993) for references and a thorough discussion of this and other issues surroundings beta], we allow for the possibility that such extra risk factors of a given firm affect the evolution of the expected returns of other firms as well.

Our modified version of the CAPM draws from the literature of spatial statistics, which deals with the measurements or observations of a particular phenomenon associated with specific locations or regions [see, for instance, Haining (2003)]. In particular, one concept developed in spatial statistics is that of spatial correlation, which aims at measuring whether the occurrence of an event at a specific point in space affects another place. Spatial dependency is usually associated with geographic proximity or contiguity.

Although spatial phenomena have been extensively studied in various research fields, such as environmental sciences, geographical epidemiology, and urban economics, the study of spatial linkages in financial markets has been essentially overlooked. [Exceptions are Villar Frexedas and Vaya (2005) and Fernandez (2007).]

In order to formulate our model specification, we resort to cross-section tools developed in spatial econometrics. Good sources on this field of econometrics are the survey articles by Anselin (1999) and Anselin et al. (2008) and the textbook by Anselin (1988).

The measurement of spatial correlation requires the definition of a spatial weights matrix, which is customarily constructed in terms of the (Euclidean) geographical distance between neighbors. In finance, however, it is not obvious how distance should be gauged. In particular, geographical proximity may facilitate financial integration, but it is not certainly a necessary condition for such an integration to hold, given that most transactions are performed electronically nowadays. Therefore, the challenge is how to define *contiguity* in the context of financial markets. In this chapter, we take the route of defining contiguity in terms of firm financial indicators.

Besides spatial interactions, we also take into consideration the heterogeneity of investors' horizons. A statistical tool recently adopted in finance for such purpose is wavelet analysis. Wavelets have several advantages over traditional statistical tools commonly utilized in finance. Firstly, given that they enable us to decompose a time series into its low- and high-frequency components, we can characterize a financial index into its long trend and the fluctuations around such a trend. Such characterization is suitable to cointegration analysis and the quantification of risk diversification. Secondly, wavelets make it possible to carry out a decomposition of a time series variance, which yields information about the most important contributors to time-series variability. Similarly, a wavelet-based covariance can be computed for paired time series. The combination of variance and covariance decompositions provide us with multiple applications, some of which are wavelet-based betas and wavelet-based VaR. For recent applications in finance, see, among others, Lin and Stevenson (2001), Gençay et al. (2003; 2005), Connor and Rossiter (2005), Fernandez (2005; 2006; 2008), Karuppiah and Los (2005), In and Kim (2006), Fernandez and Lucey (2007), and Lien and Shrestha (2007). A thorough discussion on the use of wavelets in the financial field can be found in the textbook by Gençay et al. (2002).

Our study makes use of a sample of over 100 firms belonging to Brazil, Chile, and Mexico during the period 1997 to 2006. To our knowledge, our methodological approach to VaR is new in the finance literature. Specifically, we consider four financial indicators to quantify the distance between "neighboring" firms: market capitalization (relative to firm size), the market to book, EV/EBITDA, and debt ratios.

The chapter is organized as follows. The second section of this chapter describes the methodological tools utilized in our analysis, whereas the third section describes the data and discusses our empirical findings. This chapter's fourth section summarizes our main findings.

METHODOLOGICAL ISSUES

Spatial Cross-sectional Linkages

Let us consider N geographical units that are characterized by the existence of spatial autocorrelation, that is, $\text{cov}(y_i, y_j) \neq 0$, where i and j represent observations with their corresponding locations and y_i and y_j are the values of the random variable of interest at such particular locations [see, for instance, Anselin (1988)].

Given a sample of N observations, the elements of the $N \times N$ matrix containing the above-mentioned covariance terms will not be identifiable. One way to address this issue is by assuming a particular spatial stochastic process. Specifically, we concentrate on two types of spatial regression models: a spatial lag model and a spatial autoregressive (SAR) error model.

A spatial lag model is of the form

$$y = \rho Wy + X\beta + \varepsilon \qquad (22.1)$$

where ρ is a spatial autoregressive coefficient, the element i of the vector $\mathbf{Wy}$ is given by $[\mathbf{Wy}]_i = \Sigma_{j=1,\ldots,N}\, \omega_{ij}\, y_j$, where W is a weights matrix whose elements on the main diagonal are zero.[1] Therefore, $[\text{Wy}]_i$ represents a weighted average of the dependent variable at neighboring locations. X is a

---

[1] As mentioned in the Introduction, the weights matrix is constructed on the basis of the distances between neighbors. The distance between one particular location and itself is zero.

matrix of exogenous regressors, β is a vector of parameters, and ε is a vector of spherical errors with variance–covariance matrix given by $\sigma^2 I_N$.

Given that Wy is correlated with ε, ordinary least squares applied to Equation (22.1) will provide inconsistent estimates of ρ and β. A computationally simple approach to circumvent this problem is spatial two-stage least squares. This estimation method uses WX as a set of instruments for Wy:

$$\hat{\gamma}_{IV} = (Z' P_Q Z)^{-1} Z' P_Q y$$

$$\text{Var}(\hat{\gamma}_{IV}) = \hat{\sigma}^2 (Z' P_Q Z)^{-1} \qquad \hat{\sigma}^2 = \frac{(y - Z\hat{\gamma}_{IV})'(y - Z\hat{\gamma}_{IV})}{N} \qquad (22.2)$$

where

$$\gamma = [\rho \ \beta]', Z = [Wy \ X], Q = [WX \ X], \text{ and } \mathbf{P_Q} = \mathbf{Q(Q'Q)} - 1 \ \mathbf{Q'}$$

The SAR error model is in turn given by

$$y = X\beta + \varepsilon \qquad \varepsilon = \lambda W\varepsilon + u \qquad (22.3)$$

where u is assumed to be a vector of spherical errors.

The model can be rewritten as $y = X\beta + \varepsilon \ \varepsilon = (I_N - \lambda W)^{-1} u$ (223'). If $u \sim N(0, \sigma^2 I_N)$, then $\varepsilon \sim N(\mathbf{0}, \mathbf{\Omega})$ w, $\mathbf{\Omega} = \sigma^2 (I_N - \lambda W)^{-1}[(I_N - \lambda W)^{-1}]'$, so that the concentrated log-likelihood function for N independent observations, in terms of λ, can be readily obtained:

$$\ln L \propto -\frac{N}{2}\ln(\sigma^2) + \ln |I_N - \lambda W| - \frac{1}{2\sigma^2}\upsilon' \upsilon \qquad (22.4)$$

where $\upsilon \equiv (I_N - \lambda W)(y - X\beta)$, $\hat{\beta}_{ML} = (\tilde{X}' \tilde{X})^{-1} \tilde{X}' \tilde{Y}$, $\tilde{X} \equiv X - \lambda WX$, $\tilde{Y} \equiv Y - \lambda WY$, $\hat{\sigma}^2_{ML} = \hat{\upsilon}' \hat{\upsilon}/N$.

Given that for a given value of λ, $\hat{\beta}_{ML}$, and $\hat{\sigma}^2_{ML}$ can be easily computed, the maximization of Equation (22.4) can be accomplished by searching over a grid of values for λ. Standard errors of the parameter estimates can be obtained from the first derivatives of the log-likelihood function, i.e.,

$$\text{VaR}(\hat{\theta}) = \left(\sum_{i=1}^{N} \frac{\partial l_i}{\partial \theta} \frac{\partial l_i}{\partial \theta'} \right)^{-1}$$

where l_i is the log-likelihood function for observation i and $\theta' = (\lambda \ \beta \ \sigma^2)'$.

Metric Distance

In order to compute a weights matrix, we state that its (i, j) element is given by the Euclidean distance, d_{ij}, between a specific financial indicator associated with firms i and j:

$$d_{ij} = \sqrt{2(1 - \rho_{ij})} \tag{22.5}$$

where ρ_{ij} is Spearman's correlation coefficient. Equation (22.5) defines a Euclidean distance adequately because it satisfies the following three properties: (1) $d_{ij} = 0 \Leftrightarrow i = j$, (2) $d_{ij} = d_{ji}$, and (3) $d_{ij} \leq d_{ik} + d_{kj}$ [see Mantegna and Stanley (2000, chapter 13)]. We prefer Spearman's correlation coefficient to Pearson's because, unlike the latter, the former is a concordance measure of association between two random variables. That is, it has the property of being invariant to increasing transformations of the data.

Spatial VaR in the Context of the CAPM

Let us define a spatial lag CAPM in matrix form such as

$$\mathbf{r} - \mathbf{u}_f = \rho \mathbf{W}(\mathbf{r} - \mathbf{u}_f) + (\mathbf{r}_m - \mathbf{r}_f)\tilde{\boldsymbol{\beta}} + \boldsymbol{\varepsilon} \tag{22.6}$$

where $\boldsymbol{\varepsilon}$ is a vector of spherical errors, $(\mathbf{r} - \mathbf{u}_f)' = (r_1 - r_f \ldots r_N - r_f)'$ is a vector of excess returns, $[\mathbf{W}(\mathbf{r} - \mathbf{u}_f)]_i = \rho \Sigma_{j=1,\ldots N} \omega_{ij} (r_j - r_f$ and $\hat{\boldsymbol{\beta}}' = (\hat{\beta}_1 \ldots \hat{\beta}_N)'$. This specification implies that the risk premium of one firm is a linear function of a weighted average of the risk premia on neighboring firms and on the market portfolio.

Alternatively, a spatial error version of the CAPM would take the form of

$$\mathbf{r} - \mathbf{u}_f = (\mathbf{r}_m - r_f)\tilde{\boldsymbol{\beta}} + \boldsymbol{\varepsilon} \qquad \boldsymbol{\varepsilon} = \lambda \mathbf{W}\boldsymbol{\varepsilon} + \mathbf{u} \tag{22.7}$$

Under this model specification, the micro unanticipated component of a firm risk premium is a linear function of a weighted average of the micro unanticipated components of neighboring firms. That is to say, a SAR error model assumes that the nonsystematic risk of a particular firm is affected by that of neighboring firms.

Under each model specification, one can readily define a measure of VaR. To that end, let us assume, without loss of generality, that the risk-free rate is known and that assets returns have an expected value of zero and are normally distributed. Under these assumptions, it is straightforward to show that for an N-asset portfolio with a vector of weights, ω, the VaR under the spatial lag and SAR models are, respectively, given by

$$V_0 k(\alpha) \sqrt{\begin{array}{l} \omega'(\sigma_m^2 (\mathbf{I}_N - \rho \mathbf{W})^{-1} \beta\beta'\{(\mathbf{I}_N - \rho \mathbf{W})^{-1}\}' \\ + \sigma_u^2 (\mathbf{I}_N - \rho \mathbf{W})^{-1}\{(\mathbf{I}_N - \rho \mathbf{W})^{-1}\}')\omega \end{array}} \qquad (22.8a)$$

$$V_0 k(\alpha) \sqrt{\omega'(\sigma_m^2 \, \beta\beta' + \sigma_u^2 (\mathbf{I}_N - \lambda \mathbf{W})^{-1}\{(\mathbf{I}_N - \lambda \mathbf{W})^{-1}\}')\omega} \qquad (22.8b)$$

given that Equation (22.6) can be rewritten as $\mathbf{r} - \mathbf{r}_f = (\mathbf{I}_N - \rho \mathbf{W})^{-1}$ $\{(\mathbf{r}_m - \mathbf{r}_f)\tilde{\beta} + \varepsilon\}$ and the variance–covariance matrix of ε in Equation (22.7) can be readily obtained by re-expressing ε as $\varepsilon = (\mathbf{I}_N-\lambda\mathbf{W})^{-1}\mathbf{u}$. $\omega' = (\omega_1, \omega_2, \ldots, \omega_N)'$ is the vector of asset weights, V_0 is the initial monetary value of the portfolio, and $k(\alpha) \equiv \Phi^{-1}(1-\alpha)$ with $\Phi(.)$ the cumulative distribution function (CDF) of the standard normal.

In the absence of spatial effects, $\rho = 0$ and $\lambda = 0$ in Equations (22.8a) and (22.8b), respectively, and VaR(α) collapses to $V_0 k(\alpha) \sqrt{\omega'(\sigma_m^2 \, \beta\beta' + \sigma_\varepsilon^2 \mathbf{I}_N)\omega}$. The first term under the square root accounts for systematic risk, whereas the second one term, for nonsystematic risk. As the number of assets, N, increases, the second term vanishes. This can be easily seen by assuming an equally weighted portfolio, i.e., $\omega_i = 1/N$, and letting N go to infinity.

The distinctive feature between Equations (22.8a) and (22.8b) is the treatment of risk. Our spatial lag version of the CAPM considers three different sources of risk, namely, systematic or market risk captured by the asset betas, spatial risk embodied by the risk premia of neighboring firms, and nonsystematic risk contained in the error term of the model equation. By contrast, in the SAR representation of VaR, spatial and nonsystematic risks are simultaneously gauged by the expression $\sigma_u^2(\mathbf{I}_N - \lambda\mathbf{W})^{-1}$ $\{(\mathbf{I}_N - \lambda\mathbf{W})^{-1}\}'$ under the square root.

Heterogeneous Investors

A subject, which has received attention in recent studies and which also has important implications for portfolio management, is the existence of heterogeneous investors. In a recent article, Connor and Rossiter (2005) point out that long-term traders will essentially focus on price fundamentals that drive overall trends, whereas short-term traders will primarily react to incoming information within a short-term horizon. Hence, market dynamics in the aggregate will be the result of the interaction of agents with heterogeneous time horizons. In order to model the behavior of financial series at different time spans, researchers have resorted to wavelet analysis, a mathematical tool developed in the early 1990s.

Wavelets enable us to decompose a time series into high- and low-frequency components [see, for instance, Percival and Walden (2000)]. High-frequency components describe the short-term dynamics, whereas low-frequency components represent the long-term behavior of the series. Wavelets are classified into father and mother wavelets. Father wavelets capture the smooth and low-frequency parts of a signal, whereas mother wavelets describe its detailed and high-frequency parts.

Applications of wavelet analysis usually utilize a discrete wavelet transform (DWT). The DWT maps a vector of n observations to a vector of n smooth and detail wavelet coefficients,[2] which make it possible to gauge the underlying smooth behavior of the data and the deviations from it. Given J levels, when the length of the data, n, is divisible by 2^J, there are $n/2$ wavelet coefficients at the finest scale 2^1, $n/2^2$ coefficients at the next finest scale 2^2, etc.[3] The number of wavelet coefficients at a given scale is related to the width of the wavelet function. This implies that the lowest scales will mimic the short-term fluctuations of the original time series.

In particular, wavelet analysis enables us to decompose a time series into its fundamental components, where each of them contains information regarding the variability of the data at a particular scale. Such a

---

[2] $S_{J,k}$ and $d_{j,k}, j = 1, 2, \ldots J$, respectively, where J is the total number of levels. At level $j = 1, \ldots J$, the $1/2^j$ vector of the detail wavelet coefficients d_{jk} is associated with changes on a scale of length 2^{j-1}, whereas the $n/2^J$ vector of smooth wavelet coefficients S_{Jk} is associated with averages on a scale of length 2^J.

[3] These are denominated dyadic scales [see Percival and Walden (2000, paper 1)].

decomposition is called a *multiresolution decomposition* (MRD) of a time series y(t), which is the sum of the orthogonal components $S_J(t)$, $D_J(t)$, $D_{J-1}(t)$, ..., $D_1(t)$ from scales 1 through J:

$$y(t) \approx S_J(t) + D_J(t) + D_{J-1}(t) + \ldots + D_1(t) \tag{22.9}$$

where $S_J(t)$ and $D_J(t)$ are denominated the smooth and detail components, respectively.

Wavelet scales are such that times are separated by multiples of 2^j, $j = 1, \ldots, J$. For instance, for quarterly data, scale 1 is associated with 2 to 4 quarter dynamics, scale 2 with 4 to 8 quarter dynamics, scale 3 with 8 to 16 quarter dynamics, etcetera.

EMPIRICAL TESTING OF SPATIAL LINKAGES

Estimation of Spatial Effects

Our data set is comprised of 50 Chilean, 42 Brazilian, and 34 Mexican firms, which have been selected from the *Economatica* database. Income statements and balance sheets for the three countries are available at an annual frequency. Figures are inflation adjusted and expressed in their original currency. The sample period under consideration is 1997 to 2006. By focusing on that period, we can rely on a greater number of firms, given that some sampled firms became listed in 1997. It is worth noting that *Economatica* does not keep track of privately owned firms.

In Table 22.1, we report the median values of four financial ratios of interest for each year in the sample: market capitalization relative to firm size, market-to-book value, debt ratio, and EV/EBITDA.[4] Market capitalization is rescaled by firm size in order to make figures comparable among firms across countries, given that they are expressed in domestic currency.

Over the sample period, we observe an increase of market capitalization, relative to firm size, over time, which also drove the market-to-book ratio upwards. Meanwhile, the median debt ratio remained relatively stable

---

[4] We use the median rather than the mean because it is more robust to the presence of outliers.

T A B L E   22.1

Medians of financial ratios for a sample of Chilean, Brazilian, and Mexican firms

Period EV/EBITDA	Market Capitalization/ Firm Size	Market/Book	Debt Ratio	
1997	0.683	0.839	0.226	11.10
1998	0.378	0.499	0.249	7.23
1999	0.499	0.738	0.230	8.28
2000	0.442	0.663	0.240	7.84
2001	0.408	0.696	0.251	7.37
2002	0.432	0.861	0.228	7.36
2003	0.607	1.188	0.254	9.05
2004	0.818	1.545	0.231	7.86
2005	0.787	1.463	0.214	7.60
2006	0.917	1.774	0.214	8.82

Notes: (1) Market capitalization is rescaled by firm size in order to make figures comparable given that they are expressed in domestic currency. (2) The debt ratio is defined as total debt over total assets. (3) EV/EBITDA is the enterprise value to EBITDA. Data source: *Economatica*.

over the same time period. The enterprise value (EV) to earnings before interest, taxes, depreciation, and amortization (EBITDA) ratio measures how long it would take to generate the firm value given its current operational cash flows.[5] This ratio presented a downward trend at the beginning of the sample to oscillate around 8.0 subsequently.

We select Morgan Stanley's Emerging Markets (EM) Latin America standard core index in U.S. dollars (USD) as a good approximation of the market portfolio. Given that this index is expressed in USD, we accordingly convert the stock returns into USD. The risk-free rate in USD is chosen to be the 10-year U.S. Treasury bill. Data on the exchange rates of each country and the T-bill are also obtained from *Economatica*.

We carry out the estimation process in two stages. At the first stage, we compute the beta for each sampled firm by resorting to the standard CAPM. In order to rely on a greater number of degrees of freedom, we use

---

[5] The smaller the EV/EBITDA ratio is, the less expensive the firm becomes in relative terms.

quarterly data of stock prices to compute the returns in local currency, which in turn are converted into USD. In order to compute each beta, we resort to an estimator that is robust to the presence of outliers and satisfies both consistency and asymptotic normality. At the second stage, we run a regression of the median returns of the sampled firms on the betas obtained at the first stage in order to obtain estimates of the risk premium on the market portfolio and of the parameters ρ and λ of the spatial lag and SAR error model specifications described earlier. All the computer code involved in the estimation results reported in the subsequent sections was written in S-Plus 7.0.

Four alternative weights matrix $\mathbf{W}_N$ are constructed by resorting to the annual data contained in the balance sheets and income statements of the 126 sampled firms. Such matrices enable us to have a sense of the distance between firms based on the financial ratios referred to at the beginning of this section.

Table 22.2 panels (a) through (d) report the spatial-effect estimates. For instance, for the spatial lag model based on market capitalization, a

T A B L E   22.2

Estimates of the spatial parameter ρ and λ

Model	ρ	p-value	λ	p-value
(a) Weights matrix based on market capitalization relative to firm size				
SAR error model	—	—	0.0052	0.000
Spatial lag model	0.0056	0.000	—	—
(b) Weights matrix based on the market-to-book ratio				
SAR error model	—	—	0.0054	0.000
Spatial lag model	0.0061	0.000	—	—
(c) Weights matrix based on the EV/EBITDA ratio				
SAR error model	—	—	0.0051	0.000
Spatial lag model	0.0050	0.000	—	—
(d) Weights matrix based on the debt ratio				
SAR error model	—	—	0.0051	0.000
Spatial lag model	0.0051	0.000	—	—

quarterly increase of 100 basis points in the weighted average of the dependent variable (i.e., the risk premium on a firm stock) at neighboring locations leads to a quarterly increase of 0.56 basis points in the risk premium of a given firm. The interpretation of the SAR error model is fairly different because the interaction among firms in this case is through firm-specific or micro shocks. For the market-capitalization weights matrix, a quarterly increase of 100 basis points in the weighted average of micro shocks at neighboring firms translates into a quarterly increase of 0.52 basis points in the nonsystematic-risk component of a given firm. In general, the estimates of ρ and λ tend to be fairly similar across the different weights matrices under consideration.

Value-at-Risk Computation

Once we have estimates of the spatial parameters of interest ρ and λ, we can proceed to evaluate the VaR expressions for the spatial lag and spatial error models given by Equations (22.8a) and (22.8b). Without loss of generality, we consider an equally weighted portfolio made up of the 126 firms in the sample, with an initial value of \$1,000. The time horizon is one quarter, and the confidence level is 99 percent. We also compute the VaR for a standard CAPM as a benchmark.

Our results are reported in Table 22.3. First of all, we notice that the VaR estimate for the standard CAPM and its SAR version are fairly similar. This is not surprising because λ is fairly small (i.e., around 0.01) under the different weights matrices, so that the term $\omega' \, \sigma_u^2 \, (\mathbf{I}_N - \lambda \, \mathbf{W})^{-1} \{(\mathbf{I}_N - \lambda \, \mathbf{W})^{-1}\}' \omega$ under the square root of Equation (22.8b) is approximately equal to $\omega' \, (\sigma_u^2 \, \mathbf{I}_N)\omega$. On the other hand, for any of the weights matrices, the VaR for the spatial lag model is greater than for the SAR error model, where the most sizeable difference is observed for the market-to-book ratio weights matrix. Given that the estimates of ρ and λ are fairly similar, the discrepancy between the VaR figures for the spatial lag and SAR error models is primarily explained by that between $\omega' \, (\sigma_m^2 \beta \beta')\omega$ and $\omega' \, (\sigma_m^2 \, (\mathbf{I}_N - \rho \, \mathbf{W})^{-1} \beta \beta' \{(\mathbf{I}_N - \rho \, \mathbf{W})^{-1}\}' \, \omega$. It is worth pointing out that it is not always the case that the spatial-lag-based VaR is always greater than the SAR error one. As illustrated in a forthcoming section in this chapter, for given weights matrix and betas, the discrepancy

T A B L E   22.3

Spatial VaR estimates

(a) Weights matrix based on market capitalization relative to firm size	
SAR error model	$93.6
Spatial lag model	$141
(b) Weights matrix based on the market-to-book ratio	
SAR error model	$95.4
Spatial lag model	$202
(c) Weights matrix based on the EV/EBITDA ratio	
SAR error model	$92.5
Spatial lag model	$106
(d) Weights matrix based on the debt ratio	
SAR error model	$92.5
Spatial lag model	$105
(e) Weights matrix equals I_N	
Standard CAPM	$92

Note: The VaR figures are computed by assumption an equally weighted portfolio with an initial value of $1,000. The time horizon is one quarter, and the confidence level is 99 percent.

between the two VaR figures hinges upon the number of assets, N, and the values of the parameters ρ and λ.

We next compute a wavelet-based version of the VaR of our portfolio for different investment horizons and alternative weights matrices. In order to carry out such a wavelet-based decomposition of the VaR, we reestimate the spatial lag and SAR error models by first obtaining the corresponding timescale components of the betas and the firm returns according to Equation (22.9). Panels (a) and (b) of Figure 22.1 depict such decomposition for the raw quarterly data and its scales 1 and 2 (D_1 and D_2, respectively), where scale 1 is associated with 2 to 4 quarter dynamics and scale 2 is associated with 4 to 8 quarter dynamics. The wavelet filter utilized in the computations is the symmlet 8 (i.e., least asymmetric), which is customarily chosen in wavelet analysis.

F I G U R E   22.1

Wavelet-based Decomposition of Firm Betas and Returns

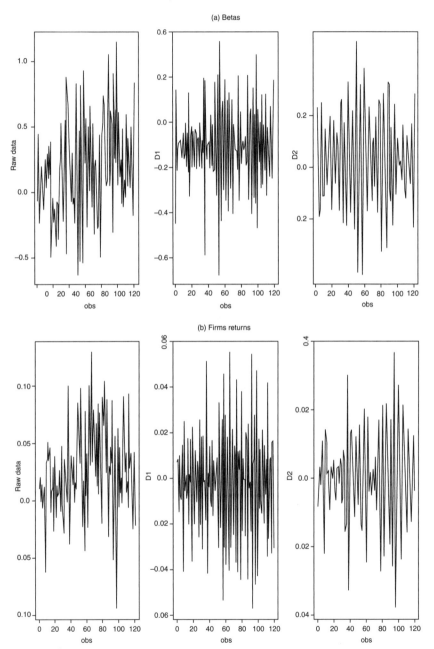

In this case, given a quarterly time horizon, the VaR at scale 1 is associated with the maximum portfolio loss, at a given confidence level, which is potentially observable at a 2- to 4-quarter investment horizon. Similarly, the VaR at scale 2 is that associated with a 4- to 8-quarter investment horizon.

Given that we rely on a relatively small sample to compute the weights matrix, it is infeasible to obtain its timescale decomposition. Therefore, we only carry out the wavelet decomposition of the betas, and the firm returns, as mentioned above; next, we compute the VaR based on Equations (22.8a) and (22.8b). Consequently, the timescale decomposition of the betas explains to a great extent the variation of the VaR across timescales. As can be seen from Table 22.4, for both models, the VaR is greater at scale 1. The reason is that the finer scales describe the higher frequency components of the data, which tend to be more volatile. Such a pattern is observable in Figure 22.1(a) and (b). On the other hand, the weights matrix does not have much of an impact on the VaR of the SAR error because, similarly to the raw data, the computed spatial parameters are relatively small. Changing the weights matrix has a more noticeable impact on the VaR of the spatial lag model because the spatial effect explicitly enters as an additional explanatory variable. Let us recall that under this model specification the vector of excess returns is given by $\mathbf{r} - \iota r_f = (\mathbf{I}_N - \rho \mathbf{W})^{-1} \{(r_m - r_f) \tilde{\boldsymbol{\beta}} + \varepsilon\}$.

At scale 2, the spatial lag model predicts a smaller VaR for every weights matrix. However, at scale 1, both models may predict a similar VaR (i.e., market-to-book ratio weights matrix) or the SAR error model may even beat the spatial lag one (i.e., capitalization relative to firm size weights matrix). In other words, the investment horizon and the way firms distance is gauged may play a role in determining which model predicts a potentially greater portfolio loss.

Extensions: Monte Carlo Simulation of VaR

In this section, we explore the impact of the number of assets on diversification. In particular, we would expect an inverse relation between the portfolio VaR and the number of assets in the portfolio. In order to confirm this conjecture, we consider five alternative portfolio sizes under the three model specifications previously considered, namely, the spatial lag and SAR error models and the standard CAPM.

T A B L E   22.4

Wavelet-based spatial VaR estimates

(a) Weights matrix based on market capitalization relative to firm size		
	Scale 1	Scale 2
SAR error model	$4.88	$2.90
Spatial lag model	$5.28	$2.77
(b) Weights matrix based on the market-to-book ratio		
Scale 1	**Scale 2**	
SAR error model	$4.86	$2.88
Spatial lag model	$4.86	$2.84
(c) Weights matrix based on the EV/EBITDA ratio		
Scale 1	**Scale 2**	
SAR error model	$4.87	$2.88
Spatial lag model	$4.67	$2.83
(d) Weights matrix based on the debt ratio		
Scale 1	**Scale 2**	
SAR error model	$4.84	$2.86
Spatial lag model	$4.60	$2.63

Note: The VaR figures are computed by assumption an equally weighted portfolio with an initial value of $1,000. The time horizon is one quarter, and the confidence level is 99 percent.

The Monte Carlo experiments are conducted as follows. The return series are generated from the standard CAPM, such that $r_{it} = \alpha_i + \beta_i \times r_{mt} + \xi_{it}$, $\alpha_i \sim U(0.005, -0.005)$, $\beta_i \sim U(0, 1.5)$, and $\xi_{it} \sim N(0, 0.0025)$. The return on the market portfolio is assumed to be normally distributed with mean and variance as in the quarterly return series of the EM Latin America standard core. We next define a metric distance based on the standardized returns. In other words, we attempt to capture return performance after controlling for volatility. After computing such a matrix distance, we evaluate the expressions of the spatial lag and SAR error VaR Equations (22.8a) and (22.8b).

It is worth pointing out that the above assumptions are made by the sake of parsimony and they are by no means exhaustive. Indeed, we basically start up with return series generated by the simplest model under consideration, and we next take account of spatial effects by means of a weights matrix, which can be computed with the available information. A more elaborate way of conducting the Monte Carlo experiment would involve defining a weights matrix from the outset. However, a priori, it does not seem obvious how to define such a weights matrix unless one would introduce some extra assumptions on the financial performance of the firms in the artificial sample.

Having these considerations in mind, we proceed by the simpler outlined route to perform the simulations. Our results are reported in Table 22.5. First of all, we observe that for a moderate level of spatial dependency (i.e., $\lambda = \rho = 0.1$) and a small number of assets (N), the three models predict similar values of the portfolio VaR. In particular, the presence of interactions between firm idiosyncratic risks does not lead to a decrease in the overall portfolio risk (i.e., SAR error model versus CAPM); whereas the interaction through firm excess returns translates into a slightly smaller potential portfolio loss (i.e., spatial lag versus SAR error and CAPM).

A distinctive pattern in the simulation results arises as the number of assets increases. For instance, when N = 40, the distance between the VaR

T A B L E   22.5

Simulations spatial VaR for different portfolio sizes

Number of Assets (N)	Spatial Lag	SAR Error	No Spatial Effects
25	$288.9	$324.9	$319.1
40	$90.0	$293	$302
80	$27.6	$285	$290
180	$5.4	$271	$273
300	$2.1	$270	$270

Notes: (1) The simulations are carried out by assuming that $\rho = \lambda = 0.1$. The number of observation of each return series is 1,100, and the number of simulations is 200. (2) The VaR figures are computed by assumption an equally weighted portfolio with an initial value of $1,000. The time horizon is one quarter, and the confidence level is 95 percent.

figures yielded by the SAR error model and the CAPM shortens, while that corresponding to the spatial lag model is noticeably smaller. The gap between the spatial lag and the other two models widens as the number of the assets gets larger. Specifically, the diversification benefit is much larger for the spatial lag model as the existence of spatial effects dampens both systematic and nonsystematic risks given the functional form of excess returns, i.e., $\mathbf{r} - \mathbf{\iota} r_f = (\mathbf{I}_N - \rho\mathbf{W})^{-1}\{(r_m - r_f)\tilde{\boldsymbol{\beta}} + \boldsymbol{\varepsilon}\}$. Such dampening effect accentuates as the number of assets becomes fairly large. For instance, when increasing the number of assets from 80 to 180, the SAR error model and the CAPM yield virtually identical values of the portfolio VaR. This means that the term $\sigma_u^2\boldsymbol{\omega}'(\mathbf{I}_N - \lambda\mathbf{W})^{-1}\{(\mathbf{I}_N - \lambda\mathbf{W})^{-1}\}')\boldsymbol{\omega}$ under the square root of Equation (22.8b) approximates $\sigma_u^2\boldsymbol{\omega}'\boldsymbol{\omega}$, which in turn tends to zero as N gets large enough (i.e., for $\omega_i = 1/N$, $\forall i$, $\sigma_u^2\boldsymbol{\omega}'\boldsymbol{\omega} = \sigma_u^2/N$. This is exactly what we observe when N = 300; all that remains is systematic risk under the SAR error model and the CAPM.

Under the spatial lag model, the term $\sigma_m^2\,\boldsymbol{\omega}'\,(\mathbf{I}_N - \rho\mathbf{W})^{-1}\,\boldsymbol{\beta}\boldsymbol{\beta}'\{\mathbf{I}_N - \rho\,\mathbf{W})-1\}'\boldsymbol{\omega}$ dominates $\sigma_u^2\,\boldsymbol{\omega}'\,(\mathbf{I}_N - \rho\,\mathbf{W})^{-1}\{(\mathbf{I}_N - \rho\,\mathbf{W})^{-1}\}')\boldsymbol{\omega}$ in the VaR expression (22.8a) for large N, as the latter becomes negligible. However, the former gets fairly small as well, implying that the portfolio risk would tend to vanish as the number of assets gets very large.

In order to carry out some sensitivity analysis, we increased the value of λ from 0.1 to 0.5. We found that the VaR slightly decreases for the portfolio sizes of 25 and 40. In the former case, the VaR becomes $302, whereas in the latter case, it becomes $291. For greater values of N, there are not quantitative differences in the computed value of VaR between the two cases. In other words, the benefit of a higher degree of spatial interaction of nonsystematic risks becomes negligible for a large portfolio as the systematic-risk component of the VaR predominates.

CONCLUSION

In this chapter, we formulate a measure of VaR in the context of a spatial version of the CAPM (S-CAPM), which accommodates for firm interrelations. Such interrelations are defined in terms of firm characteristics and a Euclidean metric distance. The existence of heterogeneous investors is accounted for by wavelet analysis, which enables to obtain a timescale decomposition of a time series. We consider two spatial functional forms for modeling VaR: a spatial lag and a SAR error model. From these two functional forms, corresponding VaR formulas are obtained and their use is illustrated by means of a panel of Latin American firms. In addition, the discussion is complemented with Monte Carlo simulations aimed at quantifying the benefit of diversification in terms of VaR reduction.

Our main findings can be summarized as follows: First, more portfolio diversification gains are attainable under a spatial lag model because spatial interactions affect both systematic and nonsystematic risks. Second, a timescale decomposition of the data will impact the value of VaR, suggesting that the investment horizon is a key element to determining a portfolio loss. Finally, a higher degree of spatial interaction in a SAR error model translates into a smaller VaR only for portfolios of reduced size. As expected, this finding indicates that nonsystematic risk becomes irrelevant as the portfolio size gets large enough.

REFERENCES

Anselin, L. (1988) *Spatial Econometrics: Methods and Models*. Series: Studies in Operational Regional Science. New York: Springer-Verlag.

Anselin, L. (1999) Spatial Econometrics. Working paper, University of Texas at Dallas, Richardson, Texas.

Anselin, L., J. Le Gallo, and H. Jayet (2008) Spatial Panel Econometrics. In L. Matyas and P. Sevestre (eds.), *The Econometrics of Panel Data: Fundamentals and Recent Developments in Theory and Practice*. New York: Springer-Verlag.

Connor, J. and R. Rossiter (2005) Wavelet Transforms and Commodity Prices. *Studies in Nonlinear Dynamics & Econometrics*, 9(1): 1–20.

Fama, F. and K. R. French (1992). The Cross-section of Expected Stock Returns. *The Journal of Finance* 47(2): 427–465.

Fernandez, V. (2005) The International CAPM and a Wavelet-Based Decomposition of Value at Risk. *Studies of Nonlinear Dynamics & Econometrics*, 9(4).

Fernandez, V. (2006) The CAPM and Value at Risk at Different Time Scales. *International Review of Financial Analysis*, 15(3): 203–219.

Fernandez, V. (2007) Spatial Linkages in International Financial Markets. Discussion Paper No.234, Institute for International Integration Studies (IIIS), Trinity College, Dublin.

Fernandez, V. and B. Lucey (2007) Portfolio Management under Sudden Changes in Volatility and Heterogeneous Investment Horizons. *Physica A*, 375(2): 612–624.

Fernandez, V. (2008) Multi-period Hedge Ratios for a Multi-asset Portfolio When Accounting for Returns Co-movement. *The Journal of Futures Markets*, 28(2): 182–207.

Gençay, R., B. Whitcher, and F. Selçuk (2002) *An Introduction to Wavelets and Other Filtering Methods in Finance and Economics.* San Diego, CA: Academic Press.

Gençay, R., B. Whitcher, and F. Selçuk (2003) Systematic Risk and Time Scales. *Quantitative Finance*, 3(2): 108–116.

Gençay, R., B. Whitcher, and F. Selçuk (2005) Multiscale Systematic Risk. *Journal of International Money and Finance*, 24(1): 55–70.

Haining, R. (2003) *Spatial Data Analysis: Theory and practice.* Cambridge, U.K: Cambridge University Press.

In, F. and S. Kim (2006) The Hedge Ratio and the Empirical Relationship Between the Stock and Futures Markets: A New Approach Using Wavelet Analysis. *Journal of Business*, 79(2): 799–820.

Jorion, P. (2007) *Value at Risk: The New Benchmark for Managing Financial Risk.* New York: McGraw-Hill.

Karuppiah, J., C. and Los, (2005) Wavelet Multi-resolution Analysis of High-Frequency Asian FX Rates, Summer 1997. *International Review of Financial Analysis*, 14(2): 211–246. Special issues in *Quantitative Issues in Finance*.

Kothari, S. and J. Shanken (1998) On Defense of Beta. In J. Stern and D. Chew (eds.), The Revolution in Corporate Finance. Malden, MA: Blackwell Publishers.

Mantegna, R. and H. Stanley (2000) *An Introduction to Econophysics: Correlations and Complexity in Finance*. Cambridge, U.K: Cambridge University Press.

Lien, D. and K. Shrestha (2007) An Empirical Analysis of the Relationship Between Hedge Ratio and Hedging Horizon Using Wavelet Analysis. *The Journal of Futures Markets*, 27(2): 127–150.

Lin, S. and M. Stevenson (2001) Wavelet Analysis of the Cost-of-carry Model. *Studies in Nonlinear Dynamics & Econometrics,* 5(1): 87–102.

Percival, D. B., and Walden, A.T. (2000) *Wavelet Methods for Time Series Analysis*. Cambridge University Press, Cambridge, UK.

Villar Frexedas, O. and E. Vaya (2005) Financial Contagion between Economies: An Exploratory Spatial Analysis. *Estudios de Economia Aplicada*, 23(1): 151–165.

CHAPTER 23

How Investors Face Financial Risk Loss Aversion and Wealth Allocation with Two-Dimensional Individual Utility: A VaR Application

Erick W. Rengifo and Emanuela Trifan

ABSTRACT

We study the attitude of nonprofessional investors toward financial losses and their wealth allocation among consumption, risky, and risk-free financial assets. Utility is derived from two sources: consumption and financial wealth fluctuations. Financial investments are narrowly framed. Loss attitudes are modeled in an extended prospect-theory framework that accounts for both loss aversion and the impact of past risky portfolio performance. Wealth allocation is determined in a portfolio optimization framework with individual value at risk as risk measure. We solve for the aggregate market equilibrium where the representative investor maximizes expected utility. Empirical estimations based on real market data suggest that the maximizers of expected utility are little averse toward financial losses in general but prefer to invest more in risk-free than in risky assets. Myopic loss aversion is mostly rejected.

INTRODUCTION

One of the common decisions in everyday life is the optimal allocation of resources among different activities that generate utility. For individuals, the first and most important source of utility is consumption. Additionally, people who are active in financial markets derive utility from their investments. This work addresses the behavior of nonprofessional investors who derive utility from both consumption and financial wealth fluctuations.

We are first interested in the *attitude of nonprofessional investors toward financial losses*, knowing that they narrowly frame financial investments and change current perceptions subject to the past performance of these investments. Equally, we analyze how nonprofessional investors have now to decide upon the optimal *wealth allocation* between consumption and financial investments in total—where the latter category offers a further choice between a risky portfolio and a risk-free asset—as a consequence of their loss attitude. We adopt the formal views in Rengifo and Trifan (2007) regarding the subjective perception of risky vs. risk-free investments—that is, the prospective value—and how it enters the wealth-allocation problem of nonprofessional investors. In this context, loss aversion is quantified by two measures: the loss-aversion coefficient and the global first-order risk aversion (gRA).

The wealth allocation is expressed by the wealth percentages dedicated to consumption and to (different types of) financial assets. It is derived from an extended version of the portfolio optimization setting by Campbell et al. (2001) that uses the value at risk as a measure of risk. This extension accounts for the subjective perceptions of nonprofessional investors, in particular for the formation of what we denote as the *individual* value at risk (VaR).

In addition, we rely on the theoretical approach of Barberis and Huang (2004; 2006) and Barberis et al. (2001), according to which investors' decisions rely on the maximization of their expected utility. The utility function is shaped in order to account for the narrow framing of financial investments and for the influence of past portfolio performance on the current perceptions of risky investments.

We analyze the loss attitude and wealth allocation in the aggregate equilibrium with a representative investor. We derive the equilibrium equations and, from them, the variables of interest, specifically the discounting factor and the prospective value. The latter serves further for obtaining equilibrium-equivalent measures of the loss attitude: the loss-aversion coefficient and *gRA*. Wealth-allocation variables can only be assessed on average.

The empirical implementation of the theoretical part consists of, first, simulating how nonprofessional investors behave in an environment where consumption and financial markets are characterized by general parameters—such as the risk-free returns and the dynamics of consumption and of expected returns—which we derive from real data. Second, we analyze various investor profiles by using different combinations of our behavioral parameters—such as the degree of narrow framing, the consumption-related risk aversion, the weight of financial utility, the sensitivity to past losses, the way of accounting for past performance.

The remainder of this work is organized as follows: The second section of this chapter builds upon the theoretical framework. We commence, however, in the first section of this chapter, by briefly reviewing of the model in Rengifo and Trifan (2007). In so doing, first we focus on variables that describe perceptions; then we address the optimal wealth allocation with individual levels of risk VaR*. Once again, this chapter's second section extends this framework in order to account for two-dimensional utility. The implementation of our theoretical model for different constellations of behavioral parameters is discussed in this chapter's third section. Finally, the fourth section of this chapter summarizes our findings and concludes.

THEORETICAL MODEL

This section presents the theoretical framework describing how nonprofessional investors perceive financial risks and accordingly allocate wealth in order to maximize perceived utility.

A One-dimensional Utility Framework: Risky vs. Risk-free Assets

One of the most important human decisions is how to allocate resources, in particular money, among different type of activities. These activities may be either necessary and/or can generate further revenues. In the latter category, investing in financial assets has nowadays become one of the most popular alternatives. This widespread trend of ordinary people turning into "investors" is due, at least in part, to the formidable accessibility of information concerning financial markets, at almost no cost and in almost real time. Under the pressure of the huge amount and intensity of such information, even nonprofessional investors may have no choice but to become "overly concerned" with their financial investments. This phenomenon of putting excessive emphasis on financial investments is denoted in technical terms as *narrow framing* or *myopia*. Under narrow framing, the central decision refers to how to allocate the "right" amount of money first to financial investments in general, then across different financial assets. In addition, financial investments are perceived as distinct and overly important generators of individual utility. This dissociates the decisions upon wealth allocation from the naturally larger context with multiple utility generators, such as consumption or other factors that do not exclusively apply to financial markets.

Drawing on this idea, Rengifo and Trifan (2007) model the attitude toward financial losses and the decision making of nonprofessional investors regarding the optimal wealth allocation among different financial assets. *Nonprofessional investors* are people whose main occupation does not concern financial investments and/or who lack the necessary knowledge, expertise, time, or any combination of them for making more sophisticated investment decisions. These investors are assumed to derive utility from financial investments only. Moreover, their attitude toward possible losses associated with financial investments depends on the subjective perception of such investments. Perceptions are modeled according to the extended prospect-theory framework by Barberis et al. (2001).

Rengifo and Trifan (2007) explain that wealth-allocation decisions often imply the aid of professional managers: In essence, nonprofessional investors are interested in how to split their money between the two main categories of financial assets: risky and risk free. The more refined decision upon the composition of the risky portfolio is committed to professional portfolio managers. Managers solve for the optimal wealth allocation among different risky assets and a risk-free one in a portfolio optimization framework based on Campbell et al. (2001), where market risk is measured by the VaR. Rengifo and Trifan (2007) introduce an individualized VaR level (denoted as VaR*), which is based on the psychological profile of nonprofessional clients and hence on their subjective perceptions of financial risk, and consider its implications on wealth allocation.

The present work extends the model by Rengifo and Trifan (2007) for the case when not only financial investments but also consumption generates utility. In the remainder of this section, we briefly review the model structure and variables in Rengifo and Trifan (2007) that serve as support for the present two-dimensional utility framework.[1]

Individual Perceptions

As mentioned above, the assignment of the individual loss level VaR* in the investor minds takes place according to Barberis et al. (2001). Thus, the subjective perception of one unit of risky investment (relative to the risk-free rate) is captured by the *extended value function v*. As in the original prospect theory (PT) of Kahneman and Tversky,[2] this value function accounts for the distinct perception of gains and losses with respect to a subjective reference point and for the higher reluctance toward losses. In addition, the extended value function is designed to capture the possible influence of past performance on current risk perceptions.[3] We apply the definitions from Equations (7) to (9) in Rengifo and Trifan (2007), that is,

$$v_{t+1} = \begin{cases} v_{t+1}^{\text{prior gains}}, & \textit{for } S_t \geq Z_t \\ v_{t+1}^{\text{prior losses}}, & \textit{for } S_t < Z_t, \end{cases} \tag{23.1}$$

where

$$v_{t+1}^{\text{prior gains}} = \begin{cases} S_t x_{t+1}, & \text{for } S_t x_{t+1} + (S_t - Z_t)R_{ft} \geq 0 \\ \lambda S_t x_{t+1} + (\lambda - 1)(S_t - Z_t)R_{ft}, & \text{for } S_t x_{t+1} + (S_t - Z_t)R_{ft} < 0 \end{cases} \tag{23.2}$$

and

$$v_{t+1}^{\text{prior looses}} = \begin{cases} S_t x_{t+1}, & \text{for } x_{t+1} \geq 0 \\ \lambda S_t x_{t+1} + k(Z_t - S_t)x_{t+1}, & \text{for } x_{t+1} < 0. \end{cases} \tag{23.3}$$

In the above expressions, R_{t+1} stands for the next-period returns of the risky portfolio, R_{ft} for the risk-free returns, and $x_{t+1} = R_{t+1} - R_{ft}$ for

---

[1] Please refer to the original paper, Rengifo and Trifan (2007), for further details.
[2] See especially Kahneman and Tversky (1979) and Tversky and Kahneman (1992).
[3] Which makes, among others, the reference point vary subject to past losses or gains.

the return premium. Moreover, S_t denotes the current value of the risky investment, while Z_t is a benchmark level for past portfolio performance. The difference $S_t - Z_t$ represents the so-called cushion of past results generated by the risky portfolio, where $S_t - Z_t \geq 0$ ($S_t - Z_t < 0$) points to prior gains (losses). The present analysis focuses on so-called myopic cushions, for which the benchmark level of past performance is taken to be identical to the last-period risky holdings $Z_t = S_{t-1}$ so that myopic cushions amount to $S_t - S_{t-1}$.[4] The parameter λ is referred to as the *loss-aversion coefficient* and should satisfy $\lambda > 0$ with $\lambda \geq 1$ indicating loss aversion. Finally, k stands for the *sensitivity to past losses*, and $k \geq 0$.

Central to the analysis in Rengifo and Trifan (2007) is the derivation of the so-called prospective value V. This variable captures the subjectively perceived utility of the risky portfolio (relatively to the risk-free rate) and hence is related to the attitude adopted toward financial losses. One goal of the present work is to determine the prospective value assessed by investors who derive utility from two main sources—consumption and financial investments—to financial investments, in the equilibrium of the aggregate market. According to Equation (13) in Rengifo and Trifan (2007) and with the probability notations in Equation (23.7), the prospective value can be formally defined as[5]

$$
\begin{aligned}
V_{t+1} &= \pi E_t \left[v_{t+1}^{\text{prior gains}} \right] + (1 - \pi_t) E_t \left[v_{t+1}^{\text{prior losses}} \right] \\
&= \left(\pi_t \psi_t + (1 - \pi_t)\omega_t + (\pi_t(1 - \psi_t) + (1 - \pi_t)(1 - \omega_t))\lambda \right) S_t E_t \left[x_{t+1} \right] \quad (23.4) \\
&+ \left(\pi_t(1 - \psi_t)(\lambda - 1)R_{ft} - (1 - \pi_t)(1 - \omega_t)kE_t \left[x_{t+1} \right] \right) (S_t - Z_t)
\end{aligned}
$$

Drawing on the idea that individual attitudes toward financial losses can be measured by means of the loss-aversion coefficient, it is interesting to compute such a coefficient $\bar{\lambda}$ that is equivalent to the prospective value $\bar{V}$ in the market equilibrium. From Equation (23.4), $\bar{\lambda}$ formally yields:

---

[4] Rengifo and Trifan (2007) analyze not only myopic but also dynamic cushions. The latter assume the benchmark to be a combination of past references and current risky investment values $Z_t = \eta Z_{t-1}\bar{R}_1 + (1 - \eta)S_t$, where the parameter η measures how far in the past the investor memory stretches, and hence result in $\eta(S_t - Z_{t-1}\bar{R})$.

[5] The two terms of the last expression in Equation (23.4) are denoted by Rengifo and Trifan (2007) as the *PT effect* and the *cushion effect*, respectively. The former stems from the value-function formulation in the initial PT of Kahneman and Tversky, while the latter effect has as its source the prior gains and losses accumulated from trading the risky portfolio.

$$\bar{\lambda}_{t+1} = \frac{\bar{V}_{t+1} - \left(\pi_t\psi_t + (1-\pi_t)\omega_t\right)S_tE_t\left[x_{t+1}\right] + \left(\pi_t(1-\psi_t)R_{ft} + (1-\pi_t)(1-\omega_t)kE_t\left[x_{t+1}\right]\right)(S_t - Z_t)}{\left(\pi_t(1-\psi_t) + (1-\pi_t)(1-\omega_t)\right)S_tE_t\left[x_{t+1}\right] + \pi_t(1-\psi_t)R_{ft}(S_t - Z_t)} \quad (23.5)$$

Note that previous research (based on PT) suggests for the loss-aversion coefficient values of 2.25.

However, the simple loss-aversion coefficient fails to capture the influence of past performance that is yet explicitly considered in the extended PT by Barberis et al. (2001). Consequently, Rengifo and Trifan (2007) introduce a further measure of the loss attitude denoted as the *global first-order risk aversion (gRA)*. It stands for risk aversion of first order in the loss domain and hence is formally defined as the first derivative of the prospective value with respect to the expected return premium. According to Equation (14) in Rengifo and Trifan (2007), *gRA* yields

$$gRA_t = \frac{\partial V_{t+1}}{\partial E_t\left[x_{t+1}\right]}$$
$$= \left(\pi_t\psi_t + (1-\pi_t)\omega_t + (\pi_t(1-\psi_t) + (1-\pi_t)(1-\omega_t))\lambda\right)S_t \quad (23.6)$$
$$- (1-\pi_t)(1-\omega_t)k(S_t - Z_t)$$

Note that *gRA* directly reflects changes in the attractiveness of financial investments—captured by the prospective value—so that higher *gRA*-values point to more relaxed loss attitudes.

Based on the perception of financial investments captured by the value, the *individual loss level* VaR* of nonprofessional investors is further taken to be the quantile of the subjective loss distribution. The following expressions underlie the probability of past gains π_t, the probability of positive return premiums after past losses ω_t and the probability of enhanced premiums of the magnitude $x_{t+1} + (1-Z_t/S_t)R_{ft}$ after past gains ψ_t:[6]

---

[6] Such premiums, which are higher than the usual return premium x_{t+1}, express raised expectations emerging from recurrent gains.

$$\pi_t = P_t(S_t \geq Z_t)$$

$$\omega_t = P_t(x_{t+1} \geq 0 | S_t < Z_t)$$

$$\psi_t = P_t\left(x_{t+1} + \left(1 - \frac{Z_t}{S_t}\right)R_{ft} \geq 0 | S_t \geq Z_t\right)$$

(23.7)

Then, according to Equation (11) in Rengifo and Trifan (2007), VaR* formally results in:

$$\mathrm{VaR}^*_{t+1} = E_t\left[loss - value_{t+1}\right] - \varphi\sqrt{\mathrm{VaR}_t\left[loss - value_{t+1}\right]}$$

$$= \lambda S_t E_t\left[x_{t+1}\right] + \left(\zeta_t(\lambda - 1)R_{ft} + (\zeta_t - 1)kE_t\left[x_{t+1}\right]\right)(S_t - Z_t)$$

(23.8)

where "loss – value" stands for the subjective value ascribed to financial losses (from the loss branches of the value functions in Equations (23.2) and (23.3). These subjectively perceived losses are assumed to follow a distribution (e.g., normal or Student's t) with the lower quantile φ. The expected return premium is $E_t[x_{t+1}] = E_t[R_{t+1}] - R_{ft}$ and the last expression in Equation (23.8) is obtained using the simplifying notation $\xi_t = \sqrt{\pi_t(1-\psi_t)}\left(\sqrt{\pi_t(1-\psi_t)} - \varphi\sqrt{1-\pi_t(1-\psi_t)}\right)$.

Once being formed in investor mind, VaR* is communicated to the portfolio manager in the form of a fixed number. Managers interpret it as a fixed risk level and incorporate it into the problem of optimal capital allocation among financial investments as a risk constraint. This problem is solved following the portfolio optimization model with VaR as risk measure by Campbell et al. (2001). Let us now shortly review this model and then show how it changes when the individual VaR* serves for quantifying market risks.

Optimal Capital Allocation with (Individual) VaR

In the setting by Campbell et al. (2001), financial assets are chosen in order to maximize expected returns, subject to a twofold restriction: budget and risk. The market risk is assessed by means of VaR. The objective of the optimization problem in their model is to maximize the next-period wealth W_{t+1}. This wealth results from what the components of the risky portfolio and the risk-free assets are expected to return. The risky portfolio consists of $i = 1, ..., n$ financial assets with single time t prices $p_{i,t}$ and portfolio weights $w_{i,t}$, such that $\sum_{i=1}^{n} w_{i,t} = 1$. Moreover, $a_{i,t}$ is the number of shares of the asset i contained in the portfolio at time t.[7] Formally, the portfolio optimization problem entails

$$W_{t+1}(w_t) = (W_t + B_t)E_t\left[R_{t+1}(w_t)\right] - B_t R_f \xrightarrow[w_t]{} \max$$

such that

$$W_t + B_t = \sum_{i=1}^{n} a_{i,t}\, p_{i,t} = a_t{}' p_t \quad \text{(budget constraint)} \qquad (23.9)$$

$$P_t\left[W_{t+1}(w_t) \le W_t - \text{VaR}^{ex}\right] \le 1 - \alpha \quad \text{(risk constraint)}, \qquad (23.10)$$

where $R_{t+1}(w_t)$ stands for the portfolio gross returns at the next trade and $E_t[R_{t+1}(w_t)]$ stands for the corresponding expected returns. Henceforth, we refer to the gross returns of the risky portfolio by "returns" or "portfolio returns."

In the Equations (23.9) and (23.10), B_t denotes the risk-free investment, i.e., the sum of money that can be borrowed ($B_t > 0$) or lent ($B_t < 0$) at the fixed risk-free gross return rate R_f. Note that the maximization in Equation (23.9) is carried over the weights of the risky portfolio w_t but *not* over B_t. The *risk-free investment* B_t results as a by-product of the optimization procedure.[8] Finally, P_t denotes the conditional probability given the information at time t, and $1 - \alpha$ is the chosen confidence level. After some manipulations, Campbell et al. (2001) obtain the *optimal weights of the risky portfolio* as

$$w_t^{opt} \equiv \arg\max_{w_t} \frac{E_t[R_{t+1}(w_t)] - R_f}{W_t R_f - W_t q_t(w_t,\alpha)}, \qquad (23.11)$$

where $q_t(w_t,\alpha)$ represents the quantile of the distribution of portfolio gross returns $R_{t+1}(w_t)$ for the confidence level $1 - \alpha$ (or significance α), i.e.,

---

[7] Clearly, $a_{i,t} = w_{i,t}(W_t + B_t)/p_{i,t}$.
[8] See the comments concerning the two-fund separation below.

$P_t[R_{t+1}(w_t) \le q_t(w_t, \alpha)] \le 1-\alpha$. Thus, the optimal mix of risky assets depends merely on the distribution of the portfolio gross returns and on the significance level α.

Equation (23.11) shows that, similarly to the traditional mean-variance framework, the *two-fund separation theorem* applies: Neither the (nonprofessional) investors' initial wealth nor the desired risk level VaR^{ex} affects the maximization procedure. In other words, investors first determine the optimal risky portfolio (i.e., the optimal allocation among different risky assets) and second, they decide upon the extra amount of money to be borrowed or lent (i.e., invested in risk-free assets). The latter reflects by how much the portfolio VaR, which is VaR$_t = W_t(q_t(w^{opt}_t, \alpha) - 1)$, varies according to the investor degree of loss aversion measured by the selected (desired) VaR^{ex} level. The optimal investment in risk-free assets can be then written as:

$$B_t = \frac{\mathrm{VaR}^{ex} + \mathrm{VaR}_t}{R_f - q_t(w^{opt}_t, \alpha)} \qquad (23.12)$$

and hence the value of the risky investment at time $t + 1$ yield

$$S_{t+1} = (W_t + B_t)R_{t+1} \qquad (23.13)$$

As apparent from Equation (23.12), the *optimal amount of money B_t to be borrowed or lent depends* on the risk level communicated by the nonprofessional client to the portfolio manager. Rengifo and Trifan (2007) work with *individual* risk levels and extend the above optimization procedure in order to account for the individual VaR* from Equation (23.8). Formally, VaR^{ex} in Equation (23.12) is replaced by VaR*, since in the view of the manager, they represent the same level of risk indicated by the client. This amounts to:

$$B_t = \frac{VaR^* + VaR}{R_{ft} - q_t(w^*_t, \alpha)} \qquad (23.14)$$

The variable B_t plays a major role for the nonprofessional investors, as their interest is in how to split their money between risky assets in total and the risk-free asset. Therefore, it also represents one of the main variables in our model and gives account of the wealth-allocation decisions of our investors in the market equilibrium.

A Two-dimensional Utility Framework: Consumption vs. Financial Assets

As mentioned above, Rengifo and Trifan (2007) consider that investors are merely concerned with financial investments and the utility they generate. In their model, nonprofessional investors exclusively aim at maximizing the subjective utility of these investments, i.e., the prospective value. Yet in practice, such considerations—that is, focusing on financial utility alone—appear to be better suited to professional investors than to nonprofessional ones. The activity of the former demands a strictly investment-oriented perspective, and their main task reduces to making money that is going to be reinvested in financial markets. By contrast, nonprofessional investors sooner regard financial investments as a source of income dedicated to covering consumption needs. In other words, consumption should be the main generator of individual utility for nonprofessional investors. However, financial investments can be perceived as an equally important source of utility. The main reason resides in the above-mentioned narrow framing, i.e., the excessive focus on financial investments, which appears to be driven by the fear of registering losses when facing financial risks.

Based on these considerations, our work extends the setting in Rengifo and Trifan (2007) by allowing for *two sources of individual utility*: financial wealth fluctuations and consumption. In essence, the wealth-allocation problem in Rengifo and Trifan (2007) is now augmented by a step splitting money between consumption and financial investments—that should be placed before partitioning the last sum between risk-free and risky assets. However, as the performance of risky investments is mostly measured with respect to risk-free assets,[9] we can formally merge these steps into a single decision. The common goal is then the maximization of total utility derived from consumption and risky (relative to risk free) financial investments.

---

[9] Recall that the reference points of the perceived value of the risky prospect in Equations (23.2) and (23.3) include the risk-free rate R_{ft}.

Following Barberis and Huang (2004), we consider an aggregate market, which lacks perfect substitution. Hence, we can focus on absolute pricing and avoid possible arbitrage opportunities generated by narrow framing. The total utility is formulated in order to account for the above-mentioned twofold origin, specifically as the sum of discounted utilities of consumption $U(C)$ and of perceived values of financial investments $\tilde{V}$, that is[10]:

$$U = U(C) + \tilde{V} = \sum_{t=0}^{\infty} (\rho^t U(C_t) + \rho^{t+1} b_t \tilde{V}_{t+1}) \qquad (23.15)$$

where ρ is referred to as the *discounting factor* and $\rho < 1$.[11] According to Equation (23.15), at each time t, the current consumption is discounted with ρ^t, while the prospective value—that encompasses subjective perception of the *next-period* performance[12]—has to be provided with a corresponding ρ^{t+1}.

In line with Barberis et al.(2001), b_t is an exogenous scaling factor designed to map the perceived value of gains and losses into consumption units. It follows the rule stated in their Equation (23.11), that is, $b_t = b_0 \bar{C}_t^{-\gamma}$, where $\bar{C}_t$ represents the exogenous[13] *aggregate per capita consumption* at time t and b_0 measures the *degree of narrow framing*. Finally, γ denotes the *consumption-related coefficient of risk aversion*.

In line with Barberis and Huang (2006), it is now possible to develop an equilibrium framework in the aggregate market with a representative investor.[14] We derive the equilibrium conditions when investors maximize expected utility. Throughout, we formally incorporate the assumptions

---

[10] Strictly speaking, $\tilde{V}$ corresponds to the prospective value V from Equation (23.4), *before* taking expectations. Recall that the prospective value stands for the perceived utility of financial investments. Being obtained from the value functions weighted by the pure occurrence probabilities of the different possible outcomes, it is equivalent to an expected value.

[11] In the applied part, we consider a finite investment duration T that is, however, sufficiently long to allow for reaching an equilibrium.

[12] Recall that the prospective value encompasses the future returns R_{t+1}.

[13] The *exogeneity* refers here to the subjective viewpoint of the individual investor. It points out the fact that b_t is independent of every individual feature related to risk aversion or loss aversion.

[14] Henceforth, we use the denominations of "representative investor" and "investors" interchangeably, drawing upon the idea that the latter stands for a group with homogenous preferences. In essence, the actions of all investors in equilibrium can be summarized by the corresponding choices of the representative investor.

of narrow framing and dependence of current decisions on past portfolio performance.

Furthermore, we are interested in the phenomenon denoted as *myopic loss aversion* (mLA). Introduced by Benartzi and Thaler (1995) and supported by numerous experimental tests, mLA refers to the fact that narrow framing (or myopia) strengthens the loss aversion, so that investors reduce their risky investments when risky performance is checked on more frequently. In view of the manifold possibilities to quantify the loss attitude, we refine the notion of mLA in the following sense: The *mLA in strict sense* denotes the enhancement of loss aversion with the evaluation frequency. According to our model, the loss aversion can be quantified either by the loss-aversion coefficient or by the extended measure *gRA*. Thus, mLA in strict sense holds if either the loss-aversion coefficient increases or *gRA* decreases with the evaluation frequency. As both loss-aversion measures are derived from individual perceptions of risky investment, we can also measure *mLA in large sense* with respect to the prospective value. We can support mLA in large sense if the prospective value falls at higher evaluation frequencies. Finally, *mLA in monetary sense* is defined as the decrease of monetary risky holdings—in percentages of the total wealth—in consequence of more frequent portfolio evaluations. In addition, we can speak about *myopic aversion toward financial investments* when the wealth percentages dedicated to consumption increase with the evaluation frequency.

The Expected-Utility Approach

We focus here on the approach of Barberis et al. (2001), where the representative investor aims at maximizing total *expected utility* generated by both consumption and financial wealth changes.[15] Moreover, we assume that this representative investor lives well beyond the VaR horizon.

We refer to the utility of consumption in the traditional CRRA terms and hence assume

$$U = U(C_t) = \frac{C_t^{1-\gamma}}{1-\gamma}$$

---

[15] As demonstrated in Barberis et al. (2001), this framework can explain the emergence of equity premiums of the magnitude observed in practice.

The utility of financial investments is measured by the prospective value in Equation (23.4). The maximization problem of the nonprofessional investors from Equation (23.15) results then in:

$$E_t[U] = E_t\left[\sum_{i=0}^{\infty}\left(\rho^i\frac{C_i^{1-\gamma}}{1-\gamma} + b_0\rho^{i+1}\overline{C}_i^{-\gamma}v(G_{i+1})\right)\right]\xrightarrow[c_t,\theta_t]{}\max \qquad (23.16)$$

where v is the value function from Equation (23.1).

Moreover, G_{t+1} represents the next-period value of the risky investment and yields:

$$G_{t+1} = \theta_t(W_t - C_t)(R_{t+1} - R_{ft}) \qquad (23.17)$$

where W_t stands for the *total wealth* and θ_t for the *fraction of postconsumption wealth allocated to the risky portfolio*.

We reformulate the Rengifo and Trifan's (2007) postconsumption wealth proportion put in risky assets θ_t, current value of the risky investment S_t, and amount of money B_t borrowed ($B_t > 0$) or lent ($B_t < 0$) in order to correspond to the total wealth W_t, which now encompasses not only financial wealth but also consumption, and obtain:

$$\theta_t = \frac{W_t - C_t + B_t}{W_t - C_t} \qquad (23.18a)$$

$$S_t = \theta_t(W_t - C_t) \qquad (23.18b)$$

$$B_t = (W_t - C_t)\frac{VaR^* + VaR}{(W_t - C_t)R_{ft} - VaR} \qquad (23.18c)$$

Thus, the postconsumption wealth fraction allocated to risk-free assets entails $1 - \theta_t = -B_t(W_t - C_t)$. In addition, the next-period total wealth results from the current financial investment and, since consumption only generates utility but no wealth, can be expressed as follows:

$$W_{t+1} = (W_t - C_t)\left(\theta_t R_{t+1} + (1 - \theta_t)R_{ft}\right) \qquad (23.19)$$

Recall however that our investors are long-lived and view financial investments as single source of wealth. It is then possible that financial investments do not produce sufficient revenues in order to cover consumption needs over the entire interval. We circumvent this potential problem by considering that at each time t, investors dispose of additional incomes I_t. Such incomes represent, for instance, the wages earned by nonprofessional investors from their main employment. They are *exogenous*, that is, they stem from outside of those investments that constitute the decision making object at hand. Under this assumption, the total wealth in Equation (23.19) results from financial investments and the additional income and yields at $t + 1$:

$$W_{t+1} - I_{t+1} = (W_t - C_t)(\theta_t R_{t+1} + (1 - \theta_t)R_{ft})$$ (23.20)

The additional income I_t may cover a part of the consumption needs of the current period, and hence we define it as follows:

$$I_t = \frac{C_t}{\alpha\delta}$$ (23.21)

where α represents possible percentages of total wealth dedicated to consumption and δ is an arbitrary constant. This procedure facilitates the numerical estimation and the choice of the parameters α and δ will be detailed in a subsequent section.

Note that the maximization in Equation (23.16) is carried out with respect to both consumption C_t and the wealth fraction invested in risky assets θ_t (and hence the value of the risky investment S_t). Thus, the corresponding Euler equations for optimality at equilibrium yield[16]:

$$\rho R_f E\left[\left(\frac{\overline{C}_{t+1}}{\overline{C}_t}\right)^{-\gamma}\right] = 1$$ (23.22a)

$$\rho E\left[R_{t+1}\left(\frac{\overline{C}_{t+1}}{\overline{C}_t}\right)^{-\gamma}\right] + b_0 \rho \overline{C}^{-\gamma} E\left[\overline{v}(G_{t+1})\right] = 1$$ (23.22b)

---

[16] See Equations (23.27) and (23.28) in Barberis et al. (2001).

According to our approach, $E[(\overline{v}(G_{t+1})]$ represents the *prospective value at equilibrium* that we denote by $\overline{V}$. Our goal is to provide an empirical estimate $\hat{V}$ of this prospective value from which we can derive the equilibrium-equivalent loss-aversion coefficient $\hat{\lambda}$ that follows Equation (23.5).

In order to perform the estimation of $\overline{V}$, additional assumptions concerning the consumption and return dynamics are necessary. In line with Equations (68) to (70) in Barberis and Huang (2006), we take

$$\log\left(\frac{C_{t+1}}{C_t}\right) = c + \sigma_c \varepsilon_{t+1} \tag{23.23a}$$

$$\log(R_{t+1}) = r + \sigma_r \eta_{t+1} \tag{23.23b}$$

$$\begin{pmatrix} \varepsilon_{t+1} \\ \eta_{t+1} \end{pmatrix} \sim N\left(\begin{pmatrix} 0 \\ 0 \end{pmatrix}, \begin{pmatrix} 1 & \sigma_{cr} \\ \sigma_{cr} & 1 \end{pmatrix} \right) \tag{23.23c}$$

independent and identically distributed (i.i.d.) over time. Thus, for a constant risk-free rate R_f, the expected-equilibrium Equations (23.22a) and (23.22c) entail[17]

$$\exp\left(-\gamma c + \frac{\gamma^2 \sigma_c^2}{2} \right) = \frac{1}{\rho R_f} \tag{23.24a}$$

$$\exp\left(-\gamma c + r + \frac{\gamma^2 \sigma_c^2 + \sigma_r^2}{2} - \gamma \sigma_{cr} \right) + b_0 \overline{C}_t^{-\gamma} \overline{V} = \frac{1}{\rho} \tag{23.24b}$$

APPLICATION

This section presents numerical findings based on the theoretical results from a previous section. We first review the general assumptions made in order to facilitate the estimation procedure. The estimation results are subsequently detailed.

---

[17] Here we used the fact that for $x \sim N(\mu,\sigma^2)$, $E[\exp(x)] = \exp(\mu + \sigma^2/2)$. Also, for $x_i \sim N$ (μ, σ^2), where $i = 1, 2$, i.i.d. over time and with covariance σ_{12}, we have $E[\exp(x_1 + x_2)]$ $= \exp(\mu_1 + \mu_2 + (\sigma_1 + \sigma_2)^2/2 + \sigma_{12})$.

Data and General Assumptions

The first data set that underlies our estimations includes nominal returns of the stock index SP500 and of the three-month Treasury bill—as proxies for the risky and the risk-free investment, respectively—from 01/02/1962 to 03/09/2006 (11,005 daily observations). These data are divided into two parts: The observations before 03/01/1982 serve to estimate the empirical mean and the standard deviation of the portfolio returns at what we consider to be the beginning of the trade, namely 03/01/1982. The second part, from 03/01/1982 to 03/09/2006 (6,010 observations), is the actual data used for performing simulations. Additionally, aggregate per capita consumption data between 01/02/1962 and 12/31/2005 sampled at quarterly and yearly intervals provide a basis for the calculation of the log-consumption mean and variance.[18] We will analyze how the recommendations of our model change for these two evaluation frequencies. Table 23.1 presents descriptive statistics of the data used.

T A B L E   23.1

Log-differences of the S&P 500 Index and of the three-month T-bill returns for quarterly and yearly portfolio evaluations

	Evaluation Frequency					
	Quarterly	Yearly	Quarterly	Yearly	Quarterly	Yearly
	S&P 500		Three-Month T-bill		Consumption	
Mean	0.017	0.066	0.017	0.073	0.016	0.052
Median	0.018	0.071	0.017	0.070	0.001	0.049
Standard deviation	0.079	0.136	0.006	0.026	0.008	0.022
Kurtosis	2.661	−0.9659	0.623	0.974	0.673	−1.084
Skewness	−0.671	−0.205	0.951	1.042	−0.018	0.165
Max.	0.290	0.345	0.036	0.142	0.042	0.090
Min.	−0.302	−0.207	0.009	0.037	−0.010	0.011
Obs.	175	43	175	43	175	43

[18] These data were provided by the Department of Commerce, Bureau of Economic Analysis and Bureau of the Census.

After smoothing out the outlier corresponding to the October 1987 market crash,[19] quarterly and yearly returns are constructed from the actual data set and used to derive the main variables that describe the loss attitude and the optimal wealth allocation of our nonprofessional investors.

In so doing, we assume that investors start by spreading their wealth equally between consumption and financial assets. The latter fraction is further allocated in equal parts to the risky index and the risk-free T-bill. Our investors are long-lived beyond the VaR horizon and are not allowed to quit the market during the trading period. Portfolio gross returns are assumed to be normally distributed, and future portfolio returns are to be estimated as the unconditional mean of past returns. In addition, the risk-free returns, the mean log-consumption, and the mean risky returns are set identical to means of the corresponding variable throughout the actual trade period from 03/01/1982 to 03/09/2006, specifically as $\hat{R}_f = \text{mean}[R_{ft}]$, $\hat{c} = \text{mean} [\log(C_{t+1}) - \log(C_t)]$, and $\hat{r} = \text{mean}[\log(R_t)]$, respectively.

Further assumptions concern the behavioral model parameters that are varied in order to study the influence of the investors' behavioral profile on the equilibrium variables. Due to the lack of space, we subsequently focus on few cases that appear to be the most realistic and entail plausible estimates. Further interesting situations are explicitly indicated.[20]

In particular, we work with different values for the initial loss-aversion coefficient $\lambda \in \{1; 2.25; 3\}$ from which we subsequently refer to the most used in literature $\lambda = 2.25$. Moreover, we rely on Barberis et al. (2001) and Barberis and Huang (2006) in choosing a risk-aversion degree in the set $\gamma \in \{0.5; 1; 1.5\}$ where higher values point to increased aversion. Our subsequent comments concentrate on $\gamma = 0.5$ as a benchmark case. Following the same authors, we also account for no, moderate, and high influence of past losses on the perception of risky investments $k \in \{0; 3; 10\}$. We also consider a wide range of narrow-framing degrees $b_0 \in \{0.001; 0.1; 0.5; 1;5; 10; 100; 1,000\}$, where the first value stands for the situation with (almost) no narrow framing since $b_0 \neq 0$ according to Equation (23.25). In the sequel, we address situations in which there is substantial narrow framing of financial investments $b_0 \geq 1$.

---

[19] This outlier is replaced with the mean of the 10 before and after data points.
[20] The results obtained for further parameter values are qualitatively consistent with those discussed in the text. They are available upon request.

In addition, our investors are assumed to assess cushions myopically as $S_t - C_{t-1}$.[21] Their additional income I_t is adjusted by means of the parameters α and δ, according to Equation (23.21). Although we work with wide ranges of $\alpha \in [0.1, 0.98]$ and $\delta \in [0.1, 100]$, we merely comment on the *average* additional income I at three qualitatively distinct levels that we denote as low, middle, and high.

The Expected-Utility Approach

In this section, we present estimates of the main variables that quantify the loss attitude and the wealth allocation in the expected-utility equilibrium. Our interest lies in how they change subject to different psychological profiles of the representative investor. We report on *average* changes of these variables subject to the ceteris paribus variation of chosen parameters.

The main equilibrium variables in the expected-utility setting are the discounting factor ρ and the prospective value $\bar{V}$. They are obtained by plugging in the parameter values assumed in the section Data and General Assumptions into the following reformulations of Equations (23.24):

$$\rho = \frac{1}{R_f} \exp\left(\gamma c - \frac{\gamma^2 \sigma_c^2}{2}\right) \tag{23.25a}$$

$$\bar{V} = \frac{\bar{C}_t^\gamma}{b_o}\left(\frac{1}{\rho} - \exp\left(-\gamma c + r + \frac{\gamma^2 \sigma_c^2 + \sigma_r^2}{2} - \gamma \sigma_{cr}\right)\right) \tag{23.25b}$$

From the expression of the prospective value in equilibrium in Equation (23.25b), we can further assess the corresponding loss-aversion coefficient $\bar{\lambda}$ according to Equation (23.5). All estimates are henceforth denoted by a ^ symbol.

Before detailing the estimation results, let us make an important remark regarding the interpretation of the prospective value in equilibrium: Combining the above Equations (23.25), we can rewrite $\bar{V}$ as follows: $\bar{V} = \bar{C}_t^\gamma / b_0 \exp(-\gamma c + \gamma^2 \sigma_c^2 / 2)(R_f - \exp(r + \sigma_r^2 / 2 - \gamma \sigma_{cr}))$.

---

[21] We also measure the cushions using a dynamic cushion defined as $\eta\,(S_t \bar{v} Z_{t-1}\,\bar{R})$ with different memory-length parameters $\eta \in \{0; 0.1; 0.5; 0.9; 1\}$ and with $\bar{R} = \text{mean}[R_t]$. The corresponding results are available upon request.

This expression is proportional to a factor that indicates the trade-off between the revenues from risk-free vs. risky investments, which is the last right-hand term in parentheses $R_f - \exp(r + \sigma^2_r/2 - \gamma\sigma_{cr})$.[22] This term *decreases* as risky investments become *more* profitable and so also does $\bar{V}$. In other words, the prospective value is directly proportional to the profitability of risky with respect to risk-free assets taken *with negative sign*. Recall that the prospective value stands for the perceptions of the benefits of risky investments—being, as its name says, a "value"—and hence it is expected to *grow* as risky assets become *more* profitable. Therefore, only the absolute values of the prospective value in equilibrium $|\bar{V}|$ can be meaningfully interpreted and our subsequent comments will exclusively refer to such absolute values.

The main equilibrium estimates under maximization of expected utility for yearly and quarterly portfolio evaluations and our usual parameter values are illustrated in Table 23.2.

First, as implied by Equation (23.25a), the estimates $\hat{\rho}$ of the discounting factor do not vary with any of our behavioral parameters b_0, I, k, or the cushion type, and hence we discard them from Table 23.2. In particular, $\hat{\rho} = 0.99059$ (0.95685) for yearly (quarterly) evaluations. The decline of $\hat{\rho}$ with the frequency of the risky performance evaluation can be intuitively explained by the fact that the notion of immediacy might change of meaning when investors check more often on their portfolios: Perceived time intervals are shorter and thus the preference for immediacy should drop. Thus, our estimates $\hat{\rho}$ of the discounting factor lie close to the value of 0.98 assumed by Barberis et al. (2001) and Barberis and Huang (2006), speaking for the validity of our approach.

Second, let us analyze the subjective utility of financial investments quantified by the prospective value. Note also that the evolution of $|\bar{V}|$ is independent of each the sensitivity to past losses k, the average additional-income levels I, and even the way in which cushions are assessed. However, $|\bar{V}|$ decreases considerably subject to higher narrow framing b_0,

---

[22] We can approximate this factor by $R_f - \exp(r + \sigma^2_r/2) \approx R_f - E_t(R_{t+1})$, which is the expected return premium taken with a negative sign. This approximation holds in our data set, since the correlation between risky returns and consumption takes a very low value σ_{cr} 0:0168 (0.0056) for yearly (quarterly) evaluations.

T A B L E　23.2

Main estimated parameters in the expected-utility equilibrium for yearly and quarterly portfolio evaluations*

			Yearly Evaluations			Quarterly Evaluations		
			$k = 0$	$k = 3$	$k = 10$	$k = 0$	$k = 3$	$k = 10$
Low I	$b_0 = 1$	$|\hat{V}|$	229.8	229.8	229.8	229.8	229.8	229.8
		$\hat{\lambda}$	0.88272	0.69103	0.52197	0.040833	−0.013175	−0.079496
	$b_0 = 5$	$|\hat{V}|$	45.961	45.961	45.961	45.961	45.961	45.961
		$\hat{\lambda}$	0.55173	0.51857	0.49687	0.098019	0.08707	0.073462
	$b_0 = 10$	$|\hat{V}|$	22.98	22.98	22.98	22.98	22.98	22.98
		$\hat{\lambda}$	0.51035	0.49702	0.49373	0.10517	0.099601	0.092582
	$b_0 = 100$	$|\hat{V}|$	2.298	2.298	2.298	2.298	2.298	2.298
		$\hat{\lambda}$	0.47311	0.47762	0.49091	0.1116	0.11088	0.10979
	$b_0 = 1000$	$|\hat{V}|$	0.2298	0.2298	0.2298	0.2298	0.2298	0.2298
		$\hat{\lambda}$	0.46939	0.47568	0.49062	0.11224	0.11201	0.11151
Middle I	$b_0 = 1$	$|\hat{V}|$	229.8	229.8	229.8	229.8	229.8	229.8
		$\hat{\lambda}$	0.61664	0.59439	0.57693	0.15208	0.14411	0.13325
	$b_0 = 5$	$|\hat{V}|$	45.961	45.961	45.961	45.961	45.961	45.961
		$\hat{\lambda}$	0.49851	0.49925	0.50786	0.12027	0.11853	0.11601
	$b_0 = 10$	$|\hat{V}|$	22.98	22.98	22.98	22.98	22.98	22.98
		$\hat{\lambda}$	0.48374	0.48735	0.49923	0.11629	0.11533	0.11386
	$b_0 = 100$	$|\hat{V}|$	2.298	2.298	2.298	2.298	2.298	2.298
		$\hat{\lambda}$	0.47045	0.47665	0.49146	0.11271	0.11245	0.11192
	$b_0 = 1000$	$|\hat{V}|$	0.2298	0.2298	0.2298	0.2298	0.2298	0.2298
		$\hat{\lambda}$	0.46912	0.47558	0.49068	0.11236	0.11216	0.11172
High I	$b_0 = 1$	$|\hat{V}|$	229.8	229.8	229.8	229.8	229.8	229.8
		$\hat{\lambda}$	0.47727	0.48285	0.4968	0.11589	0.11545	0.11465
	$b_0 = 5$	$|\hat{V}|$	45.961	45.961	45.961	45.961	45.961	45.961
		$\hat{\lambda}$	0.47064	0.47694	0.49183	0.11303	0.1128	0.11229
	$b_0 = 10$	$|\hat{V}|$	22.98	22.98	22.98	22.98	22.98	22.98
		$\hat{\lambda}$	0.46981	0.4762	0.49121	0.11267	0.11246	0.112
	$b_0 = 100$	$|\hat{V}|$	2.298	2.298	2.298	2.298	2.298	2.298
		$\hat{\lambda}$	0.46906	0.47553	0.49065	0.11235	0.11216	0.11173
	$b_0 = 1000$	$|\hat{V}|$	0.2298	0.2298	0.2298	0.2298	0.2298	0.2298
		$\hat{\lambda}$	0.46898	0.47547	0.4906	0.11232	0.11213	0.1117

* Initial loss aversion $\lambda = 2.25$, risk-aversion $\gamma = 0.5$, and using various cushion-assessment methods, degrees of past-loss sensitivity k, additional-income levels i, and narrow-framing degrees b_0.

so that a more intense focus on financial investments appears to worsen the perception of the utility they are generating. Moreover, $|\bar{V}|$ is smaller for quarterly data. Thus, the perceived utility of financial investments ameliorates when the risky performance is evaluated more often, a result that is at odds with the concept of mLA in large sense.

We subsequently turn our attention to the investor attitude toward financial losses. One variable that captures this attitude is the loss-aversion coefficient, and we denote its estimates by $\hat{\lambda}$. Table 23.2 reveals that when risk-adverse investors revise risky performance yearly, $\hat{\lambda}$ lies substantially below the value of 2.25 advanced in the original PT and in various subsequent theoretical and experimental studies. Yet, this situation changes radically for quarterly evaluations, when investors who assess cushions myopically are clearly loss averse. This holds across all considered parameter combinations and underpins mLA in strict sense: (Even) in the aggregate equilibrium, investors become more reluctant to financial losses when they check on risky performance more often.

Note also that the values of $\hat{\lambda}$ for yearly evaluations and myopic cushions are smaller than 1, speaking thus for loss-loving attitudes. Earlier findings show that such attitudes are not very likely to occur in practice. We can interpret this somewhat puzzling result in manifold way: for instance, as a necessary condition for reaching the market equilibrium under maximization of two-dimensional expected utility. Markets with investors who are reluctant to financial risks (and behave according to our model) might then not attain a steady state. It is nevertheless possible that $\hat{\lambda}$ does not accurately measure the actual loss attitude. This reinforces the potential relevance of our second loss-attitude measure, gRA, on the estimates of which we comment below.

As anticipated, having more money (from exogenous sources) at their disposal renders investors less loss averse and $\hat{\lambda}$ diminishes on average with the additional income I. However, this holds only for yearly but not for quarterly data. The frequency of performance checks appears thus to overcome the role played by the additional income and hence to drive the loss aversion. The influence of the narrow focus on loss aversion appears to be also dependent on the portfolio evaluation frequency: $\hat{\lambda}$ decreases (increases) with b_0 for yearly (quarterly) evaluations, other things being equal. In other words, it is not the importance ascribed by investors to financial investments as a utility source that changes their attitude toward possible losses but to how often they check on the risky performance. Frequent checks and high narrow framing result in pronounced loss reluctance, while even under an increasing narrow framing, seldom checks entail a lower reluctance. This corroborates with mLA in strict sense.[23]

In addition, $\hat{\lambda}$ clearly diminishes subject to higher sensitivities toward past losses k for quarterly portfolio evaluations. This is somewhat counterintuitive, since investors who behave aversely toward past losses (i.e., have a high k) should remain averse toward future ones as well (high λ).[24] The evaluation frequency plays yet a very important role also in this respect.

T A B L E   23.3

Estimated global first-order risk aversion (gRA) in the expected-utility equilibrium for yearly and quarterly portfolio evaluations

		Yearly evaluations			Quarterly evaluations		
		$k = 0$	$k = 3$	$k = 10$	$k = 0$	$k = 3$	$k = 10$
Low l	$b_0 = 1$	14,663	14,444	13,954	10,078	10,210	10,531
	$b_0 = 5$	19,317	19,098	18,608	14,246	14,378	14,699
	$b_0 = 10$	19,898	19,680	19,189	14,767	14,899	15,220
	$b_0 = 100$	20,422	20,203	19,713	15,236	15,368	15,689
	$b_0 = 1000$	20,474	20,255	19,765	15,283	15,415	15,736
Middle l	$b_0 = 1$	216,770	214,900	210,630	162,420	164,300	168,780
	$b_0 = 5$	221,420	219,560	215,280	166,590	168,470	172,950
	$b_0 = 10$	222,000	220,140	215,860	167,110	168,990	173,470
	$b_0 = 100$	222,520	220,660	216,380	167,580	169,460	173,940
	$b_0 = 1000$	222,580	220,720	21,644	167,620	169,500	173,980
High l	$b_0 = 1$	7,099,800	7,099,800	7,099,800	7,099,800	5,418,000	5,567,000
	$b_0 = 5$	7,104500	7,048,200	6,918,000	5,359,400	5,422,200	5,571,200
	$b_0 = 10$	7,105100	7,048,800	6,918,600	5,359,900	5,422,700	5,571,700
	$b_0 = 100$	7,105600	7,049,300	6,919,100	5,360,400	5,423,200	5,572,200
	$b_0 = 1000$	7,105600	7,049,400	6,919,200	5,360,400	5,423,200	5,572,200

Initial loss aversion $\lambda = 2.25$, risk-aversion $\gamma = 0.5$, and using various cushion-assessment methods, degrees of past-loss sensitivity k, additional-income levels l, and narrow-framing degrees b_0.

---

[23] Moreover, $\hat{\lambda}$ is extremely high (positive or negative) for b_0 0.001 and hence implausible. This supports our assumption that the lack of narrow framing is incompatible with the present framework.

[24] Also, the other loss-aversion measure gRA constantly falls with k across all considered parameter combinations cases (see the comments on gRA below), pointing to a relaxation of the loss attitude.

As mentioned above, we attempt to refine the analysis of loss attitudes by means of our extended measure *gRA*. Table 23.3 presents the estimates of *gRA* for yearly (quarterly) evaluations. First, note that *gRA* reflects first-order changes in the perceived utility of financial investments, and hence higher values of *gRA* point to a *more* relaxed loss attitude; By contrast, higher $\hat{\lambda}$ reveals a *smaller* acceptance of possible losses.

In almost all cases, *gRA* supports the above findings obtained when loss attitudes are captured by the simple loss-aversion coefficient $\hat{\lambda}$. The only exception regards mLA in the strict sense, which is contradicted since *gRA* grows—and thus also the loss acceptance—for more frequent portfolio evaluations. Moreover, *gRA* also varies somewhat more consistently with respect to the behavioral investor profile.

In the sequel, we turn to the problem of wealth allocation in equilibrium. We compute the average values of the wealth proportions dedicated to consumption and to different types of financial assets. The mean fractions of total wealth to be consumed $\bar{C}/\hat{W}$ and of the postconsumption wealth assigned to risky assets $\hat{\theta}$ are exemplified in Table 23.4.

For all analyzed additional-income levels *I*, investors who evaluate the financial performance once every year (three months), are risk averse with $r = 0.5$, and are loss averse with $r = 2.25$ dedicate to consumption average percentages of their total wealth $\bar{C}/\hat{W}$ of up to 14.7 percent (23.1 percent). The same investors appear to behave myopically averse toward financial investments in total: They allocate less money to financial assets—and implicitly more to consumption—for more frequent portfolio evaluations.

The computed mean percentages $\bar{C}/\hat{W}$ fall for higher additional incomes *I*, since covering current consumption needs from financial revenues becomes less stringent. Note that this decline of $\bar{C}/\hat{W}$ with *I* is extremely pronounced. Moreover, when investors are more reluctant to past financial losses, they might also allocate less money to financial ventures and proportionally more to consumption, and indeed, we observe that $\bar{C}/\hat{W}$ rises with *k*.

Finally, the corresponding percentages of *total* wealth assigned to risky investments can be obtained by multiplying $(1 - \bar{C}/\hat{W})$ by $\hat{\theta}$. Across all considered additional incomes, the average values $(1 - \bar{C}/\hat{W})\hat{\theta}$ amount to 6.7 to 13.5 percent (8.2 to 35.5 percent) for yearly (quarterly) portfolio

T A B L E   23.4

Estimated wealth allocation in the expected-utility equilibrium for yearly and quarterly portfolio evaluations

		Yearly Evaluations			Quarterly Evaluations		
		$k = 0$	$k = 3$	$k = 10$	$k = 0$	$k = 3$	$k = 10$
Low I	$\bar{C}/\hat{W}$	0.14555	0.14576	0.1462	0.14574	0.14594	0.14637
	$\hat{\theta}$	−0.034714	−0.034729	−0.034818	−0.039377	−0.039509	−0.039873
	$(1-\bar{C}/\hat{W})\hat{\theta}$	−0.029661	−0.029667	−0.029727	−0.033638	−0.033743	−0.034037
Middle I	$\bar{C}/\hat{W}$	0.020167	0.02018	0.020209	0.020182	0.020195	0.00011144
	$\hat{\theta}$	0.11555	0.11573	0.11612	0.11151	0.11165	0.11193
	$(1-\bar{C}/\hat{W})\hat{\theta}$	0.11322	0.1134	0.11377	0.10926	0.10939	0.10966
High I	$\bar{C}/\hat{W}$	0.00080024	0.00080057	0.0008013	0.00080065	0.00080099	0.00080177
	$\hat{\theta}$	0.1338	0.13397	0.13433	0.12978	0.12993	0.13023
	$(1-\bar{C}/\hat{W})\hat{\theta}$	0.13369	0.13386	0.13422	0.12968	0.12982	0.13013

Initial loss aversion λ = 2.25, risk-aversion γ = 0.5, and using various cushion-assessment methods, degrees of past-loss sensitivity k, and additional-income levels I.

evaluations and myopic cushions, showing that investors split their money between consumption and risk-free assets. The sole exception is again the case with lowest additional incomes I, where for yearly data $(1 - \bar{C}/\hat{W})\hat{\theta} \approx -3$ percent. Having more money from investment-exogenous sources at their disposal augments the investor openness toward risky assets and hence $(1 - \bar{C}/\hat{W})\hat{\theta}$ grows with I. We can hence conclude that mLA in a monetary sense does *not* hold under the maximization of twofold expected utility: Average investments in risky assets, as proportion of total wealth, increase for more frequent evaluations of the risky portfolio.

In addition, the reluctance toward risky assets is less (more) pronounced than in the one-sided utility framework in Rengifo and Trifan (2007) for yearly (quarterly) portfolio revisions.[25]

[25] According to Rengifo and Trifan (2007, Table 1), for myopic cushions and normally distributed expected returns 34.51 percent (13.42 percent) of wealth is invested in risky assets when portfolios are evaluated yearly (quarterly).

CONCLUSION

This chapter extends the work of Rengifo and Trifan (2007) by analyzing loss attitudes and wealth allocation in a two-dimensional utility framework. Specifically, we are interested in how nonprofessional investors, who derive utility from both consumption and narrowly framed financial investments, behave when faced with financial risk. We also study how these investors change their perception of losses and how they consequently split their money between consumption and risky vs. risk-free financial assets.

Following Barberis and Huang (2004; 2006) and Barberis et al. (2001), we consider an aggregate market where, in equilibrium, a representative investor maximizes subjective expected utility. We explicitly account for the narrow framing of financial investments, as well as for the impact of past performance on current perceptions. The wealth allocation is based on the portfolio allocation model of Campbell et al. (2001), which is adapted in order to account for individually perceived VaR.

The expected utility setting delivers direct equilibrium estimates of the prospective value, i.e., of the subjective utility of financial investments. Equilibrium-equivalent measures of the loss attitude, such as the loss-aversion coefficient and the extended measure gRA, can then be obtained from this variable. In addition, the expected-utility setting provides estimates of the coefficient by which utility is discounted in time.

The theoretical results are subsequently tested and extended in an applied context. The numerical findings can be summarized as follows:

First, the prospective value mostly grows with the narrow-framing degree of financial investments, showing an improvement in the perceived benefits of such investments. Moreover, we can find no evidence for myopic loss aversion in large sense, i.e., for the depreciation of the perceived financial utility in consequence of the more frequent evaluation of risky performance.

Second, the two measures of the loss attitude vary consistently with each other. Yet, they deliver different results with respect to the myopic loss aversion in strict sense, i.e., the increase in the loss reluctance with the evaluation frequency. Specifically, this holds only with respect to the loss-aversion coefficient. Relative to this coefficient, gRA appears to be better suited as a measure of loss aversion.

Third, wealth-allocation variables can be assessed only on average. The respective average estimates suggest that wealth allocation is invariant with respect to the narrow-framing degree but strongly influenced by the additional income. Investors who check on risky performance more often allocate less money to financial assets in total, so that they behave myopically averse toward financial investments in total. Myopic loss aversion in the monetary sense, i.e., the decline of the total-wealth percentages to be put in risky assets for higher evaluation frequencies, does not hold in our setting.

Note also that degrees of consumption-related risk aversion that are too high appear to be incompatible with the present equilibrium framework.

REFERENCES

Barberis, N., and M. Huang (2004) Preferences with Frames: A New Utility Specification That Allows for the Framing of Risks. Working paper, University of Chicago, Chicago, IL, and Stanford University, Palo Alto, CA.

Barberis, N., and M. Huang (2006) The Loss Aversion/Narrow Framing Approach to Stock Market Pricing and Participation Puzzles. NBER Working Paper No. 12378, Cambridge, MA.

Barberis, N., M. Huang, and T. Santos (2001) Prospect Theory and Asset Prices. *Quarterly Journal of Economics*, 116(1): 1–53.

Benartzi, S. and R.H. Thaler (1995) Myopic Loss Aversion and the Equity Premium Puzzle. *Quarterly Journal of Economics*, 110(1): 73–92.

Campbell, R., R. Huisman, and K. Koedijk (2001) Optimal Portfolio Selection in a Value-at-Risk Framework. *Journal of Banking and Finance*, 25(9): 1789–1804.

Kahneman, D. and A. Tversky (1979) Prospect Theory: An Analysis of Decision under Risk. *Econometrica*, 47(2): 263–291.

Rengifo, E. and E. Trifan (2007) Investors Facing Risk: Loss Aversion and Wealth Allocation between Risky and Risk-Free Assets

Darmstadt Discussion Paper in Economics 180, Darmstadt University of Technology.

Tversky, A. and D. Kahneman (1992) Advances in Prospect Theory: Cumulative Representation of Uncertainty. *Journal of Risk and Uncertainty*, 4(5): 297–323.

INDEX